The Awkward Warrior

The Awkward Warrior

Frank Cousins: His Life and Times

GEOFFREY GOODMAN

SPOKESMAN

First published in 1979 by
Davis-Poynter Limited.
Second revised edition published in 1984 by
Spokesman, Bertrand Russell House, Gamble Street,
Nottingham. Tel. 0602 708318

Goodman, Geoffrey
    The awkward warrior.
    1. Cousins, Frank. 2. Transport and
    General Workers Union — Biography
    3. Statesmen — Great Britain — Biography
    I. Title.
    331.88'113805'0924   HD6665.C/
    ISBN 0-85124-409-2
    ISBN 0-85124-417-3 Pbk

Printed in Great Britain by
the Russell Press Ltd
Nottingham.

To MARGIT

Without whose love and self-sacrifice
this book could not have been completed;
and to my children.

Contents

PREFACE TO NEW EDITION

I'm glad that *The Awkward Warrior* is being made available in popular form because it deserves the widest readership. The book has a special niche in the history of our Labour movement, and provides material of inestimable value to students and all others interested in the progress of mankind.

Frank Cousins was an exceptional man, and encouraged many people in challenging old policies and fossilised ideas. I was privileged to work with him in the process of changing the outlook of the TGWU, which, thanks to the ability and scholarship of Geoffrey Goodman, is recounted so well in this book.

I have written elsewhere that 'not one man but many built the Union' but Frank made a splendid contribution and the book is a well deserved tribute to his endeavours. He will especially be remembered for his contribution to the cause of unilateral nuclear disarmament. On his 80th birthday he will have the satisfaction of knowing that support for that great cause has grown beyond belief.

It is to the credit of the Bertrand Russell Peace Foundation that they are re-publishing this book; the old man would have felt proud to witness the growing popularity of his ideas on peace and to know of the part played by Frank Cousins of the TGWU.

Jack Jones

*   *   *

To outsiders, Frank Cousins is known as a former General Secretary of the TGWU and the Minister of Technology in Harold Wilson's first Cabinet. He is remembered as a relentless and brave champion

ix

of two causes: nuclear disarmament and opposition to Government pay restriction policies.

Under his leadership, the TGWU continued to exert enormous influence within the TUC and the Labour Party, as well as pressing the day-to-day demands of our members.

Inside the TGWU, Frank is associated with paving the way for a new era within the Union: an era of greater membership involvement, openness and progressive policies. The Union had come of age. Frank had set a course to adapt the Union to the new demands of the 1960s and beyond.

Geoffrey Goodman has long been an outstanding commentator on the industrial scene and I strongly recommend this biography of Frank Cousins for its insight and clear description of the man and the political battles he fought.

Moss Evans

*　　*　　*

The *Awkward Warrior* is a worthy testimonial to a man who was the original trade union standard bearer on the question of unilateral nuclear disarmament in Britain.

Nearly a quarter of a century ago, Frank Cousins, when outlining the development of our union's policy to a mass rally in Portsmouth, gave a warning "that any progressive organisation was bound to come in for public criticism until events justified its policies."

Today's growing popularity for this cause has clearly shown that events have proved that the decisions that the union took under Frank's leadership, at that time, were sound.

Frank's overall contribution to the trade union and labour movement makes this biography compelling reading in the 80th year of a man who worked for those who need and deserve a better life.

Ron Todd

ACKNOWLEDGEMENTS

A book of this character is like a huge building. There may be only one architect but there are countless builders; all, in their own way, fetching and placing the bricks without which nothing could be achieved. There are the site engineers and the providers of shelter when the inescapable storms prevent any actual construction. They were all present on my construction ground. To them all I owe a great debt of gratitude. I can only hope that the finished product offers them some small crumb of satisfaction.

A number of them are mentioned in the text. Can I add to those who are named the considerable number of Transport and General Workers' Union officials who are unnamed but who gave me such invaluable assistance.

I have had access to the archives of the late Richard Crossman including his still unpublished diaries and I would like to express my profound appreciation to his widow, Ann, the Trustees of the Crossman literary estate and Dr Janet Morgan who was working on the diaries at the time.

Throughout the several years of research, preparation and writing—indeed, since its original conception—I have received enormous encouragement and help from Michael and Jill Foot and I am deeply grateful for that. I also wish to thank Jack Jones for his considerable help and friendship.

This book was ultimately made possible as a result of my Fellowship at Nuffield College, Oxford, and the initiative of one of its distinguished Fellows, Lord McCarthy. He sponsored my Fellowship and it was that which enabled me to complete the book. I want to emphasise my debt to Bill McCarthy and his wife, Margaret. I want also to thank the then Warden of Nuffield (Sir Norman Chester) and the Fellows of the College for their generosity, stimulus and hospitality during my 15 months with them. In particular I must acknowledge with gratitude the considerable help and scholarly guidance given to me by Philip Williams, Fellow of Nuffield and biographer of Hugh Gaitskell.

ACKNOWLEDGEMENTS

I am also indebted to the Chairmen (Lord Cudlipp, followed by Lord Jacobson and Sir Edward Pickering) of Mirror Group Newspapers and to the editors and directors of the Daily Mirror. It was their exceptional generosity in agreeing to release me for a lengthy sabbatical that enabled me to take up my Fellowship at Nuffield College.

Finally, though not least, there has been the support of the Cousins' family and especially of John Cousins. His help and encouragement has been constant. Neither Frank nor Nance Cousins wanted any biography written. It was John Cousins who persuaded them to acquiesce.

INTRODUCTION

Frank Cousins was an outstanding trade union leader who came to power by the coincidence of two deaths. Arthur Deakin's sudden death on 1 May 1955 was followed later the same year by that of his successor as General Secretary of the Transport and General Workers' Union, Arthur 'Jock' Tiffin. These two deaths made possible Cousins's dramatic and unique rise to the top of Britain's largest trade union—and also to one of the most important political positions in the country.

But more important than Cousins's elevation to power is what he did with that power. His ultimate election as General Secretary of the TGWU coincided with and possibly precipitated one of the most significant and far-reaching of all post-war social and political developments in Britain : the emergence of an altogether more radical force throughout the trade union movement which has since became a major power factor in the country.

Whether Frank Cousins inspired this development or simply opened the door to impulses which were already strongly pressing against the walls of society is debatable, but it is one of the principal contentions of this book that his arrival as General Secretary of the TGWU marked a watershed in post-war labour history for Britain.

It is, however, not with the man but with his trade union that the book begins, for the story of Frank Cousins is, in large measure, the story of the Transport and General Workers' Union, the biggest trade union in Britain. We must look briefly at its life before Frank Cousins came to lead it.

The TGWU had only five General Secretaries between 1922 and 1977 : Ernest Bevin, Arthur Deakin, Arthur Tiffin, Frank Cousins and Jack Jones. Realistically there have been only four : Tiffin was a sick man when he took office and he held it for only eight months; for most of the time he was ill and away from the seat of power. To say this is no reflection on Tiffin's ability or integrity: no one can know what the outcome might have been if he had lived. Certainly there were signs, even during his few months at the top, that he wished to make important changes in the running of the TGWU and to improve on the 'image' the union had had under Arthur Deakin, Tiffin's predecessor. During Deakin's reign the TGWU had grown bureaucratic and even autocratic; many sections of the membership were in revolt, especially the dockers. Tiffin recognised this, and indeed he confided to me on one occasion that he was anxious to repair the damage. He was never given the opportunity.

Three men, then, dominated the union from the General Secretary's chair before Jack Jones. Together they made a profound contribution to the development of organised labour in Britain and also to the political Left, in the widest sense. This book is concerned primarily with the third of the trio, Frank Cousins.

His predecessors, Bevin and Deakin, have already been discussed in substantial studies,[1] but it would be impossible to discuss Cousins's contribution to the TGWU without taking into account what he inherited when he became General Secretary on 11 May 1956. However good or bad a driver he may be judged, he took over a vehicle that was roadworthy as well as powerful. It was in need of serious maintenance and repair and required new motive force and perhaps different fuel, but even so, the machine was an established institution of great power and influence in the Labour Movement, and indeed in the country at large.

No individual who assumes power in such an institution can ignore his inheritance, whatever his wishes may be. To be sure, there is no evidence to suggest that Frank Cousins wanted to ignore it; quite the opposite. But he did want to change the direction of the machine and to change it radically. He took over leadership of the TGWU with a strong sense of loyalty to its traditions, yet he was convinced that the union had slumbered too long under Arthur Deakin and that it was no longer doing its job as effectively as it could, or should. A major shake-up was required. The problem was how to go about it and in what time-scale. No matter how powerful a leader may be, how strong his convictions and how well-developed his administrative abilities, he cannot reshape an institution just by invoking slogans or by passing resolutions. It has been said that the TGWU changed overnight when Cousins replaced Deakin. In some specific ways that is true, but in the larger sense it is a gross oversimplification. There was, after all, the inheritance to contend with. So, before we continue with Frank Cousins's story

---

1. For Bevin, see Alan Bullock, *The Life and Times of Ernest Bevin*, Vol. I (Heinemann, 1960); Trevor Evans, *Bevin* (Allen & Unwin, 1946); Francis Williams, *Ernest Bevin* (Hutchinson, 1952). For Deakin, see V. L. Allen, *Trade Union Leadership* (Longmans, 1957).

let us have a look at this inheritance, which was to shape his own life as well as the history of labour relations in Britain.

A newly-elected union leader does not, of course, inherit an estate with prescribed physical assets, limited or determined by specific statutes of settlement. There is no immutable sovereignty. He does not take over a simple package of effects or a clear-cut sphere of influence defined by legal rights. It is not like succeeding to a constitutional monarchy, although a certain 'spirit of the realm' is in deed involved.

All institutions are more than the sum total of their separate parts. They collect and nourish their own *élan*, their own special and often peculiar loyalties, their own charismas and temperaments, all of which are influenced as much by the times in which they live as by their own precepts. These may be deified or despised, but they cannot be easily changed. A trade union has something more – a deep and abiding class loyalty. The members of most unions are prepared to forgive many sins of omission in their chosen leaders provided they adhere to these basic – though unwritten – tenets of loyalty. Only when leaders are seen to have broken away from their roots (which are, though vaguely, identified with class roots) are they regarded as having violated a sacred bond – like Ramsay Macdonald.

In a union, moreover, there is a constant interplay of ideas, thoughts and even instinctive reactions between members and their officials. This is frequently vicarious, but it is certainly more persistent and intense than most people assume. Democracy is given rather more than lip service inside the trade union structure, not only because of the elective processes, but even more because of the very nature of the voluntary institution. It has become fashionable to deride trade union democracy. To be sure the system is far from perfect; it is sometimes abused or, rather more frequently, exposed to abuse. Yet considering the difficulties inherent in the whole exercise of the democratic process, the unions, with the social and economic balance weighted so heavily against them in the past, have not done badly. If democracy is sometimes under-used, as distinct from ill-used, it is more often due to rank-and-file apathy – an apathy not confined to trade unions – than to autocratic leadership. With all their blemishes the unions are probably the most advanced form of institution providing for 'peoples' participation' that Britain has so far devised. This may sound a large claim, not easy to justify, yet it remains my firm belief.

In any union the inheritance of leadership can never be easy. In a union with the power, influence and resources of the TGWU the complexities loom much larger. Such an organisation must inevitably reflect the strengths and weaknesses of its leading personalities, the hierarchical structure they have created, regardless of the rule-book, and the ambience with which they surround themselves. In every respect the TGWU has been,

INTRODUCTION

and has been *seen* to be, the union of Bevin, Deakin, Cousins and Jack
Jones.

Ernest Bevin *was* the TGWU. Arthure Deakin *was* the TGWU. Both
men, of course, would have refuted such assertions. They never tired of
repeating that *they* would be nowhere without the union, without the loyalty
of the membership and the officials. All that is true, but it is impossible to
separate the powerful stamp of personality from the casting of the union's
'image'. That is what Bevin did from the outset. He cast the image.

Bevin *was* the TGWU in the special sense that it was his idea to establish
a trade union of this type. Was it an original thought? Possibly not. It seems
likely that he was influenced by his experience in the United States. (Bevin
visited the USA in 1915 as a fraternal degelate from the TUC. He paid
special attention to the system of trade departments extensively used by the
American Federation of Labour. They were, in their own way, a kind of
pattern for what eventually became the TGWU.) Nevertheless, in most of
its detail the TGWU was his inspiration. He was not just a trade union
architect. He was a man of 'power' in every sense of that much abused word.
His name stands like a monumental milestone along the path of labour
history in this century. He not only formed the TGWU but, almost at the
same time, reformed the TUC by devising the General Council system as we
know it today. He was a militant and radical union leader in the mid-1920s,
and would then have probably been described, in the language of today, as
'a rebel'. Bevin rallied support for the miners in the General Strike of 1926,
though in the end he recognised the need for the miners to make a settlement. He did not see a revolutionary socialist government as a practical or
desirable option.

Bevin was sceptical of the political wing of the Labour Movement at that
time, and was especially disenchanted by Ramsay Macdonald, whom he
heartily disliked. He was neither surprised nor crushed by the *débâcle* of
1931. He immediately set about salvaging what remained of the parliamentary Labour Party by organising trade union support for its shattered
remnants, and by that act he helped to hold the Party together. From that
time he began to assume an increasingly dominant position in the political
as well as the industrial wing of the Movement. He also moved steadily to
the Right. Bevin found himself in open opposition to men like Stafford
Cripps, Aneurin Bevan and, in the most pronounced conflict of all, with
George Lansbury, who was then 'caretaker' leader of the Party. It was
Bevin's attack on Lansbury at the 1935 Party conference in Margate which
finally defeated the famous pacifist and paved the way for Clement Attlee
to take over the leadership. All this inevitably set the TGWU in a particular
political framework. It also set Bevin in the role of king-maker – and king-
destroyer. Yet he never allowed his political loyalties to the Labour Party to
deflect him from the pursuit of industrial policies which he considered right

for his members, even if on occasion they might embarrass his political friends. He flatly refused to temper his industrial militancy in 1924 when, after the first Labour Government came to office, they asked him to co-operate. Bevin was single-minded in his conviction that the newly-formed TGWU must pursue the strongest possible industrial policies, regardless of their effect on transient Labour governments.

Bevin was not an easy man to tangle with. His handling of people was often gruff to the point of rudeness. He was impatient of critics; he spoke bluntly and sometimes insensitively. He had, in short, many of the characteristic weaknesses which so often mark men of exceptional strength and drive: impatience, a streak of arrogance and, quite often, a touch of absolute ruthlessness. This rubbed off on to the union. The TGWU's reputation with other trade unions was not exactly spotless. It acquired the label of being a 'steamroller', and kept it long after Bevin's departure and throughout Arthur Deakin's reign.

The house that Ernie built was handed on to Arthur. Whatever Deakin might privately have thought of Bevin's edifice – and he was by no means an uncritical admirer or servant of his master – he was compelled to accept *his* inheritance just as Frank Cousins was forced to use what Deakin and Tiffin bequeathed to him. He had, indeed, no overwhelming desire to make radical changes. In any event he had little chance to do so, since he took over command of the union in a 'caretaker' capacity as acting General Secretary in 1940, when Bevin joined Churchill's wartime Coalition Government as Minister of Labour. In effect Deakin held the wheel, but not the compass.

Deakin's background was similar to Bevin's. His childhood was spent in extreme poverty. His father, a village cobbler in Sutton Coldfield, died when Arthur was very young, and his mother struggled on a pittance to bring him up in Dowlais. He became a full-time official of the Dockers' Union in 1919, when he was twenty-nine, and was later absorbed with his union into the TGWU. That was in 1922, when Deakin was an assistant district secretary in the North Wales area. In 1932 he went to London as national secretary of the general workers trade group and came under the influence of Ernest Bevin. Three years later he was appointed Assistant General Secretary.

Although nominally in charge when he succeeded Bevin, Deakin was for-ever casting an anxious glance in the direction of the Ministry of Labour, wondering what Ernie was up to. For his part, Bevin, who still regarded the union as *his*, made a practice of dropping in at Transport House (TGWU headquarters) to make sure that his empire was being effectively and suitably looked after. The TGWU had already become a well-established force. When Deakin took over the General Secretary's chair the membership was 743,349; that was more than double the total at the time of the 1922 amalgamation. In 1941, Deakin's first full year as acting General Secretary, it went over the million mark for the first time. This extraordinary increase – 27.5 per cent in one year – was due to the massive intake of unskilled workers (many of them women) into the war factories.

Deakin's problem was to adjust the union's role to a totally new set of social and industrial conditions. Before the war, the TGWU, like all other unions, operated against a background of mass unemployment and repeated pressure from employers for wage reductions. Now, in wartime, the situation was very different. Of necessity Deakin had to amend the administration of his rapidly growing organisation. And Bevin at the Ministry of Labour was functioning as a kind of protector of trade union interests in general.

Union influence increased as the war-production effort developed. The TUC was brought into national policy-making as never before. Its leaders were introduced into the corridors of Whitehall power in a style and to a degree that had not seemed possible a few years earlier. In this respect Arthur Deakin's inauguration was rather more favourable than Bevin's, a generation earlier, and, indeed, considerably better than Frank Cousins was to find his sixteen years later.

At the same time, greater influence brought new and difficult responsibilities. Any act of irresponsible leadership would have caused serious harm to the war effort and to the trade unions' reputation. It was a testing situation demanding new qualities of leadership and diplomacy in handling totally new problems. There is little doubt that this period was decisive in shaping Deakin's approach after the war, when the unions were called on to continue a policy of political responsibility and economic restraint. A whole generation of union leaders, indeed, were moulded and motivated by their wartime experiences and their involvement with the State machine. War made many changes in British society and the unions could not, even if they had wished to, insulate themselves from these changes.

When Arthur Deakin took over from Bevin, the union's administration had changed little since its formation, in spite of its vastly increased membership and the problems of servicing them. Membership reached a wartime peak of 1,135,165 in 1942; there then followed three years of slight decline in recruitment until, in 1946, there came the largest intake for any single year – 254,851. This was the effect of the first wave of demobilisation. Such remarkable figures tended to conceal the serious weaknesses developing within the Union's administrative structure – weaknesses which in the late 1940s led to charges that the TGWU was 'out of touch' with its members, that it was dictatorial in is handling of affairs as between officials and members and that it had outgrown its 'natural size'.

Deakin was not formally elected General Secretary until 1945, though he had been doing the job since May 1940. Right up to the 1945 General

Election Bevin's position remained uncertain. If the Conservatives had won Bevin would not have become Foreign Secretary, and in all probability he would have returned to his old post as TGWU General Secretary, at least for a time. Indeed, during the brief spell between the ending of the wartime Coalition and the election of the Labour Government – when Churchill ran a 'caretaker government' – Bevin did return to Transport House. However, when Bevin was finally transformed into Britain's Foreign Secretary, Arthur Deakin was confirmed in office. From that moment the TGWU became 'Deakin's union'. It was a difficult time to inherit full power, in a Britain recovering from the exhaustion of war, lacking war's patriotic and political stimulus, moving slowly out of uniform into 'utility' clothing and resenting the continuation of austere wartime conditions.

In 1945 the Labour Government was armed with a programme of widespread social and economic change. This included nationalising basic industries (including coal, railways, gas and electricity), establishing the National Health Service, facing up to the dramatic closure of the Lend-Lease aid from the United States, and negotiating huge new loans to help finance the imports of food and raw materials necessary to restore a peace-time economy. In accomplishing this, the Attlee Government inevitably leaned heavily on all the support it could get from the trade unions. This meant asking their members to accept sacrifices which, in the aftermath of the war, strained the loyalties and often the understanding of the rank and file. It was an earlier form of Social Contract. The most fundamental of these sacrifices was demanded over wage restraint. It was the beginning of an era of government attempts to influence the course, and indeed the character, of collective bargaining, which remains with us today. And these strictures were imposed on unions that were manifestly weak in their administrative structure. The unions were no more prepared for the 'revolution of 1945' than – as things turned out – was the Labour Government itself.

The TGWU membership reached a record point of 1,323,679 in 1948, at the very moment that the Attlee Government finally persuaded the unions to accept a policy of severe wage restraint. We have seen from the experiences of the last twenty-five years that it is difficult enough to administer a policy of wage restraint (or, in more sophisticated language, an incomes policy) in a trade union with a compact, stable and unified membership. How much more difficult, then, to secure acceptance for such a policy in the conditions that prevailed inside the TGWU of 1948–9.

To his credit, Arthur Deakin foresaw some of the problems well in advance. At first he was wholly opposed to what was then loosely described as 'a national wages policy'. In April 1946, writing in the TGWU journal, *The Record*, after a meeting of cabinet ministers and union leaders, Deakin observed :

INTRODUCTION

> There was no disagreement with our declaration that 'wage policy' is a term so vague and uncertain that it may not mean anything but might, in a general way, at some time be interpreted as constituting a 'wage ceiling' which the Trade Union Movement is not prepared to accept. We took our stand on the inalienable right and record of the proved ability of trade unions to raise the standard of living of their members through the usual channels of negotiation.

In other words, Deakin was not prepared to sacrifice one jot of the trade union freedom to continue, as usual, with 'free collective bargaining'. He started off quite clearly by being opposed to what we now call incomes policy.

In 1947 Deakin publicly rebuked Sir Stafford Cripps – then Minister for Economic Affairs – for suggesting wage restraint. But Government pressure on the unions grew as Attlee's cabinet encountered mounting difficulties in its programme of post-war reconstruction. The TUC was brought increasingly into the Government's confidence, and the opposition to wage restraint visibly weakened – at least at the level of top leadership. By 1948 Deakin, along with the majority of the TUC Economic Committee, had been swung over to accept the pay freeze proposed by Cripps, then Chancellor of the Exchequer. There was no enthusiasm about the change, but the facts of life as presented by the Cabinet left the TUC leadership, they believed, with absolutely no option. To the last, Deakin was a reluctant convert. He knew the problems it would expose inside his own and other unions. Ultimately, however, all were driven by a loyalty to the Labour Government, though they were soon to realise that loyalty was no substitute for a carefully explained and equitably shared policy of economic sacrifice. Inside the Cabinet, Ernest Bevin unquestionably had a great deal to do with the conversion. Frequently Attlee asked Bevin to take the chair at meetings between the Government and the TUC. His arguments, on both sides of the fence, were particularly well informed, hard to resist and still harder to contest. Even so, Deakin demanded equal restraint on profits and strong government measures to keep prices stable – familiar arguments to contemporary ears. The Government promised to do all in its power, though already it had few illusions about the limitations of that power as far as profits and prices were concerned.

The wage restraint policy was launched at a special conference of the TUC in March 1948. A conference of union executives endorsed the Government's appeal for restraint – and by so doing opened up a completely new phase in the relationship between government and unions. It was, in effect, the first significant pact of its kind in peace-time Britain. But by mid-1950 the treaty was already wearing thin at the edges. Many unions were in revolt against a policy which in practice simply meant that working people were bearing the brunt of the economic crisis while other sections of the community were continuing to enjoy considerable economic freedom. The policy was overturned at the TUC conference in 1950, despite advice from the General Council and in the face of a fierce rearguard action fought by Arthur Deakin himself.

Deakin continued to support the principle of restraint in broad terms right up to his death in 1955, although in practice he permitted his officials to negotiate substantial pay increases for TGWU members. His apparent ambivalence led to increasing strains within the TGWU and, at times, to open revolt against his leadership. Mounting tensions between sections, and even within the same trade group, led to friction between Deakin and some of his national officers – in particular Frank Cousins, who then led the road haulage group.

It was at this time that Deakin also became publicly involved in a running fight with the Communists, both inside the union and on the world political stage. To the outside observer it often appeared that he was obsessed by the spectre of the Communist Dragon almost to the exclusion of everything else. It seemed to warp and distort his judgment even in relation to minor industrial issues. Any trouble inside the TGWU, however remote from the hand of Moscow or even King Street (the Communist Party HQ in London), was usually attributed to Communist plotting. No doubt Deakin was justified in believing that the Communists were bent on undermining his authority, but he heavily overplayed his anti-Communism in his often absurd over-reaction. There was, of course, a personal background to his emotional responses. When he took over from Bevin he found an increasing number of Communists and left-wing members being elected to the union executive. Aware of Deakin's sensitivities the newcomers tended to goad him deliberately, although they would not have taken the same liberties with Bevin. Deakin grew increasingly intolerant of such irritants, and there was constant friction between the acting General Secretary and the Communists on the executive – even when Soviet Russia was our gallant and respected ally. But the open break did not come until after the war, when the international situation worsened and Anglo-Soviet relations deteriorated.

Another attempt was made at that time to revive a unified trade union international by founding the World Federation of Trade Unions (WFTU). From 1942 delicate negotiations continued between the British TUC and Soviet trade union leadership after the formation of the Anglo-Soviet Trade Union Committee. At that point Arthur Deakin had little to do with the operation. When the WFTU was launched in 1945 the first President was Sir Walter (now Lord) Citrine, General Secretary of the TUC. Hopes were high that the wartime alliance with the Soviet Union would ripen and flower into a peace-time *entente* which would help to rebuild and reform the whole of Europe and beyond. Not everyone shared this sanguine view. Bevin, by then ensconced in the Foreign Office, certainly did not. His suspicions of Soviet motives were already well developed. And when Arthur Deakin was nominated by the British TUC as President of the WFTU in 1946 (Citrine having moved on to take a job with the newly-formed National Coal Board) Bevin advised him against taking the post. Deakin rejected Bevin's advice; he believed it was possible to work with the Russians and certainly felt that it was a platform he could not refuse to test.

The outcome is well known : there were deep-rooted suspicions on both sides and dubious motives were ascribed to everybody by everybody. The attempt to continue the wartime alliance collapsed as decisively in the trade union sphere as it did in the wider diplomatic one, and there is no reason to suppose that the two spheres were separable.

Deakin attempted to contain the WFTU within strictly 'industrial' issues, seeking to divert the Soviet delegation from the political tensions already developing on the world stage. It was an unrealistic attempt – and it failed. At the Paris conference of the WFTU in January 1949 he led a Western walk-out, leaving the World Federation mostly confined to the Communist bloc countries. In June he was one of the leading figures in preparing the way for a new trade union international, divorced from the Communist bloc: the International Confederation of Free Trade Unions (ICFTU), which was formed at a Constituent Assembly in London in December 1949. Thus ended the wartime alliance between the trade union organisations of the West and the Soviet Union; it was a bleak moment in international relations generally. The Cold War had started; Stalin had contemptuously turned down the Marshall Plan for the economic revival of Europe; the Berlin blockade and its counter, the Western air-lift, were in the background; and the Korean War was about to start. This period marked the peak of anti-Communist feeling in the British trade union movement, and at the TGWU's biennial delegate conference in July 1949 Deakin had little difficulty in persuading the delegates to bar Communists from holding any office in the TGWU.

The vote was 426 to 208. Nine full-time officials of the union refused to sign a document declaring that they were *not* Communists. They were sacked. (This ban was rescinded at the union's rules revision conference at Belfast in July 1968 – see pp. 561–5).

It is generally believed that the ban on Communists came naturally to Arthur Deakin, obsessed as he appears to have been by the 'Red Menace'. That is not the case. Privately, he was reluctant to take this step, even after his experiences in the WFTU. Frank Cousins himself emphasised, in conversation with the author, that Deakin really did believe in freedom of thought and expression, and would have preferred to fight the Communists openly within the union rather than expel them.

None the less, once the decision had been taken, it was exercised with ruthless and sometimes vindictive thoroughness – though not always by

Deakin himself. People were sometimes moved out of their jobs for generally leftish views, whether they were card-carrying Communists or not. Often they were replaced by men whose principal qualification was their anti-Communism. This added to the already serious defects in the union's administration and sometimes led to a manifest deterioration in the quality of service offered to its members. Unorthodox views were treated as heresy, regardless of whether they were formally Communist views or not. The over-reaction against Communists spread beyond the TGWU into other trade unions and even into the TUC itself.

It was a period in union affairs when the nonconformist, the iconoclast, the unorthodox and the plain straightforward rebel had a more than usually difficult time. This was the period when Frank Cousins began to emerge as a force, as a new name to be reckoned with, inside the Transport and General Workers' Union.

Let us go back to his emergence first of all, in 1904; to the background of his birth.

Chapter One

THE STRUGGLE BEGINS

You could say that within the thirty-two-mile radius from Clay Cross, Derbyshire, lies the crucible of the first industrial revolution. Sheffield, Derby, Nottingham, Newark, Rotherham and Doncaster all stand within this circle, which overlaps into Yorkshire, Nottinghamshire and almost up to the borders of Lancashire and Staffordshire. Just outside the circle are Manchester, Birmingham, Leeds and Leicester. Inside this area lies much of the history of the technological, economic and social upheavals which combined to produce the Industrial Revolution and later convulsions which swept through the whole of the nineteenth century. From this crucible much of England as we know it has emerged. The impact of events has carved the landscape, moulded the people and in turn affected the world.

The Cousins family drifted into the area about 170 years ago. It is not clear where their previous roots lay. The founder of the dynasty in Clay Cross was Thomas Cousins, who married Eliza Turner, a girl from Sutton Coldfield, in 1853. Tom Turner had lived at Heague, eight miles from Clay Cross, where he was a schoolmaster. He was compelled to give up his teaching job when an illness left him deformed and crippled. He became a tailor and moved to Clay Cross, where there was a greater demand for clothing than in the surrounding villages. Tom Cousins' parents, John and Rachel, appear to have moved into Derbyshire at about the turn of the last century. According to family records they both came from Kent and were descended from early Huguenot settlers, but the evidence for this is at best extremely sketchy.

Once settled in Clay Cross, Tom and Eliza Cousins made a modest living out of the tailor's shop. Four years after their marriage, a daughter, Esther, was born on 10 September 1857. She was to become the grandmother of Frank Cousins. Esther was probably the dominant, and was certainly the most prolonged, influence on the paternal side of the Cousins family.

1

She had no formal education. A rudimentary schooling system had only just begun, and this provided only for the children of employees of the Clay Cross Company itself (founded by George Stephenson). Esther was certainly not one of that privileged class. She could neither read nor write, though in later years, when she ran her own little sweetshop in the front room of her terrace house, she evolved a most complicated accounting system of her own, worked out on a slate. From an early age, though, Esther, showed an unusual independence of mind and character. Like most girls in the area she went into domestic service as soon as she could be spared from home, and by her early teens she had already worked for several of the local landed squirearchy. There is an unproven suggestion that she was at one time employed at the Duke of Devonshire's Chatsworth estate.

At nineteen, Esther became pregnant and on 3 November 1877 she gave birth to Charles, who became the father of Frank Cousins.

The child appears on his birth-certificate as Charles Fox Cousins. The name and occupation of the father are not given. The certificate is signed by Esther with an X.

Esther was known to have had an affair with the son of a wealthy farmer in the neighbourhood, though this remains clouded by gossip and rumour, and precisely how far her perambulations took her while she was in domestic service can never be known. The one man who may have shared her secret was John William Fox, whom she eventually married. 'Bill' Fox was much older than Esther, and appears to have raised no objection to marrying a girl who had already borne a child. Perhaps in appreciation of this act of generosity, Esther gave Charles the middle name of Fox, insisting that his surname must be her maiden one of Cousins. Some eight years later Esther and Bill had a daughter of their own, Eliza Ann.

By now Bill Fox had become a railwayman – a natural enough choice in Clay Cross for men looking beyond the traditional limits of farm labouring or domestic work. He was a dull though kindly man; slow moving, somewhat infirm, but an amiable and good husband to Esther.

According to E. H. Cousins, Eliza Ann once asked her father who Charles's father was. He answered: 'I was his father.' But there is strong division of opinion in the Cousins family on this point and the general view suggests that Bill Fox was a most improbable father for Charlie: 'Uncle Bill was, to put it mildly, perhaps inadequate for [Esther's] lively spirit. He was extremely passive, though a pleasant enough person.' Yet E. H. Cousins goes on to state: 'I think you can discount the story of Charlie's father being of the gentry. I knew him, and he bore a considerable likeness in physical characteristics to William Fox. He walked the same way. But facially he featured Esther.'

So the mystery remains unresolved. Frank Cousins himself had little evidence to offer, though he cast strong doubt on William Fox being his grandfather.

If there is doubt about the paternal influence, there can be none about the influence of Grandma Esther. She remained a woman of extraordinary resource until her death in 1936 at the age of seventy-nine. Frank Cousins has said that Esther was one of the three women who had most impact on him as a child – and even later in his life. The other two were his own mother, Hannah, and Hannah's mother, Grandma Smith.

Charlie Fox Cousins left school before he was twelve. In 1889 there was still no free education in Clay Cross and it cost 2d. a week to keep him at school, a waste of good money when a lad of twelve could be usefully employed in one of the local industries, bringing home a valuable contribution to the family income. His first job was in the pits, at a colliery on Whittington Moor, but after about four years the young Charles decided to try his luck in the big city of Nottingham, twenty-one miles from his home. He sounded out the possibilities of getting a job in the Colwick locomotive sheds at Carlton, Nottingham, which were opened in 1886 and gradually extended. Manpower was being drawn into the railway industry, as the word spread that it was better than working in the mines, pay being competitive with miners' wages and the work less arduous, cleaner and less dangerous. Moreover, it was a brand-new industry with all kinds of bright opportunities. Even so, Charlie had got used to working in the pits and his first move away from Clay Cross was to a mine in County Clare in Southern Ireland; but he was soon back. There was no black gold in Ireland, and not much excitement. His next job was as a fireman-driver in the engine sheds at Carlton.

Charlie Cousins had settled into the railway environment of this Nottingham district when he met Hannah Smith, the daughter of a Methodist mining family living in near-by Bulwell, with whom Charlie had found lodgings. His fireman's job was reasonably well paid by the standards of the day – about 25s. a week – and after a while Charlie began courting the daughter of the house, a fine, well-built, attractive girl. It was a long courtship. Charlie had been in Carlton for about six years when they married on 20 December 1900. Charlie was just twenty-three and Hannah nearly four years younger.

Grandmother Hannah Smith, who later lived with the Cousins family in Doncaster, is remembered as an austere, arrogant woman, who could convey her feelings with the flick of an eyebrow or the twitch of a lip. She suffered fools badly, and what she saw as irregular behaviour even more so. Her daughter, styled and named like her mother, embodied many of these characteristics, and it is little wonder that she was to become the most dominant influence in the grooming of her eldest son, Frank.

Charles and Hannah Cousins set up home in Bulwell, at 28 Minerva Street, in 1901. Minerva Street is still a typical provincial working-class street which has changed little 'in outward appearance since the Cousins family lived there. The houses were built towards the end of the last century in terraces of four, linked together, a covered arched passage-way separating each terrace and leading to back yards and gardens, which were about twenty feet long. The houses front on to the street: flat and red-bricked, the front steps scrubbed and blockstoned cream or white. Number 28 has three bedrooms, no bathroom, two rooms and a kitchen downstairs with the front parlour opening on to the street. When the Cousins family lived there, the rent was 5s. 3d. a week – tolerably expensive by the standards of the day, but Bulwell was a prosperous zone. Not only was it in the heart of a rich and developing mining area, but it had the new railway depots and an already thriving industry of hosiery and lace. Indeed it was one of the most affluent of Britain's new industrial areas. Good wages were being earned; the workers spent easily, and prices, including rents, tended to reflect the availability of ready cash.

This was the background against which Frank Cousins was born on 8 September 1904. But when Frank was three years old the family moved to Doncaster. The South Yorkshire coalfield was then expanding rapidly and Charlie felt the tug to return to the pits. It is also possible that he wanted to establish his own particular base in life away from his in-laws, the Smiths, at Bulwell, and away still further from Clay Cross, off into an area that was new and different, where he could start afresh to bring up his own family. They moved to Doncaster to settle in a new housing development at Wheatley, right on the edge of the colliery area, and Charlie signed on for work at Brodsworth colliery, then just opening up. It was the pit where he was to remain for the rest of his working life.

Brodsworth colliery was about $4\frac{1}{2}$ miles away from the Cousins's house. The only way to get there, before miners took to riding bicycles, was the special colliers' train, known as the Paddy Train, from Doncaster station. Only a minority of miners lived in Doncaster town itself (most of them having their homes in the pit villages), and travel to and from the pit was always a fatiguing task in the days before pithead baths and fast transport. The attraction of living on top of the pit was it saved the burden of dragging weary limbs and filthy clothing for long distances after a shift. But Charlie Cousins preferred to live at a distance and would get up at 4.30 a.m. to reach Brodsworth in time for the 6 a.m. shift, rather than bring up his family in the closed environment of a colliery community. Every morning he walked to the station to catch the Paddy Train – there was no formal station, merely a halt platform. Older miners in the area still recall miners gambling and fighting on pay nights while they waited for the train back to Doncaster.

It was a hard, tough school. There were certainly no frills to the routine of existence for miners or their families in the Doncaster area in those early days of the century. Here is a description of a typical miners' housing estate in the district:

> The houses were built of brick units of four or six with a brick wall round each unit. The accommodation was adequate for family needs, though the amenities left much to be desired. There was a living-room with a Yorkshire grate and a small side boiler; this had to be filled by a hand ladle (or lading can) with cold water from the scullery, and since there was no tap it had to be emptied in the same way.
>
> Leading from the living-room was the scullery with its sink and copper; there was of course only a cold water tap. The copper was filled with cold water ladled from the sink tap and heated by a coal fire underneath. The hot water for washday was obtained in this manner and again was ladled from the copper to a wash-tub. Most housewives boiled white clothes in the copper and with a copper-stick lifted the hot steaming clothes into a wash-tub of clean water to be rinsed. There was no bathroom or fixed bath in these houses and so the copper provided hot water for the men returning from work. Usually a portable zinc bath was used and this had to be filled and emptied by hand. There were no pithead baths in those early days. Some people built a wooden shed (or lean-to) near the back door and often this acted as a bathroom for the men. Womenfolk bathed in front of the fire in winter or in the scullery when the house was quiet and free from the intrusion of men and children. To reach the W.C. one went out of the back door and round the end of the house.[1]

First of all the Cousins family lived in the north-eastern district of Wheatley, at 65, St Mary's Road, and Frank began his school life round the corner at Beckett Road School. When he was ten the family moved across Doncaster to Balby, on the south-western side of the town. There were a number of reasons behind the move. Not the least was that by 1914 Charles and Hannah had increased the size of the family to six, three boys and three girls. Moreover, Charles was not a man who wanted to spend all his waking hours in a strictly mining community. He was first of all a family man and felt that it might be better to bring up his children in a less concentrated environment. In a pit village or pit dormitory area it was inevitable and inescapable to meet the men you worked with and few others. Charlie Cousins had no desire to spend the rest of his working life this way and was not enthusiastic about his children following him to the coal face. Perhaps there was a touch of snobbery in his attitude, though he was a miner down to the very grit and grime under his fingernails.

1. M. E. and A. Lawrence, 'How a Colliery Village Came into Being, 1910–1914', in *The South Yorkshire Historian*, I (1971).

Charlie Cousins's huge frame, six feet one inch tall, was proportioned like a boxer's : his chest was structured in the shape of a sinewy cage, and he never carried much surplus flesh. To his last day – he died when he was eighty-two – he never developed a paunch. His pride in his own strength was matched by a quiet, even superior, dignity. Straightforward in his dealings with other men, he was not easily roused, but when stirred he reacted like flexed steel. Charlie could, and did, drink his share of beer with his mining mates, but he did not count that as a proof of his manhood. He was proud of his children, keen to see them get on a bit better than himself, and strict without being overbearing. He was deeply devoted to Hannah, and was never once known to stray towards another woman. Frank Cousins recalls the first time his father *invited* him, a miner of eighteen, into a pub, during a day out in Sheffield. Charlie ordered two pints of beer, and as he did so a flashy girl sidled in beside him and piped up, 'And a gin for me, please, luv,' looking hard at Charlie. Frank vividly recalls his father's spontaneous reaction as he turned back to the barman and added, 'And a pint of water to pour over this cow's head'.

The Cousins home in Balby – 10, Alexandra Road – was a ten-roomed terrace house. It was altogether larger than the house in Wheatley, ample enough for the family they had then acquired, although it gradually became overcrowded as the numbers increased to ten children. Balby was more of a railwaymen's suburb than a miners' area. The new Doncaster railway works were within easy reach, and the district was being developed more spaciously than Wheatley. There was also a new elementary school in the next street, King Edward Road. Started at the turn of the century and completed in 1908, it was one of the 'new-style' single-storey, red-brick buildings springing from the expansion in State education for the children of working-class families. Frank went there in September 1914, a month after the start of World War One.

It was not exactly the most propitious moment for the ten-year-old son of a miner to be starting in a new elementary school. Classes of forty or fifty were commonplace; facilities were absurdly meagre; teaching staff was hard to come by and was soon made scarcer still by the demands of war. But Frank was lucky in his headmaster, William Richard Grundy, a devoted and hard-working teacher who did his best to secure and maintain a standard he had painstakingly set. A school of that kind was endowed with extremely limited funds, but unsparing hopefulness. Spirit and devotion never quite compensated for the lack of material support, yet they had their inspiring qualities. Grundy kept the school functioning against the odds.

The school logbook for the period contains this illuminating note :

On 20th October 1914 part of the school building was closed for the billeting of soldiers and hence all the boys were taken to Hexthorpe and Balby

Bridge Clubs [that is Trades and Labour Clubs] for their lessons. Work was done under considerable difficulties made even worse early in 1915 by a shortage of one teacher, though on 31st May 1915 all returned to the school premises when the troops had departed for the Western Front.

The current headmaster of Balby Junior School, Mr C. M. H. Bishop, notes that

October 1915 saw more difficulties due to military billeting, when the children were taught in the Great Northern Railway Mess Rooms, a considerable distance away from the school. An entry dated June 1916 by Mr Grundy noted that due to the hours of work, shortage of staff, unsuitable premises, etc., all of which were causing difficulties, the school was now unable to keep the pace of work up to the prescribed syllabus. (This was of course the era of 'payment by results' under the system of class standards.)

Frank Cousins won no distinction as a scholar, and there is no mention of him in the school log. That is not surprising, since, as Mr Bishop further explains, 'the mention of any pupil's name for good, or bad, was an extremely rare entry in those days'. Moreover, the school routine was so severely disrupted by wartime conditions that few items appeared in the logbook other than the headmaster's reflections on the difficulties of running a school at all. It was difficult enough in peace-time for a child from a working-class household to rise above his environmental limitations and move up through the State system into a grammar school, because of what we would now describe as the 'cultural poverty' of so many of those homes. They suffered from the absence of books, the sheer lack of time for parents to give their children the encouragement required to develop an interest in learning, and, perhaps the most critical of all obstacles, the knowledge that at fourteen the child would be required to go out to work without delay to help the household to survive. These have always been powerful forces militating against working-class children remaining at school and progressing through the system. It was immeasurably more difficult in the conditions prevailing in elementary schools during World War I.

King Edward Road School did develop a reputation as a 'sports academy', giving a number of notable footballers and cricketers to the Doncaster area. Frank Cousins himself was not a particularly outstanding games player. He went in for the usual things – soccer, cricket, a bit of boxing and athletics – but, though he was already a big lad for his age, there was no evidence of any special talent for a particular sport. Probably his most accomplished performances were in the school swimming teams.

· Nor did he establish any strong links with other boys at this school. This was due less to his shyness than to the economic pressures on the Cousins household. After school hours the Cousins children had to join in the co-

7

operative attempt to sustain a large household on one man's wage. Charlie Cousins was then bringing home about £2 a week, sometimes as much as £2 10s. after a good production week at the pit. That was a high wage for 1914. Few trades were then paid more than the miners. None the less it was still a struggle to maintain a family of ten children on such a pay packet. The rent of 10, Alexandra Road ranged from eight to ten shillings a week, about a fifth of a good week's pay; and Hannah was given about thirty shillings a week on which to feed and clothe the household and to try and save for the occasional treat and for the Christmas spree. There was nothing to spare.

The girls had to help with the cooking and the cleaning, the boys with the general upkeep of the household and maintenance and repair. Each boy had his particular task allocated by his father. Frank's job was to chop the firewood and get in the coals each day. George peeled the potatoes for the entire family. Brother Charlie was given the job of kneading the dough for Hannah's daily breadmaking, and was also cast as shoe-repairer; but this was not a very onerous task since frequently the family could only afford one shoe-repair a week. The jobs were sometimes switched and added to. Frank cleaned the cutlery and kept it in good shape. It was non-stop every day, and these domestic jobs took precedence over everything else: they had to be properly done before the children went out or applied their minds to any marginal activities such as reading. Charles Cousins, though a kind and fair-minded father, was none the less unbending in ensuring that the family code was strictly adhered to.

He was the dominant father figure, but at the apex of it all was Hannah, a woman of enormous character. She commanded the home with an extraordinary authority and a sharp, rugged tongue, frequently given to an expletive, but also with a motherly warmth and understanding which evoked respect and love from her children. In the minds of the Cousins family to this day, she remains the person who provided them with that special reserve of spiritual security which binds groups of people together and fortifies their instinctive behaviour.

In the home she did all the baking and made and mended most of the children's clothes. During bad weeks when Charlie's pay-packet was slim she would hawk round her home-made cakes. She produced meals for the family of twelve from the most limited resources, yet they never went short. There was never any real want in the Cousins household, though they were often near the brink. It was a constant, never-ending struggle, yet Hannah was rarely seen to be miserable. She laughed with an infectious gaiety that inspired the family and softened the hardships. She played the piano to cheer them up – not as a conscious act of showmanship to produce a false sense of well-being, but simply because she liked to 'bang about on the piano'. In fact, she was quite a good pianist.

Frank's description of his mother has its own particular flavour: 'Dad was a gentleman, firm but fair. Mother was a very dominant woman. She was frightened of no man, or woman.' Frank goes on:

Of course, there were always two sides to growing up with a man and woman like my mother and father. Mother was dominant, proud, always striving to make ends meet; buying where she could as cheaply as she could; scraping and making do with astonishing economy. Mother would always sacrifice her own welfare for that of her family.

But it was always difficult. My earliest recollections are of how difficult our life was and how little money there was to spare. I was inclined to be a serious-minded lad. Perhaps it was the constant feeling of insecurity in the economic sense. We had little to laugh about, though we tried. As a matter of fact I don't ever recall feeling foolhardy or light-hearted with humour when I was a kid. Of course I had my dreams. But I was always conscious of the fact that mother was struggling to feed us as a family. Conscious too that when I went to work, as the oldest lad in the family, I was quickly to become the principal breadwinner.

Charlie Cousins would lay down the rules of the household; but Hannah made sure they were carried out, and she could, at times, reveal quite a temper when the children were slow to obey. Father insisted that all the children should be home by 9 o'clock at the latest. Five past nine was not permissible. It was the only way to establish a system of discipline in a large family under such economic pressures.

Shortly after they moved to Alexandra Road, the fourth son, Walter, was born. He was followed, at approximate intervals of two years, by Ethel, Harry and finally Eva, who was born in March 1920. By that time Frank was almost sixteen, and both he and George were working with their father at Brodsworth colliery. Frank's eldest surviving sister, Ida, underlines the point about the age-spread of the Cousins family: 'There were really two quite separate generations among my brothers and sisters'.

Frank, George and Charlie junior were the three brothers most closely linked in age and temperament. Frank and George also spent much of their earlier working life in the same, or parallel, jobs. The three brothers usually shared the same attic bedroom at home, and often the same thoughts; and Walter was later accepted into the 'special community' of that attic life. When the family moved again, to a council house in St Peter's Road, in the near-by district of Hexthorpe, Frank, George and Charlie once again shared a bedroom, but that move came after Frank and George had left school and were working at Brodsworth. Walter and Harry were separated from Frank by age, and indeed it seems by temperament, to such a degree that they never really enjoyed a close relationship. Of course, it has to be remembered that Harry, Frank's youngest brother, was still at school when Frank married.

It was much the same with the sisters. Hannah, the eldest of the whole family, was probably the closest to Frank, both in age and temperament and certainly in political conviction. Her death was a severe blow to him. The next eldest sister, Nellie, was an ailing girl and died when she was only twenty-seven. Ida, eight years younger than Frank, still recalls the early family days at Alexandra Road with warmth. She echoes her brothers' views about the Cousins's closeness as a family unit, about the gaiety of the home, despite all the economic pressures and problems. 'It was,' she says, 'a cheerful home, and the lads, especially, had a lot of fun.' She recalls that Frank's great interests were motor-bikes, swimming, sport in general and dancing.

'He had an obsession with motor-bikes, though,' she says. 'He was always messing about with them, taking them to bits and rebuilding them.' There were few books in the house, as far as she can recall, but this did not mean that there was no reading. 'Dad was a studious man', says Ida, 'and I can recall how he would sit down in the evenings and pick up an encyclopaedia he'd borrowed from the library and read it from beginning to end. He had a remarkable memory for all kinds of things, and he was also very good at figures. I think that's where Frank got a lot of his intellect from.'

Frank Cousins left King Edward Road School in 1918, shortly before his fourteenth birthday and towards the end of World War I. Mr Grundy wrote 'Promising' at the foot of his school-leaving report which was good as far as it went. By this time Frank had a particular passion for reading. He liked adventure stories, books on astronomy and stories about science, discovery and technology. He was avid to fill his mind with knowledge, to learn new words and their meanings, to discover something of life. Yet the horizons were cramped, the opportunities virtually nonexistent and the immediate pressures inescapable. His school life had been stunted and disjointed. The wartime period had stirred his imagination and opened up his mind to new names and feelings and ideas. But it was all in an unformed state : there were no clear definitions, no standard texts against which to measure his thoughts and dreams, only the stability of the home and the omnipresent authority of mother and father. But the spare-time jobs he had taken while still at school – delivering newspapers, riding the butcher's bike to deliver weekend supplies – had all given the young Frank some sense of proportion and an early understanding of what was involved in balancing dreams and ambitions against need and necessity.

Frank was not an extrovert child. He did not seek the company of schoolboy groups or gangs; there was no Alexandra Road Lads' Brigade to attract the young Cousins. He was curiously shy and even clumsy. He himself confessed that he was 'a sensitive youngster, frightened to death of some of the things that used to happen, in and out of the home'. He would dream occasionally of becoming a tea-planter in one of those faraway parts of the British Empire about which he had learned at school. It sounded attractive, interesting, remote and utterly different from anything he could see across the Doncaster landscape. It was one of those strange, escapist childhood dreams, like being a deep-sea diver, an explorer, even an engine-driver. But 'Promising' or not, Frank went into the pit. He was the first of the sons to follow in Charlie's footsteps, treading that well-worn track, so natural in mining areas, in spite of all the silent hopes of ambitious mothers.

Brothers George and Charlie agree that Frank ought 'by right' to have gone to a secondary or even a grammar school. By all accounts he had the potential, or 'the promise'. But it was out of the question, a mere academic fantasy that had no more relationship with reality than the idea of going to Ceylon, India or Burma to become a wealthy tea-planter.

On the morning of 9 September 1918 Frank and his father cycled to Brodsworth to sign the book. The induction process was simple and clear. The introductions around the pit – 'Charlie Cousins's boy', and so on – were performed as a ritual. And then it was down the pit to see how things were done. There was also the union. Charlie was a staunch trade unionist, a member of the Yorkshire Miners' Association, part of the Miners' Federation of Great Britain. One of the first things he did was to *instruct* Frank to join the YMA. Frank Cousins tells what happened in that first week at Brodsworth:

> My dad, who was a member of the trade union and Labour Movement, made me open my first pay packet [it contained 23s. 10d.] and join the union . . . I thought he was a shocker. I wanted to take it home to Mum, you know, the way that kids do when they get their first pay packet. But Dad said to me quite clearly – this is the place where you get your protection, you go and join the union. And that was that.[2]

Joining the mining industry in September 1918 was just about as unpropitious as starting school in August 1914.

The miners were claiming a six-hour day, an increase in basic wages and national ownership of the mines. In the national interest the mines had been controlled by the Government for the duration of the war, but now the Government was anxious to return them to the colliery owners. To avoid having to make a snap decision, it offered a special commission to investigate the miners' claims. Sir John (later Lord) Sankey was appointed its chairman. The Sankey Commission came up with a new charter for the miners. Three interim reports, issued in 1919, recommended that the working day should be reduced from eight hours to seven, and that a six-hour day should be seriously considered; that wages should be increased by 2s. a day for men and 1s. for boys; and that government control over the coal industry should

2. John Freeman's 'Face to Face' interview with Frank Cousins, 15 October 1961, by kind permission of John Freeman and the BBC.

continue. In effect the Commission was proposing a form of nationalisation. The Government accepted the proposals on wages and hours, but evaded the issue of control. The strike threatening the coal industry in 1919 was averted, but only for a time.

It was a harsh enough baptism for the young Frank Cousins. Already he had begun to learn what working life was about. His first underground job was as a haulage hand on the transport system between the coal face and the supply lines to the pit surface, and it was there that he ran into his first clash with authority at work, when he flatly refused to call the underground manager 'Sir'.

Frank could be stubborn even at the age of fourteen. When the manager threatened to take the complaint to Cousins senior, Frank said: 'All right. Tell my dad.'

Charlie was disturbed when he was called into the manager's office and heard the facts, and he asked for the boy to be brought in.

'What's the trouble, Frank?' he demanded. 'Why do you object to calling the manager "Sir"?'

'I don't think you ought to say "Sir" except to those who are very old or to those you respect,' replied Frank, quite unruffled.

Charlie was a bit nonplussed. He turned to the manager with a shrug.

'Well, I don't suppose you can quarrel with that, can you?' he said.

The rebel was grooming himself at an early stage.

Chapter Two

GROWING UP AT WORK

At the outset, life in the pits was exciting and physically demanding for the young Cousins. Known as 'Charlie Cousins's kid', which was a mark of affection, Frank soon realised that the family's respect and regard for their father was widely shared: Charlie was held in great esteem at Brodsworth. The work in the underground haulage system was hard and tiring for the youngster, but there was a special thrill to the job: it was 'man's work'. Frank felt himself suddenly to have grown up. Almost overnight the world had enlarged. There was something unique about work in the pits: an instinctive fellowship, a community of spirit, a certain quality of response which it is hard to match in any other working group. It helped to compensate the young Frank for the physical fatigue, as well as the mental strain of adjusting to an adult world.

He was proud of the part he was now playing in helping to support the family. His contribution was important: almost half his father's wage. A slight euphoria appeared over the landscape and the Cousins household felt that 'things' might be improving at last. The Armistice came soon after Frank started work, and by 1919 Britain was feeling an upsurge of post-war optimism, as the 'replacement boom' swept across the country. Gradually Frank grew more accustomed to the rigours of colliery life, helped by his feeling of security in having his father working in the same pit. The youngsters tended to be protected by the older miners, although the elders often had to prevent some of the young lads risking injury in attempting to prove that they could do a 'man's job'.

Throughout the first year at Brodsworth, Frank Cousins was enthralled with this new world. There soon began the apprenticeship for more active work nearer to the coal face, and he transferred from being a plain haulage hand to a pony carrier, with the job of looking after the ponies in the haulage system. This is where he had his first pit accident. One of the ponies hauling coal wagons suddenly went wild and in a frenzied surge tried to break away from the haulage lines. The danger was acute and obvious. Had the pony dragged the wagons off the track there would have been a serious accident. Frank managed to restrain the pony but in doing so he was pinned against a pit prop, badly injuring his back, arm and hand. He was off work for some time, and the accident left him with a permanently buckled little finger on his left hand – an injury which was later to play a crucial part in determining the course of his life.

By the time the 1921 lock-out hit the coal industry Frank had worked in the pit for two and a half years. Mining had become part of his life-style, and his younger brother, George, now joined the family group at Brodsworth. The income of the Cousins family had measurably increased, but so too had their expenditure. The family was growing up, and it was no easier to feed twelve people in 1921 than it had been on a smaller income in 1918. And it was at this point that the three-month pit closure hit the Cousins family, along with the families of nearly a million other miners. The bulk of wage-earners were now insured against unemployment, but benefits were low – at the rate of 15s. a week for men and 12s. for women.

The mines, like the railways, were in the process of being handed back to their private owners who had yielded control for the duration of the war, and in both railways and mines the pressure was on to force reductions in wages because of the general state of the economy. The miners' reply to this was to appeal to the TUC and the Labour Party to launch a political counter-attack against the Government's plans. The miners wanted the Sankey Report implemented; they wanted nationalisation. But Lloyd George would not – and indeed could not – risk losing Conservative support within his Coalition Government, which remained firmly committed to supporting the employers in their policy of wage reductions. The miners also sought to revive the Triple Alliance with the railwaymen and transport workers – an alliance negotiated in 1914–15 but shelved because of the war. This was designed as a mutual-aid pact in which all constituents would support any single member under attack.

The first step by the government was an announcement that it would decontrol both mines and railways on 31 August 1921; but the date for the transfer of the mines back to their old owners was advanced five months because of the industry's heavy financial losses. The coal-owners immediately demanded substantial wage-cuts, which the miners refused to accept. On 31 March 1921, the day of decontrol, the miners were locked out by an abrupt ending of all prevailing wage agreements. The Miners' Federation called on the Triple Alliance for support. At first, the railwaymen and transport workers agreed to strike with the miners from 16 April, but because the miners broke off informal talks with the Government and refused to re-open negotiations, the railwaymen's leader, J. H. Thomas, cancelled the strike decision and the transport workers did likewise. The Triple Alliance collapsed on what has become known in labour history as 'Black Friday', 15 April 1921. But the miners stayed out of the pits, refusing to accept wage reductions, until the end of June, when they were finally compelled to knuckle under. They went back – those, at least, that the coal-owners chose to take back – defeated, dejected and bitter, and to lower wages.

Frank Cousins was not yet seventeen, but that episode had a traumatic effect on his mind, his feelings and his entire attitude to life. He was in his formative years, wide open to impressions of personal and social behaviour. What happened in Doncaster and in the South Yorkshire coalfield had a profound effect. He was not, then, a political animal of any special kind. No one, then, would have picked him out as a potential labour leader. He was one of many thousands, the kid son of a miner, a kid miner himself, emotionally damaged by the brutalities of a system which, without any guidance from academic political scientists or socialist books, was already appearing in his young eyes as absurd and immoral.

Frank Cousins reached his late teens in a period of severe depression, political confusion, and economic turmoil. The entire trade union movement was on the defensive, fighting to limit wage reductions, and there were nearly two million unemployed, as well as hundreds of thousands on outdoor relief. In some areas, during 1922 and 1923, miners' wages fell below the 1914 level. Yet Frank Cousins did not, for some time, become an active participant in either a trade union or political movement. He attended lodge meetings, but left most of the serious activity to his father. Frank was more interested in sport and his motor-bike. Belonging to the union was for him, as for all miners, an essential part of existence, an everyday fact of life like eating breakfast. The loyalty of youngsters like him to the brotherhood was never in doubt; but to imagine that union membership necessarily meant something beyond this to most miners would be to misunderstand the situation. Then, as now, union activists were fighting against apathy. Frank Cousins was not yet an activist.

There was nothing about the teenage Frank Cousins that struck either his family or outside acquaintances as being particularly precocious. He was very strong and well-built for his age : by the time he was nineteen he was as tall as his father. But there was no evidence of a pronounced or developing political conviction, nor of trade union militancy. His tastes in sport were for boxing, soccer, cricket and swimming – especially boxing. He found the YMCA a fruitful centre for sports activities and he became an active member. There was nothing religious in this decision, at least not consciously so. Neither of his parents was a churchgoer. But the YMCA in Station Road provided a focal point for Frank to meet people of his own age and to play games. No precise spiritual obligations were demanded of him and none were offered. For Frank the YMCA was a place where he could relax away from home, mix with his contemporaries – many of them young miners like himself – and use the facilities, such as the gym, where he could practise his boxing under a trained instructor.

In the South Yorkshire towns of the 1920s, with their deprived cultural and social environment, the YMCA played an often remarkable role in providing amenities not available elsewhere. Not only did it offer sporting and physical recreation, but it attempted to generate an interest in learning, in literature, art and music as well as religion, to inject into working-class life a wider sense of the joys of living, in spite of the economic depression and squalor of the age. In June 1918 the YMCA secretaries in Yorkshire towns and cities had formed what was called The Fellowship of Reconstruction, to prepare for the homecoming of the Forces and the cultural and educational rebuilding after the war. Part of their statement of principles proposed that : 'society should lavish upon all its immature members an education sufficient to equip them for living out the very best that is in them'.[1] The YMCA's objective was to work closely with the WEA (Workers' Educational Association) the adult education movement, and, where possible, with the trade union and cooperative movements in enlarging the social and cultural horizons of working-class families.

Frank Cousins was not concerned with the wider aspects of YMCA work, though he did not dismiss its religious background. He had no strong religious beliefs and did not feel the need to belong to an organised church group; but neither was he a non-believer; he was not then, and has not become, an atheist or even an agnostic. His view, as it has developed, is that no scientific or rationalistic explanation of existence sufficiently satisfies him. He believes in 'a God' in the way the scientist might believe in an 'X factor', to fill an unexplained gap in the reasoning process.

What additional benefit he derived from attending the Doncaster YMCA is again impossible to measure. He went there for the sport and for the comradeship; but he brought away more than the cuts and bruises that came from his earlier boxing experiences, although a blow to the mouth later brought him a great deal of dental trouble.

Frank Cousins was never a serious reader of the kind who would seize on a theme in history, economic theory or politics and pursue it with a relentless thoroughness. He picked up books casually, at random, although he was especially interested in mechanics, technology and science. There were few books on the shelves at home; no tradition of books existed in the Cousins household. The young Frank would find escape sometimes in thrillers or in science fiction, which later became an obsession in his reading. He was not

1. *The Equipment of the Workers* (Allen & Unwin, 1919). This was a research enquiry carried out by the St Philip's Settlement Education and Economics Research Society, Sheffield.

a gregarious youth. He did not go searching for new friends, preferring the security of his home environment.

He liked the practical, working with his hands and with tools, helping his father on the allotment. At one time he wanted to be a farmer. Like so many youngsters of his generation, he longed to tinker about with motor-car engines, but found it was cheaper and easier to get hold of an old motor-bike and renovate it by scratching and scraping round the mechanics' yards for spares. He picked up a good deal of his engineering knowledge in that way.

In 1923 the Cousins family moved again, to nearby St Peters' Road, where they had found a larger house with its own allotment where they could grow their vegetables. There was also room at the bottom of the garden to keep a few pigs. Every penny counted in that household and there was nothing to spare. The daily menu was meagre and the children learned to hide away their breakfast rations in all sorts of curious places and would get down early before anyone else snaffled them.

The same thing happened with clothes. George recalls: 'We would "borrow" each other's clothes, even pinch each other's bootlaces. The result was that the first up was often the best dressed, and usually the best fed too.' It was all done with good humour, but underlying everything was a clear enough message: for all Hannah's careful contriving there wasn't really enough to go round.

George Cousins has another revealing story of those days in Doncaster. Both the parents were keen cyclists, Hannah in particular. Cycling down-hill one day she lost control and crashed into some railings, one of which pierced her side. For weeks she was seriously ill. The family doctor even-tually called in an Indian specialist. According to George Cousins it was this Indian doctor's dedication that saved his mother's life. Frank was deeply disturbed by the incident. If anything, he was more profoundly attached to his mother than to his father. For weeks he was restless, difficult, perpetually uneasy. As his mother's condition improved, so did his mood. George believes that Frank never forgot that incident, and in particular the role played by the Indian doctor. It cannot be idle fancy to suggest that an event of such emotional importance must have left a considerable impact on Frank Cousins's mind and may well have influenced his strong views on racial harmony, views that, at the end of his public life, took him to the Community Relations Commission as its first chairman.

In the autumn of 1923, when he was nineteen, Frank Cousins was begin-ning to question whether he should stay in the pits and spend all his working life, as his father had done, groping in the darkness and dust underground and fighting the coal-owners on the surface. In developing a thirst for know-ledge he had become increasingly aware of the limitations of his education and his understanding of how the world operated. He was reading more and borrowing books from the library or anywhere he could find them. It was not disciplined reading; nobody guided him; he was carried forward by his own instincts. Tennesee Williams says: 'One's youth is a magical period partly because one is not really aware of the ugliness that surrounds you.' In a sense that is true; yet there is an awareness – not so much a profound impression about the irrationalities of life as the beginning of realisation. That beginning of realisation was now developing in Frank's mind as he felt increasingly the need to get away from the colliery. Enos Gilbourne provided the lever.

Enos Gilbourne worked in the same 'stall' as Charlie at the coal face. He had been wanting to get out of the pit for some time and had already worked out a scheme for doing so, having acquired a solid-tyre Model-T Ford truck for delivering coal to the miners' homes – the concessionary system which was part of their 'fringe benefits' from the owners. Gilbourne wanted an extra driver, a young man he could trust, and he approached Charlie Cousins's boy, Frank. How would he like to leave the pit and come into the business? Frank would like it very much; and at the end of 1923 he left Brodsworth colliery and joined up with Enos Gilbourne.

He stayed in that job for four years, delivering coal in the streets of Doncaster, where there are still people who remember 'Cousins the Coalman'. This was a worthwhile job in money terms, Gilbourne giving Frank about £3 a week, slightly more than he had been earning in the pit, and more, incidentally, than his father was earning. It also attracted Frank because for the first time in his life he could actually get his hands on the steering-wheel and drive a vehicle round the streets. That in itself was a thrill. So too was the chance to work in daylight. At first the job appeared to have few disadvantages. Gradually Gilbourne's business expanded; he bought another truck; Frank's pay went up and business seemed bright. Then came the General Strike of 1926.

By that time Frank had developed strong views. He volunteered to drive for the Doncaster strike committee, who gave him the job of ferrying supplies of fish and bread between Doncaster and Grimsby. Miners' families were close to starvation, as the pit strike dragged on for months, after the collapse of the General Strike. There was no coal for Frank to deliver because the pits were silent. In the autumn the miners were driven back to work, as they had been in 1921, their spirits embittered and their resistance broken. Like all other miners' families, the Cousinses survived as best they could. Although George left the pits to drive a grocer's delivery van, Charlie Cousins went back to Brodsworth where he was to spend the rest of his working life. Nothing was ever quite the same after the Strike. The struggle for existence took on a new edge, a sharpness and a depth of feeling that, in the coal industry, remained until nationalisation in 1947. Whole families had been disrupted, if not destroyed, by what happened during the Strike. Victimisation and 'blacklisting' at the collieries added thousands to the unemployment statistics.

Enos Gilbourne's coal delivery business was affected, like everything else. Enos was in financial difficulties and Frank had no wish to become a burden on him, difficult though it would be to find another job. He describes this period of his life that it was his 'first direct experience of capitalism', in the sense of actually being involved in its detailed effect on a two-man business. He was working for a small private entrepreneur whose success depended on the basic exploitation of a single product: a fetch-and-carry service in coal. 'It quickly became clear to me,' Cousins said of his break with Gilbourne, 'that there was not enough in the business to support two people. The money allowed by the colliery owners was sufficient to support one person but not two.'

After he broke with Enos and left the business in 1927, Frank worked with other coal-delivery firms not quite as small as Gilbourne's. At Newtons' his pay-packet was £2 10s. a week, a pound less than Enos had paid him. Then in 1928 he took a similar job with Hagans' coal-delivery firm, but left after a few weeks.

He joined the unemployed and was out of work for several months. This was probably the most difficult period in his working life. Jobs were hard to find and often harder to keep, without totally submerging one's individual character and independence of spirit. Cousins had developed both strongly. He was a hard worker; nothing was too much for him in a physical sense and he was prepared to put every ounce of strength into his job. But he always had a reputation for being 'awkward'. That brush he had had as a lad of fourteen at Brodsworth was by no means an isolated case of Frank Cousins refusing to toe the line of quiet obedience.

In the months after he left Hagans' there seemed little prospect of any job turning up. Frank reflected on his private ambitions. Farming was still high on the list, but it had now been overtaken by a new and powerful desire: to be a lawyer. He found it difficult to rationalise this secret wish, except that he felt the law was so heavily loaded against working-class people that he would like to try his hand at weighting it differently. He knew, of course, that it was an absurd dream. From where he stood in the unemployment queues at Doncaster, being a lawyer was as remote as being a millionaire. The capital required, the qualifications, the time to study . . . no, it was a futile hallucination. But what about the police? Well, he reflected, it was true that he had vaguely discussed the notion with his pal, Ernie Paling, who worked at the Co-op, and another friend, George Pope. They did not really like the idea. They did not feel any affinity for the police. On the other hand, they argued, it *was* a job. They might be able to hold it for a time, until the situation in the country improved, and it might lead to something better. And at the back of his mind Frank reflected – without mentioning it to anybody – that a job with the police might just possibly help him to realise that absurd, vainglorious ambition to become a lawyer. The three friends began making applications to the various constabularies: to Sheffield, Halifax, Huddersfield, Wakefield – all in Yorkshire, of course – and also to Louth in Lincolnshire. There were no openings. Then they heard that policemen were wanted in Wiltshire and wrote off immediately to Devizes. At last they got a response. They were invited for an interview and examination. In the meantime Pope had managed to get a job with the Sheffield police. He had one distinct advantage over Cousins and Paling: he could play the French horn – a considerable asset when competition for police jobs, as for any other kind of job, was so keen. Ability to play a musical instrument of that kind was often a critical factor, especially in the police force with its pride in brass bands. And so Cousins and Paling went to Devizes without Pope. It was the summer of 1928, and Frank was not yet twenty-four.

He passed the police test with ease and was virtually a constable. But Paling was rejected, and this greatly upset Frank, since Ernie was his closest friend. It seemed unthinkable that he should be left out, and this was probably decisive in turning Frank Cousins against the idea of joining the force himself; though his mind was finally made up for him by the chief officer, after he had passed the various tests and was about to be signed up. Sitting in front of the officer's desk, Cousins was answering the routine questions about his previous work and his family background, when suddenly the officer leaned across and tapped the buckled finger on Frank's left hand with his stick.

'What's that?' he demanded stiffly.

'A broken finger', snapped Cousins.

'*Oh,*' the officer continued, still more stiffly. 'You didn't say anything about *that* during your medical. And,' he added sharply, 'say "Sir" to me when you answer.'

Frank Cousins did not move a muscle. But inside his head and his stomach the blood raced around as if the pumping system had suddenly decided to treble its pace. He recalled that incident at Brodsworth with the underground pit manager. He remembered his father's words after he had explained that he did not think it reasonable to call any man 'Sir' unless he was very old – or unless he deserved respect. But Frank said nothing.

The officer added that the finger would have to be broken again and reset before he could be enlisted in the police force. Then Cousins reacted. He told the officer that he had no intention of having his finger mauled about; he was no longer interested in the job; and anyway he was not proposing to call him 'Sir'. That was that. Paling and Cousins went back to Doncaster and unemployment.

Curiously, in his later years, Frank Cousins is reluctant to talk about this incident. He is particularly sensitive about the fact that some of his critics regard it as a sign of his political immaturity that he should ever have contemplated joining the police in the first place, since no 'true socialist' would even consider joining a branch of the State machine charged, among other things, with the protection and maintenance of the *status quo*. I make this point because the incident is still regarded by some of Frank Cousins's old friends as an outstanding example of how in his earlier days he behaved 'out of context'. But it would be naïve to make too much of the occasion. Desperation drove many young men in the 1920s to extremes – not only in Doncaster. It would be absurd to argue that a move of that kind, when his attitudes were still developing, was the mark of a man who cannot be regarded as a serious political animal.

In many ways Cousins's next job, which followed some weeks later, was still more significant in changing the pattern of his life, for it brought him within striking distance of becoming a small-time industrialist.

At nearby Sprotborough there was a seventeenth-century water-driven flourmill, run by a solitary miller, Joe Heald. Frank Cousins learned that Heald needed a truck-driver and went to enquire. The miller wanted to know how he had heard about the job.

'I heard about it', said Cousins, testily.

'From whom?' the miller wanted to know.

'Well, look here, do you want a driver or don't you?' Frank snapped, exasperated.

'Perhaps I do. Perhaps I don't', said Joe Heald playing the same game.

'Well, if you don't know I'm sure I don't', said Frank. 'But when you've made up your mind you can let me know.'

He give his address and left, inwardly snorting. Shortly afterwards Heald visited the Cousins household; Frank found him there one afternoon, talking to his father.

'What the old blighter had done,' said Frank, 'was to check up on my family background before hiring me.' He got the job.

Joe Heald was the miller of an artist's dream : short, plump, with sparkling eyes and full rosy cheeks, there was always a thin coating of flour over his toothbrush moustache and eyebrows. Sprotborough Mill had an idyllic setting by a cutting in the River Don a few miles outside Doncaster.

The truck Frank was to drive was a vast three-ton Vulcan with solid tyres, practically a museum-piece even in those days. It took two firm hands to operate the gear-shift. But driving was a minor part of Frank's work. He operated the mill and Heald was glad to let him do it. He was getting old and had a young wife by his second marriage. He let Frank do the hard work, such as the highly skilled operation of 'dressing' the millstones, which Frank soon mastered so that he became a craftsman at the task; he must now be one of the few left in this country who can dress a millstone according to the old manuals.

In the afternoons Joe Heald would drift indoors to play his beloved violin. More and more he passed over to Frank the running of the mill and its general administration – apart from the accounts. Eventually he took Frank aside and told him that he would like him to take over the mill when he retired. It might even become Frank's own property one day. Joe had no desire to go on working much longer. He had enough cash to retire and devote himself to his wife, and now that he had found someone he could trust to carry on the mill he had no fears for the future. Heald was genuinely attached to Frank, treating him like the son he had never had, and the affection was plainly reciprocal.

Another lasting affection began to influence Frank's life at about this time. At a Co-operative dance, on New Year's Eve 1928, Frank met Annie Elizabeth Judd. He danced with her several times, but didn't take her home on that occasion, because she had come with someone else. But on that first morning of 1929, as they walked home from the dance, he told an astonished Ernie Paling: 'I've met the girl I'm going to marry.' The self-assurance was remarkable; it was Cousins's way of expressing himself. The pursuit was on. And indeed he did marry Anne Judd – or, as he decided to call her, Nance.

That New Year's Eve dance was perhaps the decisive moment of Frank's life.

Chapter Three

NANCE

Nance Cousins is a remarkable woman in her own right, gifted and articulate, with a profound political awareness and sense of direction. It would be easy to imply that she has been the intellectual inspiration behind very much of Frank Cousins's work and achievements. Indeed, some people have frequently suggested that she was always the mainspring of his activities, that she has been to Frank Cousins what Eleanor Roosevelt was to F.D.R. The point has been strongly and frequently put by many of Cousins's critics. Nor have they failed to add, with a deliberate touch of acid, that although Frank never belonged to the Communist Party, Nance, for a brief time, *was* a member. The implication was always meant to be clear : that the ex-Communist wife was really the effective driving force of the Cousins partnership. We shall, I believe, come to recognise that this was never the case. Cousins has always been his own man.

Indeed, it would be a crude and wholly inaccurate caricature of Nance Cousins's role to present it as that of a political tactician or ideologue, forever driving a husband on to deeds he would otherwise not have performed. It would, however, be equally absurd to suggest that she had not been a decisive factor in Frank's life and career; but it has been as chief lieutenant, not commander-in-chief. Nance Cousins was an extraordinary combination of a wife and mother, a political activator constantly helping Frank to refuel and recharge his own batteries, and a woman with a quite unusual capacity for assessing people, especially the motives and likely tactics of Frank's opponents. Her deep and totally committed socialist beliefs have plainly been a cornerstone on which her husband developed his own certainties. They have disagreed sometimes on vital issues of tactics and strategy, but more often on their assessments of people with Frank taking a more lenient view toward the vagaries of human behaviour.

Nance never imposed a political decision on him. She was never persuasive enough to recruit him into the Communist Party.

The remarkable feature of the role she played does not lie in any supremacy that she established, politically or intellectually, over her husband, but in her contribution to their partnership, a partnership that must be considered among the most significant to emerge in the post-war British Labour Movement.

Percy Judd's father – Nance's grandfather – had come to Doncaster from London, where his own father had been a policeman in Bow (one of the first Bobbies). Like thousands of others he was drawn by the lure of the expanding railways, but in fact his first job was as a groom to a Yorkshire landowner in the area, Sir William Cooke, the squire of Wheatley Park. Percy Judd's mother was a maid to Lady Charlotte Copley, sister of the owner of Wheatley Park. They met and married when Percy's father carried messages between the two big houses – Lady Charlotte lived in Sprotborough Hall. After they married and Percy was born Judd senior went to work in Doncaster for the Great Northern Railway Company, whose Locomotive, Carriage and Wagon Works – commonly known as 'The Plant' – was a Doncaster landmark, as well as one of the main sources of employment for the whole area. It was there that Percy started work in 1901, introduced by his father, when he left school at fourteen. At the back of his mind was an ambition to become a draughtsman, but he soon realised that this was an impossibility. It would have meant years at a technical school, which his family certainly could not afford, and would have involved buying expensive equipment running to something like £100 – all of it well beyond the means of even the most careful working-class family in Doncaster. But, after a year in the workshops, Percy decided to switch to the clerical staff when a vacancy arose, and at fifteen he was accepted for a post in the clerical department of the mineral manager's office. It was a post he was to hold, eventually in a senior capacity, for forty-five years. He was still there when he served as Mayor of Doncaster from 1947 to 1949.

In 1906, when he married Lillian Penny, Percy was earning £1 a week, a wage which increased in stages of 2s. a year. That was about the average for the white-collar employees in developing industries like railways and coal. It enabled the Judds to live well above the poverty level.

Lillian Penny's background was not dissimilar to Percy Judd's. Her father came to Doncaster from the farmlands of Salisbury, Wiltshire, her mother from nearby Cudworth. The Penny family were farmers and craftsmen, including highly skilled carpenters and wheelwrights. Lillian's father was a carpenter by trade and he soon found a job in the Doncaster railway workshops. Both of Lillian's parents were religious people, her father being an active Quaker, and Lillian was brought up in that faith. Indeed, there was probably a higher level of religious awareness in the Penny household than in the average working-class family in Doncaster.

The Judds were also a religious family, though in a more orthodox fashion. Percy was brought up along traditional Church-of-England lines and went to St George's Church every Sunday evening up to the Second World War, when he was shocked out of his beliefs by the bellicose sermons of a local archdeacon. The fact that Percy was Church and Lillian was Chapel offered a foundation of great strength for a family unit.

The Cousins home, too, was united by a personal strength and a moral code well above the average. Yet the Judds and the Pennys had already established roots in Doncaster before the Cousins family arrived. There was another crucial difference between the Judd and the Cousins families : the number of children. While Charles and Hannah struggled heroically to bring up ten children in the most testing social and economic conditions, Percy and Lillian had only four; two girls and two boys, Alfred, Philip, Doris and Annie.

Annie Judd, the future Nance Cousins, was a precocious child. Her mother recalls that she walked at nine months and was running about by her first birthday. At three she was dancing to the music of street hurdy-gurdies. She was, her mother says 'a very active, lively and clever child'. At the local elementary school she did extremely well both academically and in sports, and she won a scholarship to the Doncaster Grammar School for Girls, a remarkable achievement for a working-class child at that time. (Annie Judd was beginning her spell at the Grammar School when Frank was starting at Brodsworth colliery.) It was not easy for the Judds to finance their daughter's education. Percy was then taking home about £1 10s. a week, on which he had to keep, feed and clothe four children. It was one of the most difficult periods the Judds ever experienced. The grammar-school uniform for Annie was out of the question, and Lillian had to make up an outfit at home.

Annie did well at school, especially at sport, and stayed on until she was nearly seventeen, but the family resources would not run to any higher education. Towards the end of 1923 – at the time Frank Cousins was thinking of leaving the pit – Annie started work in the shoe department at Doncaster Co-operative, and she kept the job until she married Frank six years later.

During their courtship Annie was at once liked and instinctively accepted by the Cousins family, but the same could not be said of Frank's first experiences with the Judds. They found him much 'rougher' than Annie's previous boyfriend, a railway clerk and therefore socially a 'cut above' Frank, as well as an altogether much more commanding personality. It was some time before they warmed to him. Frank's manners seemed raw and crude to the Judds (though he was never vulgar : vulgarity was not tolerated in the Cousins household). He had the characteristic toughness of a young miner, even long after he had left the pits. In the Yorkshire idiom, he was 'rough and ready'. He would arrive at the Judds' house on his beloved motor-bike looking better equipped for an evening on the speedway track than for a visit to potential in-laws. The Judds felt uneasy with Frank. Before they really got to know him, both Percy and Lillian felt that their daughter could have 'done better for herself'. In the eyes of the railwaymen of that period miners always seemed a 'rough lot'.

But the Judds were kind and gentle people who did their best to hide their real feelings, and they tried to make Frank feel at home. All the same, the gulf between them and their daughter's friend was evident for some time. The young couple were certainly aware of this, Annie in particular. Nor was the situation eased by the straightford language of Hannah Cousins, who would quite often erupt with an exuberant 'bloody this' or 'bloody that' in front of the Judds, who were quite unaccustomed to this style of speech. Yet in spite of these distressing signs, Lillian and Percy accepted the fact that Annie was very much in love with Frank, and they refused to allow their social qualms to override their affection for Annie and their understanding of her feelings.

It would have appeared monstrously hypocritical for Percy and Lillian to have shown signs of any social squeamishness at their daughter's courtship with a miner, for the Judd household was now deeply involved in the labour and trade union movement in Doncaster. Percy had been active in his own union, the Railway Clerks' Association (now the Transport Salaried Staffs' Association), ever since he started work, and was schooled in the socialist literature of the pioneers. Though he was never a Marxist, Percy steeped himself in the writings of Shaw and Wells, William Morris, the Webbs, of Blatchford and the *Clarion* Group, in the gospel of socialism and the brotherhood of man as preached by Keir Hardie and Ramsay Macdonald. So the warm wrap of the Judd household closed softly round the ample shoulders of Frank Cousins.

Meanwhile the political education of both Frank and Nance was advancing rapidly. Not the least of the secondary influences that were helping to shape Frank Cousins in Doncaster was Percy Judd. He made Frank think about politics in a somewhat deeper and more complex way, as did Nance herself, though at that stage she was not intensely interested in politics. More significant was the effect of the dramatic events of 1929 to 1931.

During their courting days Frank and Nance began regularly attending political meetings in Doncaster. Visiting Labour stars, like Sir Stafford Cripps, Arthur Greenwood, Hugh Dalton, D. N. Pritt and George Lansbury, all had an influence on the young couple as they sat holding hands and absorbing the socialist gospel. They went to trade union meetings and heard the famous miners' leader, A. J. Cook, who had led the miners in the 1926

General Strike, and Herbert Smith, the Yorkshire president of the Miners' Federation. They attended meetings organised by the Workers' Educational Association in cooperation with the Doncaster Trades Council. They were ready to absorb everything that was offered which would give them a better understanding of the political and economic crises in which they found themselves trapped.

Although Frank and Nance met at the beginning of 1929, they did not marry until Boxing Day 1930. It was not unusual to prolong courtships in the late 1920s, especially when families had to scrape and save to launch a couple into marriage. They would have married sooner, but economic facts were against it, and Nance insisted on having a house of her own at the outset. Even had they wanted it, there was no room for a young couple in either of their parents' homes. They waited a long time for a house they could afford to rent, but eventually found one on a new estate at Dunsville, a few miles to the east of Doncaster. By 1930 Frank was well established at the Sprotborough Mill, and there was every prospect that the job would go on and even develop as Joe Heald had hinted. Yet the pattern of future developments did not work that way.

Joe Heald was a sick man at the time the Cousins married. In December 1929 severe gales swept across Britain, bringing the worst floods for twenty years. Swirling currents swept mud and river rubbish into the cutting on the River Don where Sprotborough Mill was situated. The water-wheel jammed, and in attempting to free it, working waist-deep in the water, Joe Heald was nearly drowned. He never recovered from the experience. He was ill for his remaining two years and finally died in December 1931.

This was another turning point in Frank Cousins's career. During his illness Joe had again made it clear to Frank that he would inherit the management of Sprotborough Mill – but there were problems. In the middle of 1930 the South Yorkshire Navigation Company had already undertaken big developments at Sprotborough to lessen the impact of flooding. Not only that : the mill and the adjoining cottages were endangered by mining subsidence. Joe had in fact been given notice to quit, but had ridiculed any suggestion that the mill might have to shut down. It had been occupied by the Heald family since the turn of the century, and Joe was determined that Frank Cousins should take over a going concern. Frank and Nance had, indeed, married on the assumption that they would probably finish up as the owners of the mill.

They had reckoned without Mrs Heald. On his death, Joe's young widow lost no time in selling off the mill and all the assets, to provide for her own future. Joe Heald had left no legal instructions on Frank's behalf, and nothing could be done to prevent the sale in Mrs Heald's favour. As Frank Cousins says now : 'If Joe had not died, I would never have been general secretary of the TGWU.'

Joe Heald's death and the collapse of Frank's prospects could not have come at a worse time. Frank and Nance had been married for less than a year. Their first child, John, was just born.

Frank spent some time winding up affairs at the mill and collecting debts now due to the young widow. The prospect of searching for a new job cast a fearful shadow over the New Year of 1932; it loomed against the background of the worst economic crisis to hit Britain, and the entire Western world, in the years between the wars.

By the summer of 1931 the full impact of the American depression had rolled across Europe. In Britain the pound was under pressure as confidence sank and industries, forced into recession by the collapse of world markets, began to lay off more and more workers. Unemployment figures reached 2,750,000 in July 1931. On 24 August the Macdonald Government resigned. It was then announced that the Labour leader was ready to form a new government with the cooperation of the Conservative and Liberal Party leaders. The shock waves swept across the Labour Movement at first in eddies of disbelief, then bitterness, and finally with a sullen and lasting resentment. The *Daily Herald* described the entire crisis as a bankers' ramp. It seemed that the whole fabric of capitalist society was being torn apart by world forces that were out of control.

For workers and their families the collapse of the Labour Government in 1931 was only the forerunner of harsher things to come, as unemployment continued to rise and wages were cut back still further. A report on public expenditure produced by the May Committee recommended cuts of £96 million, a huge amount by prevailing levels, with wage and salary cuts for civil servants, the police, workers in government factories and shipyards, and on top of all that, severe reductions in unemployment benefits. By the middle of September 1931, the new National Government under Macdonald was rushing through these measures. Unemployment pay was reduced by an across-the-board 10 per cent, though, in practice, when the newly introduced means test was applied, the effective cuts in benefits to families of the unemployed often amounted to double that figure. On 27 October 1931, coinciding with the birth of young John Cousins, the Conservatives decided to force another general election and appealed for support for another National Government with Ramsay Macdonald as its leader. Labour was routed at the polls. The party's vote fell from 8.3 million in 1929 to 6.6 million; the Liberals dropped from 5.3 to 2.3 million, while the Conservative vote rocketed from 8.6 million to 11.9 million.

In Doncaster, during the summer of 1931, the unemployment rate was almost one in three of the male working population – double the figure for the previous December. Wages were being cut back in all the town's industries and public services. Bus and tram workers were compelled to accept a reduction of 10 per cent in their basic wage of £2 12s. a week. Every job was hit by the twin pressures of the rise in unemployment and wage reductions. Railways, coal-mining, engineering, building and construction work, public and private transport – nothing escaped. While Frank Cousins was still at Sprotborough Mill his wage was about £3 a week, and Nance continued to work at the Co-operative until shortly before John was born. But the small savings they had accumulated were soon swamped when the mill went, and the young people were in dire trouble : a newly rented house to maintain, a baby, no job and not the slightest prospect of getting one.

One evening Frank came home from the hopeless search for work, tired, deeply depressed, helpless. It was early in 1932. Nance told him that she had decided to take a job in a local shoe shop. Her mother would look after baby John during the day. Frank had to swallow this blow to his pride. One working member in the family could bring in enough to pay the rent and keep them clear of debt, although the wage was only £1 10s. a week. It was a job, as it happened, that brought good things to the Cousins family, and eventually changed the tide of events.

Soon after Nance started the job, a man came in to buy a pair of expensive riding-boots. In the course of the transaction Nance realised that she was dealing with a man of some means. As she discovered, he was Bill Smart of the London and Southern Counties Transport Company, known in the road haulage trade as 'Spans-the-South'. Smart was in Doncaster to survey the scene before opening a transport depot in the area and was on the way to Newcastle, where another depot was in prospect.

Sensing the possibilities, Nance was bold enough to ask Smart if he might be looking for transport drivers.

'Possibly', said Smart.

'Well, my husband is a transport driver who wouldn't mind a change of job', said Nance, half-lying. She added that Frank was experienced with many types of vehicle, stressing his familiarity with the three-ton Vulcan which he had driven for Heald at the mill.

Smart was impressed, offered to give Frank a trial and finally invited him to come on the trip to Newcastle.

Frank had embarked on his career as a long-distance truck driver.

By this time, Cousins, nearing his twenty-eighth birthday, had already become much more acutely aware of the importance of trade unionism and of the wider social and economic problems facing working-class families – not least his own. His political instincts were aroused, though he still lacked any strong ideological direction or coherent thinking. He would probably have described himself as a socialist, even a militant one, yet it would have been difficult, if not impossible, to attach any label to him or to slot him into any clearly defined political category. 'Labour', yes; but so were nearly all the men he worked and lived with. That was much more a class description than a specific political commitment, a way of life rather than an intellectual choice. Frank Cousins was, like the vast majority of working people of his generation, being stirred into political awareness by the demands of everyday life. His reading was haphazard: anything from the *Daily Herald* every morning – and that had a profound influence on working-class opinion – to the odd pamphlet picked up at a WEA meeting. Frank was now absorbing all the knowledge he could come by. His brother Charlie recalls: 'He used to buy dictionaries – any number of them – to learn words and their meanings. He would buy educational books – anything he could learn from. It was as if he was trying to *devour* knowledge.'

For the men and women of that generation it was an extraordinarily hard task to try to bridge the gaps left by the inadequacies of their education. The obstacles facing working-class families have always primarily been economic. But even that is an umbrella term for what amounts to a whole range of difficulties arising from the inability to buy not only books and schooling but time, leisure, privacy and experience – the security and the style which helps to equip the mind as well as the body. Deprivation is most easily measured in economic terms, yet some factors defy calibration. How is it possible to assess the bitterness and frustration of an unfulfilled potential? How can one measure the energy and resourcefulness required for a man weighed down by the burdens of working-class life in the early 1930s to climb out of that economic servitude into intellectual freedom and political understanding? Small wonder that so many trade union leaders, in recent years, have not reached national office until they were well into their fifties.

Chapter Four

ON THE ROAD

The job with 'Spans-the-South' opened up a new life-style for Frank Cousins. For nearly eight years, since leaving the pit, he had moved from job to job without settling. At one point it had seemed that the flour-mill offered a solution as well as a reasonably secure future, but that had crumbled. His one stable relationship was his marriage and it was this factor which most worried him when he was given the chance to join the ranks of the long-distance truck drivers. The new job was bound to throw a heavy burden on Nance, who was just settling into the routine of married life with a young baby. Yet there was no real option. He was without a job. The money was desperately needed; the opportunity was there, perhaps not to be repeated. So he took it, not with much enthusiasm, but with his usual cockiness and energy, and also with a certain amount of excitement at getting not only a new job, but one that would give him the chance of handling motor vehicles under quite novel circumstances. In 1932 driving was still a cherished dream among the vast majority of youngsters. They had little prospect of driving their own vehicles – except possibly a motor-bike – and so a driving job carried with it a special attraction.

Frank was already a good, if not widely experienced, driver, accustomed to handling heavy vehicles carrying weighty and awkward loads. He had a working knowledge of the mechanical side. What he lacked was a wider experience beyond Doncaster. But Bill Smart did not regard this as an obstacle.

When Cousins reached Newcastle, on his trial run with Smart, he was sent on with a three-ton truck and a mate to East Riggs in Dumfriesshire. When he arrived there he was told to go to Aberdeen and pick up a truck-load of beef for London. Frank had not bargained for this long stint. He had yet to learn the hauliers' business, and to learn it the hard way. Drivers often worked literally to collapsing point, and accepted the conditions because the one alternative was the dole queue.

At Aberdeen Frank found a huge Leyland 'Bull' truck loaded with beef carcasses for Smithfield Market. He had never seen, let alone driven, such a truck: a six-ton vehicle nearly 23 feet long, with solid tyres, specially designed to move dead meat from Scotland to London and so compete with the railways for cost and speed of delivery. The lorry bodies were designed to carry two tiers of carcasses, and a regular service was running from Scotland to Smithfield.

It was hard work and the hours were cruel, but the pay was not bad by prevailing standards. Cousins earned £3 10s. a week, with a lodging and expenses allowance on the road. Rather than be separated for long spells, Nance and the baby moved to Castle Douglas, where 'Spans-the-South' had their headquarters in Scotland.

Driving lorries across Britain in the 1930s was one of the most hazardous and difficult jobs there were at that time; the hazards were quite unlike those Frank had faced at Brodsworth colliery, but potentially just as lethal. With no effective legal enforcement on the speed or roadworthiness of their vehicles, many firms simply pleased themselves about the condition of their trucks and the behaviour of their drivers. Cousins tells a story which illustrates the situation in the industry at that time. He brought a vehicle back to his Scottish depot one time and complained that the brakes were bad. He told the maintenance foreman that they had failed repeatedly on the return journey and explained what ought to be done before the vehicle went on the road again. The foreman cut him short and waved him away saying, 'What do you want good brakes for? The only good they do is to stop you'. As far as the foreman was concerned, speed of delivery was all that mattered. Safety came a poor second.

Before continuing with Frank Cousins's story, we must pause to take a brief look at the industry he was working in.

Life in the road haulage business in the early 1930s was closer to a Wild West film than to a major British industry, and it was no mere colourful romanticism to describe the employers, and indeed many of the road haulage employees themselves, as 'cowboys of the highway' or 'death or glory boys'. There was scant regard for working conditions, safety regulations or the maintenance of vehicles, let alone the social niceties. Governments seemed powerless to enforce their own legislation, designed to introduce some mild form of regulation. A system of vehicle licensing, introduced in 1930, was further strengthened in 1933 by successive Road Traffic Acts. It provided for the application of a 'Fair Wages' clause, which was designed to lay the foundation for a modest form of wage regulation throughout the industry. It also laid down that the Industrial Court should take account of any relevant Joint Industrial Council agreement or any other voluntary agreement in deciding what in fact constituted a 'fair wage' for road haulage.[1] But the truth was that no voluntary agreements were applicable to road haulage. The Ministry of Labour therefore set up a voluntary body aimed at providing the basis for applying the 'fair wage' provision. It was like trying to apply table-tennis rules to jungle warfare. The industry was split into hundreds of small firms whose employers, large and small, were notoriously individualistic and buccaneering. Competition was fierce and so was undercutting. There was systematic evasion of almost all regulations. And in such conditions it was self-evident that trade union membership should be low, and effective union organisation virtually non-existent. The majority of road haulage workers connived at this 'outlawry' chiefly because it was often the only way they could hold on to their jobs – jobs which were, as we have seen, better paid than those in the majority of industries at that time. In his biography of Ernest Bevin, Professor Alan Bullock (now Lord Bullock) suggests that the road haulage workers had to behave in this way : 'to earn a bribe for keeping their mouths shut or simply for their own convenience when, by driving excessive hours and breaking the speed limit, they could get home earlier'.[2]

Under the 1933 act there were three categories of vehicle licensing, A, B and C. The 'fair wage' clause was more easily enforceable in categories A and B, because these covered public service transport and local private transport on limited-distance work. Category C related to private carriers on long-distance hauls. According to an expert in this field,

Fair wages applied only to those workers whose employers were protected by the community. But in road haulage this principle divided the industry in an impractical way. A manufacturer could decide whether he would operate his own lorries or whether he would hire those of a licensed carrier. Since there was no restriction on the number of lorries of his own which he could operate A and B licensed vehicles were in direct competition with those carrying C licences. The absence of protection for workers on C licensed vehicles was bound to make it difficult to implement the 'fair wages' clause. Moreover, since three-fifths of the half-million road haulage workers worked for private carriers (the long-distance firms in the main) the protection extended to only a minority.[3]

The Government knew that if the 'fair wages' clause was to have the remotest chance of working effectively there would have to be some form of voluntary wage-bargaining system throughout the industry. So, in March 1934, the Minister of Labour set up a National Joint Conciliation Board

1. See Alan Bullock, *The Life and Times of Ernest Bevin*, Vol. I (Heinemann, 1960), p. 544.
2. *Loc. cit.*
3. F. J. Bayliss, *British Wages Councils* (Blackwell, Oxford, 1962), pp. 31–2.

for the Road Motor Transport Industry (Goods) with an independent chairman.

Every effort had been put into this experiment and Ernest Bevin himself had recommended the idea to the Minister, but it was doomed from the start. The trouble was that there were no effective ways of enforcing the agreement or of compelling employers to behave in a manner which many of them believed was not in their commercial interests. The employers' associations taking part in the new National Board represented only one-quarter of the firms with A and B licensed vehicles. Trade union organisation was no better. Local boards were created to draw employers and unions into voluntary wage bargaining in the regions, but they too were almost a total flop from the start.

The Cousins family stayed in Scotland for some eighteen months, by which time Frank had become more confident in this strange new world and could organise his working life in such a way that he could contrive to find himself more frequently in Doncaster. Both he and Nance hankered after their home town. It was cheaper there, too. They managed to find a council house in Leicester Avenue and moved in there before their second child, Brenda, was born on 1 January 1934. Frank was away from home as much as ever, but at least Nance had her parents close by and she was not so cut off as she had been in Scotland.

It was still hard going. The Judds recall that this was a particularly difficult time for the whole family, and indeed it was the strain on the domestic scene, more than anything, that finally decided Frank to change to a Doncaster-based meat-transport company, Fairclough's. He made the switch early in 1934, by which time he had been a member of the Transport and General Workers' Union for more than a year and had become an active, even a militant, trade unionist and a keen voluntary recruiting agent for the union. This, too, may have been a contributory factor in his break with 'Spans-the-South'. Frank Cousins had acquired a reputation as an activist. He was persistent in his work to recruit drivers into the TGWU, and he was threatened with the sack in 1934 for what the chairman of the company regarded as 'Bolshevik behaviour'. Specifically, the threat of dismissal came when Frank was trying to organise a trade union 'shop' at 'Spans-the-South', with the aim of pressing the company to establish a system of collective bargaining and union negotiations in line with the spirit, if not the letter, of the 1933 Transport Act.

By the time he moved to Fairclough's, the industry was a tangle of fiercely competitive groups, some already devouring each other by mergers and takeovers. His experience with 'Spans-the-South' had not only provided Cousins with a remarkable insight into how the industry functioned, it had also brought him into the TGWU and fired him with an intense enthusiasm for trade-union activity and organisation. He had become widely known as a union militant. Even before he took the job at Fairclough's his reputation was growing in Doncaster as 'Cousins, the union chap'.

The move to Fairclough's was not made primarily for the money, but to try to ease the domestic problems arising from his long spells away from home. When Frank joined, in fact, he took a cut in basic pay from £3 10s. a week to £3 7s. 6d., and this at a time when the loss of half-a-crown a week meant a real sacrifice.

His brother George joined the firm at the same time. They were told that they would get £3 12s. 6d. when they qualified as 'super drivers'.

'When will that be?' Frank asked the depot manager cheekily.

'When I decide you're super drivers', said the manager.

'We think we're super drivers already. As good as any you've got here, at any rate,' Cousins returned brassily.

The manager almost exploded. 'Do you want the bloody job or not?'

George calmed his brother by answering for both of them. 'Yes, we'll take the offer,' he said.

'I want *his* answer too,' the manager rasped. 'He can speak for himself, can't he?'

'Yes, all right,' said Frank grudgingly.

The important thing for Frank and Nance was that he was now based at home in Doncaster, even though his movements about the country were just as widespread as before and almost as unpredictable. Fairclough's specialised in meat delivery runs to London, but they also did a great deal of general cargo transportation. Trade was picking up and unemployment was falling, and the road transport industry was taking advantage of the improved economic atmosphere and expanding its field in competition with the railways, who were still having a hard time as more and more goods were being carried by road.

Inevitably this meant that the limited regulations and the unwritten ethical codes were increasingly ignored. Pilferage was rampant. Frank Cousins did not make himself the most popular of drivers by standing out, almost ostentatiously, against this practice, which had become an accepted part of a driver's 'perks'.

Cousins admits to only one pilferage in the whole of his driving career. He told me that this was something forced upon him in the early days, when a large consignment of prams had come into a certain transport depot and, by some odd statistical quirk, the number of prams on the trucks out-numbered the number due to be delivered. An organised and semi-official raid was arranged, in which every driver was invited to take his pick. John was still using a pram and one was pushed into Frank's hands and he took it home – and immediately regretted this one lapse.

Cousins now modestly observes that his reputation for iron honesty probably stemmed more from his fear of being caught than from any inflexible moral sense. This reputation as 'Honest Frank' was something of a legend in the Doncaster branch of the TGWU, and a branch official at that time, Mr Bill Goulding has testified to it. 'Off twelve fourteen-ton loads of meat', Goulding once said, 'Frank Cousins would never as much as pinch a steak.'[4] His workmates were often suspicious of this attitude, and at times they were even hostile; but Frank lived down both the suspicions and the hostility, and even those who remained his strongest critics conceded that Cousins's most remarkable feature was his astonishing honesty and integrity. His employers were just as curious about his reputation, and he was once chided on this score by a manager at Fairclough's. Cousins replied: 'If you ever sack me it won't be for dishonesty – but because you simply don't want me around here any more.' The manager understood this to mean that, if Frank were ever sacked, it would be because of his trade union activities and not for any dishonesty.

Perhaps there was self-righteousness in this posture. On the other hand, Cousins would never 'rat' on any of his fellow-drivers, no matter how horrific the pilferage. He simply did not want to become involved.

One one occasion Frank was driving home from Scotland when his co-driver, an ex-pilot, noticed an attractive concrete bird-bath in a field. Frank stopped while he had a closer look at it, but as it was broad daylight the co-driver decided to collect it on the return journey. On the following night the ex-pilot, who was at the wheel, stopped at the field and tried to carry off the bird-bath, but finding it too heavy for one man to shift he persuaded Frank to give a hand. The two men, both over six feet tall, managed to manhandle the bird-bath as far as the road, but could not get it on to the truck.

'Serves you right,' said Frank. 'You'll have to leave it here where it belongs.'

But the co-driver signalled down a passing motorist and asked him to give a hand, producing some 'documents' and telling him that the farmer who had sold him the bird-bath had promised to have it lifted on to the truck, but had failed to turn up. The motorist was not interested in the details, but willingly helped them to lift the bird-bath on to the truck.

'But suppose that had been the police?' said Frank, marvelling at his mate's audacity. 'What would you have told *them*?'

'I'd have told them that we'd found this obstruction in the middle of the road,' said the ex-pilot, 'and asked them to help us get it out of the way.'

An extravagant story? Not in the least. Whole vanloads of goods would regularly disappear from transport depots, even live sheep and cattle. Noth-

4. The *Sunday Times*, 2 October 1966.

ing was beyond the ingenuity of the road haulage workers. Few of them were uninvolved and everyone, including the management, knew fairly accurately what was going on. Occasionally there would be an attempt to stamp out the pilferage. For a week or so the tempo of stealing would slow down. Then slowly it would mount again to the usual level of larceny. All this went on around 'Honest Frank' and it was far from easy for him to sustain his own personal code of behaviour while maintaining a healthy relationship with his fellow workers. Yet these were important determinants shaping Frank Cousins's social attitudes.

Many years later, in a television interview with John Freeman, Frank Cousins was asked whether there was any particular incident that had made him aware of the human condition, any single outstanding experience that had 'made' him a socialist. He replied :

There are a number; but one stands out particularly in my mind, as a young lorry drive in the times of the Depression. I happened to be in a transport café on the Great North Road when a young couple came in with a child in a nearly broken-down pram. They were walking from Shields – Shields was one of the places that got hit in the slump . . . and they were walking from there to London because the man understood that he could get a job in London. They came into the cafe and sat down, and they fetched a baby's feeding bottle out and it had water in. They fed the baby with water and then lifted the kiddy's dress up – it was a baby, a real baby – and it had a newspaper nappy on. They took this off, wiped the baby's bottom with the nappy they'd taken off, and then picked up another newspaper and put that on for another nappy. And I think if ever I felt a resentment against the system it was on that occasion. I thought somebody ought to do something about it. I won't say I thought *I* ought to do something about it. But I thought *somebody* ought to do something about it.

We'd gone through the disputes and strikes in 1926, but here was the oppression being brought home to an innocent, defenceless child. And, oh, along with a lot of other lorry drivers, we sort of helped them on the way. But it made a profound impression on me. And I think it's one of the things I would regard as a highlight of starting in this job.[5]

Frank's brother, George, was with him on that occasion. It was in a transport cafe at Boroughbridge, near Doncaster, where they had stopped for a cup of tea and a hot bacon sandwich. The young couple could not afford more than a mug of tea. The lorry drivers passed over some food and some money, and George remembers Frank saying : 'There must be something we can do to stop this sort of thing.'

But what *could* individuals do except fight through their trade unions

5. John Freeman's 'Face to Face' interview with Frank Cousins, BBC TV, 15 October 1961.

and the political institutions of the period? Many who were politically active joined the Communist Party at that time in the belief that it was the only party capable of effectively campaigning against a rotten and – as it appeared to many – rotting system. But Frank Cousins did not join the Communist Party. *His* church was the union, through which he was becoming increasingly convinced that it was possible to fight injustice, to contest the employers' almost unchecked powers, and to establish an army of working people who could be forged into an immensely powerful force capable of changing the old order. This was certainly not a clearly formulated doctrine in Frank's mind, but simply a sense of direction, an impulse, a feeling.

Meanwhile, Cousins was doing relatively well at Fairclough's. After a year he qualified for the top-rate basic pay of £3 12s. 6d. given to 'crack' drivers. He was already regarded by his employers as one of their best men, despite his politics and trade union activity. This work for the union, on top of an exacting job, stretched Cousins. Increasingly he was spending more time on union affairs. His practice was to try to recruit new members among the drivers he met in the lorry parks and transport cafes along the trunk routes. It meant carrying forms and notebooks and reporting back on his progress to the Doncaster branch of the TGWU, where he was now a member of the branch committee. This inevitably resulted in some conflict at the depot. Very few road haulage employers were willing to cooperate with organised trade union groups. To cushion his activities as a union militant, Cousins had to make quite sure that his working record and personal conduct were beyond reproach. His relationship with Fairclough's was always slightly tense, though he regarded them as good employers; but he did his job superbly well and it would have been difficult (though not, of course, impossible) for the firm to have picked him off simply because of his perfectly legitimate union activities. His attitude on this score was clearly demonstrated when he made his first speech as TGWU General Secretary shortly before his appointment in 1955. Speaking to a meeting of BEA drivers and loaders at Hayes, Middlesex, Cousins said : 'I was very proud to be a lorry driver – I was a good driver (at least I thought I was) and a good trade unionist. I have always believed that a man who represents his fellow workers should set an example of good work.'[6]

Cousins's relationship with his chief foreman, 'Bronco' Reed, was abrasively healthy and candid. They frequently shouted at each other; they fought about wages and working conditions; they argued about politics. Yet they retained a mutual respect and perhaps even regard. They trusted each other. Each knew that when the other man promised something, then it would be done. In a way this relationship was a prototype for the kind that Cousins

6. TGWU *Record*, October 1955, p. 118.

was later to develop in his dealings with many managements when he became a full-time union official.

At about this time, Cousins first met Ernest Bevin, the General Secretary and grand architect of the TGWU. Bevin was also chairman of the TUC, having been elected to that senior role in September 1936 for the coming year. Bevin was waging a renewed battle to improve the wages and conditions of road haulage workers, a cause he had been fighting for for most of the 1930s. Chiefly as a result of his pressure, the Government had set up yet another enquiry into the industry. The committee of enquiry under Sir James Baillie, which reported in May 1937, recommended new legislation, eventually embodied in the Road Haulage Wages Act of 1938, providing for a form of statutory regulation of wages. While the enquiry was sitting, Bevin toured the regions to discuss the industry's problems with his union's members and committees. In Leeds, Bevin called a delegate meeting of road haulage drivers from the Yorkshire area to explain the union's policy and to listen to his members' views. Cousins was present. Part of Bevin's case was that a great deal of responsibility rested on the union and its members in depots to force employers to set up joint negotiating machinery. It was important to do this in advance of any future government legislation, Bevin argued. But he ran into a good deal of criticism from the meeting, because some of the rank and file felt that their General Secretary, illustrious figure though he was, did not fully appreciate just how difficult it was for trade unionists to operate in the conditions existing in most of the transport companies.

Frank Cousins has told me that several times he shouted interruptions while Bevin was speaking. He complained that the union's General Secretary 'didn't know what he was talking about'.

Several times Bevin glowered across the hall at this young rank-and-file upstart who was giving him a rough time. When the meeting was over Cousins was called by an official to see him in a room at the back of the hall.

'What's your name, brother?' asked the official. 'Mr Bevin would like a word with you.'

'And who does Mr Bevin think he is?' snapped the ever-cocky Cousins as he strutted with the official towards the back room.

Bevin heard that remark. He sidled tank-like towards Frank. Frank was a head taller than Bevin, but the TGWU leader stretched out an arm and patted him on the shoulder.

'All right, lad,' he said. 'You'll make out. You'll make out. Now tell me, what's your problem?'

In a way Cousins's 'problem' was that he felt he could do the union job better than many of the full-time officials with whom he had come into contact. His self-confidence had grown considerably; his rough, abrasive mannerisms had been somewhat smoothed and he was less defensive in behaviour. It would be wrong to suggest that he had already begun to consider actively a full-time union job. The thought had occasionally crossed his mind as a possibility, but as yet it had not rated the status of a serious discussion with Nance. After all, there was his growing family to consider. His younger son, Michael, was born on 23 November 1935, in a council house in Lime Tree Avenue, where they had moved when the home in Leicester Avenue had become too crowded for a family of five. Soon they were to move again – to 47, Keppel Road (now Ardeen Road), the first house they would set out to buy, and also the first base for Frank Cousins, the trade union official.

Chapter Five

THE FORGING OF A WARRIOR

The appointment of Frank Cousins as a full-time official of the TGWU in July 1938 was the result of a good deal of controversy at the top level of the union – important enough to have brought Bevin and his assistant, Arthur Deakin, into conflict. The executive minute which formally approved his appointment tells the facts while omitting all the dimensions of the story:

> Dealing with the question of Yorkshire organisation the General Secretary [Ernest Bevin] reported that in pursuance of the powers granted by the General Executive Council he had arranged for the employment of Brother F. Cousins on organising work in the Doncaster district on the basis of a two years guarantee [at a salary of £5 5s. per week] with an assurance of permanency at the expiration of that period if justified by the results expressed in membership.

The next minute, No. 580, refers to a Brother J. L. Jones in connection with the Spanish Civil War. The Liverpool area secretary was requesting permission to fill a vacancy on the area committee and National Docks group committee as a result of Brother Jones's going 'to Spain to join the Government forces over a month ago and there being no indication as to when he would be likely to return . . .'

That was the month in which the Road Haulage Wages Act was finally passed, and in a way it was responsible for Cousins's appointment. While the Bill was moving through its parliamentary stages Bevin prepared the union to respond to the new opportunities for building up membership in road haulage. He knew this would mean taking on more full-time officials and he instructed his area and regional secretaries to put forward their proposals for this expansion in union activity. The Yorkshire secretary, Albert Heal, suggested to Bevin that he should be allowed to do something quite unique : to take on some new full-time officials on a purely temporary basis, without the normal pre-appointment examination, to test the ground. If the temporaries succeeded in paying their way and enlisting enough recruits, then they could be confirmed as permanent appointments, again without examination. Bevin thought this was a good idea and recommended it to the union executive. But it was strongly opposed by Arthur Deakin and a number of other executive members on the grounds that Heal's proposal would depart seriously from the TGWU policy and practice of appointing officials only after a lengthy examination. Deakin particularly objected to the concept. He was a conventionalist who feared the longer-term implications of permitting random appointments. But he was overruled by Bevin who, though a strict guardian of the union's rule-book, never hesitated to break convention if he thought it was necessary in the union's interests. Speed, he contended, was now essential. That was why he was prepared to make an exception to support Albert Heal's proposal.

Heal had been informed about Frank Cousins's abilities by the late Joe Bowman, the commercial group secretary in the area. Bowman had been immensely impressed by Cousins's work in the Doncaster branch where Cousins had been elected chairman of its commercial group committee. Indeed, Bowman several times urged Cousins to apply for a full-time union post. When the Leeds office had a vacancy for a district organiser Cousins did apply, but he did not know the union's rule-book sufficiently well to pass an examination. Shortly afterwards, he applied for three jobs in the London and South-East area : at Yarmouth, Chelmsford and the Outer London area. Cousins hoped he might get the Yarmouth job. He wanted to live by the sea and have his children grow up in a seaside town. But while he was waiting to hear from union headquarters about the vacancies he had a visit from Albert Heal and Joe Bowman, in the early summer of 1938. Heal offered him a job as a temporary organiser in the road haulage section covering the Sheffield and Doncaster district, which Bowman urged him to accept. If he did the job properly, he would become a full-time official after three years without having to take an examination. Cousins asked for time to think it over. He spent that afternoon with Nance, walking slowly round the back streets of Doncaster, discussing the venture. Should he throw up his job at Fairclough's where he was now one of the senior drivers earning about £7 10s. a week – an unusually high industrial wage in 1938 – and take a drop of £2 a week in accepting the union post? The children were still too young to be left at home if Nance took a job to help out the family income.

Accepting Heal's offer meant burning their boats, since Frank would then be settling with the union for life. Mrs. Cousins has told me that she said finally: 'Take the job. You're working for the union now for nothing, because you like it. You're obviously enjoying it, so why not take the plunge and do it full-time?'

When Heal and Bowman came back to the house later that afternoon, Frank told them that he would take the job.

Cousins became a full-time union organiser in June 1938. He was based in Doncaster and simply carried on the work he had been doing in a voluntary capacity for some time. At this stage he was not concerned with wage rates or working conditions – that was left to the senior officials – but continued with the task of organising and recruiting, spreading the gospel of trade unionism, and persuading the men he had already worked with for over six years that it was in their interests to join the TGWU.

He still toured the lorry parks and transport cafes throughout South Yorkshire, which he knew well, keeping up the prescribed schedule of recruitment and indeed exceeding it. It was hard work, but he enjoyed it.

The economic improvement that had been apparent in 1934 was tailing off. In 1938 the number of men laid off rose to a total of 1,831,372, the highest for three years. The decline in road haulage was at a slower pace than elsewhere in industry and road transport was expanding despite the general air of depression. (By 1939 1,300,000 people were employed in road transport, nearly one in ten of the adult population.) Even so, Cousins had to work extremely hard to keep up his self-imposed high standards. To quote Bill Goulding, the Doncaster branch secretary at the time: 'By God he worked. That's one of the things that really lifted him . . . He's done more for the lorry driver than anyone in England.'[1]

It would be hard to imagine a more dramatic back-cloth of political events against which to begin a full-time career in the trade union and Labour Movement.

By September 1938, a year before the outbreak of World War II, Frank Cousins, at 34, was very much a 'political animal'. Every day the experiences he encountered, the newspapers he read, the books he picked up casually to scan and more often to read with a quickening pace, confirmed his belief that a socialist solution was essential and indeed inevitable. A socialist solution? What *was* that? How could it be defined? He was not hypnotised by the Soviet Union, not drawn into the conventional Marxist and Communist Party process which was then so fashionable. Cousins viewed the ultra-organised, over-simplified political solution with strong suspicion. He was not a man who adapted easily to a highly disciplined regimen. He was 'awkward' mentally, as he was large and craggy physically. Human beings,

1. The *Sunday Times*, 2 October 1966.

he would reason, were not digits. The lorry drivers he knew were no angels, just because they were working-class; they could not be slotted into pre-determined moulds of political – or any other – behaviour patterns. Cousins did not believe that life was as simple and straightforward as all that. He allowed for the element of mystery and uncertainty, perhaps even for spiritual quality.

The most important influences on Cousins at this time were two of his senior colleagues in the Sheffield District office of the TGWU, Joe Bowman and Hugh Turner. These two probably helped to shape his political attitudes more than any other single force. Bowman, in particular, was something of an idol to Cousins, combining the roles of father-figure and political mentor. He was in the great Labour tradition of self-educated, well-read, wise men who could quote Marx and Shakespeare, Shelley and the Bible, Byron and Lenin, Hegel and Shaw. He could also talk to ordinary men and woman with a warmth and a passion which evoked a special response. Such men have been dotted across the landscape of labour history everywhere, though in the main they have been anonymous.

Cousins tells a story to illustrate Bowman's remarkable self-sacrifices. During the worst period of unemployment in South Yorkshire Bowman, already a full-time union official, hired a man from the employment exchange as the district office's chauffeur. He did so against union rules and the specific instructions of his superiors. And he paid the man out of his own wages. 'It was his way of trying to relieve the distress of unemployment', says Cousins. 'It was just one man, it's true, but Bowman was just one man, too. And in Bowman's view it was the least he could do in those terrible times.'

Hugh Turner was another of Cousins's mentors. He was an organiser in the building industry and a prominent socialist in Sheffield politics. 'He taught me most of what I learned about socialist policies, then,' says Cousins.

At times Cousins would despair. His impatience and impetuousness rebelled against the routine difficulties and obstacles in the way of making perceptible progress. He became despondent about his job, sometimes wondering whether after all he had made the right decision. He toyed with the notion of giving up trade union work to enter politics and possibly contest the Doncaster seat for the Labour Party (an idea which Bevin did much to discourage when he met Cousins again during the war). He was also discouraged by the perpetual battles with employers, as he fought to recruit new members. This was particularly the case after the outbreak of war, when Cousins was given permission by Arthur Deakin to set about recruiting women workers, a task he found more demanding and less productive than he had expected. Hugh Turner nursed him through this difficult patch. When Cousins expressed despair, Turner would say : 'You can never win a fight by quitting the ring.' It is a message that still echoes in Frank Cousins's mind. Turner would take him to one side and talk to him like a father. He would painstakingly emphasise the virtues of working for the trade union movement and extol the satisfaction to be derived from assisting the victim of an industrial accident to win compensation – only one of the unparalleled opportunities which union work offered to help the underdog. Turner preached to him, and Cousins took heed. Both Bowman and Turner urged Frank to study the union's rule-book and the law relating to industrial legislation. He followed their advice, steeping himself in everything he could lay his hands on relating to trade union law and practice, and transport legislation. He became an authority on the 1938 Road Haulage Wages Act and quickly began to surprise his mentors by his capacity to absorb and understand the complexities of the trade.

Looking back on his early experiences as a union official, Cousins says that those first few years were as disenchanting as were his later experiences in the Labour Cabinet of 1964–6. Why? Perhaps because he is a man who has always been unsure of himself in new situations, lacking the deep-seated confidence to overcome his inner doubts, despite his external appearance of brashness, even to the point of arrogance. All of this may well have concealed a deeper sense of inadequacy, which only time and experience could effectively expel. Clearly the influence of Bowman and Turner was crucial at that stage in Cousins's career. 'It was men like Joe Bowman who made me,' Frank Cousins has told me. 'There were hundreds like him. And I am the product of hundreds of men with whom I grew up, on whose shoulders and by whose help and wisdom I became what I am today.'

When Frank Cousins told me that in 1966, he was still in Harold Wilson's Cabinet. That was when, after deep reflection, he defined himself as 'a kind of Marxist-Lansbury type of socialist'. A mixture, perhaps, of the scientific socialist and the idealistic dreamer, not an altogether unique combination in British socialism.

The move to 47, Keppel Road shortly after Frank became a full-time official was precipitated when the union provided Frank with a car – there was no room for it in their previous place. Keppel Road was a new development with houses for sale at under £500, with a down payment of £20 and mortgage repayments of about 14s. a week. At last they were buying their own home.

Frank's pay had gone up but it was well into wartime before his weekly pay-packet reached the sum he had been earning as a lorry driver in 1938.

When war broke out, trade union officials were classified as in a reserved occupation, but Frank joined the Home Guard and was involved with civil defence committees in Sheffield and Doncaster. The final confirmation of his union appointment in August 1940 helped Cousins to overcome his earlier anxieties about the job. He was now a fully-fledged organiser, covering not only road transport, but general trades as well, with enormous zeal and energy. His normal working day was sixteen hours, and he thought nothing of leaving Keppel Road at 8 a.m. and returning at midnight, frequently for days on end. He would travel any distance within his union province if there was the slightest prospect of recruiting new members. No longer were there periods of sustained remorse or self-questioning about whether he had chosen the right road. He had : his conviction was absolute.

For the first time since their marriage in 1930 Frank and Nance felt that their life had a sense of longer-term direction; true, their years together had been happy and sometimes exciting. They had three children. Being separated for long stretches had brought its problems, but an unusually powerful devotion to each other had helped them over those periods.

The one thing that had hitherto been lacking in their lives had been what is now called 'work motivation'. Now, in his middle thirties, Cousins had found something to match his maturing personality and temperament : the conviction that, by some means, the world must be changed. Life as a full-time trade union official gave him the sense of direction, continuity and wider significance that had so far been lacking in his career. The fact that they were now buying their own home gave the young couple a new feeling of stability and confidence.

Frank now began to see his role in a much wider setting and to cast off the day-to-day frustrations inherent in his job of recruiting new members in the face of stubborn resistance from the employers. He worked now with a greater zeal and dedication than ever. The goal was clear : to build up the union and then to fight relentlessly to secure a better society for its members and their families. That to him *was* the socialist aim.

Early in 1940, a young Scottish doctor and his wife moved into the house next door to Frank and Nance. Dr. Bertram Mann was a newly-qualified doctor and was working on a research project at the local hospital. The two families became close friends, in spite of age differences and the fact that the Manns were still childless, treating each other's homes as their own and discovering that they had a great deal in common. The Manns had been active Communists since their student days and were now working with the local Party branch, particularly with the miners' lodges where Communist influence was especially strong. Dr Mann and his wife were both generous enough to discuss this period without demur.

Dr Mann says :

I suppose [Frank] was somewhat distrustful of intellectuals – and I was one in his eyes; but he was never distrustful of ideas and debate. I bought the *New Statesman* regularly and I would pass it on to Frank and Nance, and we would gather round the kitchen table at the weekends to discuss some issue raised in the paper . . .

Frank was a strong Left-winger, but he would never join the Communist

Party. I suppose the truth is that he was never a really good party man in the orthodox party-hack sense. Frank was always a terribly difficult chap for any party to strait-jacket. He was always an individualist; he would always kick against things. I can't imagine Frank tolerating the kind of discipline expected of a member of the Communist party. His mind didn't work that way.

Dr Mann recalls Frank Cousins at that time as 'abrupt, blunt and perhaps a little audacious' in his general approach. He was sometimes 'prickly,' even in his dealings with union members. He did not suffer fools gladly – early indications of characteristics that will sound familiar to many who knew him as General Secretary of the TGWU. Dr Mann remembers that this was a job Frank had set his heart on when he first knew him :

Frank would suddenly declare that he would become General Secretary one day. At first we thought he was joking but we soon learned that he was quite serious about his aim. Nance would always try to bring him down to earth again. She would say to him : 'Oh, come off it, Frank.' Even so we all felt that Frank had a terrific potential.

The doctor, who has long since left the Communist Party and ceased to be politically involved in any way, recalls that Frank did not attend any of his Marxist classes and only rarely came to a discussion group. Nance, however, was a regular attender and became a member of the Communist Party – introduced by Mrs Mann – after the Nazi invasion of Russia in 1942. But her membership lapsed after two years.

It is arguable that until Frank Cousins came into contact with Bowman, Turner and Mann he had not really thought out a coherent political philosophy. His trade-union activity was much more an instinctive class response. True, he had listened to some of the great socialist orators; he had become involved in the dialogue about Labour Party affairs in Doncaster through the Judds; and his work within the trade union system necessarily overlapped into politics. But none of this was quite the same as developing a strong and clear political view for himself.

The relevant point about Frank Cousins's rise is that it was made possible only through the institutional framework that the unions had built for themselves. He was a classic product of the process and the times. He knew instinctively that once he had found his feet within the union system he was on the right course. The pull was immediate, if not always clear even to himself. And when Dr Mann speaks of Cousins's ambition to be General Secretary, the most likely explanation is that this was his natural response to a sudden sense of awareness that he was now part of an institutional setting where the limitations of his class, his education, his entire social background no longer mattered : a setting, indeed, where those limitations were, in a distinctive way, a special strength. This was the strength on which he was later to draw when, from the seat of power and authority in the largest of Britain's unions, Cousins gave force and direction to a new move to the Left by the British Labour Movement, a move which may have been historically inevitable, but which required the qualities – the weaknesses as well as the strengths – of a Frank Cousins to give it the necessary impetus.

In Sheffield Frank Cousins soon acquired the reputation of being 'a bit of a nut-case' – his own phrase – largely because of his readiness to go anywhere and tackle even the most intractable problem if there was half a chance of making a few recruits. This was especially true of his conviction that women workers ought to be recruited, and that the great increase in their number because of war production gave the TGWU a unique opportunity. His colleagues listened to these views with barely concealed scepticism, if not hostility. The senior officials were far from convinced, but they agreed to give Cousins his head, on the grounds that he was unlikely to make any headway, but that if he did it would be a relatively inexpensive bonus for the union. This negative attitude towards potential women trade unionists was not untypical in those early days of the war.

On one occasion there was a strike of 400 women workers at the Batchelor's pea factory in Sheffield. They were demanding union recognition by the management. The strike leader brought a deputation of six women into the TGWU office to see a union official. This official told the deputation that he would send the union's leading expert to the factory, provided that the strikers could assemble in the canteen one lunch-time with management approval. Meanwhile, he contacted Frank Cousins.

'Frank,' he said, 'I have the very job for you. There's 400 women workers at Batchelor's Peas all ready to join the union. They only want a bit of persuasion, and you're the man to do it. After all, I've told them that you're an expert on food production techniques and hygiene and all that.'

'But,' Cousins protested, 'I don't know anything about food hygiene.'

'Well,' the official replied, 'it won't take you long to read it up. I've fixed the meeting for the day after tomorrow, and I've told the management you're coming.'

So Cousins spent the next two days reading up the legislation on clean food production, hygiene in factories, the required minimum standard of protective clothing, the techniques of food-processing, and so on. He became an expert almost overnight. He went along to the factory at the appointed time, together with the chairman of the Sheffield branch of the TGWU. The canteen was crowded with women and girls, and Frank was introduced to them as one of the country's leading experts on food-processing, as well as on working conditions for women. The chairman put on a splendid performance, then called on Frank to speak. Cousins delivered a twenty-minute speech on food-processsing and the need for trade union protection and organisation in factories like this. Even his colleagues were impressed by his instant grasp of the business. He then answered questions before winding up with a final appeal to the women to join the union.

'Are there any other points you want to raise?' he asked.

Silence.

'Are you sure?' he pressed.

An attractive young blonde in the front row got up and said softly:

'Yes, love, I've got a question. What time do you finish work tonight?'

The meeting dissolved into uproars of laughter, whistles and calls of 'Answer!'.

Cousins, as red as a beetroot, nervously tried to laugh, but was too shattered to do anything but make a quick exit. He described this as one of his most embarrassing moments as a union official.

Cousins worked in the Sheffield area through most of the war years and did achieve a reputation as a diligent organiser. Wartime Sheffield was not exactly the easiest place for trade union work. Frank was there throughout the Blitz period and figured in one of those narrow-escape stories so common in wartime. There was a last-minute cancellation of a meeting he was due to attend in one of the main hotels in Sheffield. That night the hotel was destroyed by bombs.

A more amusing incident offers another glimpse of the Cousins character. Frank was sharing a fire-watching stint at the union's Sheffield office with a man called Smith. Early in the evening Smith decided to go out for a couple of hours, leaving Frank on duty alone. Cousins did not hear him come in before he himself decided to turn in. He stripped off – he always slept naked – and then was called to the WC. The door of his room shut after him and his keys were inside. There he was in the hallway with nothing on and – as he thought – alone in the building. He considered his options. He could call the police, but what kind of story could he tell them that sounded plausible enough to justify calling them out? He could spend the night on the floor of the hallway. But what about the women cleaners who would be the first to arrive in the morning? What sort of impression would *they* get? Cousins then decided to climb out of a window at the back of the building, sheltered from prying eyes, and clamber along a ledge to his room which was also on the inside wall. So, stark naked, he climbed out of the window on to the narrow ledge which was above the glass roof of a furniture showroom and groped his way along like a huge pink spider. Half way along he thought: 'Suppose I slip and crash through that glass roof, what will the coroner's verdict be? What will Nance think? What will anybody think?' His heart sank as he fumbled in total darkness along the narrow ledge, scratching and scraping his flesh on the rough brick. It was damnably cold. He finally reached his window and after manoeuvring under the black-out curtain he slithered into the room, black with grime, cut and scraped and bleeding. Exhausted, he sank into bed and slept. Next morning he showed his battle-wounds to Smith, who told Cousins that he had been in his room all the time. He had returned quite early and gone straight to bed. And, said Smith, he had keys to fit all the doors in the building.

'Thanks,' said Cousins.

The need to spread his recruiting wings into new areas, especially among women war-workers, was not simply an idealistic vision : for Cousins it was also a necessity. His work in the road haulage industry was becoming increasingly difficult and he needed new outlets for his energies, fresh fields to work on, as the road haulage firms were hit by fuel restrictions and the call-up of the younger drivers made recruiting to the union increasingly difficult. By February 1940 fuel supplies to the industry were down by about 25 per cent of pre-war levels, in accordance with the Government's policy of transferring long-distance transport to the railways. But despite the Government's vigorous attempts to tighten control over transport, it was not until the end of 1942, after two years of unbroken discussions between Whitehall and the road hauliers, that an effective system was eventually arrived at, and even then the industry remained dissatisfied. The official history of the war points out that even in 1942 'The road goods transport industry still composed a highly individualistic and keenly competitive industry. The grouping scheme imposed on the industry at the outbreak of war had not greatly diminished the rivalry between firms and there was still little unity of purpose within the industry as a whole.'[2] These difficulties naturally affected trade union organisation in road haulage.

In any event, Cousins's activities and his thinking were shifting to wider horizons. In 1943 there was a vacancy for a new secretary for the union's general workers' group in Yorkshire, a job to which he was immediately attracted. His practical experiences in the Sheffield area had brought him into close contact with a wide variety of industries, and he had already become in effect a general workers' organiser rather than a strictly road haulage man. The group secretary's job, covering the whole of the Yorkshire area, would be based in Leeds. Cousins applied towards the end of 1943, just as a second job fell vacant. A national officer was required at the union's national headquarters in London, for the Road Transport Commercial group.

Frank was not interested, and it is likely that he would have passed the job up had it not been for the persuasion of some of his friends in the Doncaster branch, and especially the pressure of Nance. The secretary of the local branch of the TGWU at that time was a veteran called Harry Blyther, a confirmed Cousins supporter who was constantly predicting that 'the lad had a great future in the union'. He even affirmed that Cousins

2. C. I. Savage, *History of the Second World War: Inland Transport* (HMSO and Longmans, 1957), p. 102.

50

would one day be General Secretary. It was Blyther who pressed Frank to apply for the national officer's job in London. Frank, however, was keener on the Leeds job. One night towards the end of 1943, with the connivance of Nance, Blyther brought Frank an application-form for the job in London and told him point-blank to fill it in. Blyther and Nance stood over him – ignoring his protests that it was too late to apply anyway (the closing date was only two days away). At about midnight Nance got on her bicycle with the completed form and handed it in in the nick of time at the post office in Doncaster.

Competition for this post was keen, since it would take the successful candidate into the very heart of union affairs, or so it appeared. In February Cousins was called to an interview in London and took Nance with him. He had a thirty-five minute interview in front of the union's finance and general purposes committee – the senior policy committee – dealing with the union's structure and rules, the road haulage industry, government legislation and the effect of wartime controls on road haulage : daunting stuff for a young and relatively inexperienced provincial official up against five others with far more experience than he had and probably more support behind them. Cousins had been well briefed by Bowman and Turner; he had Blyther's advice and good wishes ringing in his ears; but the whole thing rested on how he would stand up to the relentless cross-examination by the selection team. Harold Clay in charge of the board, was the union's Assistant General Secretary and a man of great experience who had previously held the post of national secretary of the road passenger transport group and was an authority on the union's affairs. Cousins claims now that he 'thoroughly enjoyed the examination', but it was probably not so good at the time. Clay's questioning riled Cousins.

'Now, Brother Cousins, I believe you claim to be an expert on transport law.'

'I know enough to do my job,' Cousins retorted belligerently.

Clay proceeded to take him through the hoops, firing question after question on the niceties of transport legislation. Cousins stood his ground, impressing the board with the extent of his knowledge.

On that Saturday morning Frank and Nance got back to Keppel Road to find a telegram waiting from Albert Heal asking Frank to ring him at once.

Frank rang from the corner shop and Heal congratulated him on his appointment to the national job. The news left him stunned. The other five candidates on the short-list had had paper qualifications far higher than his own. His main purpose in attending the board at all was to give himself experience when it came to applying for the Leeds job.

There was no time for the Cousins family to adjust themselves to this major development in their lives. Heal had arranged for Frank to be in

London on the following Monday morning. Frank had no idea of what the job would involve, nor of where he would live when he arrived in London. His first step up the ladder to national fame was by its very nature a step into the exciting unknown. The salary increase was in itself an indication of the importance of his promotion: a rise of more than £2 10s. a week was significant by 1944 standards.

Cousins presented himself at Transport House at 8 a.m. on 17 February 1944. The cleaners were still scrubbing the floors and the place was otherwise deserted. He sat on a bench opposite the lifts and waited. About half an hour later Harold Clay arrived.

'Hell!' he exclaimed. 'What are you doing here at this hour?'

Cousins eyed him coolly while he selected one of those characteristic replies.

'I'm here to do the job you appointed me to do,' was the truculent response.

Shaking hands, they became, as they were to remain, firm friends.

Chapter Six

NATIONAL OFFICER

Frank Cousins entered the world of national trade union affairs at about as difficult a moment as that at which he started out on working life. At fourteen, when he began work in the pits, World War I was drawing to an end; at thirty-nine, when he began his career as a national officer in the TGWU, World War II was reaching its climax and was to end about a year after he arrived in London.

By 1944 the industrial tensions and strains of wartime Britain were coming to a head. After four and a half years of stress the domestic front was showing signs of wear which were not greatly dissimilar from those in the armed forces. The physical conditions of wartime work in the factories were far from easy even in those areas outside the range of routine air attack. There was a distinct weariness and fatigue about the quality of civilian life in 1944 : a fatigue exacerbated by the build-up of consistent and extensive shift-work, limited leisure, the scarcity of goods, and the cramped character of social relations. The general social and domestic pressures of wartime life in Britain and the anxieties as well as the expectations of what post-war life might have to offer were all reaching a climax in 1944.

Obviously this tended to throw problems like wages and working conditions into sharper focus. Of course, wages improved considerably during the war years and the days of mass unemployment faded into a bleak, though recent, past. Almost overnight, those in the dole queues of 1939 became weekly wage earners, discovering a new dignity and self-respect : a disturbing commentary on the national conduct of affairs, where an insoluble problem in peace-time was clarified immediately war started, even though it was not easy for men who had been unemployed for years to adjust at once to the changed conditions. There was a legacy of bitterness and a psychological conditioning left by the Depression years that had to be overcome. Many men had become unused to the climate of regular factory

53

life and the routine disciplines of a working day. The wartime industrial communities developed their own special and unique climate with the mix of older workers, the former unemployed, the vast influx of women workers and those who were exempt from military service for one reason or another.

From the earliest days of the war some Government departments, notably the Treasury, argued for a system of statutory wage control.[1] This was opposed by other ministries, especially by the Ministry of Labour, as well as by the TUC leadership. The whole problem of wage and price control was still under discussion when the wartime Coalition Government under Churchill came into office in May 1940. Ernest Bevin became Minister of Labour and his move from general secretaryship of the TGWU to the War Cabinet was as much a turning point in terms of labour relations as Churchill's was in the overall conduct of the war effort. The new government chose the path of voluntary agreement with the trade unions and Bevin himself immediately initiated a new dimension to joint consultation between government and unions by forming a Joint Consultative Committee composed of ministers, the TUC and the employers' confederation. The previous Government had set up a National Joint Advisory Council representing the Government and the two sides of industry. But Bevin's JCC was more compact, more influential and altogether more centrally involved in policy making. In fact, it was the start of a completely new level of joint consultation between the State and the trade unions.

Although Bevin was strongly against statutory wage control and remained convinced of the superior efficacy of what he described as 'voluntaryism' (a consensus between government and unions), he knew, better than most, that the pressure for wage increases, prompted by rising living costs and the inevitable thrust of wartime inflation, would cause severe strains inside the trade union movement. For this reason he proposed a new system of compulsory arbitration which would in effect make strikes and lock-outs illegal.

At the first meeting of his newly-formed JCC, on 22 May 1940, Bevin asked the parties to consider the best means of 'removing wage problems from the field of prompt controversy'. He suggested a special tribunal to apply a uniform system of wage settlements to all industries, the introduction of an 'independent element' into wage-bargaining machinery, and the establishment of a system of compulsory arbitration to be used when the normal negotiating machinery failed to produce agreement. The unions rejected Bevin's first two proposals, but the third was accepted and formed the basis of Order 1305 – a now famous milestone in industrial arbitration which lasted until August 1951.

Order 1305, the Conditions of Employment and National Arbitration Order, established a new system of compulsory arbitration under a national

1. N. D. Ellis and G. J. Harkin, *Trade Unions and the State* (Oxford: Blackwell) (not yet published).

tribunal. The Order laid down that where there was failure to agree in any trade dispute there would be no stoppage of work. The dispute would be referred to arbitration and the decision of the tribunal would be binding on all parties. That meant the outlawing of strikes and lock-outs. Of course there were strikes during the war, almost all of them unofficial and all of them technically illegal. In the main they were small strikes of brief duration, and the pattern of industrial conflict was quite different from the pre-war situation, and indeed substantially different from the only relevant parallel, the strike picture during World War I.[2]

The relationship between the government – which in this context meant Bevin in effect – and the unions went far beyond anything that had previously existed. As Ellis and Harkin explain:

> It meant that the terms upon which the wartime 'social contract' was established could be extended to include almost any issue that the unions chose to raise and introduce into their consultations with Government. In this way the unions were able to exercise a significant influence upon policies extending well beyond the immediate issues of industrial relations including those applying to prices and profits, taxation and rationing. And because of their increased bargaining power the 'social contract' which finally emerged was closely modelled on the unions' demands.[3]

Bevin's policies were given complete support by his colleagues in Cabinet and even those who might have been 'politically disturbed' by the new power and influence of the unions were silenced by Churchill's backing for Bevin. Trade union membership in wartime rose from 6,300,000 in 1939 to 8,174,000 by the end of 1943 – the first time it had reached the eight-milion mark. This was despite the numbers of workers who had been absorbed into the armed forces, which were reaching their peak strength in 1943–4. At the time of D-Day, 6 June 1944, out of every nine members of the potential labour force in Britain two were in the armed forces and three engaged in war production. No other country ever equalled this proportion, which was maintained in Britain at virtually the same level for the three years 1942–5. Most trade unions gained membership and influence as a result of the wartime regulations introduced by Bevin and the development of joint consultation, works councils and the altogether more formalised system of wage bargaining. In 1942 TGWU membership jumped above one million – to 1,133,165 – for the first time, though by 1945 it had slipped back to a total membership of 1,019,069.

Frank Cousins arrived in London to take over his national officer's job in 1944. Part of his task was to build up the TGWU's road haulage group and

2. See V. L. Allen, *Trade Unions and the Government* (Longmans, 1960), p. 142.
3. N. D. Ellis and G. J. Harkin, *Trade Unions and the State* (not yet published).

prepare the ground for post-war development in the union's organisation. He found the scene somewhat depressing. The National Secretary, Jack Corrin, was an able organiser and a genial man, but the national organisation was a bit threadbare.

Nothing was set out for Cousins to do on his first day. There was no briefing on what his first national job would entail; no intimate introduction into the complexities of the post; no formal approach of any kind. Jack Corrin greeted him, made him feel at home and painted a gentle picture of life at Transport House. The only trouble was that Frank had nowhere to work : there was neither a desk nor a chair for him. His predecessor, Harry Nicholas – later national secretary of the metal, engineering and chemical group – was still using his old office. Frank stood around, feeling about as much at home as a polar bear in the Congo, while Corrin tried to find a corner where he might settle – eventually producing a desk of sorts and a rickety chair which he made room for in his own office. Frank was not to get an office of his own for some time to come. His start was from a stage before scratch!

Jack Corrin, as Frank soon discovered, tended to concentrate on head-office administration and national negotiations. Links between headquarters and the regions were tenuous and there was no two-way flow of information – barely a trickle, indeed. Cousins soon realised that he would have to make the job for himself by creating a completely new strategy. Corrin agreed to his scheme for travelling around the country as much as possible, rather than remaining tethered to London, and encouraged him to get around the regional offices to bring in new members. This suited Frank very well, since Nance and the children were still in Doncaster and he was in no hurry to bring them to wartime London. He himself was staying with Harry Nicholas, ironically enough the man he was ultimately to defeat for the general secretaryship. He stayed with Nicholas in Streatham until they were bombed out, when, still keeping in the union family, he moved in with Jack Corrin and his wife in New Malden, Surrey. For the rest of 1944 he moved about the country meeting local officials and building up a new organisational network : a simple, obvious administrative process in itself, but one that had never been approached before in Cousins's painstaking and precise fashion.

The leadership situation in the TGWU at the beginning of the final year of the war was as uncertain as was the postwar political direction of Britain, and for the same reasons. In the early months of 1945 no one could tell at what point the war might end. Only Ernest Bevin, a member of the War Cabinet, with access to military papers, knew that it was only a matter of time. The climax of the war was approaching – for Europe, for Britain and, in particular, for Ernest Bevin. Would he come back as General Secretary of the TGWU? Would he remain in politics? Where would the Labour

Party stand in the post-war parliament? All the evidence suggests that Bevin, like the majority of Labour Party leaders, seriously underestimated the strength of feeling that had developed in the armed forces about the need for political and social change. While the party prepared for a general election in 1945, they appeared to have no great conviction that they would get in against a Conservative party whose leader, Winston Churchill, was the unquestioned and victorious war leader. So Ernest Bevin turned his mind to a likely return to the TGWU, as its General Secretary.

Arthur Deakin was still only acting General Secretary, there having been no election when he stepped suddenly into Bevin's job in 1940. It was still 'Bevin's union', and although Bevin was absorbed in his role as Minister of Labour, he still spared a corner of his mind for the union which was, after all, still his power-base. He was kept informed of what went on at Transport House by his many friends inside the organisation. There was no overt interference, and none was necessary, since the whole fabric of the TGWU's hierarchical canvas had been shrewdly woven to Bevin's pattern. For Deakin, his wartime role as caretaker General Secretary was as difficult as it was frequently invidious. He had a tremendous regard for Bevin, but then everyone who came into contect with the remarkable force of Bevin's character – friend or foe – had such a regard. The truth is that though Deakin respected Bevin he never really liked him. Deakin would never permit his innermost feelings about his leading colleagues inside the union to overcome his profound sense of corporate loyalty. Rarely would he – and then only to his closest personal friends – relax into a confidential whisper about what he really thought of Bevin, or for that matter of anyone else within that closed circle of influence at the top of the union. To the outside world Deakin always insisted that he had suffered no interference from Bevin in the course of his work.[4] But there is strong reason to doubt this, despite the absence of clear evidence.

At any rate, in December 1944 Bevin met the TGWU General Executive to discuss the future.

He told them that his leave of absence from the TGWU would come to an end on the dissolution of Parliament, when he would return as General Secretary until his retirement at 65 in March 1946. At that time Deakin was the senior administrator after Bevin. But before he joined the War Cabinet Bevin had suggested that Deakin should exercise control in consultation with Harold Clay, who was then appointed acting Assistant General Secretary. He now said he did not think that his return need 'interfere with

4. V. L. Allen, *Trade Union Leadership* (Longmans, 1957), pp. 230–1. Allen points out that Deakin had been under Bevin's influence since he became national secretary in 1932, when he 'admired Bevin and accepted his decisions . . . He did not construe an interest in the affairs of the union by Bevin as interference nor did he see anything wrong in seeking Bevin's advice'.

the administrative arrangements then operating and that neither Deakin nor Clay should be demoted. He did not state in what way he was going to function as general secretary but he confirmed that he regarded Deakin as the chief administrator.'[5]

What happened later was as much a surprise to Bevin as to many of his union colleagues, who were quite certain that he would return to his old chair. This indeed he did, but only for the brief spell between the break-up of the War Cabinet in May 1945 and the formation of the Labour government after the election of July 1945.

There is some conflict of evidence about precisely what Bevin did in these weeks, but the account given to me by Frank Cousins suggests that he virtually ordered Deakin out of his chair :

> Deakin was made to wait in an outer office while Bevin discussed with the union's finance and general purposes committee, whether he, Bevin, would resume again as general secretary. Deakin never forgave Bevin for this. Bevin's intention was to return (assuming Labour lost the election) for a period of about 4 to 6 months and then retire as general secretary. His idea was to supervise the election of a successor (who would probably be Deakin) following which it was Bevin's intention to remain on the union's payroll as financial adviser.

Cousins maintains that his account of the Bevin-Deakin relationship is substantiated by Deakin's behaviour towards Bevin once he had been confirmed as General Secretary after the 1945 election, when Bevin was ensconced in the Foreign Office. 'Thereafter,' Cousins says, 'Deakin's relations with Bevin were always cold and unfriendly. In fact Deakin made no attempt during the following ten years of his life as General Secretary to commemorate Bevin's service to the union. There was no fund; no special gesture; and rarely even a mention in any of Deakin's utterances.'

Cousins tried to correct this when he took over as General Secretary by seeking to establish a chair in industrial relations at Oxford, naming the endowment after Ernest Bevin. He was informed by the university authorities that this was not possible. He sought a similar chair at Cambridge, again without success. Then, still trying to compensate for what he regarded as a serious omission by Deakin, Cousins discovered from Vic Feather (the late Lord Feather), that Jacob Epstein had a bronze bust of Bevin in the cellar of his London home. Bevin had sat for this work, but had refused to accept it when it was finished, telling Epstein that it made him look like a murderer.

Frank Cousins acquired the bust for a token £250 on behalf of the union, and it now stands in the General Secretary's office at Transport House. A variety of motives have been attributed to Cousins's determination

5. *Loc. cit.*

to counteract Deakin's 'aberration' about Bevin. It is suggested that he would do anything to prove to the union that he was a more honourable and reasonable man than Deakin, that this was one of his ways of seeking popularity at the expense of Deakin whose image he wanted to undermine. It is possible that such thoughts were in Cousins's mind, but in my view he was genuinely anxious to put right what he regarded as a serious error on Deakin's part in failing to honour Bevin's pioneering work for the TGWU and the Labour Movement as a whole.

For the first two years of the Labour Government there was a remarkable tranquillity on the industrial front compared with the parallel period after World War I. Demobilisation went smoothly enough and the massive task of converting industry back to a peace-time footing was carried out with surprisingly little dislocation. The lessons of the 1920s had been learned. But quite apart from that there was a totally new mood of excitement and expectancy among the returning troops as they exchanged their uniforms for a suit of 'utility', albeit good quality, civilian clothes. There was a collective determination not to be trampled on as were so many of their fathers after World War I. These were the sons and daughters of men and women who could recall the broken dreams of 1919 and the 1920s, who had heard that cynical cliché about a 'land fit for heroes'. They were the children of the thirties, many of whom had found in the armed forces a sense of community and, even amid the destruction of war, a sense of identity and security which had been quite absent in prewar Britain. Some of them had even been able to fill in some of the gaps left by the inadequate system of education available to the majority of the people. All these factors were reflected in Labour's huge majority in the House of Commons: a clear majority overall of 146 and a majority of 195 over the Conservatives – almost a complete reversal of the parliamentary position after the previous election in 1935. Labour was now in Government with real power for the first time in the Party's history. It was heralded as the dawn of a new political and social era for the British people. And in truth, it was.

The first year of the Labour Government was probably the most dramatic of any parliament in modern times. The outline of a social revolution was placed before the House of Commons and step by step during the succeeding five years many of the basic industries were nationalised: coal, railways, road haulage, electricity, gas, civil aviation and the Bank of England. Freedom and independence were conceded to India, Burma, Ceylon and Egypt. The Welfare State was raised from a system of fringe supports to the foundation stone of an entirely new approach to social affairs. In 1947 the school-leaving age was raised to fifteen. A New Towns Act of 1946 empowered the Government to begin the development of a programme of completely new towns to ease the pressure on London and other densely populated areas. And the National Health Service was born. It is impossible by simply offering a list of this kind to convey the dynamic spirit and the feeling of change which pervaded most of Britain – though of course not all – in those immediate post-war years. When Parliament adjourned for its first summer recess in August 1946, *The Times* commented: 'No Government has ever before attempted so much social change in one session.'

The observation was not entirely approving. The critics were already claiming that Labour was trying to do too much too quickly and were predicting that in the fragile post-war system of world trade and international finance the British economy would be unable to stand the strain. Severe balance-of-payments problems were already emerging and the Attlee Government leaned more and more heavily on its 'special relationship' with the trade unions, in an attempt to establish a voluntary agreement (an early form of 'social contract') in which wage claims would be restrained in exchange for a programme of social equity from the government. The abrupt ending of the wartime lend-lease programme, and the commitment of the Labour Government at the beginning of its life to huge new loans from the United States, inevitably placed serious limitations on the freedom of the Attlee Cabinet. It did not deter it from pursuing its social and economic programme, but it did mean that this new era was ushered in under a cloud of grey austerity which in the end dampened enthusiasm and tarnished the brightness of the new dawn. The full impact of this cloud did not occur until the Korean War knocked the Attlee Government completely off course in July 1950; but it was already building up as early as 1947, the year in which the Marshall Plan was launched by the United States to help Europe recover from the ravages of war. By then, British industry was already facing serious shortages caused partly by the post-war replacement and rebuilding boom and also by the shortage of capital to pay for raw materials. The enormous disparity between the American and the European economies – including Britain's – manifested itself in an acute 'dollar gap'. This had existed before the war, but it was much worse since the gulf between American and European production systems had widened with the war. The Marshall Plan was devised to help narrow the gap in the interests of both sides of the Atlantic. But it meant a tightening of belts for the British and a slowing down of the more ambitious programmes for social change; it meant a return to or a retention of wartime controls, which added to the social and economic tensions; and as the Labour Chancellor, Sir Stafford Cripps, reimposed a form of wartime austerity to fight inflation the Government inevitably ran into difficulties not only with the trade union leadership but – more electorally damaging – with its supporters and voters.

It had been plain to the TUC leadership from the start that there would have to be a change in their general approach to economic and industrial problems now that a Labour Government was in effective power for the first time. No one in the TUC hierarchy was sure what this change would involve or what its ultimate implications might be. It was simply accepted that the relationship between government and unions would inevitably be different from all previous peace-time experiences. After all there was no absolute precedent for the 1945 political situation. On the other hand the trade union leaders had already established a much closer liaison with the State machine as a result of their wartime associations, especially after having Ernest Bevin at the Ministry of Labour. The corridors of influence, if not of power, had been opened to them as never before. They had to try to exercise a degree of control over and responsibility for their members, which imposed considerable strains on them as individuals and on their organisations. There was no enthusiastic relish to continue this into peacetime, yet in reality most of the TUC leadership knew in their hearts that they had no option. Implicit, if not explicit, was the understanding that a degree of wage restraint and industrial peace would be required to enable the Labour Government to overcome the accumulation of formidable domestic and international problems that lay on the Cabinet table. The unions had successfully resisted statutory wage control in wartime and they were determined to oppose it in peace-time, notwithstanding a strong Labour Government pledged to carry out Socialist policies long advocated by the unions. In 1946 the Government held a series of meetings with the TUC General Council and its various sub-committees, especially the influential economic committee. At the beginning of 1947 the Government published a White Paper, *Economic Considerations affecting the Relation between Employers and Workers*,[6] which asked for restraint in wage demands, and in general spelled out the need for more efficiency in production methods as well as greater cooperation between management and workers in the national interest. But the TUC made it clear to ministers that its support of the White Paper was 'on the definite understanding that unions would continue to be free to submit wages applications as formerly where this was found to be necessary'.[7]

At every available opportunity the trade union leadership emphasised the absolute priority of keeping collective bargaining free from the constraints of statute. But it was clear, long before the Cripps White Paper, *Personal Incomes, Costs and Prices*, was issued in February 1948, that the Government would ask the unions to accept a period of rigid restraint. The Cripps policy was not one of total freeze though in practice it tended to come close to that. The demand was that 'each claim for an increase in wages or salaries must be considered on its national merits and not on the basis of maintaining a former relativity between different occupations and industries'.[8]

6. Cmd 7018, January 1947.
7. TUC *Annual Report*, 1947, p. 219.
8. Cmd 7321, February 1948.

The Government White Paper insisted that it was not the intention to trample on free collective bargaining. The new policy need not mean a rigid acceptance of existing wage structures. Wages could be increased against a set of criteria covering the lower paid, increased output, undermanning in key industries and industrial efficiency. It was a formula which was to become familiar as the criteria for pay restraint in the decades to follow. At first there was reluctance and even irritation and anger inside the TUC General Council – as much for the manner in which Sir Stafford Cripps handled his relations with the union leaders as for the policy itself. Cripps was not the most tactful of ministers in his dealings with the TUC, nor was he given to a warm and humble understanding of trade union internal difficulties; yet despite all this the TUC accepted the policy as essential in the national interest and out of loyalty to the Labour Government. A special conference of trade union executives held in London on 24 March 1948 voted by 5,421,000 to 2,032,000 to endorse the policy. Wage restraint became the official policy of the TUC from then until it was overturned at the Brighton TUC of 1950.

Of course, this support was always conditional on the government's imposing similar restraint on profits and prices and pushing firmly ahead with policies of the redistribution of wealth. Unfortunately these policies were not nearly as successful as the wage restraint and the effect of the Cripps 'freeze' was to reduce the real purchasing power of workers during the period. To that extent it succeeded in curbing wage inflation but not in resolving the endemic problem of the balance of payments and the 'dollar gap'. It also raised, or perhaps accentuated, other difficulties. It exposed trade union leadership to severe strains and added to the administrative problems of imposing unpopular, and in many ways ill-defined, policies on a trade union membership that had grown since the end of the war by nearly one and a half million. By 1948 the affiliated membership of the TUC was at a record level of 9,320,000, and similarly the TGWU membership reached its then highest-ever figure of 1,323,679. The sheer physical difficulties of servicing such an increased membership clearly raised their own problems. They would have been there regardless of the tensions created by wage restraint. The trade union leadership was having to fight for its credibility as well as to maintain its authority with the membership.

These tensions were manifesting themselves, as tensions invariably do in industrial relations, in strikes. Of course the strikes were unofficial: Order 1305 was still in force and the Government had no intention of withdrawing it in the light of the economic circumstances. In a sense the wartime emergency was still in existence, though the causes and the effects of the emergency were of a different order.

The TUC was already being faced with challenges by unofficial strikes and at the 1948 Trades Union Congress the President referred to the 'disloyalty and irresponsibility displayed by a minority of the workers . . . involved in unofficial stoppages'. She went on to refer to organised attempts at 'fomenting industrial strikes and a constant and deliberate campaign . . . kept going with the object of undermining the solidarity of the Unions and discrediting their elected officers'.[9]

Of course the TUC President was referring in the main to the activities of the Communist Party and the Trotskyist groups in industry who .efused to accept a continuing policy of wage-restraint. The turning-point had come with the launching of the Marshall Plan in the middle of 1947. Up to that moment the main groups of unofficial shop-floor organisations, especially the Communist Party, had supported the policy of applying wage restraint where it was felt to be in the national interest. Indeed, the Marshall Plan was just as much a watershed in domestic and international trade union affairs as it was in the general fabric of East-West relations.

Frank Cousins's first major brush with authority, as a national official, has to be seen against the general canvas of events immediately after the war. Any strike which hit at the national lifeline was then looked on almost as a treasonable offence. The trade unions, and their officials in the field, were expected to fulfil their role as spokesmen for workers' interests, but at the same time to set everything against the vital need to protect the newly elected Labour Government. There was no written 'social contract' to that effect – it was simply implicit in the whole credo of behaviour and attitudes in the Labour Movement. A considerable responsibility for ensuring a smooth transition from war production to demobilisation and peace-time industrial reconstruction clearly rested on the shoulders of the trade union movement. The TUC accepted this charge, in effect, as a continuation of its war-time role – with the added incentive that they were now operating in a completely new political climate, with a Labour Government enjoying real power for the first time in history. The mood was one of pioneering excitement and great expectations.

Cousins was already establishing himself as a national organiser in road haulage and he was quick to seize the opportunity to recruit into the union the large numbers of men returning from the forces to the industry, and the even larger number coming into the road-haulage industry for the first time, having had their grounding by driving heavy trucks in the Forces. Cousins's work in creating a stronger network of regional contacts helped to boost recruitment, and the union's road-haulage membership swept up from 105,000 in 1945 to 156,000 in 1947.

Wages and conditions in the industry were, however, still conditioned by the 1938 Act and – what was even more restricting – the war-time legacy of regulations and controls. Discontent was widespread, and men were much

9. The late Dame Florence Hancock, in TUC *Annual Report*, 1948.

less ready to accept the absolute authority of employers than they had been before the war. This change of mood had not yet registered with the upper echelon of trade union leadership, nor perhaps with others lower down the scale of command. This change of mood took another ten years or so to reveal itself in more coherent form; yet the first signs of a radical change in the industrial climate were already visible, in isolated incidents, as early as 1946. Frank Cousins happened to be in the firing line of one of these incidents, which had a lasting impact on his later performance as General Secretary.

Cousins was certainly more sensitive and responsive to the feelings of the road haulage workers, having been one himself. He was one of the few national officials at that time with such practical contact with life 'on the shop floor'. He warned Jack Corrin and even Arthur Deakin that the situation was tense and that he could give no guarantee that it would be possible to hold off unofficial strike action over a new claim submitted in May 1946, just a year after the war in Europe ended. This claim asked for a reduction in the working week from 48 to 44 hours, a modification in the way overtime was calculated, which would have the effect of increasing overtime earnings by establishing a minimum working day and an increase in paid annual holidays from one to two weeks. The claim was rejected by the employers in July, and the union then asked for the dispute to be referred to the Road Haulage Wages Board – an arbitration system built into the 1938 Road Haulage Wages Act, consisting of representatives of the unions, employers and an independent section with an independent chairman.

After much delay the Board announced, on 31 December 1946, that it had rejected most of the workers' claims. On 6 January 1947 an unofficial strike began, called by lorry crews and shop stewards in East London. The Road Haulage Association suggested that the dispute had been started 'by a handful of malcontents',[10] yet by 9 January the strike was involving about 15,000 men and affecting all London's main markets and the docks. It was also spreading to the main provincial centres. By 15 January, the day before the strike was called off, the total of those on strike was about 30,000 and it was still spreading rapidly. From the start, the TGWU and the road haulage employers, under strong pressure from the Government, tried to find a formula to resolve the dispute. The Ministry of Labour was aware that there had been an unjustly long delay in negotiations and that, had the strike not started, the Minister might have used his powers to intervene and call on the Wages Board to reconsider their rejection of the claim. Even so, the employers were adamant in sticking to the Board's decision. Mr R. W. Sewill, director of the Road Haulage Association and Frank Cousins's former boss at 'Spans-the-South', declared that the employers would not deviate from the terms of the proposed award.

10. The *Daily Telegraph*, 7 January 1947.

Cousins was convinced that the men were justified in their demands, although he had to suppress any instinctive desire to associate himself with the strike. It was, after all, in defiance of the union's policy and instructions and strictly speaking a violation of the law. But Arthur Deakin believed that Cousins might have had a hand in fomenting the explosion, which he (Cousins) had been predicting for some time. Cousins denies this, though he was probably aware of the strike plans being hatched by the unofficial leaders. Deakin also knew and accepted that the lorry drivers had genuine grievances and had been subjected to absurdly long delays. But his view, endorsed by the union's finance and general purposes committee, was that the men should resume work and allow new negotiations to begin free from duress.

What was proving most difficult in the informal discussion between the union and the employers was the strikers' demand for a completely new negotiating system. The strike leaders – and again Cousins was in strong sympathy with them – wanted the Wages Board system to be scrapped and replaced by a National Joint Industrial Council, free from the casting vote of an independent group, some of whose members tended invariably to side with the employers. The road hauliers resisted this demand at first and the strike seemed likely to be prolonged and bitter, with the prospect of the Government's using troops to transport essential foodstuffs and raw materials from the docks, and the almost certain chain-reaction of a dock strike. On the weekend of 11–12 January the Government cancelled leave for the troops and the outlook was ugly. Deakin himself stayed the Cabinet's hand by asking the Minister of Labour, George Isaacs, to intervene and bid for more time, while he, along with Cousins, addressed a mass meeting of the strikers in London. He urged them to end the strike on the understanding that the union would take over their case officially and back their demands in negotiation.

That meeting was held in East London on Sunday 12 January. The troops were due to move into the docks next day. But the Government agreed to hold back while Deakin fought for a peace formula with the Road Haulage Association, though some troops were used to move perishable foodstuffs.

The strike leaders refused to call off the strike at that stage, but no great efforts were made to extend it, and by Tuesday a formula had been reached for a settlement, which in effect conceded most of the men's demands, as well as a proposal to set up a new National Joint Industrial Council.

On Wednesday 15 January, at 9 a.m., the TGWU finance and general purposes committee met the strike leaders and put the formula to them. A mass meeting had been arranged for later that morning, at which Deakin wanted the strike leaders themselves to recommend a resumption of work. But the strike committee was reluctant to take the risk until the new deal was signed and sealed. It was suspicious of the employers – and to some extent of the union leadership itself. So Deakin said he would put the formula to the mass meeting, at the Memorial Hall in Farringdon Street.

Deakin was given a very rough reception by the lorry drivers. In the end, unable to put his case for a resumption of work, he left the platform in anger and stalked out of the hall. After a hasty meeting the strike committee announced to Deakin that the meeting was prepared to have two union officials on the platform, provided that Frank Cousins was one of them, since they wanted him to put the union's case. Deakin was beside himself with fury. He had always suspected Cousins of playing a double game in support of the strikers and this seemed to justify his belief. Cousins and Deakin clashed immediately. It was made no easier when Cousins challenged his General Secretary: 'Well, do you want me to go in there to speak to them or not?'

Deakin glowered, but he controlled himself and told Cousins and Corrin to go back to the meeting. Cousins won the lorry drivers' support for the peace formula which was not, at that moment, public knowledge; nor was it being publicly admitted by the employers. So this was a difficult and delicate situation to sell to the strikers. But they trusted Cousins, who had staked his position on getting the formula endorsed by everyone concerned, and they voted to end the strike.

Of course, this was the last thing that could enhance Cousins's reputation with Arthur Deakin. Indeed it made a bad situation much worse, since a comparatively junior official had succeeded where his General Secretary had failed. It was a serious blow to the dignity, not simply of Deakin himself, but of the office he held. Deakin understood that clearly enough, though at the time Frank Cousins did not. His cocky confidence overcame his sense of understanding. His view in simple terms was that he had succeeded in getting the men back to work; he had helped to secure for the road haulage workers a remarkably good deal; and the trade union's position in the industry had been greatly strengthened by the creation of a National Joint Industrial Council, of which he, Harold Clay and Jack Corrin would represent the union, and of which he was joint secretary. All these gains were, in Cousins's view, an ample justification for what had happened. In his eyes Deakin's continuing hostility after the dispute was settled seemed unreasonable to say the least. With the exception of their claim for two weeks holiday the lorry drivers got everything they asked for out of the new NJIC. Even the holiday claim was partly met by conceding an extra half a week, making one and a half weeks paid holiday. The whole package was an outstanding achievement at a time when a driver's basic pay ranged from £4 17s. to £5 10s. for a 48-hour week.

Yet Deakin's authority and dignity had been challenged and put to a severe test. And this had been done by someone about whom Deakin had already become somewhat suspicious. Cousins was known to keep company with avowed Communists as well as other less committed left-wingers. This had been reported to Deakin, who was always kept informed of the general behaviour as well as the political attitudes of his national (and often local) officials. The combination of what he knew and what he believed to be true was already conditioning Deakin's prejudice against Cousins, and in spite of his national officer's achievements in the road haulage dispute Deakin felt bound to report critically on Cousins's conduct to the next meeting of the union's finance and general purposes committee and the general executive council, where an inquest took place on the lorry drivers' strike. Deakin accused Cousins of 'seeking personal favour' for the way he behaved at the Memorial Hall meeting and indeed generally throughout the strike.

It was a serious charge in trade union terms, since it offended against the corporate well-being of the organisation, and when a General Secretary makes such an allegation against a member of his staff it is taken seriously by the executive. Deakin did not press the point, however. He made the report; he criticised Cousins; the executive noted the situation; but there was no prolonged inquest nor lasting recrimination. It was mostly put down to Cousins's inexperience. He was helped by his popularity among the rank and file. Yet the black mark was against his name and as far as Deakin was concerned the black mark remained. Cousins himself was deeply upset by the incident and told Corrin that he felt like resigning. Corrin told him to 'forget it'. The ever-encouraging avuncular National Secretary took a much more relaxed and philosophical view of Deakin. In any event he probably had some sympathy for the General Secretary's predicament. Corrin liked Cousins and admired his tenacity, his dedication and his candour. But he also looked on his national officer as a somewhat green recruit to the big game of union officialdom. He did not lecture Cousins. Instead he sought to console him and dissuade him from taking any precipitate action. 'Arthur's like that', he would tell Cousins soothingly. 'We all catch the edge of his tongue sometimes, but he doesn't really mean it and he doesn't sustain his grudges.'

In general that was true. Deakin did not carry his prejudices to extremes of personal behaviour – with two exceptions. The first was against Communists and people he regarded as 'fellow travellers' of the Communist Party, to whom he rarely showed any mercy. The second was to people around him in the union whom he suspected of disloyalty to the organisation. He had difficulty in slotting Cousins into either category and, in a way, that infuriated Deakin still more. Cousins was not a Communist – though Deakin was probably never completely persuaded of this to his dying day; nor was Cousins ever guilty of disloyalty to the union or culpability in his administration. None the less, the road haulage strike of 1947 left an indelible scar on relations between the two men. It probably swayed Deakin against Cousins more than any other single incident.

Yet in retrospect Cousins's view is surprisingly sympathetic towards Deakin. He now admits that what he did to Deakin – albeit unintentionally – was an unforgivable act in Deakin's eyes:

> It is easier now for me to understand Deakin's view. Here was a young and unknown official upstaging him in front of his own members and other national officials. I have often tried to put myself in his position since then. I have tried to ask myself what I would have done, as general secretary, confronted with a similar situation. And I cannot guarantee that I would have acted differently from Deakin. I would like to think that I would; but I am not sure. It was a blow to his dignity. I can understand that, now. I would probably have behaved exactly the same way myself, although I know it to be wrong. But when a junior official does something like that to his general secretary, what can you expect?

Frank Cousins now believes that his clash with Deakin was (in his own words) 'the last straw' in their already fractious relationship. Although the two men were to work together – and frequently to clash again – for the next eight years, it is doubtful whether Deakin ever forgave Cousins for that Memorial Hall 'success'.

Frank Cousins was always noted for his aggressiveness as a trade union official. His commanding physique added to the power of his forceful argument, augmenting an unusual arrogance of manner and style that sometimes made him appear more angry and formidable than he intended. The belligerence was also a reflection of his boundless conviction that *he* was correct, even where he acknowledged that there were, perhaps, some merits in an opposing view. He was also noted for making dramatic, not to say unexpected, gestures of defiance. One remarkable story illustrates this tendency, especially in the psychological sense of providing a dramatic challenge to himself – another of his characteristics. During a meeting of the road haulage industry's newly-formed National Joint Industrial Council, in July 1947, Harold Clay pushed a packet of cigarettes across the table towards Cousins, inviting him to take one. It was a normal, routine gesture. Cousins was a heavy smoker, averaging anything up to fifty a day. He had just stubbed out his previous smoke.

'No thanks,' Cousins told Clay. 'I don't smoke.'

Clay looked at him quizzically. 'What the hell's wrong with you?' he asked. 'Aren't you feeling too well?'

Cousins had a cold and had not been his usual healthy self that day.

'No, I'm all right,' he told Clay. 'It's just that I don't smoke.'

Clay practically exploded. 'But you're the heaviest smoker of all of us. Is there something wrong with *my* cigarettes or something?'

'No,' Cousins told him earnestly. 'I don't smoke. I've just stopped.'

And he has never smoked since that day.

Later that week Cousins went out to buy some tools for carpentry with the money he reckoned he had saved by giving up smoking, and he turned his mind, seriously, to perfecting his already well-established ability for working with wood.

Something similar had happened years before, in 1938, shortly after he became a full-time official of the union. On that occasion the dramatic gesture, the deliberately invoked personal challenge, was against his sustained gambling on horses. Coming from Doncaster, living and working in a mining community, he had absorbed the miner's love for a flutter. This was virtually a way of life. It was never a lot of money that was staked; he did not have much to bet with, anyway. But in relation to his weekly earnings he would still spend quite heavily with the bookies, winning and losing with a balanced frequency. Then on St Leger Day 1938 he backed in every race and lost the lot. His deficit for the day was over £4, a great deal of money by his standards. As he walked away from the race-course that day, he decided never to gamble regularly again. He has maintained that pledge to himself except for an odd day at the races with Nance and the collective sweep-stake among his colleagues at union headquarters.

In March 1948, when the TUC's special conference of executives finally accepted the policy of wage restraint, Frank Cousins knew that the National Secretary, Jack Corrin, would be retiring later in the year. He prepared himself for what he was already convinceed would be a stiff test – succession to Corrin.

It was the accepted custom and practice that the national organiser succeeded the national secretary in the ladder of promotion up the union hierarchy. In Cousins's case, however, nothing could be taken for granted. Since he wanted to succeed Corrin (and Corrin wanted him to) Cousins had to make sure that his credentials were unmatched and his knowledge of the union invincible. Even so, in the summer of 1948, when he appeared before the union's 'selection board' – the finance and general purposes committee – with Arthur Deakin in the chair, Cousins knew he would be stretched. He was. Deakin tried every trick in the book to corner Cousins. He carried on a continuous barrage of questioning for nearly an hour – an unusually long time by the normal standards of union examinations – covering details of the TGWU rule-book, the road haulage industry and general policy. Cousins answered consistently well. It was only towards the end of his ordeal that it dawned on him that the questioning would probably continue until he failed to answer accurately. Cousins takes up the story.

Arthur Deakin kept up his bombardment quite mercilessly. He was obviously determined to catch me out. So I decided to deliberately fluff an answer. He asked me what I knew about the Baillie Committee. [The Baillie Committee reported in 1937 on the problems of the road haulage industry and put forward proposals for new legislation which were embodied in the Road Haulage Wages Act of 1938.] I thought about it. I hesitated and slowly shook my head. There was silence in the room as Arthur waited for the answer. 'No,' I feigned. 'I'm afraid I can't remember what that was for.' Deakin looked satisfied and said he had no more questions.

He got up from his chair and was about to leave the room when I suddenly announced that I had remembered the answer. I quickly told the committee what the Baillie Committee had been concerned with. Deakin looked as if he could have killed me. He knew he'd been beaten at his own game.

On 7 October 1948 Cousins was formally appointed to succeed Jack Corrin, and on 1 November he took over as National Secretary of the road transport (commercial) group.

The next seven years were to be no less difficult than his first four as a national official. But his growing experience helped Cousins to cushion the worst irritations in his relationship with Deakin. There was never any significant improvement; but there was a form of unwritten and undiscussed agreement between the two men to try to live together without too much tension and fury. In many ways Deakin admired Cousins, though he never came within any measurable distance of actually *liking* him. There were occasions when Deakin was asked who might succeed him in the years ahead, and he would privately confess that he regarded Frank Cousins as one of his most able national officials. (Deakin is reported to have said this to Sir Frederick Leggett, one-time Permanent Secretary at the Ministry of Labour.) But Deakin would always qualify this by claiming to have doubts about Cousins's politics. He frequently tried to pin a specific charge of membership of the Communist Party on Cousins, not because he ever had any valid evidence of this, but because the rebellious Cousins would consistently be found opposing Deakin's policies, industrially and politically, and often in the most challenging way.

On the other hand, Deakin gave Cousins considerable freedom and latitude. When the question came up of appointing a successor to the job he had vacated – as national organiser for road haulage – he asked Cousins whether he had anyone in mind. Cousins named his personal choice, Fred Eastwood, who was a local official in the Manchester area. 'Well,' Deakin said, 'you'd better make sure he gets the job, hadn't you?' Cousins protested that he assumed the job vacancy was open to competition. Deakin waved this aside by making it clear that if Cousins preferred Eastwood to anyone else, then it was up to him to ensure that Eastwood got the job – and Deakin would not interfere. In one sense this can be interpreted as a sign of Deakin's confidence in Cousins and his readiness to accept his judgment in affairs of his concern. Another interpretation – one which Cousins favours – is that it was Deakin's way of telling Cousins that the union hierarchy usually got the man they personally desired, regardless of the 'open competition', in union appointments – that the 'mafia system' usually triumphed.

Eastwood was indeed appointed as Cousins's deputy and new national organiser. Some time later, when Cousins was away from London on union business, Deakin asked to see Eastwood. He knew, of course, that Cousins and Eastwood were personal friends, but he began by asking the new appointee never to repeat to Cousins what he was now about to tell him. Eastwood was reluctant, but under Deakin's pressure agreed to the confidential discussion. Deakin asked him, 'Is Frank a Communist?' He demanded to be told candidly. Eastwood told him : 'No, I don't think so, in fact I'm pretty certain he isn't. To begin with, he's much too independent-minded to be a Communist, Arthur. He wants his own way far too much of the time for the Communists to tolerate him, or for him to tolerate the Communist Party. You should know that, Arthur.'

Deakin appeared to be impressed, if not wholly convinced, by Eastwood's answer. In practice, however, it made no perceptible difference to the relations between the two men. In 1949 and in the early 1950s, when Cousins had consolidated his position as National Secretary and was continuously opposing many of Deakin's policies, the MacCarthy mentality had crossed the Atlantic and was seeping into sectors of British life. Deakin was preparing to introduce a ban on Communists' holding office, which indeed he carried at the union's biennial delegate conference in July 1949. In readiness for that move he wanted to know more precisely where he stood in relation to Frank Cousins; hence the questioning of Frank Eastwood. It was an almost ceaseless cat-and-mouse game between the two men; but Deakin never succeeded in getting Cousins to cooperate with him in the anti-Communist inquisition – nor was he ever able to satisfy himself that he would have been justified in openly charging Cousins with Communist allegiance.

That confrontation never came.

Chapter Seven

THE TREMORS OF THE FIFTIES

Industrial conflict on the scale witnessed in the 1970s is a new phenomenon in Britain. While strikes were frequent in the 1920s and 1930s there was only one occasion – the General Strike of 1926 – when an industrial challenge threatened the stability of the system and held out a potential threat to Government. It was not until the late 1960s and into the 1970s that the power of organised labour, drawn from a quite different generation (to some observers it seemed as if it were sometimes a different species) and under the guidance of a different national leadership, not only threatened Government but actually precipitated the fall of an administration. There is now no doubt that the miners' strike of 1974 led to the collapse – or should it be the surrender? – of the Heath Government. It is still too soon to be quite clear about the deeper causes of this change in the attitudes and postures of organised labour. What is recognisable is the existence of a new dimension of workers' militancy today.

The contrast between the mood of the late 1960s and early 1970s and that of the mid-1950s when Frank Cousins was elected General Secretary is a staggering one. They appear almost as two quite different ages. Yet all history is a product of itself. The Cousins era in the TGWU and in the wider Labour Movement spans that period of remarkable change and it is difficult, if not impossible, to appreciate the full significance of the Cousins era without taking account of the social and political ethos prevailing in the 1950s.

It is my belief that we must examine the 1950s to trace some of the strongest roots of the social revolution that has since developed into a compelling force in contemporary society. Perhaps the most important element influencing the attitudes of the 1950s was the mood of war-time hangover.

Much of that post-war decade was a projection into an uneasy peace-time society of habits, attitudes and institutional behaviour which had grown up and matured in conditions of war-time Britain. Similar disciplines were called for by Government from the trade unions and by union leaders from their rank and file. The same kind of political and industrial loyalties were expected and in some instances demanded. The responses were never absolute, any more than in war-time Britain. Yet they were invariably pre-dictable and usually orthodox.

The trade union bureaucracy felt bound my ties of loyalty and tradition to a Labour Government, and its instincts for self-preservation seemed sufficient to justify a continuation of policies of wage restraint and industrial disciplines, all of which could reasonably be rationalised and explained in terms of national survival as well as of loyal support for the Attlee Government.

The problem was that the style and the thinking of the trade union leader-ship had become so closely identified with established Government think-ing that the tension between the leaders and the led began perceptibly to increase sometimes to the point of explosion. It was at this time, in the mid-fifties, that a new dimension of tension began to develop on the shop floor; unofficial strikes increased sharply and many of them were as much a protest against what was increasingly seen as a remoteness of trade union officialdom as they were demonstrations against the traditional foe, the employer. A new degree of shop-floor assertiveness was growing, and as it developed it infected the younger generation of workers with a fresh sense of awareness and confidence.

The separation of post-war industrial relations into two distinct categories was in the process of birth. There was the national and the so-called 'official policy' of collective bargaining at the higher level and, below that, a much more authentic system of plant and local bargaining. This 'split-level' system, though not unknown between the two world wars, grew to considerable pro-portions in the late 1950s and, by the 1960s, it had become the major factor in the British system of industrial relations, as Lord Donovan's Royal Com-mission recorded.[1] Its virtue, if that is the right word, was that it enabled the trade union hierarchy frequently to face both ways. It was a useful, though a deceptive, safety valve.

Plant-level bargaining produced a steady increase in earnings at a time of full employment, often through excessive overtime payments and doubt-ful productivity agreements – mostly designed to suit local and particular circumstances. During the period of official wage restraint in the early 1950s national trade union leadership frequently averted its gaze from local deals which certainly helped to increase living standards. Where this local bar-

1. Report of the Royal Commission on Trade Unions and Employers' Associations, June 1968

gaining led to disputes and, occasionally, difficult strikes, the national union leaders would frequently condemn the stoppages in public, while privately accepting the inevitability of what they knew was going on at shop-floor level. This tendency, one of the most prominent features of the 1950s, produced a situation described by some sociologists as 'institutionalised conflict'.

(This is a description given to the development of organised and systematic militancy on the shop floor. There is plenty of evidence that shopstewards, like trade union leaders and all other hierarchies, become infected by bureaucratic tendencies as they are drawn more and more into trying to direct and control the impulses of their rank-and-file members. Indeed there are numerous recent examples of where shop-stewards, even the most militant ones, have been unable to control their still more rebellious rank and file members.[2])

In some instances – such as the TGWU dockers' section – the challenge from below was so strong and persistent as to threaten the fabric of the union. Frank Cousins was always a man to react strongly against the frustrations imposed by authority, any authority. He was also quick to sense the mood of rebellion. Long before the office of General Secretary came within his sights he felt by experience and instinct that the leadership of the TGWU, under Deakin, was deeply out of touch, and sometimes hopelessly out of sympathy, with the developing impulses of the rank and file. Cousins was strongly aware of this gap between leadership and led – a gap which he saw widening all the time. He worked within this developing situation of the early 1950s and in turn he was thrust forward, in the union, by its very existence.

The 1950s began with a General Election in which the Labour Government under Clement Attlee was returned – but with its majority reduced to nine. This was a huge swing to the Conservatives and a far cry from the glorious and jubilant days of 1945. Five years of austerity, controls, food rationing, shortages, five post-war years of greyness and utility, induced gloom and fresh frustration in a people already tired after six years of war. There is little doubt that the corporate reaction to that ambience was a major factor in the swing against the Labour Government in 1950 – regardless of the quite remarkable social and economic changes which the Attlee Government had started. It is, of course, easier to appreciate and understand those achievements in retrospect than it was for the electorate of 1950 to respond to them at the time. By 1950 the post-war strain was at its most tense.

Consider the scene. The gigantic task of switching over from war time to peace time was now effectively accomplished in terms of the mechanics.

2. This development has been touched on in the 'Survey of Workplace Relations' carried out for the Donovan Commission. See also W. Brown, *Piecework Bargaining* Heinemann, 1963).

Millions had been turned out of uniform into civilian clothes, the machinery of war had been wound down and the factories turned towards the 'Export-or-Bust' syndrome. A vast programme of social and economic reform had been put on the statute book, but as yet had made little direct impact on the daily life of the majority. Yet *that* majority had nursed its dreams and visions of a post-war world, and these dreams were wearing thin although they had not yet broken down into shattered illusions.

The British economy moreoever had scarcely scrambled to its feet when the Korean War and the worsening international scene propelled the Attlee Government into a new and huge rearmament programme which it could neither afford nor adequately administer. The strains inside the Labour Government also began to open up into a public argument and, in the end, it snapped into a public slanging match and bitter discord. Aneurin Bevan's resignation in April 1951 was the real political turning point for the post-war Labour Government. Bevan recoiled against Hugh Gaitskell's Budget of 1951 – the Budget that imposed charges on Bevan's brain-child, the National Health Service. Those charges were admitted as a contribution towards the cost of the rearmament programme. It was the first shot in a prolonged war of intense bitterness inside the Labour Movement – a war that continued up to the death of Aneurin Bevan in July 1960 – and indeed beyond that to the death of Hugh Gaitskell in 1963. It was a struggle for the soul of the Labour Movement and one in which, later, Frank Cousins became deeply involved almost entirely on the side of Aneurin Bevan.

Yet in those first bitter moments in 1951 there was no doubting where the TGWU stood; firmly beside Gaitskell. Arthur Deakin resolved to destroy Bevan and the Bevanites. Deakin took personal command of the operation although he had with him a team of Praetorian guardsmen from the trade union establishment who readily and eagerly pledged themselves to help in the destruction of Bevan, the Bevanites and all that Bevanism represented in the Labour Movement.

As Michael Foot writes in his biography of Bevan: 'From Scarborough 1951 [the Labour Party conference was in session there that year] until the day of his death Arthur Deakin was a man with a mission – to exterminate the infamous Bevan.'[3] The hatred of Bevan by the trade union 'establishment' was unqualified and obsessional. As far as it was concerned, Bevan had committed the worst crime in the catalogue of political criminology: he had shown disloyalty. And by that they meant, quite simply and un-ashamedly, that he had challenged the *accepted view*. As Michael Foot says, Deakin's dream of democracy was that 'leaders must be loyally followed'.[4] That was the doctrine he demanded from his own members and he saw no

3. Michael Foot, *Aneurin Bevan*, Vol. I (Davis-Poynter, 1973), p. 353.
4. *Ibid.*, p. 353.

reason to fall below such standards in his relations with the Labour Party. When Bevanism spread with speed and enthusiasm throughout the local Labour parties and expressed itself at the Labour Party conferences in the early 1950s, Deakin looked upon this rank-and-file revolt in the same way that he regarded any revolt from the shop floor against the policies of his – or any other – union leadership. First crush it – then ask questions. The miners' President, Sir William Lawther, the steelworkers' General Secretary, Sir Lincoln Evans, and the General Secretary of the National Union of General and Municipal Workers, Sir Tom (now Lord) Williamson, combined with Arthur Deakin to form a formidable quadrumvirate, not only against Bevan and his political platform, but also in support of Hugh Gaitskell's rise to the leadership of the Labour Party following the retirement of Attlee in 1955. For the whole of that period the battle between Deakin and Bevan was conducted with relentless fury.

Labour lost the General Election of October 1951 and Winston Churchill came back into office at the head of a Conservative Government that was to remain in office, under three subsequent leaders, Eden, Macmillan and Douglas Home, for thirteen years. Perhaps sensing the potential industrial dangers implicit in the return of the first postwar Conservative Government, Churchill shrewdly appointed Sir Walter Monckton as his Minister of Labour. He was a man of great charm and urbanity with a will for peaceful compromise. Monckton's era at the Ministry of Labour is regarded by many as a period of unqualified passivity towards the trade union movement. It was not quite like that, but the myth lingers. The view gives less credit to Monckton than is due. More than some of his Whitehall advisers, Monckton sensed the development of new moods and stirrings on the workshop floor, though he was unable to define what he sensed. He also wanted to give the TUC leaders a sense of continuity in their relationship with the Government – Conservative as well as Labour – and his mission as Churchill's 'special ambassador' to the trade union *leaders* worked extremely well.

Of course this also had the effect of still further deluding some of the leading trade union figures about what was actually happening at shopfloor level. The TUC leaders got on extremely well with this new Conservative Minister of Labour; they also found that the corridors of Whitehall remained open to them despite the change of government. They were reconciled to a continuation of their now routine relationship with the State apparatus, which was precisely what Churchill wanted. Yet the feelings on the 'lower deck' were hardly allayed by the knowledge of such accord between the Churchill Government and their national leaders, and it so happened that the 1950s became one of the most strike-prone decades of the postwar period with a gradual increase in the number and extent of stoppages from 1951 until the strike figures reached a peak in 1957 with a major national engineering and shipbuilding wages dispute.

Certainly, in terms of working days lost, the 1950s was a decade of greater industrial strife than the 1960s. Apart from 1956, the working time lost increased annually during the fifties. The 1957 figure of 8,412,000 days lost was the worst post-war year for strikes until the explosion of the early seventies.[5] The pressures from below had already begun to force reluctant union executives to develop more militant postures. Prices rose, not as a result of external economic factors, but because in Britain the demand for goods that had been unobtainable (or perhaps even unknown) in the previous ten years produced a period of unmatched post-war boom. The first few years of the Conservative Government in the 1950s were years of domestic excesses, the abandoning of controls and the restocking of home larders on a huge scale. From the beginning of 1952 to the middle of 1954 the Conservatives benefited from a remarkable swing in terms of trade in Britain's favour. Prices of basic materials and the foodstuffs that Britain bought from abroad fell by one quarter between 1952 and 1954. At the same time our exports continued to fetch higher prices in a world still hungry for British manufactures, even though there was a decline in the volume of exports. The domestic output rose rapidly and people in Britain were able to go on a tremendous buying spree for a couple of years.

It was self-indulgence on a massive scale by a Conservative Government determined to prove that 'Tory freedom works'. It did work – though at a price. The level of Britain's investment in new and developing technology or even routine industrial regeneration did not expand at anything like the same rate as that of our main competitors. The result was that by the 1960s Britain was already lagging significantly behind Western Germany, Japan, Scandinavia and elsewhere. The boom of the 1950s was the spree before the storm.

On the other hand it was perfectly understandable for a nation to want a taste of honey after so much strain, tension, drabness and sheer exhaustion. There was a distinct yearning for relief, for gaiety and some colour to life after years of war and austerity, and this yearning spread across class barriers. Even so, the economic policies pursued in the early 1950s were to have a disastrous result for the nation's industrial strength in later years. The whole decade, in this sense, was very much a saga of wasted years. Curiously enough, the TUC leaders were ready to discuss some form of continuing wage regulation with the Government, provided the Churchill Cabinet was also prepared to maintain controls and to continue the Attlee philosophy of 'fair shares', instead of letting everything rip in a gigantic free-for-all. Yet the Government was perfectly content to let things rip – including wages, if necessary – rather than perpetuate the old policies of control and austerity. So, in effect, the unions were themselves driven away

5. See Department of Employment Labour Statistics, Table 197.

from a policy of wage moderation by the determined efforts of a Conservative Government bent on creating a new atmosphere of economic freedom.

By the mid-fifties the number of motor vehicles licensed was almost double the 1938 figures. Television sets were creeping into an increasing number of homes – at first in a slow trickle, soon in a torrential flood. The BBC 'monopoly' existed until 1955 when it was broken by the decision to allow television advertising under a new public body, the Independent Television Authority. From that moment television penetrated into more and more areas of life and it gradually became apparent that it was having a profound – if unclear – effect on the social and economic habits of the nation. The world was brought on to the tea table in every house along Coronation Street and the next man's strike became as intimate as one's own. The sale of books fell and commercial libraries closed.

In 1954 only one child in four saw a TV set at home; by the end of the decade the figure was nearer three in four. It is not possible accurately to assess the impact of these changes on attitudes and habits at home or in the factory in terms of industrial, or wider social, relations. But from what evidence is available it would seem to have been far-reaching. It is hard to challenge the impressionistic view now widely held that television has had a substantial and disturbing effect on industrial relations in the sense that its immediacy has aroused and developed expectations on an altogether new scale. It has provided visual stimuli drawn afresh from other people's actions and experience. Moreover, the post-war young generation in the 1950s was increasingly weaned on a diet of this immediacy. They entered working life with value judgments that were different from those of their fathers. Young men and women expected more from life, and they demanded more. They were less overawed by authority, less bound by traditional or family loyalties. A new breed emerged from the schools feeling more, not less, frustrated than their elders about the inadequacies of an educational and social system that remained, despite all the claims of the post-war social reformers, strongly biased in favour of the middle classes. This new generation came into industry prepared to attack the older conventions and to invade the tranquillity of fixed assumptions embedded in the older social fabric. Yet there were the inevitable contradictions : they comprised the raw material not only for a new and quite different style of left-wing militancy but equally and paradoxically for a brand of political apathy which affected the Labour Party and the unions as it did most other institutions.

Indeed some of them joined forces with the younger middle classes who voted in their battalions for Harold Macmillan's 'Never-Had-It-So-Good' prospectus in 1959. They saw the Conservative Party as the political expression of their own acquisitive drive. Macmillan was surely accurate in his assumption about the relative affluence of the late 1950s. In many ways, and despite the darkening shadows of an economic crisis yet to burst, the

Britain of 1959 had never had it so good, in a superficial sense. It was candyfloss; but many people liked candyfloss.[6]

The working class was not immune from this affluence, yet the country remained deeply divided, socially. There was little evidence of any basic redistribution of wealth or of social privilege. Public services were starting seriously to deteriorate and the Health Service was already showing signs, even in 1959, of undernourishment because of insufficient resources and attention. There was a continuing shortage of housing, schools were over-burdened, and teaching standards starting to decline. There were growing social tensions in the New Towns where the bright new social horizons of post war became as clouded and darkened as some of the brickwork. The 1950s were in a very real sense a post-war watershed for Britain. Some look back, today, as if that decade was a kind of final 'golden age' before the bubble burst after the débâcle of Suez. It was the period when the enormous changes in social and industrial behaviour that have since transpired were in their chrysalis.

The Permissive Society had not yet bourgeoned; the Pill was still in the test-tube. The open and confessed challenge to, still less the violent denunciation of, authority, whether in the shape of Government, Management, Schoolmaster, Trade Union Leader, or Family Unit was still at the drawing board stage. Above all a new cultural trend was already perceptible with the explosion of a popular culture based essentially on dissent – almost as a conscious protest against all that had gone before as well as a manifestation of the new dreams of young people. It came in a torrent in the form of music, clothing, hairstyles, teenage behaviour and social relationships. The Beatles and Mary Quant; Teddy Boys and Skinheads; groups of youngsters leaping around on motor-bikes finding emotional relief by gang wars on the beaches of quiet coastal towns. Some of this did not burst publicly until the early 1960s but it was brewing and fermenting in the 1950s.

It was not, of course, all violent stuff. The popularity of the Promenade concerts reached new peaks in the late 1950s and the demand for university education from working-class homes compelled local authorities and central Government to recast their education budgets.

In the 1950s scarcely any sphere of life in Britain remained significantly untouched by some aspect of the developing social revolution – least of all the workshop floor.

6. During the 1959 General Election I toured the country with Aneurin Bevan. I particularly recall a comment he made at a crowded election meeting in West London, answering Harold Macmillan's claim about the 'Never Had It So Good' society. It would have been astonishing, Bevan pointed out, for any prime minister to have made any other claim. 'Of course we are better off than a year ago, or ten years ago. That had nothing to do with Conservative policies but a great deal to do with the nature of social, economic and scientific developments.' The question Bevan posed was not whether we were having it so good, but how very much better we could have it.

Chapter Eight

PRELUDE TO POWER

Frank Cousins's ambition was to become General Secretary of the TGWU. This distant and improbable goal fired his imagination from a quite early stage in his career as a full-time union official, though it is hard to tell when the objective was first aroused, even as a passing thought. All men harbour dreams, though some dreams are more fanciful than others. It is quite probable that something began to stir in Cousins's mind from the time he decided to make trade unionism his life work. He clearly listened to the encouraging noises that were made by his mentors, all of whom believed that he was the kind of material from which general secretaries are hewn, though that is a far cry from suggesting that any of them actually saw Cousins as someone with an outstanding chance of ascending to the pinnacle of trade union power. Even so, a hint or a marginal comment such as, 'You'd make a good secretary, Frank,' would be picked up by the self-assertive Cousins and stored away. His strength and his vanity were inevitably flattered by such attention.

The moment when he perhaps realised most strongly the potential that was within his grasp was when he moved to London to take on the job of national organiser for the road haulage workers; and this sense of the possible certainly became more pronounced when he succeeded Jack Corrin in the national secretaryship of the road haulage group in 1948.

Sir Harry Nicholas told me of a conversation he had in 1944 when Cousins first came to London and was staying with Nicholas. Frank Cousins made it clear that it was his ambition to become General Secretary of the union.

With his own particular brand of arrogance, Frank Cousins felt he could do the job of General Secretary at least as well as the incumbent or any of his likely successors. At the same time he became increasingly aware of the improbability of his ever getting the chance. Quite apart from his conflict with Deakin during the 1947 road haulage strike, Cousins knew the power set-up inside the union well enough to recognise that the likelihood of his becoming General Secretary appeared quite as remote as his chances of, say, becoming Prime Minister. The road to succession after Deakin's retirement seemed blocked to anyone with radical and unorthodox views, even if there was still uncertainty about who would eventually succeed.

Even so, when an opportunity arose early in 1948 to test the ground, Cousins, no doubt rather presumptuously, decided to throw his hat into the ring. Some seven months before he succeeded Corrin as a National Secretary he actually applied for the post of Assistant General Secretary. He knew he was throwing sand at the sea, but he saw it as a worthwhile gambit for two reasons: first, it demonstrated to the union's hierarchy, as well as the membership, that he had ambitions beyond the ordinary ranks of trade group officialdom; second, he believed it would strengthen rather than weaken his chances of succeeding Corrin. Of course, Cousins knew that he was already in a strong position to take over the union's road haulage section. None the less, he was determined to leave nothing at risk. He calculated that Arthur Deakin would make him fight every inch for the National Secretary's job when Corrin retired, later in 1948; and he also calculated that having first stood for the Assistant General Secretary's vacancy would probably impress the selection committee when it came to choosing Corrin's successor. He was right in both those calculations.

The Assistant General Secretary's post fell vacant in March 1948, when Harold Clay was appointed to the newly-formed Road Transport Executive – the body charged with the task of running nationalised road haulage. It was indeed a crucial choice because Deakin was due to retire in seven years, and all the potential candidates knew that the union executive would, in effect, be choosing the man to succeed Arthur Deakin. The successful candidate would become Crown Prince of the TGWU. Deakin himself had no doubt about who this should me: Harry Nicholas, who was then national secretary of the engineering group, itself a key post. The second favourite was William Tudor, the secretary of the Power Workers' Union. Certainly the man who was eventually appointed, Arthur 'Jock' Tiffin, was regarded as no more than an outside possibility when the contest opened. He wasn't even a national official of the union, but a London regional official, which amounted to assistant to the regional secretary.

Deakin did not particularly like Tiffin. True, Tiffin wasn't a radical; on the other hand, he had not shown any particular responsiveness to Deakin's policies, even though he was a willing and reliable lieutenant. Deakin wanted – and was quite convinced he would get – Harry Nicholas as his number two. Nicholas was professionally and emotionally prepared for the appointment, and felt that provided he could outshine Tudor the job was virtually his. It was at this moment that an extraordinary discovery was made by the union officials doing the routine check on candidates' credentials, prior to the closure of nominations. They discovered that Nicholas was 'out of compliance' with his union card and was therefore ineligible. The union's rules stress that anyone standing for national office must have a card that has been in full compliance (that is, with no arrears break) for a clear two years. Unfortunately, during a period of domestic stress while his wife was in hospital Nicholas had inadvertently missed a payment. It was an almost absurdly trivial slip. Deakin was stunned. He called in Nicholas for an explanation but Nicholas too was stunned. There was nothing Deakin could do to save Nicholas, who had lost the job for a trifling omission, and probably with it any hope of succeeding Deakin in the future. The General Secretary was the custodian of the union's rule book and it was characteristic of Deakin's faithful adherence to the rules that he stuck to the book even when events swung against him. Whatever Deakin's personal preference, he knew he dare not brush aside Nicholas's lapse, however accidental, since it would inevitably be discovered and seen as a clear act of favour toward one particular person. All Deakin could offer was consolation to Nicholas with the reassurance that he would remain in a very strong position when, once again, the Assistant General Secretary's post became vacant. After all, Deakin consoled, Nicholas was still a young man, then in his early forties. Time was on his side – or so it seemed at the time.

With Nicholas out of the running in 1948, the name of Tiffin thrust itself forward as a powerful contender despite Deakin's preference for Tudor. Tiffin had several factors to his advantage. He was an older man and could therefore be regarded as 'a caretaker' by the senior members of the TGWU executive who might wish to appoint someone with a briefer reign ahead of him rather than commit themselves to a younger man. That is often a significant consideration in any institution when new men are being appointed (or even elected) to the hierarchy. In a union like the TGWU where the power to appoint future leaders comes only rarely to the influential finance and general purposes committee – the union's senior sub-committee of the executive and its examination and selection board – the temptation to choose older men is almost irresistible.

But neither Tiffin nor Tudor were to have a free run. To the surprise of most people, five additional men offered themselves as candidates for the number two job: Frank Coyle, C. E. Ackroyd, Tom Hodgson – none of them with much hope of success – and two other equally improbable candidates, not least because of their known hostility to Deakin – Frank Cousins and Jack Jones, then a district secretary in Coventry.

On 13 May 1948 the seven men were examined by the finance and general purposes committee. It was, as is usual, a strenuous test. The committee members put searching questions to each candidate on the state of the union, its policies, its rules, its agreements, and then asked each individual to pronounce on wider issues of political and economic policy. To everyone's surprise Bill Tudor did badly. His performance before the 'examination board' deeply disappointed Deakin. Frank Cousins produced a competent performance without being outstanding. Jack Jones's response was, by all accounts, quite the best. Tiffin's was quiet and authoritative. The names of Tiffin and Jones went forward with a recommendation to the union's full executive committee that Tiffin should be appointed to the job 'as being the most outstanding candidate'. And he was duly appointed by the executive on 31 May 1948. Jones returned to Coventry and his district office. Cousins, whose all-round ability had surprised all members of the finance and general purposes committee, since he was still an 'unknown quantity' at that level of the union, was more than content with his showing in the contest. He had emerged from the trial better than anyone had expected; he had gained valuable experience in competition with some of the top names in the union. It had clearly helped to bolster his confidence. And this was a powerful asset when he again appeared before the 'examination board' for Jack Corrin's job. Even Arthur Deakin's guile, and pressure on the finance and general purposes committee, did not succeed in undermining Cousins's determined confidence on that occasion. Cousins was appointed to succeed Corrin and he took over as national secretary of the road haulage group on 1 November 1948.

Taking full responsibility for a trade group in the TGWU is rather like becoming General Secretary of a medium-sized union in its own right. The membership of the commercial road transport group was almost 155,000 in 1948, larger than the majority of unions affiliated to the TUC. Moreover, it was a particularly difficult section to administer because its membership was so dispersed. To add to the complexities, road haulage nationalisation was in its honeymoon period. Straightaway Cousins had to tackle the reorganisation involved in the transfer of men and vehicles to the Road Haulage Executive.

This was generally a period of intensive reorganisation in private road transport, post-war industrial reconstruction, nationalisation of part of the industry, and of economic problems across a wide front of national affairs. The wage-restraint period had begun. It was scarcely the most propitious moment to draw up completely new agreements covering wages and working conditions for a newly nationalised industry. This, however was the task facing Cousins when he took Corrin's chair. As the official war history observes : 'One thing is fairly clear; the problems of restoration and organisation which faced British inland transport when the war ended was scarcely less formidable than the transport problems encountered in the most difficult war years.'[1]

1. C. I. Savage, *History of the Second World War: Inland Transport* (HMSO and Longmans, 1957), p. 639.

The first thing Cousins did after his appointment was to secure the assistance of Fred Eastwood as his national organiser. His friendship and working cooperation with Eastwood dated back to Cousins's early days as a national organiser when he was touring the country seeking to improve the union's organisation in road haulage and, on the basis of that improvement, to boost recruitment. He and Eastwood understood each other's working methods, and shared a common purpose : to strengthen the union's organisational power and win better pay and conditions for the road haulage workers. Together they formed a formidable team.

Throughout the first half of 1949 Cousins was involved in negotiations with the Road Transport Executive, working to establish a constitution for future collective bargaining in the nationalised sector. It was finally achieved at the end of July with the setting up of a totally new system for joint negotiation. This consisted of a National Joint Council and a series of national and local joint negotiating committees, with their own built-in disputes procedures. At that time it was one of the most up-to-date and elaborate collective bargaining mechanisms in British industry.

Cousins's work in this field did not prevent Deakin from continuing his bullying campaign. A member of the TUC staff at the time recalls a meeting of the TUC's nationalised industries committee, at which both Deakin and Cousins were present, to discuss the future of nationalised road transport.

> At one stage during the discussion Frank Cousins intervened with a comment but was immediately told to shut up by Deakin. Deakin made it clear that Cousins's role at the meeting was to sit there and say nothing. If anyone was going to speak for the union, Deakin told Cousins, it would be the general secretary and no one else. That was typical of the Deakin 'reign of terror' in the union at that time.

The bulk of the union's road haulage membership was still in the private sector, where negotiations were hard and organisation patchy. Among the strongest organised groups were the oil-tanker drivers, the men who took petrol from the refineries to the filling-stations. Normally, relations between the petrol companies and the unions were outstandingly good, and wages and conditions were among the best in the industry. One of the warmest tributes paid to Frank Cousins by an employer came to me from senior management in the Esso Company. Mr Kenneth Proudman, a senior executive, remembers negotiating with Cousins in 1949 shortly after he became National Secretary. Proudman was then a junior official in the industrial relations division of Esso, involved with the group of petroleum companies in negotiations over drivers' pay. Cousins was presenting the union's case for a pay increase. Proudman said :

His case was well argued and well documented. It always was. But I was a novice and I clearly underestimated Cousins. I interrupted him during his presentation of the union's case because I thought I saw a flaw in his argument. Yet halfway through my own counter-argument I suddenly realised the fallacy in my own case – and I could tell that Cousins had seen it too. His smile widened as I continued. Still, I decided to take the onslaught that I presumed was certain to follow. But it didn't. Cousins simply retorted: 'Well, I'm sure Mr Proudman realised that what he was saying is not exactly correct...'

He let me down so gently I was astonished, and I had a respect for him ever since. Of course my chief told me later that Cousins behaved that way because he was shrewd enough to realise that he would have to deal with me again and he didn't want to make an enemy from the start. The other thing my chief told me was that it was a characteristic gesture from Cousins. He was a tough negotiator, but also a nice man.

Proudman also tells an amusing story of his chief, Eric Frost, once complimenting Arthur Deakin on having such a competent and effective national secretary as Cousins.

'Ah,' Deakin replied contentedly, 'I know how to pick 'em.'

With the break-up of the World Federation of Trade Unions in Paris in 1949 the cold war spread throughout the international trade union movement. Arthur Deakin led the British TUC walk-out from the WFTU, and from that moment he was determined to crusade against Communist influence on the domestic as well as the international trade union scene. He followed up by banning Communists from holding any office in the TGWU, a policy carried by a large majority at the biennial delegate conference in 1949. And as we have already seen, the campaign against the Communists spread in its effect across the whole spectrum of left-wing opinions – much of which could in no sense be described as fellow-travelling or even sympathetic to Communist policies or objectives. It was a blanket offensive against left-wing opinion and radical thought, attacking anyone or any group with the temerity to question the practices and attitudes of the established leadership. Cousins was already under suspicion from Deakin, and no amount of reassurance could convince the TGWU General Secretary that his road haulage secretary was not a political embarrassment.

Moreover, the economic picture had become much blacker following the devaluation of the pound in September 1949. This first post-war devaluation came as a serious shock to national morale and to the Labour Government's plans. In many senses it was the watershed point of Attlee's two administrations and led, perhaps inevitably, to the defeat of 1951. The pound was devalued from four dollars and three cents to two dollars and eighty cents – a drastic measure that opened the gates to more inflation and intensified pressure from wage-earners. What really saved the economy from a much more serious collapse was the success of the export drive and the maintenance of full employment. The growth in productivity was prodigious at this period, with the reconstruction effort reaching a new pitch. At the same time, home consumption was severely restricted not only by wage restraint but by physical controls, a grim reminder that wartime austerity was still very much a characteristic part of post-war Britain.

The Government's problems were to some degree shuffled off on to the trade unions, as they were called on to maintain wage restraint despite the pressure of increased import prices. There were signs that this imposition of restraint or, as it turned out in some instances, a period of near freeze, was causing severe strain on the relations between the rank and file and union officials.

In his report to the TGWU executive in December 1949 Arthur Deakin referred to the grave problems facing the unions but added: 'Any failure to maintain a policy of restraint in these critical days would, in my view, create those conditions which would make for a repetition of the economic disaster that overtook us in 1931 ...'

By this time Deakin viewed any criticism from the Left as mainly Communist-inspired in order to disrupt Britain's economy and pave the way to social disorder.

Deakin was far from insensitive to the difficulties of his membership or the problems facing his officials. It will be recalled that he was not an enthusiastic supporter of restraint when it was first mooted and took some persuasion before he embraced it. He was always aware of the tensions that it created for trade unionism. But he was prepared to avert his gaze from these tensions in the wider national interest. As he said in his 1949 report:

I appreciate that it may not be easy for our people to understand the reasons which force us to say that we have got to exercise restraint, or in other words, to consolidate our position for a period of time. But the facts are there and our task must be to see to it that they are made crystal clear. The key to the future, whether it is in this country or in any other, turns completely upon the productivity of the workers in industry. If we are to live better then we can only do so by producing as efficiently and in as full a measure as we can those things which are necessary to improve the standard of living of the people everywhere.

These problems invaded Frank Cousins's newly-inherited sphere as they did all other sectors of British industry. Cousins was under heavy pressure from his road haulage members to submit a new wage claim in the winter of 1949–50, and his national trade group committee – which was, in effect, a mini-executive committee for the road haulage section – proposed a pay demand for 10s. a week extra throughout the industry. It was not an excessive demand, yet it was still too high for the union's national executive to condone. Deakin himself proposed that the claim, which required prior approval by the national executive, should be referred back. He argued that the union could not accept the resolution from the road haulage trade group, because it not only flew in the face of the wage restraint policy but also came from an industry whose workers could not 'be regarded as being amongst the more lowly paid'. Such were the atmosphere and the conditions under which trade union officials had to operate at that time.

Of course Frank Cousins found it irksome, as did so many of his colleagues inside the TGWU and other unions. There was constant friction not only between officials and membership but between officials and their national leaders. It was altogether an exceptional period of stress for the hierarchy of trade unionism. Yet the practice of restraint was never as rigorous as the precept. Between April 1948 and April 1950 – the main period of restriction – average hourly rates of pay and earnings increased by about 5 per cent and 7.5 per cent respectively,[2] and it was already clear that the strain of holding the unions to a policy of formal restraint would soon become intolerable. With the outbreak of the Korean War in July 1950, and the consequent rapid rise in raw material prices throughout the world, the inflationary pressures on the domestic economy intensified and the task of holding back union wage demands seemed to be impossible. It was scarcely surprising when the 1950 Trades Union Congress overturned the General Council policy on restraint. Yet the rejection brought anger and dismay to the majority of the TUC leadership, particularly to Arthur Deakin, who tended to attribute the 1950 defeat to Communist inspiration.

To some extent Deakin was right. The wage restraint policy was defeated on a motion from the Electrical Trades Union, then Communist-led, which was carried by a majority of 220,000. But there was considerable support for the ETU's motion from unions who were neither Communist-led nor Communist-influenced. The driving force behind the General Council's defeat was a recognition that it had become an untenable position for a union to resist the mounting pressure from its members for pay increases to match rising living costs. This did not mean the wholesale abandonment of pay restraint, since quite apart from any other considerations the main groups of employers were by no means ready to discard tough wage bargaining simply because the TUC had failed to carry their policy for continuing restraint. Deakin himself told his General Executive Council at its November meeting that although the TGWU would accept the rebuff of the 1950 Congress,

2. *British Labour Statistics, 1886–1968* (HMSO, 1971), Department of Employment Tables 28 and 46.

We must also recognise that it does not mean the end of wage restraint. It simply means a shifting of responsibility. Instead of the TUC having to accept an overall responsibility it now becomes the responsibility of each individual trade union executive to pursue that policy of restraint best suited to the needs of its own membership or, alternatively, just allow a policy of drift to operate with an inevitable collapse of the nation's economy.

And in fact a policy of restraint was maintained for the remaining years of Arthur Deakin's reign as General Secretary, often in the face of increasing militancy from some sections of the union, especially the docks, but also from other groups who had no reputation for militancy.

Frank Cousins recalls an amusing incident from the 1950 period which illustrates the tension that existed between Deakin and himself, not only over wage claims but over disputes in general. Deakin had made a speech in which he declared it TGWU policy in the event of redundancies to give protection first of all to trade unionists. He said that 'all things being equal' non-unionists should be declared redundant rather than trade union members where dismissals became unavoidable. At the time, Deakin was much criticised in the Press. Shortly after this speech a margarine factory in West London – a subsidiary of the Unilever group – declared some redundancies and included a number of trade unionists in the list of those to go. Some were in Frank Cousins's section and they called on him to support an official strike in protest against the redundancies. The drivers quoted Deakin's speech to Cousins, who went to discuss the situation with the TGWU leader. Deakin exploded at the suggestion of union support for an official stoppage and told Cousins to forget it. Cousins quoted Deakin's own words back to him, but Deakin denied he had made such a speech and accused the Press of misrepresenting him. Cousins pulled some newspaper cuttings from his pocket and put them in front of Deakin.

'This is the section the shop stewards are quoting to me, Arthur,' he said, pointing to a particular passage from Deakin's speech.

Deakin shifted his ground slightly and according to Cousins replied, 'Well, all things are *not* equal in this case' – meaning that he suspected that some of the active trade unionists listed for dismissal were men the firm wanted to get rid of because they were trouble-makers and possibly even Communists.

'In that case, Arthur,' retorted Cousins, 'You'd better go down there and tell them that yourself.'

This had precisely the same effect as lighting a stick of dynamite under Deakin's chair. The two men had a verbal slanging match for several minutes, Deakin instructing Cousins to return to the margarine factory and tell the men there would be no backing from the union for any strike. Cousins flatly refused to do this. Then, producing his ace, he accused Deakin of being scared to defend himself in front of these members. That challenge goaded Deakin, as it was intended to. He went down to see the men next day and decided their case was so strong that he changed his mind completely and backed a short stoppage. Yet such 'successes' in Cousins's dealings with Deakin simply made their relationship more, not less difficult.

Deakin was always irritated by the company Cousins kept – frequently with officials whom Deakin regarded as near-Communists, if not actual party members. The banning of Communists from holding office at the 1949 TGWU conference had been passed by a large majority (426 to 208) and by the end of that year nine full-time officials of the union who refused to sign a declaration that they were not members of the Communist Party (or any fascist party) were dismissed. The protests against this action rumbled on through the union for months, even years, afterwards, but Deakin would never be shifted from his conviction that he had done the right thing.

None the less, it is fairly certain that some officials who were close to the Communist Party (if not actual members) did sign the declaration and therefore remained on the union's payroll. In other cases where Communists were not full-time officials – or even lay officials, since they too were barred from holding office – the 1949 decision seemed simply to drive them to use less open tactics to attack the leadership. For his part, Arthur Deakin increasingly regarded *any* rebellious expression in the union as the work of Communists or their supporters. Attitudes on both sides became embittered and polarised, and it was almost impossible to raise an issue of substantial challenge to the union's policies in the industrial or political sphere without being suspected, or openly accused, of Communist sympathies. As V. L. Allen has written, the ban on Communists

> removed some assiduous officials from office but still left them in the branches eager to press their points of view and to get them accepted as resolutions. In a less material way it influenced opinion on the union. Officials who gave vent to dissident expression drew attention to themselves and sometimes cast a reflection on their own integrity.[3]

It was this situation that affected Frank Cousins. We have seen how Deakin sought to convince himself that Cousins was either a Communist or a fellow-traveller; how he attempted to embarrass Eastwood into a candid confession; and how he remained to the end doubtful of Cousins's political attachment. Yet he did not confront Cousins with a direct challenge, as many believed at the time. There was a story in circulation, which Cousins denies, that Deakin did once put it to him in typically blunt terms that he was a member of the Communist Party, and that Cousins's reply was a string of unprintable four-letter words. I can find no evidence to support such a story. The point is

3. V. L. Allen, *Trade Union Leadership* (Longmans, 1957), p. 288.

that it was never necessary for Deakin to question Cousins in such a direct form. Each knew instinctively what was in the other's mind. Both circled round each other preparing for a showdown that never materialised.

Frank Cousins frequently attempted to proffer the hand of brotherly sympathy, if not outright friendship, but the hand was never gladly accepted. He tells of occasions when he would visit Deakin on union business and find him looking rather tired and strained.

'Hello, Arthur, what's the matter?' he would ask with genuine sympathy. 'You're looking a bit pale. Aren't you feeling very well?'

Deakin would bridle and flush. 'I don't want anybody's sympathy – certainly not yours,' he would reply.

Cousins would return an acerbic comment, such as : 'I'm not offering you any sympathy. I was simply asking how you are.' Whereupon the two men would slip, easily and naturally, into a totally irrational argument.

Cousins, of course, took advantage of Deakin's weaknesses. He knew that the General Secretary had a habit of standing on the steps of Transport House at 9 o'clock in the morning, casually checking if his staff were arriving on time. It was a quirk which Deakin would try to conceal by strolling round the ground-floor corridors. Cousins, always an early arrival, would take particular pleasure in chiding his chief by joking irreverently about his 'spying' tactics. He knew it would inflame Deakin, and it did.

Yet, in spite of the extraordinarily tense relationship between the two men, there was also a strange mutual respect. Perhaps each, in his way, recognised, however reluctantly, the power and the sensitivity of the other.

It was Deakin who came to Cousins's aid in one of the two big strikes in which Frank was involved as National Secretary. This was a dispute in May 1951 involving drivers employed by the newly nationalised British Road Services. Ten thousand lorry-drivers, from some fifty depots in the London and South-Eastern areas, struck at midnight on Sunday 27 May in protest at what they described as 'snoopers' employed by BRS to 'spy' on drivers' working activities. The Road Haulage Executive, under its chairman Major General G. N. Russell, had introduced five patrols and was planning a further eleven, to check on drivers' routes, parking practices, speeding, and carrying passengers in their driving cabs, as well as the costs of overnight accommodation and the facilities available.

The strike threatened to develop rapidly into a national – albeit unofficial – stoppage. The drivers claimed there had been insufficient consultation about the 'snooping' scheme between the Road Haulage Executive and their union. Deakin himself had not heard of the plan and was furious when he discovered what had happened. He began by rebuking Cousins for not having ensured adequate consultation, then discovered that Cousins had not been to blame. Then the Government moved in. The Minister of Labour, Mr Alfred Robens (now Lord Robens of Woldingham), intervened on the third day of the strike, and when he called the sides together Arthur Deakin came to Cousins's defence in remarkable and unusual style. In the Minister's room, Deakin, flanked by Cousins, attacked the Road Haulage Executive and Major General Russell for trying to impose 'little Hitlers' on the road. He told Russell and Robens that he wouldn't have it. Deakin threw his support behind the strike – although he insisted that this should not be reported to the strikers: even when he sympathised with a strike Deakin could scarcely bear to admit it publicly. Yet Deakin's tacit support for the strike was sufficient to persuade Robens and the Government to back the union against the Road Haulage Executive.

Subtly, Robens played his trump card. He told Russell that although it was not his responsibility to ensure that essential transport services were maintained (that was Russell's job) he must nevertheless report to the Cabinet on what steps were being taken by the Road Haulage Executive to provide alternative means of transport should the strike become worse. Russell knew he was beaten and agreed to drop any further development of the road patrol scheme. It was one of the rare occasions when Cousins found himself not merely in agreement with Deakin but actually being supported by his General Secretary in a major dispute.

By 1951 the pressure of work on Frank Cousins's life had greatly increased. Nance and the family rarely saw him except at weekends. He had almost as much travelling to do as when he was a truck driver. It was an unusual event for him to spend a week-day evening at home. When he did he would often take off to his allotment, where he found complete relaxation and an environment in which he could more easily unwind, in silence, among his vegetables and flowers. Nance frequently prepared him a jug of tea and a few sandwiches to take there instead of a set meal, especially in the summer evenings. Even in his early years in Doncaster and Sheffield, Frank had had little time to devote to the routines of family life, much as he loved to do when he could. Now he had less time than ever before. He was absorbed in his job, almost to excess. Frank was a perfectionist, and like all perfectionists he had an exaggerated fear of failure and an inner distrust of merely moderate success. A brilliant negotiator, outstanding in committee work and debate across the negotiating table, he spent a great deal of time preparing his case and making sure of his facts. And he went to endless trouble with his 'homework'. He was determined not to be caught napping by an employer on some fact concerning his industry or over the interpretation of some aspect of legislation. His special quality was his capacity to focus on a particular point of detail, usually central to the case he was arguing. Whatever Frank Cousins did he had to do well; whether it was gardening, carpentry, driving a car or negotiating a union deal.

In spite of everything, however, family life went on. In July 1951 Frances Anne, the fourth child, was born – while Frank was at the union's biennial delegate conference at Whitley Bay. Frances was later to become a centre of attention because her father often referred to her during the national controversy over nuclear disarmament. At particularly emotionally charged moments in the debate Cousins would speak of his youngest child and her generation growing up under the shadow of the nuclear war threat. Observers at the ringside on these occasions frequently felt that he was over-dramatising the picture; he probably was. Perhaps because she was the last and the youngest of his children there has always been a special place for Frances in Frank Cousins's emotions. Most people who know him closely stress his affection for all children and his ability to establish a *rapport* with young people, even total strangers.

During the early 1950s it became clear to the activists in the TGWU's road haulage group that they had, in Frank Cousins, someone who was not in the orthodox mould of union leadership. Cousins's reputation for being a 'rank-and-filer's man' was widespread, while at the union's HQ it was generally known that he was a thorn in Arthur Deakin's flesh. Cousins was not concerned with that. He was striving to build up union membership in road transport and to steer the drive for better wages and working conditions – two processes that were obviously closely linked. By the beginning of 1952 Cousins had pushed the membership to a record level of 166,581, though even this was still only a modest increase compared with the potential recruitment.

As always with road haulage organisation, the difficulty was that the main growth of membership occurred among small traders who owned two or three vehicles, rarely more than half a dozen. These hauliers generally paid union rates, yet strongly discouraged union recruitment. They did so for a variety of reasons: political or emotional prejudice; a determination not to let 'outside' bodies interfere with their freedom of action; and self-protection, since union recognition would inevitably involve them in raising the general standards of their vehicles, maintenance and working conditions for their drivers and staff. Some of these firms managed by working their drivers beyond the legal limits, a practice which offered the drivers a great deal of freedom, with the opportunity to boost their earnings above the average levels for the industry. Despite all the regulations imposed on road haulage many traces of pre-war practices survived well into the 1950s and well beyond.

Nor were the industry's problems confined to the smaller firms. In 1953 a serious dispute broke out in the petrol distribution sector which reflected a whole range of difficulties inherent in road haulage. This was a strike of tanker drivers working for the big petrol companies, the thriving giants of the industry. It brought together the questions of wage restraint, union recruitment (including the closed shop), the industry's own organisational problems, and other issues such as productivity and costs. As in so many disputes, the main elements of the trouble had been smouldering for months before the explosion occurred. It required a flash-point of some kind to bring all the issues together in one emotive conflict. This came when five men at the Fulham motor-repair depot of Shell-Mex BP refused to join the TGWU.

After much pressure from the rest of the men a strike of the depot's 250 workers began on Monday 19 October, and spread within twenty-four hours to involve over 2,500 tanker drivers throughout the London area. All the major petrol companies were affected. The preparations by the unofficial strike leaders had been excellent and their planning perfect. Within a few days the whole of the London area, covering a radius of thirty miles from the city's centre, was plunged into a petrol famine which threatened public and private transport alike. By the Saturday morning the situation had become critical. The Government decided to send in troops to distribute petrol to essential services and industry, and this intervention sent up the strike figures to about 3,000. It looked as if the strike might escalate into a national shut-down. But Cousins and Eastwood managed to persuade the London drivers to return to work so that negotiations about all their grievances could continue.

What was the root of the trouble? Deakin, as usual, tended to blame the Communists for exploiting grievances which he believed could have been easily resolved without a strike. And, indeed, one of the men who led the strike was a well-known Communist, and a former member of the TGWU executive, Bert Slack. He had no reason to feel warm towards Arthur Deakin and it may well be that he took this opportunity to try to teach Deakin a lesson. Be that as it may, there was also a range of genuine grievances that had remained unresolved.

The strikers made four main demands: that workers not belonging to a union should be dismissed and re-engaged only after accepting union membership; that the practice increasingly being adopted by the petrol companies of sub-contracting work to smaller haulage firms should either cease or be governed by conditions of work and pay operating in the larger companies; that the employees of the sub-contracting firms must belong to a union; and that the oil companies should grant a pay rise of 10s. a week back-dated to August.

The strikers argued that the pay and conditions offered by the sub-contracting agents were inferior to those of the major oil companies, and they suspected that the retention of non-unionists would weaken their bargaining power. They already knew that in return for a pay increase the companies were asking for the phasing out of drivers' mates. Clearly all the ingredients were there for a major conflict.

Deakin issued orders to Cousins and Eastwood that they must not enter into any negotiations to resolve the disputed issues until the men were back at work. He also instructed them not to attend any meetings called by the unofficial strike committee. The only meetings they could attend were those called officially by the union. The General Secretary was determined not to have a repetition of the 1947 situation, when the striking lorry drivers and his national officer appeared to have such a close understanding. This time Cousins went to Poplar Town Hall on the fourth day of the strike to a meeting called by the union where he simply conveyed the instructions of the TGWU executive and Arthur Deakin. *The Times* reported after that meeting: 'Mr Cousins is a popular figure in the union and the strikers were clearly disappointed that he had brought nothing but the uncompromising order to stop the strike.'[4]

After a week of intensive activity in which Cousins and his deputy Fred Eastwood worked ceaselessly to find a formula, the drivers did return to work, on 27 October. The pay claim was, however, referred to arbitration, following another failure to agree, and when the award came in December, it failed to improve on the employers' original offer of 5s. 6d. a week extra. (At the time drivers' minimum rates ranged from £7 5s. 6d. to £7 14s. 4d. for a forty-four-hour week.) It was no one's victory, then, except in token terms: the drivers had made their point about contract labour.

The importance of the tanker drivers' strike was that it contained many new ingredients of industrial conflict – ingredients which were to become of increasing importance during the later years of the 1950s. The whole question of rationalisation and consequent redundancies was still in its infancy as an issue of industrial conflict. The drivers' case against the method of sub-contracting proposed by the oil companies was also an early indication that workers were becoming much less disposed to sit back while their jobs – or their concept of job security – slipped away. It was also an important dispute because it once again spotlighted the flaw in the attitude of trade union officialdom. In the early 1950s there was little comprehension of the real nature of the redundancy problem. Indeed, it did not become a major factor in trade union thinking until July 1956, when the then British Motor Corporation declared redundant 6,000 workers in their factories in the Midlands, Oxford and South Wales – an action which shocked the entire industrial community and indeed the Conservative Government of the day.

Yet if the unions can be criticised for lacking an understanding of what was developing (or likely to develop), management must carry an even larger share of the blame. The cosy relationship that had been established between senior management and many trade union officials inevitably blurred the perspective. On both sides of the negotiating table there was a distinct tendency to accept the status quo in industrial relationships as a lasting one, or at least as one that would change only slowly. 'Trouble' was easily and all

4. *The Times*, 23 October 1953.

too casually ascribed to Communist instigation. This was a seductive trap for both management and union hierarchies, who frequently walked into it with a lack of both sensitivity and awareness that may seem astonishing to contemporary eyes. There was much of all this in the tanker drivers' strike of 1953. The distinguished columnist of the *News Chronicle*, A. J. Cummings, one of the great liberal journalists of his day, wrote a post-mortem on it in which he questioned the prevailing view that the Communists were at the bottom of it all.[5] 'This short answer is not enough,' wrote Cummings. 'It takes no account of whether the strikers had a real grievance; whether it was considered rationally and sympathetically by the employers; whether official trade union leadership has played its part adequately from the beginning.'

Cummings argued that neither the employers nor the trade unions had done their job properly, and concluded that in his view 'these unsatisfactory affairs are due very largely to the workers' impatience at the clumsy internal machinery which causes interminable delay.'

Frank Cousins certainly found himself in an embarrassing situation during the tanker strike. His sympathies were with the strikers, even if he did not wholly approve of their tactics. He spoke at official meetings with his tongue in his cheek, and in the main the men guessed his position. He was deeply frustrated at the role he was called upon to play. Both he and Fred Eastwood knew perfectly well that the Communist Party was active in using the situation to twist Deakin's tail, but they also knew that an explosion of some kind had long been in prospect because of the unresolved grievances that had been building up among the tanker crews. The strike was a brief one, but in its way it contained many more pointers towards things to come than many of the more dramatic and lengthy stoppages of the period.

Frank Cousins was not a conspicuously political animal during his period as a National Secretary. He concentrated almost exclusively on industrial affairs, and these kept him fully stretched. Fred Eastwood recalls that he and Cousins rarely discussed political issues in any depth. The two men were close friends, on family visiting terms, yet Eastwood says he cannot remember one specifically political discussion with Cousins, except in so far as their industrial and trade union activities overlapped into politics. 'Politics were never very much in Frank's mind until he became General Secretary,' Eastwood says. 'He was concerned with trade unionism and industrial questions, first and foremost.' Throughout the whole time that Eastwood worked closely with Cousins, he says, 'I never had the feeling that Frank put industrial questions second to political ones.' Obviously political questions played an increasingly important part in his calculations about union

5. The *News Chronicle*, 27 October 1953.

policy. That was inevitable. Yet, despite the reputation he acquired of being the TGWU's 'most political general secretary', Cousins remained to a large extent, like Bevin and Deakin, 'only a labourer in politics' – in the phrase of Dr V. L. Allen.[6]

The degree to which this was true was not to become fully apparent until Cousins entered the Labour Government of 1964-6, but it is worth emphasising here that though he was a political figure of a special kind in the trade union world of his period, he remained throughout his public life essentially a *trade union* leader. It can be argued that this was a basic flaw when he moved into Parliamentary politics, since there is a sharp distinction between the trade union politician and the political politician. If one may generalise and draw a dividing line between these two kinds of man, one might describe the distinction between them as one which contrasts the 'doers' with the 'talkers'. Trade union officials certainly see themselves as 'practical men'. They are drawn into their trade union by a conviction that 'things need to be done', rather than to be discussed endlessly in some public forum. They tend to be impatient with intellectual debate for its own sake, or with the questing after theoretical perfection. The politician may scoff at this simplistic attitude among union officials, and may even regard it as something less than democratic. And to be sure there is an authoritarian streak in every successful union official. In many respects the unorthodoxy of Frank Cousins came from the fact that he combined the qualities and the defects of both schools. He tended to stand out as a political figure among his trade union colleagues, while being very much a trade union emperor among the politicians. He was a democrat among the authoritarians and, sometimes, an authoritarian among the democrats. He wanted to 'get things done'; but he profoundly wanted to do them differently.

At the 1954 Labour Party annual conference Frank Cousins took up his strongest political challenge to date against the established view, and he did so on the most emotive issue of the period – the proposition that the Labour Party should support the rearmament of West Germany. A divided Parliamentary Labour Party had been finally won over to the view that Germany should be allowed to rearm, within NATO, in the interest of Western defence and to assist the reintegration of Western Germany into the European community. The late Herbert Morrison (Lord Morrison of Lambeth – the Foreign Secretary in the previous Labour Government) was the driving force behind this view and had been for some time. And although the issue cut across the normal Left *v.* Right loyalties, the whole question of German rearmament inevitably became meshed into the Bevanite row. The Left were solidly against German rearmament on the grounds that it would further embitter East-West relations, make *détente* more difficult, split the

6. V. L. Allen, *Trade Union Leadership* (Longmans, 1957), p. 154.

Labour Movement unnecessarily and inflame xenophobic emotions less than ten years after the end of World War II.

Aneurin Bevan led the campaign against the Morrison case, and the issue therefore became inextricably interlaced with the whole struggle for supremacy within the Party leadership. Those on the Right who had the deepest doubts about German rearmament were none the less driven into line by the knowledge (and the fear) that to vote against Morrison on this issue would lead to accusations of siding with the Bevanites. Some in the middle of the road, between the two camps, shuddered at the prospect. The trade unions were divided along similar lines. The giants of the Establishment, marshalled by Arthur Deakin, fought tenaciously to make sure that the Bevanites were crushed – and with them, all opposition to German rearmament. In his winding-up speech to the Party conference at Scarborough in 1954, before the final vote was taken, Morrison told the delegates that they were about to vote on 'one of the greatest decisions we have made in the history of the Party'.

To add to the volcanic atmosphere in Scarborough in that late September, Nye Bevan was challenging Hugh Gaitskell for Party Treasurership for the first time. Bevan had resigned his secure seat in the constituency group of the Party executive in order to challenge Gaitskell to a vote by the entire conference – which in effect meant the trade union block vote. The trade union majority was already committed to Gaitskell, and the right-wing union establishment, led by Deakin, Williamson and Lawther, left nothing at risk to ensure that Bevan was crushed in his bid to defeat Gaitskell. By a curious irony of circumstance, voting figures for the new executive were announced immediately before the debate on German rearmament; they showed that Hugh Gaitskell had romped home as Treasurer with 4,338,000 votes to Bevan's 2,032,000.

Despite this two-to-one majority, the trade union establishment was not satisfied that it was a sufficiently humiliating defeat for Bevan. The following year, union membership affiliations were increased with particularly substantial increases in the affiliated membership of the TGWU and the National Union of General and Municipal Workers. This helped to produce a result at the 1955 Labour Party conference in which Gaitskell defeated Bevan by 5,475,000 to 1,225,000.

The bitterness and fury at Scarborough was, if anything, even more pronounced than at Morecambe the previous year. The acrimony had become almost wholly personalised and unrelenting. And it was in this cauldron of strife that Frank Cousins took his first open political stand alongside Bevan. Before every Party conference the union delegations spend the weekend deciding their policy towards motions on the agenda. Each union calls together its delegation for a formal meeting to discuss union policy in relation to the various resolutions. The TGWU delegation – one of the largest in attendance, as well as the holder of the largest single block vote – met on the Sunday morning, to decide how it would vote on German rearmament, among other things. There was never any doubt about how the union would cast its huge block vote (then 835,000). Even so, Cousins was determined to challenge the leadership and at least force the delegation of forty to debate the issue. He moved that the TGWU should *oppose* German rearmament. It sounded such an absurd proposition to most of the delegates present that some of them told me later that they thought Cousins was either joking or had misunderstood the point. He did neither; he was deadly serious in his challenge to Deakin.

Cousins put the case against German rearmament in both emotional and political terms : it was morally wrong for the Labour Movement to encourage it, and it would make the chances of a disarmament agreement with the Russians infinitely more remote. This was, of course, a futile protest, since the heart of the issue was no longer the merits of the case but the playing out of the internal feud between Right and Left in the Labour Movement. Cousins's protest was dismissed; he picked up only two supporters from the delegation of forty.

The outrageousness of Cousins's challenge on German rearmament is further underlined by what he knew was happening behind the scenes to ensure that the Party proposals were carried by the conference. Earlier that month the TUC had approved of German rearmament by only a very small majority. Everyone recognised that this vote stood in danger of reversal at the Labour Party conference, because the majority of constituency party voting was known to be against German rearmament. Moreover, some right-wing unions in the TUC, who had voted in favour at the Congress, were not affiliated to the Labour Party. The absence of their votes clearly seriously jeopardised the outcome at Scarborough. During that eve-of-conference weekend in the hotel rooms of the Yorkshire resort, the slide-rules and micrometers worked overtime trying to calculate the result as word came through from each trade union delegation meeting. It was finally discerned that the outcome would hinge on the vote of one small union – such as the Amalgamated Society of Woodworkers (now part of the Union of Construction, Allied Trades and Technicians). The Woodworkers had voted against German rearmament at the TUC, which was in line with the decision taken at their own conference that year. None the less, under pressure principally from Arthur Deakin, but also from others including Morrison, the Woodworkers' President, George Brinham, agreed to switch his union vote (of 122,974). That was sufficient to secure a majority for the 'required' decision by 3,270,000 to 3,022,000.

It was also sufficient to ensure an explosion of bitter recrimination against the power of the trade union hierarchy, probably surpassing anything known at a Labour Party conference before or since. In an ironic way it justified

Bevan's attack on 'the trade union bureaucracy', as well as vividly demonstrating the response to Bevan's tauntings.[7]

Major objectives were of course at stake – notably the leadership of the Labour Party. Attlee was on the point of retirement. Deakin was coming close to his own retirement, and knew that if he didn't act decisively in 1954 and 1955, then Bevan might snatch the initiative. The group of union leaders around Hugh Gaitskell was single-minded in its determination to ensure that he should succeed Attlee. Morrison had been abandoned as the great 'white hope' against the Left because of the manner in which he had stepped aside for Arthur Greenwood – a generous act in the best traditions of the Labour movement, but one which finally destroyed him in the eyes of the trade union hierarchy.

The conference at Scarborough in 1954 therefore promised melodrama on a grand scale. Everything was at stake – or so it seemed to the actors on that particular stage. Within a year, however, a crack appeared in the edifice of the traditional power complex. Frank Cousins became Assistant General Secretary of the Transport and General Workers' Union. It was an event which was slow to yield its full significance, except for a few who quickly appreciated the amazing turn in the wheel of fate.

7. See Martin Harrison, *Trade Unions and the Labour Party* (Allen & Unwin, 1960), p. 195–261.

Chapter Nine

GENERAL SECRETARY

The death of a potentate always induces a wave of trauma, though it soon ebbs away. It is hard now to recapture the feeling of shock, even disbelief, in the trade union world and the Labour Movement when Arthur Deakin died after collapsing at a rally at Leicester on May Day 1955. He would have reached the retirement age of 65 that November.

In the few months before his sudden death Deakin had experienced a gruelling time. Thousands of TGWU dockers were breaking away to form a new dockers' union, based on the small Stevedores' and Dockers' Union. This action put Deakin under tremendous pressure and was unquestionably a serious emotional shock to him. He had been deeply involved with the TUC in settling major disputes in the newspaper industry and on the railways; on the political front he was continuing his campaign to ensure Hugh Gaitskell's succession to the leadership of the Labour Party; and he was also preparing the ground for the TGWU election which would elevate Tiffin to the succession. All these activities combined put a severe strain on Deakin, especially since he was not well, although he had often made it plain that he was not looking forward to his approaching retirement. The union had been his life for forty years.

This outwardly hard, ruthless, blustering, bully-like man was indeed a strange mixture. It would be untrue to say that Arthur Deakin inspired devotion in many people, yet he somehow managed to convey a strong impression that behind the iron mask there was an unexpectedly sensitive and generous human being. He was not a man of profound wisdom or pronounced intuitive understanding. Most people who worked around him feared his wrath and observed his mediocrity; they testify to his narrowness, but they also acknowledge his quiet kindnesses and unobtrusive gestures to help people. Publicly he roared like a wounded bull; privately there are numerous testimonies to a warm spirit trying to break through the hard exterior image.

Frank Cousins himself has told me of the discoveries he made when he became General Secretary, which revealed to him for the first time Deakin's many private acts of generosity. There was never any question of publicity because Deakin, like many trade union leaders, distrusted showmanship. He took great care to make sure that no one, outside a very small private circle, got to know of the warm gestures he consistently made. Another reason for this secretiveness was, of course, to discourage any belief that he might be 'a softy at heart'. Maintaining a hard, seasoned outer shell was very important to Deakin. His flaws were almost always on public display and he never apologised for them. His warmer, more human qualities were concealed.

Deakin's early life had been scarred by the death of his father, a cobbler, when Arthur was a small child. His mother remarried and the family went to live in Merthyr Tydfil at the turn of the century. The deprivation in the valleys was overwhelming. Arthur started work at thirteen for 4s. a week at the Guest, Keen and Nettlefold plant at Dowlais. No school was harder, and the bitterness of those years left their rutted marks on his personality. He became a full-time official of the Dock, Wharf, Riverside and General Workers' Union when he was nineteen, after moving from South Wales to Shotton in Flintshire. His education was snatched at night schools and from the preachings of the pioneer socialists like Keir Hardie, to whom Deakin was drawn when he lived in South Wales. When Bevin founded the TGWU he incorporated the union to which Deakin belonged, so he became a full-time official of the Transport and General Workers' Union from its inception. In a very real sense, therefore, the union *was* his life, his emotional base, his university.

Nothing came easily to Deakin, not even gaiety. In later years it is doubtful whether he felt himself a happy man. He seemed to attract conflict as much as to stimulate it. He was conditioned to a certain order, an accepted code of discipline and fixed loyalties which were cardinal and, in his view, immutable. Change he recognised was inevitable, but he wanted it to be, if possible, very slow.

On his death, Attlee spoke of the 'great shock' to the Labour Movement, referring to Deakin as a man who 'at all times . . . showed great courage and was always resolute against Communists and other irresponsible agitators . . . His death leaves a great gap.'

There was an almost Czarist-like quality about Arthur Deakin's cremation on 5 May: the choice of Frank Cousins as one of the six coffin bearers provided a twist of macabre irony.

Sir Winston Churchill, who had only just handed over Downing Street to Sir Anthony Eden, described Deakin as 'a great servant of the nation as a whole'. *The Times* said he was 'not a clever man, but he was determined, obstinate, courageous and intensely loyal to his union, to the Labour Movement and to his country'. But the paper also noted that 'his most serious weakness was his inability to understand the point of view of his own members when they rebelled against the authority of his union'.

The following day *The Times* returned to the subject in an editorial, but this time trying to analyse what Deakin's death implied for the balance of power in the trade union and Labour Movement. It pointed out that the old guard leadership in the TUC was now reduced to one man – Sir Tom (now Lord) Williamson. Sir Lincoln Evans had already departed to join the Steel Board set up by the Conservatives to help denationalise steel. Sir William Lawther, the miners' President, had retired in 1954. Williamson was the only survivor of the 'quadrumvirate' which for much of the post-war period held the leadership of the Trades Union Congress largely in its hands. *The Times* detected 'powerful forces straining against the present pattern of union policy', but it wasn't at all clear what these forces were. The elements it perceived were : a growing demand for higher wages; the development of white-collar trade union pressures; a shifting of forces within the trade union movement itself; and the claims of skilled workers arguing for wider differentials. 'The task of the new leaders will be not to resist such a shift of emphasis too long', *The Times* concluded, 'but to guide it carefully.'

The ballot for Deakin's successor commenced on 18 April, several weeks before his death, and the result was announced in June. Arthur 'Jock' Tiffin was elected as everyone knew he would be. He was already acting General Secretary, a decision made by the union's general executive council on the death of Deakin, so that the outcome was a foregone conclusion. The only thing in doubt was the size of his majority over his strongest rival, Charles Brandon – the secretary of the TGWU Region No. 1 (London Area) and the man to whom Tiffin had once been an assistant. Brandon, known in the union as 'The Mandarin', was, in terms of his power-base, the second strongest figure in the union after Deakin. Even so, Frank Cousins fancied his own chances and he was nominated along with Tiffin, Brandon, William Tudor, Harry Nicholas and Tom Hodgson. In fact, Cousins thought his chances were so strong that he sought to persuade Brandon to stand down in his favour, believing that he could attract more support from the Left and therefore mount a harder campaign against Tiffin – the man with the 'Deakin machine' behind him. Brandon didn't accept this view and told Cousins so in blunt terms. His account of these conversations does not square with Frank Cousins's version. Cousins suggests that Brandon at least seemed ready to consider the idea of standing down but was persuaded against it – on the basis that he, Brandon, would have more chance of recruiting Communist and left-wing support than would Cousins. The Cousins version claims that Brandon received a pledge of support from certain leading Communists, inside and outside the union on the understanding that if he were elected General Secretary he would remove the ban imposed on Communists becoming officials by Deakin at the 1949 conference. Brandon told me there was no such pact, but he admits that he was approached by some leading members of the Communist Party who promised support provided he agreed to scrap the ban – a promise, he claims, that he refused to give. He says:

> I didn't want the ban to go on; I fought against it at the time because I thought it was the wrong thing to do. On the other hand if I had become general secretary I would not have fought to get the ban removed. I would have let things remain as they were – although if there had been a spontaneous move from below for its removal then I would not have opposed it. But I would not have taken the initiative.

This would not seem to invalidate Cousins's claim that there may well have been a private undertaking by Brandon – or at least an implicit understanding. Not that Brandon was sympathetic towards the Communist Party. He was a staunch Labour Party supporter; but he also believed that Deakin had carried the anti-Communist campaign to absurd extremes and in the process had damaged the union.

The situation in the union, he says, was desperate when Deakin died. 'Deakin was sitting on a powder keg which would have blown up in any case – no matter who would have become general secretary.'

Brandon insisted that he did not at first intend to contest the election against Tiffin but was pressed to do so against his original wishes. Again, this lends some weight to Cousins's claim that Brandon might at one point have been ready to stand aside. In any event, it is doubtful whether a Brandon-Cousins pact would have made any material difference. Tiffin would still have won.

The result of the election was:

A. E. Tiffin	267,019
Charles Brandon	146,366
Frank Cousins	74,217
William Tudor	57,078
Harry Nicholas	44,215
Tom Hodgson	26,972

Even if Brandon's vote is added to Cousins's, it still leaves Tiffin safely in the lead. There were suggestions that some of the election returns were not above suspicion and that voting figures from various branches and areas had actually exceeded their registered membership, but there is no evidence of malpractice as far as I can establish. From Cousins's point of view the result was satisfactory, since he had finished an honourable third, in front of two men who were known throughout the union to have been favoured by Arthur Deakin – Harry Nicholas and Bill Tudor. For Nicholas the result was a bad omen of what might happen in the selection of a new Assistant General Secretary, the job in which he was principally concerned. The smallness of his vote was a major surprise. He was national secretary of the engineering group of the TGWU, which then had a membership of 218,277, and by any calculation he ought to have polled better than he did. Cousin's road transport group at that time had a membership of 169,913, which means that even if he drew no support from any other section he had collected a much higher proportion of votes from his own trade group than Nicholas had from his.

Within a month of Tiffin's election applications for the vacant post of Assistant General Secretary were called for. Short-listing was scheduled for 21 July, the examination by the finance and general purposes committee for 11 August, and the appointment was to be made formally by the full executive the next day. Cousins was on holiday when he submitted his application but he had signalled his intentions. Inside the union hierarchy there were already signs that the end of the Deakin era had registered. There were few illusions about the new General Secretary. Most of the senior staff knew Tiffin to be a kindly, quiet and precise man, but not a strong leader. Moreover, there was already a doubt about his health. He went into hospital for an examination shortly after his election. Yet no one knew – certainly not Tiffin – just how seriously ill he was.

Behind the scenes in Transport House in that summer of 1955 there were frantic manœuvrings prior to the appointment of a new number two. Harry Nicholas remained convinced that at last he would succeed to the post so long earmarked for him by Deakin. Tudor had given up hope after so many disappointments, but others moved into the running, including Ron Mathias, the able and radically minded regional secretary from South Wales. It was clear that the field would be wide and the competition intense.

When the jostling and jockeying was at its height, Frank Cousins received an unexpected morale-booster from one of the key men inside the union's establishment : the chief administrative officer, Alf Chandler. Chandler says that he told Cousins he was 'the best man for the job in the long-term interests of the union'. This was a remarkable move, because Chandler was probably the most influential man inside the hierarchy after the General Secretary. Moreover, he was known to be a man of the Left. He had grown up with the union and was virtually built into the superstructure. For Cousins to be given tacit support from such a source was the most unexpected, and clearly the strongest, encouragement any candidate could possibly receive. Especially so since it was Chandler himself who traditionally submitted the list of questions from which the finance and general purposes committee chose their points to put to candidates for union office.

Why was Chandler impressed by Cousins? It is not easy to answer such a fundamental question. Partly the answer is that he had been increasingly attracted by Cousins's work for the union, his administrative ability, his courageous stand against Deakin's bullying and his general posture of independence and integrity. Chandler thought that Cousins was 'head and shoulders' above the rest. The other part of the answer is that he had become deeply disenchanted by the Deakin regime and believed it had brought the union close to the point of serious disintegration. In every respect Chandler's motives were to save the union by using what influence he possessed in favour of a quite different type of leadership.

He had wanted a change in union policy for some time before Cousins became Assistant General Secretary. He believed the union had swung too far to the Right, that there was a serious lack of democracy in the organisation, and a lack of industrial drive. He wanted a more militant wages policy and a union leadership prepared to fight for it. He believed Cousins best fitted these needs.

Other leading members of the TGWU regarded Chandler as a man of the Right. Bill Jones, the London busmen's leader and former Communist, who returned to the executive during Frank Cousins's period of office, has described Chandler as someone who had always been 'out to do the Left'. Even so, when Chandler retired, Jones spoke of him warmly as a man dedicated to the union.

The final list of candidates was : Tom Birkett (national secretary of the waterways and fisheries group); Tom Healy (national secretary of the agricultural and flour milling section); Jack Jones (recently appointed engineering secretary in the Midlands region and former Coventry district secretary); Ron Mathias (South Wales regional secretary); Len (now Sir Len) Neal (general workers' district officer, London region); Harry Nicholas (national secretary, engineering group); E. A. White (clerical and supervisory trade group secretary, Bristol region); and Frank Cousins.

Cousins did outstandingly well before the examining committee and Nicholas ran him a close second. The two men were short-listed for a final round, which consisted of a short speech. The committee then asked them to leave the room while they voted. The eight members split four to four. It was in fact the vote of the committee's chairman, a Bristol coach-driver, Ted Fryer, who had been regarded as a Nicholas supporter, that paved the way for Cousins's eventual success. The dead-heat vote meant that the committee had to submit both names to the full executive of thirty-nine members which met the following day.

Each was called on to make a ten-minute speech. Nicholas spoke about the problems in the engineering industry and how he proposed they should be resolved. Cousins made a remarkable speech. He ranged across the whole field of union policy and criticised the way things had been done in the past.

Audaciously, he even criticised the executive for being 'bad employers'. Cousins accused them of consistently refusing to give sufficient power to their officials or to back them in the immense task of resolving the problems facing the union. A great job of change and reconstruction was required, Cousins continued and added that, in his view, he was the man to help them achieve that objective. They agreed; the general executive council voted overwhelmingly for him. It is said that only six votes went to Harry Nicholas, although I have been unable to confirm this with either Nicholas or Cousins. The vote was not recorded, because it was so overwhelming for Cousins.

The Cousins appointment astonished everyone – with the exception of Alf Chandler. That day, the headquarters of the TGWU echoed with the sound of incredulous whistles as the news spread from room to room. Few had doubted that Nicholas would triumph over 'the outsider'. The enquiring outside world, especially the Press, wanted to know who 'this man Cousins' was. What was his background? How was it possible that someone labelled as a Leftist had triumphed in this way? Where had the slip-up been made, and how could it be accounted for? The amazement was no less widespread inside the Parliamentary Labour Party when it was discovered that a pronounced Leftist would shortly represent the TGWU – that bastion of the orthodox establishment – on the Party's National Executive Committee. (It was always the role of the Assistant General Secretary to sit on the Party's Executive Committee while the General Secretary sat on the TUC General Council, the routine priority given by most unions who are also attached to the Labour Party.)

When Frank Cousins came out of the executive committee room after his appointment three men were waiting in the corridor hungry to hear the outcome. They were Tom Healy, Ron Mathias and Jack Jones. Healy and Mathias was stunned to silence when they heard the news. They did not appear over-eager to congratulate the 'outsider'. Only Jones spontaneously welcomed the news by declaiming loudly, 'That's marvellous. It's as good as me getting the job.'

Cousins and Jack Jones had known each other for a long time and were good friends. They shared a common view on a wide range of issues and, broadly speaking, common left-wing political attitudes. Jack Jones was the first of Cousins's colleagues to recognise the dramatic significance of his appointment as Assistant General Secretary.

Harry Nicholas later congratulated the victor at the executive meeting and spoke of his readiness to work with the man who had defeated him – a gesture typical of the loyalist Nicholas always was. No man could have been more deeply disappointed and inwardly dejected than Harry Nicholas that day. Twice he had seen the door to power slammed in his face when everything seemed set for him to walk through. Yet he took it all with a quiet and stoical dignity. On 16 August, in minute No. 513, Frank Cousins was formally appointed Assistant General Secretary. His salary was fixed at £1,193 11s. rising to £1,343 11s. in two yearly increases of £75.

He was one stride away from the seat of supreme power in the union, the seat he had for so long coveted.

Tiffin was well enough to attend his first (and as it turned out his only) biennial delegate conference as General Secretary, held in Blackpool in July 1955. He at once sought to inject a greater degree of free debate and flexibility into the proceedings. He was acutely aware of the dangers threatening the union and of the urgent need for new and more enlightened policies. Although he felt constrained not to demonstrate his satisfaction too openly, he was in fact pleased by the appointment of Frank Cousins as his deputy.

At the September meeting of the executive Cousins took his place alongside Tiffin as the union's number two. He had already spoken for the TGWU at the 1955 Trades Union Congress when he moved a resolution calling on the Government to speed up the repayment of post-war credits. That was the first time he moved a motion at the TUC, though nobody noticed. The name Cousins was still without any special significance. But at the general executive council meetings which began on 19 September the members of the executive *did* notice, because half-way through the week Frank Cousins took charge of the union – and remained there. Tiffin looked a sick man on the first day of the executive, but stayed through the session. By Tuesday he was worse, yet persisted in remaining. But on Wednesday morning when Cousins came into Tiffin's office he found the General Secretary slumped behind his desk, looking pale, weak and much worse. Cousins put his hand on Tiffin's head. It was cold and moist.

'I feel rough,' Tiffin said.

Cousins exploded. 'Christ, you look ill, mate!' he cried. 'Why don't you go home?'

Tiffin protested that he couldn't desert the executive in the middle of their week. Cousins took control. He told Tiffin that whether he liked it or not, he was going home. The executive would get by, and in any event there was nothing left on the agenda that Cousins couldn't take care of.

Tiffin was sent home that day. He never returned to Transport House. Shortly afterwards he went into Manor House Hospital and died there of cancer three months later on 27 December.

Meanwhile Frank Cousins has started his round of country-wide speeches as Assistant General Secretary: the ritual to which a new incumbent must submit.

'We believe', he told his first meeting, 'that in this new age there is an even greater need for joint consultation between men and employers.' He spoke about the growth of automation and the threat of redundancies as a result of technological change. The union, he pledged, would do everything to protect the security of its members, and he voiced an early warning about the problems of developing technology :

> There will be no industrial peace despite the introduction of pension schemes and other forms of welfare if you ignore the fact that a whole range of people exist to whom the benefits of automation cannot be directly applied. It is something we cannot dodge – will people be the servants of the machine or the machine the servant of man?

This was an early indication of Cousins's interest in and concern about developing technology. That autumn there were other indications of things to come in later years – for instance, on the question of legislation to curb strikes. It was on this issue that Frank Cousins made his first major contribution to a Labour Party debate, at Margate in 1955. Throughout the summer there had been a campaign in a number of newspapers, echoed by some Conservative politicians, calling for legislation to control strikes and reform industrial relations. The Government, under Eden, had been quick to react to this by reassuring the trade unions that no such legislation was contemplated, or, in their view, desirable.

None the less, the Labour Party conference in 1955 had before it a composite motion demanding total resistance to any legislation which might interfere with the right to strike – resistance which, it was specified, would include industrial action. Cousins spoke on this motion, telling delegates the Government must be reminded that the trade union movement 'was not to be played with' and warning of the danger of interference 'by any political party in relation to industrial rights'.

At the close of that conference Cousins was elected to the Party's National Executive Committee, replacing Tiffin who had held the place before becoming General Secretary. His first executive meeting was at Margate on 13 October – a formal meeting chiefly to assemble the new executive, which then included Attlee, still leader of the Party, Gaitskell, Morrison, Harold Wilson, James Griffiths and Richard Crossman. Dr Edith (now Baroness) Summerskill was in the chair to welcome Cousins. Nye Bevan was not present.

It was during a private session at the conference that Frank Cousins had his first significant experience with Bevan – one he would gladly have forfeited but which he could not have avoided. The issue was Party organisation, finance and the whole relationship between the Party and the unions. This was based on a report by a Party committee headed by Harold Wilson which had proposed far-reaching improvements in what it described as Labour's 'penny-farthing' organisational set-up. The TGWU naturally had a strong view on this and Cousins as leader of the union's delegation had to state the view. But in the process of doing so he stuck his neck out and invited Bevan and the Bevanites to forget the old differences and work together for a united Party.

It was a brave, if futile, gesture for a man in his position. He could offer no more than hints; and he was sensitively aware that his union had been committed to voting against Bevan for the Treasurer's post long before Cousins's appointment as Assistant General Secretary. There was nothing he could do about that. The Cousins gesture came to nothing. A bitter and angry Bevan came to the rostrum later to attack the trade unions and their tactics in terms as fierce as any he had used before – and again not without justification. Bevan threw out the challenge that it wasn't so much the Party organisation that was at fault as the absence of socialist conviction in the Labour Movement; and he drew particular attention to the posture of the trade unions in this respect. The unions resented the attack; they knew at whom the barb had been flung. Frank Cousins knew it as well as anyone in the hall. But he was still powerless to influence the atmosphere. His modest attempt lay in the waste basket.

When Cousins attended that first routine meeting of the executive he was elected to sit on a number of its principal sub-committees, including the important home policy committee. In turn this led to his appointment to a series of study groups which the home policy committee set up to prepare a comprehensive new programme for the next General Election. This would take three years to complete, since no one expected another election until 1959 or 1960. After two successive electoral defeats the Labour leadership were now starting to redraft and redefine a socialist policy for contemporary Britain.

Cousins was elected to these important study groups just nine days before Attlee resigned the leadership of the Party. It was in fact the beginning of a new period in the development of the Labour Movement, as well as an inaugural period for a new generation of leaders.

A few weeks later, in December, Hugh Gaitskell was elected Party leader with Bevan and Morrison in second and third places: the result for which the Right wing of the Labour Movement had worked so hard and so long. Now, Gaitskell's supporters concluded, it was a question of elaborating his views and establishing his policies throughout the Labour Movement. That Christmas, as Michael Foot recalls, Aneurin Bevan retired to his farm 'to brood'.

Frank Cousins was also in a brooding frame of mind. News of Tiffin's decline in health came to him daily. He had already taken over the General Secretary's commitments and was speaking regularly at union rallies throughout the country. The message coming through from his speeches was distinctly different and already transmitting warning undertones. He continued to refer to the threat of redundancies resulting from automation and

109

the union's determination to fight for the rights of workers. He put increasing emphasis on the need for higher wages, especially for public service workers like busmen. Talk of wage restraint was now becoming a common feature of the economic dialogue. The Government was clearly looking for support from the TUC and had good reason for believing that some kind of cooperation would be forthcoming. It came as a profound shock, therefore, when the December meeting of the TGWU executive, with Cousins in the General Secretary's chair, came out with a blast against wage restraint, the autumn budget and the whole economic policy being pursued by the Government. The TGWU executive accused the Government of reversing the policies on which earlier wage restraint had been based, and thus ruling out any chance of cooperation with the unions while it followed such a course. Writing in the union *Record* (January 1956) Frank Cousins declared:

> There must be no dubiety as to where we stand as a union. While prices rise wages must rise with them. In other words, wage increases that result from rising output are the workers' share of the extra wealth they are helping to create. To re-state our position as a union in a single sentence: we are not prepared that our members should stand still whilst the Government continually hand out largesse to those who are more favourably placed.

That declaration on wages policy is now regarded as the turning-point in TGWU affairs although, at the time, it was invested with less signficance.

Five days before Christmas 1955 R. A. (now Lord) Butler resigned as Chancellor of the Exchequer and was replaced by Harold Macmillan. The threads were being drawn together for a period in which the names of Macmillan, Cousins and Gaitskell would increasingly dominate the news columns.

Arthur Tiffin died in hospital on 27 December, while Frank, Nance and John Cousins were at Kempton Park races. On their way home to Worcester Park, Surrey, they stopped to telephone Manor House Hospital and were told that Tiffin was dead. Frank Cousins's mood on the drive home through the Surrey lanes on that darkening December afternoon was a turbulent mixture of melancholia and jubilation, with a deep inner feeling of fatalism at work, as he reflected how two men's deaths had opened the door for him to take over a position of unrivalled power in the trade-union movement.

He felt he was driving away from the past into a future which was enthralling; but which, he was comforted to realise, he could in no way foretell.

On 2 January 1956 a special meeting of the TGWU general executive council appointed Frank Cousins acting General Secretary at a salary of

£1,878 14s. 2d. a year. At the same time, they once more set in motion the process for electing a General Secretary and appointing an Assistant General Secretary – for the second time in less than a year.

The election of a new General Secretary began in February with a call for nominations. Ten people came forward to challenge Cousins, but by the time the ballot commenced on 26 March nine of the competitors had withdrawn, leaving a straight contest between Cousins and Tom Healy, the national secretary of the union's flour milling, agricultural and allied trades group. By then no one in the union – or indeed outside it – had any doubt that Cousins would win. It was taken for granted that, as the night follows the day, the tradition of the TGWU and every other union – that the sitting incumbent is confirmed in power – would be maintained, even though the incumbent was a most unusual and unorthodox figure.

Meanwhile, Cousins continued his work with the Labour Party executive while he waited for the outcome of the election. But at the February meeting of the executive it was reported that he had been elected to fill the vacancy on the TUC General Council caused by Tiffin's death, and at the March meeting he formally resigned from the Labour Party executive. He attended only four meetings, but they were enough to demonstrate to the Party leaders that the TGWU was now under new management and that the Assistant General Secretary, should he become General Secretary, would be a quite different political animal from his predecessors. Richard Crossman noted in his diary early in 1956, after Tiffin's death, that Frank Cousins seemed to him to be 'determined to show that he wasn't a Deakin, and was a real militant'.[1] He added later : 'He seemed to be a nice, vigorous man who was obviously going to intervene on every kind of issue but wasn't terribly well informed.'[2] This was a characteristic Crossman view; he rarely conceded that any of the trade union hierarchy, Right or Left, were 'well informed'.

In January Cousins attended a meeting of the National Council of Labour – the body comprising the leaders of the Labour Party, TUC and Co-operative Movement. The occasion was largely a set-piece for Hugh Gaitskell to celebrate his election as Party leader, enabling him to outline the prospects and strategy for Labour, as he saw them, over the following four years. Gaitskell accepted that Labour would almost certainly be in opposition for that period, and he dealt with the chief features necessary in his view if Labour was to return to power at the next election.

On general policy he said that the Party executive was now engaged on a three-year programme, and declared : 'Time and careful thought would be given to the study of the kind of society Labour wanted and how it could

1. Richard Crossman, the unedited diaries, (to be published by Jonathan Cape and Hamish Hamilton in ? 1979).
2. *Ibid.*, August 1956.

be achieved. When the programme was completed at the end of three years it should be an up-to-date version of Labour's socialist faith.'³ There was an implication in Gaitskell's message that the unions would need to play a responsible and constructive role. Audacious as ever, Cousins chipped in to point out that this was all very well, but the unions – and certainly *his* union – were going to press for better wages. There was going to be no collaboration with the Tory Government on wages policy while the living standards and conditions of his members declined or remained so low. An observer at the meeting recalls a certain iciness in the atmosphere after that intervention, though is was passed over quickly with polite gestures all round. Even so, it was a warning shot and an omen of a kind. It certainly seemed to confirm the anxiety already being felt in some of the right-wing sections of the Labour Movement about the advent of Frank Cousins to the leadership of the TGWU.

The result of the election for General Secretary came on 11 May. Cousins's vote was 503,560 against Healy's 77,916. This was the largest ballot return in the history of the union, whose membership at the time was 1,329,600. It was also the largest majority ever registered in a General Secretary's election.

It has been alleged that the voting figures were 'deliberately enlarged' to give the impression of mass participation, but there is no evidence to support this.

Democracy at work plus an extraordinary turn of fate had produced a result that, a year earlier, would have been inconceivable. A year and ten days after the death of Arthur Deakin, Frank Cousins sat in the chair from which Deakin had so often tormented and mocked him. He himself found it hard to believe. And so did other people who realised, if only vaguely, the significance of what had happened.

This was a manifestation of the change beginning to take place inside the trade union movement. It was a reflection of the vibrations occurring on the shop floor, for no matter how rigid and conformist the institutional systems of the powerful unions were they could not completely insulate themselves against the changes at the roots. If it hadn't been Cousins, then it is almost certain that these changes would ultimately have thrown up someone else who would have understood the impulses of the moment and would have been able to respond to them.

Cousins had no doubts at all about his ability to tackle the immense challenge that lay ahead of him. In his election address he had concluded : 'I have no doubts as to my ability to lead the union in the difficult days ahead and it is in that spirit and on the basis of my past record that I submit myself for election.'

3. Minutes of the National Council of Labour, 18 January 1956.

Shortly after the result was announced[4] the union's chairman, Edgar 'Ted' Fryer, the Bristol coach-driver who had played such a crucial role in his appointment as Assistant General Secretary, came to see Cousins. Avuncular, chunky and homespun, with a West Country burr, Fryer said that he had come to offer Frank some fatherly and friendly advice. He didn't wait to be either encouraged or discouraged.

'Frank,' said Fryer, 'surround yourself with people you can trust. Clever buggers, you can buy 'em, twelve a penny.'

Good advice : not easy to follow.

4. TGWU, Minutes of the Finance and General Purposes Committee, Minute No. 294, 11 May 1956. Frank Cousins's salary as General Secretary rose to £2,000.

Chapter Ten

THE FIRST IMPACT

When Frank Cousins took over the Transport and General Workers' Union it was already in an explosive state. He did not create the conditions for a substantial change in the policy and direction of the union: he inherited them.

Cousins inherited a power base that was, on paper, the strongest in the trade union and Labour Movement and at the same time one that was ripe for new leadership. This was an enviable combination, especially at a time of significant political and social change. On the other hand the inheritance, as we have seen from earlier chapters, was extraordinarily difficult. The machine established by Ernest Bevin and consolidated by Arthur Deakin was cast in a particular mould. It was rigidly conformist; it had created its own characteristics and tradition; it had a political and industrial reputation in the Labour Movement which attracted both loyal support as well as bitter opposition.

The great majority of the union's full-time officials – at that period there were about 600 of them throughout the country – were men appointed and sustained by the Bevin-Deakin regimes who were not on the whole disposed to welcome sudden and dramatic shifts of policy, industrially or politically. They were set in their ways and attitudes. They tended to have a strong vested interest in the *status quo*, and those who were ready to welcome change were reluctant to move either as swiftly or as boldly as Cousins wished. This aspect of his inheritance was a huge and discouraging handicap, only partly offset by the advantages he held.

At the same time the shifts at the grassroots of the unions were a reflection of deep changes in society as a whole, and certainly in the methods, technology and economics of British industry. World competition was beginning to have a sharpening impact on management and its reaction towards labour problems. Wider social changes in the attitudes of Britain's workpeople were pressing the unions to take up a more aggressive posture. This tension was not yet reflected in any marked political move to the Left; there was certainly no indication of any substantial gain by Labour in public support. What *was* changing was the traditional readiness to comply with established social disciplines and the fixed economic relativities of the past. Workers were saying 'No' in greater numbers and with what seemed like a new collective will. This mood helped Cousins as much as his rise to power reflected it.

Frank Cousins did not take over with a clear-cut design for a reconstruction of the union which had been carefully worked out in advance, though he knew what he wanted in general terms. All his reflexes responded to the mood he had long sensed and which was now revealing itself so strongly among the union's rank and file. He wanted to give the ordinary member more freedom of expression; he wanted the union's machine to be reconditioned so that it would react more quickly and sensitively to the needs of the individual member; he wanted to use the TGWU's great authority and assumed power to force employers and government to concede more to working people in terms of wages, working conditions, social improvements in general and he wanted to exploit the unparalleled influence of the TGWU inside the TUC and the Labour Party and to use it, this time, on the Left by trying to push the Labour Movement toward 'more socialist policies'. He saw no need at that time to be too specific about the definition of those policies.

Cousins calculated that it wouldn't be very difficult to steer the union in a more radical direction, since it could scarcely have been less radical in the past. At that stage, therefore, there was no obligation to enunciate a clear and precise doctrine of what his left-wing philosophy involved. This was just as well, because Frank Cousins never claimed to be a political philosopher; he was always a doer rather than a thinker, a man who did not require to have his socialist faith explained in terms of reasoned argument but felt instinctively that the faith was self-evidently rational and ultimately would triumph.

Cousins viewed the immediate task ahead as a strictly practical one. The union was in poor shape organisationally; its morale was low, and the gulf between full-time officials and rank and file had widened dangerously during the Deakin post-war era. In some areas, like the docks, the situation was serious enough to threaten the whole structure of the TGWU. Nobody doubted the urgent need for a spring-clean and a new sense of direction and purpose. In that context the union's latest decision to fight for higher wages became a priority. It was seen by Frank Cousins and his closest advisers – like Alf Chandler – as the starting-point for the change in policy, partly because it would galvanise the membership and help to revive faith in the union, and partly because it was seen to be necessary in its own right.

Wages in British industry were far too low, especially among the majority of workers represented by the TGWU: the semi-skilled and unskilled workers.

Frank Cousins did not, however, take over his seat of power with too many illusions. At the March meeting of the union executive, before his election result was formally known, he reported that the TGWU would be: 'confronted with an extremely difficult position during 1956, calling for all the foresight and judgment of which we are capable'. He was referring to the general political, economic and industrial situation in the country as well as the TGWU's internal problems. More specifically, on the situation in the docks section Cousins told the executive: 'I think we have to face the fact that it is going to be a long and difficult task, but here again given full cooperation between the officers and a determined approach we should eventually succeed in recovering the lost membership.'

Recalling those first days as general secretary, Frank Cousins views the remarkable turn of events which brought him to the top with great modesty:

I don't think I converted the feeling of the union when I became general secretary. All I did was to give expression to feelings that were there. We were at a stage where things were beginning to fall apart – particularly in dockland. The union was ridden with unofficial movements because there was very little identity between leadership and rank and file.

The political campaign against the Communists had left serious weaknesses and Frank Cousins found, he says, that during Deakin's secretaryship, 'People were put into jobs in the union simply because they were anti-Communist and because they were politically "safe".' In addition, much of the administration was hopelessly run down.

At the same time, he knew that many senior officials were hostile towards him and resentful that he had reached the top in spite of all the well-laid plans of the Deakin regime. A number of leading officers disliked Cousins both personally and politically – so there was much point in Fryer's avuncular advice to the new boy that he should surround himself with people he could trust.

In this respect Cousins had one great advantage: Alf Chandler was his chief lieutenant inside the organisation. (The appointment of Harry Nicholas as Assistant General Secretary was not made until 21 June 1956 and it became effective on 2 July that year.) There is no lack of appreciation of this from Frank Cousins. He told me:

Alf Chandler was ready, able and willing to ensure change in the union. And he was a man of tremendous capacity. He had influenced me greatly when I was a younger official and he taught me much about the political and industrial background of the union. I should say that at that time he was one of the men who made it possible for me to understand what this union meant in the whole scheme of the working-class movement.

Chandler guided the inexperienced Cousins through quicksands and whirlpools, encouraging him and protecting him from many minor irritations. A year later, after Cousins had taken charge of his first biennial delegate conference, Chandler wrote in the union's journal:

> I myself have never had any doubts as to [Cousins's] character and ability based solely on our socialist beliefs. Nevertheless his baptism was something to be seen to be believed. He showed a remarkable grasp of the essentials of every problem he was called upon to handle with repeated flashes of real brilliance . . . In my time I have attended many union conferences but in all sincerity I am bound to say that I have never seen a personality and leader of men of quite the same calibre as Frank Cousins. To move up from the lower level to the general secretaryship of our great union in a single stride, to meet the supreme policy-making conference just in a matter of months and to command such respect and confidence is really something. He stands high now but I would prophesy that given a continuance of the forthright and virile approach which was in evidence at Torquay he will when he reaches the end of his term of office rank amongst the foremost trade union leaders of our generation.[1]

That was a remarkable tribute from a man like Chandler who had grown up with the TGWU from its birth; who had been on terms of the closest relations with Bevin and Deakin; and was in so many ways the embodiment of the union.

The new General Secretary was, of course, understandably uncertain of himself when he took over. There is a world of difference between acting as General Secretary and being confirmed in power, for when the word 'acting' is removed the real impact of the loneliness of high office becomes truly apparent. It is then that men have to face themselves and their own inner doubts, their feelings of inadequacy and insecurity, while the outside world sees only the external protective image of a man in power with muscles braced to face the challenges.

At first Frank Cousins told his national officials that the General Secretary's office would in future have an 'open door'. He wanted to sweep away the bureaucratic oppressiveness of the previous regime. But he was soon to discover that although the 'open door' policy was an attractive principle, it

1. TGWU *Record*, August 1957, p. 27.

was a demanding and difficult practice. Charles Brandon recalls the first days of Cousins's rule with some asperity :

> He was very immature at the outset. At his first meeting with full-time officers at Transport House Frank Cousins said that he would not be bound by anything his predecessors had said or done. Bevin, he said, had been a great man; Deakin may have been a great man. But he was Frank Cousins, and his policies would be his own – and no one else's.
>
> The reaction to this was not entirely favourable. It was in my view a tact-less thing to say if you have before you men who had worked for years with Bevin and with Deakin and then you say to them, in effect, 'Well, here I am —but don't think I'm going to be like your old mates, Bevin and Deakin; I'm Frank Cousins.' He was a tactless man.

Brandon's claim is that Cousins started off on the wrong foot; that he 'threw his weight around' because he was so uncertain; and that often he insisted on change for its own sake rather than carefully considering the wider implications for the union. This was a view shared by a number of the old guard officials. The retrospective judgment on this suggests that most of this kind of opposition to Cousins came from men who would have resented change in any event, but were still more determined to resent it when it was promoted by someone they regarded as a 'young upstart' or by someone whose political attitudes they resisted, as most of them did.

Even if the change of direction was certain to be slower than Cousins imagined and hoped, they knew that it would, none the less, be sharp. Given the new leader's determination, there was only a limited amount they could do to stem the new tidal wave.

Compared with this largely negative approach it must be said that there were officials in high places who, while disapproving of Cousins (or at least not yet committed to him) were prepared to give him the benefit of the doubt and accept what the future had in store, out of loyalty and dedication to the union. Harry Nicholas was in this category. He pledged his full sup-port and loyalty to Frank Cousins and he always maintained it, even when he obviously did not agree with the new policy. Why, for instance, didn't Nicholas challenge Cousins for the general secretaryship after Tiffin's death? Nicholas's answer to this is revealing :

> I didn't stand because I regarded the man who was assistant (and then act-ing) general secretary as having a basic right to expect promotion when the premier job became vacant. I also knew that Frank Cousins had a great deal of support behind him from a great many people who felt the union ought to change from Right to Left. In addition I was probably regarded as being too closely associated with Bevin and Deakin; and as a Right-winger. This was rubbish – but there it is. I have always regarded my first loyalty as

being to the general secretary in all the difficulties he experienced. That was perhaps why people regarded me as being of the same views as Bevin and Deakin.

This again, is a characteristic response from a man of Nicholas's loyalties. And he added that his feelings towards Frank Cousins after he became General Secretary did not alter simply because Cousins had thwarted the ambition of his lifetime:

> I never allowed any of these things – the unfortunate things in a way – to stand between me and the sort of job I thought I had to do for the union. Loyalty has always been very important to me. We never had any arguments on the issue of loyalty; we did have arguments about attitudes. But we never fought about the job. Of course I would have loved to have been general secretary. But basically I wanted to do the best I could for the union – whether it was being run by Bevin, Deakin, Tiffin or Frank Cousins. Mind you, I found more problems with Frank – but also more basic friendliness with Frank than with any of the others.

The union that Cousins took over was, structurally, almost exactly the same as the machine that Bevin had built and launched in 1921–2. It was divided into thirteen geographic regions – now reduced to eleven – with each region operating a comprehensive mini-TGWU in its own area. The regional secretaries in charge of these sectors of the empire are powerful figures in their localities and in the politics of the union as a whole. Parallel with this geographic structure, into which are slotted branches and district committees collectively governed by a regional committee, there is an industrial structure. This divides members into national and local trade groups, according to their jobs.

Although Frank Cousins could be exceptionally helpful and considerate to his colleagues, there has always been a deep reserve beneath all the personal relationships. He has always been a very private person. He has all the hall-marks of the real introvert. So he did not make friends easily, nor did he ostentatiously assist his enemies to overcome their prejudices against him. At times he was accused, rightly, of insensitive behaviour to his officials, which would have been avoided by a more confident and experienced manager of men. His confidence in his own convictions and in his policies was overwhelming; but it was not matched by a confidence in his personal relationships. He was not given to the smooth or diplomatic approach: indeed that particular style is not among the routine arts of trade union leadership. Neither Bevin nor Deakin were any different in this respect, but they operated in a different political climate and inside an institution which, by and large, responded more readily to leadership. This was not the case with Frank Cousins. For the most part he was acting, both politically and personally, against the grain of the union's style. He was pushing for change, exhorting the rank and file to demands which many full-time officials did not believe in. To have conducted that kind of operation without provoking the hardened opposition of men brought up in quite different traditions would have required the touch of a saint.

It would be wrong to give the impression that Cousins was faced with enemies and opponents wherever he turned. He had important friends and allies inside as well as outside the union. There were people like Jack Jones, who was by then Midland area engineering secretary; and there was Fred Eastwood. The Cousinses, the Eastwoods and the Joneses were on family friendship terms. Fred Eastwood, who had taken over the road haulage section from Cousins, remained a personal friend until the time he left the union, and gave him constant, if not uncritical, support. He was one of the few national officials who could sense, and deal with, Cousins's moodiness. He had worked with Cousins long enough to know, by instinct, how to handle his General Secretary even in his most spiky mood.

'I would sometimes go into his office in the morning,' Fred Eastwood has told me, 'and see Frank sitting there, tense and tight-faced. I would notice a red patch in the middle of his forehead and I knew, immediately, he was in a bad mood. That red patch always depicted that Frank was in a bad temper so I would fight shy of any encounter with him at that point. I would go for a walk round the block and come back perhaps an hour later to see if the red patch had gone. It usually had. He was often in a bad temper in the early morning. Of course he would get very frustrated at other times of the day, as well.'

As a young official, Eastwood knew Bevin and idolised him, and in Cousins he saw a replica. 'There was a strong parallel between the two men,' Eastwood claims. 'Both had great strength of will and in many respects they had the same kind of temperament. Both men insisted on winning: neither of them could stand the emotional risks in losing. Both were good human beings – but neither could really openly confess to a failure, a mistake or a substantial error. Both men found apologising very difficult indeed. Deakin was different,' Fred Eastwood asserts, 'He was a bully because he was *not* such a big man and he was also under the shadow of Bevin. Frank Cousins was straight and immensely loyal to friends. He was a trusting man – often, in my view, too trusting.'

Eastwood knew Cousins's parents and he recalls a conversation with Frank's mother, Hannah, to whom Frank was especially devoted.

'Fred,' Mrs Cousins asked Eastwood on one occasion, 'if ever you see our Frank's head getting too big, will you please do me a favour?'

'What?' Eastwood inquired.

'Just tell him,' she demanded.

After the death of Mrs Cousins Fred Eastwood told this story to Frank, who seemed a little shocked and surprised. He could not imagine that he could be guilty of excessive vanity or of the kind of self-importance for which he in the past had criticised his predecessors. Yet the fact is that such vanity is the occupational hazard of all prominent national figures, even the most .radical and socialist of trade union leaders.

Eastwood, like so many others who knew Frank Cousins intimately, reckons that his General Secretary was at his best and his happiest in the garden or with children. 'That was where he could be completely natural – where it was never necessary to strike any postures,' Fred Eastwood says.

Part of Cousins's problem in establishing close relations with his officials was that he desperately needed to trust people, yet he was always uncertain about the degree to which he could depend on the system and the matrix he had inherited from Deakin and Tiffin. Emotionally he was a man who leant naturally towards trust and who found satisfaction in loyalty to friends and loyalty from friends. One senior official of the union claims that Cousins had few friends among his fellow national officers 'because there was no other senior official who shared the strength of his political convictions or the strength of his desire to change the direction of the union's policy'. This is almost certainly an exaggeration, but there is truth in it. There were officials – senior men such as Easwood – as well as men like Chandler who *did* share Cousins's general outlook. They were as convinced as he was that the union needed to change direction and urgently needed a new style of leadership. Yet it was also true that the degree of Cousins's commitment to change was stronger than that of anyone else, and he was less prepared to compromise, less willing to pull back from the brink, in pursuit of that change, than any of his national officials. Because of this, because he was so clearly 'a new kind of animal' in the seat of power, and because he appeared to be such an odd egg in the TGWU nest, he was not an easy man to work with. Some of his colleagues found him somewhat overbearing and have described him as 'bigheaded' or 'aloof'; they had seen him as an aloof man even when he was national secretary in charge of road haulage. He did not socialise much or spend a lot of time gossiping in the pub; he never found chat either about the weather or his colleagues' sex lives an absorbing pastime; there was no easy-going, casual conversation with his fellow officials, the great majority of whom were, of course, Deakin's hand-picked men.

It was much the same inside the TUC General Council. There was the predictable, one might say almost natural, resentment toward the man who comes in from the outside and immediately sets about overturning the table. 'Oh well, if that's his game . . .' they seem to have said to themselves, with few exceptions. The TUC establishment felt affronted by Cousins's manner and style as much as by his policies. It scarcely needed a row over the Cohen Council[2] or cooperation with the Government to precipitate a hostile reaction to Frank Cousins. His brashness and disregard for conventions were sufficient in themselves to alienate many of his TUC colleagues; and they were pleased to point at what they saw as personality defects to support their general hostility to Cousins's views and policies.

Yet it was far from all unfavourable, even inside the TUC. The staff of Congress House welcomed the wind of change coming from the top man in the TGWU. The TUC staff, in Deakin's days, had felt themselves to be in a form of intellectual bondage. They saw the emergence of Cousins as a liberating force. One middle-ranking member of the staff has described the situation to me in these terms :

> Previously the attitude taken by the TGWU was predictable which in turn meant that the attitude of the General Council was predictable as was the attitude of Congress itself. It was not that Cousins was Left of centre which introduced a new dimension so much as that he could not be taken for granted – or rather the support of the TGWU for a particular line of policy could not be taken for granted in advance. This meant that the stability of the General Council was disturbed and both TUC staff and other GC members were forced to recognise that they had to 'negotiate' with Cousins.

While Sir Vincent Tewson remained General Secretary of the TUC the old guard had at least a focal point around whom they could group. But this was to be shattered later when George Woodcock succeeded to the general secretaryship of the TUC and, as we shall discuss later, established a working relationship with Frank Cousins which had a profound influence in reshaping TUC policy between 1959 and 1964 when Cousins joined the Labour Government.

The launching of Frank Cousins on the national scene also occurred at a time of unusual and even dramatic events both in industry and government economic policy. The watershed had been reached in post-war industrial relations, and management were beginning to react against the unions in a more aggressive style. The sequence of events is worth considering in some detail since it illustrates a quite new development in industrial and economic strategy, with the major employers' organisations taking the initiative in advance of the Government, to be followed six months later by a Ministerial offensive for wage restraint.

2. The Cohen Council, sometimes known as the 'Three Wise Men' was the Council on Prices, Productivity and Incomes set up in August 1957 under the chairmanship of Lord Cohen. The other members were Sir Dennis Robertson and Sir Harold Howitt. The Government intention was to set up a Council with an independent status but whose authority would carry conviction. It was asked to consider all aspects of economic policy relating to prices, productivity and incomes and report periodically. In fact it was the first of a series of bodies, permanent, quasi-Governmental institutions, whose remit was to inform and influence public opinion on prices and incomes policy.

The employers' offensive actually began in September 1955 when the British Employers' Confederation (now part of the Confederation of British Industry) issued a declaration of policy entitled *Britain's Industrial Future.* This called on both sides of industry and on the Government to take immediate action to restrain inflation. The task of keeping costs and prices stable so that exports could be expanded, the BEC argued, could only be achieved by higher and more efficient production and by firmly checking internal demand and curbing wage increases. No doubt this declaration was well timed to follow the emergency measures the Government had been compelled to introduce in July to tighten the credit squeeze. It also helped fortify the Government's resolve to introduce still tougher measures in the mini-budget of October. But these measures, tough though they were when measured against earlier Government philosophy, of giving economic freedom its head, were still not strong enough for the employers. The BEC specifically called for a deliberate policy of wage restraint allied to a possible dividend limitation. And they made it quite clear that at least part of their motive was to provide a 'challenge to the Government to produce their own statement'.

In November the powerful Federation of British Industries (also now incorporated in the CBI) added their authority to the plea, and in March 1956 the Government published a White Paper – *The Economic Implications of Full Employment.* This was an undistinguished document, full of platitudes and generalisations. It was a defensive publication : it emphasised that the Government was not attempting to 'interfere with the system of collective bargaining' nor seeking to determine what incomes people ought to be receiving. None the less, the message was clear : the pressure for higher wages could threaten the policy of full employment which had been a basic principle accepted by both the major political parties since the war.

The White Paper was also a confession of failure by the Government, and so it had to be projected in subdued tones. It was in effect a U-turn in Conservative post-war policy, since it marked its reluctant acknowledgement that Conservative 'freedom' was not entirely the panacea it had been claimed to be. Although the call for restraint was made in moderate tones, it was essentially a return to the policies of the late 1940s, and it sought the kind of agreement with the unions that had been established, after so much difficulty, between the Attlee Government and the TUC. But even if there had been no change in trade union leadership or in the mood of the rank and file it would have been almost impossible for the Conservative Government to have recreated that earlier concordat after a four-year period in which the virtues of economic freedom and the evils of controls had been so loudly proclaimed. No doubt the Cabinet recognised this. At any rate, while their response to the employers' initiative was muted on the wages front much more direct and stronger action was taken to control the financial policies of the nationalised industries. Ministers intervened to prevent price increases in transport, electricity, coal and gas. In this way the Government was not only forcing the nationalised boards into serious deficit; it was also compelling the State industries to bear the brunt of labour trouble which was bound to result from limiting the freedom of the boards to negotiate freely with the unions. It was a form of back-door intervention, yet no less effective and dangerous for that.

Frank Cousins took his seat on the TUC General Council on 22 February and was later appointed to seven of its committees, the most important of which was the economic committee. It was this commitee that met the Prime Minister, Eden, and the new Chancellor, Harold Macmillan, on 5 March to protest against the new economic policies and their unequal impact on working people compared with the wealthier sections of society. This was Frank Cousins's first experience of confrontation with the Government as a member of the TUC, and he was far from impressed by the vigour of the protest mounted by his TUC colleagues.

The meeting took place before the Budget, and the TUC were promised a further meeting with the Prime Minister in May, which in fact materialised the day before the formal announcement of Cousins's election on 10 May. At that meeting Eden, flanked by R. A. Butler (Lord Privy Seal), Harold Macmillan (Chancellor) and Iain Macleod (Minister of Labour) put the formal appeal to the TUC leaders for wage restraint. The TUC shuffled inconclusively. They refused to give their cooperation, but at the same time said they would need to consider the Government's view since they accepted the fact that a 'wage-price spiral is a bad thing'. On the day of his election Frank Cousins told *The Times* that the TGWU had already made its position on wage claims quite clear : the union would press the interests of its members 'in a reasonable way', but they would be pressed. He also made it quite clear that he would fight the policy of restraint, and he hoped the rest of the trade union movement would do likewise.

That same day, Prime Minister Eden speaking at Perth made his first major public appeal for wage restraint, and *The Times* displayed his appeal alongside the story of Cousins's election as General Secretary.

The campaign and the conflict were now gathering some momentum. On 25 May at Newcastle Mr Macmillan came out with the strongest warning so far that the Government intended to fight on the wages issue as hard as possible. The Chancellor declared that another round of wage increases like that of the last two years could endanger Britain's competitive position in world markets. He was careful to explain that the Government was not asking for a rigid policy of wage control; there was no objection to wages rising with productivity and greater efficiency. But another pay round without such matching benefits could not be repeated without disaster. It was because the Government saw this danger that he and the Prime Minister had been engaged in talks with the TUC and employers, whom the Government had asked to keep prices stable.

Frank Cousins replied to Macmillan next day. Speaking at a union rally in Coventry he retorted: 'We are not very impressed by his telling us that if there are no wage increases for twelve months everything will be all right.'

And at his first executive meeting following his election he reported the economic situation in this way:

> We are now seeing very pointedly the results of the free-for-all into which the Conservatives plunged the country on the plea that there would be plenty for all coupled with a progressive reduction in prices. What is more, it seems certain that unless the Government institute some form of controls the position will continue to worsen. This, however, would appear to be unlikely, as we now have a spectacle of the Chancellor of the Exchequer in his Newcastle speech again returning to the philosophy of wage restraint as the answer to the problem. Hardly a word is directed towards the employing interests and the higher income groups except the customary half-hearted appeal, without any definite Government action. Once again, apparently, it is the workers who are to stand still while the cost of living continues to rise.

Cousins did not question the seriousness of the economic situation, but insisted that the only way it could be tackled was by spreading the burden equitably across the whole community.

> It is not sufficient to maintain the cry of higher production and still higher production as representing the solution to all our ills. Certainly it is a very important factor but it cannot just rest in that setting and I therefore submit that until such time as the Government are prepared to accept the principle of a common sharing of the burden, our attitude must remain steadfast based upon the policy statement issued in December of last year.

At that stage in the early summer of 1956 it appeared that the whole industrial scene was about to explode. The TUC General Council could scarcely find it credible that the General Secretary of the TGWU was speaking in such extraordinarily aggressive tones. The TUC was at the time preparing a policy statement for its annual Congress, to be held at Brighton in September. The switch in Government policy had already complicated the situation, but the main reason for the growing confusion inside the General Council was the emergence of this vigorous, outspoken leader of the country's most powerful union. His attacks on Government policy introduced an altogether new stridency into relations between Whitehall and the trade unions.

When Cousins took his seat at the February meeting of the Council there

125

was no question of his playing himself in gradually. The custom and practice for freshmen to the TUC hierarchy had always been to remain discreetly on the sidelines for two or three meetings before a gingerly placed contribution, usually on their own specific speciality. Not so Frank Cousins. At his first meeting he spoke twice, vigorously and without hesitation. He caused a minor sensation by mentioning the word 'socialism' – a word then only rarely used at the illustrious level of a General Council meeting. The Boilermakers' Society leader, the late Ted Hill (Lord Hill) who was usually an isolated left-wing figure at TUC meetings, was seen to be nodding his head in vigorous and even astonished agreement with this newcomer from the TGWU.

Cousins caused a good deal of irritation among the stolid old guard at subsequent meetings by his persistent questioning and probing; his challenges to the authority of the General Secretary, Sir Vincent Tewson; and his seemingly arrogant contempt for the usual ritual deference towards seniority. He had calculated that he had to make a quick impact and a decisive one. There was no point in delaying this by adopting the manicured tactics he so much despised in others. So he plunged in at once, and the effect was dynamic. If it caused fury and anger among the right-wing and moderate groups on the General Council, it also brought him the delighted approval of the tiny minority who constituted the Left of the TUC leadership in those days – men like Ted Hill and Robert Willis, the London print workers' leader. Yet Cousins did nothing to encourage their devotion. He made it clear – often embarrassingly clear – that he was not seeking acolytes or clandestine groupings; he was not setting out to establish a group-within-a-group or a Cousins-faction. He began as a distinctly single-minded, individual force, and he remained a loner for the duration of his career on the General Council. There was only one exception to this : his loose and often seemingly contradictory partnership (if it can be so described) with George Woodcock in later years.

A partnership which might have stuck was the one he began to establish with Jim Campbell of the National Union of Railwaymen. Campbell and Cousins had known each other before and during the early years of the war when they were young officials in the Doncaster area.

When Campbell's tragic death brought Sidney Greene to the leadership of the NUR, he and Cousins touched a mutually hostile chord almost from the first. John Newton, the Tailors and Garment Workers' leader, was another member of the tiny left-wing minority who would have wished to work with Cousins if there had been anything equivalent on the TUC of the Bevanite grouping in the Labour Party. But there was not.

Several members of the TUC staff have told me of their mixed reactions to Frank Cousins. Those who accepted the conventional political and industrial position of the TUC leadership were immediately hostile to him. They considered him to be overbearing and inconsiderate. They objected – like General Council members – to his insistence that he should sit on the important committees from the start. The tradition was that new members should serve their apprenticeship on relatively less important sub-committees. There was also a feeling that Cousins's general dislike of the TUC leadership, as it was then composed, extended to staff members.

Cousins was also reluctant to be told, or even advised on, how the TGWU might conduct its affairs. There is an early story of how Lionel (Len) Murray, now General Secretary of the TUC and then secretary of the economic department, submitted a paper proposing that the unions might do more to expand their interest in fringe-benefit claims. Cousins was not wholly convinced that they should take precedence over pay claims and suspected that a switch to fringe-benefit claims might be an undercover method of encouraging a policy of wage restraint.

Murray assured him that there was a good deal of evidence to show that rank-and-file trade unionists were interested in winning extra fringe benefits. He cited his experience at a recent weekend school where he had met shop-stewards, including – he added injudiciously – TGWU shop-stewards who *were* enthusiastic about fringe-benefit claims. Frank Cousins drew himself up to his full height and turned on Murray.

'When I want advice on how to run the TGWU,' he said : 'The last person I would come to would be the secretary of the TUC's economic department.'

Murray regarded this as a sign of Cousins's deep distrust of the TUC establishment and of his belief that the TUC, like the TGWU hierarchy, was still full of people schooled in and conditioned by the attitudes of Arthur Deakin. Indeed to Frank Cousins, at that time, the world was full of Deakins seeking to perpetuate Deakinism. Of course, from his unaccustomed position on the bridge at the TGWU it was an understandable fear.

Yet not all the TUC staff were hostile or fearful of the abrasive new master of the TGWU. A substantial minority silently welcomed the wind of change, and in their own discreet fashion let it be known.

In Cousins's first few pioneering months as a member of the TUC General Council the main policy issue was the trade union reaction to the Government's increasing pressure on wage claims and the growing clamour for wage restraint. Some members of the General Council would have been ready to go along with a policy of restraint, provided they could have secured concessions from the Government on prices. A policy document on economic affairs was produced for the June meeting of the economic committee which set out some tentative ideas on restraint. Cousins savaged the document and its authors (members of the TUC economic department and Sir Vincent Tewson). The document went back for redrafting. It came up again in August, again to meet a Cousins demolition performance. It was thereafter shelved. The General Council knew they were in for a difficult Congress that year.

Other serious problems were looming up for the TUC, all of them adding to the drama. An automation dispute at Standard Motors raised new and fundamental problems of job security. In April Standard announced that there would have to be large-scale redundancies that summer as a result of the introduction of automatic machinery in the tractor factory, which was being completely reorganised. The company had bought German-made automated machines capable of reducing manpower by up to 75 per cent. When the machines were fully operative six men could do the work once carried out by twenty-eight men. For some months before this announcement the management and the shop-stewards had been in negotiation about how best to cushion the impact of this huge reorganisation. The stewards wanted a guarantee that no one would be sacked and that the company would introduce a system of universal short-time working, and allow men to drift away voluntarily. The management rejected this policy of 'shared misery' and argued that it would be economically self-defeating for the company and its workforce. When it was clear there would be no agreement the company announced its redundancy proposals : 2,900 workers would be laid off for varying periods during the summer. There was no guarantee that any of them would be re-hired. At the end of April 11,000 Standard car workers started an unofficial strike, including 5,000 members of the TGWU.

Nine unions were involved in the stoppage and their officials immediately set about trying to persuade their members to return to work so that negotiations could be resumed with the company. Meanwhile, wholly against previous practice, the TGWU decided to pay dispute benefit to their members on strike, despite the fact that the strike was still unofficial. This was a remarkable departure from the days of Arthur Deakin, and Frank Cousins's first significant success in persuading the union's executive to reverse former policy. The strike lasted seventeen days before the unions persuaded the men to suspend action while negotiations were resumed. But at the end of May, after fruitless discussions to reduce the numbers of workers affected, Standard insisted on dismissing 2,600, with a £15 compensation payment offered to each worker. Originally the company had wanted to lay off 3,500. Negotiations had saved 900 jobs. What made the unions' task infinitely more difficult was the deteriorating world market for British cars and vehicles. While negotiations with Standard were in mid-stream Australia announced new import restrictions. The credit squeeze on the home market further depressed prospects. Union leaders sensed that the whole industry would soon be caught up in a new cold wind of economic change. They fought for the best compensation terms they could get from Standard before yielding to the inevitable.

For their part, the Government kept out of the debate as much as they possibly could. Ministers argued that the whole problem was something for the motor industry to sort out for itself, between management and unions.

There was no doubt in the minds of the headline writers about what had caused the sackings. The *Daily Mirror* described it as 'The Robot Revolution', and the *Daily Herald* of the same day[3] headlined its main page-one story : 'Automation Firm Sacks 2,600 men'.

The Standard automation dispute certainly caused great bitterness – and profound shock – through the Midlands, and a great deal of surprise in the country as a whole. Despite the discussions between the management and union officials, which had been going on for some months before the final decision to sack so many workers, the company's firm stand still surprised the unions. It raised the whole spectre of automation more vividly than ever before.

Up till that moment, automation existed as a nagging fear : a dark shadow on the horizon which might one day become a nightmarish reality. The American experience was well known – and disturbing. But in Britain the question had hitherto been confined largely to discussions in academic circles, and even in trade union circles to academic terms. The Standard dispute of 1956 turned that academic issue into what seemed a dramatic threat to the security of almost every British worker. In retrospect one can see that the drama and the fears were exaggerated, but that was not how it appeared at the time.

The Government sought to play down the anxieties. Nevertheless, Ministers were privately seriously alarmed, and the Cabinet decided to set up an inter-departmental inquiry into the implications of automation's threat to British industry. The Minister of Labour, Iain Macleod, made speeches inside and outside parliament urging the unions and their members to adopt a calmer view of the prospects ahead. He stressed that workers had more to fear from industry being out of date than they had from the modernisation of Britain's factories. It was a not too convincing attempt to reassure the men on the shop-floor. Macleod took an each-way bet by inviting both sides of industry to meet him, and other Ministers, to discuss the whole problem.

The talks had scarcely been launched when an even bigger shock-wave broke across the entire Midlands car industry. On 27 June British Motor Corporation (as it was known before the merger which brought into existence British Leyland Motor Corporation) sacked 6,000 of their workers from twelve factories, with the axe falling most heavily on the main Longbridge works at Birmingham. The remainder of the company's employees were told that they would switch to a three-day or four-day week at the same

3. 31 May 1956.

time. There had been no warning, and no prior consultation with union officials either locally or nationally. Even the Government had been given only the briefest of advance notice – and then only on an informal basis. The first reaction was one of total disbelief. When it became clear that the company meant precisely what it said the shock was profound. Even Iain Macleod appeared to be shaken.[4] As Frank Cousins observed later in his union journal, it was as if 'The British Motor Corporation has not fully appreciated the date and age in which it is operating.'[5]

One must conclude that BMC had decided, quite deliberately, to shock the unions, and perhaps the nation, into recognising that the motor industry was over-manned and under-equipped to compete in world markets against the rapidly rising and highly efficient competition from European car producers (the Japanese had not yet begun to swing into full-scale world competition). It is also fairly clear that BMC took the opportunity to follow the initiative taken by Standard Motors while the unions were still reeling under the impact of the Coventry sackings. The unions were weaker than they dared to admit publicly. They were uncertain about the response to a massive strike call to defend redundant jobs; and the majority of union leaders recognised that it was unrealistic to make a blanket demand that all redundancies should be resisted either by short-time working or by a refusal to accept sackings until alternative work had been provided. The shop-stewards were themselves divided on the issue, and the employers knew this.

On the other hand, the unions had little choice but to resist, at least by putting up a strong initial fight. First, however, the leaders of the fifteen unions with members at BMC sought to persuade the company to change or modify its policy. They asked for reinstatement of the 6,000 pending negotiations; they sought an extension of short-time working; they claimed substantial compensation when all else seemed to fail; and they asked, as a palliative, for a pledge that there would be adequate warning and consultation before any future dismissals.

On 19 July BMC issued a detailed defence of the dismissals, claiming that the state of the car industry left them no choice. Between January 1954 and March 1956 they claimed they had increased their workforce by 16 per cent while the redundancy represented *only* $12\frac{1}{2}$ per cent and that 75 per cent of those being dismissed had less than three years' service with the company. The unions challenged all these arguments. When it became clear that no satisfactory compromise could be reached, the leaders of the fifteen unions reluctantly gave notice of an official strike from 23 July. Most of the drive behind the demand for a strike came from Frank Cousins. Most of the unions went along with the strike call not because they felt any convic-

4. For a detailed account of the BMC sackings see Hilda Kahn, *Repercussions of Redundancy* (Allen and Unwin, 1964), pp. 21–38.
5. TGWU *Record*, September 1956, p. 98.

tion about winning, but in the belief that they had got to show some fight, if only for their own self-respect.

The strike was less than a week old when Iain Macleod intervened and brought the two sides together again for negotiations. Yet it took nearly a fortnight of intensive talking to produce a patched-up compromise and to force BMC to make concessions which enabled the unions to scramble out of the crisis with at least some small achievements.

Work resumed on 13 August after the company agreed to pay a modest compensation to the dismissed workers and gave a pledge to consult the unions in the event of any further dismissals. It was the minimum that could have been expected – or accepted. None the less, even this apparently modest success was a landmark for British trade unions. Two new principles had been established – the principle that employers must give reasonable notice of dismissal, and the still more substantial principle that there should be compensation for those who are sacked.

It is difficult to believe, now, that such principles were unregistered – even if not altogether unknown – as recently as 1956, and that the most powerfully supported official strike since the war had to be waged before they were established. In his assessment of the extraordinary affair Frank Cousins later claimed in his union journal, perhaps half defensively :

> The unions had endeavoured to reach a settlement by peaceful means – it is never our desire to bring men out if it is possible to find a solution to the problem around the conference table – but no union could have allowed a situation to go unchallenged as a result of which thousands of workers were cast out of work without regard to normal, decent industrial practice.[6]

It was one way of describing an experience – his first major industrial exploit as General Secretary – which had ended in neither victory nor defeat. Not that Cousins had anything to be ashamed of. It was not because he was new to the job that the result was so limited; nor that he was inexperienced in handling situations of such complexity. It was because the Standard and the BMC disputes contained far wider political, social and economic implications than the union had faced in any previous industrial explosion since the war, raising issues that were – or so it seemed at the time – well outside union control.

Even the Government was temporarily stunned. Many Ministers were fiercely critical of both Standard and BMC, and said so privately and publicly – the more so because the Government appeared impotent to cushion the impact of the sackings. The companies concerned seemed themselves to be in a confused state of mind. There was a mixture of managerial panic and despair induced partly by the serious turn in world markets, the

6. TGWU *Record*, September 1956, p. 99.

erosion of confidence in domestic economy and the fear that if management consulted the unions in advance and sought a joint approach to an acute industrial problem then they might get nowhere.

In retrospect, there is little doubt that the BMC dismissals in particular had a deep and lasting effect throughout British industry. The resentment lingered on for many years and did a great deal of damage to industrial relations in the car industry. No company ever attempted anything quite like that again.

Three days after the BMC announcement of the 6,000 sackings the entire political and economic atmosphere in Britain was transformed by the news that Egypt's President Nasser had seized the Suez Canal and, without any international consultation, nationalised it.

Israel invaded the Sinai Peninsula at the end of October 1956 and this was followed a few days later by the Anglo-French landings at Port Said and Suez. Shortly afterwards the British and French troops withdrew, leaving the whole Suez operation as an unfinished fiasco, because the United States refused to support the venture.

This is not the place to do more than mention the Suez episode, but events that followed in its wake had fundamental effects on the whole range of British policy, both domestically and internationally. No other incident since the end of World War II so explicitly indicated a new and lesser role for Britain in world affairs.

Meanwhile Russian tanks had moved into Hungary, and many people believed that World War III was about to start.

In May Britain exploded her latest nuclear weapon on the Monte Bello islands in the Pacific. Four days later the United States exploded her first air-dropped H-bomb in the Central Pacific.

It is significant, in the context of Frank Cousins's career, that these events came at the moment he was taking over in the TGWU. Looking at the Press pictures of the mushroom cloud, the new General Secretary reflected sadly on the evil turn in the development of science and technology. What a wonderful world it might be if the genius of man could be applied to creative enterprises rather than destructive force; what a role there was for a country like Britain, which, he thought, might encourage such a transformation of energies . . . if only the imaginative political leadership were there.

As he toured the union's regions – he visited each one in turn after becoming General Secretary – he made a point of picking out international affairs for a special mention. This showed Cousins's serious interest in foreign affairs, always allowing for his disclaimer that he was simply a novice in the field. Frank Cousins's main theme at all these union events, however, was an attack on the Government's economic and wages policies. Each speech emphasised ever more strongly that the TGWU policy *had* changed;

there would be no truck with a Conservative Government on wage restraint. The union, he kept repeating, was not seeking any industrial confrontation with the Government: it wanted conciliation. Nevertheless, he stressed: 'We shall not be apologists for the Conservative approach.'

Throughout the summer of 1956 as he went from region to region, from trade group to trade group, the message was repeated loud and clear: there would be no wages deal with a Tory Government because a Tory Government was simply not politically willing, or able, to offer the unions the kind of deal that would be acceptable. It was, as it turned out, a warning given as much for the benefit of his TUC colleagues as to the Government and the employers.

Shortly before the September Trades Union Congress Harold Macmillan called the Press to the Treasury for a carefully prepared on-the-record briefing about the Government's view on the general economic and industrial situation. He again emphasised the need for wage moderation and introduced a phrase which later became famous by calling for a 'plateau' in wage and price levels. The Chancellor even offered to travel to Brighton to speak at the TUC if he was invited. It was a cheeky, audacious and even facetious proposal, since he knew that the TUC had never invited a Conservative politician to speak from a Congress platform. The TUC leaders have indeed always been somewhat reluctant to yield their platform even to a Labour politician, in or out of Government. The very notion of a Tory Chancellor lecturing a Trade Union Congress on the virtues of wage restraint certainly gave some scope for the cartoonists; Macmillan's little joke did little to help the moderates inside the TUC General Council who, privately, would not have been averse to some understanding with the Government if they had felt it possible to carry their membership. That was not to be.

The central issues at that Congress were the worsening economic climate, the fear of growing unemployment (underlined by the outbreak of automation redundancies in the car industry) and the Government's pressure for wage restraint. The unions knew they were being pushed back on the defensive, and the natural caution of the General Council majority was reflected in the speech by Wilfred (the late Sir Wilfred) Heywood, the neat, precise General Secretary of the National Union of Dryers, Bleachers and Textile Workers, a moderate man from Bradford who was chairman of the TUC economic committee. He counselled caution and moderation: a predictable posture. He acknowledged that 'in the present temper of unions' the Congress would not accept any Government-sponsored wage restraint, 'but,' he said hopefully, 'I have sufficient faith in executive committees to believe and indeed, I think, to know, that they will act with responsibility.'

Of course Heywood had a shrewd idea of what was to come. The General Council had already spent several days discussing the TGWU resolution opposing wage restraint, and arguing with Cousins. Heywood knew that Cousins would not be shifted from his militant position. This was the essence of the motion that Frank Cousins moved: 'Congress asserts the right of Labour to bargain on equal terms with Capital and to use its bargaining strength to protect the workers from the dislocations of an unplanned economy. It rejects proposals to recover control by wage restraint and by using the nationalised industries as a drag-anchor for the drifting national economy.' But it was really Cousins's speech which opened a new era in TUC politics.

He dismissed Harold Macmillan's suggestion that he might come down to Brighton to explain Government policy with a whiplash reply: 'What does he think it is – a film festival? We will welcome a Chancellor of the Exchequer, but we will wait for one – we will wait for a Labour Chancellor of the Exchequer.' He challenged the Government to 'go ahead with their freedom': 'We have told them where it will take them. It will take them straight into the arms of the next Labour Government. But in the intervening period we are not prepared to sit down and see our members' conditions worsened. The economic problems in our opinion are caused by the Government.' He referred to the pressure the Government was now putting on the nationalised industries, especially the Transport Commission, and warned that his union would not shrink from fighting for its members' interests if a fight was unavoidable. But he was not, he emphasised, looking for a confrontation:

> We are not going out on a rampage. We are not going to use our organisational strength to prove that the TGWU are first – and the rest can get where they like. What we are saying is that there is no such thing in this country as a place where you can say: 'Wage levels stop here' – and that we ought to be content even if things remain unequal.

So much for the Macmillan 'plateua'. Then came the phrase which echoed after Frank Cousins throughout his career both as TGWU General Secretary and as a Cabinet Minister: 'In a period of freedom for all we are part of the all.'

Cousins had spent most of the time with his union delegation in the main body of Congress delegates and not, as was usual, with leading members of the General Council on the platform with the TUC leadership. It was an open, symbolic gesture of where his priorities lay. The reception of his speech was almost hysterical, partly because it was unique, coming from the TGWU, but chiefly because of its belligerent style. No delegate present had heard the leader of such a powerful union talk publicly like that before. It had not happened since the General Strike. To some ears on the far Left it sounded like a bugle-call to battle, though they learned later that it wasn't meant to be quite that. To the majority of General Council members the Cousins speech sounded more like a knell. The old alliances were in ruins. The 'certainties' which surrounded the old guard of TUC leadership in the days of Arthur Deakin had been demolished. Even those who strongly opposed the Cousins militancy felt themselves being swept along by the tidal wave of support he was receiving from *their* own rank and file as well as junior officials. Cousins, however, had been careful to warn that he was not offering hostages to fortune. His speech and his challenge covered the whole trade-union movement, hinting plainly that the TGWU would be ready to back other smaller unions caught up in the web of Government economic policies. But he still cautioned that 'no union wants to throw its gauntlet down and turn round to see who picks it up. That is not the issue.' Still, he pointed out, the gauntlet *had* been thrown down by the Government, and added: 'We have said we do not want it, but if it is there we will not refuse to pick it up if we are compelled to.'

No one who was present at that Congress will forget the moment of slightly bewildered awe as Frank Cousins stepped down from the rostrum in the Dome conference hall and strode, heavily, back to his seat among the TGWU delegation.

It was much more than the end of the economic truce that had existed between the Conservative Government and the TUC leadership. Churchill had forged that truce in 1951 and the Eden Government inherited it, under more testing economic conditions. The majority of those in the Cabinet and on the TUC General Council would have preferred to have continued with it despite all the difficulties. The emergence of Frank Cousins made that impossible. This was the end of an epoch.

Seventeen months later on, the *Observer* said of this Cousins speech: 'For most people it is Mr Frank Cousins, general secretary of the TGWU, who has symbolised "the unions". Many regard his speech against wage restraint at the 1956 TUC as the main cause of what they consider a marked change in the attitude of the trade unions to wages policies over the last two years.'[7]

Harry Nicholas has told me that he believes the 1956 speech represented Frank Cousins's most dramatic and most lasting impact on British trade union affairs – a view that is valuable not only because Nicholas was as close to Cousins as anybody in his working life but because he was detached enough, politically, to see him in perspective. Cousins himself recognised the importance of his achievement. He reported to his own executive council afterwards that the 1956 TUC could be

> regarded as setting a changing pattern in the industrial field based upon the policy which we initiated as a union in December last and subsequently crystallised in the motion tabled on the Congress agenda . . . The Govern-

7. *Observer*, 9 February 1958.

ment can now be in no doubt as to where the Movement stands, and one can only hope that this will mean a change in their course of action as an alternative to what would otherwise seem inevitable, namely, a far- reaching industrial upheaval throughout the country.

The Cousins speech was different because it was in fact a major *political* speech. It was directed as much at the leadership of the TUC, and the Labour Party establishment, as at the Government. It was Cousins's signal that from then on things were going to be different and that neither the Government nor the Opposition should any longer take the unions for granted. Political speeches at the TUC in the past had been either muted with caution or identifiable as standard Communist attacks on the TUC (or Labour Party) establishment. This time there was a fundamental political challenge from the non-Communist Left; a challenge that could not be ignored, because it came from the General Secretary of the country's largest trade union.

The late Richard Crossman, who was present at the Brighton TUC, observed later that the speech marked the end of 'Butskellism' as far as the organised trade union movement was concerned. Crossman also noted that the speech would be 'enormously invigorating to the Labour Party – though it will probably have the simultaneous effect of scaring off middle-class voters and recreating a sense of class tension.'[8]

A few weeks later at the Party conference, when Frank Cousins led his delegation for the first time as the fully-fledged General Secretary of the TGWU, he was feted by most of the rank-and-file delegates as a new prophet of socialism – a kind of trade union equivalent of Aneurin Bevan. It was also the occasion of his first real meeting with Nye Bevan – in Crossman's room on the Saturday evening before the conference opened. According to Crossman it was not a particularly auspicious encounter. He has recorded how they immediately started arguing about the TUC's attitude to public ownership and the lack of ideology inside the trade union movement. Bevan was never impressed by the quality of trade union understanding about the role of public ownership in a socialist society. In Cousins, however, he found someone who *did* understand that role, though he still believed that trade union independence was essential in terms of representing their members' interests, whether the industry concerned was public or private. Bevan did not see it in quite those terms, and he frequently expressed to me the view that Frank Cousins's attitude on this harked back to the syndicalist views of the turn of the century.

Shortly after the 1956 TUC I had a long discussion with the late Sam Watson on the significance of the event for Labour politics in general. Watson, at that time perhaps the most influential trade union figure in Labour

8. Richard Crossman, the unedited diaries, 1956–8, Ref. sheet 874.

politics, was the Durham miners' leader, chairman of the Labour Party's international committee, and a close confidant of Hugh Gaitskell as well as numerous other distinguished men of power. He was a kind of Metternich of the Labour Movement; immensely shrewd, far-sighted, and, despite his confirmed right-wing stance, surprisingly fair and sensitive to the Left, especially to Aneurin Bevan.

Watson told me :

The Party seems to be shifting towards the Left. This is probably inevitable at the present time though it is hard to see how it will all work out in the end. The country is going through a difficult time. At such times the Party naturally tends to follow the lead of the TUC – so if the TUC moves to the Left the Labour Party is bound to follow that lead. Much hinges on the power of the big unions, especially the TGWU. Their big card vote is vital; if the TGWU decided to switch their views on foreign policy the whole fate of Europe could be changed. This is therefore of very great importance.

Watson also said :

One or two Labour Party leaders have been talking to Frank Cousins urging him to steady his hand on wages. An outright assault on the economic front could have disastrous effects on the nation at home and abroad. The first impression of these talks with Cousins is that his attitude privately is less militant than it appears on the rostrum. But it is hard to tell. One will have to wait to see how he shapes in the next year. He might make a very good general secretary of the TUC itself. He could give leadership and direction.

Watson indicated that ideas were afloat to tempt Frank Cousins with a big job of that kind, if he developed a responsible sense of his role, but he also added that if the whole Labour Movement 'went Left', with Bevan and Cousins linking up, then 'there might be a very great deal of trouble ahead and no one can predict how it may end . . .'

On the other hand, Watson continued, the influence of Cousins and his left-wing views might provide 'a kind of third force inside the Labour Movement which would weaken the Communists. The initiative in the trade unions so far as the Left is concerned has been for too long in Communist hands. Cousins could alter that . . .'

After the Brighton Congress, Cousins continued to emphasise that he was not going out looking for trouble with the Government or private employers. He told the annual meeting of the Institute of Directors that he was a patriot and wanted to see the nation prosper economically and to adopt sensible industrial policies. 'The trade union movement', he assured the assembled tycoons, 'is not entering a recklessly militant period of industrial relations. Indeed I believe that a most fruitful period lies ahead in which we shall see a great development and diversification of good relations between employers and employed.'

That was moderate enough; yet the sting remained when he reminded the directors that this should not be interpreted as implying that he was 'going soft on wages or that the resolution passed by the TUC at Brighton was window-dressing'. He continued: 'Those of us who believe good industrial relations are important to the nation's economic health must take a firm line in establishing a wages policy which is independent of – though not necessarily opposed to – *any* government's policy. He concluded by emphasising his attitude to wages policy whatever party was in power:

> I hope it is appreciated that an independent wage policy is as essential to a democracy as any other feature of independence. Because if you once put it under the State, then you must accept the corollary that goes with it. The State must determine the measure of your ability. We are willing to be full partners in industry, but we have no desire to be sleeping partners.

An illuminating story about this speech indicates the impact he had already made as 'the big red bogeyman'. When Sir Richard Powell, then the Institute's Director General, invited him to speak at the Albert Hall conference it was the first time the Institute had invited a left-wing trade union leader to address them in public. So profound was the disquiet at Sir Richard's move that Lord Bracken, then one of the Institute's senior dignitaries, resigned and wrote to Sir Richard: 'How can you invite a man like that – a man who is opposed to everything that you and I believe in? If you have him, I'm off.'

Sir Richard didn't cancel the invitation and Lord Bracken left the Institute, never to return. Sir Richard – who now lists Cousins as one of the men he most admired in public life[9] – recalls that he took a lot of trouble over his speech, and adds:

> And it was good. He was a trifle nervous till he got into the swing of it; indeed his first joke, because he didn't deliver it well, didn't click; actually it was rather a good one. 'Gentlemen,' he said – there were no lady directors in the audience in those days – 'Gentlemen, the dockers *I* represent . . .' Sir Bernard Docker had just been kicked off the BSA board after one of the most fiery special general meetings I ever remember. But that's another story . . .

The Suez debacle left Britain's unhappy economy in a far more serious condition. The trade unions moved into 1957 aware that they were entering a

---

9. Sir Richard Powell, in *The Director*, October 1974.

period of industrial stress and tension that would be greater than at any time since the end of the war.

The employers' offensive, started a year earlier, now not only appeared to have a great deal more logic in it but the Government, at first hesitant, had thrown in its support. The nationalised industries were looked upon as the keystone. The private sector assumed that it would be able to rely on the State sector holding the line on wage restraint. A number of pay claims were already in the pipeline, and several were being negotiated when the Suez crisis broke. The railwaymen and the municipal busmen were awarded pay rises of 3 per cent in November and December – roughly equal to the rise in living costs during the previous year – and this was eventually accepted, though with reluctance. Indeed, the railway unions decided to submit a new claim as soon as they had settled. Still, the Government regarded the 3 per cent figure as a kind of unofficial and acceptable norm. One of the major test-cases in the public sector was the outstanding claim for the London busmen, an important unit in Frank Cousins's union. They were in no mood to settle for 3 per cent especially as living costs were escalating because the Suez crisis had sent up petrol prices and touched off a chain-reaction of further price increases. The impression grew – an impression not based on statistical fact – that living costs were 'soaring' as a direct result of Suez, and that compensating wage rises were therefore entirely justified. As against this, the nationalised industries were trying to operate Mr Macmillan's price plateau by keeping down their charges.

In January 1957 Frank Cousins personally took over the negotiations with London Transport on behalf of his busmen and came out with a 5 per cent increase, a good deal more than others had received – and somewhat more than he himself thought likely at one stage in the talks. London Transport had certainly stepped outside the 'official ring' to settle with its busmen. Even without straws in the wind of this kind there were other indications that the Suez crisis had reduced the enthusiasm for a showdown with the unions that existed in private industry as well as inside the Government. Nevertheless the Engineering Employers' Federation still seemed prepared to fight the unions' claim for a 10 per cent all-round rise. The employers' first reaction to this, at the end of 1956, was total rejection. The engineering employers rejected the claim on 29 November and the ship-building employers on 11 December. But before these dates the Government ran into its post-Suez political crisis : Eden resigned the Premiership and Harold Macmillan succeeded him, with Peter (now Lord) Thorneycroft becoming Chancellor.

There were clear signs that a serious industrial conflict at that juncture could have precipitated an even worse economic and political crisis at home, linked with a collapse of confidence in sterling. The fear of devaluation was strong and widespread in Whitehall and in the City of London. Yet when negotiations between the unions and the engineering and shipbuilding employers resumed in February there was still no hint of compromise. But events had moved on since the November pay settlements of 1956 and all the signs suggested that the unions would not accept 3 per cent. Nor did the employers favour arbitration, especially since they already suspected that the Government was backing away from a fight with the unions. So they chose to fight it out – on their own.

By the beginning of April some 1,500,000 engineering and shipyard workers were on official strike, with plans prepared by the unions to double that number by the following week. It was the biggest industrial stoppage since the 1926 General Strike. The Government clearly could not let the dispute escalate any further and the attempts at conciliation, started hesitantly by the Minister of Labour, Iain Macleod, were brought to a climax by the appointment of a Government court of inquiry under the chairmanship of Professor Daniel Jack.

In the meantime, the engineering and shipbuilding employers had stepped down by offering a range of pay increases tied with a list of conditions on working efficiency and a twelve-month standstill on any further rises. The shipbuilders offered slightly more than the engineers – 5 per cent as against the engineers' 3 to 4 per cent. With these offers dangled before them, and the court of inquiry appointed, the unions met to consider calling off the strike. Frank Cousins was opposed to this until something more precise, substantial and acceptable had been wrung from the employers. He was backed by a string of unions on the Left, but opposed by the President of the Amalgamated Engineering Union, the late William (later Lord) Carron. The engineers' executive had split three against three and Carron decided that there was no virtue in pursuing the strike in view of the court of inquiry, and the clear readiness of the Government to buy peace. He used his casting vote accordingly.

And so the strike was called off, though not without a great deal of interunion rivalry and even bitterness. Cousins remained wholly unrepentant about voting for a continuation. He was attacked in the Press for 'playing to the gallery' when he knew the aggregate vote would be for calling it off. Yet he had made his position quite clear several days before the delegate conference of unions. In speeches at Southampton and Bristol the previous weekend he said: 'We don't want [the strike]; we want to get out of it as soon as we can – when we have won. We don't want to get out of it just to get out of it; we need a just and proper settlement. If we don't win this one, we won't win the next one.'[10]

Cousins regarded the challenge by the engineering employers in particular as a crucial test for its trade unions and their future wages policy. He

10. TGWU *Record*, May 1957.

knew that although the Government had backed away from a formal confrontation with the unions on wage restraint they were still looking to the engineering employers to extract the maximum advantage from their fight. In fact, the settlement that was eventually reached on the basis of the inquiry's report produced increases of $6\frac{1}{2}$ per cent in engineering – with 'strings'. After further prolonged negotiations an even better settlement was reached for the shipyard workers. The employers had lost the battle. They blamed the Government for having shirked a fight with the unions.

The effect of these engineering and shipyard strikes transformed the industrial atmosphere in 1957. That spring and summer there were many more strikes. Commentators described the situation as the worst since the General Strike. There were strikes of provincial busmen, dockers, market porters in London's Covent Garden – all of them members of the TGWU, so that Frank Cousins was constantly being called on to intervene. In the Covent Garden dispute he returned from holiday to persuade the porters to accept the terms they had previously rejected. This was a highly unpopular decision, and Cousins was barracked and jeered as he left the meeting after the return-to-work vote. He was offered – but refused – police escort when the scene began to look ugly. That was an unusual experience for Frank Cousins, who had rarely tasted such rank-and-file resentment since his days as an official in road haulage.

There was a paradox here, right enough. Far from strenuously promoting militancy wherever he went, Frank Cousins sought to find solutions and avoid trouble – so long as he could win substantial concessions by negotiation. He did not court confrontation, but he did excite greater expectations among his members. He did not go into the negotiation-ring with his fists raised, but he did radiate that impression to such an extent that his opponents were often waiting for him with *their* fists raised. On the other hand he sensed that it was only a matter of time before he would find himself in a head-on clash of some kind with the Government. He has told me since : 'After the settlement of the engineering strike it was clear that the Government would do everything they could to curb wage increases and would seek to impose their policy by choosing the weakest possible link in the trade union armour – at a point where the country's economic interests would not be vitally at stake.' He did not then perceive where that 'point' might be.

In January 1957 he had persuaded the London busmen to abandon their strike threat on the grounds that the union had enough problems on its hands. He looked on the settlement with London Transport as a major 'breakthrough' in wages policy. At a speech in Leicester that May he said : 'Our stand against the London Transport Executive in the first instance was the one that broke down the attitude of the employers.' This may have been an exaggeration, but it was indeed the first public sector settlement to exceed 3 per cent that winter. And it caught the Government off balance when their political vitality was at its lowest ebb after Suez. He also told the Leicester audience of his pride in having been personally involved with the engineering and shipbuilding strikes :

> I am proud to have been associated with that particular period of trade union history; because we did not *have* to bring them out. The biggest job we had to do was to keep those in who we did not want out. Men showed that if their standard of living is trifled with, if there is a class approach to their problems, then they are just as ready to fight for their rights as their fathers were thirty years ago.[11]

No doubt that passage was a characteristically jumbled Cousins sentence. Yet these were the authentic tones of a man who believed he was fighting for something more than the percentage points of wage increases in any particular industry : a man who already saw his role as that of a tribune of working people's interests in a much wider and more general sense; fighting for a new sense of social and economic justice with an old-style fervour and dedication.

11. TGWU *Record*, June 1957.

Chapter Eleven

THE BEGINNING
OF THE BOMB

By the time the TGWU held its biennial delegate conference at Torquay in July 1957 – Frank Cousins's first as General Secretary – it was already clear that the world had moved into a new period of international tension over nuclear weaponry. Scientists in the West and the Communist blocs, drawn into a vastly expanded military-economic complex, were working at a phenomenal rate to outpace each other in developing the latest and most devastating instrument of mass destruction, the hydrogen bomb. By 1957 testing of 'new devices', as they were described with banal indelicacy, had reached new levels of intensity. The USA and the USSR were almost ostentatiously engaged in a vast, macabre arms race.

In April Britain exploded her first H-bomb, in a test carried out at Christmas Island in the Pacific. That was the effective starting-point for the Campaign for Nuclear Disarmament, although CND as such was not formally launched until January 1958.

From the moment the announcement of the test was made there was a wave of protest and revulsion in Britain. Increasingly it came from a wide cross-section of public opinion, regardless of political or social grouping. Anti-bomb protest movements sprang up all over the country, representing Church organisations, political parties, trade unions, youth clubs, local bodies of all kinds and varieties. An H-Bomb Campaign Committee was formed to try to co-ordinate the activities of these various groups. It was all highly spontaneous, if tentative, and the movement was gathering momentum by the time the TGWU delegates gathered at Torquay that July.

It was also evident, though not yet public knowledge, that the Labour Party conference in October would be dominated if not overwhelmed by the H-bomb issue. When the conference agenda was published shortly after the TGWU had met, 127 motions out of the total 443 called, in some form, for the 'banning of the bomb'. Never before in the history of Labour Party conferences had one issue so dominated the agenda. It obscured, indeed almost obliterated, such traditional subjects as economic affairs, social and welfare issues like housing, pensions and education, and nationalisation. This in spite of the fact that the 1957 Labour Party conference had to debate a new and important statement on public ownership, from the National Executive Committee 'Industry and Society', in which a system of partnership between the State and private enterprise was being proposed for the first time.

Many of the 127 motions demanded a great national and international crusade, led by the British Labour Movement, to rally opinion at home and throughout the world behind a campaign to 'Ban the Bomb'. They came from all sections of the Labour Movement – local parties primarily, but with a substantial degree of trade union support even at that early stage. The rumblings of this unique explosion of feeling, quite obviously, had been apparent to the trade union leadership as well as the Labour Party hierarchy well in advance of the agenda, and it was no surprise to find more than a dozen motions on the TGWU conference agenda calling for the banning of the H-bomb.

For Frank Cousins it was at once an opportunity to show where he stood personally and, a rather more difficult exercise, to test the sympathies of his delegate conference, where in the past the orthodox view on international affairs and defence policy had prevailed easily against any criticism from the Left. Not that opposition to the H-bomb was exclusively a left-wing issue; it was not. Nor was it, at that early stage, supported by the Communists. What was clear was that this was something likely to bring together people whose motives for protest were not generated primarily by their party allegiances. It was not a Left v. Right question in the old sense, or one on which it was easy to stick any of the conventional labels of the hustings. Indeed, it already showed signs of becoming a unique crusade.

The H-bomb question was an issue of such immensity that inside the Labour Party some of the leading figures were beginning to adopt positions that, perhaps inescapably, resulted in a dividing line being drawn between Right and Left. That was partly because the issue involved the defence of the country and therefore the whole question of Britain's relationship with the United States and NATO. Yet such considerations were far from clear in the minds of people attending trade union conferences in 1957, nor were they yet seriously taken into account by the majority of those who joined the early protest movement against the H-bomb. From the start this movement was an emotional, spontaneous reaction by thousands of people who simply saw the mushroom cloud hovering above the world as an evil in absolute terms; an evil to be opposed regardless of any qualifications suggested by conventional political thinking.

Few, at that juncture, stopped to ask how such a process might affect Britain's international alliances; or how it could affect the balance of terror in international relations; or whether it might put the Western powers at a serious military disadvantage against the Soviet Union; or whether a British protest could have any practical influence on American policy – and therefore any lasting value in terms of political power and Realpolitik. These were not debating points that July when the TGWU conference met in Torquay.

That summer the United States exploded over Nevada the most powerful 'atomic device' ever fired. Khruschev asked for an East-West understanding to curb the arms race.

At Pugwash in Nova Scotia a group of distinguished nuclear physicists from Communist and non-Communist countries urged the nations to suspend tests immediately, as a first step towards an international system of control and safeguards.

The Nevada test had been justified on the basis of the development of what was euphemistically called a 'clean bomb' – which meant experiments were being made to contain 'dangerous' fall-out. Khruschev derided President Eisenhower's claims about the development of such a 'clean bomb', and this point was picked up by Frank Cousins when the TGWU conference debated the H-bomb on 11 July. Cousins pleaded for the Labour Party to give the nation, and perhaps the world, a lead by abandoning all the talk about 'clean' or 'dirty' bombs and by launching a great crusade to stop the tests – and then to move on to ban manufacture of the bomb. That resolution, carried unanimously, is especially interesting in the light of subsequent events because it was *not* a call for unilateral nuclear disarmament but, in effect, a proposal for multilateral disarmament. After an immediate cessation of H-bomb tests by all the Powers it called for 'the total abolition of the H-bomb on a universal basis both in manufacture and existing stocks', and the 'direction of all researches into nuclear energy along peaceful lines for the ultimate good of all peoples, irrespective of race, creed or colour . . .'

At that stage there is little doubt that this was as far as Frank Cousins wanted to go, and certainly as far as he felt he could carry the union. Privately, he believed that Britain ought to give a lead, by suspending both tests and manufacture herself. Publicly, while Frank Cousins called for Britain to give a lead he did not spell out in detail what that appeal might involve, nor was the doctrine of unilateralism a clearly argued issue at the conference.

It would be quite wrong, however, to give the impression that Frank Cousins's first biennial delegate conference as General Secretary was dominated by the beginning of the H-bomb debate. The biggest ovation that he received at the conference came on the second day when the delegates debated wages policy and nationalisation. It was here that the change of policy inside the union became most blindingly obvious. From Deakin's outright scepticism, if not open hostility, to an extension of public ownership, and Tiffin's passive acceptance of the status quo, Cousins switched the union's attention to what the conference resolution described as the 'imperative' development of public ownership. He left absolutely no doubt where he stood; socialism to his mind was not possible without it, in the interests of the community. This was the case he had argued at the Labour Party's conference the previous autumn when he described himself as a firm believer in 'the old type of socialism'. That was the flag he nailed to the TGWU mast at the Torquay conference. He received an ovation for it from the delegates, many of whom were already beginning to look on Cousins as a kind of liberator.

Yet even this was overshadowed by the rapturous applause Cousins received shortly afterwards when he supported a motion rejecting 'the principle of wage restraint in any form', reaffirming the need 'to take such steps, industrially, as will ensure that wages keep pace with rising costs'. He ridiculed those people, even inside the Labour Movement, who appeared to think that the union's function was to act as spokesman for the Government. He denounced the proposed independent council to review prices, productivity and incomes (which eventually became the Cohen Council). The delegates were brought to a state of enthusiasm unknown at any previous TGWU conference for at least a generation.

On issue after issue the Torquay conference turned TGWU policy in a quite new direction. Even where the direction was not different, the motive power and force driving the union was seen in a completely new form.

Long before Hugh Gaitskell's attempt in 1959 to delete Clause 4 from its pivotal position in the Labour Party constitution, there had been a persistent campaign to downgrade the concept of public ownership as a foundation stone of socialist belief. Personality differences aside, this was always one of the principal causes of friction between Herbert Morrison and Aneurin Bevan.

The sub-committees of the Labour Party's National Executive had been working since the 1955 election defeat on a set of new policy statements. Of these the most controversial was certainly the one on future nationalisation policy. Frank Cousins had briefly been a member of the sub-committee while he was on the Party Executive, but afterwards he worked through Harry Nicholas, who replaced him there. When the statement was eventually published in July 1957 it was widely interpreted as signalling a significant retreat from old-style nationalisation. 'Industry and Society', as it was called, was in fact the first Labour Party document to call specifically for 'a new and closer relationship between the large firms and the State'. It pointed in the direction of considerably more public ownership and control – including the control of the five hundred most powerful private companies – and it was meant to do precisely that. That section was drafted by Peter Shore, who was then head of the Labour Party's research department. But the conclusions were muted and unclear. They referred to the State acquiring shares in the leading private companies both to improve the efficiency of their firms and to establish greater economic equality through the nation sharing in the capital gains of private enterprise. In some instances, the document stated, it would be more appropriate for the State to take over a single company or even a group of companies. The statement attempted to combine the interests of capitalism and socialism, and inevitably this opened up the entire debate to the widest interpretations.

The Left regarded 'Industry and Society' as a milk-and-water attempt to follow the traditional doctrines of the Labour Party without making any precise commitments to take over specific industries: the only ones listed were steel and road haulage, both of which had been or were in the process of being nationalised when Labour lost the election in 1951. Yet although the Left were, by and large, highly critical of 'Industry and Society' some prominent Leftists thought it could be used by a Labour Government for a much greater extension of public ownership than anything the Party had previously considered. And indeed this was a view taken up by some Conservative critics and by several newspapers who saw the scheme as a 'backdoor attempt' to nationalise Britain's leading companies. Hugh Gaitskell left the issue in limbo, admitting that a good deal more thinking must be done before the Party could be specific. The right wing of the Labour Party regarded this vagueness as an asset.

Frank Cousins had already made his position clear at the 1956 Party conference. He emphasised his belief in 'old style' socialist public ownership at the Torquay conference; and at every opportunity he lined up with Aneurin Bevan to demonstrate his conviction that socialism in Britain required a new injection of zeal.

Yet Cousins was in no mood to split the Labour Party conference – or the TUC – on the subject. He knew Bevan felt the same way and was anxious to give his support. Bevan had been away, in India and the Middle East, during the closing stages of the executive discussions on 'Industry and Society'. He had in fact been less than diligent in attending the discussions and he was clearly embarrassed by his association with a policy statement which appeared, to the Left at least, to water down the Labour Party's commitment to nationalisation. Indeed, his own wife, Jennie Lee (now Baroness Lee) attacked the statement in ferocious terms.

Frank Cousins was largely responsible for ensuring that the nationalisation debate at the 1957 Trades Union Congress was a muted affair. He persuaded the General Secretary of the NUR, the late Jim Campbell, to soft-pedal his furious opposition to 'Industry and Society', while he [Cousins] kept out of the public debate on the floor of Congress. Frank Cousins was concerned that the Left should not split over the new nationalisation policy. He was already working, with Bevan, for a compromise that would support 'Industry and Society' provided Gaitskell and the rest of the leadership fully recognised that the 'share buying' concept would not become a substitute for outright nationalisation and that target dates should be established for the complete take-over of specific industries.

In several other senses the 1957 TUC was an anti-climax for Frank Cousins after the huge impact he had made a year earlier. He continued to concentrate his fire on government wages policy and again he moved the principal motion calling for the rejection of any form of wage restraint, pledging the unions to 'take such steps industrially as will ensure that wages keep pace with risings costs'. Yet by now this was an almost predictable stand for him to adopt; rebellion was expected of him. By this time the Government had appointed Lord Cohen and his committee of inquiry on wages, prices and productivity. The TUC's official position was one of disdainful uninterest. They 'noted' its appointment and the Government's assurance that it would not 'interfere' with the system of collective bargaining, and they reserved their position as to whether the TUC would offer any evidence or views to the Cohen Council. Frank Cousins's view, in moving the main wages motion at the Congress, was that the committee was an irrelevance. 'If the Government want a committee to advise them, that is their affair,' he told the delegates. 'We from our union – and I want to go no further than that because it was our motion in the main – do not want a committee to advise us how to handle the affairs of our members' interests.' That declaration, emphasising that Cousins was speaking for himself and his own union, reflected the tensions and divisions inside the General Council about how far non-cooperation with the Government over wages policy could be carried. The row had gone on inside the TUC's economic committee throughout the summer months. Several senior members of the General Council saw nothing objectionable in the TUC offering their views to the Cohen Council. They argued that in doing so the TUC would not be committing itself to any support for the Government's economic policies or to wage restraint. On the other hand, by absenting themselves from any discussions on or with the new body the TUC, it was argued, stood in danger of appearing in public eyes as a wholly negative organisation.

The issue came up finally at the August meeting of the General Council just prior to the Congress. The proposal that the TUC should reserve its position came from Charles (now Lord) Geddes, General Secretary of the postmen's union. Cousins fiercely condemned this view as tantamount to offering the Government the hand of cooperation. The late Alan Birch,

General Secretary of the Shop and Distributive Workers' Union, tried to find a midway position, but failed. Geddes's motion was carried by 13 to 10, despite the outraged opposition led by Cousins. It was the second successive time that Cousins's opposition to the Cohen Council had been defeated by 15 to 9.

At least the August vote reflected a narrowing of the gap and a growing support for Cousins's view that the TUC was being baited into a trap by the Government. But it was difficult if not impossible for Cousins to win a majority on the Council. There was a basic hostility to his political position and his attempt to politicise the role of the TUC, and personal friction was growing between him and most of the longer serving members of the General Council. They were determined to oppose him wherever possible. And the more they goaded him, the more he fought back with a stubborn disregard for what he knew to be their private intrigues. A few senior members of the General Council had for instance already decided, by early 1957, that Cousins must be kept away from a position of influence on the TUC's international committee.

Several years later, even when Cousins had obtained sufficient seniority by conventional TUC standards to become chairman of the international committee, he was prevented from occupying the chair by a backstage 'plot'. It was in the autumn of 1963, before he joined the Wilson Government. The chairmanship of the committee had fallen vacant and Cousins was a strong candidate. His opponent was the right-wing Fred (later Sir Fred) Hayday of the General and Municipal Workers' Union. At the first attempt to vote in a new chairman the result was 5 to 5, so a decision was put off for the following meeting. In order to make sure that all possible Hayday supporters attended that meeting Bill (later Sir William) Webber of the Transport Salaried Staffs' Association personally phoned round all the potential anti-Cousins members the night before to make sure there was a good attendance. Webber has told me himself that he was determined to do all he could to stop Cousins getting the job. This bitter anti-Cousins feeling developed directly out of the H-bomb controversy.

They feared Cousins's 'soft line' on the Communists and his readiness to accept an invitation to lead a TGWU delegation to the USSR, though it was then TUC policy not to make official visits to Communist countries. On his side, Cousins seemed to delight in demonstrating to the TUC that the TGWU was now under very different management to that of the past. His opponents could scarcely understand, let alone appreciate, what had gone wrong with the union they had until so recently viewed as the essence of orthodoxy and as a repository of established wisdom. It is not difficult to appreciate their dilemma, yet it produced an opposition to Frank Cousins which was largely sterile. There was little attempt to understand his feelings, his views or his impulses.

THE AWKWARD WARRIOR

Until George Woodcock took over from Tewson as General Secretary the TUC establishment tended to regard Cousins as an aberration. Instead of seeking to integrate him into the machinery of the TUC, the first instinct of the majority was always to resist him. It was inevitable therefore that prejudice was met with prejudice and hostility with hostility. This was the situation Cousins was to find himself in with a frustrating consistency in the years ahead, regardless of the weight of his argument or the power of his union, and, sometimes, even regardless of the subject. He became virtually locked in a minority position on the TUC General Council from the beginning, and only on rare occasions was he able to sway the majority of his colleagues, despite the fact that his union's huge vote could almost guarantee to swing a Congress majority in his favour. Indeed, his General Council colleagues resented, as much as anything else, Cousins's appeal to their own rank and file and delegates – an appeal which frequently embarrassed and sometimes weakened the position of other general secretaries. On an issue as emotive as wages policy he knew he would have the mass of the Congress behind him, in spite of the coolness of the General Council majority : and so did that majority. At the 1957 Trades Union Congress the situation, in retrospect, seems almost absurd. The central debate on wages policy was over in about an hour. Only three other members of the General Council supported Frank Cousins : the late Sir Dan McGarvey, of the Boilermakers; the late Sir Tom O'Brien, Theatrical and Kine Employees; and Sir Fred Hayday, General and Municipal Workers. The expressions on the faces of most General Council members when Frank Cousins moved his motion illustrated clearly how disturbed they felt, and how glad they were to get the debate over as quickly as possible. I wrote at the time : 'There was no debate in the accepted sense since there was no opposition to the Cousins line. In effect it was a Cousins resolution, a Cousins debate and a Cousins decision.'[1]

The truth was that the trade union establishment was still under the thrall of the old attitudes toward cooperation with Government. The spell had been broken, but the memory lingered on. It was difficult for them to accept a new posture of militant opposition to Government policies; they were attuned to it neither psychologically nor practically, in terms of the problems involved in reconstructing the running of their unions. They also objected to Frank Cousins having the audacity – as well as the power – to brush aside the conventions of at least two generations of trade union leadership in such a cavalier manner. Their resentment burned deeply and it showed even in social relationships. Cousins did not seek the company of his General Council opponents and they did not encourage him to do so. In 1956 he had already begun to show his independence of mind by staying at

1. The *News Chronicle*, 6 September 1957.

a separate hotel from the rest of the TUC General Council. He did so primarily because he had always believed it to be unnecessary ostentation for the TUC leaders to stay at the best place in town. No doubt this was an unfair imputation, since the General Council required facilities for their meetings which smaller hotels were not able to provide. But Frank Cousins registered his view by staying elsewhere, usually at a modest family-style hotel. This made his colleagues accuse him of 'playing to the gallery', 'calculated publicity seeking' and 'pandering to the Left'. He knew what they were saying about him. It made not the slightest difference to his style, but it did make these already tense personal relationships even more brittle and sensitive. Frank Cousins, after only two congresses, was certainly not a popular figure with his fellow TUC General Councillors, despite his immense popularity with the rank and file – or, perhaps, because of that.

Observing the TUC scene at the time, Richard Crossman noted that 'the power was passing probably to Cousins'. A week later, in conversation with Sam Watson, Crossman reported him as saying: 'The establishment in the trade unions has completely disintegrated.'[2]

Sam Watson, a close friend and ally of Hugh Gaitskell and a long-standing and successful opponent of the Left, was especially concerned about the defence and international policies of the Labour Party. He was chairman of the Party's international committee. Even at that early juncture he sensed the way Frank Cousins was moving; and he didn't like what he sensed.

Not surprisingly, Cousins was charged with vanity and arrogance by the Press, and with worse things by his political opponents. A great deal was made by some newspapers of the sale in the conference foyer of Toby jugs bearing his image, in aid of the union's convalescent home fund. This enterprise had nothing to do with Cousins, but he was blamed personally for an exercise in vanity. One newspaper headlined him 'King Toby' to emphasise its judgment that Cousins was a vain, bossy man largely consumed by a desire to promote his own ambitions as well as his objectionable left-wing political views. He was also rebuked in the Press for hogging the conference. Journalists carefully noted the number of times he spoke or intervened in debates, because he did seem to be jumping in incessantly.

The curious feature of these comments is not that they were necessarily inaccurate, but that they were put forward as if the phenomenon of leadership domination was unusual. It had been a longstanding characteristic of TGWU general secretaries to dominate, if indeed not to overwhelm, their delegate conferences. Bevin was the outstanding promoter of the process. He overshadowed the union assemblies and rarely delegated any authority on

2. Richard Crossman, the unedited diaries, 12 and 20 September 1957.

the important issues of the day. He set the tone and the policy, and left not the slightest doubt in any delegate's mind that he was in complete control of the levers of power. Deakin was a dedicated pupil of this art of dominating a union conference, and his performances were no less convincing than Bevin's – although he was far less impressive in execution. Both men, as we have seen, issued executive statements' as an overture to all-important motions on the conference agenda. This was an instrument by which persuasion, if not control, was exercised. Yet when Frank Cousins picked up the instrument and, quite legitimately, used it to focus the union's attention on different objectives (or at least different perspectives) he was charged with 'dictatorship', and much worse.

It seemed that what was permissible in the hands of Bevin and Deakin became objectionable in the hands of Frank Cousins.

As to the feelings of the rank and file, and of a large number of officials, the general view was summed up in Alf Chandler's eulogy in the TGWU journal (see p. 117). Other officials, far less sympathetic to Cousins in the personal or the political sense, have since confided to me that what he started at Torquay helped to save the TGWU from serious internal disruption, that he ventilated the pent-up frustration of years – a frustration which had developed a seriously explosive state inside the union.

Even if the name of Frank Cousins had never been heard of, it would have been essential for someone, even of less militant views, to have liberated the union from its previous condition and turned it in new directions. The union was poised to respond to new leadership and new policies, and the undercurrent of support that Frank Cousins felt from the reaction of the Torquay delegates both inspired him with additional energy and convinced him that he was right in his policies and views, if not always in his tactics.

Cousins was particularly sensitive to the role of leadership in the TGWU. He understood its power as well as its pinpricks. He had suffered under it more than any of the union's senior officials, and although he is not a vindictive man it would have been more than flesh could stand for him to have successfully resisted all temptation to take advantage of his own position. There are officials, now retired, who claim that Cousins behaved to some as he had accused Deakin of behaving to him – with bluster and bullying. Yet as they tend to object as much to Cousins's political views as to his personal characteristics it is difficult to distinguish the principal influence in their minds. Cousins knew that to take over a union with the leadership traditions, as well as the previous policy commitments, of the TGWU would require a long period of settling in; he had no illusions about that. Nor did he have many illusions about the strength of feeling among those full-time officials who disagreed with him and his policies. He never doubted that he was in for a long and difficult fight, in which he would require all his tenacity and pugnacious nerve to overcome the obstacles around him.

One move for which Cousins was much criticised was the pressure he brought on the late Dame Florence Hancock, the TGWU women's officer and a senior member of the TUC General Council, to resign from the board of the *Daily Herald*, on which the TUC had four directors. This happened in the spring of 1957. Cousins was anxious to occupy the seat on the *Herald* board, as Deakin had before him. He felt strongly that the paper ought to be more vigorously directed and more socialist in policy. All four directors on the board were from the 'old guard' of the union establishment. They were complacent about the *Herald* which had again run into serious financial difficulties. After persuasion from Cousins, Dame Florence resigned from the board, but he was defeated in his attempt to replace her. The General Council spiked his move by voting the late Sir Tom O'Brien on to the board in her place. O'Brien received 11 votes, Cousins only 8. It was a severe blow to Cousins's pride. He knew the TUC majority sympathised with Dame Florence; but he reckoned they were motivated primarily by a desire to spite him. However, in July, with the *Herald* crisis at a new peak, the proprietors, Odhams Press, asked the TUC to relax the formal connection between the paper and the TUC. To consider this proposal the General Council appointed a special negotiating committee of four to strengthen the four standing directors. Cousins was elected as one of the additional four.

Cousins possessed a great asset in his knowledge of the union and his understanding of the mood of the rank and file. He also knew the importance many old-established members attached to the traditions of the TGWU and the reputation of Ernest Bevin. This was one reason why Cousins sought ways by which to commemorate Bevin's memory. He believed that Deakin had quite deliberately failed to do this because of his deep grievance about Bevin's behaviour to him. Whatever the reasons and motives, Cousins determined to do all he could to correct the omission. The attempt to establish a Chair of Industrial Relations at Oxford was only the first bid. He followed it by an endowment to Churchill College at Cambridge, and the resurrection of the Epstein bust. An Ernest Bevin Library, at Churchill College, Cambridge, was opened by Frank Cousins and Harry Nicholas on 12 November 1965. Cousins was then Minister of Technology in Harold Wilson's Cabinet and Nicholas was acting General Secretary of the TGWU. The Bevin Library was sponsored by the TGWU, which gave £50,000 for its construction, and the Epstein bust of Bevin stands at the entrance.)

He spent hours rummaging through the archives in the cellars of Transport House looking through old papers and policy documents from the Bevin period. The more he read, the more he became fascinated by the contemporary value of so much of the work that Bevin had done in the union's early years and of the validity it retained for solving many of the modern problems the TGWU was then facing. He marvelled at Bevin's prescience and imaginative, fertile mind. He was especially struck by Bevin's attitude to relations between unions and government, and his unswerving belief that the unions must never allow themselves to become wholly subservient to *any* government. This had a powerful and lasting influence on Frank Cousins's own thinking. His research into the Bevin tradition also made a valuable contribution towards his own understanding of the TGWU, its strengths and weaknesses. On the other hand, although he never lost his respect and admiration for Bevin he remained convinced that Bevin had allowed the TGWU to drift far too much to the Right and by doing so he had left Deakin with little option but to continue the operation – to the detriment of the union. There was therefore a note of jubilation when Cousins was able to declare that the TGWU was now 'on the Left'.

Cousins also began the task of bridge-building between the TGWU and Aneurin Bevan, who had, at last, been elected Treasurer of the Labour Party at the 1956 conference. Frank was among the first to congratulate Bevan and to pledge a new and hopeful future for their relationship. This was in spite of the fact that the TGWU vote that year had already been committed to supporting George Brown (now Lord George Brown) for the Treasurership. Everything seemed set, then, for a remarkable new axis between Bevan and Cousins, uniting the Left in the Labour Party and the trade unions with the objective of changing the power structure inside the whole Labour Movement. That was certainly how it appeared in 1956; and how it continued to appear until the H-bomb cloud descended.

Two conferences in the last twenty years, above all others, stand out as decisive events in the life of the Labour Party. They are those of 1957 and 1960. Both concerned the H-bomb. Both featured Frank Cousins as a leading figure. Both involved moments of terrible inner conflict and emotional torture for men at the top of their party – Aneurin Bevan in 1957, Hugh Gaitskell in 1960. The Scarborough defeat of Hugh Gaitskell on unilateral nuclear disarmament is generally regarded as the most traumatic moment in post-war Labour history. Yet in a sense the 1957 Brighton conference was even more crucial, because of the role in which Nye Bevan had been cast. Here was the greatest hero of the socialist Left opposing his own supporters on the issue which, almost without dissent, they all agreed was the biggest moral and political question of our time: the banning of the H-bomb and the need for the Labour Party to take an unqualified stand in demanding that action. Nothing was the same after the Brighton conference, as James Cameron wrote in the *News Chronicle*: 'I was there to watch the metamorphosis of a great man, the very moment of transformation . . . the star of Aneurin Bevan skipped in its course . . . and at least one aspect of politics can never be the same again.'

Frank Cousins had his own special problems at that unforgettable conference. He was committed by his own union conference decision to support a multilateralist resolution. On the other hand the phraseology of the TGWU commitment was open to wide interpretation; it could at a pinch be stretched to support a unilateral declaration. And it is at least arguable that the TGWU's Torquay motion was unilateralist in spirit if not in the letter. At their delegation meeting on the Sunday morning before the Brighton conference opened the TGWU recognised that there was some difficulty in deciding precisely in which category their motion stood; so they agreed to listen to the debate, especially to what Nye Bevan had to say, and vote accordingly. But Frank Cousins's speech, made towards the end of the debate and shortly before Bevan replied, left the majority of delegates with the clear impression that he would cast the TGWU vote for unilateral nuclear disarmament. Indeed, he pointedly explained that his own unions conference at Torquay 'had in front of it a similar type of resolution', and went on to demonstrate the parallel as he saw it, between the Norwood resolution and the one his own conference had passed (the Norwood CLP Motion called for unqualified unilateralism).[3] 'We are in considerable danger', he went on, sensing that there would be objections to such a parallel, 'of becoming lost in the words of resolutions.' Cousins repeatedly referred back to his Torquay conference and to the enthusiasm displayed for the protest against the Bomb. And he then declared his own position :

> This country, if no other will do it, ought to take the moral lead. Of course we do not want to limit the ability of our own Foreign Secretary when he takes that office in anything he may have to say to other people. But I would remind you that it is not a set of trade union negotiation in which we are engaged. There is a moral power behind a man who is speaking for his people, of their belief in something which outweighs any weapon we possess . . . We must say that this nation of all nations, great or small, however we may like to think of ourselves, does not approve of the maintenance and manufacture, either by ourselves or anyone else of this idiot's weapon. There is no compromise with evil.

In that section of his speech Frank Cousins took both the unilateralist *and* the multilateralist view in his stride. In a sense he both bridged the gap and confused the difference; he could be accused either of leaving his options open, or of wanting it both ways. But all who knew his mind and feelings on the issue were aware that he was trying to square his own deep convictions with a still unclear mandate from his union conference and a still uncertain

3. Labour Party Annual Report, Brighton conference 1957.

belief in just how far he could carry his membership with him. Yet he concluded: 'I say on behalf of my union . . . as well as myself – I say to the NEC : in this thing you cannot go too far or too fast for us.'

If the words meant anything at all this passage, linked with what he had said earlier, indicated that Cousins was prepared to take his union firmly into the unilateralist camp. Certainly the speaker who followed him believed that Cousins's speech was in support of the Norwood resolution. She spoke in support of it too.

One more speaker contributed to the debate before Aneurin Bevan rose to deliver what was without doubt the most painful speech of his career. There is no point in traversing that ground again here except to remind the reader that Bevan, in the middle of his speech, arguing and counter-arguing with himself as he went along, referred to Frank Cousins's appeal for a moral lead and echoed his sentiments : 'I agree with Frank Cousins and all who have spoken this morning that it is a high moral question, too.'

He then went on to tell the conference why, in this case, morality was not enough. Frank Cousins had heard this from Nye in their private conversations before that debate; he knew the arguments Bevan had been tormented by; he knew the internal Party pressures that had been exerted to persuade Bevan that it was unthinkable for him to support the unilateralist line, not least because the sponsors of the Norwood motion were known to be associating quite openly with the Trotskyist groups within the Party – groups that were later expelled. Cousins also knew that powerful influences had been brought to bear on Bevan by men like Sam Watson – a former miner, like Nye himself – who, though he differed so much from Bevan in his political views, none the less had an unusually persuasive effect on him.[4] And Cousins also recognised that the Bevan speech to some extent reflected the pressure for party unity, a pressure which had persuaded Cousins himself to accept 'Industry and Society', despite his own doubts and the strong attack on it from most of his left-wing friends and allies. The complex of political expediency, party loyalty, emotional pull, tactical momentum and simple common sense is such an amalgam of cross-currents and contradictory forces that the final decision, when it has to be made, is rarely satisfactory, least of all to the man who has to make it. It can be summed up as a compromise; but that tells nothing of the fearful strain that has gone into reaching the final decision.

As Frank Cousins listened to Nye Bevan struggling with himself that day he sensed all this turmoil; hardly anyone who has had power, or the possibility of wielding power, could fail to sense it. Yet there was no doubt

---

4. Sam Watson told me on two occasions earlier in 1957 that he regarded Nye Bevan as a natural, and a great, future Foreign Secretary. Watson believed that a combination of Gaitskell's leadership with Bevan as effective No. 2 would give Labour an unbeatable team at the General Election. He was wrong.

where Cousins's spontaneous reactions carried him : he wanted to support the Norwood resolution. His union chairman, Ted Fryer, was ready, poised with the union's card vote of one million, to cast in support of motion No. 24. At that point the senior member of the TGWU delegation, Charlie Brandon, stretched out his arm and grabbed Cousins.

'You can't do that, Frank,' he rasped, as he saw Frank nodding approval to Fryer to hold up the union's vote in opposition to Bevan.

Cousins, sitting immediately in front of Brandon, bridled, but hesitated. He prodded Fryer and demanded to know why he wasn't preparing to hold up the TGWU card vote. Fryer nodded towards Brandon.

'Charlie says they [meaning the delegation] won't stand for it, Frank.'

Cousins felt trapped, with no time to do anything about it. He rose on a point of order after Bevan had concluded and asked the chairman for an adjournment, so that delegations could consider their position in the light of Bevan's speech. In any case, he pointed out, it was almost time to break for lunch. Why not take the vote after lunch, to give delegates time to think? The chairman agreed.

During that lunch interval Cousins called his union delegation together in the empty gallery of the Brighton Ice Rink. It was a brief meeting, but a tense and nervous one. Brandon spoke against Cousins's attempt to swing the union behind unilateralism, arguing forcefully that this would be against the letter as well as the spirit of the Torquay resolution. Robert Mellish, MP supported Brandon. Cousins allowed his opponents the floor without attempting to contest their case. His view was that he was in the hands of his delegation : they knew where he stood – it was up to them now to decide. They voted to cast the TGWU block vote for Bevan and against the Norwood resolution. There is some doubt as to what that vote was. In two books the figure of 16 to 14 is mentioned.[5]

No figures were officially disclosed, but Charles Brandon believes the vote was 14 to 13, while Frank Cousins himself recollects a vote of 12 to 11, with several abstentions. In any event there were no more than two votes in it, possibly one.

Recalling the moment, Cousins has since told me that although he felt he could have swayed his delegation over to his own view, he had to weigh the consequences of doing this so early in his leadership. He also felt that it would have been emulating Deakin to have dragged the union behind his own personal opinions regardless of the views not only of his delegation but also of the huge unknown factor – the rank and file. In short, had he tried to steamroller the TGWU vote behind the Norwood resolution he would have been guilty of committing precisely the same error of which he always accused Deakin, albeit in a different political direction. (Another, simpler

5. See Michael Foot, *Aneurin Bevan*, Vol. II, p. 577; and Margaret Stewart, *Frank Cousins* (Hutchinson 1968), p. 33.

explanation given by some in the union is that Cousins knew he couldn't win over the delegation, so he quietly backed down.) He vowed, then, to do all he could to reverse the position so that next time he would have the union indisputably behind him. He saw his task for the next two years as one in which he had to argue and persuade. And he set his target to win over his own union to a policy of unilateralism by their 1959 biennial delegate conference.

From the moment it began to leak out of the meetings of the Labour Party Executive that Nye Bevan was in conflict with some of his supporters inside the executive about the H-bomb and that he would speak in the debate in opposition to unilateral nuclear disarmament the Brighton conference of 1957 was transformed into a political *danse macabre*. To that extent Bevan was right, in his speech, to describe the scene as 'an emotional spasm'. The shock waves penetrated every corner. Nye Bevan's attitude to the H-bomb had, in fact, previously never been clearly spelled out. He had been ambivalent about whether Britain could – let alone should – disentangle herself from the Bomb without dropping all her international alliances and obligations and, most of all, without throwing away her bargaining cards at the international negotiating table.

As Michael Foot explains in a brilliant chapter in his biography of Nye, Bevan's style was to argue constantly with himself as well as his friends on the major issues of policy and political action.[6] I was walked up and down the Brighton promenade for nearly an hour by Nye on the day before the H-bomb debate : an hour in which we argued and counter-argued about the political, moral and practical implications of a unilateral renunciation – not only by the Labour Party, in Opposition, but by any British Government in office at that time. He was wholly convinced, as he said in his speech the next day, that for the Labour Party to have committed itself to unilateralism would have been to make a declaration of impotence. He accepted, almost without demur, the moral case for such a renunciation and for a British lead. But irrespective of whether he was to become Foreign Secretary after the next election (he was then Shadow Foreign Secretary) he could see no practical alternative to negotiating the H-bomb out of existence; or at least not throwing away any card that Britain might hold *in advance* of entering the conference room. Michael Foot confesses ruefully that he was still hopeful even on the eve of the H-bomb debate that 'much would be salvaged by the way [Bevan] would speak'.[7]

I had no such hopes after that extraordinary promenade with Nye in which, I knew, he was practising his speech for the following day. He was by then quite convinced that the motion for unilateral nuclear disarmament, from the Norwood Labour Party, must be defeated. He was aware in every nerve

6. Michael Foot, *Aneurin Bevan*, Vol. II, p. 549.
7. *Ibid.*, p. 571.

of what that meant, both to himself and to those who were closest and dearest to him personally. Yet it was a measure of his remarkable courage that he was strong enough to override all these considerations. Peggy Duff argues that Bevan was never a unilateralist, nor did he oppose the original manufacture of the H-bomb; and she points out, as if to substantiate the logic of her case, that Bevan was a member of the Attlee Cabinet which decided to make the A-bomb.[8] But this is an unworthy oversimplification. As Michael Foot illustrates in his chapter on 'The Bomb', Bevan made several speeches during 1957 which might have been interpreted as placing him alongside the unilateralists; he publicly called for Britain to give a moral lead; he never ceased to deride those who believed that evil could be defeated by greater evil. He continually echoed the sentiments of all those who called for a British lead on nuclear disarmament, by whatever name or phrase it was labelled. Yet in the end, faced with the moment of truth, he left his political allies at Brighton in a state of bewildered disbelief; not least of them the man with whom he had begun to establish such a new and complete concordat – Frank Cousins. Michael Foot has described the aftermath :

> At Brighton they gathered in clusters and waylaid Ian Mikardo, Barbara Castle, myself and others and asked over and over again : 'Why has he done it? Why, why, why?' And the only answer was to point to the speech itself. But that was no balm for wounds such as these and indeed there was no balm to be offered. I myself never asked him why; it would have been an insult.[9]

When the Party conference vote was taken at 2.15 p.m. the Norwood motion was crushed : 5,836,000 to 781,000. There were cries from the hall of 'Shame', 'Carve-up' and 'Block vote'. Delegates accused Cousins of a last-minute cowardly retreat and of 'doing a Deakin'. He was bitter and disappointed, but, characteristically, unwilling to say much to the Press who were hunting for his story. At a Press conference that day he simply commented : 'The vote is that of the union, not of Frank Cousins; there is nothing dramatic about being democratic.' But of course there was, especially in the TGWU, and the Press was not slow to recognise the drama. It was one of the unhappiest experiences Frank Cousins had at any conference.

Nor was this the only strange event at that strangest of Labour Party conferences. The Party statement on nationalisation, 'Industry and Society', was approved by a huge majority of 5,309,000 to 1,276,000. Yet this happened only after extraordinary scenes in which right-wing and left-wing speakers agreed with each other; in which Left argued with Left, and Right con-

---

8. Peggy Duff, *Left, Left, Left* (Allison and Busby, 1971), p. 70.
9. Michael Foot, *Aneurin Bevan*, Vol. II, p. 577.

tested with Right. The original concept of the State buying its way into private companies and forming a partnership and a pattern of control by intervention was certainly not regarded in 1957 as the great blue-print for socialism that it became in the 1970s.

A remarkable moment in that debate was when Herbert Morrison (later Lord Morrison of Lambeth) and Manny Shinwell (later Lord Shinwell) spoke *against* the Party policy and in favour of a much more full-blooded approach to nationalisation. Jim Campbell, the General Secretary of the NUR (tragically killed in a car crash in Soviet Russia later that year) moved the main motion against the Party statement, as he had always planned to do. Frank Cousins, on the other hand, though a close personal friend of Campbell, as well as a political ally, spoke in favour of 'Industry and Society'. Aneurin Bevan believed that the policy statement went as far as it was possible to push the Labour Party at that time, under Gaitskell's leadership. But his wife, Jennie Lee, speaking from the floor of the conference, attacked the document in passionate terms.

The 1957 Labour Party conference was as much a watershed for Cousins as it was, in a different sense, for Bevan.

At the peak of his authority and influence in the socialist forum, Bevan faced the classical conflict between political popularity and political courage. Cousins, still new to the Labour Party's power games, tried to balance on a tightrope with his feet pointing gingerly in two directions while his heart urged him only one way. He had yet to establish his clear authority even within his own union, let alone in the central theatre of Labour politics, while being exposed to the ridicule and tricks of the practised tacticians, as Crossman's diary reveals. In a passage about the 1957 conference Crossman illustrates his own arrogance and intellectual snobbery rather more vividly than, as he intended, Cousins's naïveté. He was speaking to the conference that week on Labour's pension plan and was nervous about the likely reaction to the scheme, so he confesses that he found solace in the figure of Frank Cousins, seated in the middle gangway at the head of the TGWU delegation. Crossman wrote in his diary: 'Fortunately I saw Frank Cousins sitting right in the middle – the ideal WEA 3-year tutorial class member, a long not very intelligent face which nods when it's got it, at last. So I talked to him throughout . . .'[10] This attitude, reminiscent of Beatrice Webb, frequently and visibly infects the intellectual socialist approach to the lesser minds of the trade-union world. It is an attitude that Cousins was to find even more infuriating in later years, when it was apparent in the patronising sycophancy of people like Crossman. Cousins learned to recognise the trait and to flick off its irritation with his own arrogant contempt for some of its practitioners, but it always angered him – more for political than for per-

10. Richard Crossman, unpublished diaries, 4 October 1957, p. 1006.

sonal reasons. He saw in it the contempt that so many public-school figures cherished for the common people, despite their political posturings.

After the conference there were more immediate issues for Frank Cousins to tackle – such as the Government's increasing pressure to curb wages, and the difficulties already being encountered in negotiations in the public sector. Late in October the Chancellor, Mr Peter (later Lord) Thorneycroft, met the National Joint Advisory Council, a body consisting of Government, trade union leaders and senior representatives from both private industry and the nationalised boards.

It was the first time in four years that a Chancellor had attended a meeting of the Council and his message was startlingly clear : the economic squeeze was to begin in earnest. Bank rate was to be increased, public lending cut back, and expenditure axed. The union leaders were left in no doubt that they would find it extremely difficult to get wage increases of more than 3 per cent out of their public sector negotiations. The TUC was plainly stung. The chairman of the economic committee was the late Alan (later Sir Alan) Birch, who challenged the Chancellor's arguments about the need to curb wages to stop inflation getting out of hand. But Birch's protest was muted compared with the fiery response of Frank Cousins who, brushing aside the diplomatic protests of his colleagues, attacked Mr Thorneycroft and the Government with vigour and announced on the spot that his union, for one, would not accept the Government's policy. This, of course, didn't endear Cousins to Birch, or to the majority of his TUC colleagues. It started, indeed a sourness between Cousins and Birch that grew later into something close to mutual detestation.

At the November meeting of the economic committee Cousins demanded a clear statement of where the TUC stood on the question of giving evidence to the Cohen Council. He wanted an open declaration of hostility, while others still felt it was necessary to agree to some contact, if only an informal meeting. To Frank Cousins's surprise he was supported by Bill Carron (the late Lord Carron). Indeed, when the TUC finally went to see Lord Cohen and his committee on 8 January 1958, the three members of the economic committee who boycotted the meeting were Carron, Willis and Cousins. A month after the Chancellor had warned the unions of the horrors to come, the Government acted by putting a veto on a 3 per cent increase that had already been agreed for 40,000 hospital workers. The TUC exploded with an immediate cry of 'unwarranted intervention', and demanded to see the Prime Minister. Macmillan refused to meet them. In his union journal Frank Cousins left no one – neither the Government nor his TUC colleagues – in doubt about where he stood if the Government were to precipitate a fight :

The present Government represents the party of parasites. The Tory Party is largely made up of wealthy non-producers who rely on the Party for protection and get it in full measure when the Party is in power. But the workers, the articulate workers, are no longer prepared to go short in order that others may surfeit; and they are articulate enough to make their determination palpable.[11]

It was already clear that an open conflict was developing and the only question that remained unanswered was: where would the battle of words explode into open industrial war? How long, it was asked, could the leader of the country's largest trade union continue to attack the Government in such unusually bellicose terms without being drawn into a real trial of strength? The answer was soon to come.

Whatever depressions settled over Frank Cousins in the aftermath of Brighton, 1957, and in his early conflicts with his TUC colleagues, he always had one outstanding private consolation: unfailingly he could go home with his problems and discuss them with a uniquely sensitive and understanding wife. Nance kept the domestic fortress unassailable. Her patient awareness and, perhaps even more critical at that point, her political grasp and sympathy, were rarely more in demand. Cousins was already feeling that acute sense of loneliness which comes to leaders, especially to leaders who seek change and who take unorthodox directions. He felt this loneliness even more inside the TUC General Council. There were some potential allies, and others who would have been ready to offer a more specious kind of aid, given the slightest encouragement. Frank Cousins was neither the easiest of allies nor the kind of man to encourage obsequious support. Almost ostentatiously he exhibited an arrogant independence; but it was the arrogance of shyness and uncertainty, not yet of convinced authority.

Clearly, this arrogance did not encourage allies or recruit neutrals. It simply consolidated opposition to anything that even faintly suggested the influence or inspiration of Frank Cousins. Contrary to a popular belief at the time, Cousins did not go out of his way to court disfavour; he was quite normal in his desire for approval if not affection from the people he worked and lived with. Yet by his manner, which contained a good deal of prickliness, as much as by his unorthodox policies, he tended to build a barrier around himself. Only at home did the barrier disappear. The Frank and Nance partnership, as we have already seen, contained qualities and reciprocal forces that were not in the routine mould of marital relationships. They were, in fact, both ordinary and extraordinary: homespun, Yorkshire earthiness was blended in Nance with unusual political sensitivity and responsiveness. Astute observers were already commenting that it was difficult to make an assessment of the TGWU's new leader without taking her influence into account. And in his home life the emotional, as well as intel-

---

11. TGWU *Record*, December 1957.

lectual, protection that this partnership provided was of crucial importance to Frank Cousins as the external pressures on him mounted.

The glare of publicity which he attracted from the start dazzled his eyes, though not his senses. It would have required a superman to have remained unmoved under the piercing brightness that was suddenly switched onto him. He was vain enough to feel important, though his awareness of this also irritated him; but he also found the experience offensive, not only because the publicity was sometimes extremely hostile and prejudiced but equally because, on occasion, he regarded the whole operation as an obtrusive crudity. The family retreat therefore became a fortress of even greater importance to him. He could, and often did, slip behind its walls and simply disappear from public view. At moments of great stress he would stay at home and dig the garden, refusing contact with colleague or opponent, friend or foe. He would hide behind the therapeutic stems of his favourite gladioli and delve into the web of botanical experiments which he liked to weave around himself, as if to form a protective cloak. Every man needs an escape; a refuge into which he can retreat, sometimes from himself as much as from others. The garden was one such place for Frank Cousins. Here for hours, sometimes days, he would seek solace, and even inspiration. Not merely in the conventional forms of garden-lovers' activities but in remoter, more scientific work of seed blending and nurturing his own special varieties of plants and flowers. It was not sufficient for him simply to grow things; he needed to grow and develop exhibits that were unique in themselves. Gardening to him was not just a refreshing weekend pastime; it became a science and sometimes even an obsession.

The Cousins house was not, of course, exactly a monastic retreat. The children were now adults, apart from Frances. John the eldest was an airline steward and married; Brenda, twenty-five, was also married; and Michael, twenty-two, was at Selwyn College, Cambridge, a year away from graduating in physics (he later went on to secure a doctorate in crystallography). Frances, almost seven, had started school when the family lived in Worcester Park. They had by now moved on to Beech Grove, Epsom Downs. Later, when Frank was in the Government, the family moved to Sutton, where they lived in a block of flats called The Firs. Later still they moved to Pine Walk, Carshalton Beeches. Nance describes the constant moving process as 'flitting from tree to tree'. She adds, 'We have always seemed to live in trees,' and muses that there was probably 'something psychological about it.'

Chapter Twelve

THE BATTLE OPENS

In 1958 the 50,000 busmen of London went on strike for seven weeks. The strike was a major test for Frank Cousins: in retrospect, it may be seen as *the* test in his work as a trade-union leader. He himself would not dissent from this: quite the contrary. Looking back he is satisfied that it was the most important single milestone in his career as General Secretary of the TGWU. Arguments still rage about whether he was right or wrong; before examining them, we must tell the story of that strike.

The London busmen have traditionally been a highly independent group within the TGWU. They gave Ernest Bevin a great deal of trouble in 1937, with the 'Coronation' bus strike, and since that dispute they have had their own special and direct access to the union's executive and to the General Secretary in person, bypassing the national secretary for the union's passenger transport group. This involved a further concession: the union's Assistant General Secretary normally led their negotiations. Because of this exceptional status, wage claims from London busmen tended to receive somewhat special attention, and when they ran into difficulties the General Secretary invariably found himself involved.

On 17 October 1957 the TGWU submitted a claim for an extra 25s. a week for some 50,000 bus workers employed by the London Transport Executive. On 25 November the Executive rejected the claim and suggested that the union should reconsider it. In the meantime the three railway unions had also submitted claims for substantial increases for their members in both British Railways and London Transport.

The busmen had been pressing strongly for a new claim ever since the 11s. a week award to provincial busmen the previous summer. Before the London claim was submitted Frank Cousins tried to persuade their leaders to change the pattern of their wage bargaining by joining with other sections of the union dealing with provincial private and municipal bus workers.

Cousins wanted to unite all three groups within a joint wages policy. This, he felt, could strengthen their bargaining position and avoid the charge of constant wage-claim 'leapfrogging'. But the London busmen saw this as a diminution of their 'special status'. They refused to accept Cousins's plan. He was disappointed and said so, but accepted the rebuff and proceeded with a separate London claim.

In early December a delegate conference of London busmen rejected an official union recommendation to submit the claim to arbitration – by 105 votes to 25. They instructed their officials to return to the LT Executive for further discussions and, failing a satisfactory outcome, to seek 'plenary powers' from the union's general executive. That, in effect, meant strike powers. Frank Cousins's deputy, Harry Nicholas, was in charge of the negotiations, and both he and Cousins tried to head off the conflict by appealing informally to London Transport's chairman, Sir John Elliot. Two days before Christmas 1957 the London Transport Executive met the busmen's negotiating committee and agreed to a joint submission to an arbitration tribunal or a joint request with the union to the Minister of Labour requesting a committee of investigation – which, in effect, amounted to a form of court of inquiry. But the busmen's leaders were not prepared to accept either course. With the situation at deadlock, both sides sought the help of the Ministry – and the Minister's Chief Industrial Commissioner, the late Sir Wilfred Neden.

Neden, who was popularly described as the 'Government's chief industrial peacemaker', was a man of exceptional experience in industrial relations, highly respected by both sides of industry. His reputation for probity and absolute integrity in handling the most delicate and difficult situations was accepted without question. He had immense patience and took meticulous care over every detail in any dispute. He recognised that one of the principal features of industrial conflict is frequently not the purely economic argument but a clash of emotional attitudes. He regarded his role as that of a mediator seeking to cushion the impact of these strong emotions, to find a practical and perhaps face-saving formula which would preserve 'dignity', so that neither side would feel intolerably defeated nor overbearingly victorious. Neden's philosophy, and, he thought, the Ministry's role, was to cushion and if possible avert conflict by sensible compromises. But at that crucial juncture this was not, as it happened, a philosophy politically acceptable to a Government committed to curbing wage inflation.

On 10 January Neden met Harry Nicholas and Mr Anthony Bull, the labour director of London Transport, to try to find a way out of the impasse. This meeting was to have an historic importance far beyond the immediate issue of the busmen's pay dispute. It ultimately raised a question-mark against the entire role of the Ministry of Labour and its future as a mediating department. Neden had it in mind to offer the two sides some form of court of inquiry, though he had not yet decided on precisely what form this might take; nor had he discussed it in any detail with his Minister, Iain Macleod. That morning, shortly before he was due to meet Nicholas and Bull at the Ministry, he received a completely unexpected telephone call from the Minister of Transport, Harold (now Lord) Watkinson. Watkinson instructed Neden in the plainest possible terms that he was not to give the union the slightest encouragement to believe that they could get a penny out of their wage claims. This, he said, was a Cabinet instruction. No concession must be made to the busmen.[1] It was an astonishing move by the Minister of Transport who was, in effect, going over the head of his Cabinet colleague the Minister of Labour by instructing a senior civil servant in another department how to behave. The Ministry of Transport had an overall financial responsibility for all the nationalised transport undertakings, and Watkinson was possibly within his rights in a strictly constitutional sense in making his position clear. But it was done without tact, not to say in violation of Whitehall convention.

Neden tended to disbelieve that the Minister of Transport was acting under Cabinet orders, and said so, as tactfully as possible. Watkinson angrily insisted that this was so – to which Neden retorted that such an instruction would make his role as industrial commissioner difficult if not impossible. He protested to Watkinson that he could hardly go in to a critical meeting with Nicholas and Bull and tell them outright that there was not a penny to come; nor that the Government was, in effect, refusing to conciliate since London Transport was under instruction to make no concessions. But Neden's telephone conversation with Watkinson ended abruptly and Neden immediately reported to Iain Macleod. Until then, astonishingly, Macleod knew nothing of Watkinson's intervention.[2]

Neden explained to his shocked and uneasy Minister that he saw no point in meeting the two sides under the terms of Watkinson's instruction. He therefore proposed to go ahead, meet Nicholas and Bull, and offer them a board of conciliation or a committee of investigation – any name for what amounted roughly to a court of inquiry, without actually using that label. Macleod, according to Neden's description, hesitated; he seemed uncertain of his step. But he did *not* instruct Neden *not* to offer an inquiry. As Nigel Fisher explains in his biography of Macleod :

The Minister of Labour's position was anomalous. He had to reconcile his responsibility as a member of the Cabinet for implementing the Govern-

1. I have this account on the authority of Sir Wilfred Neden personally, and it has been confirmed in subsequent conversations with Lord Watkinson who told me : 'I don't deny that Neden was told that there was nothing to come.'
2. Nigel Fisher states : 'Remarkably this instruction was conveyed without Macleod's knowledge.' He does not disclose that the instruction came from Watkinson. Nigel Fisher's *Iain Macleod* (Andre Deutsch, 1973), p. 124.

ment's policy of wage restraint with the traditional role of his department to act as an impartial conciliator in industrial disputes . . .[3]

Neden went ahead with his proposal and Nicholas, armed with what appeared to be a substantial concession from the Government – since he knew nothing of what had happened behind the Whitehall curtain – summoned a delegate conference of busmen a week later. This in itself was a difficult path for Cousins and Nicholas to tread, since the previous delegate conference had rejected arbitration. But Nicholas felt that the status of arbitration prescribed by Neden, and accepted by London Transport, would enable him to persuade the delegate conference to accept. Even so, he had to fight for it against strong opposition. It took Nicholas six hours to swing the vote in his favour, persuading the delegates to reject an immediate call for an overtime ban or strike action. The London Transport Executive accepted the proposal and agreed to cooperate in a committee of inquiry. Everything appeared set for a compromise. Then Iain Macleod announced that there could be no separate inquiry into the London busmen's pay dispute. At a stroke, albeit fourteen days later, the Minister repudiated the proposal of his Chief Industrial Commissioner. It was a staggering blow to Cousins, Nicholas, the busmen's leaders, even to London Transport; but most of all to Neden himself.

This repudiation was contained in a letter sent on 24 January to Frank Cousins and Sir John Elliot, stating that it would be 'inappropriate to set up a committee for the purpose suggested', although the Minister did not 'rule out' the possibility of a wider and more general inquiry into the wages situation in the whole of the road passenger transport industry.

Iain Macleod must have realised that this proposal would irritate Cousins, after the busmen had turned down his own earlier proposal for a united approach on bus wages; and Macleod must also have known it would be quite unacceptable to the union at that stage in the negotiations. Indeed, the added irony was that no pay claim for the provincial busmen had been submitted by the union.

The letter was signed by Neden. Macleod had offered to write it himself, sensitive as he was to Neden's deep embarrassment; but Neden insisted on writing it – for his own self-esteem and dignity. He felt it was better that he should expose himself in this way quite openly and honestly rather than hide behind his Minister's authority. It was the act of a very courageous and honest man caught in an impossible situation.

This letter shocked Sir John Elliott as much as it angered Frank Cousins. Elliot was not the tough, unrelenting boss that he was often made out to be. Privately he felt that the busmen had a good case for more pay and, without Government interference, he would have negotiated an increase with

3. *Ibid.*, p. 124.

the TGWU. He certainly did not seek any showdown with the union. He has since confessed to me that 'The whole thing was laced with politics; we had no written instructions, but we were not free agents.'

Macleod's letters brought a predictable avalanche of criticism from Frank Cousins. 'This must be the first time in the history of British industrial relations where two sides in a dispute have accepted a proposal from Ministry officials aimed at seeking a solution only to find it turned down by the Minister himself.'[4]

On 28 January Cousins and Macleod met in a face-to-face confrontation at the Ministry of Labour which was not a pleasant occasion for either man. Cousins was accompanied by Nicholas, and Macleod had Neden in the room – the Ministerial room on the second floor at St James's Square. The Transport Union leader told the Minister that his action in overruling Neden's proposal was 'without precedent' and he asked him seriously to reconsider that decision. There was no question, Cousins said, of the union accepting the wider inquiry which the Minister had suggested. Cousins demanded to know :

'Who altered the instructions?' (Meaning Neden's proposals.)

'I did,' snapped Macleod.

'Well,' Cousins replied : 'If you can alter them once, you can put them back again, can't you?'[5]

Macleod accused Cousins of 'arrogance' and 'irresponsibility'. It didn't assist in smoothing the tension and the abrasive atmosphere of the meeting.

Then Sir Wilfred Neden spoke up in defence of the union's position and the personal dilemma of Harry Nicholas, with whom Neden had agreed the committee of inquiry. Neden pointed out to his Minister that Nicholas had acted perfectly legitimately in taking the proposal for an inquiry to the busmen's delegate conference. 'That is what I had proposed,' declared the courageous Neden, in front of Cousins and Nicholas. Macleod had previously sought to argue that no firm offer had been made by Neden. It was rare indeed for a senior civil servant virtually to call his Minister a liar so flatly, in front of the injured party, but Neden was bitterly angry, and he never forgave Macleod for that incident.

Frank Cousins has since expressed to me his profound respect and admiration for Neden. He has said : 'I have never had such respect for a civil servant as I felt for Neden on that occasion.' This was in spite of the fact that Cousins and Neden did not warm to each other in their general relations. Neden regarded Cousins as an impulsive, emotional and unpredictable trade union leader : a man out of the general pattern of leaders he had been accustomed to deal with.

Neden subsequently told me that in his view it was the repudiation of his

4. Report from the *Daily Telegraph*, 27 January 1958.
5. This is how Frank Cousins recalls the dialogue.

promise to Nicholas which in the end caused the strike. He was – and remained – convinced that Macleod himself was overruled in Cabinet. He puts it this way :

.Clearly Macleod was acting on a Cabinet decision to stop the rising wage inflation. Certainly I had no evidence that Macleod was fighting inside the Cabinet. Nor did he fight for the special role of the Ministry of Labour. He admitted to me that he was a man wearing two hats : that of a political Minister and that of the traditional Labour Minister – as an industrial peacemaker.

The Government's policy, according to Neden, was that the busmen should not emerge with anything that could be attributed to 'weakness' on the part of the Ministry of Labour. They were determined to use the busmen's pay dispute as a block to the growing pressure for wage increases.

'London Transport wanted to make concessions,' Neden claims. 'But the Government wouldn't hear of it.'

In Neden's view, Macleod's reversal of that arbitration decision marked 'a very important change in Government policy in regard to industrial relations; indeed, in my view it marked the end of the role of the Minister of Labour and his officers as conciliators in industrial disputes.'

This may seem too drastic a view in the light of more recent events, but the fact remains that it did mark a watershed, and was the breaking-point in the dialogue of trust that had hitherto existed between the Ministry and the TUC. It was to be many years before the trade union leaders turned again towards St James's Square in the hope of finding a sympathetic ear.

Why did Iain Macleod behave in the way he did? His reputation inside the Cabinet was strong. He was not fighting for his place in the senior hierarchy of the Government. He was an established figure and it was already being prophesied that he would ultimately become leader of the Conservative Party and Prime Minister – a prophesy that would probably have been fulfilled but for his death in 1970. Macleod insisted at the time – and subsequently to me – that the decision to overrule Neden was his own, though he had 'consulted Cabinet colleagues'. Yet this was not quite the case. Neden believed that Macleod was himself overruled by a Cabinet decision.

Nigel Fisher suggests that this Cabinet decision was unanimous.[6] It may well have been; but at an earlier Cabinet committee meeting there was no unanimity and it was in that earlier meeting that Macleod was defeated on the question of a committee of inquiry. Ministers believed that such an inquiry would almost certainly come out in favour of a substantial rise for the busmen and that this would open the floodgates for similar pay rises –

6. Nigel Fisher, *Iain Macleod* (Andre Deutsch, 1973), p. 125.

a considerable queue of pay claims in other industries having formed up behind the busmen. Such a development, it was argued, would put the Government's entire policy in jeopardy. Macleod's instinct, as Fisher states, 'was for conciliation', but once the Cabinet majority had made up its mind the Minister of Labour had no option 'but to implement this directive or resign'.[7] Fisher reveals that Macleod did in fact consider resigning and discussed the possibility with Alfred (now Lord) Robens, then his shadow Minister, who urged him not to. Macleod, Fisher reports, was saddened and depressed at having to treat both Frank Cousins and his Chief Industrial Commissioner in the way he did; yet he saw no alternative.

There is no doubt that Macleod was under the greatest pressure inside the Cabinet. One has to recall that several weeks earlier Peter Thorneycroft had resigned from the Chancellorship, taking with him Enoch Powell and Nigel (now Lord) Birch. He resigned because he had not been able to secure majority support in the Cabinet for a policy designed to cut public expenditure and bring down the level of wage settlements. None the less, Ministers were still anxious to show that the resignation had done nothing to weaken the Government's resolve to fight wage inflation. Moreover, the Prime Minister, Harold Macmillan, was out of England on a Commonwealth tour. He had departed immediately after appointing Mr Heathcoat-Amory as Thorneycroft's successor. R. A. Butler was left in charge of the Government which, in Mr Macmillan's memorable phrase, had run into some 'little local difficulties'. Inside the leaderless Cabinet strident voices were raised against any conciliatory move by Macleod, and Butler did not feel disposed to challenge these voices. There were serious tensions inside the Conservative Party which might have been exploited had the Government appeared to have weakened under union pressure. It is arguable that Mr Macmillan might have thrown his weight behind an attempt to conciliate, but other strong voices inside the Government were totally committed to the strategy of fighting the busmen. They included the Minister of Transport; the late Lord Mills, Minister of Power and Mr Macmillan's personal 'adviser in industrial affairs'; and the new Chancellor, Heathcoat-Amory.

There was another aspect, too: the chance to demolish Frank Cousins. Several members of that Cabinet to whom I have spoken contend that there was never a moment when Ministers sat down and decided: 'We are going to get Cousins.' Obviously not. Government doesn't work that way. Yet it is hard to believe that Ministers were not tempted to regard the opportunity as heaven-sent. They clearly saw Cousins's predicament; they knew he was trapped in a situation scarcely of his own making, but one from which he could not honourably retreat. They knew the weakness in his armour. However bravely the London busmen fought they were scarcely as indispensable

7. *Ibid.*, p. 169.

to the national economy as, say, the electricity, engineering or railway workers. The Cabinet calculated, quite rightly, that they could take on the busmen and Frank Cousins, and score an important political as well as an industrial victory against the man who was now their most vocal and perhaps their most powerful opponent. It was a temptation, as Oscar Wilde might have said, too promising to resist.

The only weakness in the Government's armour was the railwaymen : if they joined forces with the busmen, then the Government would be compelled to retreat. So the obvious tactic, Ministers concluded, was to separate the two forces by trying to coax the railway unions into a settlement when the time came. It was an astute and, as it turned out, extremely successful manœuvre.

Not surprisingly, the demand for strike action from the busmen grew louder after Macleod's refusal to set up the committee of inquiry which the delegate conference had accepted, in preference to an earlier strike call. It seemed unlikely that Frank Cousins could hold back his members much longer, and the predictions were for an iminent strike decision. Yet to everyone's surprise he *did* hold them back. He suggested that the dispute should be referred to the Industrial Court for arbitration – hardly the action of a man who was actively searching for a showdown with the Government. The Industrial Court was a forum for arbitration independent of Government which could be used by common agreement between the two sides to any dispute. Its decisions were not binding and left the sides free to negotiate beyond the Court award if they so chose, or to reject any recommendations outright. On 3 February Cousins and Nicholas tried to persuade the busmen to go to the Industrial Court. At first it seemed they had failed : a strike vote was carried by 83 votes to 48. Yet that was ruled non-operative because it failed to satisfy the two-thirds majority rule required to carry a strike decision. After nearly twelve hours of argument a vote of 92 to 40 finally took the busmen to the Court. The next day the *Daily Express*, in an editorial, proclaimed the busmen's vote as : 'a triumph for Cousins's power of persuasion. He has given a fine, courageous demonstration of trade union leadership.'

The Court reported on 13 March. The three-men tribunal under the chairmanship of Sir John Forster recommended an increase of 8s. 6d. a week for the 36,000 central bus crews, but nothing at all for the remaining 14,000 covered by the union's claim.

Before either side had time to comment Harold Watkinson (the Minister of Transport) declared that the cost of any increase arising from the award must be found within London Transport finances. The Government, Watkinson emphasised, was not prepared to help in any way.

In effect he was telling Sir John Elliott that he had to finance any pay rise out of cuts in services and manpower – in short, make the workers pay for their own wage rise. This declaration scarcely encouraged a promising negotiation on the basis of the Court award. Behind the scenes there were furious rows between the Minister of Transport and the Chairman of London Transport, on whom the pressure was now almost intolerable.

Frank Cousins had an inkling of what was going on behind the diplomatic curtain of Press statements and Ministerial announcements. He did not, at that stage, know the full story, but he guessed that London Transport were prisoners in a fight between the Government and his busmen's claim. Even so, he made one last bid for a peaceful settlement. He appealed to Sir John to modify the Court award by spreading the sum involved across the board to all 50,000 bus workers covered by the union's claim. The union calculated that this would produce an all-round increase of 6s. 6d. a week against the original claim of 25s. This was a daring attempt at compromise by Cousins because his own negotiating committee, a strong and militant group, had made it clear that they would not settle for less than 10s. 6d. a week all round, despite the Court award. Nevertheless, Cousins took the risk and offered to do a deal with Sir John. But the LT chairman refused on the grounds that such an amendment 'would have been quite contrary to the Industrial Court decision'.

Events then moved swiftly. The busmen's negotiating committee rejected the Court award and put forward their formal demand for a 10s. 6d. a week across-the-board pay rise. Endorsing this, a delegate conference decided by 128 votes to 4 to call on the executive for strike powers to enforce the demand. On 2 April the union's finance and general purposes committee gave Frank Cousins the powers to call an official strike of all London busmen. The union formally tendered one month's notice to London Transport of a withdrawal of labour from 4 May.

In the month that followed various attempts were made to bring the two sides together again, but it was clear that the Government was prepared to let the strike happen – indeed some Ministers positively *wanted* it to happen. Iain Macleod weathered the storm of criticism in Parliament for his failure to intervene. The Minister of Labour steadfastly refused to lift a finger to alter the award – which he knew well enough was unacceptable to the union and, privately, was also regarded by London Transport as quite unfair and unrealistic. There is a story of a Cabinet committee held towards the end of April, shortly before the strike deadline was due to expire, when Harold Macmillan felt it necessary to test out the TUC for help. The Prime Minister had been impressed by views expressed to him by several senior civil servants, who argued that if the Government defeated Cousins and the busmen this would lead to serious problems in relations between the unions and the Government. It would sour the entire atmosphere. Macmillan agreed that this was possible, and deputed a senior civil servant to discuss with the TUC General Secretary Sir Vincent Tewson the possibility of the

TUC persuading Cousins to accept a compromise.[8] Macmillan put his own Prime Ministerial car at the disposal of this civil servant, who went to TUC headquarters on a strictly private mission. But Tewson did not feel there was anything useful the TUC could do to persuade Cousins to alter course.

On 28 April in a final meeting between Frank Cousins and Sir John Elliot the chairman of London Transport offered to review the pay of the Green Line busmen and those workers excluded from the Court award 'in the autumn', provided that the union accepted the award as it stood. Cousins left the meeting with the announcement: 'This is the end of the talks.' It was. His next move was to mobilise his own troops and ensure they were in good heart for the fight, but, even more important, that they knew precisely what were the odds stacked against them. Cousins, perhaps then at the most critical point of his career, knew that this was the moment of truth. It was a truth he had to share with his busmen who were about to go into battle.

On 2 May, 48 hours before the strike was due to commence, the TGWU called a mass rally at the Empress Hall, Earl's Court, crowded to the doors with 6,000 London busmen. Cousins excluded the Press because he wanted a candid meeting between himself and the rank and file. He did not want any publicity-seeking gestures from anyone. He had already decided to put it to the busmen that they were virtually on a losing wicket, but it was up to them whether they wanted to strike or not. He told them, in what he himself has described to me as the most demanding speech he ever made as General Secretary, that he had no illusions about the difficult path ahead. If they chose to strike he would back them but there was no promise of victory at the end of the road.

He told them that he was entering the strike with a heavy heart. They might well be alone in the struggle, which could drag on for weeks with little support from other unions and very little from the general public. He told them that even at that late stage he would be willing to go back to London Transport to try again, if they wished to have second thoughts about the strike. He later said to me:

> I could not have given them a worse picture of their prospects. I have always taken the line that if the men and women involved wanted a dispute they could have one. But they must understand the facts of the situation. I do not believe in starting a strike and then telling people that they are on strike.

At the end of his speech Cousins asked for a vote on the strike. Then he declared how proud he was of their courage and their convictions. He bolstered their morale by insisting that they were now engaged in a fight not

8. I have been given this account by the civil servant who actually went on the mission from Macmillan to Tewson.)

simply for their own pay claims but for all trade unionists, against the wages policy being imposed by the Government. It was a view he maintained throughout the subsequent seven difficult weeks of the strike, in the face of widespread hostility not only from the Government and most public opinion but, worst of all, from many colleagues inside the TUC General Council. It is a view he maintains to this day. During his many moments of gloom and depression, as he contemplated the prospect of the stoppage dragging on endlessly and probably to ultimate failure, he nourished himself with the deep conviction that he was fighting a battle for the entire trade-union movement. It may be argued that this was his own form of rationalisation to justify what others saw as an impossible situation and plain pig-headedness on his part, but it is my view that he *was* fighting for the unions as a whole : not on a battleground of his own choosing. Who in his right mind would have selected the London busmen as the issue on which to fight at that time? But this was an issue on which Cousins found himself forced in the end to take up arms.

His critics have maintained that had Cousins been a trade union leader of guile and wisdom he would soon have realised that he was trapped by Government policy, and would have 'shown leadership' by shrewdly negotiating himself out of the impasse. That, it has been said, is what Bevin or Deakin would have done. Precisely so. Deakin would never have allowed himself to lead a wages fight against the Government, but he might well have found that his busmen were following the example of the dockers and breaking away from the union, as they sought to do in 1937, when Bevin partly rescued the situation by first backing the strike and then, shrewdly, coming to terms. No two strike situations are exactly parallel. Time changes the ethos and the impulses behind industrial conflict, as with all else. Cousins's purpose in the London bus strike was as much to rescue the union from its own internal strife and erosion of purpose as it was to fight a wage claim for the busmen – or for the trade union movement as a whole. Having recognised the need to give the rank and file more say in the affairs of the union he could not retreat when the going became tough or even painful. Leadership is not to be measured simply by guile, shrewdness, the capacity to avoid defeat, if not to win : it has also to be measured by a sense of purpose, integrity and honour.

In any event Cousins was also banking on a united front with the railwaymen – a tactic not exactly without an element of shrewdness, as well as a touch of simple faith. As the bus talks were reaching their climax at the end of April the pay claim by the three railway unions was also coming to the boil. On 10 April the railways' own arbitration system (the Railway Staff National Tribunal) had rejected the claim for a 'substantial' increase. By a curious quirk of circumstance the chairman of the RSNT was Sir John Forster, who had conducted the inquiry into the busmen's dispute. But the

RSNT split on the question of giving the railwaymen more pay. Sir John and the employers' nominee were opposed to any increase. The third member of the tribunal, the trade union nominee, was Edwin Hall, the Lancashire miners' leader, who submitted a minority report recommending a rise of 3 per cent. It was clear enough that if the Government backed the tribunal majority, as the logic of their general economic policy would have suggested, then the nation would almost certainly have faced a railway strike. The Government had to think and act quickly if it was to isolate Cousins and his busmen, and prevent what would otherwise have been a major retreat from the wages policy so far adopted.

Mr Macmillan was now back in town. With characteristic shrewdness the Prime Minister invited the Chairman of the British Transport Commission (which had then overall control of all nationalised transport – British Railways and, effectively, London Transport as well), the late Sir Brian (later Lord) Robertson to meet him, together with the leaders of the three railway unions. The meeting took place on 22 April, some five days *after* the busmen's leaders met to start discussions on their plans for the forthcoming strike. They gathered at No. 10 Downing Street at 3.45 in the afternoon of 22 April: Sir Brian, Sidney (later Lord) Greene (NUR), William (now Sir William) Webber (Transport Salaried Staffs Association) and Albert Hallworth (ASLEF, the locomotive men's union). Mr. Macmillan was already convinced of the need to avert a railway strike – almost at any cost. He circulated a paper to his Cabinet colleagues proposing ways in which a new pay deal for the railwaymen could be linked with a capital programme to modernise the railways and improve their efficiency through manpower economies as well as capital expansion.

At Downing Street that afternoon Supermac gave a superb performance. He told the union leaders of his affection for railways and railwaymen; he reminded them of his own past associations as a director of the old Great Western Railway; he gave them whisky: 'a good deal was consumed,' he records;[9] and in a final display of his skills he took the union leaders on a conducted tour of the Downing Street gardens. The spring sunshine softened and mellowed the mood. Of course he also told them that, if the Government agreed to let the Transport Commission make an offer, they would have to cooperate by accepting some redundancies and reducing restrictive practices and consider any proposals to help speed up the modernisation of the railways. It was a quo to go with the quid. But the two sides went away convinced that a compromise was within reach and that the Government was prepared to back it.

The Transport Commission was now permitted to offer the railwaymen a 3 per cent all-round pay increase, with the further promise of a full-scale

9. I refer the reader to Mr Macmillan's own description of these events in his memoirs, *Riding the Storm* (Macmillans, 1971), p. 711.

review of the pay structure. This culminated in the famous Guillebaud Report, which established a new basis for railway pay. The deal was in fact clinched between Sir Brian Robertson and Mr Harold Watkinson on the very eve of the London bus strike. It was concealed behind Ministerial assurances to the public that the railwaymen would have to find the extra money by economies from within their own industry. Yet the fact was that the Government was already financing a railways' deficit to the tune of over £200 millions (at 1958 prices) to meet current and capital charges. So despite the rejection of the rail pay claim by the arbitration tribunal, the railwaymen got their rise without a strike, but the London busmen did not. The Government had succeeded in isolating Frank Cousins.

> My pig-faced kingdom with tongues of wrong
> And an historical gait of trial and error,
> Under whose bridges Time, faster than rivers,
> Bears individual and event along
> Into a past overloaded with souvenirs . . .
>
> George Barker 1943

Chapter Thirteen

THE BUSMEN'S STRIKE

The scene was now set for a showdown between the Government and the largest trade union in the country. It was a situation unique in post-war industrial relations. Until the miners' strikes of 1972 and 1974 it remained the outstanding example of a Government decision to take on a union in the public sector in an attempt to force through a general policy of wage restraint.

But, of course, the busmen could never hope to wield the economic and industrial power of the miners. Indeed they were in a particularly exposed position and their main hope lay in trying to mobilise support – moral, financial and, if possible, in a more active form – from other sections of the Labour Movement. The railwaymens' pay dispute was central to this hope. Cousins always believed that a united front of railwaymen and busmen could defeat the Government, especially if they could draw on the moral support of the TUC. There were other cards Cousins could use if the TUC support was not forthcoming though he recognised these would be less effective. The TGWU strength lay less in the power of its numerical membership than in the diversity and breath of its vast industrial coverage. In the last resort Cousins knew he could probably persuade the dockers, the power stations workers and even the oil-tanker drivers to join the fight beside the busmen. But he was reluctant to do this. Partly because he recognised that it was a dangerous and risky path to tread but more so because he knew he would be running against the grain of TUC attitudes.

In that situation if he were to be forced back on to his last line of defence, compelled to bring in his other troops to rescue the busmen *without* the support of the wider trade union movement then he knew he would be driven relentlessly into a bleak and lonely isolation. It would also amount to a confession of political, as well as industrial, failure. Cousins therefore never shifted from his central objective – to win the support of his TUC colleagues. But, of course, he could do this only by convincing them that the London busmen found themselves in confrontation with the Government in a battle on behalf of the entire trade union movement; and that it was a battle not of their own choosing but one into which they had been trapped by a skilful, wily Government bent on isolating a weak link in the political-industrial chain of the Labour Movement. It was indeed the only broad strategy that made sense; but Frank Cousins failed to win his General Council colleagues to his view. And above all it was that failure which, finally, compelled him to fight a rearguard, defensive and ultimately hopeless action. In that exposed position he was almost inevitably outmanœuvred by forces quite beyond his single-handed powers. And indeed by forces within his own brotherhood that were willing accomplices of a Government bent on destroying Cousins's influence.

It is true that, at the outset, the Government itself was not certain of victory. Even Macmillan was anxious and worried about the possibility of a national rail strike although his intelligence system must have informed him that this was improbable. Macmillan and his senior Ministers were also concerned about a possible extension of the bus strike into the docks and road haulage industries. In fact there was a strike of lorry drivers at London's Smithfield meat market which began at the end of April and which appeared, to Government eyes, to have all the signs of a test-bed operation from which there might be a serious extension of the bus strike.

The market lorry drivers' strike also brought sympathetic action from London dockers and as the dispute rumbled on through May, alongside the bus strike, it looked like a potential rallying base for a wider spread of sympathetic strike action. Yet Cousins refused to exploit the potential. He was under constant pressure to do so both from within the TGWU and from militant forces outside the union and his refusal to be budged brought a great deal of criticism on his head. The truth was that he did not want to get the two disputes combined together bacause he feared it would weaken his bid for the TUC's 'political' support – which, to be sure, it would have done, slender though his chances were of getting such support at any time.

The Government was never quite sure of its step during these complicated shufflings around the focal point of the busmen's strike. One false move by Ministers might easily have provoked an explosion of anger from several other sections of the industrial front. It was only by the most careful, judicious handling of the whole situation by that master of tactics, Harold Macmillan, that the Cabinet was steered away from the risk of a much wider confrontation with the unions.

In fact Macmillan himself was always strongly opposed to pushing a policy of deflation too far. He feared the kind of social divisiveness such a policy might invite. Nor did he want to deliberately court an industrial crisis which could upset his longer-term political strategy. So there were clear contradictions within the Government and its own policies. It wanted to 'stand firm' against the unions and maintain its policy of wage restraint; but it also wanted to do this at the lowest possible cost both in political and economic terms. Provided the London busmen could be isolated, this strategy could be achieved. No doubt if the busmen had been able to count on the support of the TUC and more particularly the railway unions, then the Government would have been forced to find an acceptable formula for a compromise settlement. The pressure on London transport would have been eased. But it was not to be. Cousins and the busmen were left to the mercy of the Government in what eventually became a grim war of attrition.

In his memoirs Mr Macmillan observes: 'While I was ready to accept the bus strike in London and even in the provinces I was determined to find some concession which would bring a settlement on the railways.'[1]

It was true, as Macmillan admits, that some Ministers wanted the showdown to include resisting the railwaymen as well as the busmen, but he regarded such pressure as imprudent, if not plain silly. In fact the Prime Minister himself was personally responsible for steamrollering the railway pay settlement through the Cabinet. The shrewd Supermac, backed by Butler and, significantly, Iain Macleod, made quite sure that the Cabinet approved his formula for 'buying off' the railwaymen by offering them a compromise settlement. Macmillan wrote later: 'Some Ministers were very reluctant to agree to my proposal [on settling the rail pay claim] and did so only out of loyalty.'[2] There were rumblings of complaint inside the Tory Party as well as the Cabinet, but Macmillan was as dismissive of these rumblings as he was of the stringent Treasury doctrines which, despite Thorneycroft's resignation, still lingered. He records: 'The Treasury now seemed especially wedded [to a tough wages policy] and some Ministers revered with almost Brahminical devotion . . . that there should be no advance of wages unless it could be got out of economies.'[3]

In fact Macmillan used this doctrine cleverly to secure the railway settlement. He stood the doctrine on its head by persuading the Transport Commission to devise ways of making savings equivalent to a 3 per cent all-round increase in pay which, in any case, he knew the Treasury would have to guarantee since so much railway debt was already underwritten by the Government. Harold Macmillan was fudging the books. In fact any savings, if they were made at all, added up to a highly dubious balance-sheet. Still, the device enabled Mr Macmillan to divide the unions, settle the railway dispute and isolate Frank Cousins. And Cousins could only stand by helpless while he did this.

Mr Macmillan has since described to me his own reflections on that

1. Harold Macmillan, *Riding the Storm* (Macmillan, 1971), p. 714.
2. *Ibid.*, p. 714.
3. *Ibid.*, p. 714.

period. He knew that he and the Government were in a very strong position and that Frank Cousins was in a weak one. People, he has since told me, don't worry if they can't get a bus for a few weeks : 'It's an inconvenience, but not a disaster' for a Government.

Once the strike began, Cousins recognised that his chances of averting a long-drawn-out and costly stoppage hinged on getting decisive and continuing support from the TUC. Equally the Government knew that it must play every card in its strong hand to ensure that the TUC's 'Establishment' (whom Mr Macmillan knew well) were made aware of Ministerial 'thinking'. The Government was determined – increasingly as the dispute dragged on – not to let Cousins off the hook, and in this they received a surprising degree of private encouragement from some members of the TUC hierarchy.

At first the TUC gave the busmen its full and sympathetic support – – indeed in its first public statement it blamed the dispute squarely on the Government.

This declaration, issued three days after the strike began, gave Frank Cousins some hope. But he misjudged the balance of power inside the TUC leadership. The statement was drafted and issued by George Woodcock, who was then second in command to Sir Vincent Tewson, and temporarily in charge. He was impressed by Frank Cousins. Far from sharing in the general resentment of the emergence of this new force, he welcomed it.

Woodcock had a good deal of sympathy with the busmen's case and with Cousins's personal predicament. He felt that it was the TUC's duty to help a union in such difficulties, especially when it was so obviously the victim of a deliberate Government strategy. Unlike Tewson and most of the old-guard TUC leadership, Woodcock was not wedded to the concepts of the *status quo* in relations with the Government. Nor was he an unquestioning admirer of much of the official thinking in the TUC at the time. Privately he shared some of Cousins's own attitudes towards his General Council colleagues; attitudes which, when Woodcock became General Secretary of the TUC, were to bring the two men together in a working relationship. But that was in the future. There was little more that Woodcock could do at that time. He could not commit the TUC too strongly or too far. In Tewson's absence he had to choose his ground with great care. The authority of the General Secretary at the TUC has always been supreme in the hierarchy. Positions are held with a zealous regard for seniority. And in any event there was little affection between Woodcock and Tewson.

Cousins had written to the TUC, on the day the strike began, asking whether there was 'any proposal at TUC level to give further consideration to the position'. Woodcock understood precisely what that meant and what lay behind the question. It was also necessary, in Woodcock's view, to counter the strong hints in several newspapers that the TUC would in effect disown Cousins and his busmen. Some members of the General Council had already been making their views known, privately, to pressmen. At that early stage what Frank Cousins required, and what Woodcock gave him, was a strong declaration of moral support. He did not ask for direct support, financial or otherwise, nor did he want the TUC to intervene with the Government to try to secure a resumption of direct negotiations. He knew that would have been a futile gesture. But he did want his senior colleagues on the TUC to show they were with him in spirit. He told the finance and general purposes committee on 7 May that :

> an attempt . . . was being made particularly by the Press to present the dispute as against the public and as one with which his colleagues on the General Council and affiliated unions had no sympathy. He knew that none of the insinuations was correct. The busmen themselves were in full support of the action taken though they had been told by the union that the strike might be a long one and that they must fight the issue on their own. The only support that the union asked for at this time was the moral support of the trade union movement which could be properly expressed by the General Council.[4]

Yet the scene shifted sharply within the next week. On 10 May, with the strike about to enter its second week, the TGWU again wrote to the TUC. In this letter Cousins asked whether the TUC might sponsor a 'national appeal for collections to supplement strike pay'. When he put his appeal to another specially convened meeting of the General Council he explained that he had already received some £3,000 in gifts from other unions, trades councils and local Labour parties. The union, he told the meeting, regarded this as a sign of spontaneous support for the busmen and as 'proof of a widespread recognition' that the busmen's strike was 'a fight for the whole trade union movement'. In these circumstances he wondered whether the General Council would consider themselves 'to be the most appropriate body to initiate and operate a national appeal'.

It was a shrewd move by Cousins. In effect he was seeking to follow through and test the declaration of support made a week earlier. But the majority of the General Council did not want to get deeply involved. They demurred at Cousins's request and questioned its validity. After all, General Council members taunted Cousins, the strike involved only a comparatively small number of the TGWU's membership. And, they added, might it not be that a TUC appeal launched so early in the strike would leave the public with the impression that the TGWU's case was a weak one? Cousins was riled; he was meant to be. Angrily he rounded on his TUC colleagues with a retort that he was not asking for charity. His busmen, Cousins said, were in battle for the whole trade union movement, not just for themselves. They

4. TUC *Annual Report* 1958, p. 129–30.

were fighting, in particular, to try to establish some justice for lower-paid workers, to whom the TUC were always offering lip-service. He was not asking other unions to fight his battles for him, he reminded the Council; he was merely giving them an opportunity to show that they were with the busmen, at least in spirit. His tone was bitter as the words burst out. Yet, he concluded, the fact that he wasn't asking for their help should not be interpreted 'as an indication that it would be right for everyone to sit back and wait for the strike to succeed – or collapse'. The debate switched from one of principle to one of timing. Cousins agreed that it might possibly be too soon to issue a fully formalised TUC circular appealing for money. Even so he thought there ought to be a clear recommendation to the next ordinary meeting of the General Council on 21 May. That was agreed, though with a marked degree of grudging acquiescence which left behind a sour taste.

The appeal was sent out after the meeting of 21 May and the results surprised everyone, including Frank Cousins. Large sums of cash were offered on interest-free loan by many unions, even by the union leaders who had strongly criticised Cousins inside the General Council. But the TUC appeal for funds was a muted one, and if the money that poured in later was more than Cousins expected, that was hardly due to any encouragement from the TUC.

I have been told that the cross-examination to which Cousins was submitted at the special meeting of the General Council on 14 May was part of a carefully worked out strategy to cover the TUC's retreat from the position taken up on 7 May.[5] Several senior members discussed this privately with Sir Vincent Tewson and agreed to halt what they feared might develop into a headlong confrontation between the TUC and the Government. These old guard members had sympathy neither with Frank Cousins's general policies nor with his handling of the busmen's dispute. Privately they criticised the licence he allowed to his busmen's negotiating committee because it was dominated by left-wing militants, including several Communists. They believed he was allowing himself to be dragged along by 'extremists' and had in effect become a prisoner of the left wing of the busmen's committee. They criticised him for failing to impose on the busmen's leaders the kind of determined and 'responsible' leadership which they themselves sought to impose on their own members and which they had become accustomed to seeing exercised in the TGWU by Arthur Deakin. Cousins's critics simply could not understand what impelled him to give his rank and file so much of their own head, unless it was sheer irresponsibility on his part. This conviction was held by all but about half a dozen of the General Council members – that minority who sympathised with Cousins's political

5. My information has been provided anonymously by people who were senior members of the TUC General Council at the time.

views, admired the way he challenged the conventional wisdom and welcomed the injection of industrial democracy he was giving to the TGWU.

The state of tension between Cousins and his TUC colleagues did not improve as the strike dragged on. He now knew he would not get their support, except as a cover for a retreat. He knew that the TUC feared the consequences of accepting a united challenge to the Government because, as they saw it, it could lead the TUC into a form of 1926 General Strike situation. Even so, the TGWU leader strenuously denied that he was seeking to challenge the Government as such. He stressed the point in his union journal when the strike was at its peak.

The argument about the bus strike being a 'challenge to Government' is not a particularly rewarding one to assess. Any serious challenge by a trade union in the public sector of the economy can now be regarded as a challenge to the authority of the Government. Most major strikes can be regarded as 'political strikes' in the broadest sense of the term. This is now widely accepted as a fact of life, but it was not yet in 1958. The somewhat fuzzy and unrealistic demarcation between an 'industrial dispute' and a 'political strike' still existed. It was wearing thin but, because the Government had not hitherto sought so palpably to apply a wages policy by resistance to pay claims in the public sector, there was still a good deal of confusion over the rights of a union to challenge such a policy. Today, the role of Government in modern industrial relations is so powerful that almost any major industrial conflict is equally a matter of major political importance. It is no longer a prerequisite for a union to be motivated by political hostility towards a Government in order to turn a strike into a political challenge.

The importance of the London bus strike was precisely that it took place at the turning point of this change in emphasis. One can therefore understand the anxieties of the TUC leadership as well as the over-defensiveness of Frank Cousins in his insistence that it was *not* a challenge to the Government. It was part of his difficulty that he had no useful guidelines. In practically every way he was breaking new ground. He was violently breaking with the traditions of his own organisation by leading such a strike; he was, despite all that was said, challenging what he knew to be Government policy to contain wage increases in the public sector – albeit on good grounds of social justice; he was bringing into question the entire corpus of TUC thinking and forcing his colleagues, against their wish, to consider aspects of political and industrial policy which they had never faced up to before. It was an unpleasant experience for them, as well as for Frank Cousins.

Towards the end of May it became clear that the bus strike was having only a minimal effect on the life of the capital. In Harold Macmillan's incomparable phrase it was 'an inconveniece'. And it was not even a serious inconvenience for many. The real problem was the railway settlement, which was in its closing stages. The normal running of the London Underground trains seriously undermined the busmen's strike, reducing it in some instances to an irrelevance. The busmen's negotiating committee was quick to spot its weakness and it put increasing pressure on the General Secretary to do something about it – through the TUC if possible. Yet what could Cousins do at the TUC? His relations with his General Council colleagues were frigid; nor did he have any rapport with the new General Secretary of the NUR, Sidney Greene. Unlike his predecessor Jim Campbell, Greene was unsympathetic to Cousins and was quickly recruited as an ally by the TUC Establishment.

By the end of May the busmen's negotiating committee was demanding swift action – preferably by involving the union's membership among London petrol-tanker drivers and workers employed in supplying electrical power to the Underground trains. On 27 May Cousins sought to stall on this by informing the Minister of Labour that he and his officers were ready to meet the Minister for talks and were ready to resume negotiations with London Transport as soon as LT wished. Macleod came back with a flat rejection. No useful purpose could be served by a meeting at that stage. In effect he was asking Cousins to surrender. On 28 May Cousins decided to make a decisive move to bring the dispute to a head. He and his deputy, Harry Nicholas, went to see Sir Vincent Tewson at the TUC. They warned him that they were now under exceptional pressure to spread the strike. The pressure was so strong and the provocation so great (he cited Macleod's ostentatious rejection of his peace feeler) that it would be impossible for the union's leader to resist it for much longer. The moment for decisive action had arrived, Cousins told Tewson. The TUC General Secretary understood the message and summoned a special meeting of the General Council for the next day. At this meeting they appointed a committee of five to mediate with the Government. It consisted of the TUC chairman, the late Sir Tom Yates, Sir Tom (now Lord) Williamson, Harold (now Lord) Collison, Robert Willis and Sir Vincent Tewson. (George Woodcock as Assistant General Secretary, also went with the team.)

Their first move was to see Iain Macleod to ask him to intervene and help restart negotiations. Macleod refused once again – on the now routine grounds that he could see no useful purpose in resumed negotiations until the TGWU was ready to accept London Transport's terms. The TUC immediately asked to see the Prime Minister.

The next day, 30 May, the TUC committee went to 10 Downing Street. The purpose of the exercise was primarily to find a way out of the impasse by some skilfully drafted formula which could permit Cousins and the busmen to get off the hook (as the TUC saw their predicament) and to allow Sir John Elliot and London Transport a little more room to negotiate, while at the same time preserving the Government's policy more or less intact. There was not much difference between the Government and the TUC in this attitude – except for Robert Willis and George Woodcock who, as Tewson's deputy, did not really have a voice in the dialogue.

Macmillan knew he would have no substantial problem with the TUC. He knew this well before the meeting on 30 May because of the informal contacts which had taken place between them from the beginning of the bus strike. Without Cousins's knowledge, several senior members of the TUC maintained a regular and informal dialogue with the Prime Minister. Not until some months after the strike ended did Cousins realise the full extent of what had been going on behind his back. Several times Mr Macmillan had been assured by senior TUC men that they would contain Cousins; that there would be no TUC support for the busmen; that there was no desire among the majority of the TUC leadership to get into any confrontation with the Government. Indeed the Prime Minister was actively discouraged from showing any signs of agreeing to settle on Cousins's terms, because some of his TUC colleagues feared the sequel of a demonstrable success for the busmen. Iain Macleod told me years later that during the bus strike TUC leaders came to see him privately to urge that the Government should not submit to Cousins's demands : 'They wanted Cousins taken down a peg. They didn't like him. They wanted to ensure that the Government didn't cave in to him, because it would have made their job that much more difficult.'

Frank Cousins himself kept a sporadic diary during the London bus strike. In it he noted on 25 May 1958 :

In the presence of Bob Willis, Tom O'Brien advised me that Harold Macmillan and Winston Churchill asked him at 10 Downing Street, on the eve of the bus strike, whether Frank Cousins was trying to start a civil war or a revolution . . . Also mentioned the visit of Sir Vincent Tewson to Downing Street to see the Prime Minister and advise him that attitude of TUC would be to NOT give support to the busmen . . .

To this day there is a bitterness in Cousins's attitude toward some of his TUC colleagues for their behaviour at that period. He felt they let him down – but, more to the point, they let down the busmen and a great many other loyal trade unionists. His objection is not that they differed from him in political or industrial attitudes, but that they deceived him and conspired behind his back.

Not all of this was clear to Frank Cousins at the moment when the TUC's special team trooped into 10 Downing Street on 30 May to see Harold Macmillan and his Transport Minister Harold Watkinson. It was a bright May morning and Mr Macmillan was at his stately best, duly grave and saddened by the whole unfortunate business. Another 'local difficulty'. How tiresome it all was. The rituals proceeded. The Prime Minister recounted the whole story from the time of the arbitration award. He also took them through the railway settlement and dwelt on his own handling of that dispute, describing with heavy implication how the railway union leaders had helped him to reach a settlement 'which was generally approved by all moderate people'.[6]

Sir Tom Yates reported to the Prime Minister the events of the General Council meeting the previous day and of Cousins's warning that the strike might be extended. Yates pleaded for a Government initiative to leave London Transport free to resume negotiations and, perhaps, in a position to offer those busmen excluded from the Industrial Court award some increase in the future. Macmillan refused to bring pressure on London Transport or, to put it more accurately, to release the pressure already firmly placed on Sir John Elliot. But he offered a formula on which, he argued, fruitful negotiations could be resumed. The Macmillan plan was for :

1. Acceptance by the TGWU of the 8s. 6d. award for Central London busmen.
2. The inclusion of the Green Line busmen in this settlement.
3. Negotiations between London Transport and the union to fix a definite date for a pay review for the remaining men not included in the award.

In short, a promise of more pay for the excluded men without actually fixing an amount or an operative date for implementation. Towards the end of the meeting Macmillan turned on the pressure by emphasising that the Government was not prepared to allow London Transport to negotiate under the threats that had been made of extending the strike to petrol-tanker drivers and workers in power stations supplying London Underground. He told the TUC that the Government would take steps to ensure that oil supplies were maintained. He hinted that weekend leave for troops might be cancelled as a contingency – and indeed later that day to the TUC's surprise the Government announced publicly that leave was being cancelled.

The TUC had assumed that the Prime Minister would keep that move up his sleeve, at least until they had a chance to discuss the situation with Frank Cousins.

At another meeting of the General Council, after they had seen Macmillan, the TUC leaders put it to Cousins that he ought to pick up the Prime Minister's formula as a basis for negotiation. There were concessions in it, but he wasn't impressed – since, to him, it didn't appear to offer a major concession. But he agreed to put it to his busmen's committee. The next day the busmen agreed to reopen talks with Sir John Eliot; but after two days of further haggling, in which they sought to pin down Elliot to a precise offer and a date, the talks broke down. The union put it to Sir John that they could not recommend a return to work without some offer to the

6. Harold Macmillan, *Riding the Storm*, p. 717.

excluded busmen – even a token offer. They suggested a payment of 4s. a week as an immediate increase, with an unspecified further rise after the pay review. London Transport refused, because they knew this would be unacceptable to the Government. It was back to total deadlock. In the meantime the NUR and ASLEF had told Frank Cousins that the most they were prepared to do in support of the busmen was to refuse to work any extra trains put on to cushion the impact of the bus strike. That apart, they would work normally.

On 4 June the TUC mediators saw the Prime Minister again; it was touch and go whether Cousins would now bring out the petrol-tanker men. Macmillan urged the TUC to do all it could to dissuade him from this action.

'Give no support to Cousins,' Macmillan warned the TUC, as he made it clear that he neither could nor would urge Sir John Elliot to go beyond his formula of the previous meeting.[7]

There followed yet another meeting of the TUC General Council, where the mediating group reported on its meeting with the Prime Minister. This time they did not pull their punches nor conceal that, in their view, it was the end of the road. There was no point, they told Cousins, in any further meetings with Macmillan. It was now up to him to retreat as best he could. They put it to him with brutal candour. Cousins was equally candid. He demanded to know from them: 'How soon was this strike going to be developed into something that somebody was going to take notice of?'

The time had come, Cousins told them, where the strike must either be extended or ended. The TGWU could – and were prepared to – bring out their members in oil distribution and power stations. But what he demanded now to know from his colleagues, he declaimed, waving his arm round the oval arrangement of tables in the General Council chamber, was how much support he could expect from his fellow trade union leaders. Would they follow normal trade union practice if *their* members became involved – a practice which would, in effect, mean support?

'What is your attitude?' he finally demanded.

They told him their attitude: they were simply not prepared to see the bus strike extended. Indeed, they wanted the strike settled as quickly as possible, on the best available terms. It was now up to Cousins to accept the inevitable. That was their answer. An extension of the strike, they told the TGWU leader, would mean a direct conflict with the Government which would end in failure with disastrous consequences for the whole trade-union movement. Sir Tom Yates told Cousins flatly, 'You might as well settle now. We are not prepared to back you in an all-out strike.'

He echoed Macmillan's warning that if the oil-tanker drivers were called

7. Harold Macmillan, *Riding the Storm*, p. 717.

out, then the troops would move in and shift supplies. The NUR leader Sidney Greene confirmed that his underground members would not come out in support of the busmen. Cousins had no cards left. He was isolated and embittered. Tewson asked him to stay behind after the meeting to help draft a Press statement.

'Why?' snorted Cousins. 'Are you ashamed of what you've done?'[8]

The terse Press statement simply stated: 'The General Council decided to advise the Transport and General Workers Union against any extension of the stoppage to other groups of workpeople.'

Talks between London Transport and the union were resumed the next day, but there was still deadlock, because Sir John Elliot remained adamant against committing himself to a precise cash figure for the excluded busmen. In fact he personally wanted to make such an offer as a gesture of goodwill, but he knew he dare not. Sir John has told me how he saw the Chancellor to try to persuade him of the need to make some gesture, but it was another ten days before the Government allowed Elliot any room for manœuvre. On 6 June Frank Cousins called a delegate conference of busmen to inform them of the TUC position. He also reported that their negotiating committee had voted by 7 to 6 to extend the strike to other groups in the TGWU. Cousins told the delegates that it was now up to them; but he warned them that if they did spread the strike within the union they could expect no support from other unions nor from the TUC. It was true, he reported, that local leaders of the London Underground – members of the NUR – had voted to strike each Monday in support of the busmen. But Sidney Greene had instructed his membership to ignore that strike appeal. Cousins himself opposed the recommendation from the busmen's committee to extend the strike and the delegate conference accepting his warning voted by 71 to 60 against spreading the dispute. Yet they voted unanimously to reject the latest terms for settlement offered by London Transport and agreed to continue the strike. Cousins commented after that meeting: 'There has never been anything like this in the history of the British trade union movement for the last thirty years. There has not been one word raised of wavering or fear or desire to go back.'

None the less, the climax had been reached. It was now a question of time. The days trickled by as Cousins sought a dignified retreat. He saw Macleod and suggested again that London Transport be allowed to name a token figure. But the Minister of Labour was not averse to rubbing salt into the exposed wounds. He ostentatiously remained unhurried about getting negotiations restarted.

On 12 June, the day before Cousins summoned his bus delegates again for what was scheduled to be the finale, the TUC agreed to ask other unions

8. Frank Cousins's own description to the author.

to put borrowing funds at the disposal of the TGWU, which had already spent over £1 million on the bus strike. The TGWU had ample resources, but was anxious not to sell off its investments in a hurry since that would have involved a considerable financial loss. The unions responded generously to that appeal, especially as they knew the end was in sight.

On 13 June the negotiating committee put a recommendation before a delegate conference proposing a return to work. Frank Cousins addressed the rank-and-file busmen's conference, wearied, saddened and bitter. He listed the catalogue of disappointments: the TUC's refusal to support an extension of the strike; London Transport's stubborn resistance to any concession proposal; the Government's determination to fight; the isolation of the busmen.

'In view,' he told them, 'of the forces ranged against us,' it would not be in their interests to continue the struggle. He hinted that once the strike was off it would probably be possible for Sir John Elliot to make an offer to the country busmen excluded from the original award. Elliot had told Cousins that once work was resumed he would be in a stronger position to make some offer. An end to the strike, he thought, would take some of the Government pressure off him. At least that is what Elliot assumed. Cousins fastened on to that hope, and the delegate conference voted by 94 to 32 with six abstentions to call off the bus strike.

It seemed to be the end – but it wasn't. To everyone's astonishment – Government, TUC, London Transport and, it must be said, Frank Cousins himself – the garage-by-garage vote rejected the decision of the delegate conference. The depot votes were announced on 17 June, and the result was stunning: 54 garages voted to return to work, 64 to stay out. The strike was to continue – after six weeks of bitterness and what appeared to be a forlorn struggle. Some national newspapers had already taken it for granted that the strike was over and were left looking rather absurd. Why did so many garages vote like this, against all the odds? Partly because of a London Transport notice posted in all depots announcing that there would be severe cuts in bus schedules once work was resumed. It was inept and crude and it certainly backfired against management. It added to the feelings of bitterness and frustration among the busmen who, with a remarkable tenacity, decided that even if they were facing defeat they were not going to accept ignominious surrender terms. Mr Harold Macmillan noted this demonstration by the busmen as an 'illustration of the fact that the Englishman did not know when he was beaten'. It made him, he said, 'feel a genuine if somewhat reluctant admiration for their doggedness.'[9]

The final stages of the strike were to be still more filled with drama. On 19 June a formula was issued by London Transport which carried the pledge

9. Harold Macmillan, *Riding the Storm*, p. 718.

that the country busmen would receive an 'agreed increase' from the resumption of work and that other excluded grades would have their pay reviewed – a retreat from their earlier position. London Transport also toned down its earlier statement about cuts in bus services. Originally it had specified a 10 per cent cut; this time no precise figure was mentioned. Even so, there was an explicit warning that London Transport's serious financial problems, and the fall in demand for its services, would involve cuts. On 19 June the terms were put to another delegate conference. This time the vote was 113 to 15 (with 4 abstentions) for acceptance. The depots confirmed this vote on the clear understanding 'that the country busmen were to get a pay rise no less favourable than that of the Central London busmen. Buses were back on the London streets on 21 June.

Yet within hours of the first bus leaving its depot Sir John Elliot and Frank Cousins were locked again in a fierce dispute about the terms of the settlement. The dispute over figures continued through July before the TGWU, finally exhausted, accepted with resignation the London Transport offer of 5s. for most of the country busmen, with an extra 7s. 6d. for those country service (Green Line) busmen driving single-decker buses. Cousins and the busmen's negotiating committee regarded this as a serious breach of a pledge by Sir John Elliot. Cousins maintains that the original promise – on which the strike was called off – was for increases ranging from 6s. 6d. to 7s. 6d. a week for the busmen excluded from the original 8s. 6d. award. The evidence strongly suggests that Sir John intended to pay this, but was forced to withdraw his private offer under the severest pressure from the Government. In fact it almost led to Sir John's dismissal from the chairmanship.

Sir John Elliot issued a public statement denying that any figure had been mentioned in the final stages which led up to the ending of the bus strike. This is not how Frank Cousins recalls it. Nor indeed does it square with a point put to me by Iain Macleod who, though absent from Britain during the closing stages of negotiations, recalled vividly that Sir John was ready to go beyond the Government's prescribed limit in order to settle. This occurred immediately after the bus garages surprised everyone by voting to continue the strike. 'We almost sacked him, there and then,' Macleod told me later. Sir John himself has admitted to me that he ran into serious trouble with some Ministers during the closing stages of the strike. Sir John and Sir Brian Robertson jointly approached the Chancellor to urge a Government concession to the busmen. But the Chancellor wouldn't accept this view. He was accompanied by Harold Watkinson, who felt no less strongly that the Government must resist the busmen then than he had at the very outset. Heathcoat-Amory was finally persuaded that London Transport should make a token offer, privately, to test the temperature. He proposed 3s. 9d. extra. The Chancellor told Robertson and Elliot that the Government had no intention of letting Cousins off lightly: 'We feel he must be taught a lesson,' Heathcoat-Amory is alleged to have told the two chairmen. But Sir Brian and Sir John persuaded the Chancellor to think again and consult the Prime Minister. This he did, and later that night he telephoned the London Transport chairman to say that he withdrew his figure of 3s. 9d. He left it to Elliot to decide the appropriate amount, but warned him that it must be kept below the 8s. 6d. offered to Central London busmen by the Industrial Court.

'We were under every kind of pressure from Downing Street not to concede,' Sir John has told me with great frankness. 'The whole thing was laced with politics. They [the Government] were gunning for Frank Cousins. We had no written instructions, but . . . we were not free agents.'

Lord Watkinson has also told me that in his view the man who suffered most in the London bus strike was Sir John, because he was sandwiched between Government and union. The former Transport Minister admits that he frequently clashed with Elliot during the strike because the London Transport chairman would have been prepared to settle, but was told by Watkinson that if he did he would get no help from the Government and indeed would find himself in serious difficulties.

There is little doubt in my own mind that figures of 6s. 6d. and 7s. 6d. were mentioned in the informal talks between London Transport and the TGWU leaders in those final, fateful days. There was no bitterness between Elliot and Cousins as men; they were locked in an artificial battle with each other. Both of them knew the real arbiter was the Government. Elliot had considerable sympathy with Cousins personally and with the busmen's case. He desperately wanted to find a suitable compromise, but he was trapped from the beginning, rather like Cousins himself. Even at the end of the strike, having put the formula in which no figures were mentioned and having won an acceptance for it from Cousins and the busmen's delegate conference – after all that, Elliot was almost sacked for refusing to claim an outright victory over Cousins. He merely described the end of the strike as 'a victory for the London public', and when pressed to go further he refused to exult. This, allied to the fact that Ministers were convinced he had offered 'over the odds' to Cousins, brought Sir John a savage scolding from the Tory 1922 Committee. It called upon Macmillan to sack him. Elliot himself believed his departure from London Transport was imminent and consulted his old friend Lord Beaverbrook, who agreed to talk with Macmillan to get the affair smoothed over – which he did.

On 17 July, in a last despairing cry of anguish at the manner of their treatment, the TGWU leaders called off their attempt to get the settlement for most of the country bus workers raised above 5s. A long statement approved by a delegate conference complained that the union had in effect been sold a pig in a poke.

'This conference is convinced', it declared, 'that the membership would not have called off the strike' on the basis of London Transport's interpretation of the settlement terms. It continued : 'We finally wish to record our opinion that the treatment of our wages claim allied to the now known news of the alarming proposals of the LTE to drastically reduce services and close garages makes it virtually impossible to have any beneficial form of cooperation with the LTE in the future.' Sir Wilfred Neden was again called upon to try to patch up the quarrel, but to no avail. The London bus strike of 1958 ended on the same note of bitter and frustrated discord that had echoed throughout its seven weeks.

At the Trades Union Congress in Bournemouth later that year Frank Cousins refused to conduct an inquest into all those weeks of internal strife. He preferred to offer his thanks for the help he received and to resist the temptation to recriminate. Yet behind the guarded phrases and the evaded criticism every delegate knew how Cousins felt about his treatment by the majority of his TUC General Council colleagues : resentful and exasperated : 'We spent a lot of money on the bus strike and we were very grateful, I repeat, to those who helped us to bear that burden. We think we have never spent any money better since we have been in the union.'[10]

The total cost to the TGWU of the London bus strike was £1,170,000, which included strike pay and other financial assistance given to members and their families. The various appeals raised £193,000, which included substantial sums from within the TGWU itself as well as from other unions and the TUC's appeal. There was also a total of £364,000 loaned to the TGWU, on an interest-free basis, by other unions. The largest of these loans came from the General and Municipal Workers' Union, which offered £250,000. All were subsequently repaid.

What, then, is the verdict of time? Was the bus strike of 1958 an absurd and ill-thought-out adventure by Frank Cousins? Was it avoidable? Could he have achieved the increases he eventually secured for the country busmen without such an exhausting and embittered struggle? Was it poor judgement, misplaced zeal, an exaggerated view of the importance of rank-and-file decision-making? All these criticisms were thrown at Cousins then, and have often been repeated since. It is easy to recognise that there may be elements of truth in some of the charges, but they all miss the point. Of course the bus strike could have been avoided if Cousins had agreed to capitulate on principle at the outset; of course he might well have extracted a concession for those excluded from the arbitration award, had he played the Government's game and woven his tapestry differently. But given the man and his credo, given his set of principles and political attitudes, no other road was conceivable or acceptable.

10. TUC *Annual Report*, 1958, p. 434.

THE BUSMEN'S STRIKE

After the bus strike I wrote in the *Daily Herald* that Frank Cousins was 'stronger than ever'. That suggestion was strongly challenged by some of Cousins's critics, who regarded the bus strike as having been one of his major failures, if not *the* main mistake of his career. I remain unrepentant and still believe my original assessment to have been correct. Why? It does not seem to me that even with hindsight one should unnecessarily complicate or over-intellectualise the reasons. The fact is that Cousins emerged stronger as a man. The TGWU emerged as a healthier and more vigorous organisation. And there was evidence of a feeling of greater self-respect not only among the busmen themselves but among most of the active rank and file of the union. It is worth noting that despite the length of the strike, the odds poised against them from the start, and the disappointments which repeatedly hit the busmen throughout the stoppage, only 3 per cent of the 50,000 busmen left the service by the end of the strike, although job opportunities in the London area were plentiful. Even by standards of the normal 'wastage' of manpower that is a significantly low figure.

Nor can the bus strike be regarded as just another industrial conflict. It was a very special dispute which helped to change, irrevocably, the relationship between leadership and led in the TGWU. The union Cousins had inherited was, as we have seen, an organisation with a long tradition of autocratic leadership. The strike decisively marked the end of that tradition. It is true that tears in the old fabric were already appearing before the bus strike. But it was Cousins's action in leading that strike which saved the TGWU from being weakened still further by internal conflicts and, in the process, also helped to lay the foundations for a period of internal repair. Cousins the socialist, Cousins the democrat, was pledged to change the old order which had reigned for so long in the TGWU, and although the bus-strike was very far from offering the ideal occasion there was no real choice, in the end. If he had failed to pick up the challenge, if he had continued to apply the old pattern of authority, his subsequent career would have been gravely damaged. His TUC speech of 1956 would have been regarded as empty rhetoric and his claims to champion a new democracy within the union would have been ridiculed as demagogic double-talk. It was, in short, a challenge he could not duck even if he could not win. It was also an act of great courage.

The price he paid may have been a high one; but the cost of inaction would have been much greater. I quote my own assessment, again in the *Daily Herald*, at the time : 'You can't inject democracy at the drop of a hat and expect calm responsibility from men who have for years felt the needle pricks of frustration . . . the bus strike has been a remarkable exercise in trade union democracy as well as an epic wages struggle.'

I remember calling on Frank Cousins at a critical moment towards the climax of the strike. He sat tired, somewhat dejected and looking terribly lonely, in his spacious office at Transport House. The bust of Ernest Bevin stared down at a pile of letters on his desk – some of them containing contributions to the strike fund, others full of abuse against Cousins, his family, the union and the busmen. I ventured to ask him whether the whole exercise had been worth it. He looked at me through his lenses. 'I happen to believe in democracy,' he said quietly. 'It's as simple as that.' It would be easy to deride that simplicity. Many of his critics did so at the time, and have done since. I have asked Frank Cousins for his candid view on whether the bus strike was, from his own personal point of view, a 'necessary strike': was it necessary, for instance, to establish an authority for himself and his new policies in the TGWU? Was it necessary in order to administer a psychological shock to the union, groomed and grounded as it had been for so long in different attitudes, to expect different responses from its leaders? Was it perhaps necessary as an act of open defiance of the conventional wisdom and trade union orthodoxy; or again to convince Government and employers that Frank Cousins really meant to practise what he had been preaching? Cousins denies that these motivations were predominant or even significantly present in his mind at the time. He was faced with a particular industrial problem; he believed his members had a right to a greater voice in determining policy; and he saw the busmen's cause as a morally just one as well as industrially correct.

The fact that it was also loaded with political dynamite, fraught with complicated strategic difficulties; that it would lead him into a possible confrontation with the Government as well as his TUC colleagues, did not loom large at first. Perhaps it ought to have done; perhaps he ought to have thought through every possibility and every likely pitfall. He did not do that. His reactions were perhaps too instinctive, too much lacking in the traditional cunning and caution of the long-distance negotiator. But that was his style. He acted on the basis of what he thought to be right and against what he profoundly believed to be wrong.

'After the bus strike,' he has since told me, 'the union became more mature. The men themselves also became more mature. And, in my view, the whole British trade union movement became more mature.' In that sense he was also admitting that he too became more mature.

'Of course no one in the TUC would accept that view – but it is my belief. One of the good things that came out of that dispute was an awareness of the importance of trade unionism: an awareness that had not been there for some time previously.'

Frank Cousins probably underestimated the impact the bus dispute *did* have on TUC thinking. Several members of the TUC staff of that time have told me that both the strike and the personal impact of Cousins's views inside the General Council had a traumatic effect on the entire TUC establishment. They claim that the strike changed the basis on which the

TUC had conducted its relationship with Government since the war: it transformed the declaration of October 1951 in which it pledged that it would 'seek to work amicably' with whatever Government was in power and that its function was to work for the improvement of the 'general condition' of Britain even under a Conservative Government. This attitude dominated all TUC policies until Frank Cousins arrived on the scene. It was the London bus strike of 1958 that changed it.

Bernard Dix, a member of the TUC staff at that time, has suggested to me: 'Cousins managed to force from the General-Council the recognition that there was a direct inter-relationship between industrial affairs and the philosophical content which determined a Government's economic policy.' In Mr Dix's view the London bus strike was much more decisive in influencing the TUC, both in terms of internal staff attitudes and the policies of the General Council, than the great H-bomb dispute which exploded in the trade union movement the following year. And this view is shared by a wide range of people, many of whom were opposed to Cousins's policies throughout. Frank Cousins himself accepts this evaluation of the bus strike:

> If I were to say, out of all the things I have done what was best for the working-class movement, I would say the London bus strike. It was a fight against injustice. We had a wage freeze; we had said we weren't going to accept it. We kept our word. After our strike the road haulage men, the miners and the engineers all had settlements . . .

He told me he was convinced of that at the time and he sees no reason to change his mind now. One might recall the claim made in the TGWU *Record* at the moment the strike was ending, though before the final wrangling on the cash settlement had been resolved:

> Whatever the actual outcome may be in the monetary sense this can be said in all truth: the London busmen have won a victory for every trade unionist with a wage claim pending. By their determination they have at least placed a brake on the Government policy which has sought to ensure that wages shall not rise with the cost of living.[11]

The Press treatment of the bus strike and of Frank Cousins personally was almost entirely hostile, with notable exceptions like the *Daily Herald*, the *Daily Mirror* and the *Morning Star*. Indeed, the Labour Correspondent of *The Times* in his summing up of the strike observed:

> From the beginning [Frank Cousins] looked upon the strike as a struggle between the Government and the workers as a whole. He seemed to picture

11. TGWU *Record*, July 1958, p. 32.

himself as a sort of Prometheus defying the gods of the Establishment on behalf of ordinary men and at times almost to welcome the prospect of noble defeat with the Press eagles picking at his liver. Engrossed in this role he may have neglected to use all the mundane arts of the negotiator.

More down-to-earth union leaders say he could have got as much for his men without a strike and, for most of them, got it earlier. This is as may be. In any case he might answer that there is a long-term gain in showing the Government they cannot impose a wages policy on the unions without a struggle.

The *Daily Mirror* more succinctly declared:

> After nearly seven weeks the London bus strike is over. For the strikers' leader Frank Cousins it has been seven weeks of abuse. He has been accused of arrogance and self conceit. He has been painted as a man out to 'challenge' the Government. He has been held up as a troublemaker whose schemes were designed for political ends. All these attacks have proved to be without foundation . . .

To the active adversaries of the day – like Macmillan and Watkinson – Cousins subsequently appeared as a man of great integrity, goodwill and idealism, though not very realistic. He tried to change the ball game when he was not in possession of the ball, and that, to the Ministers of the day, seemed an absurd waste of energy and enterprise. Sir John Elliot has reflected:

> The truth is that Frank Cousins had no hope of winning that strike. I told Frank that the public would beat that strike by walking; after all it was May, not winter. But of course he was pushed into the strike by his busmen's committee. It was the tail wagging the dog and Frank was beaten by London Transport standing firm; the public who walked and the Government who were determined to have his head on a platter . . .[12]

As for the busmen themselves Sir John has remained on their side. He believed their claim was a just one, even if impracticable in that political climate; and he was, and is, full of admiration for their spirit and behaviour during the strike. 'Do you realise', he asked me, 'that not a single pane of glass was broken in any of the L.T. garages throughout the whole of the strike?'[13]

Iain Macleod accepted that the London bus strike was the turning point in post-war industrial relations. Up till then the Ministry of Labour (now the Department of Employment) had tried to carry out an anomalous role

12. Sir John Elliot to the author.
13. *Ibid.*

of neutrality as between Government economic policy and the routine operation of industrial life : its role was that of an arbiter on what was reasonable and fair within the context of some unwritten code of industrial justice
– a code that had become more or less universally accepted in post-war
Britain. It was Monckton's role as Minister of Labour to sustain that code
after the Conservative victory of 1951. But it was Macleod's role to change
it.

He regretted what he felt he had to do to Cousins, and he insisted to me
later that there was no intention, at the start, to use the strike as a weapon
with which to beat down Cousins personally – though eventually that is
what it became.

Be that as it may, there is no doubt that the Government eventually used
the strike to the maximum to try to damage Cousins; and used the antipathy
of Cousins's colleagues on the TUC General Council as part of their justification. Macleod told me : 'Cousins didn't fit in to the TUC Establishment
– just as, later, he didn't fit into the Cabinet Establishment. He isn't the
type.' In Macleod's view Frank Cousins was 'a loner', a man who tempera-
mentally liked to play a lone role : 'a simple purist', as Macleod described
him to me. 'Not an ambitious man in the political sense; but a man who
identifies himself with the people he comes from.'

The political sequel to the bus strike became one of the major controversies
both inside and outside the Labour Party throughout 1959. After Labour's
defeat that October many of Cousins's old critics resurrected their criticisms
by alleging that the bus strike had seriously damaged the whole Labour
image. They attributed to him the reputation being acquired by the trade
unions, especially in the eyes of middle-class public opinion, of being the
'bully-boys' of the Labour Movement. Certainly the Conservatives attacked
the Labour Party in Parliament for their defence of the bus strike and for
associating themselves so completely with Cousins's attack on Government
wages policy. Macleod in particular rebuked Hugh Gaitskell for defending
the unions, especially the London busmen. It was the clear purpose of the
Conservative attack to demonstrate to public opinion that the Labour Party
was so wedded to the trade unions that their Parliamentary leaders dare not
criticise the major unions even when, as it was shrewdly implied, they did
not really agree with an issue such as the bus strike. The public opinion polls
in the summer of 1958 showed a substantial shift towards the Conservatives
and reflected a big rise in Macmillan's own popularity. As Richard Crossman's diaries note, Hugh Gaitskell was 'gloomy' and felt depressed about
the situation and about growing criticism within the Labour Party of his
own role as Party leader. A number of Gaitskell's supporters in the Labour
Party and the TUC suggested to him that part of the decline in Labour's
public standing must be due to the bus strike and to Frank Cousins himself.

Crossman noted at the time : 'When Frank Cousins threatened to pull the petrol lorry drivers out Nye [Bevan] offered to go with him to Frank Cousins and tell him it would be utterly disastrous.'[14] And Crossman records a conversation he had with Gaitskell at the time in which the Labour Party leader observed : 'Of course we lost a lot by supporting that strike and we got no kudos within the TUC because they hate Cousins.'[15]

No doubt the Labour Party's 'image' was dented by the bus strike at the time, but it is hard to sustain the claim that it had any measurable effect on the election result of October 1959. There may be more validity in the accusation that it was affected by Frank Cousins's opposition to the H-bomb, which had reached a new peak that summer (and was already threatening to split the Labour Party). But the election came sixteen months after the London bus dispute. By then the conflict had slipped from the front of the public memory and there is no evidence to show that even where it was recalled it had any adverse effect on Labour's electoral potential. The third successive Conservative election victory of October 1959 was not so much an election lost by Labour as one won by Harold Macmillan and a successful Tory team. They profited from a national mood of economic well-being, rising wages, rising output, rising profits, stable retail prices – a period so often described as the most successful, if brief, period in British post-war economic history. Britain was then what John Kenneth Galbraith called an affluent society.[16] Mr Macmillan assured the British public that it had never had it so good.

If the strike ended in a defeat for Cousins it is arguable that it was his fellow TUC leaders rather than the Government who were mainly responsible for his failure. With support from the railwaymen the London busmen would certainly have won a concession after a brief strike. With stronger moral support from the senior TUC men there is equally little doubt that Macmillan would have been ready to find a compromise formula to enable Sir John Elliot to settle at a much earlier stage – and on more favourable terms. It was primarily the political, rather than the industrial, challenge which undermined Frank Cousins's chances of success – success at least, in the clearly perceptible sense. His was the forerunner of the great challenges to Government and managerial authority which in the later 1960s and the 1970s were to become so much a part of our changing social and industrial pattern. He stepped out of line and refused to accept the traditional values and practices of his period. In present-day terms what he achieved at the time might seem puny compared with the rewards of more recent industrial conflicts. But that is the price the pioneer must always be prepared to pay.

It is interesting and not a little instructive now to read the remarks of

14. Richard Crossman, the unpublished diaries, 11 July 1958.
15. *Loc. cit.*
16. J. K. Galbraith, *The Affluent Society* (Hamish Hamilton, 1958).

Jack Jones, Cousins's successor as TGWU General Secretary, at a TGWU rally held in June 1958. The bus strike had reached its climax and the end was in sight. Frank Cousins told the union rally that the TUC had, in effect, failed him. They had failed to recognise, he claimed, that the bus strike and its political implications was 'the most serious problem the trade union movement had faced since 1926', and Jack Jones, who was then secretary of the Midland region of the union, accused the TUC of being in a 'conspiracy' with the Government: a conspiracy, he declared, which had isolated Frank Cousins in a way which compared with the TUC's treatment of Arthur Cook, the miners' leader, in the General Strike of 1926. Jones accused the TUC leadership of having become 'apologists for the Government's policies, rather than trade union spokesmen on behalf of their members'. It was a bitter comment on a bitter episode. In its way the London bus strike of 1958 was as much a watershed in the development of trade unionism as the General Strike of 1926 – or the miners' strikes of 1972 and 1974. It was a power struggle between a Government and a great trade union; something that is now a rather familiar pattern but which was unique in the late 'fifties.

Chapter Fourteen

THE BOMB EXPLODES

From 1956 to 1958 the impact of Frank Cousins on the industrial scene sent violent shock-waves through the entire trade union movement. From 1958 to 1961 his impact politically had a similar profound effect throughout the Labour Party. This was mainly, though by no means wholly, due to his stand against nuclear arms. No event in Britain since the war has stirred such a national response as the campaign to ban the H-bomb. The Ban-the-Bomb cry became a slogan which seemed to symbolise almost all radical dissent. It expressed a mood, rather than a programme of action: the cumulative moral reaction to and rejection of the creeping cynicism of post-war world affairs and its influence on domestic political values. It was an eruption of passion and anger against 'things as they were', rather than a clear, far-sighted policy or even rational examination of what might be politically feasible. To this extent Nye Bevan's famous description of the scene at the 1957 Labour Party conference as an 'emotional spasm' contained more than a grain of truth, though it came oddly from the man who, more than any other British politician, had a matchless capacity to assess and articulate the emotional moods of contemporary society.

The Campaign for Nuclear Disarmament was born in January 1958 at a meeting held in the home of Canon John Collins of St Paul's at 2, Amen Court, underneath the shadow of the Cathedral. Frank Cousins was not there; nor did he attend the public launch of the campaign a month later, on 17 February, at the Central Hall, Westminster; and he took no active part in CND activities during 1958. He was preoccupied with industrial problems, notably the London bus strike. He knew what was going on and had already established contact with Canon Collins, but had no intention of publicly associating himself with the campaign at that stage. With Nance he was in Trafalgar Square at Easter 1959 for the finale of the second Aldermaston march, yet when Canon Collins, speaking at the plinth of the Nelson Column, invited them to join the platform, they declined.

Cousins still had to persuade the TGWU to support nuclear disarmament. The test would come at the union's biennial delegate conference in July 1959. Until then he felt obliged to concentrate his activities on the committees now at work in the Labour Party and TUC seeking to persuade the Party leadership to go beyond the commitments of the 1957 conference decisions. He told Canon Collins at an early stage in CND's life that he preferred to remain in the background for the time being. But his mere presence in Trafalgar Square that Easter was an augury, enough to set all the alarm bells ringing again. Indeed, it was meant to be a warning message that since his efforts in the joint Labour Party-TUC committee on nuclear disarmament appeared to be getting no further he was poised to lead his union in defiance of official policy. But we are jumping ahead.

Cousins's reluctance to get too deeply involved in the CND campaign in the year of its birth, because of his preoccupation with industrial problems, was certainly not due to his belief that his industrial and political activities were mutually exclusive – quite the opposite. Indeed he was frequently criticised at the time, even more strongly later, for mixing politics and trade unionism too freely. The critics included a number of his own union officials and even some vocal rank-and-file members; but the more open criticism came generally from politicians (including leading figures in the Labour Party) and from the Press, which by now had come to see Frank Cousins as the big bogeyman of the 'wild left'. In a way he had taken over that mantle from Nye Bevan who, since his Brighton speech of 1957, was being increasingly fêted as a responsible statesman and even a potential national leader.

Yet Frank Cousins was enough of a Marxist to hold the view that the socialist can never separate his trade unionism from his political action, or *vice versa*. It has been said of Cousins that he, more than any other trade union leader, was more of a political animal than an industrial leader. Yet he could not understand why his critics made what he regarded as such a false distinction. He saw himself first and foremost as a trade union leader, because that is where he had his power base, but to pretend that the leader of the country's biggest trade union was not (or ought not to be) a political figure of considerable significance was, to his way of thinking, an absurdity. Moreover, he was a deeply committed socialist who saw his role in the union as parallel to his political objectives and ideals. To be sure, there were many occasions when the two paths were separated by the routine practicalities of life around the negotiating table. The detailed processes of industrial relations leave no room for politics in the routine sense of the term. Yet this did not mean that Cousins ever went into industrial negotiations without a political dimension to his thinking. It was always there, ready to be used in support of his industrial case. In the wider political arena he saw his role as much more than that of a typical trade union official whose concern was primarily to add a few more pounds to the pay packets of his members. He always saw himself as being involved in the wider task of changing society. He regarded social change as fundamental to a real and qualitative improvement in life for his members and all working people. Without such a change the trade-union function, vital though it is to an extension of a living democracy, would become sterile and restricted by the market values of a capitalist society. Cousins believed that these wider objectives, and the great dreams, could be realised only by an attack along the whole of the political battle-line. Any separation, therefore, between his role as a political and a trade union animal was to him a distinction without a difference : a matter of emphasis, not one of principle. He was in the business of social and economic change, and he wanted to use all the instruments and weapons he could grasp hold of.

Certainly there were no contradictions in his mind between his industrial and political objectives after the London bus strike. He was determined to press forward with his campaign against wage restraint and to try to secure higher living standards for his members. At the same time he wanted the TUC, as the collective institution of organised labour, to recognise that there was a more general and cooperative role to be played. Cousins wanted it to raise its sights above the routine functions of month-to-month industrial affairs, to consider a longer-term and altogether broader, even philosophical, approach. He asked his TUC colleagues, shortly after the Congress of 1958, to reflect more deeply on the whole political and social perspective now opening up. He suggested that they might consider setting up a small group of TUC leaders to form a kind of 'think-tank' on future policy and perspectives. His idea was that this special group should be separate from the normal sub-committees of the TUC General Council, and kept as small as possible so that it could get down to a working programme. This could then be put to the rest of the General Council for discussion and ultimately debated at a future Congress. It was the Cousins plan for thinking out and then acting on a programme across the entire political and industrial spectrum. He proposed three headings for discussion as a starting point : 1) wages policy for the future; 2) the role of public ownership in British industry and union relations with the State; 3) international affairs – which he saw as inextricably bound up with future domestic social and economic development. At that stage he was, incidentally, by no means hostile to the general concept of the Common Market.

His imaginative proposal, linking as it did the whole chain of contemporary political and industrial affairs, could have developed into a dialogue at the top of the trade union movement which would have been unique and might have led to a far more coherent policy. But the Cousins Plan was rejected, indeed dismissed almost out of hand. Some of his General Council colleagues thought the idea would simply duplicate work already being done by existing sub-committees. Others undoubtedly regarded it as a potential danger to the existing balance of power inside the General Council, since they saw it as a process by which Cousins might well increase his own influence and authority, which they were determined to contain. Writing in his own private diary at the time Frank Cousins observed : 'Clichés come fast and furious from both sides [meaning right- and left-wing members of the General Council] but there is no long-term thinking.' He despaired of his TUC colleagues ever getting down to it.

But he had no such inhibitions. At the Labour Party conference at Scarborough in 1958 he plunged into a major debate on education policy, the sequel to a debate that had gone on inside the Party throughout the year. And he did so with all the enthusiasm of a concerned father as well as a social critic.

Frank Cousins linked himself with those who were demanding an end to the public-school system which he believed to be one of the most divisive features of British society. The Labour Party's national executive had put before the conference a new policy statement on education which was designed to bring Party thinking up to date and to prepare an attractive policy on education to put before the electorate in 1959 – the year when it was already being assumed that Harold Macmillan would go to the country. But to Cousins's disgust this policy, 'Learning to Live', contained no significant references to the private sector – nothing about taking over the public schools. At their pre-conference meeting the TGWU delegation supported his proposal that the policy should be openly challenged and, if possible, made to include a demand for the ending of educational privilege. They agreed to support a composite motion calling for the abolition of fee-paying schools and their integration into the State system. The Party executive refused to be shifted from its policy as published, despite the frontal challenge from the TGWU; so the education debate, scheduled for the opening day, became the major talking-point on the eve of the Scarborough conference. On the morning the conference opened the newspapers were full of the Cousins challenge, already predicting a full-scale revolt led by the new bogeyman.

Frank Cousins's speech was in fact a modest and brief intervention, in which he sounded almost embarrassed to be questioning the Labour Party's fidelity to socialist principles. He confined himself to supporting the mover of the composite motion – Fred Peart, then MP for Workington [now Lord Peart], who made a particularly eloquent plea for educational equality. The essence of Cousins's case was that the public schools were not merely a system for buying educational privilege for a minority but, much more divisively, they were a cornerstone for the perpetuation of that privilege later in life. The public schools, he argued, fed and sustained the very privilege which supported them. 'We are facing the real issue,' he said, 'that this country's economic, international, political and industrial affairs are in the hands of a privileged group who pass privilege on from place to place.'

The Peart amendment was defeated, though by an extremely narrow margin (3,544,000 to 3,067,000), mainly because it would have meant sweeping the Party's carefully prepared education policy to one side and starting again from scratch. The next morning the *Daily Express* cried, in banner headlines across eight columns of front page : 'Cousins Rocks The Boat'. It was that man again. But he was a popular figure with the Party's rank-and-file delegates. Increasingly he was seen as a spokesman for the radical and left-wing idealism of the Labour Party, as well as a militant trade union leader who was ready to fight the Tory Government. When he went to the rostrum at the start of that Scarborough conference he was given a sustained welcome of applause before he uttered a word – a demonstration of the conference's feeling about the London bus strike (later in the week, during the economic affairs debate, Cousins paused to thank the conference for its many warm references to the busmen's fight).

We cannot leave that conference without noting Cousins's speech in the economic debate, because it was to become, in retrospect, a warning signal of what a future Labour Government could expect from the TGWU in terms of wage restraint. It was a muted reference, because the one thing he did *not* want to do at the 1958 conference was to 'rock the boat' or be accused of doing so. There were high hopes, not without reason, that Labour would win the anticipated 1959 General Election, and so the old question of a Labour Government's relations with the trade unions was a major topic. Informal discussions had been taking place between the Labour Party and TUC leaders, and Frank Cousins had already told Hugh Gaitskell and Harold Wilson that he was not prepared to accept wage restraint even under a Labour Government. Cooperation, caution, help and comfort – yes; but formal wage restraint? It was not on.

Cousins's attitude had still further upset several of his senior colleagues on the TUC General Council, notably the late Sir Alan Birch, the Shop and Distributive Workers' leader, who was also chairman of the economic committee and a close friend of Gaitskell. Cousins and Birch were increasingly coming into conflict on almost all aspects of TUC policy. During the bus strike Birch had made it clear to Cousins that nothing would induce him or his union to break any of their agreements in order to support the busmen. Birch certainly played a prominent part in destroying any hopes Cousins might have had of winning stronger backing from the TUC, and an almost obsessive hostility was now developing between the two men. It revealed itself at the 1958 Trades Union Congress in the manner in which they interpreted TUC economic policy in quite different ways : Birch was for moderation, Cousins for a continuing attack on the Government. It was repeated at the Scarborough conference, although Cousins leaned over backwards not to offend Gaitskell or seem to be challenging the Party's general economic policy. Even so it is worth recalling a part of Cousins's speech in 1958 because it does show quite clearly how his mind was working on the crucial issue of wages policy under a Labour Government:

> We have said that we do not accept and would not accept a policy of wage restraint, a transference of the economic problems of the community onto the shoulders of the organised and unorganised workers, merely as a means by which the economy could be balanced.
>
> We would not recognise that that was the way of solving the economic ills of the community. I have been a member of the TUC delegation who have seen the Chancellor of the Exchequer and the Prime Minister of the Conservative Government from time to time on this subject and that is the view we have expressed. And we do not change our views on the entitlement of the workers by a transference of Government from one Party to another.
>
> If we did we would be entitled to be accused, as certain sections of the community do describe us, as an adjunct, an industrial mouthpiece, of a political party. We are not that at all. We are the trade unions representing the workers, and we shall continue to do that whatever Government is in power, because that is democracy . . .

This was the basic issue which was to crop up again and again between then and 1964, when Frank Cousins joined the Wilson Government. It was the issue over which Cousins ultimately resigned from the Labour Cabinet. And there it was – the warning signal clearly flashed, as far back as the 1958 conference. Hugh Gaitskell's response when he wound up that debate at Scarborough was discreet. He knew Cousins's views; but he recognised there was no mileage in having an open row at that time. Moreover, he was relieved by the moderation of Cousins's speech and his palpable desire to paper over any cracks. Cousins, indeed, went out of his way to compliment Gaitskell on his approach to economic affairs, and to defend the Party leader from some conference critics who had raised a question mark against what they felt had been the rather tepid support given to the busmen's strike by the Parliamentary Labour Party. Cousins scolded these doubters and, perhaps with a touch of theatre, praised Gaitskell's handling of the busmen's strike in Parliament.

Indeed the Scarborough conference dispersed in an atmosphere of accord which surprised many and brought sceptical doubts from the commentators, who were more than ordinarily surprised at the harmony. But, of course, both Left and Right wings of the Labour Movement felt that 1959 would bring a Labour Government to power with Gaitskell as Prime Minister.

Economically there were many indications that the Macmillan Government had run out of ideas as well as steam. Production was falling, prices rising, wages pressure mounting and unemployment growing at a disturbingly rapid rate. The balance of payments situation was getting worse, with British exports running into increasing competition in world markets. To overcome the depressed state of industry the Government lowered Bank Rate to 4 per cent in November 1958, but the stimulus appeared to be too late and too little. By February 1959 unemployment had leapt to 620,000, the highest level since 1940, except for the special case of the 1947 fuel crisis.

It was in this atmosphere and at this time that the great debate over nuclear disarmament again began to splutter and eventually to explode into a conflict that was to dominate Labour politics almost completely for the next two years. At times all other issues seemed to be utterly submerged under the shadow of the Bomb; everything appeared obscured by the clouds of anger and recrimination, charge and counter-charge. The leadership and the whole future of the Labour Party was at stake.

In January 1958, under pressure from Frank Cousins, the TUC international committee saw Harold Macmillan and Selwyn Lloyd to urge that Britain should make a clear declaration that she would not be the first to use nuclear weapons. The Prime Minister and Foreign Secretary were courteous, understanding, even sympathetic in a patronising way. They assumed the TUC would recognise that Britain had no intention of being the first to use the Bomb the nuclear deterrent, they assured the TUC, was a defensive wall against the Russians. But of course, Selwyn Lloyd pointed out, if the Russians with their immense superiority in ground forces were to overrun Europe and threaten Britain, then we would have no option but to use our nuclear deterrent. That was why in the Government's view the TUC's proposal was quite unrealistic. The TUC committee went away like admonished schoolboys, having been given a lesson in first-principle military logic. But Cousins was far from assuaged. He still demanded TUC pressure for the declaration they had requested from Macmillan. Principally as a result of his agitation a joint meeting of the international committees of the Labour Party and the TUC was held at Transport House on 6 March. It was one of the longest meetings of all the many joint sessions between the two bodies held over the following two years. But it ended, as so often on this issue, in deadlock.

The argument was between Hugh Gaitskell, backed by an overwhelming majority, on one side, and Nye Bevan and Frank Cousins on the other. Bevan and Cousins, operating in harness, demanded that the Labour Party and TUC should come out with a clear and categorical declaration that Britain would not be the first to use the H-bomb. Gaitskell stubbornly resisted, never once shifting from his conviction that to make such a pledge would be tantamount to saying that 'we were prepared to have the H-bomb as a deterrent against nuclear attack but never as a deterrent against conventional attack, even if overwhelming. He could not accept such a commitment. It was very difficult when in opposition to commit yourself to what you would do in all circumstances but he had no doubt that a commitment never to use nuclear weapons first removes the only deterrent we have against a large-scale conventional attack'.[1]

In effect Gaitskell lined himself with Selwyn Lloyd, and this provoked Cousins to ask what the difference was between the Tory Government's defence policy and the Labour Party's policy.

Bevan, who at times seemed to be somewhat retracing his steps from Brighton, was passionate and vehement in his advocacy. He declared that he was utterly convinced the Russians had no intention of overrunning Europe; but even if he was wrong about that he did not think it was possible 'to combat an evil with an evil which is greater than that which is being combated. He would prefer to be overrun by the Communists than have civilisation extinguished.'[2]

Gaitskell drew most of his vocal support from Cousins's opponents on the TUC side : Tewson, O'Brien, Webber, Williamson, Yates and Hayday. Cousins had only one supporter among his seven TUC colleagues – Robert Willis. At one moment, exasperated by Gaitskell's stubborn resistance to any compromise and Crossman's tortuous arguments on the metaphysics of defence policy, Cousins exploded. It was, he said, as if 'we seemed to be discussing H-bombs as though they were bladders on sticks . . . Britain was pretending she could match two great powers in destructive power, which was nonsense. Militarily we have only a nuisance value. But we have a tremendous moral value. Russia has told us that in future war will be economic and idealogical, not military. We are still talking as if the right thing to say is "If you attack us we will retaliate with H-bombs." We are carrying out a Conservative policy by saying that unless the Russians do what we want we will throw H-bombs at them.'[3]

But it was to no avail. The passion and the anger drained away. The weary meeting ended with a decision to launch 'a national campaign' to explain Labour's existing policy. This was that Britain should stop all nuclear tests, if necessary unilaterally, and then go all out to seek a summit conference on nuclear disarmament. The statement also contained demands for stopping all US air patrols by aircraft based in Britain carrying H-bombs, and also postponing the construction of US missile bases in Britain – at least until a summit conference had been tried. In effect this statement was the first specific reference to multilateral nuclear disarmament as distinct from unilateralism : a fundamental distinction, of course, and one that was to become crucial in the years ahead.

But the meeting from which the statement emerged produced no signifi-

1. Official minutes of the National Executive of the Labour Party joint meeting with the TUC, 6 March 1958.
2. *Ibid.*   3. *Ibid.*

cant change in policy. As Gaitskell was reported to have said, 'It brings Brighton up to date.' This is precisely what it did – no more.

Even before the declaration was issued, however, the row inside the Labour Party had erupted in full force, as a result of an initiative in a most unusual quarter, the *Daily Herald*. The *Herald* had only recently secured a loosening in the terms of its agreement with the TUC as the official organ of the TUC and the Labour Party. There was now a much less binding agreement with Odhams Press (then its publishers) designed to give the *Herald* greater freedom of action to compete on commercial terms with its main Fleet Street rivals. A less formal link with the TUC and Labour Party was thought to be an essential part of this development, though the Odhams management had given a clear pledge that the paper would continue its support for the Labour Party and the trade-union movement. On 26 February, however, the *Herald* astonished the Labour Party, the TUC and most of Fleet Street with a front-page editorial demanding that Britain should give the world a lead by ending the manufacture, as well as the testing, of nuclear weapons. Under the title 'A policy for Staying Alive' the *Herald* went well beyond official Labour Party and TUC policy with what amounted to a clear declaration in favour of unilateralism. It was pure CND. 'We will get peace only by general disarmament. And we alone can give a decisive lead', the paper declared. Inside the *Herald* office, where I then worked as Industrial Correspondent (and later as Industrial Editor) the enthusiasm among the majority of the journalists for this unique departure from the Party line was uncontainable. The editor, the late Douglas Machray, after consulting half a dozen of his leading colleagues and others on the staff (including myself) believed that the paper should come out with a clear lead on the most important issue of the day, for Britain and for the world. With great courage he rejected friendly warnings that he was heading into a tornado. He was convinced that it was right for the *Herald* to go ahead, and positive that what the *Herald* was saying was the right policy for the Labour Movement. The next day the storm broke. Morgan Phillips, General Secretary of the Labour Party, was on the telephone first thing demanding space in the paper to attack and rebut the *Herald*'s audacity; Sir Vincent Tewson, the TUC General Secretary and a director of the paper, was beside himself with fury. But the *Herald* continued its campaign with yet another long editorial (albeit this time on page 4) repeating its advocacy of the previous day and inviting readers' views. Their response was amazing: over 13,000 letters poured into the office, most of them in support. Never in the paper's history had a policy campaign evoked such a swift reaction.

The *Herald* also published a letter from Morgan Phillips denouncing it for 'appearing to undermine the Party by such over-simplification of what is undoubtedly the main challenge of our time – that of human survival'. The editor hit back in a footnote: 'The intention of our present campaign is not to undermine but to invigorate the Labour Movement to which this paper is dedicated.' The battle continued until the official policy statement on defence came out in March.

The *Herald* editor came under exceptional pressure to tone down the campaign and at one stage came close to resignation. He was under crossfire from the leadership of both the Labour Party (including Hugh Gaitskell) and the TUC (except for Frank Cousins, who congratulated the *Herald* and Douglas Machray on their stand). Clearly the campaign could not be sustained at that pitch against the organised opposition of the Party and the TUC 'establishment'.

Douglas Machray recognised that he could not take the paper 'outside the limits of the TUC and Labour Party conference decisions'. But, he said, 'Not until I became convinced that the whole Labour Movement (or so I thought) was moving rapidly to a condemnation of the nuclear arms race and would be prepared to declare for unilateral action did I decide to take a stand in the paper.'

The paper organised a poll on the subject. On the morning that it appeared the managing director of Odhams Press phoned Machray to report that Hugh Gaitskell had been in touch with him to complain. The chief of Odhams demanded that Machray should 'discontinue the poll'. Machray refused and it went ahead as planned. Surrey Dane, then the editorial director of Odhams, phoned Machray subsequently to ask if he was prepared to justify his attitude to the TUC representatives on the *Herald*'s board of directors and to Gaitskell. Dane said he was prepared to stand by him, though he disagreed with Machray's views and attitude. Machray agreed to meet the *Herald* directors, including some TUC leaders and Gaitskell, at a luncheon in St Ermin's Hotel, Westminster.

In a rather bare, downstairs room of the St Ermin's, 'with a spare bar in one corner', Machray was confronted by Gaitskell, Dane and three TUC leaders: Tewson, Williamson and O'Brien, who jointly demanded to know whether he was aware of 'the split I had accentuated in the Movement'. Gaitskell, according to Machray, speaking in his 'gentle, modulated tones', attacked him and his motives. He accused Machray of 'ignorance of the Party policy', and suggested that he was 'under the influence of irresponsible elements in the Party'. He also referred to Machray's handling of the affair and, by implication, his 'thoughtless pacifist behaviour'. This riled the *Herald* editor to an explosion against the Party leader.

Douglas Machray had every reason to feel aggrieved. He had a distinguished war record: he fought in Burma, and was decorated by the French after the North Africa liberation. He says: 'I thumped the table and said, "You can call me what you like, Hugh, but don't call me a pacifist. I have my medals in the war to prove you're wrong. Do you want me to show them to you?"[4] Gaitskell apologised. But he continued to attack the *Herald*'s line. It became clear that the *Herald*, like Cousins, was isolated from the TUC and Party leadership.

At the March meeting of the TGWU's general executive committee Frank Cousins sought to strengthen the union's policy on the issue of nuclear disarmament, but he knew it was impractical until the next delegate conference in July 1959. So the TGWU policy statement remained roughly in line with the 6 March declaration, although its wording reflected the direction of its General Secretary's thinking and convictions. Indeed in a speech at Bristol on 23 March Cousins went on record, quite specifically, as being totally opposed to the manufacture of the H-bomb by Britain. Although the following year was dominated in his work by the industrial confrontation, he was still consumed with the belief that the Labour Movement ought to offer a decisive lead on the Bomb, and he became more and more convinced that he should play a leading part in trying to persuade it to do so.

The opportunity to bring the issue back to the boil come in April 1959, when Macmillan admitted to Parliament that nuclear fall-out had doubled in the previous year due to tests of H-bomb 'devices'. The unions were alerted and annual conferences, such as the engineers', began to revive demands for stronger action by the Labour Party. At the end of May the TUC took the initiative – again under Cousins's prodding and pressure – to re-open the unfinished dialogue of March 1958. It told the Labour Party that the time had come to revise the 15-month-old declaration in the light of major developments in nuclear weaponry and the alarming dangers resulting from the latest series of tests. It is possible that the time-scale for a resumed joint meeting of the Party and TUC leaders might have been slower had it not been for a phenomenal development.

Early in June the ultra-moderate General and Municipal Workers' Union, to the astonishment of everyone including their own leaders, voted for unilateralism at its annual conference in Scarborough. By 150 votes to 126, with 75 of the delegates either abstaining or absent (having tea), the GMW urged that the next Labour Government (expected at any time) should take 'unilateral action in ceasing to manufacture nuclear weapons'. This extraordinary incident has been put down to a fluke; a momentary lapse by the GMW leadership who had no idea that they were in such danger; or due perhaps to the fact that so many delegates were at their tea-break. My own view (I was there) is that these explanations are an over-simplification. They do less than justice to the wave of feeling that was beginning to sweep through the ranks of active trade unionists, as well as other sections of the Labour Movement – even in those unions with an unbroken record of conforming to orthodoxy. The fact is that the anti-Bomb

4. As told to author by the late Douglas Machray.

campaign was not confined to the radical Left, as many critics of CND alleged at first. It was already collecting wide support across the whole political (and indeed non-political) spectrum of British society.

Nevertheless, the General and Municipal Workers' vote stunned almost everybody, not least Hugh Gaitskell, who was a member of that union. That vote, rather more than Frank Cousins's continuing insistence on a new policy statement from the Labour Party, concentrated the minds of the Labour leadership. They knew they could no longer delay a resumption of talks between the TUC and the Party executive in an attempt to draft a fresh document on nuclear policy and disarmament. So a meeting that had been fixed for the end of July (timed to take place *after* the Transport Union's biennial delegate conference) was advanced to 23 June. Moreover, it was equally obvious, after the GMW vote, that some fresh development was necessary to raise the Labour Party's policy above the programme set out in March 1958. The formula devised was the concept of the non-nuclear club – an idea that had been floating around the international scene for some time and one which attracted a good deal of support in Britain because its central proposition was the attempt to check the manufacture of the H-bomb. It appealed to some on the Left of the Labour Party as well as to those on the Right; it even had adherents inside the Conservative Government and Whitehall; and it had won respectable support from academics in military studies.

But was it sufficient to satisfy and appease those who wanted Britain to go much further and give a distinctive moral lead? Was it enough to head off the groundswell of support for a clear declaration in favour of nuclear disarmament? The Labour leadership had few illusions about this. They knew it would not do that; they certainly knew that it would not neutralise the support for bodies such as CND; and they were also beginning to realise that it was unlikely to appease Frank Cousins. None the less, priority was to get something on paper that could divert the revolt spreading among more unions, even hitherto 'safe' unions like the GMW. There were also other key trade union conferences due in July, such as those of the miners and the railwaymen. So it was decided to press ahead quickly with the concept of the non-nuclear club, which a Labour Government would sponsor if the Party won the General Election. And it was this proposal that became the centrepiece for a joint meeting between the TUC and Labour Party leaders on 23 June.

The central issue was to try to unite the Labour Movement in readiness for the General Election (which Gaitskell and Bevan believed would almost certainly be in the autumn) and to present a policy statement which would head off the simmering revolt among the trade unions. To avoid Press leakages, great secrecy surrounded the circulation of advance drafts of the new document. The secrecy was far from successful, but even so the TUC leaders did not receive their copies until 10 o'clock in the morning of 23 June when they arrived at Congress House. The ten-page draft was difficult to absorb at such short notice and that in itself became an irritant. Yet the main point emerged quite clearly: every country except the United States and the Soviet Union would be invited to join the 'club' and asked to sign an agreement, preferably under the control of the United Nations, not to test, manufacture or possess nuclear weapons.

This agreement would be subject to international controls to ensure that the pledges were being honoured. And the Labour Party plan set out the promise that a Labour Government would, under such an international agreement, stop making nuclear weapons and even give up those that Britain already possessed. The first stage would be a limited agreement for a standstill on the development and production of nuclear weapons. The declaration stated that Britain did not deny that in taking such a dramatic initiative, with the support of other nations such as France, it 'would leave Russia and America as the sole nuclear powers [and] we should be making some sacrifice in power and influence'. It went on to reject categorically the go-it-alone solution of the unilateralists. No concessions at all were made to their demands for a moral lead by Britain in advance of all other nuclear powers. 'There is not the slightest evidence', the draft statement insisted, 'that if we were to take this step it would induce America or Russia to follow suit or in any way influence the policy of General de Gaulle or the Chinese Government.' It would also be tantamount to a withdrawal from NATO – and, the statement declared, 'nothing could be more dangerous.' That was the policy, piloted carefully by Hugh Gaitskell and Nye Bevan, which was put before Frank Cousins and the TUC leaders. It did nothing to persuade Cousins that the Labour Party attitude had shifted in any significant way.

Bevan introduced the policy and was immediately challenged by Robert Willis, who was TUC chairman that year. Willis said he could not see what sacrifice there could be in proposing the non-nuclear club, since Britain would be protected by America. Making no bones about his hostility to the new policy document, Willis then opened up the meeting to questions and discussions.[5]

All eyes turned toward Frank Cousins. He waited to see if others might speak. They waited for him. There were seconds of complete silence. At last Cousins accepted the inevitable. Turning to Nye Bevan he said he fully understood and sympathised with Nye's primary aim of unifying the Movement. Then he added, with a determined thrust of his jaw: 'But this document will not unite the Movement. It will divide and demoralise it.' He challenged its wording in several places. It was weak on the issue of stop-

5. My account of the meetings between the Labour Party and TUC is based on the official minutes; access to the diaries of Richard Crossman; and conversations with some of those who took part.

ping H-tests. It talked only of suspending them. Why not state specifically and categorically that a Labour Government would 'stop' tests, and leave it at that? Why not say frankly and clearly that we would never be the first to use these terrible weapons? And why, he asked finally, pretend about the non-nuclear club when it was simply a manœuvre? Any fool, Cousins added acidly, could see that a power like China would refuse to join. Did anybody imagine the French would agree? It wasn't a question of semantics, as far as he was concerned. It was a question of the integrity and the meaning of the Labour Party's policy. This was a sharp and devastating opening to a fierce meeting.

Bevan retaliated. He scorned Cousins's lack of understanding of what was politically possible in the world of international affairs. He even derided the unions. Trade unions, he said, according to Crossman's diary, had useful functions, but were a poor place for making serious decisions. He would rather get out than be told by the trade unions what to do in the Foreign Office.

There have been several accounts of that bitter exchange between Bevan and Cousins – two men who shared so much of the socialist ethos, yet could attack each other with such violence. Some reports tend to be more dramatic than others, but all who were there recall it as an extraordinary battle between the two giants of the Left. Crossman notes that Bevan in a final bitter remark shouted at Cousins: 'I have led more controversies and rebellions than anyone else here – but whenever elections approach I call for unity against the common foe.'

He told Cousins that if he persisted and carried the division still further he would ensure Labour's defeat at the General Election. It is hard to think of a more searing rebuke to a political ally.

Cousins was not moved. He replied that the Party leadership were underestimating the shift that had taken place in opinion both inside and outside the Labour Movement. There was no evidence, as he saw it, that a clear-cut moral lead from Labour would become an electoral liability.

The next day the Party's National Executive and the TUC General Council met separately to approve the new statement. The minority in both bodies again pressed for amendments. Anthony (now Lord) Greenwood, Ian Mikardo, Tom Driberg, Barbara Castle and Edwin Gooch (the farm-workers' representative) supported the unilateralists' programme for the re-nunciation of all H-tests, for all time and an immediate pledge that Britain would never be the first to use nuclear weapons and that under a Labour Government Britain would stop manufacturing the Bomb. But they were so heavily outnumbered that Greenwood was persuaded not to press his amendment to a vote. At the TUC there was a vote against Frank Cousins of 16 to 7. His six supporters were Robert Willis, John Newton (Tailors and Garment Workers), Lionel Poole (Boot and Shoe Operatives), Harold Hewitt

(Pottery Workers) plus the two other TGWU members of the General Council, Len Forden and Ellen McCullough.

The lines of battle were now drawn. Only a miracle could avert an open confrontation at the TGWU conference in Douglas on the Isle of Man, due in a fortnight. Immense pressure was put on Frank Cousins to change his mind or at least modify his stand. He was warned, cajoled, courted, attacked, advised and even threatened by friends and opponents. Some of his trade-union colleagues, even those who supported his stand, advised him to 'play it softly'. Labour MPs urged him to put Party loyalty above his own personal views, regardless of the strength of his convictions and the moral correctness of his attitude. They warned him, as Nye Bevan had, that an electoral defeat would be blamed on him. The Press, with the exception of the *Daily Herald*, attacked him ceaselessly, ridiculing the right of a union leader, no matter how powerful, to seek to determine the nation's foreign policy in this way.

The strain was far greater than anything Cousins had previously experienced. Outwardly he remained resolute and determined to continue his opposition; inwardly he had deep reservations about how far he should push the confrontation. Pressure mounted daily as the TGWU conference approached.

A week before the conference Cousins asked to see Bevan privately. They met in Bevan's room at the House of Commons and talked for several hours. He pleaded with Nye to think again; Bevan pleaded with Cousins to do the same. Cousins said that his was *not* a completely unilateralist stand, since he was not proposing the abolition of Britain's nuclear stockpile as a go-it-alone gesture. Bevan said that this made no difference. If the Party were to accept Cousins's proposals they would wreck their chances of winning the election, and he warned again that if Cousins pressed his claim it would split the whole Movement. Cousins told Bevan he could not understand why Nye had moved away from the position they had both held in March 1958. He had never thought he would live to see the day when Nye Bevan would be lined up on the same side as the Right wing of the TUC and the Labour Party, as well as the Communist Party (who were then opposed to unilateralism), with himself on the other side. Bevan replied: 'Well, that's your fault for putting yourself in that position.'

He did confess at this meeting that he had tried to persuade Gaitskell to accept at least two of the three points Cousins put forward – on stopping the tests and pledging that Britain would not be the first to use nuclear weapons. But the Party leader resolutely refused to accept either point in those categorical terms. Having failed to convert Gaitskell, Bevan reconciled himself to the fact that it was more important for Labour to win the election than for him to fight to get his way with Gaitskell – possibly risking a major split at the top of the Party on the eve of the polls. It was because he himself had made such a compromise that he was doubly angered to find Cousins attacking him on issues over which he actually agreed with the Transport Union leader. Moreover, Bevan clearly expected Cousins to accept his good faith on these two crucial points and to recognise that if he ever became Foreign Secretary then he would use all his influence to persuade a Labour Cabinet to carry out two of the points – though not the third – for which Cousins was pressing.

This meeting between Bevan and Cousins resolved nothing. Gaitskell made no attempt to seek a meeting with Cousins, who felt alone and exposed. I recall meeting him in the company of Michael Foot shortly before he left London for Douglas. He made it clear he was prepared to see the whole thing through. Despite all the pressure he would not give up. He did not believe that the Labour Party would go down to electoral defeat if it offered the country a moral lead, yet he had by then reconciled himself to the fact that even if that turned out to be true then he would rather Labour should lose the election than sacrifice principle on this paramount issue.

What Cousins did fear, as he told me on that occasion, was that he might well be fighting an isolated battle. He knew then that attempts were afoot to arrange for a recall conference of the General and Municipal Workers, so that the anti-Bomb vote at their Scarborough conference could be reversed in the light of the latest Labour Party policy. And he was quite convinced that none of the other big unions would join him in his outright opposition to nuclear weapons.

On 26 June Cousins decided to make one last attempt to put his case to the Labour Party leaders. He sent a personal and private letter to Hugh Gaitskell, addressed to Gaitskell's home in Hampstead, rather than his office at the House of Commons. The letter is so important in terms of setting out clearly where Cousins stood on the issue which was to divide the Labour Movement that it is worth recording it in full, along with Hugh Gaitskell's reply.[6]

Frank Cousins wrote :

Personal and Private
                                                                26th June, 1959.
My dear Hugh,
    The complex nature of the problem facing the world today, increased immeasurably by the development of the hydrogen bomb as a possible weapon of mass destruction, inevitably creates grave issues for all of us to face. In such circumstances it is not surprising there are differing shades of opinion within the Labour Movement as to the method which should be used to try to rid the world of this danger.

6. I am indebted to Dr Philip M. Williams of Nuffield College, Oxford, for this correspondence. Dr. Williams is the official biographer of Hugh Gaitskell.
[Yet to be published]

We do, I am sure, agree that the objective of all reasonable persons must be identical, namely, to bring to a definite and permanent end the testing of nuclear weapons and to take progressive steps towards full and comprehensive multilateral disarmament.

The proposal which the Labour Party have just made for the creation of what has become loosely known as the 'non-nuclear bomb club' with the suggestion that the Government should be prepared to announce that, if the nations who do not now possess nuclear weapons but are capable of manufacturing them will pledge themselves not to test, manufacture or possess nuclear weapons subject to full and effective international controls to see that this is carried out, that Great Britain would not only cease the manufacture of nuclear weapons but would also deprive herself of their possession, does not appear to me to take us anywhere along that road.

There is such an ambiguity in the wording of the proposal that many interpretations are already being made, but that is not the main objection.

It is fairly evident that some countries are unlikely to be influenced in any way by the proposal, nor be greatly concerned with decisions which may or may not be taken by European countries.

This is particularly so in the case of China, whose attitude towards the need for self-possession of the H bomb is apparently related to her fears regarding the relationships between herself, The United States of America and the Nationalist Chinese forces on the one hand, and a desire to be in nuclear parity with Russia on the other.

As this position must be quite well understood by those of our party leaders who are projecting the idea, this makes the proposition appear to me to be a little unreal.

Whilst recognising the justification for trying any new methods which may have the intention of providing a policy of containment of the nuclear bomb I feel that the full facts concerning the unlikelihood of the acceptance of such a proposal by all the nations involved should be emphasized and clearly understood within the Party.

We have always prided ourselves on the honesty with which we portray our proposals and I am sure it would be very unwise to depart from that principle on such a major issue.

So far as is possible I have avoided allowing my natural detestation of the horrifying nuclear bomb to influence my approach to the question of the joint statement of the Labour Party and the Trades Union Congress, in the firm belief that our objective was the securing of the greatest measure of common understanding on what should be said irrespective of differing views of the relative place of this weapon in our overall defence policies. It has, therefore, come as a complete surprise to me to find during the past few days an atmosphere developing in which, apparently, the main objective of the exercise has been to create a background in which the anticipated views of the General Secretary of the Transport and General Workers' Union could be defeated.

It may provide a measure of satisfaction in some quarters if the Transport

Workers' Union can be isolated and the views of our forthcoming conference, whatever they may be, made less effective. But I very seriously suggest this cannot be in the overall interest of the Movement, nor expected to provide the greatest degree of unity in the team who will be required to undertake the task of winning the electorate to a support of Labour Party policies.

Unfortunately, for a number of reasons, particularly because we are both so excessively busy these days, it has not been possible for us to meet for some time and probably this is a contributory cause towards the difficulty which now exists.

I am sure you will understand my concern that there are apparently quite a number of our Labour Party and trade union colleagues who are holding the mistaken view, and in some cases saying publicly, that I am leading an opposition to yourself with a campaign for unilateral renunciation of the hydrogen bomb and discontinuance of our association with N.A.T.O. This, as you are aware, is absolute nonsense and one wonders whether it arises from those who are so unsure of the correctness of their own actions and the political consequences, that they are preparing their excuses for defeat at the polls before this happens.

So that you can clearly recognise my position I say that notwithstanding my doubt regarding the value or even the real political honesty of the 'non-nuclear club' proposal. I would not make an issue on that, but I do feel very sincerely that the three points which I made at the joint meeting of the Party and the T.U.C., all of which have been publicly stated in various places by leaders of the Party as the official policy of the Party if returned as a Government, should have been clearly stated in the policy document. These were, as you know :

(a) Stopping of tests to mean no re-starting.
(b) A declaration that we will not use the nuclear bomb first, nor allow it to be used from our territory first.
(c) A re-affirmation of the statement previously made by Nye Bevan that 'the suspension of tests means a suspension of production'.

This view I shall continue to hold and express, in the firm belief that ambiguity on any aspect of our defence policy would be the most damaging thing in our approach to the electorate.

On Wednesday, at the T.U.C. General Council, your colleague Douglas Houghton said something to the effect that a feeling was developing in some quarters that I was becoming the keeper of the conscience of the Labour Party and that policy decisions were being taken by one or two big unions and not by the Labour Party N.E.C. and that this was resented. You, of course, more than anyone else, will be aware that the suggestion is both untrue and unfair. One thing must be said, however, whilst having no wish to look after the conscience of the Party I certainly reserve the right to look after my own. Douglas Houghton made his comment in a semi-public place so I am sure he will not object to my reference to it, in this personal setting to you.

217

It is quite unusual for me to write to you, but I felt it desirable that you should have at this time a clear expression of my views in order that the possibility of misunderstanding should be reduced to a minimum.

Trusting that our deliberations will, in the ultimate, bring us to the decisions which are in the best interests of our party and the country.

      I remain,

           Sincerely,

              Frank Cousins.

Gaitskell's reply was as follows:

Personal and private

                                     30th June, 1959.

My dear Frank,

Thank you for your long and interesting letter of the 26th June in which you set out your views on the new joint declaration on nuclear policy. I am very glad that you wrote. As you mark your letter 'Personal and Private', I do not propose to show it to anybody else. I assume that you will treat mine in the same manner.

I could not agree more on the emphasis you place on the fundamental aim of all round, comprehensive, multi-lateral disarmament. As you know, we have particularly underlined this in the statement where we describe it as our paramount objective and the first priority of the Labour Government.

I should like to emphasize also that the so-called 'non-nuclear club' is not in any way a substitute for this major aim but, as we hope and believe, an important step and contribution towards it.

I am sorry however that you take such a critical view of the 'club' itself. I am sure you would not deny that the danger of the spread of nuclear weapons is real and increasing or that the world will be a far more dangerous place if ten or twelve Governments instead of two or three produce and possess nuclear weapons of their own. Indeed it seems to me hard to exaggerate this. There is not only the fact that some of the newcomers will have less responsible governments but that this spread is bound to make any comprehensive multilateral agreement much harder to reach.

But I am sure it is not necessary for me to argue this point. The real question is, 'What is to be done about it?' You take the view that there is no hope of reaching agreement. Of course, you may be right, and I would not deny for a moment that China is a tremendous problem. But I have been encouraged by the fact that during the last few days three people as different as Bertrand Russell, Adlai Stevenson and Gladwyn Jebb have all expressed approval of our project. Certainly I think there is a real hope that in the case of France their desire for national prestige may be satisfied if they find themselves on the same level as ourselves. This was the impression I received when I saw de Gaulle in January and Gladwyn Jebb confirmed to me that this was his opinion.

How China will react is almost impossible to say. Any hope of her entering into such an agreement must be ruled out, unless we can get her into the

United Nations. But since we want to do that anyhow, I do not regard this as an insuperable obstacle. Some people who have been to China think that the prestige point is also very significant for them – not only the danger of war with the U.S.A. or nationalist China. I think the attitude of the Soviet Government will be very important. On the one hand they will hardly be interested in helping China to develop her own nuclear weapon production. On the other hand, they must be ready to stand by her in the event of any trouble with the U.S.A. The position does not seem to me to be so very different from that of the U.S.A. and Western Europe.

In any event, I really do not think the charge of dishonesty is a fair one. I have never for a moment denied the difficulties. Nor does the declaration. Indeed, it goes out of its way to emphasise them. But are they a real reason for not trying? What alternative, which is more likely to succeed, has anybody suggested?

I can understand the Tory opposition as expressed, for example, by Hailsham last week. They will no doubt beat the big drum and declare we must be on a par with America and Russia and that we cannot, therefore, give up our nuclear weapons unless they do too, even if the rest of the world were to agree to our proposals. We must surely fight this jingoistic line. We must point out that even if, as I would admit, the possession of these weapons does at present give us some influence and power in dealing with the United States, it is completely outweighed if, by giving them up, we could stop the spread of nuclear weapons.

I find it harder to understand the opinion of those who urge that unilateral action by ourselves is the right course. This simply does not seem to me to add up. If we cannot persuade other countries to agree to give up nuclear weapons by negotiation, why should it be thought that the same countries will just follow an example?

As to the position of the Union and yourself, I can assure you that at no time have I ever thought that you were, to quote your own words, 'leading an opposition to yourself with a campaign for unilateral renunciation of the hydrogen bomb and discontinuance of our association with N.A.T.O.' I know you far too well to suppose that you would do any such thing. What has happened is that the Tory Press has played up anything that looks like a row or disagreement in the Party, hoping as the *Express* clearly does, that it will lead to a complete split.

Before I deal with the three points on which you criticise the declaration, I should like to say two things.

Firstly, as Leader of the Party it is obviously my job to stand by the declaration absolutely. That I intend to do. It would be quite wrong for me to put glosses on it of my own or to give special interpretations.

Secondly, I have inevitably to be particularly careful about precise commitments about hypothetical situations which might have to be fulfilled when we come into power. Naturally we accept a good many commitments but I have to ask myself all the time when I am pressed to accept a certain form of words, 'Am I quite sure I am not embarrassing a future Labour

219

Government? Is it possible that I should find myself in a year or two hence unable to do something which I believed to be right for the country because of some commitment I have made now?' I ask you to appreciate this because I know that if you were in my position you would behave in exactly the same way.

Now about the three points :

(1) The stopping of tests. As you know the word 'stop' was not the word used in the official policy statement last year. The phrase was 'suspend tests of thermo-nuclear weapons for a limited period'. That was as far as we went. In the policy statement at Scarborough, the same words were used. In neither was the word 'stop' used, still less was it suggested that under no circumstances would there be any restarting.

In his speech at Scarborough, Nye used the word stop but in relation still to hydrogen bomb tests. As far as I am aware no one took the view that this signified a change in policy.

In the debate on April 27th last, however, he went further and said, 'We shall stop all hydrogen bomb and atom bomb tests at once', and in a television interview shortly afterwards, in reply to a question by William Clark, he said, 'I can conceive of no circumstances in which we would want to renew them.'

In order to make my own position clear, I should add that Nye used these words 'off-the-cuff' without discussing them with me first. For my part I have all the time stood by last year's declaration and used the word 'suspend'. Nevertheless, I did not make an issue of this. For I know that Nye regarded it as largely a matter of words.

Subsequently, in the discussions which took place on the draft of the new declaration we had a long argument out of which emerged the final phrasing of the document. This goes a considerable distance further than the formula used last year. I was prepared to accept that, partly because one must be willing on some points to compromise for the sake of unity and partly because it is in the highest degree improbable that we should resume tests, and in the case of H-bomb tests which pollute the atmosphere, almost inconceivable.

I honestly do not feel it is reasonable to ask me to go further. I cannot as Leader of the Party, pledge a future Labour Government – whatever the circumstances in the world, however terrible the international situation, however many other countries might be developing nuclear weapons, whatever our relationship with the United States, and even if, as is extremely likely, tests could be carried out without any danger of poisoning the atmosphere – never to undertake them.

Quite frankly, I would have liked in many ways to have said as much but, as I did not want to widen any differences between us, I deliberately refrained from doing so.

The difference is surely a very narrow one. We have gone to the limit in implying we should not resume tests, short of absolute commitment. That I really do not consider would be right. I hope that in the circumstances you will agree to leave the matter as it is.

Now for your second point – which concerns the proposed declaration that we will not use the nuclear bomb, nor allow it to be used from our territory first. I do not think this has yet been said in any policy document or, as far as I know, by Nye, myself, or any other leading figure in the Party. The reason is that, since in Western Europe the N.A.T.O. armies are heavily out-numbered in conventional forces by the Soviet Union and the other iron curtain countries, we might have to balance this weakness by the use of tactical atomic weapons. If we come out with the declaration that we will never use these first, we say in effect that we are prepared to accept a position in which the Russians are subjecting us to defeat with superior conventional forces and we simply allow this to happen.

By saying it we run at least the faint risk of encouraging them to do so. That is the difficulty about the pledge of the kind you want. Moreover, if we were to make it, we would certainly be asked whether in order to restore the balance in conventional forces in Europe, we were prepared to reintroduce conscription. I certainly could not commit the Party to this without a great deal more discussion.

These objections do not apply in the same way to H-bombs, which I do not think we could or should ever use first. This was the point made in the *Times* leader where a distinction was drawn between tactical and strategic weapons.

As to whether, however, a declaration of this kind, limited to not using the H-bombs first, would be worthwhile, I am rather doubtful. I am afraid that it would lead to too much confusion. For all these reasons, I think it is better that the whole question should be looked at first by our defence sub-committee.

Your third point that Nye's statement that 'The suspension of tests means a suspension of production' is rather different. I have looked up his speech at Brighton. It is clearly a statement of fact, not of intention so far as a future Labour Government is concerned. It could not possibly be understood in this way since, as you will remember, Nye was speaking against a motion for a unilateral decision not to manufacture nuclear weapons. Taken as a fact the meaning that I have always given to it is that if you suspend tests you cannot make new nuclear weapons. Otherwise, it just seems to me to be untrue.

Let me say that I fully appreciate the deep emotion which motivates you in all this business. I know you will do me the justice of believing that I too have deep feelings on the subject. I should be only too glad to talk with you further about it all and I share your regret that we were unable to do so in the limited time before the declaration had to be settled.

Finally, although it is absurd to expect us all to use exactly the same language, I know full well that you will appreciate the great importance of presenting, as far as we are able, a united front at the moment.

One can hardly overstress the significance of this correspondence. It was highly unusual for Frank Cousins to put such a lengthy statement of his personal position into a letter at all and, as he pointed out, equally unusual for him to write to Hugh Gaitskell. But he sought to demonstrate, in the three propositions he put to Gaitskell, that he was some way from being a complete unilateralist. Cousins believed, and hoped, that he might yet establish some lifeline of compromise with the Party leader which might help to avert the looming confrontation. Nothing in Gaitskell's reply, however, helped in this direction.

The Party leader's letter was sent to Cousins at the Isle of Man, where he had set up base in readiness for the biennial delegate meeting. The great volume of motions on the agenda paper demanded that the union should declare itself wholly against the Bomb, and many went further than Cousins himself. He could not, at that late stage, rein back the conference, he had no option but to go ahead with the fight – or throw in the towel. On the eve of the conference I wrote in the *Daily Herald* :[7]

He is ready to risk an open showdown with the Party chiefs to demonstrate his faith in the moral gesture of abandoning the nuclear weapon. It is a phenomenal decision. He will be assailed for it. But he will also be seized on by many as a new potential leader. This aspect, it seems, has never really entered into his calculations on the H-bomb. For him it is a simple burning faith; he believes he is right and the Party leaders are wrong.

Frank Cousins knows that if he continues to oppose Labour-TUC policy on the H-bomb and takes his massive 1,266,000 vote with him, as he will, it could split the Party on the eve of an election. If Cousins won it would place Mr Gaitskell as well as Mr Cousins's old friend Mr Bevan in an impossible position. They might have to quit and leave a divided party to Mr Cousins himself.

That was not an improbable postulation. Plenty of people inside and outside the Labour Party believed that Frank Cousins's motive in driving ahead with his anti-bomb campaign was to secure the leadership of the Labour Party. This was the theme of several newspaper attacks on him at the time of the Isle of Man conference. But he had recognised he must steel himself against all the pressures. He was now quite alone at the top of the Labour establishment in his stand, comforted only by the deep conviction that a great many people in Britain supported his arguments even if these were rejected by his own Party leaders and TUC colleagues. One main criticism of Cousins's action was (and remains) that he was unrepresentative; it was suggested that he did not genuinely speak for the majority of his rank and file union members, despite the votes at the TGWU conference. Perhaps there was some truth in this, though it was never put to the test. Undoubt-

7. *Daily Herald*, 2 July 1959.

edly it was the power of Cousins's leadership and the overwhelming strength
of his conviction that swung the once-orthodox union to the opposite extreme
in defence policy, as in so much else.

This is what made the union's stand on the H-bomb so different from,
say, its policy on the London busmen's strike. In that strike Cousins accepted the will of the rank and file and to a large extent was himself led by it.
In the H-bomb controversy the reverse was clearly the case. It was Frank
Cousins who led the union and led it, as far as nuclear policy was concerned, against the opposition of the majority of his national officials –
though *not* against the wishes of the union's executive.

The other charge made against Frank Cousins was that a trade union had
no right, anyway, to meddle in subjects it did not properly understand. This
is still a typical elitist attack on unions which want to raise any issue beyond
wages and working conditions. Yet it had even been touched on by Nye
Bevan himself at the joint meeting of the Labour Party and the TUC, so
it was not simply a ploy of Tory journalists, politicians and academics.
Cousins's answer was characteristic: a trade union is a public institution,
representing a wide cross-section of ordinary people who often have no voice
at all except through their union. It was therefore fully within a union's
rights to express its views and campaign for policies on issues of such universal importance as possible nuclear destruction. This right was, to Frank
Cousins, a self-evident one; it was implicit in his concept of trade-union
democracy.

The Isle of Man conference of the TGWU was the most extraordinary
trade union assembly I have witnessed. It was a collector's piece in conferences; a remarkable demonstration of rank-and-file participation in a
public debate. This debate took place towards the end of the conference
week, after days of speculation, prophecy, and preliminary dramatisation.
Cousins was anxious to clear away most of the main industrial issues before
the conference concentrated on the Bomb. So the first three days were spent
on industrial affairs, but with a foretaste of what was to come. On all the
main issues Frank Cousins showed that he was well to the Left of the
majority of his colleagues in the Labour Party and TUC leadership. He
repeated that he would continue to fight wage restraint. He re-echoed his
demand for a more full-blooded programme of public ownership and a new
socialist dimension to Labour Party economic thinking and policy. Indeed
this brought him telegrams of congratulation from several Labour MPs,
including Herbert Morrison (not slow to see Cousins's campaign as a further
blow against Hugh Gaitskell) and Manny (now Lord) Shinwell as well as
George (now Lord) Wigg.

On Thursday it was time for the Bomb. No one present is likely to forget
that day. It was taken up entirely by the debate on a seven-point motion

submitted by the union's executive and moved by Frank Cousins – a Frank Cousins looking distinctly nervous as he stood on the platform, jacketless and mopping his brow.

The seven points covered all the issues debated for so long in previous months : a complete end to all H-tests; a pledge that a Labour Government would never be the first to use a nuclear weapon; a promise that stopping all tests also meant stopping production of H-weapons; stopping all planes carrying nuclear weapons from using British bases for their patrols; a renewed objection to the existence of any missile bases in Britain; restoring political as distinct from military control over the use of weapons of mass destruction; and urging a drive for world disarmament through the United Nations. It was an omnibus of a motion, yet it implied, rather than explicitly stated, the unilateralist case.

The debate ran throughout the entire day, resuming after a midday break. There were 58 speakers from the floor, each a rank-and-file delegate. I cannot recall attending any trade union conference when so many delegates spoke on a single issue. In the end out of 763 delegates only 50 hands were counted against the seven-point motion. In his wind-up speech Cousins was at his most passionate, repudiating the suggestion that he would split the Labour Movement, ridiculing Nye Bevan's phrase about going into the conference room naked. 'These phrases,' said Frank Cousins, 'should never be used.' But he resisted any attack on Nye. 'Believe me,' he pleaded, 'I do respect Nye. But he's as likely to be misguided as any other man; as likely as Frank Cousins is to be misguided . . .'

Perhaps the most controversial item in that concluding speech was Cousins's reference to the possible damage the union's decision might do to Labour's election prospects. It was to be quoted back at him many times. 'I have never believed,' he said, 'that the most important thing in our times was to elect a Labour Government. The most important thing is to elect a Labour Government determined to carry out a socialist policy.'

The Isle of Man vote brought a frenzied reaction – inside the Labour Movement, as well as outside, though it was far from unanimously hostile. There was much praise for the moral stand taken by the TGWU. A sizeable number of Labour MPs hailed the Cousins stand as one of great courage, though the majority thought he was wrong and unwise. And the Press, with rare exceptions, screamed at Cousins for his outrageous behaviour. The *Daily Sketch* prophesied : 'COUSINS LOSES THE ELECTION'. The *Daily Mirror*, quick to admonish, was headmasterly : 'COUSINS GOES WRONG'. The *Sunday Express*, not averse to the smear, demanded : 'IS COUSINS A DANGER TO BRITAIN ?' – and, not surprisingly, decided that he was.

Hugh Gaitskell knew that the Labour Party now faced a critical situation. Official policy on disarmament could still be defeated at the TUC and the Labour Party conferences – unless an election intervened. There was now a serious and ever-darkening shadow over the election, which Gaitskell knew was imminent for the autumn. It was still possible for Cousins to rally a good deal of support, especially if unions like the General and Municipal Workers could not reverse their decision. Moreover, the Party leaders knew that Cousins had given new impetus to grass-roots feelings; the TGWU stand on the H-bomb had revived the spirit of idealism in local Labour Parties and touched on a sensitive nerve which brought responses from all over the Movement.

In the week-end following the TGWU conference Gaitskell took an immediate opportunity to hit back at Cousins. In a speech at Workington he pledged that a Labour Government would never be committed by the block vote of any trade union conference – nor, by inference, would a Labour Government become a prisoner of any vote at a TUC or Labour Party conference. 'Policy,' Gaitskell declared, 'will not be dictated by one man.' And he went on :

> Our Party decisions are not dictated by one man whether he be the leader of the Party, our spokesman on foreign affairs [Aneurin Bevan] or the General Secretary of the Transport and General Workers' Union. It is not right that a future Labour Government should be committed by conference decisions on every matter of detail for all time.

That was a clear enough warning that Gaitskell was not prepared to be bound by conference decisions, an issue which caused such deep and grave misgiving after the Scarborough Party conference of 1960. In that Workington speech Hugh Gaitskell repeated that a Labour Government simply would not unilaterally abandon nuclear weapons. There was no question about it, in his mind, and he emphasised that the nation should be in no doubt either. A Labour Government certainly would seek an international agreement to try to outlaw the Bomb, but no risks would be taken with the nation's defence. This was not only a reply to Frank Cousins and the TGWU. It was also a pre-election speech to the nation, in an attempt to make it perfectly clear that a Labour Government under his leadership would be a responsible one, not given to adventure at the behest of a trade union block vote. Gaitskell remained quite unmoved in his support for multilateralism. There would be no compromise on that.

Gaitskell and Cousins were obstinate men. Both were wholly convinced they were right. Both pleaded – and were sincere in their pleas – that they were acting in what they held to be the best interests of their country, their party and their own private consciences. Of course, there was animosity between the two men. It would be idle to pretend that no unfriendly thoughts crossed their minds when they reflected on each other as men and Labour leaders. Hugh Gaitskell no doubt saw Frank Cousins as an egocentric leftist who was determined to pull the Labour Movement further to the Left, regardless of the damage he did to the Movement and its prospect of governing Britain. No doubt there were times when Gaitskell believed – or some of his advisers urged him to believe – that Cousins was further to the Left than he in fact was, and that the TGWU leader was bent on 'wrecking tactics'. There was also a personality conflict between the two men, as there was between Gaitskell and Aneurin Bevan. Cousins, a man of strong working-class origin, saw Gaitskell as a middle-class reformer rather than as a socialist. Quite apart from the H-bomb controversy – indeed well before it – Cousins had already sensed Gaitskell's resistance to public ownership, and this was a litmus test of the genuine socialist as far as Frank Cousins was concerned. Nevertheless, it would still be wrong to regard the conflict as a purely personal one; personal conflict there undoubtedly was, but it was secondary to the deep difference of political attitude, approach and, perhaps as much as anything, the different chemistry of the two men.

The scene was set for a full-scale confrontation on the eve of the election : a bitter and depressing prospect for all Labour supporters. The spotlight was now turned on Cousins. His every move and shift was noted and publicised. He is a shy man, who for all his physical presence, towering frame and dominating thrustfulness always had a profoundly self-conscious reaction to public situations. He did not like the glare of the lights, even when he felt flattered by their presence. He was vain about the attention he commanded, yet resented its intrusiveness. In this way he was like Nye Bevan, though he lacked Bevan's unique capacity often to turn such a situation to his advantage. Frank Cousins seemed to be less subtle, more obviously prickly, though no less aggressive and pugnacious.

As he came increasingly under fire Cousins retaliated with a hammer-like force. One such incident occurred in the week after the Isle of Man conference. Crossman was then writing a regular column for the *Daily Mirror*. On 14 July 1959 he charged into Cousins with lances poised in both fists. Far from damaging Labour's chances at the General Election, Crossman wrote, the Gaitskell-Cousins clash actually strengthened them :

Hugh Gaitskell is already emerging looking fitter and stronger than ever before . . . Mr Cousins delivered himself into Mr Gaitskell's hands by the clumsy tactics he adopted. He could loyally have urged his Transport Workers Union to accept the new Labour Party-TUC document on the H-bomb despite his own grave personal doubts. Then he could have pleaded that it should be amended at the Labour Party Conference. This tactic would have put Hugh Gaitskell and Aneurin Bevan in a quandry. As it was, by launching an incoherent all-out attack on the Labour leadership Mr Cousins gave Mr Gaitskell a chance to show his strength. Up till now many

Labour sympathisers and middle-of-the-road voters have been in doubt whether Mr Gaitskell – as a middle-class intellectual – is strong enough to discipline his own supporters and take the tough and often unpopular decisions required of a British Premier ...

Crossman then asserted that by his resounding rebuke to Cousins and his declaration that he would not be deterred by the block vote of even the most powerful of British trade unions Hugh Gaitskell had strengthened his position in the Labour Party and in the eyes of the British electorate. It is doubtful whether Gaitskell himself was as convinced of that as Crossman seemed to be, but that is beside the point. At any rate, the Crossman column provoked a searing letter from Frank Cousins. Written on the day the column appeared in the *Mirror*,[8] it was addressed to 'Dear Mr Crossman' (not 'Dear Dick'), and complained that :

Only in the completely right-wing Conservative section of the press has there been anything which approached the biased and prejudiced comment you make and it will I am sure be felt by many of our trade union colleagues to be a further example of your much too frequently displayed anti-trade union attiude.

Fair comment and difference of opinion is never objected to but your article has so misrepresented the position that the effect can only be likely to cause real harm to Labour Party and trade union relationships.

If you are intending to continue in this strain you should, I think, ask our leader Hugh Gaitskell, whether this form of attack is approved by him. Nothing said in our TGWU debate could be regarded as personalising the issue and we do not thank you for your attempt to bring the question to such a level.

As a person I resent your inference regarding my loyalty to the Labour Party and would suggest that your comment as to methods I could have used to place Hugh and Aneurin in a quandry indicates only your complete lack of understanding of the issue involved.

There is one thing about which you may be assured, however the debate at the Labour Party may go, whether I am able to get support or not for the views I hold on this subject there will not be two different speeches in my pocket in case circumstances change during Conference week.

> Yours,
> Frank Cousins.

Crossman's reply was equally caustic. He began by addressing Frank as 'Dear Frank', with the immediate comment, in parenthesis : 'I don't see why however angry we are with each other, we should add the insult of Mr. !' He then continued :

8. 14 July 1959 }
9. 16 July 1959 }　from the private correspondence between the two men.

If you were disturbed by my article in Tuesday's *Mirror* I was disturbed by your letter of the 14th. Of course I didn't expect you to like the article. But I did assume that you would regard it as fair comment and it does therefore disturb me that you should feel, in your own words, that I have 'so misrepresented the position that the effect can only be likely to cause real harm to Labour Party and trade union relationships'.

Let me clear one secondary point out of the way first. Nothing I wrote was meant even by implication to throw any doubts on your personal integrity, your socialist faith or indeed your loyalty to the Labour Party. What I do question is the wisdom of the tactics you employed and the leadership you gave in the Isle of Man. It looked to me, as I wrote in my article, that you were challenging Gaitskell's and Bevan's leadership of our Party, throwing doubts on their socialist integrity and indicating that you had so little trust in them that you felt bound to try to tie them up before they got to Downing Street. In my view this challenge compelled Gaitskell to take the line he did including his reference to 'dictation'. In particular, in spite of your letter, I do not understand why you repudiated the whole idea of a non-nuclear club. I can see that it can be regarded as unrealistic or insufficient by someone who wants to go further. What I cannot see is why you should have felt it necessary to reject it so contemptuously . . .

Crossman concluded his letter by restating his conviction that he had not been unfair to Cousins:

> In all my life as a journalist . . . it is my guiding interest first and foremost to represent the situation fairly and squarely as it really is.

He told Cousins that he had never been afraid to speak his mind but if he had misrepresented anything or anyone he was always ready to put things right in print.

Writing in his diary shortly after this exchange Crossman disclosed that George Brown told him he had agreed a draft of a new policy statement on disarmament with Frank Cousins at an early stage in the June discussions.[10] This draft, according to Brown, contained a form of words which met Cousins's requirements about Britain not using nuclear weapons first. Brown thought it was satisfactory from the Labour Party point of view and brought it back to Gaitskell, who turned it down flat. Brown then told Crossman:

> From the first Hugh manœuvred to isolate Cousins. He didn't want an agreement. I can tell you that. After all I'm not likely to offer Cousins compromises which are very extreme on this issue. I warned Cousins he was going out on a limb and Hugh would lick him but he wouldn't listen. Hugh has certainly won. But will it pay him in the long run if he loses the election? I think he's started something very serious indeed with Cousins leading a new Left.[11]

10. Richard Crossman, the unpublished diaries, 13 August 1959.   11. *Ibid.*

This was an interesting and perceptive comment by George Brown. And in the very next item in the Crossman diary there is from George Brown an equally significant observation about Nye Bevan :

> We agreed that Nye has been quite soft and ineffective throughout this crisis. We also agreed that he had done nothing to put Cousins's points to Hugh and that Nye could have overthrown Hugh during this crisis quite easily by insisting on having his way on the two points Cousins wanted. 'But he hasn't the strength left,' said George.[12]

Not long after that conversation with George Brown Crossman had the opportunity to test Brown's statement with Gaitskell himself. The Labour Party leader told Crossman 'he is determined to smash Cousins,' and added 'he has accepted the General and Municipal Workers reversing themselves though he wasn't formally asked whether he wanted it.'[13]

Indeed the GMW *did* reverse its anti-Bomb vote on 21 August at a special conference, where the voting was 194 to 139 in support of Labour's newly-drafted policy incorporating the non-nuclear club. This vote made it certain that the Party policy would be carried easily at the Trades Union Congress and at the Party conference if one were held. By then only the TGWU among the major unions was ranged against official policy. The engineers, miners, railwaymen and distributive workers had all voted to support it. The reversal by the General and Municipal Workers Union simply completed the isolation of Cousins. None the less, it is interesting to reflect that none of the commentators who had been so strenuous in attacking Cousins and the TGWU for their 'bullying' and 'undemocratic' behaviour attacked the GMW for an extraordinary about-face which scarcely did credit to trade-union democracy. Almost everyone knew there had been a good deal of squalid, behind-the-scenes manœuvring to get the GMW vote switched. It was an illuminating example of the application of double standards. No doubt the GMW leaders could – and did – claim that a new situation had arisen since their Scarborough vote, but so, too, could the bulk of other unions who had held their conferences before the Labour Party revised its policy. None did.

Even so, everyone predicted a trial-run confrontation at the Trades Union Congress in Blackpool that September. It was seen as a dress rehearsal for the Labour Party conference, due to follow three weeks later – and it would have been, but for the announcement on the Monday congress opened that there would be a General Election on 8 October. Harold Macmillan's timing of the announcement meant there would be no Labour Party conference as arranged. Instead Hugh Gaitskell was invited to Blackpool, so that he could

12. *Ibid.*
13. *Ibid.*, 13 August 1959.

use the opportunity of the Congress as a platform from which to open the election campaign. And this effectively muffled any explosions on the H-bomb row.

The scene at Blackpool was full of tension. The TUC headquarters was established at the Imperial Hotel, at the north end of Blackpool, which had become the traditional centre for all the main political conferences in the town. Cousins preferred to stay with his wife at a small family hotel at the south end. His motion on nuclear disarmament based on the seven-point policy agreed at the Isle of Man conference, also stood apart, on the agenda. He was against it being composited with any other motion. When it came before the General Council at its pre-Congress meetings it was voted down by 28 to 5. That was no surprise to Cousins; the voting inside the General Council on the issue never varied by more than one or two votes, depending on whether one of his left-wing supporters was absent from any given meeting. Ted Hill was absent that morning. Cousins's most prominent supporter was still Bob Willis, that year's Congress chairman. Still there was no chance that the TGWU motion would succeed. Everyone, including Cousins, knew it.

By the evening of the first day the Congress atmosphere was dominated by the election announcement and the news that Hugh Gaitskell would address them on the Thursday – the day after the H-bomb debate. Into Blackpool for the occasion had already come the Labour Party's General Secretary, Morgan Phillips, as well as the Party chairman, Barbara Castle. The hotel lobbying was furious. Cousins was still under pressure to soft-pedal his assault on defence policy, but he stood firmly by his motion. When it finally came, the debate was something of an anti-climax, confused not only by the shadow of the impending election and the imminent arrival of Hugh Gaitskell but by the existence of three, rather than two, opposing motions on nuclear disarmament. The official policy was supported by the Amalgamated Engineering Union (now the AUEW), backed by most of the big unions. Then came the TGWU motion supported by a number of smaller unions, and, following a last-minute decision, by the then Communist-led Electrical Trades Union (the first indication that the Communist Party was moving in to support the anti-bomb campaign). There was also a third motion, sponsored by the Supervisory Staffs, Executives and Technicians (forerunner of Clive Jenkins's ASTMS) and the Fire Brigades Union, demanding clear-cut support for unilateral nuclear disarmament – as distinct from the Cousins compromise policy. They were all debated together.

Almost all his TUC General Council colleagues were ranged against Frank Cousins – mostly in sorrow rather than anger. When Cousins came to the rostrum he repeated his insistence that 'there are no personalities involved in this, no question of whether it is Carron against Cousins or Gaitskell against Cousins. We are all seeking the same thing; we are seeking peace and the abolition of this terrible weapon. We are seeking progress for our social beliefs and we are seeking freedom; and any steps that any of us is taking are in that direction'[14]

Here then was a Cousins arguing strenuously for his view but palpably aware of the need to contain and restrain the argument; and not offering any hostages to anyone who might be tempted to accuse him of 'splittng' the Labour Movement at that crucial hour. His two speeches, presenting the TGWU motion and in reply to the debate, were studies in tightrope walking. Yet he did not flinch from forcefully presenting his central case that Britain under a Labour Government must give a moral lead and that anything short of that would be tinkering around with the strategy of destruction. His scathing criticism of the non-nuclear club concept was in no way muted – if anything, he had become increasingly hostile to it. Acceptance of it, he told the Congress, would be 'stretching credulity to its breaking point'.

Ironically the next speaker, Harry Knight, General Secretary of the Association of Supervisory Staffs, Executives and Technicians (ASSET), criticised the TGWU motion as itself 'a compromise'. Mr Knight was moving the motion which called for a completely unilateralist policy, and which Frank Cousins did not accept. The essence of the Cousins case at that time was that the logic of the Party's *own* policy must inevitably lead to what he was proposing. If it did not then it was not due to any flaw in the logic of his reasoning but to a doubt about the nature of the Party's policy and possibly even its integrity. Stopping the tests, Cousins argued, meant what it said : to stop them and be finished with them (as he assumed Nye Bevan to have repeatedly assured him) implied that manufacture would also be suspended, since one process was contingent on the other. The sticking point was the pledge on whether Britain would ever be the first to use nuclear weapons. Here semantics appeared to give way to emphasis and perhaps even intent and trust. There was no question at that stage of Cousins and the TGWU demanding a unilateralist policy.

The result of the voting at the Blackpool Congress was the predicted overwhelming defeat for the TGWU motion – by 5,133,000 to 2,795,000. The engineers' motion supporting official policy was carried by 5,214,000 to 2,690,000; and the unilateralists' motion was defeated by a huge majority on a show of hands. The prelude was over ...

The next day Hugh Gaitskell arrived in Blackpool, to be greeted by a standing ovation at the Congress. Everything was now submerged beneath the waves of election fervour. In his speech to the TUC Gaitskell touched only briefly on the nuclear debate by referring to his recent visit to Moscow, where he and Nye Bevan met members of the Soviet Government. Gait-

14. TUC *Annual Report*, 1959, p. 402.

skell told the Congress that both Khrushchev and his Foreign Minister, Andrei Gromyko, appeared impressed by the concept of the non-nuclear club. The Russians, he added, also wanted an agreement to stop all nuclear tests. Indeed, they went even further by telling Gaitskell and Bevan that they would not make any further tests unless and until 'somebody else starts them up again'.

In effect the undertone here was to demonstrate the unrealism of those who wanted Britain to go it alone. It was Gaitskell's way of saying to the Left, 'Look, even the Russians think you're dotty for pushing such a proposal'. But of course this was what Cousins had been saying. His was not, as some then argued, a 'Communist-inspired' policy: quite the contrary, because official Communist policy was at that time opposed to the unilateralists.

Still, Gaitskell did not dwell on the nuclear row. Having set out the Labour Party policy and justified it, he then concentrated on using the opportunity to launch the election campaign, which he did with great skill and confidence. He made it clear that a future Labour Government would not be committed by any conference decisions – trade union or otherwise.

> Let me state very plainly what, as I see it, the true relationship is between the trade unions and the Labour Party. It is quite simple. We are part of the same great Labour Movement of Britain. We are comrades together but we have different jobs to do. You have your industrial job and we have our political job. We do not dictate to one another. I should get the brush off pretty quickly if I started trying to dictate to Bob Willis [sitting in the chair of Congress beside Gaitskell]. And believe me any leader of the Labour Party would not be worth his salt if he allowed himself to be dictated to by the trade unions.

Gaitskell was determined to go into the election campaign with a clear declaration of the Party's independence from the trade unions. The Conservative Press and the Tory leaders had already made much of the insinuation that Gaitskell had become a prisoner of the unions and even of men like Cousins. It was a demonstrably absurd charge, and known to be so by all who understood the relations between the two men. None the less, it was the kind of accusation which tended to sway the uncommitted voter suspicious of the Labour Party's ties with the trade unions. The TUC departed from Blackpool, as did Gaitskell, confident that the Labour Party stood an excellent chance of winning the election. Their worst fears that Frank Cousins might undermine Labour's electoral prospects had certainly not been borne out. In fact the controversy, including the nuclear debate, had been conducted in an atmosphere of surprising tolerance and sophistication.

In the meantime Cousins had left for America to attend the Convention in San Francisco of the American Federation of Labour Congress of Industrial Organisations. Here indeed was a piquant situation. Daniel was in the lions' den. Cousins had been to the United States once before with an Anglo-American productivity team soon after the war. Then he was a national official. Now he was there for the second time in a somewhat different capacity, as leader of Britain's biggest union. He was introduced by George Meany, President of the AF of L-CIO, a man who was the arch upholder of American conventional wisdom on foreign policy and who would in British terms almost certainly be classified as a conservative. Outside America the name of George Meany was – and remains – synonymous with power and influence in international trade union affairs.

Cousins offered the usual courtesies, at the start; but then quickly developed a radical theme which quite plainly embarrassed the President. None of Meany's executive members would have dared speak in this vein : Cousins with his typical impishness and courage swept on into a condemnation of the nuclear arms race. Meany became increasingly restive. Cousins spoke about his union wanting an end to all nuclear tests and manufacture of the Bombs. 'We want', he told the convention, 'an agreement that we would not be involved in using this terrible weapon first, because we do not think there is any moral justice in using this kind of weapon.'

Many delegates actually stayed in their seats to listen to this unusual Englishman, who was offering views of a kind they had not heard before. For delegates to an American trade union convention to remain in their seats to listen to anyone except their own groups is decidedly unusual and certainly a tribute.

Cousins was back in Britain in time to carry out a series of speaking engagements in the election campaign, though he did not play a prominent part in it. It was a strange campaign in that warm October sunshine of 1959, when Britain seemed to be basking in a climate of unaccountable self-satisfaction. Unemployment had fallen from 621,000 at the beginning of 1959 to slightly above 400,000 by September. The balance of payments appeared healthier though this surface reading understated the dangers ahead and drew heavily on the exploitation by the Conservative Party of the national mood of self-indulgence. None the less, Hugh Gaitskell was confident that Labour could win the election. He did not seem to think, then, that the great nuclear controversy had done serious harm to Labour's prospects. Indeed he expected to win right up until the day before the election, when the public opinion polls – especially the one in the *Daily Mail* – shook his confidence.

In the event, it was a sweeping victory for Harold Macmillan, the third successive Tory success. The Conservatives had a majority of 107 over Labour, with 6 Liberals and one Independent. This was a shattering, staggering blow to Gaitskell, to Bevan, to the whole Labour Movement. It was the prelude to a bitter inquest and to an even more destructive year of recrimination which came close to tearing the Labour Party apart.

Chapter Fifteen

1960

The General Election of 8 October 1959 gave the Conservative Party its largest post-war majority. The Macmillan Government were returned to power with a Parliamentary authority which no Conservative Government had possessed since the early 1930s. Macmillan was at the peak of his influence. In one sense it was the last General Election conducted by a generation of politicians schooled in pre-war Britain and still unused to the techniques demanded by exposure to mass TV. It was an election fought in a climate of acute social change; though in retrospect this was a change which can be seen to have had more to do with fragmentation of traditional certainties than with the crystallisation of new ones. In so many ways 1959 was the end of an era not just the end of a decade.

The impulse for change was not limited to the trade unions or the Labour Movement. A younger generation of politically uncommitted people found that they were able to exploit the "Opportunity State" of the Macmillan period with a latitude which surprised as well as impressed them. British society had grown accustomed to full employment, economic growth, the increasing spread of mass consumption and TV. The attractions of the tinsel society, now on full display, were underestimated by the Labour Party. On the shop floor there was a growing revolt against authority, alongside the break-up of the old regime of leadership inside the trade unions. The campaign against the H-bomb overlapped social and class frontiers. It became the focal point of an emotional protest against the old order of things. As it grew in size it seemed to offer the opportunity to express dissent across a wide spectrum of affairs without involvement in a precise 'programme' of detailed reform. It was outside party politics, and frequently appeared to be outside the normal parameters of economic and social problems. To a large extent this accounted for its appeal, as well as its weaknesses. It appealed to an innate instinct for survival rather than a necessarily rational view of the military and political realities of world affairs.

235

The majority of the nation, as the election result demonstrated, clearly felt safer and more secure on the whole under Macmillan Toryism than with the Gaitskell alternative. The Conservatives' play on the prosperity theme was immensely successful : the electorate was probably in no mood to listen to forecasts of gloom. Hugh Gaitskell, speaking at the Labour Party's inquest conference at Blackpool in November 1959, mocked those in the Labour Movement who had referred to the mood of smugness. He compared this view with Oscar Wilde's celebrated remark that : 'the play was a great success – but the audience was a failure'. Yet, in historic terms, the feeling that the electorate had somehow missed the point – perhaps even consciously – could not be excluded from any analysis of that remarkable Tory victory. Harold Macmillan appeared to sense the mood with an almost supernatural instinct. Whatever may be said by his critics, no post-war Prime Minister can claim a more remarkable achievement in the management of public response than Macmillan in October 1959.

With all this in mind it would be extremely difficult to draw any precise deductions about why Labour lost the 1959 General Election. Yet there were many on the Right wing of the Labour Movement who blamed Frank Cousins for having scared off the middle-class voters. Gaitskell himself believed, at one time, that the busmen's strike had been very damaging to the Labour Party, though there is no evidence that it had any great effect at all. The H-bomb, however, is a different matter. Claims have been made that the Cousins rumpus lost much potential support for Labour among the 'floating voters'. In her book on Frank Cousins, Margaret Stewart says with conviction : 'the much publicised and deepening fissure over defence undoubtedly contributed to the Labour Party's defeat in 1959'.[1] It may be. It cannot be proved either way. It can be argued that in the margin of electoral opinion the feeling that the Labour Party was split over defence policy assisted Macmillan to consolidate opinion behind the 'prosperity and security' theme of the Conservatives. All I can offer by way of evidence to the contrary is that I found no trace of this at all during my own travels around Britain in that campaign, when I accompanied Aneurin Bevan on his extensive national tour. Throughout that entire tour there was no sign that the defence row inside the Labour Party was influencing people's thinking or potential voting. Here was the man who, more than anyone else in the country, was at the centre of that controversy. Yet there was no significant mention of the H-bomb row. It was a surprise to both of us : as if the issue was almost too big to be encompassed within the routine language of the hustings. Naturally Bevan sought to bring in foreign affairs and often concentrated on them by demoting domestic policy to brief passing references. He attacked the Macmillan Government's record on Suez, on Cyprus,

1. Margaret Stewart, *Frank Cousins: A Study* (Hutchinson, 1968), p. 99.

in Africa and over disarmament. Always he set out his message against the background of socialist philosophy. Yet when it came to audience response the range of questioning was overwhelmingly concerned with domestic issues – economic and social policy – not with foreign affairs nor the H-bomb.

All those crowded meetings were significant for the numbers of young people in the audience. It helped to inspire Nye with the belief that Labour would win, and he did not seriously question this until the day before polling when Gaitskell promised that there would be no increase in taxation under a Labour Government in order to pay for the extra social benefits promised in Labour's programme. I was with Nye when he heard of the Gaitskell speech and he exploded. Turning to me with anger in his eyes, he said, 'He's thrown it away. He's lost the election.' That promise may have had a profound influence in those last two decisive days : no one can tell. But in Nye's eyes the Gaitskell gaffe (which was how Bevan saw it) was more damaging than anything thrown up by the defence controversy. Gaitskell himself certainly expected to win. Lady Gaitskell has told me : 'He thought so until the very day before polling, when he saw the *Daily Mail* opinion poll. Then his hopes sank. Perhaps it was that promise about no increase in tax despite all the extra benefits. We thought at the time that it was right for him to say that, but perhaps it wasn't.'

Having said that Nye Bevan expected to win (he was certainly shocked and surprised by the size of the Tory victory) I must make a qualification. Throughout that campaign he impressed me as a deeply saddened and introspective person fearing, as it were, that the prospect of effective power was slipping away from his grasp. Perhaps it was the beginning of his illness, which, within the next nine months, was to take away this incomparable figure. All the time during my conversations as we travelled around there was a brooding gloom in Nye, a certain despair at the immensity of the task ahead. In retrospect it is difficult to resist the feeling that he had already begun to sense what fate might have in store.

There was never any real doubt about Nye's attitude towards Hugh Gaitskell. He was almost unremittingly critical of Gaitskell both as the leader of the Labour Party and as a socialist. 'He is no socialist,' Nye would repeatedly insist to me. Yet he saw no way of overthrowing Gaitskell's leadership, although he regarded it as 'a tragedy' for the Labour Movement, because of the balance of power in and composition of the Parliamentary Labour Party. But Bevan also admitted that if Labour lost the election he would, perforce, have to challenge Gaitskell. He had no clear notion of how this was going to be done, or what the result might be; but he felt there would be a necessity to do it. And he was already talking about the 'new forces' inside the Movement that would need to be rallied to such a cause – forces reflecting the changes taking place at the roots of the Party and the unions, of which, in his view, Frank Cousins was a clear manifestation.

Bevan told me: 'If we are defeated we must discuss the next steps not so much within the Parliamentary Labour Party machine but outside – with those trade unions and other forces who can be brought in.' In this context he particularly referred to Frank Cousins, whom Bevan saw as a figure of fundamental importance to the kind of changes he believed were necessary, and indeed, inevitable, within the Labour Movement. Yet Bevan was puzzled and confused by some of Cousins's attitudes. He thought the Transport Workers' leader had strong tendencies towards 'syndicalism', of which Bevan disapproved. Cousins was a breath of fresh air to Bevan, after his experiences with union leaders like Arthur Deakin, yet he still felt that Cousins did not sufficiently recognise, or accept, the need to fit the trade unions into a socialist programme. It would be a gross over-simplification to claim (as some have done) that this reflected Bevan's latent authoritarianism and his conviction that a socialist economy, to be effective, must have a strong central core. In this sense there was as much of the centralist in Frank Cousins as there was in Nye Bevan. Equally there was in both a profound rejection of authority and a searching for a combination, within the socialist ethic, of centralism, in the form of a philosophic direction for society, combined with a widening of democratic freedoms.

Bevan's attitude towards the unions was not, of course, based solely on the philosophical question marks he placed against their structure and process. He had strong reservations about their political basis, seeing them as creatures of the capitalist system, institutions conditioned by the necessity to react against the pressures and demands of such a system rather than as a 'creative' force. In this he was not in conflict with Frank Cousins. But Nye Bevan had other factors to contend with when he contemplated the trade unions. He bore all the emotional scars of having done personal battle with the union 'junta' (as he often regarded the hierarchy) for most of his parliamentary life. In his experience it had almost always been on the Right of the political spectrum and, by his standards, politically unimaginative and negative, true of the TGWU under both Bevin and Deakin. Indeed the conflict between Bevin and Bevan had been as constant as it had been frequently ferocious. There is a famous story dating from the time that they were members of the Attlee Cabinet. After one particularly unpleasant slanging match a third Cabinet Minister said to Bevin, 'You know, Ernie, the trouble with Nye is that he's his own worst enemy.' Quick as a flash Bevin replied, 'Not while I'm alive he ain't . . .'. Bevan's relationship with Deakin was, as we have already seen, no better. So he had an automatic tendency to regard both the TGWU and its General Secretary with deep suspicion and misgiving. He was all the more astonished to find that the union had thrown up to the top a man like Frank Cousins, and Bevan, like so many others, at times still found this almost unbelievable. Moreover, Bevan and Cousins had been reared in different schools: the Parliamentary and the trade union. However, they had both started out as miners, from mining families; both had been reared in that special atmosphere of dedication to the general philosophy of the Labour Movement, and both possessed that special almost instinctive impulse for sweeping political change which has been so deeply rooted in mining communities. Yet they articulated differently not only because they were men with different chemistries but because of their contrasting 'schools'. Aneurin Bevan, for all his disillusion with the Parliamentary Labour Party machine, was still deeply committed to Parliamentary institutions and the concept of legislative authority vested in Parliament. Frank Cousins, schooled and conditioned in industrial bargaining, was more sensitive to the need to take account of the vagaries of rank-and-file moods and reactions.

Cousins has always seen the role of trade unions as basic to the needs of working people to express themselves where the social and economic conflict bites hardest – at the point of production. He was always suspicious of attempts to muzzle the unions or to impose conditions on them which might subordinate them to a strong central authority, even if that authority was a socialist Government. Bevan reacted to this by describing Cousins's attitude as 'syndicalist', and perhaps it was. But Cousins defended his position first on the basis of democracy and secondly on the sheer practical grounds that no society, even the most tyrannical, can for long suppress the instinctive drive for a better working life that it is the natural role of trade unions to express.

The role of the unions in a socialist system is something that has never been satisfactorily resolved. The Webbs in their classic study at the end of the last century expressed the belief that with the inevitable growth of collectivism a method of legal enactment would gradually, if not entirely, replace the system of collective bargaining. This was, and to a large extent remains, a perfectly valid view. But collectivism has *not* replaced collective bargaining; it has simply made it more difficult and in some areas more obviously contradictory. There can be no absolute formula for relations between trade unions and the developing role of the State – not even within a system which can be described as socialist. It is not commonly accepted that one of the main factors helping to discredit claims by Communist countries to be democracies is the almost completely subordinate role allocated to unions by the State machine – that is, if you believe a union's function is to provide working people with the means of expressing and advocating their particular interests, even where those interests would seem to conflict with the wider public interest. Unions may, of course, be severe irritants in any managerial conception of neatness, efficiency and perfection, whether in a capitalist or a socialist economy. They can be, and usually are, awkward and obstinate obstacles for the designer of theoretical blueprints. They can be a frustrating brake on what is regarded as progress and rational planning, just as much as they can frustrate the forces of the market place. Unions are the institutional voice of the worker on the shop floor and, not infrequently, that voice can be infuriatingly stubborn, conservative and even selfish. Frank Cousins's view on this has always been quite clear : the need for these irrationalities to find an effective expression is just as important in the socialist State as in any other, though he recognised that crucial changes would be necessary in trade union relationships within a Socialist State. What he would never accept was that unions should be required to surrender their right to protest in such a State – that they would automatically be expected to become the acquiescent instruments of authority, however benevolent that authority might be. This gave an awkward edge to Cousins's socialism and led him into conflict with both Left and Right wings. It was also the basis of his rejection of wage control even under a Labour Government, even when he became part of such a Government.

I have dwelt on this issue at some length at this stage because the Cousins concept of the unions' role and their place in a democratic and socialist system is central to the development of his policies and actions over the decade which followed Labour's election defeat of October 1959.

Nothing since the Labour collapse of 1931 had such a traumatic affect on the thinking of the leadership of the Labour Party and the trade union as that third successive electoral defeat. Morale was badly damaged, if not shattered. Recrimination was not only in the air but publicly voiced with amazing candour. The 'inquest' conference at Blackpool in November produced Hugh Gaitskell's famous call for the amendment of the Party constitution in which the historic allegiance to public ownership was to be severed. Gaitskell's view was that the specific reference in Clause 4 of the Labour Party constitution to the 'common ownership of the means of production, distribution and exchange' was now out of date. He also concluded that nationalisation had lost votes for Labour during the election and that the old conception of public ownership was a liability to the Party.

For months before the election there had been agitation from right-wing members of the Labour Party, not all associated personally with Hugh Gaitskell, to pull away from the old concepts of socialist dogma. The argument advanced was that the traditional allegiance to nationalisation was neither relevant to a modern mixed economy nor essential to a programme for radical change and greater equality. Tax reform, it was argued, could do the job more effectively and excite less electoral hostility. The call to abandon the old ideological commitments was loud and clear among the Right wing of the Party well before October 1959. To my knowledge it was indeed already a topic of serious consideration as early as June 1958, after the settlement of the London busmen's strike.

I was at a luncheon in St Ermin's Hotel on 27 June 1958 given by the

Daily Herald for Hugh Gaitskell. It was a small, private luncheon at which Douglas Jay, Patrick Gordon-Walker and Harold Wilson were present, along with the editor of the *Herald*, Douglas Machray. Gaitskell was in a passionate mood as he reflected on the Labour Party's failure to make an impact in terms of public opinion poll-ratings compared with the Tories. Why, he inquired, aren't the public reacting against the Conservatives? He believed it was because the Labour Party had not departed sufficiently from its old 'working-class attitudes'. People in Britain, he reflected, were in the main 'radical' but not socialist; they wanted a 'left of centre radical party' which would make social changes without being revolutionary or authoritarian. More and more, he believed, the 'Keir Hardie image was becoming a dim and distant feature of the past'. The Labour Party had to find some more modern image if it was to be a successful force. There was now a feeling of prosperity among the working class, he observed, and this was turning the British electorate into a largely middle-class vote.

Douglas Jay supported this view, but went still further in proposing changes. It would be a good idea, said Jay, to change the name of the Labour Party – 'though I realise that this is not possible at present'. He believed it would be better electorally for the Party to rename itself – either as the Liberal Party, in a new form, perhaps by adding the label Liberal Democratic Party, or some other such title. This he felt would help to recruit much more support from the centre of British politics and present a real alternative to Tory rule. On the other hand, Jay recognised that his proposition would not be accepted within the Labour Party, and was not anxious for his views to be made known outside that gathering.

Gordon-Walker appeared himself to share the Jay view. Harold Wilson plainly dissociated himself from Gaitskell and Jay, partly by silence and partly by an open difference of opinion. Both Machray and myself were stunned by the force of the Gaitskell-Jay view. It has to be remembered that this was still some fifteen months before the 1959 election campaign and more than two years away from the Scarborough conference of 1960 where, after the split over nuclear disarmament, *The Times* said there were 'two Labour Parties' – one of the Left, another of the Right. The ideological fissures had become palpable long before.

At any rate it came as no thunderous shock to discover that immediately after the 1959 defeat there were discreet soirees at Hugh Gaitskell's home in Frognal, Hampstead, where the reformers gathered in some strength to plan the rebirth of the Labour Party, possibly under a new name but most certainly with a new constitution relieved of its fundamentalist socialist commitment. The date of the first formal assembly of the Reformers, according to Michael Foot in his biography of Bevan, was Sunday 11 October.[2]

2. Michael Foot, *Aneurin Bevan*, Vol. II (Davis-Poynter, 1973), p. 630–2.

On the following Friday Douglas Jay published a famous article in the weekly *Forward* (the Right wing's answer to *Tribune*) in which he publicly called for a new name for the Labour Party and the abandonment of further nationalisation proposals. Everyone who was anyone in the Labour Movement was in full cry with his or her analysis of the lost election weeks before the Party conference gathered in Blackpool.

The speech then delivered by Hugh Gaitskell, committing him firmly to a fundamental revision of the constitution (though not a change of name), had a carefully prepared text, worked on for many weeks, and it came as no profound surprise to anyone with an ear to the groundswell of political gossip. None the less, it turned the Blackpool conference into a bitter affair which, in retrospect, can be seen to have had much to do with the split that in 1960 came near to smashing the Party. It is almost impossible to disentangle the campaign against the H-bomb, as it developed inside the Party, from Gaitskell's attempt to redirect the Labour Movement away from its traditional socialist commitment. Cousins himself sought to keep the two issues separate, but inevitably they frequently merged in his mind. Gaitskell's speech at the 1959 conference undoubtedly deepened Frank Cousins's mistrust of the Party leader and the coterie around him, and fortified his own conviction that the right-wing attempt to shift the whole pivotal balance of the Labour Movement had to be resisted, come what might.

Cousins's speech at Blackpool came on the second day, sandwiched between Gaitskell's and Nye Bevan's magnificent wind-up speech, which so many observers have said was one of the greatest of his career. Certainly Bevan can be said to have saved the Labour Party from leaving Blackpool in a condition of total disarray if not open warfare. At the same time the great weight of opinion in the speeches from the rostrum was hostile to Gaitskell and his revisionist concepts. And in this sense Cousins's speech summed up the feeling on the Left when he declared :

We can have nationalisation without socialism – we cannot have socialism without nationalisation. Those who make any other form of approach are doing a disservice to the Labour Movement ...

Cousins then went on to attack Gaitskell directly :

My views are different from Hugh's. I do not think we portrayed ourselves sufficiently well as a Party in opposition to the Tories. Let us give over pretending we have to get half a million Tory people to change their allegiance to us at voting time. There are five million or six million people who are socialists in embryo waiting for us to go out and harness them to the power machine we want to drive, and the sooner we get on with that job the better for all of us ...

Cousins rebuked Gaitskell for putting his proposals to the conference before having discussed them with the Party's National Executive. That seemed 'a bit peculiar', he observed. What, he wondered, was Gaitskell afraid of:

> If the idea is that all we need to do is to add something to our constitution there could be something to be said in favour of that. But if, as I gather, Rule 4 is likely to be revised to make a different reference to our attitude towards public ownership I would suggest with the greatest possible respect to our Leader that no way – Douglas Jay's or any other way – is going to change that one.

And Frank Cousins at once ranged himself alongside those who prepared to fight to the last to prevent any significant change in 'that one'.

His own private thoughts were set down in another of those brief diaries which he kept from time to time. These diary notes are quite remarkable for their perceptiveness. Unfortunately they were sporadic. He kept them when the mood captured his imagination or when his political spirits were unusually low. A batch of notes kept between 3 October 1959 and 29 April 1960 ended as abruptly as they began. Yet they contain some fascinating commentaries on events.

After the General Election of 1959 he wrote of Douglas Jay's article in *Forward*:

> My feeling is that D. Jay has done us all a disservice, but I hope we can also recognise that he is only expressing publicly views which have been known to be held for a long time by some of the leadership of the party including Hugh Gaitskell, Patrick Gordon-Walker, Tony Crosland, Roy Jenkins and Douglas Jay himself. Most of the party policy statements during the past three years have tended to display that kind of thinking, particularly those on industry and society, control of industry and education. We are probably running into a bad period, and I hope the unions and their leaders can retain their balance.

Cousins had little faith that the union leaders would be able to retain what he called 'their balance', by which he meant a radical attitude. His diary of 7 November noted sardonically that the TUC leaders felt it necessary 'to display to the country our responsibility and statesmanship' regarding strikes by taking a tough line against all unofficial strikes:

> The recent attitude in the national press of describing all strikes as 'wildcat strikes' is having an effect on some members of the General Council. They are wanting to institute investigations and prepare reports. My feeling as expressed to our TUC colleagues is that we should not become involved in this, as it is only playing into the hands of the enemies of the trade union movement. I am afraid, however, they will go ahead with it . . .'

And they did.

A week before the Blackpool 'inquest' conference Cousins was one of a group of TUC leaders who met Gaitskell and Bevan to discuss the future. They met for dinner at the Euston Hotel on the night of 22 November. The following day Cousins noted in his diary that he was accompanied by Carron, Williamson, Greene and Webber, all of them right-wing and pro-Gaitskell union leaders as well as anti-Cousins (and anti-Bevan).

> The first noticeable thing was that the election has left its mark on Hugh, he seems tired and older but perhaps this will only be a passing phase. A disturbing thing is that the two of them [Gaitskell and Bevan] do not appear to have anything in common. Whilst the meeting was not in any way an inquest on the election, obviously we could not avoid talking around it. Hugh feels that nationalisation was a vote loser at the polls. Nye thinks it was a vote winner when tackled boldly, and says if it lost votes anywhere it was because we shied away from it. Hugh says association with trade unions did not affect results, Nye disagrees and says we will never make real progress whilst we have a man like Tewson, who is completely non-political, at the head of the TUC. Also says unions should give more money to Party and allow some of it to be spent at the discretion of the Parliamentary Party leaders ...

Referring to the forthcoming Blackpool conference, the diary notes that he is horrified to learn that the three main speakers there, Gaitskell, Bevan and the chairman, Barbara Castle, were all preparing their separate speeches in isolation and without any mutual consultation. 'How daft can we all become?' he asks.

Cousins was in fact glad to be away from Blackpool and its tensions. A few days after the conference he visited the TGWU's Oxford area and noted in the diary that it was 'a treat to be able to visit our Oxford pressed steel branch . . . and to mix again with *real* trade unionists who still believe in themselves and their ability to do some of the things which still need to be done'. In that same entry, 6 December, he also revealed that:

> there has been a lot of pressure lately from the Left wing of the Labour Party asking me to go into Parliament and to challenge Hugh for the leadership. They seem to be surprised when I tell them I have no desire to be in the House nor wish to be the Leader. I really want to help a leader by using our trade union beliefs to establish socialism.

Nevertheless the same entry added: 'Very grave doubts are in my mind as to whether Hugh Gaitskell has either the wish or the fire to achieve that.'

Cousins' returned to the theme of his 'grave doubts' in his diary the following spring. On 26 March 1960 he wrote, regarding the moves being made to revise the Labour Party's constitutions, that there was now a determined move on the part of the right wing 'to sacrifice our principles for the sake of securing an election victory'. He went on :

> The importance of this move is that the particular group of politicians of the Gaitskell, Crosland, Wyatt, Jay, Callaghan, Gordon-Walker, type are really trying to secure the removal from the constitution of the Labour Party the reference to those aspects of policy in which they do not have any belief. They are reformists with a main purpose to secure political power for themselves, quite satisfied to maintain the existing structure of society with kindly alterations.

Cousins would never accept that there was any political morality in proclaiming socialist doctrine and refusing to face up to the ideological consequences. He totally rejected Gaitskell's reasons for dismissing nationalisation and positive economic control – just as later, when he was in the Wilson Cabinet, he rejected the compromises Wilson embraced on these issues. Increasingly Cousins came to believe that the transformation of the political system which he believed to be necessary (and which was, in his view, inevitable (anyway) would have to be carried out by political leaders who rejected such compromises and were prepared to face the consequences. But that was not for 1960.

The whole of 1960 was dominated by the battle for the soul of the Labour Party, punctuated by the immense disaster of Bevan's death in July, when the whole Labour Movement seemed to be balancing on the edge of a precipice. Other elements of the deepest emotional kind were involved in Frank Cousins's life at that time, when everything around him seemed to be building to a climax. In January 1960 he and Harry (the late Lord) Douglass the steel union leader, went to India to represent the TUC as guests of the Indian National TUC. But in the middle of the visit Cousins received news that his mother had died, and he immediately flew back to attend the funeral. Hannah Cousins had been ill for some time, and her death was no sudden shock, yet it still had a profound effect on Frank. He had always felt closer to his mother than to his father. Her passing was an emotional landmark affecting him more than he realised at the time. Her example, her courage and her forceful character had moulded Frank from his childhood. Even when she died at the age of 78, Frank still looked on his mother as a prime influence in his life. She was proud of her son, the lad she had seen grow from her simple home to become one of the most important names in the land. He was conscious of her pride and, subconsciously always felt the urge to justify it. After her death Frank was ill for several weeks, partly a chill after the India visit, partly a strained back from heaving a bag of concrete, but at the root, perhaps, as a psychosomatic reaction to Hannah's death. The cord was broken.

Apart from personal and political problems, Cousins had many battles on the industrial scene in 1959 and 1960. After the 1959 Congress the General Council, after persistent criticism by the Press, agreed to hold its own inquiry into unofficial strikes and the powers of shop-stewards within each affiliated union. Sir Tom (now Lord) Williamson was put in charge, but Frank Cousins made it clear from the start that he didn't agree with the motives behind it. He opposed the inquiry inside the TUC and spoke against it publicly. He also refused the TGWU's cooperation, on the grounds that the whole concept was misconceived. Of course, there was an increase in 'shop-floor power'; but that, he argued, was not due to any sinister political plot by shop-stewards or Communists. It was due principally to the changes taking place in industry, the pressures of new technology, the widening horizons and broadening aspirations of workers. If the TUC wanted to hold an inquiry into those factors, then he would certainly cooperate, but he wanted to have no part in what seemed to him an essentially negative investigation into whether unofficial strikes were a bad thing in themselves and how best they could be curbed. 'We have believed,' he told a Bristol meeting in November 1959, 'that the weapon of withdrawal of labour should be the last resort of men and women to pursue their legitimate claims. If you use it wildly, it has not the same value as when you use it properly.' Disputes generally arose from legitimate grievances, he stated, and some were deliberately allowed to develop by bad management. Nevertheless, the prerogative of calling strikes rested with the union's executive. The fact that he was known to be opposed to the TUC's inquiry, Cousins explained, should not be interpreted as indicating that he was in favour of wholesale stoppages, official or unofficial. 'We only want to take this step [to stop work] when it is useful to do so,' he added. Indeed what he really resented about the inquiry was the presumption behind it that the tension in industrial relations reflected some sinister political plot rather than a growing conflict of interest and, as he saw it, a strengthening of working-class conviction that they now had the potential to protest, and protest vigorously, against injustice real or assumed. Frank Cousins believed that the TUC's attitude was far too narrow and its understanding of what was happening on the shop floor was extremely limited.

Although there was so much to occupy his mind later in 1960 he continued to attack those who sought to make the strike issue a stick with which to beat the unions. In Leicester at the end of May he said:

> We do not think that striking is the best way to solve our problems but on some occasions it is the only weapon that we have to use. We are not willing to forgo our strike weapons in a world where employers themselves want to

retain their rights of dismissal or repudiation of the principal of negotiation when it suits them to do so.

The TGWU's membership started to climb towards the end of 1959, reaching in 1960 a new peak of 1,340,000, from which point it rose steadily throughout the 1960s. In 1960 there was the biggest single annual increase the union had experienced since 1946, when demobilisation brought a huge post-war surge to its ranks. One can only guess at how far this reflected the militant policies pursued by Cousins, both industrially and politically. The improved economic climate undoubtedly played as significant a part in increasing membership as the previous slump had contributed to a decline. Nevertheless it is reasonable to conclude that Cousins's policies gave a new impetus to the recruitment drive, especially since membership of the TGWU was increasing at a higher rate than most of the other unions.

There was never a time during 1960 when the row over Clause 4 and the continuing fight over nuclear weapons could be separated, in the minds of the principal contestants or their followers. On the other hand, they were kept quite apart from each other in the formal processes of politics. Hugh Gaitskell was anxious to push his case for a revision of the Party constitution immediately after the Blackpool conference, and he raised it at the December meeting of the Party's National Executive. A special meeting was arranged for early in 1960 and by February the debate was in full swing, but by then Gaitskell had picked up an increasing number of warning signals and was in fact beginning to retreat from his Blackpool position, under pressure from some of his own supporters who began to realise, somewhat late in the day, that they had made a serious error in underestimating the emotional reaction throughout the Labour Movement to any watering down in the terms of the founding faith. Moreover through Jennie Lee, Nye Bevan (who was dying) passed on to Hugh Gaitskell his feeling that nothing should be done to undermine Party unity by scrapping Clause 4. Gaitskell appreciated the debt he owed to Bevan for that Blackpool speech in which Nye had probably saved Gaitskell's leadership. But apart from that the Party leader was under pressure from all quarters in the Party to drop his insistence on amending Clause 4. He was warned by Morgan Phillips, that if he pursued his campaign irreparable damage could be done to the Party. So the retreat began almost before the bugle was sounded for the second time.

Gaitskell conceived a compromise that would leave Clause 4 as it stood, but would augment it with an additional Statement of Aims setting out the Labour Party's philosophy in more modern terms. A draft of this statement was put before a special meeting of the Party's National Executive on 16 March. In effect it consisted of a twelve-point 'new testament'. One of the

main points – Section J – set out the need for public ownership, but qualified this by proposing that in future the character of such ownership ought
to take varying forms, including state-owned industries and firms, producer
and consumer cooperatives, municipal ownership, public participation in
private companies, and so on. It also recognised that both 'public and private
enterprise have a place in the economy . . .' That was Gaitskell's own phrasing.

A crucial amendment was proposed to Section J by Jennie Lee. She
argued that the preamble should include Nye Bevan's memorable phrase,
which he used at the Blackpool conference, about 'the commanding heights
of the economy' coming under public ownership. Gaitskell didn't demur; he
accepted Jennie Lee's suggestion at once, grasping at an obvious life-line.
There were other amendments, too, though none was as significant. Morgan
Phillips proposed that there should be a 'link phrase' to illustrate that the
new statement was *not* an amendment to Clause 4 but an amplification.
He suggested that the 'link phrase' should be : 'The following is the re-state-
ment and amplification of Party objects adopted in 1960 in the light of post-
war developments and the historic achievements of the first majority Labour
Government.' That was designed to help Gaitskell out of his dilemma. But
Harold Wilson succeeded in further amending this proposal by deleting
all words after 'is' up to and including 'objects' – which was accepted,
though it did not please Gaitskell.

By the time the meeting had finished with the Gaitskell draft the original
concept was left in a battered and almost absurd state. Indeed in one sense
the document eventually issued was irrelevant, while in another sense the
inclusion of the crucial Bevan phrase strengthened rather than weakened the
attachment to public ownership.

Only one hand was raised against the revised Statement of Aims at the
close of the meeting – that of Harry Nicholas. He was under instructions
from the TGWU executive to resist any attempt to water down the original
Clause 4. In the event he was therefore committed to oppose even the
Statement of Aims, innocuous though it was. Still, the Party executive had
registered clearly and firmly that there was to be no retreat from the basic
tenets of the Party's faith. Gaitskell himself had been forced to accept a
major defeat.

The question which remained to be decided was how the new Statement
of Aims would be presented to the Party's annual conference at Scarborough
that year – and in what relationship it would stand to the original Clause
4. In fact it was simply included in the annual report to the conference as
an appendage to Clause 4 and the other clauses in Labour's aims. Then it
was debated against a collection of motions, all of which confirmed Labour's
commitment to public ownership and socialism. The whole episode became
a rather elaborate and banal face-saving formula to enable Hugh Gaitskell

(and those who originally supported his case for a revision of Clause 4) to escape from a still worse embarrassment – defeat at the Party conference. Indeed at Scarborough Gaitskell publicly confessed that he had misjudged the feelings of the Party and that, to his surprise, 'it became obvious that there were throughout the movement strong feelings about the 1918 Constitution [the constitution incorporating Clause 4].' Equally confessional was his candid admission that one reason he agreed to drop his original idea was that it became 'quite clear we were going to have a major division over defence, and we did not want to add to the divisions in the Party unnecessarily'.

There is no doubt that had Gaitskell chosen to stick to his original plan to amend Clause 4 he would have been heavily defeated at the Scarborough conference and the margin of his defeat would almost certainly have been larger than the defeat over nuclear disarmament. In the spring of 1960, when union conferences began to line up behind the TGWU on the H-bomb, there was a clear trend to link this with opposition to any tampering with Clause 4. The engineers, the shop and distributive workers, the boilermakers – all voted for the unilateralist policy on nuclear arms and, at the same time, opposed Gaitskell on Clause 4. But more significant was the tendency for those unions who supported the official policy on defence to oppose any amending of Clause 4. For instance, both the miners and the railwaymen voted against Cousins on the H-bomb at Scarborough, but they equally opposed any watering down of Clause 4.

It is now generally accepted that Gaitskell made a major error of judgment over the Clause 4 controversy. He himself conceded that he had made a tactical error, but he never saw it as one of principle. Baroness Gaitskell has told me that both she and Hugh regarded the whole affair as a bad mistake. It should never have been brought up at the Blackpool conference, she says, and she is in no doubt that it made him 'less popular in the movement.' She adds:

I think that in the end he realised that, too, although he never doubted that he was right in principle. He was never a great nationaliser, he never regarded nationalisation as an end in itself, only a means. He was in favour of various forms of State intervention in the economy but he never regarded nationalisation as a major principle at any time in his life. Hugh was a reformer, never a revolutionary socialist.

But of course the sense of outrage that was felt throughout the Labour Movement, and consistently reflected by Frank Cousins at the time, did nothing to help Gaitskell quell the rising storm over nuclear arms policy. That is why it is difficult to disentangle the two issues when one considers the emotional explosion of 1960. Bill Simpson in his book on the Labour

Party's relations with the trade unions refers to Gaitskell as being 'routed by emotion as well as by good common sense' over Clause 4.[3] Simpson, who was elected to the Labour Party Executive in 1962 and has always taken a moderate political position, writes that Gaitskell made a 'political blunder [in 1960] which for me cast doubts on his judgement and his basic rapport with the rank and file of the party'. He explains:

> The Clause 4 controversy need never have happened. It had not been a factor in the 1959 election. If it had been, Labour with the same consti- tution would not have been elected in 1964 and 1966. The public despite the importance given the matter by the papers treated the argument with indif- ference spiced with a dash of bewilderment. The members of the Party, how- ever, fought among themselves like political tigers and in a few weeks a political party which had been healthy and united in the election was trans- mogrified into a dialectical shambles.[4]

Simpson over-rates the 'unity' that existed during the election, yet his account of the morale-shattering impact of that Clause 4 row is certainly no exaggeration. In fact it can be argued, perhaps to the disadvantage of Frank Cousins, that the nuclear disarmament campaign might never have succeeded at Scarborough if Gaitskell had not made such a major political blunder over Clause 4. By his Blackpool speech he helped to erode the sup- port of people who might very well have been on his side in the defence row under different circumstances.

The unilateralist campaign inside the trade union movement reached its peak in the spring and summer of 1960 as conference after conference swung over. The first to move into the Cousins camp was the Union of Shop, Distributive and Allied Workers (USDAW) at their conference in April, despite the appeals made by their General Secretary, Sir Alan Birch. Less than two weeks later the Amalgamated Engineering Union (now the AUEW) followed suit, again in the face of desperate appeals by their Presi- dent, the late Bill (Lord) Carron. Both Birch and Carron were among Gait- skell's closest allies in the hierarchy of the trade-union movement. Their appeals for 'common sense' were swept aside, and the USDAW vote at the end of April made it imperative that the Labour Party and TUC leaders should meet again to redraft their joint policy on defence in the hope that a modified statement might stem the tide of support for unilateralism. Frank Cousins had been pressing for such a meeting for some time, though it was not until USDAW and the AEU swung away from official policy that Gaitskell decided to move. One week after the engineers' vote the Labour Party international committee met in London to review the crisis. It heard

---

3. William Simpson, *Labour: The Union and the party* (Allen & Unwin, 1973), p. 111.
4. *Ibid.*, p. 111.

Hugh Gaitskell reaffirm in the strongest possible terms his determination to fight the anti-bomb campaign, insisting that whatever happened at the TUC or Party conference that year the Parliamentary Labour Party would never accept the CND policy – come what might. It was perhaps the first ominous hint of the 'fight, fight, and fight again' speech . . .

From the end of May, when the joint meeting between the TUC and Labour Party leaders took place, until the Trades Union Congress met in September there was a non-stop series of meetings of all shapes and sizes. Most were informal and private, some were clandestine, but all strained at every conceivable formula in an attempt to avert the impending disaster, which loomed larger as each summer day passed. For his part Frank Cousins, while wanting to avoid an open showdown if possible, did not deviate from his campaign, not only on nuclear weapons but across the whole political and industrial front. In spite of Gaitskell's retreat on Clause 4 Cousins continued to make public speeches warning that he would fight any attempt to move the Labour Party away from its fundamental attachment to the concept of public ownership. It was a long and bitter summer.

The joint meeting of the TUC and Labour Party executives at the end of May appointed a Committee of Nine to draft a new statement on defence. It included Cousins, who was in fact quite isolated, although unexpectedly he found a modest ally in Crossman, who tried hard to find yet another formula which might somehow bridge the gap between Gaitskell and Cousins. For his pains Crossman was sharply rebuked by Gaitskell, and relations between the two became exceedingly strained.

Speculation at the time, and in accounts since 1960, suggest that the Committee of Nine came very near to an acceptable agreement. Certainly this is asserted in the Crossman diaries.[5] Crossman wrote at the time that he was convinced that agreement could have been reached but for Gaitskell's stubbornness. The committee was at work on a draft agreement on 1, 2 and 3 June with Crossman and Brown trying to persuade Gaitskell to make some concessions to Cousins in order to avert the inevitable confrontation at Scarborough. But it was clear that there was never any real hope of achieving this. Speaking at the General and Municipal Workers' conference at Yarmouth two weeks earlier Gaitskell had already declared his uncompromising opposition to any retreat from the fundamentals of official defence policy – the retention of nuclear weapons. He had also repeated his determination not to be 'dictated to' by the trade unions or even the Party conference (still to come). The Parliamentary Labour Party would decide, he insisted, and they would not be deflected by the votes of any conference on such basic issues as defence and national security. That was a passionate, immensely frank and unswerving speech which was probably the best

5. Richard Crossman, the unpublished diaries, 1 June 1960.

speech Gaitskell made on the issue until his Scarborough marathon performance. In it he explained that the Labour Party would now be ready to amend its defence policy by agreeing to drop the insistence on Britain possessing her own independent nuclear strike force. He admitted that he did not himself much like this policy change, but the situation had been transformed by the Conservative Government's decision to scrap the Blue Streak missile. This, said Hugh Gaitskell, made it plain that within a few years Britain would not be in a position to maintain an independent nuclear deterrent; independent, that is, of the Americans. The whole missile race had become too expensive for Britain to support a deterrent of her own, he admitted. The cost of the US missile programme he estimated was equal to the total cost of Britain's entire defence system. On the other hand he wanted Britain to maintain her contribution to a NATO defence force which would be based on nuclear weaponry. There could be no escape from the logic of that position as far as he was concerned.

That was the line he laid down with absolute conviction in advance of the joint meetings with the TUC and before the Committee of Nine began work. Yet both Crossman and George Brown thought they saw the opportunity of some compromise formula as a result of the fundamental shift in Britain's defence policy – a shift which had already compelled the Labour Party officially to change its stand. George Brown in particular came out strongly against any further attempt by Britain to manufacture her own independent nuclear deterrent and pre-empted Gaitskell on this, much to Gaitskell's fury. The situation was further complicated by the astonishing collapse of the summit conference in Paris, where Nikita Khruschev walked out on Eisenhower on the grounds that the American 'spy plane' incident – in which a U2 reconnaissance aircraft was shot down over Soviet territory – had shattered any confidence the Russians might have had in such a conference. The temperature of international tension was raised to a new level and inevitably cast a cloud over any campaign for disarmament.

To be sure, there was now a great deal of confusion as to what the Labour Party's defence policy really was, though there was no confusion in Hugh Gaitskell's mind as to what he wanted it to be. He remained totally committed to NATO, to a firm British contribution to the Atlantic alliance, with at the same time a strengthening of political control over the NATO bureaucracy. He insisted that this must be the basis on which any Labour Party defence policy had to rest. The attempt at a compromise in the Committee of Nine collapsed into recrimination, renewed bitterness all round, and quarrels between Gaitskell, Brown and Crossman. Nothing had been resolved, though things could hardly have been made worse.

On 3 June the TGWU executive, which had been in session at the same time as the Committee of Nine, finally announced a unanimous reaffirmation of its stand on nuclear weapons. Cousins reported to a Press conference afterwards that the differences between Hugh Gaitskell and himself 'were basic'. 'We were endeavouring to see if we could get a compromise,' he said, 'but it appeared that not only at the beginning but at the end of the meeting there were fundamental differences between us on the approach to the defence question'. The TGWU, he stressed, was against the testing, manufacture or use by Britain of nuclear weapons and against missile bases in this country. He did not think the new defence situation or the inter-national tension materially changed that position.

The new defence policy of the Labour Party – essentially based on reli-ance on NATO and the American 'nuclear umbrella' – was finally approved at a meeting of the National Executive on 22 June. Four voted against : Harry Nicholas, Barbara Castle, Anthony Greenwood and Tom Driberg. At the TUC General Council on the same day no decision was taken, because the draft of the new policy statement arrived after the meeting began. This absurd situation enabled Frank Cousins and Bob Willis to sup-port a move for deferment of any vote, though they made it clear they would oppose the policy when it eventually came to a vote. No doubt that was a frivolous gesture, but it reflected the anger felt by the union leaders (even those who supported the official policy) at being treated by the Party as a rubber stamp. By 12 votes to 8 (15 TUC leaders were absent) they voted to postpone a decision for a week and call a special meeting of the General Council. It was then approved by the usual overwhelming majority. Cousins and four other members of the Council comprised the by now routine minority.

Looking back at the phraseology of the Labour Party-TUC defence state-ment and comparing it with the stated policy of the TGWU it is perhaps difficult to understand fully why the differences – so slender in terms of phras-ing – should have led to such a bitter rift. The new official policy, issued on 22 June, even went as far as declaring that a Labour Government would press for a review of NATO strategy to ensure that 'the West shall never be the first to use the H-bomb nor base its strategy on threatening to do so' – a pledge which, at an earlier stage, might have satisfied Cousins as a demonstration that there *was* a genuine will to compromise. But it was too late. Gaitskell's style and manner in the Committee of Nine convinced Cousins that there was no real intention to bridge the gap; Cousins himself would never go cap in hand, especially having seen the way Gaitskell had dismissed the attempt at compromise by Crossman and Brown. At that stage nothing could be done to slow down the headlong dash to con-frontation. Whatever may be claimed in hindsight there is little doubt that too much mistrust, mutual suspicion and recrimination existed between the two men for either to have stopped in his tracks at that late stage. Frank Cousins told a conference of the Scottish TGWU at the end of June that there was no 'mortal conflict' between Gaitskell and himself: 'I have no personal antagonism towards the leader of the Labour Movement at all and I am sure he has none towards me'. The issue, he insisted all the time, was essentially one of 'socialist philosophy'. I do not doubt that both Gaitskell and Cousins genuinely believed that their conflict was entirely over policy. But it is equally clear to me that there were profound personality differences, and that these unquestionably contributed to the mutual bitterness. It is impossible, psychologically, to become embroiled in a conflict of such magnitude, with so much at stake, without personality factors becoming a dominating influence. And indeed to that extent the personality conflict between Gaitskell and Cousins was no less manifest than it was between Gaitskell and Bevan. Baroness Gaitskell has told me:

Hugh did not hate Frank or anything like that. He never hated anybody. There were very few people against whom Hugh felt real hostility. Frank was not one of them – but I think Frank *did* dislike Hugh. Frank, I think, always felt that Hugh was never really a socialist at all. He clearly felt that Hugh was an intruder in the Movement. Frank was one of those who felt that you couldn't be a true socialist unless you were working-class. Hugh wasn't working-class, and he never pretended to be, either.

Lady Gaitskell is probably right in this assessment, though Frank Cousins denies any deep hostility towards Gaitskell. In retrospect he says he regarded Gaitskell as an 'intellectually honest man who may have been driven to extremes by the force of his own case – as I too sometimes was'. Indeed there was an incident at Scarborough after the nuclear disarmament debate which supports Cousins's contention that he respected Gaitskell personally, though he was wholly out of sympathy with the policy the Labour Party leader was advocating and pursuing. When the two men claimed that their bitter conflict of 1960 was entirely one of policy they were not being wholly devious, though somewhat self-deluding and even naïve.

By July 1960 the scene was firmly set for the most dramatic Trades Union Congress and Labour Party conference of post-war years. The TGWU resolutions for the TUC and Party conferences were both direct challenges to official policy on defence. Each motion contained six points: complete rejection of any defence policy based on the threat of the use of strategic or tactical nuclear weapons; permanent cessation of the manufacture or testing of nuclear weapons; the cessation of aircraft patrols carrying nuclear weapons and operating from British bases; opposition to missile bases in Britain; a strengthening of the United Nations to improve conditions for world peace; and, finally, a call for the reopening of international talks on world disarmament. It was this motion which George Brown, immediately before the Scarborough conference, insisted was not in fundamental conflict with official policy and could, therefore, be accepted by Gaitskell. Of course it was an absurd claim – or, more charitably, the wish was father to the thought. Clearly the TGWU motions were *not* wholly unilateralist, nor were they pacifist. Crossman in his diaries noted that George Brown, by going around the country defending Labour's defence policy, was also 'pointing out the truth, which is that Frank Cousins's executive has not permitted him to put in a downright unilateralist resolution and that the generalities he has been allowed to put in are perfectly harmless'.[6] But at the same time Crossman noted it was quite clear that Gaitskell had no intention of coming to terms with Cousins. There was indeed a great deal of self-delusion as well as confusion all round in those days, which was understandable enough.

Nor was this the only curious episode involving George Brown. Frank Cousins relates a story of Brown's approach to him, at the end of 1959, suggesting that he should consider coming into the House of Commons as a potential challenger to Gaitskell. According to Frank Cousins the argument put forward by George Brown was that since Cousins was such 'a politically minded trade union leader' he ought seriously and urgently to consider making a clear bid for the Labour leadership. This occurred towards the end of 1959 when George Brown and his wife, Sophie, visited the Cousins home at Epsom. By then relations between Brown and Gaitskell had already become strained. Brown told Cousins that he no longer regarded Gaitskell as the right man to lead the Labour Party, and he believed the Party leadership was wide open for a take-over bid. It is certain that Gaitskell had some inkling of what George Brown was thinking and saying at the time, although it is doubtful whether the Party leader actually knew of Brown's approach to Frank Cousins. He may have suspected it without ever having the precise details. In any event there was an increasingly sharp tension between Hugh Gaitskell and George Brown which was never wholly resolved before Gaitskell's death.

Brown's relations with Cousins, as with so many of his friends and colleagues, contained an equal mix of love, hate, anxiety, rebellion and almost maudlin affection. But he did have a rather special love-hate relationship with Frank Cousins. They were constantly fighting each other when they were in Cabinet, yet each had a strong affection for the other, an emotional bond which is hard to define but easy to sense. In unguarded moments George Brown has told people that his admiration for Frank Cousins was of an altogether different order from any affection or respect he may have felt toward other members of the Wilson Cabinet in 1964–6. In a sense they both came from the same 'club', they were in the same union, as officials, they both had exceedingly hard lives as youngsters, without any formal higher education or training in the orthodox sense. George Brown never

6. Richard Crossman, the unpublished diaries, 20 September 1960.

lost his chip on the shoulder about this, and perhaps he resented the way Frank Cousins had managed (or so it appeared) to overcome any sense of inferiority about his background. There was another strong emotional link between the two men : Cousins knew George's father who, like Frank, was a meat lorry driver and later a member of the TGWU executive. George even claims to have ridden, as a youngster, in the same driver's cab as Frank and his own father. These may seem tenuous links, sanctified in a reservoir of sentimental memory. Yet they are important to all men, especially as they grow older and move into areas of deeper emotional and intellectual stress – such as Government. Nothing is more attractive or easier, then, than to recall and sentimentalise the past.

Could it then be said that there was anything to George Brown's idea, except an absurd aberration? Cousins as a political leader – was it a runner? It was certainly never a serious possibility in Cousins's mind. He was still a long way from seeing himself even as a member of a Labour Government, let alone a Party leader. To be sure, he had developed a 'political style'. His power as a trade union leader gave him an automatic political authority. By 1960 he was already singled out as the most political of any of the major union leaders since Bevin. There had been nobody quite like Cousins on the post-war stage of trade union leadership, and not even Bevin had flouted the established leadership of the Party in quite the same manner. Yet none of this impressed itself on Cousins's own mind as opening up a gateway to the Party leadership, nor did he show any inclination to want it. He was first and foremost a trade-union leader, *not* a politician, and in his mind there was a clear and marked distinction between the two.

Certainly he wanted to politicise the trade union movement; to make the whole fabric of trade unionism more politically conscious and active; to use the immense power and influence of the trade union movement to help radicalise British society, and indeed, inject some socialist red blood into the Labour Party. To that extent he was, as we have already discussed, very much a political animal, but not necessarily a Parliamentary politician, as we were to see when he went into Government. He was not impressed and certainly not seduced by George Brown's idea.

Moreover, Frank Cousins's *political* leadership of the TGWU had its problems. As the H-bomb row intensified during the summer of 1960 several sections of the union – including some London busmen's branches – criticised Cousins for spending too much time on political affairs. They claimed that this was having a detrimental effect on the union's industrial affairs. Some full-time officials, including national officers, were also critical – mostly in private, although some of them did not prevent their opinions becoming public knowledge. There was also some opposition from rank-and-file members both to the anti-H-bomb policy and, more vocally at local levels, to the union's challenge to the Party leadership. It was hardly possible for Frank Cousins to prevent this criticism becoming exploited and widely known, and it is impossible to assess just how representative it was of the great mass of opinion inside the TGWU.

I have been told by men who are now full-time officials and who were then on the shop floor that the majority of their fellow-members were opposed to the Cousins line of the nuclear disarmament. Equally, I have been assured the opposite was the case. The opposition never became an embarrassment to Cousins though he was, at the time, prickly and defensive when the question of internal opposition was raised. In retrospect, he now concedes that there was both opposition and apathy among his rank-and-file members which *did* embarrass the TGWU leadership at the time. But it did not deter it from pursuing a policy it believed to be right and which, Frank Cousins still insists, was supported by the majority of *active* members. The rank and file responded, Cousins claims, but the drive, the initiative, the force of the argument did not come from the bottom. It came from the top.

The furious attack mounted against Frank Cousins – in the Press, among supporters of official Labour policy and orthodox opinion in general – was at its height in the autumn of 1960. Nowhere was it stronger than among his colleagues on the TUC General Council. As the Congress drew near they could see that it was destined to be a full dress rehearsal for the Scarborough Party conference and also the scene of a most devastating split among the trade unions. The anti-Cousins majority on the Council contemplated the approaching Congress with a mortifying foreboding. Several felt a positive hatred for the Transport Workers' leader, and this was displayed in a variety of unconnected and often spontaneous ways. For example, in July there was an undignified fracas at the conference of the International Transport Workers' Federation in Berne, where Frank Cousins was President. This was a post he had held since 1958, and it had been held by his predecessors. Yet, astonishingly, at the 1960 conference Cousins was defeated for a place on the executive Board of the ITWF by Sidney (now Lord) Greene, the leader of the NUR. Cousins even had to put up with the indignity of announcing his own defeat from the Presidential chair at the conference. Ostensibly the reason given by his critics for rejecting Cousins was that the TGWU was not really entitled to the seat on the executive although it had had one for some years; by a previous tradition, it was claimed, the place 'belonged' to the railway unions. In fact this was a piece of pure vindictiveness reflecting in the international areas the tensions that had reached boiling point on the domestic scene. Yet that demonstration of bitterness was as nothing to the warfare which flared, privately and publicly, at the Trades Union Congress in Douglas in September.

There in the Isle of Man, the personal bitterness reached an altogether new level: there was, indeed, a large element of hysteria in the air. Other factors were involved. Aneurin Bevan's death in July had been followed in August by the loss of Morgan Phillips, left crippled by a serious stroke. Phillips was a superb organiser, with a sensitive and profound understanding of the Movement, and he had already been a powerful emollient influence. His illness appeared, with Bevan's death, to have robbed the Labour Movement of the two men who might conceivably have bridged the widening gulf between Gaitskell and Cousins.

At the July meeting of the Labour Party's national executive Morgan Phillips presented a huge, 7,000 word report to the Party leaders which he entitled 'The State of the Party'. It was in fact his last major work for the executive before he was stricken down. This original draft, subsequently amended as well as retitled, started off by stating: 'The morale of the Labour Party judged by such evidence as we have is today at an all time low. Both in the House, and in the constituencies there are clear signs of demoralisation'.[7] Since the 1959 election, the Phillips document continued, the Labour Party had been racked with internal disputes: 'The debate on Clause 4 touched on the most sensitive tenet of Labour's faith; the argument on nuclear weapons raises the biggest issue of our time'.[8] And the document went on to propose that the Party executive should withdraw its revised statement on Clause 4 (the one agreed in March) and consider the whole issue more fully and carefully in 1961 or 1962. Instead of revising Clause 4 Morgan Phillips suggested that the Labour Party should draw up a programme of reform to put before the electorate for the election of 1964. The Phillips document also raised the whole question of relations between the Parliamentary Labour Party, the Party conference and the NEC and proposed: 'some new machinery for consultation that will bring into regular contact the different decision-making centres of the Party'.[9]

There were three separate sections to the Phillips memorandum, and it was so extensive, so frank and so self-critical that the Party leaders decided that it could not be published as it stood.

It was decided that Part 3 of the document, dealing with relationships between the Parliamentary Labour Party and the conference would be left out and that other sections should be amended and pruned to delete the contentious areas. The objective of the statement, which was later issued as 'Labour in the Sixties', was to set out the purpose of modern socialism.[10]

But of course the Morgan Phillips document had accurately assessed the state of the Labour Movement and had shrewdly anticipated the crisis looming if the Party conference and the TUC voted for nuclear disarmament – in defiance of Gaitskell, the NEC and the wishes of the Parliamentary

7. Minutes of special meeting of the Labour Party's NEC, 13 July 1960.
8. *Ibid*.
9. *Ibid*.
10. Minutes of Labour Party NEC Meeting, 27 July 1960.

Labour Party. This imminent danger was clearly in Morgan Phillips's mind when he drafted that unpublished candid analysis.

So, as the 1960 Trades Union Congress drew nearer and when observers (without the advantage of a sight of the Phillips memorandum) claimed that the whole Labour Movement was in the midst of its greatest internal crisis since 1931, it was hard to quarrel with that assessment.

The feeling of hostility and friction between members of the TUC General Council on opposing 'wings' – Left, Right, or whatever labels may seem appropriate – has never been more intense in my memory than at that September conference. Neither group had any effective communication with the other; it was as if a trench had been dug between the two factions. They even stood at different ends of a bar in the same hotel or, more usually, stayed in different hotels. Frank Cousins could count on about seven votes in the General Council, against a majority of twenty-three or twenty-four certain opponents. But in the Congress itself Cousins knew that he was poised to win a big majority on nuclear disarmament regardless of what the General Council members decided, because the individual union leaders were already committed by their own conference decisions, and the tally of unions lining up with Cousins had swollen to a majority of the Congress voting strength.

Some of the unions, like the engineers and the shop workers, were led by men wholly opposed to Frank Cousins's policy, yet they were committed to cast their own union vote for it. This did nothing to lessen the bitterness and friction between Cousins and men like Carron and Birch. Rancour spilled out from those who saw themselves as 'loyalists', rather than necessarily 'right-wingers', at the mere mention of Cousins's name. These 'loyalists' ('loyal' to the official Party policy) saw him as a blustering, obsessional and perplexing figure, apparently intent on wrecking the Labour Party with his 'fixation' (as they openly described it) over the H-bomb. Not unnaturally the Left did not share this view. It regarded Frank Cousins as a heroic figure who, somehow, had produced a miraculous transformation of the whole scene of Labour politics. He had, quite amazingly, emerged as the leader of the most powerful union in the country – at the head of a union with a long tradition of right-wing and orthodox leadership; he had overthrown the conventional wisdom on industrial relations, albeit with a guarded programme; he had loosened the iron grip of the right-wing inside the TUC General Council; and here he was now leading a moral crusade on nuclear arms which brought a sense of spiritual revival to radical temperaments. There were two utterly contrasting and conflicting attitudes towards Cousins, and it was these two views – labelled for simplicity, if not absolute accuracy, Right and Left – which collided at the 1960 TUC, as indeed they did again three weeks later at the Party conference in Scarborough.

In such a charged atmosphere there was something comic and even far-cical about the sensational event which burst upon the Congress delegates, on the eve of the 1960 TUC. The AEU somehow managed to get itself into the position of supporting both official policy on defense *and* the Cousins proposals. Put to the supreme test of trying to rescue Hugh Gaitskell, the AEU President Bill Carron devised a formula by which he persuaded the AEU delegation of 33 to back a motion supporting the Labour Party's latest official policy as well as the Transport Workers' resolution. This announce-ment stunned everyone, in both the pro- and anti-Cousins camps. Indeed if anything there was a greater anger among the anti-Cousins majority of the General Council, because most of them regarded Carron's action as likely to bring the trade-union movement into greater disrepute in the public eye. But Carron stubbornly, even insensitively, defended his tactic, believing that it had at least provided Hugh Gaitskell with an unexpected breathing-space. Explaining his logic Carron told the Press:

> We made no attempt at our delegate meeting to vary our National Commit-tee (annual conference) policy on unilateral nuclear disarmament. The line we have taken is consistent with that policy. We feel that it is consistent also with the new official policy which says that Britain should stop manufactur-ing nuclear weapons but says nothing about our allies having them. The new defence policy contains many facets and we felt that the Transport Workers resolution was somewhat in line with our own.

Few of his TUC colleagues shared Bill Carron's view, because they knew that whatever words and phrases were contained in the resolutions the real gulf between Gaitskell and Cousins's views was too wide to bridge by argu-ments on semantics. None the less, there were echoes of the Carron view later that month when on the eve of the Labour Party conference both George Brown and Dick Crossman reached an opinion not greatly different from that of Bill Carron. Indeed Anthony Wedgwood Benn actually resigned from the Labour Party's National Executive Committee because he failed to persuade Gaitskell and Cousins that their opposing policies were, in truth, not all that conflicting. So, absurd and incomprehensible as Carron's logic may have appeared, it was not without some foundation as well as guile. What it overlooked of course was the 'spirit' of the two opposing poli-cies, and there was no possibility of bridging that gulf. For although the Transport Union's motion was still not unilateralist in phrasing it was cer-tainly that in spirit, and ultimately, in intent.

The debate on nuclear weapons took place on Wednesday 7 September at the TUC, and resulted in the Congress, like the AEU, 'facing both ways' – adding total confusion to total crisis. Nothing was resolved, although most observers read the signs from the voting figures. The Transport Workers' motion was approved with a majority of 1,143,000 while the official policy (thanks to the AEU) had a majority of 690,000. Measuring instruments of all kinds were taken out to assess the potential threat now hanging over Gaitskell, and the calculation was that the Party conference would assemble in Scarborough with the opposing forces divided almost evenly.

That was the statistical picture; the emotional one was somewhat different. No Trades Union Congress in modern history can have reached such a pitch of excitement or hysterical fervour as the 1960 conference, during which the debate on the Bomb reached very high standards of oratory as well as drama. By common consent Frank Cousins probably made the best speech on the issue that he ever produced in public. He was always a commanding speaker; his rapid-fire style on the rostrum made with a machine-gun-like delivery. But he was not a theatrical speaker. He rarely practised his pauses or even his cadences. His mind raced ahead of his words and he frequently became entangled by his sentences. Cousins achieved his effect by conveying a sense of personal power as well as organisational strength. He was not a talented orator in the usual sense yet he made an especially powerful impact at the 1960 TUC. No doubt the occasion was such that everyone, speaker as well as audience, were captured by events and the over-hanging drama.

From the outset Cousins emphasised that he was not concerned with any play on words or phrases. In his opening speech he underlined the meaning behind the TGWU motion – 'we are opposed to any *idea* of basing our defence policies on nuclear strategy or the threat of the use of nuclear weapons'. This appeared to most observers to be a clear and uncompromising declaration; and in essence it also seemed contrary to British membership of NATO.

Cousins told the Congress:

> I say, so that there shall be no misunderstanding about our attitude in the TGWU, that we do not accept the kind of atmosphere that has been created by the Press during the last few weeks. We do not regard colleagues who have a different opinion from our own as bloodthirsty warmongers. Nor do we regard ourselves as pacifist or Communist stooges . . .

He described the Labour Party's official policy as 'a document of expediency' which tried to hide the real problems. He went over all the well-worn arguments about the dubious political and military value of nuclear weapons, and then came to what was in fact his central case: the moral argument which in his mind was synonymous with 'the socialist case against the Bomb: it was an evil in itself and there could be no compromise with evil.' He declared:

> The moral case is unanswerable. You do not have to think whether I am a Christian when I say things about the moral aspects of this issue. Those of

you who are preaching for the right to retain this weapon against the imagined threat of the overwhelming power of the Communist States want to remember that it was a very deeply religious man, the late Pope, who made clear his feelings on this matter. I would, if I may, because I do not want to say anything that he did not, quote what was said : 'if the ABC warfare – a ware of atomic, bacteriological and chemical weapons – involves such an extension of evil that it completely escapes human control then its use even in defence must be rejected as immoral' . . .

Cousins quoted the Pope; he used Churchill to fortify his argument that nuclear war was such as to remove it from the realm of normal military conduct; and he quoted Lord Hailsham (then Minister for Science) who had said that to go on stockpiling nuclear weapons at the prevailing rate would be the road to annihilation. And finally he took the Labour Party's official policy, set it alongside his own, and compared the fundamental difference as he saw it : 'We say we will not have nuclear weapons, they say we should.'

When the vote was taken yet another sensation followed, it appeared that the Transport Workers' motion had received only 255,000 votes compared with a majority of 690,000 for the official defence policy. It was then discovered that the AEU's vote had not been counted. One of the tellers had overlooked the AEU's card vote of 908,000, which Bill Carron held in his pocket. An immediate inquiry was mounted to discover the missing votes and after a further check the TUC General Secretary, Sir Vincent Tewson, announced that the result had in fact been a vote for the TGWU motion of, in fact, 1,143,000. That night Cousins predicted that the Labour Party would go the same way as the TUC – and more decisively. By this he meant that at Scarborough there would be no repeat of the AEU's tactic of voting both ways. He sensed accurately that even his most embittered opponents would not wish to re-enact the ludicrous situation of two votes, on the same day, on the same issue, pointing in opposite directions. He was partly right in his predictions, though the majority at Scarborough was substantially *less*.

The next day, at the TUC, the Clause 4 controversy was dismissed in an almost perfunctory manner. The debate lasted a mere 34 minutes and involved only five speakers, including Frank Cousins. The whole issue was dispensed with as if it was an embarrassing triviality which ought never to have come before the Congress for reaffirmation. To be sure, that is how many regarded it, and by that time even those who silently agreed with Hugh Gaitskell's challenge to the Ark of the Covenant decided to remain discreetly unobtrusive. Without opposition Clause 4 was confirmed and the Press reported that Frank Cousins had notched a further triumph on the road to Scarborough.

The 1960 Trades Union Congress was a decisive landmark in the shift to the Left. Its importance lay not merely in the dominance of the H-bomb debate, nor the ignominious rebuff handed out to those who wished to modify Clause 4. It was much more general. There was a feeling abroad among most delegates that they were witnessing a profound change in attitudes. And as if to symbolise this change Sir Vincent Tewson, though not yet sixty-five, had announced his decision to retire after that Congress. George Woodcock was to be his successor. Tewson had been General Secretary of the TUC for fourteen years, bridging the gap between the pre-war period of Citrine and Ernest Bevin and the 1960s. He had continued with the policies established in wartime, consecrated during the post-war Labour Governments and then accepted, with little significant challenge, by the majority of unions and their leaders. His was the period of Deakin, Williamson, and Lawther: a period of predictability, continuity, with most of the old certainties still on the landscape. Woodcock's assumption of the TUC leadership seemed even then to have a special symbolic quality.

Chapter Sixteen

SCARBOROUGH

Between the Trades Union Congress and the Scarborough Labour Party conference of 1960 there was an interregnum of twenty-four days: it was by any standards an extraordinary period. The drums of war were never silent. Partisan groups met constantly, though rarely in the same place twice. Every day the Press was full of the 'great conflict' between Gaitskell and Cousins. Their names were hardly ever absent from the front pages of the national newspapers. *The Times* during the TUC week referred to Cousins as someone whose name was 'a household word. Hardly anybody in the country is more written about, interviewed, analysed, criticised'. This was true. Cousins was under attack in the Press as never before, and probably never again to such a concentrated degree. In some quarters he was seen as a man who was about to set alight the revolutionary furnaces which could consume the nation. There was rarely anything in Cousins's public utterances which seemed to diminish these fears, nor did he allow the Press campaign to intimidate him. He openly declared that he was not solely concerned with 'Banning the Bomb', but with a wider issue, a fundamental shift in the political attitudes of the Labour Movement. In an interview with the *Daily Mail* Cousins told the paper's industrial editor Leslie Randall: 'My aim is to give the Labour Party a socialist policy'. He was bombarded by a continuous single theme of questioning. Was he seeking to remove Gaitskell from the leadership of the Labour Party? Was the campaign against the Bomb simply a pretext to 'get at' Gaitskell and his style of leadership, as well as his general political policies? Was it a personal vendetta rather than an issue of principle? What did he hope to achieve, even if he defeated the Labour leadership on nuclear disarmament? To the *Sunday Times* Cousins declared: 'I don't feel I must support Hugh Gaitskell because he's a friend of mine. I support him only if he's carrying out policies I approve of – socialist policies. Then I can say to my members – "This chap's doing things we want – we'll support him".'

264

Arrogant, tough, uncompromising? Yes, to be sure there was no whiff of compromise in Cousin's attitude, and none was intended. He knew it was a bitter fight to the finish. There was no purpose, as he saw it, in seeking some form of sloppy, patched-up agreement which would satisfy no one even if it could be offered to the world to demonstrate that the Labour Party had papered over its divisions (which was unlikely). Neither Cousins nor Gaitskell could now pull back, and both of them knew it. The division between them was absolute. Cousins continued to deny that he had any intrinsic personal hostility towards the Labour Party leader :

> It is not a personal matter between Hugh Gaitskell and myself. It is a question of differences of views and ideas, policies not personalities. That is the real question, no other. And it is nonsense to talk, as some do, of this controversy breaking up the Labour Movement. Anybody would think that the TGWU resolution was the only one of its kind on the agenda for the Labour Party conference.

In her book on Frank Cousins, Margaret Stewart suggests that 'the fundamental conflict between him [Gaitskell] and Cousins was not over any semantic definition of Socialism but over the issue of nuclear disarmament which came to overshadow all others between 1959 and 1961.'[1]

To my mind this is a considerable over-simplification. The conflict between the two men went much deeper, though nuclear disarmament was the dominant and emotionally symbolic issue. Nevertheless it *was* a symbol; the sweep and magnitude of this one immense problem carried within it many of the differences between the two men's basic political philosophies. We have already discussed their contrasting political 'chemistry' across a whole range of political ideas. Cousins was a socialist, a collectivist, in a way that Gaitskell never was, and Cousins's response to the impulses behind nuclear disarmament, to Clause 4; to the general revolt against the Establishment was geared by a fundamentalist approach to socialist doctrine which Gaitskell didn't possess, or which, if he had possessed it at an earlier stage, he now rejected. This view is certainly shared by Dora Gaitskell, who says : 'The real difference between them was precisely over their interpretation of socialism. Frank was in favour of more nationalisation, etc. C.N.D. came later – but the other difference, that was *the* major difference.'

In his later more considered view of Gaitskell, Frank Cousins does not substantially alter his attitude – except to be much warmer in the strictly personal sense. He still maintains that he was not antagonistic towards Gaitskell 'as a man', although he does not show the same charity towards many of Gaitskell's supporters – especially those who in late 1960 and 1961 formed the anti-Left organisation, Campaign for Democratic Socialism, which was

---

1. Margaret Stewart, *Frank Cousins: A Study* (Hutchinson, 1968), p. 113.

to play a prominent role in overturning the unilateralist campaign at the 1961 Party conference. Cousins's retrospective view of Gaitskell is in the classical tradition of a worker's view of a middle-class intellectual:

> I have always recognised that it is one thing for working-class people to rise and to acquire some education and expression. But it is much more difficult for someone from the upper classes trying to reach down and sympathise with working-class aspirations. That is what I think Gaitskell had to do – a very difficult task emotionally and in other respects. So I always had an admiration for him, and for anyone else attempting that difficult process . . .

In 1960 Gaitskell still considered that he had a slender chance of reversing the unilateralist vote at the Trades Union Congress and defeating Cousins at the Scarborough conference. His optimism was based partly on statistical calculations that the trade union vote at the Party conference might divide evenly, especially if the AEU voted for official policy (as well as unilateralism) as it had done at Douglas. Secondly, Gaitskell believed that the majority of local Labour Parties would vote for him and against Cousins. But obviously the key to all these calculations lay in securing a reversal of policy by the engineering union, and no one was more active in this attempt than George Brown. Shortly before the Scarborough conference Brown arranged a dinner party at his London home to which he invited Hugh and Dora Gaitskell and Sir William and Lady Carron. The issue: could the AEU deliver its vote for Gaitskell at the Scarborough conference? Carron explained his difficulties, and they were formidable. He pointed out that the AEU delegation at the Labour Party conference was likely to be more left-wing than had been the case at the TUC. Moreover, the AEU was firmly committed to support for the unilateralist policy, which had been laid down at its annual conference. Even so, Carron agreed with George Brown that there was indeed now a narrower gap between the *wording* of his own union's motion (as well as the TGWU's) and the official policy on defence. Carron thought it might be just possible to persuade his delegation to repeat their tactic of voting both ways, on the grounds of the compatability of the two motions.

George Brown, it is said, was greatly heartened by this – though Gaitskell did not warm to the thought of being 'saved' by such dubious manœuvres. Still, Brown reminded the dinner party that the first priority was to save Gaitskell and stop Frank Cousins from winning an outright victory at Scarborough. Brown turned to Carron, insisting that the future of the Labour Party depended on this and, as if instructing the engineers' President, declared: 'You must deliver the vote, Bill. If you don't, we're finished.' Bill Carron, cautiously hopeful, replied that he would try; it might be possible, but he was far from certain. In the event he failed, though he did consider using his Presidential authority to instruct his delegation to follow the same pattern of voting as at the TUC. He was dissuaded from this by one of his senior colleagues, a political ally, on the grounds that he would never be able to get away with it and that it would inflict a lasting harm on the union's reputation.

It is quite impossible to guess how many such private gatherings took place in those weeks between the TUC and the Labour Party conference, as stratagem and counter-stratagem were tested out for potential effectiveness. At the same time, Hugh Gaitskell consistently and courageously exposed himself to the firing-line of public debate. He sought to persuade the Labour Party throughout the country that a vote for unilateralism would be tantamount to accepting a neutralist policy for Britain and that would mean an end to her world role and influence. Gaitskell argued that this would mean opting out of our alliances, such as NATO, and would lead to the country being left dangerously vulnerable in the event of attack. Time and again he repeated that he would never be party to such a policy. The implication was clear that if he was heavily defeated at Scarborough, then he would find it difficult to remain leader of the Labour Party.

Throughout this phase one of the most persistent advocates of compromise was Dick Crossman. All summer he had been supporting George Brown's view that the Transport Workers' motion was so confused in its phraseology that Gaitskell, if he wished, could have smothered the conflict under a modest concession. Crossman's view was that Gaitskell was being stiff and stubborn and determined to be uncompromising against Cousins. Neither Crossman nor Brown was able to persuade Gaitskell, because he was convinced, as was Cousins, that the differences were far too fundamental to be brushed aside by such semantic conjurings. Still, Crossman persisted, and at at a meeting of the Labour Party's international committee on 21 September he produced his own memorandum outlining why the Party leadership could, in his view, accept the Transport Workers' motion at Scarborough. Crossman's document explained that nowhere had the TGWU motion used the precise phrase 'unilateral nuclear disarmament'. He further argued that since Labour's entire defence policy had been recast following the abandonment of Blue Streak, there was surely a real chance to establish a common policy with Frank Cousins and the majority of those who had previously opposed official defence policy. Gaitskell remained wholly unimpressed; he wouldn't budge. Crossman, furious with his leader's relentlessness, stalked out of the meeting. Yet, of course, Gaitskell was right. There wasn't the remotest chance of a compromise by way of the Crossman-Brown formula. Three days before Crossman put that memorandum to the Labour Party's international committee Cousins, in an interview with me for the *Daily Herald*, made it clear that he was in no mood to haggle over words :

I am not dodging any issue. My union's resolution is clear. We say we are not going to have anything to do with nuclear weapons. We've said so several times. And we want the Labour Party to base its policies on a resolve not to use nuclear weapons. That seems clear enough to me.

Did this mean a withdrawal from NATO?

If NATO didn't want to follow our policies then it would be up to the other countries to make their own decisions on it. This is no pacifist policy. It is a policy against the use of H-bombs. It does not mean our country would not be defended against any invader.

It would be hard to interpret those sentiments in any other way than that Frank Cousins was lining himself alongside the unilateralist case, if not in words then in thinking. Of course, it was still not a strictly orthodox unilateralist line. There were ambiguities here, and what Crossman and Brown were doing was seeking to exploit the ambiguities, partly in the hope that this might produce a compromise or (rather more likely) expose the TGWU motion as going further than its words implied.

At no time even during this period of intense political backstage work was Cousins free from other pressures. His London busmen were again on the warpath – this time over staff shortages, poor conditions in the depots and the generally run-down state of the capital's transport services. The busmen were by no means indifferent to the union's campaign against the H-bomb, or to the Clause 4 issue. They have always been among the most politically active of the TGWU membership. But there was a strong feeling among their leaders that Cousins was neglecting some of his industrial obligations. A week before the Scarborough conference a group took a petition to Cousins himself which they claimed had been signed by some 20,000 busmen (then, almost half the total workforce) – demanding union action to force a public inquiry into the state of London Transport. It was not an issue which Cousins could, or wanted to, duck. He gave the campaign his support, and it was eventually turned into a public petition which secured over 150,000 signatures. This was subsequently put to the Minister of Transport, Ernest Marples, but he turned down the request.

There were also at this time the first signs of a new recession in the car industry. Car accessory firms were beginning to lay off workers and the TUC was already knocking on the Government's door requesting easier credit facilities to stimulate demand.

There was nothing peripheral about any of these problems; yet Cousins refused to be diverted or distracted from his central objective – the Battle of Scarborough. The Press still thundered at him and questioned his motives, continuing to accuse him of running a personal campaign to destroy the leader of the Labour Party and virtually conspiring to usurp that leadership for himself. Gaitskell's leadership was, of course, under attack. His style, manner and policy were challenged to a degree which must be without parallel in modern politics, as Roy Jenkins observed in his profile of him in *The Times* (20 January 1973). But what was at stake in 1960 was not just the leadership of Gaitskell but the entire direction of the Labour Party and its relationship with the unions. Had either side in the controversy taken its position to its ultimate logical outcome the Party would have been split. When one considers the trilogy of defeats which Gaitskell suffered before and at the Scarborough conference the remarkable feature is that he did survive – enough to regain his grip a year later. He was already defeated on Clause 4 when he went to Scarborough – and he had gracefully accepted that defeat and withdrawn; he was overruled on the very eve of conference when the Party Executive, against his advice, voted 12 to 11 to accept a motion which – in words, at any rate – committed the Party to accept the ruling of conference decisions; and then finally he was defeated, albeit narrowly, on the central point of nuclear disarmament.

At the head of the 'Opposition' was the leader of the most powerful union in the country whose predecessors had a reputation both for making and unmaking Party leaders. The clamour against Gaitskell at that moment was just short of overwhelming, because of the strength of his base in the Parliamentary Labour Party. Yet, if the unions *and* the conference had forced the issue to the point of absolute insistence, then Gaitskell could not have survived. That they did not was partly due to the fact that they could not without gravely weakening themselves. This is the secret of the resilience of the Labour Movement and the reason why those who press for absolute adherence to conference decisions cannot hope to succeed – except at the expense of an irreversible split. The Labour Party, being a federation of interests and covering a coalition of quasi-Liberals, radical reformists and Marxist socialists, tacitly – if often grudgingly – accepts this situation. It has always suffered from internal strain and always will. But it will break only if these interests feel it is politically necessary, inevitable or desirable so to do. On balance it has been in the wider political interests of the various strands within the 'Labour coalition' to recognise that they have rather more to lose than to gain by a fundamental fragmentation. Certainly it is this acceptance of what one might call 'the greater unity of purpose' which enables the Labour Party to survive so many crises, and which provides its unique qualifications to represent the broadcast interests of working people as a party of the Left.

The problem which Frank Cousins faced in 1960 was to reconcile his acceptance of this – and he *did* accept it – with his conviction that the Labour Party had for too long been pulled too far to the Right, that there was now a need to respond to new and younger radical impulses in British society, demanding more dynamic socialist leadership and policies, and that the institutional relationships within the Labour Movement – between the Parliamentary machine, the Labour Party in the country and the trade unions – had become too cosy, too dominated by the concept of 'fixing things', too unresponsive to the new pressures revealing themselves among the rank and file. That is why Scarborough amounted to a great warning, an explosion of frustration. It was as vivid a signal as has ever been given by a Labour conference to its leadership. Much has been written over the years about the courage of Gaitskell; the memorable character of his 'fight, fight, and fight again' speech; his stalwart rejection of what was described elsewhere as the 'emotional spasm' of nuclear disarmament. It is not the purpose of this writer to diminish the stature of Gaitskell's performance, his courage or his subsequent achievement in reversing Scarborough. But too little has been said about the significance of the revolt *against* the leadership and the nature of the frustration which it represented. Too little has been credited to the idealism, the fervour, the sincerity and the integrity of those who actually won the vote at Scarborough. Gaitskell was superb in defeat; Cousins was by no means belittled by his victory.

We have already seen how Gaitskell received a shattering blow at the meeting of the Party's National Executive Committee on the Sunday before the conference opened. The executive vote in effect committed the Parliamentary Labour Party to accepting a motion that conference decisions were, in the final analysis, the ultimate authority. The motion was almost as crucial as the issue of nuclear disarmament itself. Its wording was concise and specific :

> This conference reaffirms that the policy of the Labour Party to be pursued nationally and in Parliament on questions of principle shall be determined by Annual conference. While acknowledging that the day-to-day tactics in Parliament must be the job of the Parliamentary Labour Party this conference declares that Labour Party policy is decided by the Party conference which is the final authority.

That motion was put to the conference on Tuesday – the day before the nuclear disarmament debate – and was carried by 3,586,000 to 1,874,000, after a warning by the late Len Williams (then Deputy General Secretary and standing in for Morgan Phillips) that its acceptance must not be read by anyone, inside or outside the Labour Party, as implying that conference could 'dictate' to the Parliamentary Labour Party. None the less it *was* a signal to the PLP that it could not ignore the will of conference and the mood of the rank and file. The relationship, like the British constitution itself, was imprecise and unspecific but each sectional interest knew by instinct, if not by rule, precisely how far they could go without violating the unwritten code which bound them all together.

To revert to that eve-of-conference executive meeting: the usual routine of considering conference motions was its principal business and, of course, the majority of the Party executive, like the TUC General Council, were opposed to the Transport Workers' motion on nuclear disarmament. They were also strongly opposed to any compromise along the lines advocated by Crossman and Brown. But Anthony Wedgwood Benn now proposed that a fresh approach should be made to Frank Cousins and the TGWU to 'ascertain and clarify the point of difference between resolution 60 [the TGWU motion] and the policy statement on defence'. This was yet another way of trying out the Crossman-Brown compromise formula. The Benn proposal was voted down by 14 to 5, whereupon Tony Benn resigned from the executive. He had already attempted a direct appeal, earlier in the day, to both Gaitskell and Frank Cousins, but had received no encouragement. He found both men in a totally unyielding, mood monumentally distrustful of each other and even of Benn for making the approach. Dora Gaitskell recalls Benn's visit to the Gaitskell room at the Royal Hotel that Sunday:

> I remember him trying to persuade Hugh not to press with his argument but to seek a compromise. He begged Hugh to change his mind. Well, perhaps in that sense Hugh was inflexible. But he would not compromise on what he regarded as an issue of great *principle*. Nor did he have any illusions about what was at stake.

Benn found Cousins in no more receptive a mood than Gaitskell. Indeed he regarded both as 'obsessional'.

After Benn's resignation the executive went on to vote on the TGWU motion and by 13 to 7 agreed to oppose it. From outside the Royal Hotel that afternoon, while the executive was sitting, the cries and chants of a huge CND march and demonstration could be heard echoing through the hotel rooms and corridors. It was led by Canon Collins of St Paul's (Frank Cousins was not one of the demonstrators), heading a mass of people, many of them chanting 'Gaitskell Must GO' – the slogan which embittered Dora Gaitskell against CND more than any other single incident at that conference. Canon Collins was then in the midst of an internal fight, with Bertrand Russell over the question of direct action, which Russell had swung over to support. Collins and some CND supporters were against the civil disobedience campaign which Russell was advocating, and the Canon had already persuaded Frank Cousins to appeal to Russell in a letter urging the philosopher to postpone any direct action, at least until after Scarborough. This Russell agreed to do, although in the end it probably made little practical difference either to CND, Russell or the Scarborough decision.

The final preliminary drama was the meeting of the AEU delegation in the Scarborough public library on the Tuesday night, the eve of the nuclear disarmament debate. A meeting which lasted nearly three hours finally voted, by two to one, to uphold the union's policy on nuclear disarmament and to reject Bill Carron's attempt to switch support (if necessary by repeating the two-way vote) to official defence policy. That clinched the issue. It was then certain that Gaitskell would be defeated. The only thing that remained to be decided was the size of the majority. On the day of the debate, 5 October, some newspapers were already speculating on Gaitskell's resignation and his possible succession by Harold Wilson – the man who had remained very much on the sidelines throughout the whole bitter controversy but who had made it known that his central and overriding concern was to protect the 'unity of the Labour Party', the man who had drawn the scorn of all Gaitskell supporters by having pointed out the dangers inherent in ignoring conference decisions.

Sam Watson introduced the official statement on defence policy and was followed by Len Misledine of the AEU moving his union's resolution, which was much more specifically unilateralist than the TGWU motion. Ian Mikardo seconded it, then Frank Cousins moved the Transport Workers' resolution. It was not one of his most memorable speeches. Indeed, one had the impression that Cousins, by then, was so overwhelmed by the trauma of the occasion that he found it difficult to mount new or electrifying arguments against the Bomb. And when he sought to answer the challenge that had been put to him so frequently in the past about his attitude to NATO he had little time left to articulate his reply :

'When I am asked if it means getting out of NATO', he said at the very end of his speech, 'if the question is posed to me as simply saying, am I prepared to go on remaining in an organisation over which I have no control, but which can destroy us instantly, my answer is, Yes, if the choice is that. But it is not that.' He left the rostrum under that cloud of ambiguity. It was as if he had posed the question almost completed an answer which began to add up to 'No', and had then said, 'Yes, if the choice is that.' The impression he left with the conference – intended or not – was that he was no supporter of NATO but that he did not intend to be lured into saying so publicly.

A much more concise speech came from John Horner, General Secretary of the Fire Brigades' Union, who seconded Frank Cousins's resolution. In one phrase he seemed to catch the mood : 'H-Bombs and a Socialist foreign policy for Britain are inconsistent. Today a free Labour Movement has an immense opportunity. Let us seize it.'

The debate stretched into the afternoon. It included a great array of speakers, many from the unions, some from the local parties. Finally Hugh Gaitskell wound up in mid-afternoon. The Spa Grand Hall was a cauldron of tension as he reached the final phrases of that memorable speech, possibly his greatest public oration. He had spoken already for 45 minutes. White-faced, his puckered brow covered in sweat, and a sprig of white heather clinging to his left lapel, Gaitskell turned to the issue of his leadership.

> I would not wish for one day to remain a Leader who had lost the confidence of his colleagues in Parliament. It is perfectly reasonable to try to get rid of somebody, to try to get rid of a man you do not agree with, who you think perhaps is not a good Leader. But there are ways of doing this. What would be wrong in my opinion and would not be forgiven is if, in order to get rid of a man, you supported a policy in which you did not wholeheartedly believe, a policy which, as far as the resolution is concerned, is not clear . . .

The crackle of interruptions pierced the atmosphere. They increased as Gaitskell taunted and ridiculed his opposition and questioned their motives.

To the unilateralists he challenged:

> It is not in dispute that the vast majority of Labour members of Parliament are utterly opposed to unilateralism and neutralism. So what do you expect them to do? Change their minds overnight?

The uproar of interruptions was now reaching the proportions of an artillery barrage as Gaitskell went on to challenge the conference, in advance of the vote which he knew would go against him:

> Supposing all of us like well-behaved sheep were to follow the policies of unilateralism and neutralism, what kind of an impression would that make upon the British people? You do not seem to be clear in your minds about it, but I will tell you this. I do not believe that the Labour Members of Parliament are prepared to act as time servers. I do not believe they will do this and I will tell you why – because they are men of conscience and honour.
>
> People of the so-called Right and the so-called Centre have every justification for having a conscience as well as people of the so-called Left. I do not think they will do this because they are honest men, loyal men, steadfast men, experienced men, with a lifetime of service to the Labour Movement.

Gaitskell went on to pummel and punch at his critics assembled in the rows in front of him. Frank Cousins sat angry and flushed – but silent – in his seat in the body of the hall, looking hard at Gaitskell. 'Do you think we can simply accept a decision of this kind?' Gaitskell continued, unmoved by the uproar of heckling. 'Do you think that we can become overnight the pacifists, unilateralists and fellow-travellers . . .' – the rest of his sentence was drowned under a huge wave of booing, yelling and shouting from all sides

273

of the hall, as delegates rose to their feet, waving their papers and demanding a retraction of the last phrase which so many deeply committed pacifists as well as unilateralists profoundly resented. To be called a 'fellow-traveller' in that way was in effect to be branded a Communist; it was a bad blunder by Gaitskell and in later moments of cooler reflection he admitted his error of judgement. But he was carried away in the transports of his own perroration. It was several minutes before the hubbub died down, as Gaitskell swept on through his prepared speech. To quell the storm of protest he tried to explain the lapse. 'You know,' he shouted back at those delegates who were on their feet howling protests at him, 'You know, I have been subjected to some criticisms and attack and I am entitled to reply.'

He moved towards the famous closing passage of his speech :

In a few minutes the conference will make its decision. Most of the votes, I know, are predetermined and we have been told what is likely to happen. We know how it comes about. I sometimes think, frankly, that the system we have by which great unions decide their policy before even their conferences can consider the Executive recommendation is not really a very wise one or a good one. Perhaps in a calmer moment this situation could be looked at!

I say this to you : we may lose the vote today and the result may deal this Party a grave blow. It may not be possible to prevent it but I think there are many of us who will not accept that this blow need be mortal, who will not believe that such an end is inevitable. There are some of us, Mr. Chairman, who will fight, fight, and fight again to save the Party we love. We will fight, fight and fight again to bring back sanity and honesty and dignity so that our Party with its great past may retain its glory and its greatness.

Four separate votes were taken at the end of Gaitskell's speech. Each one provided a defeat for the leadership. The official policy statement was rejected by 3,339,000 to 3,042,000 – a majority of 297,000. The Transport Workers' resolution was carried by 3,282,000 to 3,239,000 – a majority of 43,000. The AEU motion, which was much more specifically unilateralist than any other, was carried by 3,303,000 to 2,896,000 – a majority of 407,000. And a final motion, sponsored by the Amalgamated Society of Woodworkers (now part of the Confederation of Building Trade Unions) which backed official defence policy, was rejected by 3,331,000 to 2,999,000 – a majority of 332,000.

The extraordinary array of voting figures concealed the fact that some unions, and local party delegates, deserted Frank Cousins's motion partly (they alleged) because of its ambiguity, partly because they suspected that Cousins's motives were dominated more by anti-Gaitskell feeling than anti-H-bomb, and partly, it must be said, because there remained a good deal of resentment against the Transport Workers' Union as such because of its dominant position, both politically and industrially. A great many mixed motives were criss-crossed in that Scarborough voting pattern. Some old personal scores were traded off and some lasting feuds were rekindled. For instance, the National Union of Railwaymen voted *against* official defence policy, but also against Frank Cousins – though they voted *for* the AEU motion. Anyone trying to unravel the cross-currents of motivation would require the help of a panel of psychoanalysts rather than political scientists.

At the end of that five-hour debate in the Spa Grand Hotel delegates struggled out in a state of physical as well as mental exhaustion. There can have been few British political conference events this century to match it in drama, tension, and the traumatic impact of its final moments. It may have been, as some repeated afterwards, echoing Nye Bevan, an emotional spasm. But it was one which shook the Labour Movement to its foundations.

The sequels of that day reverberated through the Labour Movement for years to come. They persisted well beyond Gaitskell's death, and even found echoes when Frank Cousins became a member of Harold Wilson's Cabinet in 1964. There are still people, in the higher echelons of the Labour Movement, who look back to 1960 as 'the great dividing point'. It was a peak achievement for the Left and the anti-Establishment forces. It focused attention on the question of conference powers in an altogether different context from anything that had happened before, even though conference motions had previously been passed in defiance of the leadership, when Labour was in Government. It brought the crisis over Gaitskell's leadership to a point at which it almost broke him. Indeed, there are those who assert that he never fully recovered his authority or his poise after Scarborough, despite the fact that he succeeded in reversing the nuclear disarmament issue in 1961. The Press comment next day was predictable in one sense – almost without exception the newspaper commentators wrote off the Labour Party as a viable Opposition for years ahead; they saw a divided and shattered Party, lying exposed and helpless, ready to be pushed to one side if the Macmillan Government chose to exploit the situation. Yet within four years Labour was again in power, albeit with a small majority.

At the same time, some of the more perceptive commentators saw a rather wider political perspective. They realised that the issue of the H-bomb *was* a genuinely profound question for British society; they admitted that the Labour Party was the only major political movement that had attempted seriously to debate it – even at the risk of self-destruction; and to that extent they recognised that no great political movement could debate a question as momentous as this honestly, openly and democratically without exposing itself to bitter personal recriminations. For all these reasons the more enlightened commentators did not seek to trivialise or sneer at the Labour Party's dilemma – they accepted it for what it was: an extraordinary demonstration of conscience-searching, an illustration of democratic debate at its highest, as well as sometimes possibly at its lowest; a manifestation of all that is best in an open, liberal democracy.

The Times observed, perhaps with a slightly patronising air :

> The debate, however damaging in the short run to the Labour Party, was of no small service to general political argument in the country. The issue of unilateral nuclear disarmament has been fogged by fear, by genuine emotion, by the subtle distortions of Communist pressure, and latterly by the hopeful pretence in the Labour Party that the issue could not be shirked . . .

The *Daily Mirror* took a rather more adult view of the scene. The paper's political editor, Sydney Jacobson, gave this summary of the scene after the battle :

> Labour has recoiled from the brink of disaster. The Party is still split wide open over the H-bomb. Still faced by grave perils. Still looks like a sitting duck if the Tories should spring a snap General Election. But the ardour and brilliance of yesterday's H-bomb debate has undoubtedly inspired the Labour Movement throughout the country. It has made politics exciting. And Labour can succeed only when politics are exciting.

Jacobson went on to observe that the principal question now was not whether Gaitskell would remain leader of the Labour Party :

> Anyone who opposes him seems likely to get a derisory vote from Labour MPs, who elect the leader. The big question is whether Gaitskell will use the time he's won by his triumph here yesterday [meaning the impact of his speech and the narrowness of the unilateralists' majority] to try to bridge some of the gaps in the Party. He will not abandon his principles on defence. He made that clear yesterday. But many Labour supporters here feel that there is urgent need for Gaitskell and his principal opponent Frank Cousins to get together despite their continuing and deeply sincere differences over the Bomb. These two big men, it is being argued, will sooner or later have to work in harmony if Labour unity is to be restored.

Meanwhile on that same day in *The Times* the Labour Party was being effectively written off for the time being :

> Scarborough has done more than put the Labour Party in a state of civil war. It has removed, certainly for this session and possibly this Parliament, any hope of their being an effective Opposition. It has also opened up new prospects, uncertain as they still are, for the Liberal Party to create an alternative of its own to an indefinitely prolonged period of Conservative Government.

Even as early as 1960 *The Times* editorials were already hankering after a realignment in British politics around a revival of the Liberal Party. However things were not to work out quite like that. Not that any commentator could be greatly blamed for believing, in the aftermath of that H-bomb debate, that a revival in the Labour Party's fortunes would require years of soothing treatment. The personal hatreds, recriminations and slanging matches were being ventilated in every hotel room, lobby and bar. It was open war between Right and Left.

By one of those characteristic flukes of circumstance it so happened that on the night of the debate the Transport Union held its traditional conference dinner – in the headquarters at Royal Hotel. Invitations had gone out to the TGWU delegates with their wives, the union's MPs and certain other guests, usually the leaders of other unions. By tradition it is also the practice to invite the leader of the Party, and the deputy leader, to the various union functions at the Party conference. That night in Scarborough this particular custom provided a uniquely embarrassing problem, for host as well as guest. It was resolved in an unexpectedly dramatic manner. Both Gaitskell and Cousins were much in demand that night in the BBC television and radio studios of Scarborough. Both had commented at length about the day's events; both sought to reject that the result of voting meant that the Labour Movement was irrevocably split. At the end of the series of interviews Gaitskell and Cousins found themselves together in the BBC's television studio. According to Frank Cousins this is what then happened:

> Gaitskell looked so lonely and dejected as he sat there, in the studio after the discussion. So I went over to him and said: 'Hugh, don't take it this way, for heaven's sake. Come down to our union dinner and have a drink and let's forget about it for a while. After all, we've still got to work together to get a Labour Government.'
>
> Gaitskell replied, 'That's very nice of you, Frank, I'd be happy to come. Can Dora come too?' 'Of course she can,' I said.

When Cousins walked into the TGWU dinner party accompanied by Hugh and Dora Gaitskell the evening was well under way. George Brown, as a TGWU MP, was sitting next to Nance Cousins. When Frank came into the room with the Gaitskells Brown turned to Nance immediately and demanded, 'Come on Nance, stand up, come and receive your leader.' About half the people in the room were already on their feet and sporadic applause was rippling along the tables. Nance Cousins, flushed and angry, turned back on George Brown and snapped: 'Not on your bloody life. Receive my leader? Over my dead body.' George Brown stormed back at Nance using language not normally exchanged on such public occasions. She was not one to crumble under such verbal assault: she gave Brown as good as she

277

got. The top table by this time was in some confusion and uproar with people standing and clapping, others standing and silent, and Nance Cousins firmly seated in her chair, white and tense. She refused to stand, and refused to speak to the Gaitskells. And later that night, when the last guests had departed, she and Frank had one of their very rare clashes. She was so incensed that Frank had brought the Gaitskells to *that* dinner, *that* night, that she turned on him with the bitter comment: 'I thought it was disgusting of you to bring him here, and I will never go anywhere with you if you do that to me again.'

Nance, even in retrospect, does not attempt to diminish that incident. She neither apologises nor retreats, although she recognises that it was a deeply embarrassing moment for both of them and an unprecedented conflict in their marital relationship. Her explanation for her behaviour is that she could not forgive Gaitskell for his slur about 'fellow-travellers'. She claims that this was a clear implication directed towards Frank, insinuating that he was fellow-travelling with the Communists and, she suspected, an imputation about her own earlier association with the Communist Party. She regarded that remark as a shameful innuendo unworthy of any leader of the Labour Party, regardless of political differences, and certainly unworthy of that Scarborough occasion.

Gaitskell's own explanation of his attack on 'fellow-travellers' was that he was convinced that some of the unions were under a mainstream of Communist influence to remove him as leader of the Labour Party and that the nuclear disarmament issue was being used to that end. He insisted that he was not referring to Frank Cousins or the TGWU. Still, like everyone else Gaitskell was carried away by the drama of the entire occasion. Moreover, he knew he was fighting for his political life as never before. He recognised that if he lost heavily it was the end of him as leader of the Labour Party. Dora Gaitskell says that before Hugh Gaitskell made his 'fight, fight and fight again' speech he did not know what the final outcome would be:

> He certainly had no idea that the voting would be so narrow. He expected a much heavier defeat and he had no illusions whatever about the outcome of such a defeat. He would have had to quit as party leader and go to the back benches. This was a real possibility at the time.

There seems little doubt that this would have been the case because that year Gaitskell lost all his major battles inside the Labour Party. He retreated almost totally on the Clause 4 issue; he had even been rejected by the Party executive (a body on which he was normally assured of a majority) over the question of conference decisions; and a large majority against him on nuclear disarmament would have been the final and possibly the fatal blow. As it was, he survived by what many regarded as a moral victory in the nuclear disarmament debate; he lived to fight again another year.

Despite Gaitskell's retreat on Clause 4 Frank Cousins was still suspicious of the new Statement of Aims because of the ambiguity of Section J. This was the paragraph which set out, in more detail, a qualification for the original – and still intact – Clause 4. It was the section in which Gaitskell accepted Nye Bevan's phrase 'the commanding heights', but which still contained a list of the varied forms public ownership might take, including public shareholdings in private enterprise companies. Cousins objected to these phrases; he believed they could, and no doubt would, be used against the case for a programme of more outright public ownership which he supported. So the Transport Workers moved 'reference back' of Section J – only to be told by the platform that they could not refer back one section – there had to be an acceptance, or a rejection, of the entire Statement of Aims. Cousins was incensed at this, and made it very plain indeed that he regarded it as a piece of sharp practice by the Party leadership to isolate him and his objections. Gaitskell denied that this was the case; he argued that Frank Cousins was quibbling over words and phrases – since there did not appear to be any difference of major substance between their intentions. Cousins, Gaitskell noted, was not demanding the nationalisation of every corner shop; he wanted control over the big monopolies of British industry – and that, Gaitskell insisted, was his own position.

No doubt it *was* a quibble about phrases. Yet at the root of it all was the deep suspicion, held not only by Cousins but by a broad spectrum of Labour opinion, that Gaitskell's retreat from his bid to amend – or delete – Clause 4 was temporary and tactical and that it was therefore essential to contest even the slightest suggestion of any move back in that direction. Cousins pressed his reference back to a vote but he lost – by 4,153,000 to 2,310,000. The size of that defeat was undoubtedly a conference reaction against Cousins. In the eyes of some trade-union leaders he had preseed his case too strongly and too adamantly. There was, in their view, an undertone of personal antagonism against Gaitskell in the Transport Workers' insistence on opposing Section J. But the size of Cousins's defeat was also due to the platform's insistence that there could be *no* separate vote on any one item in the Statement of Aims – it had to be all or nothing, and few of the delegates wanted to throw the whole package back to the executive for yet another redrafting. That was the last major debate at the memorable Scarborough conference; there has been nothing quite like it since.

In the aftermath of Scarborough a great wave of apocalyptic gloom spread inside the Labour Movement about the whole future relationship between the Party and the unions. At all levels the Movement was in a state of ideological chaos, mentally confused and spiritually depressed. The victorious nuclear disarmers were not cock-a-hoop despite their success, since they had few illusions about the difficulties of sustaining it. The vanquished supporters of the official policy were bewildered, soured and embittered, but determined to follow Gaitskell's invitation to fight, fight and fight again.

Ten days after Scarborough a pro-Gaitskell group was formed, consisting of Labour MPs, academics, local Party moderates, and some trade union leaders, with the object of launching a national campaign throughout the Labour Movement to fight the Campaign for Nuclear Disarmament. Its nominal organiser was William Rodgers, a former General Secretary of the Fabian Society (and now Labour MP for Stockton), helped by Denis Howell, MP and Alderman Frank Pickstock of Oxford. The group named itself the Campaign for Democratic Socialism (CDS) and drew heavily on the right-wing establishment of the Labour Movement, nationally and locally. They organised a series of campaign meetings – sometimes with Gaitskell as the main speaker – throughout the country and also tried to match the organisation of the Left by informal 'lobbying' within trade unions and local Parties. They were helped greatly by a natural desire, throughout the Movement, for a healing of the wounds and a reconciliation; and they were also assisted by the tensions and divisions within the CND itself, where the defection of Bertrand Russell to the camp of extreme protesters and the civil disobedience movement confused and fragmented the nuclear disarmers. CDS was formed on 18 October 1960 – almost before the dust of Scarborough had had time to settle. And before the end of the year it was clear that they were making substantial progress in their campaign of persuasion to swing the Labour Movement behind Gaitskell and his policies.

Frank Cousins was at an obvious disadvantage. It was not his role to campaign equally actively against CDS. He stuck firmly and passionately to his views on nuclear weapons and to his demand that the Labour Party leadership should honour – or at least not openly flout – conference decisions. He was angered by the tendency in the CDS campaign to single him out as the main villain. Much later, when he and Gaitskell were reconciled to working with each other, Cousins never forgave the Gaitskell acolytes in CDS for their personal vilification of him. The campaign to restore the authority of Gaitskell's leadership – for that is basically what the CDS was all about – found support in all corners of the Labour Movement and in the most sober of academic circles as well as in virtually every national newspaper. One of the main arguments was that it was intolerable that the policies of a major political party should be determined by a handful of powerful trade union figures in command of huge block votes. Again, one might recall that no such qualms about the block voting system or the 'handful of trade union oligarchs' had been expressed when the votes were used to support, instead

of challenging, the accepted wisdom. But of course these *was* a problem.
Put in its crudest and most emotive form – and by and large that is how it
was put – it might well appear objectionable that great decisions on momentous issues should be determined by the casting of block votes based on
narrow (or not so narrow) decisions of small delegate meetings which may
be unrepresentative of the mass of union members. The late Allan Flanders,
one of the most sensitive and shrewdest of observers of the industrial relations scene wrote, early in 1961 :

> The unions, or rather enough of them to command a majority of votes, have
> told the Labour Party how to do its job on a political issue, the most impor-
> tant political issue of all – the defence of the country. Whatever position one
> may hold in the great debate on a unilateral versus a multilateral approach
> to disarmament, whether one favours pacifism, neutralism, or support for
> the Western Alliance, the traditional terms of the marriage between unions
> and Labour Party have, for the time being, been thrown into the melting
> pot.
>   Maybe they can be rescued and restored. Then the crisis will be over
> although fierce debates over policy will continue within the Labour Party as
> indeed they should. Before this year is out we should know for certain
> whether that rescue operation is likely to succeed. If not, then no one should
> deceive himself about the seriousness of the consequences. A marriage can
> continue very happily for a long time, even a marriage of convenience, as
> long as each of the parties continues to behave in the way the other expects.
> But if one of them suddenly breaks their mutual understanding anything
> can happen. The situation can rapidly go from bad to worse until – who
> knows? – divorce is the only acceptable solution . . .[2]

Flanders, a supporter of Gaitskell, was voicing a fear strongly held at the
time – that there was a real danger of a divorce between the Party and the
unions if the 'Cousins rebellion' could not be halted and reversed at the
1961 conference. The view – propagated if not conceived by the Press –
found all kinds of echoes, even inside the TGWU, where the criticisms of
Frank Cousins for having adopted a 'too political' role were not abated
after Scarborough – quite the contrary. Within the union Cousins had to
fight a continuing battle not only against the conventional opponents of
nuclear disarmament but, rather more, against the old forces of Deakinism
which were still strong among the full-time officials and which had been
given fresh impetus to oppose Cousins during his great confrontation with
Gaitskell. There were some union branches – encouraged, no doubt, by the
CDS campaign – who questioned, for instance, the right of Frank Cousins
to support the AEU resolution at Scarborough, since that went further than
TGWU policy. This pressure led to the union issuing a special circular to

2. Allan Flanders, *Management and Unions* (Faber and Faber, 1970), p. 36–7.

all branches, constitutional committees and permanent officers of the TGWU, setting out the arguments to justify the union's policy at Scarborough. The circular pointed out, a little defiantly, that the explanation was necessary because 'of "a press campaign" against what they choose to call the "Cousins policy". In fact they are attacking a policy decided by your representatives and to which expression has been given wherever and whenever a suitable opportunity has presented itself.'

The circular then went on to deal with the criticism that Frank Cousins had been too absorbed in political activities:

It is also suggested in some quarters that the industrial interests of the membership are being subordinated to political activities. What hypocrisy! If the union had pursued a policy of support for nuclear weapons these critics would have praised our 'good sense' and 'statesmanship'. Their praise is worth as much as their criticism. It is not the fact that we are concerned with politics that so annoys our opponents in the press world; it is because we pursue successfully policies of which they do not approve. In fact their concern for the industrial well-being of our members would carry more weight if there was evidence that they have ever supported us in our constant pursuit of this aim. Of course the opposite is true as was demonstrated during the London Bus dispute in 1958.

The circular went on:

Obviously there are those who do not agree with the policy laid down by the Douglas biennial delegate conference [of 1959]. Yet hundreds of letters have been received from members of the union both collectively and as individuals endorsing the stand we have taken. Members of the general public, religious and other organisations have similarly written asking that the struggle should continue as vigorously as ever.

The circular, facing up to meet whatever challenge was coming from branches, concluded:

The General Executive Council has always taken the view that the concern for the well-being of the members cannot be restricted to purely industrial matters. Peace concerns us all and we have a duty to make our views clear. The policy we have put forward can provide a means of breaking through the existing dangerous nuclear impasse towards world peace on a permanent basis.

It was a powerful – and candid – response to the internal pressures and to the Press campaign directed against the union and particularly against Frank Cousins himself. There was no attempt to apologise or to be mealy-mouthed about a union's right to indulge in debates of this character. The TGWU case was quite simple : the threat of nuclear war was of such overwhelming importance to every citizen in the country that a trade union had the duty as well as the right to raise its voice. Moreover, the TGWU had gone to exceptional lengths to test – and to mobilise – the opinion within its ranks; arguably more than any other single institution, political or industrial. If the critics were right in arguing that it had tested only a small proportion of its membership – or, as it was alleged, an unrepresentative proportion – then how much more true was this charge against other organisations, whether they supported or opposed nuclear arms? The system of trade union democracy then – as now – was far from perfect. But it was, and is, more democratic than that of most comparable institutions. Those who challenged a union's right to use its institutional power within the Labour Movement to make policy on nuclear arms could ultimately justify that challenge only on elitist grounds – that is to say, unions and their members have neither the knowledge nor the responsibility to be allowed such powers. One could understand Labour's opponents holding that view and being prepared to sustain it intellectually. What was surprising in 1960 and 1961 was the degree to which the view was held within the Labour Movement and, especially, within the Parliamentary Labour Party. No doubt the Labour MPs were influenced by the strong current of public comment in the Press and elsewhere that the Party was in danger of becoming merely an instrument for trade union power – and left-wing power, at that. Some newspapers said it was time the Party and the unions ceased to have such a close relationship : a view endorsed not surprisingly by many Conservative MPs and, more surprisingly, by a number of Labour MPs as well.

The tumult inside the Parliamentary Labour Party was reaching a new pitch when it became clear that Gaitskell would be challenged as leader when the new session of Parliament began. There were already strong hints that the challenger would be Harold Wilson or even Anthony Crossland, and that the basis of the challenge would be the need to take account of conference decision. Shortly after Scarborough Greenwood pulled out of the Shadow Cabinet on the grounds that in his view Party unity was 'no longer possible' under Hugh Gaitskell and he therefore had no confidence in Gaitskell's leadership. This increased speculation that Greenwood would challenge Gaitskell for the leadership. But a week later, on 20 October, Harold Wilson announced that he would stand, and Greenwood withdrew from the contest. In a public statement Wilson declared : 'the issue facing us today is not defence; it is the unity, indeed the survival, of this Party.'
ment of policy which covered the following issues.

Wilson set out his programme for re-establishing unity, a four-point state-

1. A compromise on defence taking into account conference decisions but also agreeing on a policy which could be accepted 'with dignity by Labour MPs'.

2. A repudiation of the demand for 12 months 'civil war' in the Party – which was a clear attack on CDS.

3. Agreement to make all major pronouncements on policy or the conduct of the Party in collective agreement with the National Executive Committee and the PLP.

4. A 'repudiation of the campaign now being waged in certain sections of the Press for a major change in the democratic and socialist basis of the Movement' – which was an attack on those advocating a break with the trade unions.

Harold Wilson had already brought upon himself the scorn and derision of the entire Gaitskell wing of the Labour Party because of his fence-sitting at Scarborough. While never a unilateralist, Wilson had studiously avoided attacking the campaign against the Bomb, and had perhaps even occasionally flirted with the notion of joining it. It was a posture bitterly resented by all the Gaitskellites, and carefully observed by Frank Cousins. It did more than anything else to draw Cousins's attention to the potential in Harold Wilson as a left-of-centre future leader of the Labour Party.

But when Wilson challenged Gaitskell in November 1960 he was easily beaten – by 166 to 81. One of Harold Wilson's closest colleagues, Fred Lee, MP, also ran for deputy leadership against George Brown with Jim Callaghan as a third candidate. On the first ballot Brown polled 118 to Lee's 73 and Callaghan's 55; then on the second ballot Brown beat Fred Lee (now Lord Lee) by 146 to 83.

Everything was now prepared for Gaitskell's counter-offensive, with the big majority of the Parliamentary Labour Party marshalled to fight with their leader to reverse the Scarborough decision. While these frantic preparations were going on Frank Cousins was leading the Transport Union's first post-war delegation to the Soviet Union – a break with tradition for the TGWU and a break with previous TUC policy, which had been to discourage unions from exchange visits. Some unions had ignored the TUC's ruling, but it was rather different for the country's biggest union to do so, and, as events turned out, the Cousins delegation to Russia broke the ice for what was to develop into a widespread exchange of visits. The awkward man at the top of the TGWU had started yet another hare . . .

Chapter Seventeen

TO MOSCOW AND BACK . . .

Frank Cousins had now led the TGWU for five years. In that period the face of the British Labour Movement had changed in a manner which few would have thought possible, let alone predictable, within such a short span. The political balance of the Movement had shifted convincingly, though not yet decisively, to the Left, and in so far as the leadership was concerned that shift occurred primarily because of the emergence of one man at the top of one trade union. Even his most persistent critics would not have denied that this was the impact produced by Frank Cousins in his first five years.

This large claim does not take account of the new forces of militancy, shop-floor awareness, and response among a younger and far less deferential generation of rank-and-file activists. The relationship between that grass-roots development and the rise of Frank Cousins has already been recognised. Nevertheless, the effect of a single change in the leadership of one powerful trade union went far beyond the routine interplay between the forces of the led and the leadership; it had an extraordinary influence on the whole power structure at the top of the Labour Movement and, eventually, on the relations between the rank and file and the leadership in many other unions. However, it was one thing to break through the chain of the old command system – but quite another to reconstruct an alternative system of priorities. It was one thing for Cousins to begin loosening the grip of Deakinism inside the TGWU, the TUC and the Labour Party – but quite another problem for him to replace, within the span of his own period of office, an entire framework of officialdom, as well as supplying new policies for old ones. That remained his constant challenge to the end of his period of office, a challenge which many of his critics, and even some of his friends and supporters, believe he failed to meet effectively.

After five years in the General Secretary's chair Cousins knew he had made only a small dent in the traditional fabric of the union. He knew that although he had pointed the nose in a new direction, the deeply instinctive resistances within the TGWU were still pulling against a rapid movement in his new direction. He also knew that the *next* five years would be even more critical in this respect. He had somehow to keep up the momentum of his new policies in an increasingly difficult political and economic climate; and at the same time he had to try to reconstruct the union from within. Cousins had no illusions about the task ahead. He knew that the fight to radicalise the trade union and the wider Labour Movement was a much bigger task than winning conference votes or conference debates. It was a task of far greater magnitude than could be encompassed within the phrasing of resolutions or in Labour Party and TUC documents which sought to explain socialist doctrine in contemporary terms.

The political mix of Frank Cousins was a mix of the pragmatist and the romantic; the down-to-earth trade union bargainer and the socialist dreamer; the Christian socialist and the Marxist. His socialism was rooted in a kind of instinctive rather than an intellectual Marxism and, at the same time, it was always modulated, shaped and conditioned by a profound belief in the democratic capacity of working people to respond to new opportunities without the bludgeon of authoritarian control. He was attracted to the use of power and he used power; but he used it to greatest effect, and with most satisfaction, when he felt he was inducing others – especially his own members – to use *their* own power for *their* own wider political and social development. He was desperately anxious to open the door to rank-and-file power, to give his members the opportunity to use their energies and talents in order that they might create an entirely new environment in industrial relations. Like Bevan he recognised that 'the purpose of getting power is to be able to give it away'. But he did not delude himself that this could come about without central direction, central signposting and, perhaps, some pushing of the corporate body (sometimes against its will) in *his* new directions.

In his own union, and in the wider union movement, Cousins now faced the task of persuading men and institutions to change their social and ethical *mores*; it was the task of constructing the pyramid of the future, brick by practical brick, on ground that was constantly shifting. He had few illusions about the mountainous problems ahead. He knew he would have to lean more heavily on his authoritarian streak than on his romantic socialism. He possessed the capacity to close his eyes to his own degree of ruthlessness, though in many ways this was more of an unawareness than a conscious insensitivity. In these respects he was like Ernest Bevin – but then it is arguable that an organisation like the TGWU (or indeed any of the powerful unions) must inevitably mould leaders and potential leaders to that particular pattern. The uniqueness of Frank Cousins was that, having been moulded and chiselled by the TGWU processes, he rebelled against the mould and set about refashioning the template itself.

From 1961 onwards Cousins's objective was to develop still further the radical process he had opened up in his first five years. The ground had been cleared by the dramatic break with previous policies, yet there still existed wide areas where the remains of the past stood out like giant warning signals to Cousins, reminding him that he could only travel at the pace determined for him by external factors as well as by the forces of opposition which remained rooted within the union. The London busmen's strike, the campaign against the Bomb, the fight against wage restraint and the economic policies of the Macmillan Government, as well as the demand for more vigorous socialist policies from the Labour Party – all of these activities, to be sure, had released a great deal more rank-and-file enthusiasm in the TGWU than ever before. Cousins's policies did galvanise and activate the union both in his favour and in terms of opposition – but especially in generating the feeling that the union was, at last, taking the initiative and 'doing something'. By the early 1960s the TGWU was a more dynamic force in British trade unionism than at any time since the pre-war campaigning days of Ernest Bevin. Its huge membership put great strains on the limited administration, which was still inadequate to the tasks facing the union, and on its full-time officials. Cousins was not as successful as he would have wished in replacing the 'old guard' of officials and he frequently felt himself curiously reluctant to push his power in this direction, perhaps because he still retained that old uncertainty behind his mask of self-confidence. Yet the TGWU did make significant progress and, not surprisingly, Cousins put this down at least partly to his new and radical policies. At the end of 1960 membership had risen to an all-time peak of 1,340,357, which was an increase of 62,047 on the figure at the end of 1959. That, in itself, was an interesting commentary on the policy the union pursued during 1960.

The invitation to the TGWU to visit Russia came from the Motor Transport, Highways and Communications Workers' Union of the USSR. It had originally been made before the Russian invasion of Hungary in 1956. Frank Cousins had cancelled the trip then, but in the past year he had been seeking a suitable moment to take up the proposal, renewed by the Russians. Cousins was keen to go partly because he had never visited Soviet Russia, but also because he sought an improvement in relations between the trade unions of the East and the West. He believed in the value of resuming the exchange of visits between union delegations because he saw in this approach a road to a wider international rapport, and he also believed it was possible to influence the Communist governments in their domestic policies. He was especially keen to visit the USSR to see for himself at first hand what conditions were like and, in particular, what constraints were imposed on trade unions. In fact the Cousins visit turned into a major international event when he became the first – indeed the only – British trade union leader to talk at length with Nikita Khrushchev.

Cousins was impressed but not seduced by what he saw. He was critical of the relationship between the State machine and the unions, and said so, bluntly, to his Russian hosts. At the same time he was ungrudgingly approving of the Soviet post-war reconstruction and many of the social and economic priorities in the Soviet Union. The Russians, with characteristic hospitality, did the delegation proud. From their point of view it was an important diplomatic success to welcome such a powerful trade union team from a Britain still in the chill air of the Cold War. The Soviet reception on that occasion was, indeed, on a grander scale than Cousins experienced when he went later to Moscow, several times, as Minister of Technology and a member of the Cabinet. Even so, Cousins did not expect to meet Khrushchev. He told his Soviet hosts that he would like to, but that was more of a formal gesture than a serious expectation that anything would materialise. After all, Khrushchev had only lately returned from the United Nations and he was known to be immersed in high-level critical international negotiations about the future status of Berlin. But suddenly one evening Cousins was told that Khrushchev would be glad to see him the next morning in the Kremlin.

When the door of Khrushchev's room was opened at 11 a.m. next day Cousins looked in on a huge salon, like a Czar's parlour, with a large desk at the far end. In front of it stood Nikita Khrushchev, smiling broadly as he advanced down the long room, hands outstretched to welcome the General Secretary of Britain's largest union.

'It was a bit like a Sam Goldwyn production,' Cousins says. 'We met in the centre of the huge room, smiling at each other and shaking hands for what seemed like several minutes.' The two men began a lengthy discussion about world affairs and Cousins found Khrushchev exceptionally well-informed about what he and the TGWU had been up to in Britain. At an early stage in the meeting Cousins went on to the offensive by telling Khrushchev that many people in Britain feared Soviet intentions; there was, he told the Russian leader, a deep and genuine suspicion in Britain about Soviet motives in Europe and a conviction that the Russians wanted to spread Communism by military force if necessary.

Half-mockingly Khrushchev replied: 'What do we want to take over Britain for? We've got enough problems of our own. Anyway, you can't even feed yourselves, so why should we want to take on that responsibility?'

Cousins accused Khrushchev of having no respect for anyone except those who held real power.

'Not so,' Khrushchev replied with a laugh. 'I respect you – and you are only a trade union leader in a capitalist country.'

Cousins chastised Khrushchev in a friendly manner for his behaviour at the United Nations Assembly, particularly that incident when he took off one of his shoes to rap the table with.

'You know,' Cousins told the Soviet Premier, 'that is just not done . . .'

'It is now,' laughed Khrushchev.

When he learned that Cousins, like him, had been a miner in early life Khruschev started reminiscing about his own days in the pits, in the Donbas region. 'Happy days in so many ways,' he reflected to Cousins, nostalgically. He recalled his prowess as a soccer player for his pit team, playing left-half. The two men increasingly warmed to each other; they seemed to discover chemical as well as political attractions in each other's personality. Both were powerful, strong-willed men, highly charged emotionally, each in his own way trying to change the power structure within his own sphere of activity and, in different contexts, to liberalise it. Clearly they felt some kinship. Khrushchev, busy as he was, cancelled his later engagements and insisted on Cousins staying in the Kremlin for lunch. The original meeting had been scheduled to last about an hour. In fact the two stayed together for 3 hours and 20 minutes, the longest session that Khrushchev ever gave to any foreign trade union delegation.

One of the oddities of that meeting was that Cousins did not raise with Khrushchev the issue of nuclear disarmament. His explanation is that the Russians knew precisely where he stood on the whole question of Britain giving a moral lead – after all, it was only a matter of weeks after Scarborough. He says he did not want to engage in any diplomatic negotiations with Khrushchev on defence or wider issues of foreign policy. 'It would not have been proper for me to do so.' Still, it is surprising that the issue did not arise. One might suspect that Cousins was wary of raising it because of Khrushchev's previously reported views that, as far as the Russians were concerned, it mattered nothing either way whether Britain had the H-bomb or not. If that was Khruschev's view, then a Cousins question might well have provoked its repetition in the company of the TGWU delegation – hardly the most encouraging Soviet reaction to take back to Britain. At any rate, according to Cousins, the issue did not arise. Yet he did press the Soviet leader on many other delicate issues during their long lunchtime discussion – a lunch which was attended by members of his delegation as well as several of Khrushchev's Politburo colleagues.

The dialogue between Khruschev and Cousins – or that part of it recalled by Frank Cousins – went like this :

FC : Why don't you let your people come out to visit the West ?

NK : It's all a question of currency. We just don't have the foreign currency.

FC : No, no . . . that won't do, come on. Tell me the real truth . . .

NK : (looking hard at Cousins) Well, all right, the truth is that they wouldn't come back to the Soviet Union.

FC : That's not a very good advertisement for your system after all these years of communism.

NK : No, you are right, it isn't. We know that we are behind you in our living standards at present. But give us another 15 to 20 years from now and you will be beginning to envy our system . . .

FC : What kind of society are you aiming at?

NK : We want a society that doesn't want to hoard things; reflect on that . . . I've never yet met a man who wanted to wear two suits at the same time.

For Cousins his long meeting with Khrushchev was one of the most memorable occasions of his life. He was deeply impressed by the Russian leader, his candour and his readiness to accept criticism of Soviet life.

While he was in Russia Frank Cousins's younger son, Michael, was having some difficulties on account of his father. Working as a young scientist recently out of Cambridge he was engaged at the Windscale plant of the Atomic Energy Authority; but not, as he tried to assure constant Press inquirers, on nuclear weaponry or the production of plutonium. His was experimental work on the industrial application of atomic power. This was an explanation which failed to convince the Press, which continued to hound him to such an extent that he was eventually compelled to quit Windscale. Moreover, before he did so his apartment was broken into by newspaper photographers in search of pictures which might reveal this son of the unilateralist Frank Cousins as a manufacturer of the H-bomb. The incident was reported to the Press Council while Frank Cousins was still in Moscow, but Cousins himself did not pursue it when he returned. He simply registered the experience as another reason why he could not learn to love the Press, another part of the price he was obliged to pay for voicing unpopular views on critical issues.

Cousins returned from Russia to find his own agenda pad full of the problems he had left behind – and more. The British economy had already entered a state of recession with the prospects of still worse to come as the Government tightened the credit market, under the pressure of a worsening balance of payments. Unemployment was growing rapidly, particularly in the car industry. By January 1961 unemployment was 419,000 throughout the country. By current standards that figure is not high, but it was at the start of the 1960s. The 1950s had been a decade of developing affluence and rising standards. There was an assumption that full employment and the Welfare State were irreversibly built into the foundations of post-war British society. It was in 1961 that the British economy first began to feel the tremors of a fundamental shift in the terms of trade and balance of payments that was increasingly to expose the economy to internal and external inflationary forces. In fact by March 1961 the Prime Minister, Harold Macmillan, was noting in his diary that a combination of internal and external pressures had produced the most concentrated crisis of his Premiership so far – 'the worst I remember since the days before Suez.'[1]

Macmillan listed the financial crisis that spring as one of the major icebergs in his path, a crisis, he suggested, which threatened to end in the 'collapse of sterling'. This was the final blow on top of his other preoccupations – such as the general international tension, the developing breakdown in relations with South Africa and Rhodesia, and the wars in South-East Asia. It finally convinced a divided Cabinet to turn seriously towards interventionism in economic affairs. This time the interventionism was to be more general than ever before attempted, affecting the whole management of the British economy. By the time the Chancellor, Selwyn Lloyd, introduced his 'mini-budget' in July – and with it a new policy of wage restraint – the Cabinet had already made up its mind to establish a new planning body which, eventually, became the National Economic Development Council, NEDC. This was an extraordinary step for a Conservative Government taken only after long and terrible heart-searchings by many members of the Macmillan Cabinet. The birth of NEDC really dated from Selwyn Lloyd's Budget speech of 25 July 1961 in which he invited the cooperation of both sides of industry in a new planning exercise. Two weeks later Lloyd invited the two sides of industry to join a national planning council on which they, with the Government, would jointly attempt to guide the management of Britain's economy. The Council was formally established at the end of 1961 though it was not until January 1962 that the TUC finally agreed to serve on it. The concept of NEDC stemmed from private talks among a group of leading British industrialists on the need for more coherent economic and industrial planning. At a conference sponsored by the Federation of British Industry (forerunner of the CBI) at Brighton in November 1960 the FBI leaders and Selwyn Lloyd unveiled their planning concept. But there was still much opposition from within the Macmillan Cabinet.

It is worth recalling that at this early stage the main objection by a majority inside the Cabinet was that such a joint planning body would usurp the role of Government if it was to be an effective body. Ministers objected that it would cut across Government views, their decisions and Cabinet responsibility by removing from Government, or at least Parliament, a decisive responsibility. By a curious irony this was the very argument levelled against NEDC by Frank Cousins and others inside the TUC, as well as by the majority of left-wing opinion in the Parliamentary Labour Party. It took a great deal of persuasion to get Cousins to change his mind and support TUC involvement in NEDC (including his own membership of the new body). And it was only achieved after much cajoling by George Woodcock.

Woodcock was then in his first year as the General Secretary of the TUC.

1. Harold Macmillan, *Pointing the Way* (Macmillan, 1972), p. 297.

He entered the battlefield at the moment when it was mined as never before. Tewson handed over after the 1960 Trades Union Congress, when the bitterness and strife inside the General Council was at an all-time peak of intensity. Woodcock has told me that he himself was deeply shocked at the extent to which this bitterness penetrated everything in which the TUC leaders were concerned. 'I do not remember in all my experience at the TUC [which dates back to 1936] such personal bitterness and animosity.' Individual members, Woodcock recalls, brought their personal feelings into General Council affairs to a degree which had never happened before : 'There were some members who were in a state of frenzy at Cousins over the H-bomb issue, and what I feared was that this feeling of personal strife was in danger of becoming so profound that it might jeopardise the industrial work of the TUC.' George Woodcock realised that this was his major challenge as soon as he took over. He had somehow to ease the tension and remove the H-bomb issue as the central point of all TUC business. He himself had no strong views on nuclear disarmament either way : he was not a nuclear disarmer, but he felt no marked objection to their views or policies, though he regarded them as unrealistic. He realised that he had to act quickly to prevent still greater damage. Moreover, he knew there was no one else, no one so well equipped and placed, to play the role of conciliator in this intensely emotional conflict. There was no other man of influence in the trade union movement who could persuade Frank Cousins to take a less abrasive course inside the TUC General Council; and no other figure who, having succeeded in doing that, could virtually demand that Cousins's opponents should respond. That was Woodcock's remarkable achievement. He did it by persuading Cousins that the focal point of the H-bomb debate must be shifted from the TUC General Council into the arena of the Labour Party. Many observers at the time, and since, have wrongly assumed that Woodcock's objective was to take the TUC out of politics altogether. This was not his purpose at all. He was certainly less firmly wedded to the traditionally close structural relationship with the Labour Party, because he felt the TUC should have more freedom to operate whatever Party was in office. But he neither wanted – nor had any illusions about the possibility of achieving – any break with the Labour Party in the wider political sense. Woodcock was never indifferent to political realities, nor was he 'anti-Labour' as was sometimes suggested. What he felt was the need to take the TUC out of the cauldron of Party strife both for its own sake and for the benefit of a wider development in the growth of the trade union movement.

His long-term objective was to open up the ranks of the TUC to white-collar, professional and more civil service unions, to strengthen its role as an authoritative body with the ability and capacity to speak on equal terms with Ministers and Government departments. He wanted the TUC to play an increasingly influential role in working with the Government to shape, plan and determine social and economic priorities. Woodcock felt that these aims and objectives would be more easily attained if he could provide the TUC with a public image that at least appeared to be less closely identified with everything the Labour Party did and said.

· Against this background of Woodcock's thinking the Government's developing interest in some form of joint planning board offered the TUC leader an ideal opportunity to do two things : firstly, to grasp the opportunity as the first significant bridgehead in establishing the new type of association with the Government he wanted, and secondly, to extricate the TUC from the obsessional and, as he saw it, introverted controversy over nuclear disarmament. Indeed Woodcock became so enthusiastic about the concept of the NEDC that the form of the organisation which eventually emerged was largely based on his blueprint. Selwyn Lloyd wanted a different set-up which, in effect, would have been an extension of the Treasury. The Chancellor's original proposal was that the NEDC Director General should be a Treasury appointment and that the new body should be entirely subject to the Treasury writ. Selwyn Lloyd did not conceive of the NEDC having its own independent research staff, but preferred to have it serviced by the Treasury. He also wanted an equal number of 'independent' members of the new body as TUC and CBI representatives. Woodcock fought him on all points – and won. And what is now the structure of NEDC probably owes most to George Woodcock's insistence, at the very beginning, that the new body must be outside the Government machinery, with its own independent system of contacts with industry and the trade unions, as well as with Whitehall. In any event Woodcock knew that without such conditions he would have been unable to persuade the TUC (and especially Frank Cousins) to accept the NEDC concept. So did Selwyn Lloyd.

How did Cousins respond to this Woodcock strategy?

He was far from easy to convince. He had an instinctive and immediate distrust of the Government's proposal and of its 'conversion' to the principal economic planning. He did not believe it was a genuine shift. He also believed it might well lead to wage restraint by another route, and the trade unions could well find themselves outmanœuvred by Macmillan and Selwyn Lloyd. He did not necessarily share some other criticisms of the Left – such as that setting up the NEDC would be removing an important area of economic debate from Parliament and shunting it into closed and private committee rooms outside Parliamentary control. Cousins accepted that the TUC had to become 'more involved' in the economic planning process, but at the same time he wanted to keep the Government, certainly a Conservative Government, at arm's length. It was the characteristic 'trade union' attitude; he wanted to have a voice – even a strong voice – in what the Government was doing, but he did not want to accept the responsibility, even in part, for their actions. Woodcock succeeded in persuading him that even allowing for all these reservations it would be extremely difficult for the TUC to reject the invitation to join the NEDC.

In part Woodcock succeeded because he was the one man in the TUC hierarchy (or, for that matter, the Labour Party establishment) whom Cousins would trust; the one man for whom Cousins had a deep and genuine respect. Woodcock belonged to no faction within the Labour Movement; he abhorred the cliques and the groups of plotters-and-planners, of Right or Left. His intellectual stature was commonly accepted by all sides to be out-standing, and he suffered fools badly, often very badly. The worst charge his critics could level at him was that he was 'aloof, remote, and difficult'. Cousins found none of these 'flaws' in Woodcock. Each man discovered complementary features in the other, and a working partnership was established from the beginning – not by formal agreement or even informal collusion, but almost by a process of natural selection. The Woodcock-Cousins link was to become the most important factor in the development of TUC policy during the years preceding the 1964 election. It certainly laid a fresh foundation for trade union cooperation with the Government and for an altogether wider development of trade union thinking and activity.

At the same time, Frank Cousins hardly needed to be reminded – by George Woodcock or anyone else – that it was important for him and the TGWU not to become over-committed to the nuclear disarmament controversy to the extent that they would find that in the end they could not control it. Cousins sensed that he would be defeated at the 1961 Labour Party conference. He sensed this not simply because of the frenzied activities of the Gaitskellite Campaign for Democratic Socialism but also because the general international situation worsened as East-West tension rose to a fresh peak. It could hardly have been a less encouraging back-cloth for a campaign in favour of unilateral action by Britain, irrespective of the logic behind that campaign. By the early months of 1961 Cousins felt the tide was running against him.

The first sign that the Gaitskell counter-offensive was gathering strength came as early as November 1960, when the Labour Party Executive decided to hold a fresh round of talks with the TUC. It was proposed that this time there would be a virtual 'Assembly of Labour' with the Shadow Cabinet, the full Labour Party Executive and the TUC General Council joining forces. Moreover, the NEC decided that, despite Scarborough, they should *not* recommend acceptance of the conference decision on the H-bomb but, instead, merely present a 'situation report'. A contrary proposal that the NEC should 'act as the advocates of annual conference on defence' was rejected by 17 to 9. Gaitskell made it perfectly clear right from the beginning that he regarded his overriding task as fighting the Scarborough conference decision, reversing it and preparing the way for that reversal by redrafting a defence policy which yielded nothing to the unilateralists. His leadership was at stake, indeed, at serious risk – and he meant to win.

At the 'Assembly' of the Labour leadership on 24 January 1961, held in the TUC headquarters at Congress House, Gaitskell proposed a completely new joint statement on defence. The main features of his proposals were that the Labour Party must make it clear to the British people that the Party stood unreservedly for defending Britain, that Britain must remain in NATO, though we could no longer sustain a role as an independent nuclear power, and that any disarmament programme must be based on a multilateral and not a unilateral policy. Frank Cousins found himself fighting Gaitskell with all the old ferocity. He was beside himself with fury at Gaitskell's nerve. The minutes of that extraordinary meeting show him urging the 'Assembly' to face up to the fact that what Gaitskell was proposing as a new defence policy was precisely the same as that which had been rejected at Scarborough. Cousins said he

accepted the need for defence, but did not accept this meant that we must stay in NATO under all circumstances. He did not accept that we should have nuclear weapons in the West unless Russia's satellites had them. He did not accept that a base for Polaris-carrying submarines should be provided in Britain. He did not agree that the policy agreed at Scarborough would be electorally disastrous.

His reference to NATO was probably the closest he had come, till then, to stating his readiness to quit the North Atlantic Treaty Organisation, and it provoked Harold Wilson to say that for the bulk of the Parliamentary Labour Party the continued membership of NATO must remain 'the sticking point'. But Wilson also stressed that 'we must take account of conference decisions, too.'

The meeting then dissolved into a contest between Wilson and Crossman trying for a compromise with Cousins, pitched against Gaitskell and George Brown who were jointly determined to yield nothing. Wilson proposed a six-point policy which he believed could have united the Labour Movement:

1. Britain should abandon nuclear weapons as a matter of policy as well as on economic grounds.

2. Britain should remain in NATO but insist on reforming the organisation (by reducing the power of the Generals).

3. NATO should not become a nuclear power.

4. There should be no nuclear bases in Britain.

5. Germany should not have nuclear weapons.

6. German troops should not be trained in Britain.

Gaitskell and Brown would not have it. Unable to agree, the assembly appointed a Committee of Twelve to try its hand at drawing up a draft policy. The Committee included all the main contestants : Gaitskell, Cousins, Brown, Crossman, Sam Watson, Denis Healey, Jim Callaghan and Walter Padley. There were four representatives from each of the main sections – the Shadow Cabinet, Party Executive and TUC. In addition to the eight listed, there were also Tom Driberg, MP, and three others from the TUC, Sir Alfred Roberts, Fred Hayday, and William Webber. It was from this committee that Dick Crossman vainly tried to salvage some unity and compromise. But his lucid arguments and gifted logic were to no avail.

That committee held four meetings, but when it concluded on 15 February it was no nearer a consensus. Crossman and Cousins worked together throughout the period trying to produce a compromise draft which Gaitskell might accept. At one point Crossman, who acted as the liaison between Gaitskell and Cousins, believed he had succeeded in finding the magic formula. He persuaded Cousins to make significant concessions which in effect amounted to a retreat from the TGWU's agreed policy on nuclear disarmament. It was clear evidence, certainly to Crossman, that Cousins was looking for a way out of the impasse and of avoiding a further confrontation at the 1961 conferences. The essence of the Crossman formula was the rejection of a NATO strategy 'based on the threat to use [nuclear weapons] first'; an end to US nuclear bases in Britain; and the creation of a nuclear-free zone in Europe as part of a plan to offer the Russians a programme for controlled disarmament. Implicit in this was, of course, the fact that Britain should give a lead in seeking to break the nuclear deadlock. Crossman and Cousins went through this draft item by painful item, comma by comma. Finally Cousins told Crossman, 'Yes, I will accept that.' A jubilant Crossman believed he had at last found 'the bridge' to end the great split. He rushed to see Gaitskell, almost crying out, 'It's peace in our time.' But Gaitskell wouldn't have it. Cousins hadn't gone far enough. It must be total surrender, or nothing.

Crossman afterwards confessed that he was utterly dismayed and exasperated by Gaitskell's refusal to compromise, by his determination to defeat Cousins and reverse the Scarborough vote, come what might. As a result Crossman found himself moving closer to Cousins, which only intensified Gaitskell's fury with Crossman. The relationship between Gaitskell and Crossman was always a puzzle. For a time, after Crossman's break with the Bevanites, he was closer to Gaitskell than almost anyone else in the Parliamentary Labour Party – or so it may have seemed. Yet, as with a number of his other personal relationships, it was difficult for this one to survive the turns and twists of Crossman's fertile ideas. Once seized by a train of thought, however much at variance with his previous thinking, Crossman would pursue it with a relentless logic and a disarming candour, often at his own expense. It was a trait as endearing to those who admired his enormous intellectual agility as it was infuriating to those who suffered from his changes of direction. Gaitskell looked for predictability and mostly, an unquestioning loyalty from his associates. As Crossman fought to find a compromise with Cousins, so he became somewhat 'suspect' in Gaitskell's eyes. There had, indeed, been a Gaitskell-Crossman 'problem' since they were together at Winchester School. They were not contemporaries – Crossman was two years senior, the outstanding boy of his generation at the school. He easily out-shone Gaitskell as a scholar, a sportsman and an authority among his own contemporaries. The same was true when the two were at Oxford later. In political life the roles became reversed when Gaitskell rose rapidly in the Parliamentary Labour Party and into the Cabinet, leaving Crossman far behind as a back-bencher. Crossman retained a strong reluctance to accept Gaitskell's seniority and the authority of his arguments. No doubt this pro-duced a powerful psychological barrier to any effective accord between the two men, quite apart from other disagreements over the Labour Party's policy on nuclear disarmament and the character of Party conference decisions. Crossman convinced himself that Gaitskell was 'impossible' to deal with at that time – and he may have been right. Certainly Gaitskell believed that the only way he could reassert his authority as leader of the Labour Party was not merely to get the conference votes for his defence policy but, more important still, to ensure that Frank Cousins was roundly defeated and seen to be defeated. Nothing could shift Gaitskell from that objective, be-cause he was convinced that his political future depended on it. And he was probably right to think so.

On the other hand Crossman had no doubts that the Left would accept his compromise draft and that this could have led to an end of the great rift. Even some of the leading CND spokesmen declared themselves ready to accept a compromise in the interests of Labour unity, and a letter to this effect was published in the *New Statesman* early in 1961 (signed by Kingsley Martin, Ritchie Calder and Benn Levy). Yet nothing would per-suade Gaitskell to think again. Crossman noted in his diary: 'The whole atmosphere is more depressing than ever – if that is possible.'[2] And a few weeks later, still in despair at the collapse of his attempts to secure agree-ment on a compromise, Crossman observed: 'These incredibly dreary manoeuvrings are making this Labour Party conflict more and more insigni-ficant in the public eye and making our own party people more and more impatient of those of us who seem to be squabbling at the top.'[3]

On 22 February the Labour Party's national executive considered the final drafts – the Gaitskell policy, which had been drafted by Gaitskell, Denis Healey and Sam Watson; the Crossman compromise plan, which had been agreed to by a number of multilateralists including men like Walter Pedley,

2. Richard Crossman, the unpublished diaries, 8 February 1961.
3. *Ibid.*, 21 February 1961.

MP, who was then the President of the Union of Shop, Allied and Distributive Workers (USDAW), and a third draft which had been submitted by Frank Cousins himself.

The Cousins draft was virtually the same as the Crossman paper, though a little tougher in its phraseology, with fewer concessions made to Gaitskell's views. Crossman himself was in the chair at the meeting (he was now Party chairman) and he pressed his compromise formula with great vehemence. In fact he came close to a remarkable and wholly unexpected success, when one vote tipped the scales against him. The proposal was defeated by 15 to 13, an indication that there was a strong impulse for compromise even inside the largely pro-Gaitskell executive. The Cousins document was easily defeated by 16 to 7, and finally Gaitskell's draft was approved by 16 to 10. That was the turning-point in the battle: the fight for the Blackpool conference vote was now the main, indeed the only, objective. The scene had been set to persuade the trade union conferences, beginning at Easter, to switch back behind official defence policy and desert the unilateralists – and, in particular, to defeat the TGWU and Cousins, who had now become the grotesquely caricatured targets for establishment attack.

The year 1961 was one in which the TGWU was holding a biennial delegate conference, and in March the union's executive rejected the new defence policy and reaffirmed its faith in the anti-bomb campaign. At the same time Frank Cousins publicly admitted that there was opposition to the union's policy from 'some branches', which was hardly surprising in view of the weight of Press comment against Cousins and the force of the Gaitskell campaign. When the agenda for the TGWU conference appeared in May it revealed the extent of the revolt against the anti-H-bomb policy. Out of 658 motions on the agenda 185 dealt with nuclear disarmament. Of these 63 backed Cousins, while 77 were critical of the union's stand for a variety of reasons, often contradictory. Some wanted Cousins to go further than he had done and commit himself unreservedly to a totally unilateralist policy; others concentrated on the need to repair the damage in the Labour Movement; some were openly critical of Cousins and pro-Gaitskell. Of one thing there was no doubt: the active membership of the union (and even the not-so-active) were aroused as never before. Nothing quite like this had happened before in the union's history. Never before had the conference agenda been so dominated by one single issue, and indeed never before had there been so many motions on one subject. The Brighton conference of the TGWU promised to be of even more dramatic stuff than the TUC and Labour Party conferences later in the year.

However, by the time the TGWU delegates met the issue had been virtually settled. Union after union swung back behind Gaitskell, starting with the AEU at its conference, where the unilateralists were defeated by 28 to

23 (with one abstention). Another unilateralist union, the Shop and Distributive Workers, reversed its position by supporting the call for unity. And in July, shortly before the Transport Workers were due to meet, two more unions, the Miners and the Railwaymen voted to support official policy. The Transport Workers were once again isolated. Of all the major unions they alone remained opposed to the British possession of nuclear weapons. Cousins went to his Brighton conference aware that he not only had a fight on his hands (a fight he was confident of winning) but also painfully aware that he was destined to go down to a heavy defeat at the TUC and Labour Party conferences. Scarborough, a bare ten months earlier, now seemed a long way off.

It was an oddly assorted platform of speakers who gathered in a theatre beside the Brighton Dome on the Sunday evening of 9 July 1961, before the start of the nineteenth biennial delegate conference. In characteristic style, George Brown, having failed to persuade Frank Cousins and the union's executive to allow him to address the conference on the subject of nuclear disarmament, arranged a protest meeting on the eve of conference. Brown's dream, as he came on to the theatre stage that night, was to have every seat filled; to see the theatre crowded with hundreds of TGWU delegates, to persuade them to overturn the policy of Frank Cousins on the Bomb, to marshal the country's biggest trade union behind Hugh Gaitskell and orthodox policy, and – though he may never have intended it – to undermine if not to overthrow the present leadership of the TGWU, his own union. That was the dream, or perhaps the midsummer madness, on that quiet Sunday evening in Brighton – the dream not only of George Brown but, perhaps even more, of the Campaign for Democratic Socialism. The Campaign distributed leaflets outside the theatre, denouncing unilateralism and urging support for the Gaitskell policy under the heading of 'Ten Points On Defence and Disarmament'. Not once was the name Cousins mentioned. Neither was there any reference to the TGWU or the Brighton conference. That was unnecessary. The tenth point of the CDS leaflet declared :

> Unilateralism also means electoral suicide at home. Ordinary men and women don't believe in it – as public opinion polls have shown. In recent Parliamentary by-elections they have voted firmly against it. If Labour is unilateralist there will never be a Labour Government to implement the decision.

Inside the theatre George Brown assembled his platform, consisting of a group of TGWU-sponsored MPs (it included G. Deer, G. Jeger, G. Oliver and Reg Prentice). In the chair was Charles Pannell, MP, representing the trade union group in the Parliamentary Labour Party. Oddly enough, he was a member of another union, the AEU – not exactly the most tactful choice on the eve of the TGWU conference. Perhaps Brown's biggest catch was Phillip Noel-Baker, MP, whose record of work for disarmament for over forty years was second to none among Labour MPs. All came to try to influence the TGWU delegates to overthrow their union's policy against the H-bomb.

This attempt turned into a fiasco. About 30 delegates turned up (out of 771) and most were hostile to what they perceived as George Brown's attempt to override the conferences' authority and the union's leadership by devious and even dubious means. There were as many pressmen present as members of the audience. This may have accounted for the fact that the absence of a sizeable audience did not prevent George Brown from making a long and passionate speech against the TGWU policy, and in favour of the multilateralist policy. Even then he denied that he was interfering with the union's democratic right to decide its own policy. The Parliamentary Party's policy must be put to the union, he said, in doing that, he was doing no more than his democratic duty. He also rejected the charge that he was trying to organise any putsch against the TGWU leadership, least of all against his friend Frank Cousins. 'I regard Frank Cousins as a very great personal friend, and I hope he regards me in the same way,' George told the few scattered faces in the theatre. It was not what Cousins regarded as the most sensitive way of demonstrating their friendship. The effect of this theatrical event was, if anything, to strengthen Cousins's hand. Even his staunchest opponents inside the conference were outraged by George Brown's meeting. Several said so from the rostrum when the H-Bomb was debated later that week. Without exception they appeared to think that George Brown's intervention had been counter-productive for Gaitskell as well as himself. It had achieved nothing except to illustrate that Cousins, despite a stronger opposition than a year earlier to his nuclear policy inside the TGWU, remained in an unassailable position. Nor was any of that surprising. Indeed the surprising thing was that anyone with George Brown's knowledge and understanding of the trade union and Labour Movement should have considered that he could have achieved anything beyond a fiasco.

Cousins himself handled the delicate issue with dignity, though he was clearly bitter and angry at Brown and the other union MPs. When the conference opened on Monday 10 July he quietly thanked the delegates for 'staying away from the meeting on Sunday night'. Later in the week when the H-bomb was debated he appealed to all delegates to 'dismiss from their minds' any thoughts of disciplining TGWU – sponsored MPs who had flouted the union's policy. A number of motions were on the agenda calling for 'action' to be taken against those union MPs who had engaged in a deliberate campaign of opposition to TGWU policy. Though he was enraged, Cousins was totally opposed to any such reprisals. Yet the pressure was on him as never before : in a sense it was more intense than in the period between 1959 and the Scarborough Labour Party conference, when he was leading the assault on official defence policy. The stress and the strain were showing during that week at Brighton, when Cousins was nervous and tetchy behind his mask of continuing aggressive self-confidence. The emotional pressure spread to his family. Michael Cousins, Frank's younger son, speaks of it being 'a terrible emotional period for the entire Cousins family. We were all in a pretty fearful state.'

It was late in the week before the H-bomb was debated : Thursday was chosen, for quite specific reasons. Cousins wanted to demonstrate that he was not obsessed by the nuclear issue at the expense of the union's industrial role, as some of his critics were suggesting. He wanted the conference to give priority to debates on wages policy, internal union affairs, nationalisation, industrial health and safety, race prejudice in some sections of the union (such as the London busmen), and even the Common Market. All these were debated before the conference reached the H-bomb motions. There was another sweeping declaration against wage restraint and Government economic policy, and a further emphasis on full-scale public ownership coupled with an attack on the Labour Party's latest policy statement ('Signposts for the Sixties'), which did not go far enough in Cousins's view to committing the Party to a substantial extension of nationalisation. The conference was gradually wound into a mood of preparedness for the great debate on the H-bomb. The delay helped to soothe, but it also led to impatience. When Thusday came, it was far from an anti-climax. For five hours the delegates went over all the old arguments : they examined the defence postures of Right and Left with a minuteness which would not have disgraced any military academy; they searched world horizons for hope and encouragement; and they delved into their own souls to try to rationalise a case which the majority already felt was a lost cause as established Labour Party policy.

That Brighton conference saw Cousins fighting for his policy as never before. His speech – one of the best he ever delivered to his union conference at any time – was the speech of a man who knew he was fighting a lost battle yet who nevertheless fought with all the passion and instinctive honesty of a total belief in his cause. However fractured the sentences, there was no mistaking their meaning. He echoed Hugh Gaitskell's 'fight, fight and fight again' phrase by promising that regardless of the vote at the TUC and Labour Party conferences later in the year he would continue to argue the case against the H-bomb; and to seek a response through the people of Britain. He showed that he still deeply resented the Gaitskell reference in the Scarborough debate to 'fellow-travellers'. He criticised other unions (and named them) which had shifted their ground on the go-it-alone vote. He was neither deterred nor dismayed by the prospect ahead and he said :

Our union has been in the forefront of policy-making in this movement for a long time. We had to take the lead on questions of economic affairs. We are the biggest union in the country and we are entitled to take the lead in every question that affects us...

So much for those who argued that trade unions ought to stay out of defence policy.

The opposition to Cousins concentrated almost exclusively on the argument that to continue the divisions over defence would reduce the Labour Movement to political impotence, and hand political victory to the Conservatives yet again. A string of delegates appealed to Cousins to accept a compromise with Gaitskell in the interests of unity. This, Cousins replied, was precisely what he had been trying to do throughout the year. He explained how he and Crossman had actually agreed on a compromise formula only to have it brushed aside by Gaitskell, and added: 'I want a Labour Government more than any of you in this room because there are some things I can't do without a Labour Government.' But then he gave this warnings, which offended some ears both inside and outside the conference hall:

We are big enough and powerful enough to bring our pressures on this issue whatever Government it may be. You will drive me, if you are not careful, in this kind of talk, to go and debate with the Conservative Party on disarmament, because there are some people in the Conservative Party who are ahead of some of those in the Labour Party on this issue.

He added that he regarded those who took the view that principle should be sacrificed in the interests of party unity as taking 'a dastardly approach'.

After nearly five and a half hours the chairman, Len Forden, brought the debate to an end; 88 delegates had spoken, 52 in favour of the union's Ban-the-Bomb line, 35 against it. Everything pointed to a narrow vote, but on a show of hands there was at least a three-to-one majority to continue opposition to the Bomb. Two years earlier the majority had been fourteen to one. The majority was larger than Cousins had anticipated, and it was undoubtedly the impact of the man rather than the argument, however persuasive that may have been, that triumphed. Seen against the sweep of the tide away from unilateralism, the growing strength and confidence of Gaitskell's position in the Parliamentary Labour Party as well as the country, the unanimity of the Press against Cousins, the world scene, which could hardly have been less promising – viewed against all this, Cousins's achievement in keeping the TGWU to its anti-Bomb policy with such a large vote was a substantial personal success. It was unthinkable that he would have been defeated on such an issue by his own conference, but his majority might have been wafer-thin and such a narrow vote would certainly have been interpreted as a 'moral defeat'. As things turned out, even Cousin's most derisive critics found it hard to question his hold over the TGWU. He had swayed the Brighton conference by the force of his views and the power of his conviction after another marathon debate.

At the end of that conference the delegates rose to give him a standing ovation which lasted about half a minute. Cousins was deeply moved. As the acclamation subsided he climbed slowly to his feet and in an almost whispered voice thanked the delegates: 'I don't think I shall ever attend a conference which moved me more than yesterday's debate on the H-bomb.'

That August, just two weeks before the Trades Union Congress met at Portsmouth, East Germany's Communist Government erected the Berlin Wall. A week later on 20 August the United States moved reinforcements into West Berlin. The tanks rolled along the *autobahn* to Berlin, and the ominous clatter echoed all across Europe. On 31 August the Soviet Union resumed nuclear tests, President Kennedy having already indicated that the US was prepared for a 'limited action' over the Berlin crisis. Little wonder that the debate on nuclear disarmament at the 1961 TUC was as perfunctory as its outcome was a foregone conclusion.

The TGWU's anti-Bomb motion was rejected by 5,571,000 to 2,048,000; the Gaitskell defence policy was carried by an even larger majority of 5,733,000 to 2,003,000. It was a crushing defeat for Frank Cousins and his union's policy.

Frank Cousins remained unapologetic. The fight would continue, he pledged, until the policies were accepted by the Labour Movement. He could scarcely say less. In fact, that Congress, the first with George Woodcock as General Secretary, was less acrimonious than either of the previous two. The dominant issue was the expulsion of the then Communist-led Electrical Trades Union. But on the other major items like wages policy, whether the unions should cooperate with the Government and employers in setting up the new economic planning board the policy towards the Common Market (a cautious wait-and-see line) – on all these there was an unusual degree of unanimity, or at least a reluctance to indulge in public brawling. It was as if the nuclear disarmament issue had exhausted the contestants to such a degree that, having apparently got it 'out of the way' for the time being, no one was prepared to open up a new battlefront. It was much the same at the Labour Party conference.

How was it possible, one must ask, for such a transformation to take place within a year? Was it that the 1960 vote at Scarborough was a complete aberration, a fluke, a temporary lapse, brought about by the views and the determination of a handful of men in control of, or positions of influence, within, the trade union machine? Was it all due to a rush of blood to the heads of a substantial sector of the Labour Movement? Or was it that the 1961 'transformation' owed more to the skilful planning and even 'plotting' of an establishment that had successfully regrouped and reorganised itself after being profoundly shaken by the sweep and speed of events in 1960? After all, those who voted in 1961 at the Labour Party conference by and large were the same people in the same places. Had they, and those they spoke for, genuinely changed their minds on the defence issue and the role of nuclear disarmament? Had the international situation, deteroriating monthly as it did, turned people against the belief that a gesture by Britain could influence world events and the nuclear policy of the super-powers? Or was it, as some cynics suggested, simply that the old balance of power inside the Labour Movement had been restored?

Even now it is impossible to be certain about the answers to these questions. What 'evidence' there is suggests that at root it was the fear (a perfectly genuine fear) that to have continued the fight and to have defeated Gaitskell for a second year in succession would not only have destroyed Labour's most credible leader at that time but would have fractured the Party as a serious political force and as an alternative Government. This view was seriously held even among people on the Left, although not by Frank Cousins himself. He remained convinced that, given a more rational appreciation of the realities of world power and the defence situation, given a less hysterically orthodox reaction by the Press and other media, then his arguments could have persuaded the majority of public opinion. No one can say he was wrong, since the proposition was not put in that way – and probably never could have been.

Peggy Duff has her own convinced views on why the 1961 Labour Party conference overturned 1960. She does not share Canon Collins's belief that the Russell civil disobedience campaign harmed CND and helped to undermine support for it in the Labour Movement. Her views is that 'the Left, in the Labour Party was unused to winning and neither the Left nor CND really knew what to do about their victory.'[4] She admits that the swing behind unilateralism in 1960 had been partly irrational, and had been fanned by the general excitement of such unusual militancy inside the organised Labour Movement. Peggy Duff also claims that the support for CND in local Labour Parties and trade union branches had been based on small majorities and these were vulnerable to the highly organised campaign run in 1961 by the Right Wing of the Labour Party. Once Gaitskell had made the nuclear issue a test of his own leadership, the 'unity' of the Labour Movement became an overriding factor.

When he opened the Labour Party conference at Blackpool, the chairman, Richard Crossman, suggested in his speech that what really decided the swing

---

4. Peggy Duff, *Left, Left, Left* (Allison and Busby, 1971), pp. 191-2.

away from unilateralism was 'the extraordinary eruption of rank-and-file feeling last spring' (meaning local Party and trade union conferences held up and down the country). He went on :

> Countless active members all over the country suddenly reached the same conclusion at the same time — that the arguments had gone on long enough and the time had come to stop talking and come to a decision. I must admit that in the course of the winter I had sometimes begun to wonder whether our democracy was not going to destroy us. But then there came that sudden imperative from below which is real democracy in action.

Yet Crossman acknowledged that the great H-bomb debate had been essential and even unavoidable, and that it had helped to convince a younger generation of political sceptics that the Labour Movement had not abandoned its idealism. Crossman was strongly aware that the CND campaign had drawn to it thousands of younger people who had lost faith in the traditional political scene and had even become sceptical of the processes of Parliamentary democracy itself. He argued, in that curtain-raising speech at Blackpool, that this sense of 'powerlessness' and 'creeping impotence' was due to the ten years of Conservative rule and that under a new Labour Government 'building socialism, democracy will come alive and ordinary people will feel they count again'.

The scenario was not to work out quite like that. Indeed, Crossman was further away than Frank Cousins in gauging the strength of feeling (not only among the young) against the conventional political wisdom. Nevertheless, the demand for 'unity' was so overwhelming that it swept aside all other considerations. Even Ted Hill voiced the feeling with surprising candour at that Labour Party conference when he made the fraternal speech as the TUC's official spokesman (he was the retiring TUC chairman that year). Hill was himself a strong supporter of unilateralism and of Frank Cousins, yet at Blackpool he demanded an end to the feuding, particularly between Cousins and Gaitskell. Unity of purpose was absolutely essential, he said, if there was to be the return of a Labour Government : 'It goes for Hugh Gaitskell and Frank Cousins, it goes for Ted Hill and Jim Matthews. I am always ready for a truce and I am sure all of us can rise to the occasion to get that unity of purpose . . .'

That was the authentic voice of the rank-and-file feeling – and it came from one of the most vigorous of left-wing union leaders.

Ted Hill's speech upset Cousins. He referred to it when the Labour conference debated the H-bomb by recalling that Hill had not only supported unilateralism throughout the years of debate inside the TUC but had actually been 'voted off' the joint TUC-Labour Party committee on defence *because* of his strong views on the Bomb. Clearly Cousins meant this to illustrate his surprise at Hill's speech; in fact it only underlined the powerful current that was running in favour of 'unity'. It was, however, an unrepentent Cousins, speaking in the face of even more difficult odds than Gaitskell the year before, presenting himself before the Labour Party conference. This was a Cousins under the shadow of certain defeat making a poor speech – poor because it tried to encompass too much detail, too much explanation of those interminable committee wranglings, too many minutiae on a subject which at that moment required emotional appeal rather more than military (or internal party) logic. At one stage he became so involved in the inner-party argument (and in his condemnation of the CDS campaign) that he seemed to lose track of the main issue and for the first and only time at a Party conference he experienced booing and a slow handclap – countered, it is true, by cheering and clapping from his supporters. Still, it was apparent that the majority in the conference simply weren't prepared to go on with the fight within the Movement. To his supporters Cousins cried out: 'Be not dispirited by any vote that is taken here today. It will mean as much, or as little, as apparently in some circles the vote did that was taken last year.' No one required to be reminded against whom that barb was flung.

It was comparatively simple for Hugh Gaitskell when he summed up an uneven, low-key, debate. He spoke for 47 minutes of almost uninterrupted silence (a striking contrast with 1960). At the end he received a great ovation. But it was less the ovation than the votes that pleased Gaitskell. His defence policy was approved on a card vote by 4,526,000 to 1,756,000 and Frank Cousins's motion defeat was by 4,309,000 to 1,891,000. Yet even then there were still curious paradoxes. A motion opposing Polaris submarine bases in Britain (the retention of which was an essential ingredient in the Party's defence policy) was carried, against the leadership, by 3,611,000 to 2,739,000. It was as if the last echoes of Scarborough were still rumbling, uncertainly, through the corridors of the conference.

There were, of course, other moments at that conference when Frank Cousins was able to hold his ground – on public ownership, over which he demanded a more vigorous policy and attacked the weakness and ambiguity of 'Signposts for the Sixties' dealing with the public control of industry; on wages policy, over which he thundered out renewed warnings to the Macmillan Government: 'We are not willing to accept in any form, shape or disguise, wage restraint'; and, during a private session of the conference, when he pledged his union's full support to a new fun-raising campaign to help the Labour Party, a pledge which brought a tribute from Gaitskell and which, even at that unpropitious moment was seen as a fragile signal of the healing of wounds and a possible reconciliation of the two men. It was to take another year for that to flower into a quite improbable alliance between Gaitskell and Cousins against the Common Market. Meantime, in

the wake of Blackpool 1961 there was only a grim and embittered acceptance by Frank Cousins that the tables had again been turned on him. .

The Press was for the most part jubilant that Gaitskell had defeated
Cousins – since the issues were almost always presented in those emotive,
personality terms – and it was satisfied that Gaitskell had finally established
beyond any reasonable doubt his authority as Party leader.

On the day after the defence debate the *Herald* published an editorial
under the heading 'The End of the Affair', in which it concluded : 'Mr
Gaitskell has emerged from an immensely difficult year with great authority
in the Party. More important, perhaps, his stature in the country has
grown.' *The Times* agreed about Gaitskell's new authority, but was somewhat more understanding of the deeper moods within the Labour Movement and much less final about 'the affair' :

> The dialogue or altercation between Right and Left is a permanent feature
> of Labour politics. It cannot be otherwise for a party of the Left in a two-
> party system . . . Unity within the Labour Movement does not therefore
> depend on identity of view. It depends on sufficient concentration of power
> and influence in the right place. Blackpool has seen this happen with the
> revival of the authority of Mr Gaitskell and his parliamentary colleagues and
> the comparative isolation of Mr Cousins – the main focus of the challenge.
> There is nothing either absolute or permanent in the present distribution of
> power. The constituency voting this week gave some evidence of growing
> support for Mr Gaitskell's critics, while the fact that the leader of the party
> and the leader of the biggest union in the country are scarcely on speaking
> terms is anything but a guarantee of stability . . .

That comment was a recognition that the Leftward shift in the mood, the
temper and the undertow of the Labour Movement, had certainly not been
demolished by the Gaitskell victory on defence policy – a recognition that
while the desire for Party unity, and the feeling that the nuclear split was
corroding the whole fabric of the Movement, were the chief reasons for the
switch between 1960 and 1961, the Leftward shift none the less remained a
powerful force and one with which the victorious Gaitskell establishment had
to reckon. At the same time it was the end of the major political challenge
on nuclear disarmament. Frank Cousins knew in his heart that it was improbable, to say the least, that Scarborough would be repeated – or even
attempted again in that form. That did not mean that the TGWU abandoned its policy. But it was going to mean that other events would crowd
in and overtake the defence split : events which no one could have foreseen
at that juncture, but which were to completely change internal relationships
within the Labour Movement and indeed to change the leadership as well.
Gaitskell himself, after Blackpool, was confident that there would be no
repetition of the nuclear challenge within the Labour Party. In a BBC inter-

view that October he told me, answering a question as to whether the controversy might be fought out again :

> Well, naturally, those who lost this year were bound to say that they would continue the fight and I don't doubt that some of them will attempt to do so. But I don't think it will be a very serious attempt. And I don't think the vast bulk of our Party members will have any sympathy with their attempts to do so . . . we've settled our argument.

Frank Cousins *was* dismayed by Blackpool. Not surprised, nor converted by any of the arguments he had heard ranged *against* his policy, nor even shaken by the strength of feeling that had flowed in the opposite direction after Scarborough. He understood the powerful appeal of unity. He was dismayed by what he feared might be a dissipation of the campaign against the Bomb as a result of internal friction and splits *within* the CND movement itself and the breakaway by Bertrand Russell to form his direct action Committee of 100 (a breakaway he had tried, and failed, to prevent). The failure to hold the Labour Party and the trade union movement behind the campaign without question resulted in a fundamental setback. Yet if it had ended in failure on nuclear disarmament the Cousins campaign had certainly roused the entire Labour Movement to a pitch of moral indignation it had not known since the pre-war days of anti-fascist protest and Spain. It had awakened the spirit of radical dissent throughout the Labour Movement as nothing else before or since. The challenge was not simply to the details of a particular defence policy but to a whole way of thinking, to a style of leadership as well as a concept of policy. Nothing was ever quite the same again.

Cousins took his defeat with characteristic dignity. There were so many other issues ready to absorb him. There was the Government's 'pay pause', which was already threatening to cause a confrontation between the Government and the unions, following Chancellor Selwyn Lloyd's ruling that pay increases for Government employed industrial workers should be frozen. There was the still unresolved question about whether the TUC should cooperate with the Government in setting up the NEDC. The industrial scene was never still. Increasingly it demanded – and received – most of Cousins's time and attention. He had little opportunity for self-pity or morose reflections on the Blackpool defeat. In any event he was not made that way. He remained utterly convinced that he had been right and Gaitskell wrong ; it was a conviction which at that moment was a vital psychological support.

One must recall his philosophy of leadership as he explained it, two years earlier, when in an unusually expansive *Daily Mail* interview he said :

> What you need to be a leader of men is, first of all, a deep-seated belief in the rightness of the thing you are trying to do. You need a bit of courage to

face the inevitable ups and downs. You have to recognise that people are more ready to remember your failures than your successes. And you have to learn to accept that the things you work for will only be achieved very, very slowly.

You must not be discouraged by setbacks. You've got to believe, and believe that what you fight for will be achieved eventually.[5]

That was the spirit which helped him to bandage the wounds of 1960 and 1961.

5. *Daily Mail*, 28 October 1959.

Chapter Eighteen

HEALING THE WOUNDS

To any observer of the political scene in 1961 it would have seemed absurd to have even remotely considered the chances of a concordat between Hugh Gaitskell and Frank Cousins. The prospect of such a compact was not on the agenda of political possibilities after the Blackpool conference of 1961. Bitterness was intense on both sides, mistrust almost total. The two men realised they would have to work together in the future. Each looked forward, with optimism, to the next General Election, reasonably convinced that Labour would, at last, unseat the Conservative Government despite the deep divisions inside the Labour Party. But it was a blind hope. Neither saw his way clearly through the next few years, which threatened a continuation of ideological sniping if not a massive explosion inside the Labour Movement. Gaitskell's victory on nuclear disarmament in 1961 confirmed and consolidated him as the leader, but it had not resolved any of the deeper conflicts on policy. He was still distrusted by the Left, and the likelihood of that distrust melting was as remote as the prospects of a personal reconciliation with Frank Cousins.

Shortly after the Blackpool conference Cousins was interviewed on TV by John Freeman,[1] who had some personal experience of conflict with Hugh Gaitskell over defence policy (As a junior Minister in the Attlee Government, he had resigned in 1951 with Nye Bevan and Harold Wilson over the rearmament programme and the Gaitskell budget.) Freeman pressed Cousins strongly on his views concerning the leadership of the Labour Party after the Gaitskell victory. Did Cousins think the question of the Labour leadership was settled? Was there a chance that the Party would unite under Hugh Gaitskell? Cousins replied:

Well, I'm not in the Party, of course, other than as an individual member. I suppose you're talking about the Parliamentary Party when you talk about

1. 'Face to Face', BBC TV, 15 October 1961.

the Labour Party. I happen to have been working all the way through for the return of a Socialist Government. Anything that helps towards that has our support, very fully. But whether the Parliamentary Party are any happier now than they were twelve months ago I really wouldn't know.

Which was a polite way of answering Freeman's question with a fairly clear 'No'.

Freeman pursued him: 'Would you prefer, for instance, to see a trade unionist like your own George Brown, as leader of the Party?' Cousins responded without hesitation, without committing himself to a specific name, 'I'd prefer to see a trade unionist in leadership of the Party.' Not unnaturally this led Freeman to ask Cousins whether he himself would be prepared to go into Parliament in pursuit of such an aim. That brought forth an immediate: 'Oh, no. No.'

'But surely,' Freeman persisted, 'you must have considered this when you campaigned against Hugh Gaitskell. Supposing you'd brought him down, you might have been faced with the possibility of leading the Labour Party.'

Cousins replied:

Well, two things. First, let's get this clear. I didn't campaign against Hugh Gaitskell. I have no interest in campaigning against Hugh Gaitskell. I put forward policies which we in the Transport and General Workers' Union believed in. I hoped that we would be able to persuade the leadership of the Labour Party that these were policies they could support. I said this on many, many public occasions. But I have no idea or no intention or wish to be in Parliament. I could have been in Parliament many years ago,[2] it's quite obvious that I have no wish to be there. I think there's quite a job of work to be done in the trade union movement because of my belief that there needs to be co-operation between the trade union and political wings . . .

There was nothing false in that reply. Cousins at that time certainly had no Parliamentary ambitions or even thoughts. He simply could not have considered himself working with Gaitskell in the Parliamentary Labour Party, and he had no illusions about the obstacles in the way of a direct challenge to the Parliamentary leadership from outside. In practical terms he therefore dismissed any romantic visions of being able to unseat Gaitskell, although he appreciated to the full the power of a TGWU General Secretary to wage war against a Party leader and his policies. The example of Bevin, in this respect, against both Ramsay Macdonald and George Lansbury, was rarely absent from Cousins's mind. Yet he was perfectly sincere in his reply to Freeman that the nuclear campaign had not been, explicitly, a campaign

2. A reference to the time he was offered a nomination for various safe Labour seats in Yorkshire when he was still a young trade union official in Doncaster. In 1938 and in 1939 he was tempted to accept a nomination for the Doncaster seat and for Clay Cross but was dissuaded by Ernest Bevin, who was always opposed to his best young talent moving from the trade union to the Parliamentary scene.

against Gaitskell personally. It just happened that Gaitskell chose to make the issue one of total war inside the Labour Movement and a vote of confidence in himself as leader; at least, that is how Frank Cousins saw it. At any rate the prospect of this conviction fading, with time, into a preparedness to work positively with Gaitskell (as distinct from sullenly and reluctantly accepting his leadership) was utterly improbable at the turn of 1961.

Yet, within a year, this is precisely what occurred. To be sure, the possibility of an early General Election powerfully concentrated people's minds: the pre-election mating season had already begun by the end of 1962. By then both Gaitskell and Cousins fully recognised the need to try to work with each other, though neither had shifted his ideological stance. It was not a true meeting of minds in the political sense, but a realisation that the time had come to draw a curtain across the internal warfare within the Labour Party and to start repairing the damage to the Party's system and morale, both of which had been ravaged to the point of despair and near destruction.

The compact, when it came, was based essentially on one issue : resistance to British entry into the Common Market. Each reached the point of resistance from different directions, each man had different motives for opposing the application to join the EEC, made by the Macmillan Government in July 1961, when Harold Macmillan announced the application as 'a turning point in our history'. Gaitskell and Cousins were responding to a different collection of impulses when they suddenly and, certainly in Cousins's case, unexpectedly found themselves to be allies for the first time. Each grasped at the opportunity of a reconciliation, not with enthusiasm but with a cautious reluctance dominated, no doubt, by the belief that they had both been presented with a unique chance to find common ground in the interests of a wider unity within the Labour Movement. In short, it was the right psychological moment, and the issue, opposition to the Common Market, appeared to supply the right combination of emotional and rational argument to satisfy both men. That in itself was a novel experience for them.

An equally interesting point about the attitude of Gaitskell and Cousins on the Common Market is that both had shifted their ground. Both had started out with an open mind on British membership. More than that, both had, on the whole, favoured some form of British association with the EEC, if not absolute membership under the terms of the original Rome Treaty. Gaitskell thought the economic advantages were roughly balanced by the economic disadvantages, but he saw some considerable attraction in a political association with the Western European countries, so long as such an association did not hamper British political initiative. Gaitskell was never actively hostile to the Common Market concept and did not share Aneurin Bevan's instinctive distrust of the whole notion. As early as 1957 Bevan was condemning the concept as an intrinsically anti-socialist alliance.

Gaitskell's view was more practical than ideological. He believed firmly in Britain's association with the Commonwealth and he was not ready to negotiate away *that* 'special relationship' for the uncertainties of EEC membership. But there was no strong commitment against the Common Market and his criticisms of the Macmillan Government's application had at the time been chiefly confined to the manner and style with which Macmillan was applying for membership. The Parliamentary Labour Party's motion criticising the Government's application in July 1961 complained that the Government would be conducting the negotiations 'from a position of grave economic weakness' (Selwyn Lloyd had just introduced his emergency Budget in a bid to cushion a balance of payments crisis), and specified that Britain should enter the EEC only 'if this House gives its approval and if the conditions negotiated are generally acceptable to a Commonwealth Prime Ministers' conference and accord with our obligations and pledges to other members of the European Free Trade Association.'

Gaitskell himself remained uncommitted, prepared to remain on the fence to see what happened to the Macmillan application. It was a position similar though not parallel to the one which Frank Cousins had held for some years, and it irritated and angered many of Gaitskell's closest friends and political allies, who felt he should have committed himself clearly to the concept of British membership.

Cousins's original view, which he held quite strongly in his early years as TGWU General Secretary, was that Britain should have sought a close association, perhaps even full membership, with the EEC from the outset. He based this on a belief that British membership might have strengthened the socialist forces in Western Europe and organised labour throughout Europe. The British trade union movement was unique in Europe in that it was united within one institution, the TUC. Cousins believed that British membership of the EEC could have materially contributed to building a powerful and perhaps a united trade union force in Europe – a force that might have played a significant role in developing a political shift to the Left throughout the Continent. He held this view when the British Government helped to fund EFTA (the European Free Trade Association) where, of course, he found allies in the strong Scandinavian trade union movement. Cousins believed a similar pattern could have been developed with the original six members of the Common Market. By the summer of 1961 he had not entirely abandoned his belief that there was some potential value in the EEC. He told his 1961 conference at Brighton that he had originally favoured a close association between the 17 European countries but that the Government had delayed and delayed until, in 1961, they had finally plunged in with their application at a most difficult time. The Common Market, Cousins told his conference that July, was now 'a going concern – largely controlled by non-Socialist forces.'

As a Socialist, he said, he had no objection in principle to Britain 'giving up some of its sovereignty – at some stage that might be necessary'. But it was questionable whether the Common Market as then constituted was the body to which, 'to surrender power over our political and economic future'. The conference was persuaded by Cousins not to commit itself finally, to await the outcome of the negotiations, which had then not yet started, and to avoid taking up a rigid stance on such a complex question. Above all, Cousins pleaded, it was important to prevent another Labour split on this issue.

Inside the TUC General Council he had also shown his hand in trying to keep open the door to Europe. Most of the trade union leadership were at best sceptical and in general hostile to the EEC, because they saw in it an immediate and quite serious threat to the jobs and security of their members. Even those who had traditionally taken a politically moderate, or even right-wing view, still had strong reservations about the Common Market. The late Sir Alan Birch found himself again opposed to Cousins – but this time Cousins was taking what might be called in the political cliché of the time the right-of-centre view and Birch the left-wing view, for the latter was strongly opposed to British membership of the Common Market. Only Cousins and the steelworkers' leader, Harry (later Lord) Douglass – again an unusual alliance since Douglass normally was regarded as a right-winger – favoured a positive examination by the TUC of the *advantages* of British membership. But by 1960–1 Cousins was already pulling away from the European concept, which he increasingly saw as a 'rich man's club' dominated by Conservative Governments and powered by strong free-enterprise economies. By the end of 1961 he had shifted to the position taken up by Nye Bevan in 1957, and regarded the whole fabric of the EEC as basically anti-Socialist. This was his attitude at the very moment when Gaitskell's indecision was at its peak, and when it was already becoming clear that the odds were lengthening against Labour coming out strongly in favour of the Common Market.

It is not possible to be certain which clock struck first. The British application in July 1961 was obviously the moment when minds became concentrated. But at the time both Gaitskell and Cousins were still deeply embroiled in the nuclear disarmament battle and were not to be diverted from that until after the Blackpool conference. Moreover, there were serious and immediate problems on the domestic front which kept Cousins fully stretched at the turn of 1961 and into the early months of 1962. The British economy was again in serious trouble. It was to take a further decade to illustrate more graphically the seriousness of the situation, yet even by 1961 there were few analysts who doubted that something of a fundamental shift was taking place in Britain's economic relationships with the rest of the world. Indeed, this was one of the strongest arguments behind the British application to join the EEC. A majority of academic economists certainly held the view that future economic and industrial strength would hinge on a British capability of establishing industrial bonds with Europe through the Common Market. It was put to me at the time by a member of the Macmillan Government that once Britain was a member of the European Community she would come to have a dominating influence. Some Conservatives saw in the Common Market the pathway towards the re-establishment of a latter-day imperial dominance by the British – a vision which may well appear absurd today but which was then seriously cherished in some quarters. Membership was seen half as a kind of rescue operation, half as an opportunity to recapture old glories. At the same time, the Macmillan move towards Europe corresponded with a quite remarkable shift in Conservative thinking towards Government intervention in domestic economic planning, including a desire to recruit the TUC leadership to the inner conference tables in Whitehall and the development of more sophisticated methods of wage control.

The starting point of Government intervention in wage bargaining lies deeply buried in the web of relationship between Government and industry over the past 50 years and in some ways goes back to the beginnings of taxation itself. The influence of the State has always existed, albeit indirectly. What we are concerned with here is the change in the form of intervention, especially after Cripps's failure during the Attlee Government. For a Conservative Government to become attracted to institutional intervention of the kind considered in 1961 and established in 1962 was unprecedented. The Cohen Council of 'Three Wise Men' had been a singular flop in the late 1950s. Yet Whitehall refused to see it in wholly negative terms. They argued that the experiment had at least demonstrated the limitations of a 'touch-line' approach to wages intervention. More direct influence was necessary. The next step was to develop a more permanent, full-time wages tribunal more closely identified with Government and Government thinking. That is how the National Incomes Commission, NIC (or Nicky), was born. This was the machinery devised to take Selwyn Lloyd out of the wages clamp he had introduced, especially in the public sector, in his July 1961 crisis Budget. The whole strategy was to some extent linked with the application to join the Common Market. In particular, Macmillan was anxious to persuade de Gaulle that the British were seriously trying to get a grip on their domestic, economic and industrial situation. One of the attractions in setting up the NEDC was that it could be seen to be styled on the French 'Commissariat du Plan', which co-ordinated the investment plans of French industry and had secured a high reputation for its contribution towards France's industrial recovery. In these respects, the launching of NEDC, the application to join EEC and the creation of a National Incomes Commission all connected.

On 24 January the TUC finally voted to join NEDC. By 21 to 8 the General Council brought to a close six months of negotiating with the Government over the form NEDC should take, its membership and its independence of action and authority.

Frank Cousins voted against the decision, though he knew it was a foregone conclusion. Despite the pressure of George Woodcock's persuasion and Woodcock's conviction that the trade unions could use a central planning machinery to their advantage, Cousins was far from convinced. He was deeply suspicious of the Government's motives; he felt that the entire concept was being devised to trap the unions into accepting wage restraint by the back door. His suspicions were reinforced by the way Selwyn Lloyd and the Treasury were using the 'pay pause' in the public sector, which Cousins was already fighting on behalf of his members in Government factories and industrial establishments. His objections led to the TUC specifying important conditions to their membership of NEDC: a clear refusal to accept the Government's policy of wage restraint; the right of the TUC representatives on NEDC (there were to be six TUC places) to report back fully to the TUC and to their own unions; and their freedom to raise any issue they thought fit for discussion by the new body – a demand which was seen to carry an implied threat that the TUC would walk out of the NEDC if they weren't satisfied with the way it was being run. Selwyn Lloyd was glad to have the TUC accept his invitation, almost regardless of their terms. He raised no objection to the conditions, just as he had accepted George Woodcock's design for the final shape of NEDC.

Within the trade union movement, and particularly within his own union, Cousins raised another objection to membership of NEDC. First of all, he argued, it might cut across the role of Parliament – a view strongly held by the Left in the Parliamentary Labour Party; and secondly, if the union leaders made a success of the planning mechanism under a Conservative Government this very fact might prejudice the Labour Party. Cousins explained this to his union members in an article in the TGWU *Record*:

> If we make a success of planning, and it will be the intention of the TUC representatives to do that, if at all possible, one can visualise the election propaganda trying to show that the Government, Big Business and the trade unions can do a better job for the community than would be the case if we allowed the Socialist planners to come in and interfere with the proposals already under way.[3]

Cousins was ambivalent about the entire project. His instincts were against joining, yet as he knew that he would be unable to carry his opposition inside the TUC he felt that if it were to accept the Government's invitation he

3. TGWU *Record*, March 1962, p. 32.

had better be a member of the TUC 'six'. It was a difficult double-edged policy for him to pursue, but he faced it with characteristic candour. He explained his position to the TGWU members in this way :

Once the decision to join had been taken your General Executive Council and I took the view that a union such as ours was too big to contract out. Whether we were represented or not any decisions taken would affect us and therefore we must be involved in the discussions and try to influence the conclusions reached. If the Council fails it will be because the planning idea is not really accepted by the architects of the NEDC – but it would be foolish to offer anti-trade union interests the opportunity of finding an easy scapegoat for any failure simply because we refuse to participate.

Cousins saw the dilemma clearly enough. He wanted a direct role in the planning mechanism, even if it was a Tory design, because he believed that the very nature of capitalist development in the Britain of the 1960s must inevitably lead to a much greater degree of State intervention. He recognised that the drive to rationalise industry, to introduce new technology and maximise output would require investment capital on a scale that could not be provided by industry as it was then structured. Private industry would be led inescapably toward greater involvement with the State, as well as into more and more mergers. The unions had the choice of remaining passengers in this process, or of moving closer towards the centre of decision-making through institutions like NEDC. At the same time Cousins also knew that NEDC would not provide the kind of planning mechanism he believed was necessary for genuine socialist planning. That was why he objected to the NEDC concept in political terms – but, recognising realities, he accepted the inevitable by joining the new body. He was accused of duplicity, and he was sensitive enough to the thinking behind that charge. Yet he believed he had no alternative.

To reassure his members that the fight against wage restraint would be maintained with his old vigour, Cousins promised unremitting opposition to Government policy so long as 'private interests continue to control the economy'.

The TUC leaders knew that the Government was planning some form of continued, and extended, intervention in wages. Yet at the time they agreed to join NEDC no one – least of all the members of the Cabinet – had any precise notion of the form this might take. Selwyn Lloyd and the Treasury had been working on a series of ideas and documents since the July 1961 'pay pause' and the White Paper on incomes issued in February 1962 proposed that money incomes should not rise by an average of more than $2\frac{1}{2}$ per cent for each worker per year.[4] The statement was, in the words of one

4. 'Incomes Policy: The Next Step', Cmnd. 1626, February 1962.

observer, 'a triumph of obscurity'.[5] It did nothing to allay the suspicion that the Chancellor had little real grasp of the problems involved in trying to establish an incomes policy, which, even if dubiously effective, ought at least to contain an intellectually persuasive argument.

The White Paper coincided with the biggest wave of official token strikes in Britain since the war. Twice in a month, on 5 February and 5 March, a one-day stoppage of some three million workers in engineering and ship-building was called by the Confederation of Shipbuilding and Engineering Unions (including the TGWU). The strikes were in support of a claim for a £1 a week rise plus a reduction in the working week from 42 to 40 hours – both claims having been rejected by the employers. At that time average earnings in engineering were about £15 a week, and the basic wage for a skilled worker in engineering was £9 15s. 2d.

In fact that White Paper was the beginning of the end for Selwyn Lloyd. Appalled by his Chancellor's general incompetence in handling the incomes policy problem, Macmillan decided the time had come for him to take a personal hand in trying to draft a more effective policy – in short, to give it a touch of the Macmillan panache. He turned his mind to drafting a document and a scheme on which the National Incomes Commission was ultimately based.

From the spring of 1962 through to July Macmillan worked on a broad strategic canvas which embraced his views on Britain's economic and indus-trial development, NEDC, incomes policy and, of course, the entire relation-ship, with Europe, assuming that his application for membership of EEC would be successful. Yet in May his diary was already reflecting his own inner anxieties :

Worked all the morning on the two great issues –
    (1) Britain and Europe in the light of my visit to de Gaulle next Satur-day and Sunday.
    (2) British economy and an incomes policy. Both intractable, obscure and baffling problems.[6]

On the second of these 'problems' he added with wry humour as well as irony :

On (2) our Incomes Policy; the colleagues (in Cabinet) are all confused – so is the Party in the House. We must try to work out something rather more imaginative than we have done so far.[7]

5. Samuel Britten, *The Treasury Under the Tories* (Secker and Warburg and Pen-guin Books, 1964), p. 239.
6. Harold Macmillan, *At the End of the Day* (Macmillan, 1973), pp. 90–1.
7. *Ibid.*, pp. 68–9.

The industrial front, generally, was in a state of barely concealed revolt. After the engineering stoppages the dockers were on the warpath against the $2\frac{1}{2}$ per cent wage ceiling, and in May the country came to the very brink of a national dock strike, which would have been the first official stoppage in the ports since the General Strike of 1926. Everything was set up for a full-scale confrontation after the port employers had turned down the unions' claim for a $4\frac{1}{2}$ per cent wage increase and a reduction in the working week from 44 to 40 hours. The employers offered a 3 per cent rise, beyond the Government's 'norm', as well as a cut in working hours to 42 the following January. The dockers' delegates would not have it, though Cousins would have been prepared to compromise by negotiating around that mark. The strike was due to begin on Monday 14 May and instructions were already being issued to 70,000 dockers throughout Britain. It had all the appearances of an unavoidable strike. The Government was scared, not only by the signs that its attempts at curbing the rise in wages was about to be swamped but, even more, by the disturbing thought that the country faced the most menacing industrial situation since the war. No one knew quite what would be the impact of a national dock strike. So Macmillan alerted the troops and appointed a special Cabinet committee under Iain Macleod to prepare to send the troops in. Again there was pressure inside the Cabinet to take Cousins on – at least to test the national reaction to a dock strike. It was a view that did not appeal to Macmillan, though he saw no way out except by a further concession to the dockers, which would collapse the Government's wages policy.

Memories of the 1958 London busmen's strike still rankled with the Government as well as the union side. John Hare (later Lord Blakenham) had replaced Macleod at the Ministry of Labour, but the conflict between Government wages policy and economic strategy on one side and the conciliation role of the Ministry on the other remained as Macleod had left it – that is to say, the conciliation role was subordinate to wider Government policy. Two days before the strike deadline Frank Cousins and his national docks secretary, Tim O'Leary, called a delegate conference to try to persuade the dockers to postpone the strike date, possibly for a week, so that the union's negotiators could have more time to try to reach a deal with the port employers. It was a strange proposal, carrying all the obvious manifestations of union uncertainty and weakness. Not surprisingly, the delegates threw it out by 48 votes to 32. Again Cousins showed his unsureness in handling the docks and revealed a kind of schizophrenia about his own militancy. It was as if he had a built-in breaking mechanism which suddenly brought him to a stop when qualifications and reservations began to crowd in on him. At such moments trade union leaders are like generals on the eve of battle, filled with doubts about their judgement, their timing, their overall strategy, the strength of their forces matched against the foe

– the moment of greatest self-questioning always comes as the countdown to battle stations draws nearer. As with the busmen's strike, Cousins wanted to make quite certain that his troops were fully aware of the implications, political as well as industrial. He knew as well as the Government that a national docks strike would be a move into uncharted territory. A stoppage in the docks would quickly paralyse the national life-line and might well lead into another General Strike, since it would be bound to involve other sections of the transport industry and, within a week or so, the bulk of TGWU membership. This was a situation that Cousins was anxious to avoid, if he could But if he could not, well, there it was – he was ready to face the battle. His attempt to get the strike postponed at such a late hour brought sneers and jeers from his critics and even some of his supporters. They saw it as clear evidence of what they had always suspected in Cousins – an indecisiveness at critical moments and an unsureness about his own judgement. Others saw it as proof that Cousins was not the militant of his public posture. The *Guardian*'s Labour Correspondent observed the day after his plea for postponement had been rejected :

> The behaviour of Mr Cousins yesterday ought finally to dispel the false belief that he is an unthinking militant in industrial matters. His own speeches must bear a large part of the blame for this unfair public image for, as in the case of the London bus strike, his actions have again proved him less bellicose than his enemies, and even some of his friends, think.

The truth must lie somewhere between all these views. Cousins was never an 'unthinking militant'. He never saw the strike weapon as something to be used with indiscriminate abandon, certainly not with pleasure. But he never shrank from using it if he had to. He did not want a national dock strike, which he knew would almost certainly produce a serious political backlash against him, his union and the Labour Movement generally. He had enough experience to recognise that 'taking on the Government' was not a pushover, even though the dockers were a far greater threat to the nation's economy than the busmen. His reasoning was neither cowardly, uncertain nor unrealistic; if he could squeeze the port employers to improve their offer, then the objective could be achieved without a strike. So why not try?

On Saturday 12 May at the Ministry of Labour, Cousins and the employers' chairman, Sir Andrew Crichton, fought out their last-ditch attempt to negotiate a way round the strike for nearly nine hours. The Minister, John Hare, stood by but made no attempt to conciliate. He was under a Cabinet instruction *not* to do so.[8] Macmillan was in Scotland when the dockers' conference rejected Cousins's appeal for more negotiating time. He can-

8. See Harold Macmillan, *At the End of the Day*, p. 66.

celled his speaking engagements and returned immediately to Downing Street to prepare for the strike and to finalise Government plans to keep the ports open with troops. It was a show of firm government which was not entirely decorative. Macmillan certainly must have known that the port employers would yield something extra at the last moment; what he did not quite expect was the extent of their collapse.

Shortly before midnight on the Saturday, after about four hours of fruitless talking, Cousins and Crichton led their respective teams to a pub near the Ministry building in St James's Square. They occupied opposite ends of the bar and divided over their sandwiches and drinks as they had over their dispute. Then Cousins, spotting that Crichton's team had run out of sandwiches, pushed across a fresh supply to his opponents. Out of such gestures battles are won, and lost. The two sides returned to the Ministry, and concluded a deal which gave the dockers increased rates only a little short of their original $4\frac{1}{2}$ per cent claim plus a cut in working hours from 44 to 42 from the end of August (that is, four months earlier than the employers had offered earlier).

In overall wages costs it was double Selwyn Lloyd's 'guiding light'. Andrew Crichton described the 'awful dilemma' they had faced – the choice between making this generous concession, as he agreed it was, or facing a national dock strike which, he added, would have been disastrous. He praised Cousins for his 'statesmanlike attitude'. Peace had been bought with less than 24 hours to go. Crichton later recalled the avuncular words of Macmillan in summing up the experience :

My dear fellow, I am so sorry for you, the dockers are such difficult people, just like the fathers and the sons, the uncles and the nephews. So like the House of Lords, hereditary, and no intelligence required, and so hard on the 'Cousins' don't you think?

There was less of the burlesque touch about Macmillan's own private musings on that 'sell-out' (as he regarded it) by the port employers. The settlement was, he said :

a great blow to our incomes policy – and makes it difficult to see where we go now . . . It is not easy to disguise the fact that it was the Government's own employees who were having to bear the brunt of wage restraint while private employers, wherever it suited their interests, gave way to the full demands.[9]

Still, the Government persisted in the search for a viable incomes policy. Macmillan, who commanded the operation, insisted that a 'formula' must

9. *Ibid.*, p. 66.

be found, a formula that would be credible to the public without being politically damaging to the Government, a formula that would get away from the aridity of the Selwyn Lloyd concept.

In Macmillan's mind the absence of a credible incomes policy and the Chancellor's personal failings were closely related. At the moment that he was sacking a third of his Cabinet Macmillan announced the establishment of a National Incomes Commission, Nicky. A new set of initials was added to the expanding Whitehall catalogue of Enid Blyton titles. But it was the first really formalised attempt to put some institutional flesh onto the bare bones of wage restraint and incomes policy. On 26 July, in a full-dress debate in the Commons, Macmillan explained that for 'this new phase there must be some new commanders'. He had dismissed about a third of his Cabinet, including Selwyn Lloyd, Watkinson, Eccles, Kilmuir, Maclay, Charles Hill, and he had taken over full personal command of 'Operation Incomes Policy'. This was, in itself, part of a much wider and an altogether more remarkable departure into economic planning and State intervention than had ever before been attempted by a Conservative Government in peacetime.

Intervention on the scale now proposed was not only new to a Conservative Government; it also threatened acute strains and conflicts within the Whitehall machine. We have already seen how the Treasury resented, and resisted, the idea of NEDC falling outside its immediate control and authority. Planning systems were still seen in Whitehall as new and dangerous toys which, in the 'wrong' political hands, could undermine if not destroy the traditional processes of Government decision-making. Tensions inside the Cabinet during the gestation period of NEDC were symptomatic of the ideological anguish with which many Conservative MPs regarded Macmillan's slide towards 'pink socialism'. The mere notion of 'economic planning', even in such a passive and 'indicative' form, was deeply offensive to many inside the Conservative Party at all levels. To all this must be added the confusion inside Tory ranks about Britain's relationship with Europe and the growing uneasiness about sinking our national identity. The groundswell of Conservative opposition to the Market was under way. The momentous years between 1961 and 1964 brought a new sweep of events into British political and economic affairs: changes in style and attitude which not only determined the pattern of affairs for a decade and more but perhaps even indicated the path Britain might follow to the end of the century. The Macmillan Government in the early 1960s became inextricably, if reluctantly, involved in planning, in trying to mould incomes policies, and in industrial interventionism. They did so in response to the seemingly insoluble problems within the domestic economy. It was all part of the wider jig-saw of events pushing and jostling at Britain, on a world as well as a European scale. The realities with which Macmillan was now grappling were the same as those facing Hugh Gaitskell and Frank Cousins.

The launching of the National Incomes Commission at the end of July was perhaps a little premature, though from the Government's point of view it was unavoidable. Not until November did NIC have a chairman and terms of reference. By then it had been denounced by the TUC as an unworkable absurdity.

On the very day of Macmillan's announcement the TUC met the Prime Minister. After the meeting George Woodcock condemned NIC as 'impracticable, a none-runner . . . based on an illusion.' He knew that there would be nothing but hostility from the trade union movement to the Government's ideas on incomes policy and he was not disposed to waste any time trying to persuade his TUC colleagues to consider a proposal in which, in any event, he had no faith. As far as Woodcock was concerned the primary consideration was to secure TUC support for NEDC. Having got Cousins's reluctant acquiescence in that, he had no intention of walking into a Government trap on incomes policy. It was the wrong time and the wrong Government for that. 'My view,' said Woodcock, 'is that it [NIC] will die a natural death. I can't see that it will have any useful life at all'. He was to be proved right.

Not that the Government's action came as a surprise to the trade union leadership. No union leader could have been under any illusion that the Government would not come forward with some form of plan for an incomes policy. There were few other options open to them if they were to extricate themselves from the Selwyn Lloyd pay pause and wage curbs of the previous year. On the other hand the Government could have had few illusions about the TUC's reaction. Macmillan knew that Cousins would never accept the concept of NIC, that he would fight any attempt by his Government to curb the power of union freedom in collective bargaining, and that with Cousins now playing a dominant role inside the TUC leadership, forming a close alliance with Woodcock, there was no prospect of any deal with the TUC.

Woodcock, moreover, had another powerful argument in his intellectual armoury. 'You cannot isolate wages from the economy as a whole,' he told the Press after his talks with the Government that July. 'And you cannot expect the TUC to put on handcuffs in the wages field. If the Government wants the TUC's advice in wages it must open the gates to *all* questions.' That was the first time a TUC General Secretary implicitly offered a Conservative Government such a bargain. In effect Woodcock was saying, 'Open all your books, take the unions into your confidence, and then let us see whether you are prepared to take action across the whole range of society. Given that situation, the unions would not be able to duck the issue of wages.' But Woodcock was in advance of his time. Whatever private thoughts Macmillan may have had on the attractiveness of such a concept, he was as trapped within his own Party's prejudices and vested interests as was Woodcock within the ethos of trade union thinking.

The Government saw the National Incomes Commission as a specific instrument of intervention in wage bargaining, not as an instrument to be used for wider social purposes. Its role was to act as a permanent and statutory standing commission on wages, not as an ad hoc arbitration board. It would publicly examine and pronounce judgments on the relative merits of different claims (or settlements), bearing in mind the 'national interest' as defined by the Government's range of economic priorities. It would always take account of the 'guiding light' norm of $2\frac{1}{2}$ per cent and, though its 'advice' was not to be binding, nor carry any statutory obligation, the Government certainly saw it as a platform from which it would be able to influence the whole range of collective bargaining. Macmillan regarded NIC as a public 'watch-dog' on pay which would have a moral effect on the private sector, but of course, a more direct and immediate impact on public sector wage bargaining. It was, indeed, a precursor of the Prices and Incomes Board. The Government also saw NEDC and NIC as twin pillars of a single strategy: control of inflation, the pursuit of economic growth and the more efficient use of resources and the maintenance of full employment. They saw the new instruments as significant aids in tackling the balance of payments problem and preparing the way for entry into the EEC.

It was a catalogue of hope and aspirations which became all too familiar in the years to come. And despite the TUC's unanimous and continuing hostility to the NIC there is no doubt that Macmillan was right to claim that his plan, and the developments leading up to it, laid the foundations for what we now know as an incomes policy. Along with NEDC the strategy compelled the trade union leadership to take seriously the challenge of economic planning, even if it was a pale, shadowy form of planning under a Conservative Government. It enabled Woodcock to present his powerful case to the 1962 Trades Union Congress. Woodcock was able to do this only because he was by then satisfied that he had the confidence of Frank Cousins – if not his wholehearted support on all fronts. It was the 1962 Congress that in a practical sense cemented their partnership, opening up a new strategy for the trade union high command.

The consensus of Press comment about Frank Cousins and the 1962 Trades Union Congress was that a 'new Cousins' had emerged from the shadows of the nuclear cloud. For the first time since he became General Secretary of the TGWU he was no longer openly at loggerheads with the majority of his General Council colleagues. This was not because either side had suddenly discovered hitherto unknown bonds of affection. Most of all, it was the catalytic effect of George Woodcock that helped to change the atmosphere. Cousins dismissed with prickly irritation all suggestions that he had 'changed' in any way, or that his 'image' was being repolished. This kind of personalised politics was an irritant that brought out his most intolerant side. He felt that he was being 'got at' in a sophisticated way and that his principles were being impugned. He would never accept that such journalistic treatment was the inescapable fate of all rebellious public figures, whose every minute shift on the platform of political life was an invitation for attack. Cousins regarded such an approach as further evidence of the superficiality of Press comment. He was not always wrong.

None the less, the 1962 'shift' was of wider significance than he admitted at the time. It was also something of a tribute to the impact he had already made within the TUC, as well as outside. Despite his detractors' hostility he had plunged on like an embattled tank thrusting forward in the face of intensive cross-fire, heading onwards toward a distant goal always shrouded and obscured by the smoke of battle. The Transport Union leader had not changed his views. He adhered to his belief in nuclear disarmament with undiminished conviction, and had taken part again that year in the Aldermaston March. Indeed the TGWU Executive at its meeting in December 1961 had actually gone further than before in reaffirming support for CND policy, despite its defeat at the Blackpool conference. Nor had Cousins toned down his opposition to wage restraint. Nowhere in his socialist stand was there any sign of weakening. His change of view on the Common Market had been if anything toward a more traditional left-wing line rather than toward what might be regarded as supporting the 'conventional wisdom'.

On the other hand, it could not be claimed that others on the TUC General Council had changed their views, either. The balance of forces inside the TUC leadership remained roughly the same. There had been a modest shift to the Left following the death of Sir Alan Birch, Cousins's long-standing and perhaps most ardent opponent inside the TUC. He was succeeded by Alfred (now Lord) Allen, who was to the Left of Birch, though by no means an uncritical admirer of Frank Cousins.

So what had changed?

Macmillan's sacking of a third of his Cabinet and the developing balance of payments crisis had weakened the Government's standing in the country, and the trade union leaders felt that a General Election could not now be too far away. After eleven years of Conservative rule the fatigue of the Government, noticeably in many of its older and most eminent figures, was plain to see. The 'conversion' to planning methods and the introduction of NEDC were seen by Cousins as defensive measures by the Tories. Defensive in that they were seen as a bid to draw the unions into a greater involvement with Government processes in order to conceal the cracks appearing in the Cabinet. Perhaps it could also be said that Cousins, after his gruelling experiences of the previous three years, was beginning to feel the tug of responsibility as well as the opportunity to play a constructive role inside the magic circles of power. He certaintly sensed that the time was opportune for him to take a positive initiative within the TUC.

Yet it was the emergence of George Woodcock which persuaded Frank Cousins that there was inside the TUC hierarchy someone he could work with and trust: a figure who was neither associated with any political grouping in the narrower sense, nor involved with any of the personal cabals with the trade union and Labour Movement. Woodcock, like Cousins, was something of a loner. It was a natural alliance: if not of opposites in the absolute sense, then of two men who needed each other's qualities in order to balance their own flaws.

Woodcock could not have succeeded in persuading the TUC to work with NEDC without Cousins's support, and Cousins would not have been able to recover so quickly from his nuclear battles without Woodcock's support. When they quarrelled over basic policies they found they could do so without rancour or the suspicion that one might exploit the situation to the other's disadvantage. In my own view this, more than any other single factor, helps to explain the emergence of a so-called 'new image' Frank Cousins at the 1962 TUC. Years later Woodcock made this remarkable observation to me:

> Frank was the most outstanding member of the General Council in my time. There was no one else to compare with him. He did his homework. He came prepared. When he said something I knew that I could depend on him. I did not always agree with him – but that was not the point. I had trust in him and, unkind though it may sound, there was no other member of the General Council in whom I felt I could have the same trust.

Woodcock saw many parallels between Cousins and Bevin, Woodcock's first and perhaps greatest hero in the trade union movement. As far as Cousins was concerned he reciprocated Woodcock's trust and confidence in a way that he showed to no other top figure in the trade union or political arena at the time.

In any event, the 1962 Trades Union Congress at Blackpool marked another turning-point in Frank Cousins's career. If there is a specific benchmark from which one might begin to chart his gradual movement towards the Cabinet post, I would single out this conference, though at that stage even the closest scrutiny of his speeches or analysis of his public attitudes offered no positive clues. In retrospect it is interesting to note that the fraternal delegate from the Labour Party that year was Harold Wilson. He was then newly in the role of Foreign Affairs spokesman in Hugh Gaitskell's Shadow Cabinet. Another Labour Party leader present at that Blackpool TUC as an 'observer' was James Callaghan, who had taken over Harold

Wilson's job as Shadow Chancellor. Both witnessed Frank Cousins stepping out in his new role and saw the TUC itself under the distinctly and distinctively new management of George Woodcock. Indeed Wilson, perhaps a little perturbed by the way the Tories were embracing the unions, spoke on the first day of the Congress issuing a warning, almost in Cousins's style, urging the unions not to be taken in by the Tory Government's 'conversion' to planning, and warning them that the whole NEDC (and NIC) operation might well be a piece of Macmillanesque manœuvring to prepare the way for a General Election.

He said :

> I do not say the Tories are against all planning, but so far for eleven years now their planning has been directed not to safeguarding Britain's industrial future but to keeping themselves in office and their anonymour paymasters in control of the industrial machine. It is a form of planning that means manœuvring the industrial system and men's livelihoods so that after three years of stagnation they can bring the economy just nicely to the boil in time for a general election and then back into stagnation again. Real planning for them is impossible, because planning means priorities and to make priorities effective you have to have physical measures to hold back the less essential, the over-profitable, the speculative, so that the country as a whole can go steadily and purposively forward.[10]

There was also a trailer for future crises and conflicts within his own 1964 Cabinet when Harold Wilson stressed the need for wages to be related to productivity and economic growth : 'Economic rewards cannot for long outstrip national production . . .' It was a brief, almost casual reference, buried away in his speech. Perhaps Wilson was making a passing observation; or perhaps he was harking back to the reply Cousins gave John Freeman in that celebrated TV interview in October 1961 when Freeman inquired whether Cousins would be prepared to accept from a Labour Government policies which, in the short term, he disliked, such as wage restraint. Frank Cousins's reply was not encouraging to the Labour Party leaders :

> No. I've talked with the leader of the Labour Party about this on a number of occasions and at one meeting of the National Council of Labour I had to make clear that the attitude of the Union would be that if the political party created the circumstances in which it was not necessary for us to press for wage adjustments we should be happy to co-operate with them in making a success of . . . whatever efforts they were making in the economic field. But if they retained the sort of position that exists now and left us in the unprivileged position we should fight against them just the same as we would against any other party.[11]

10. TUC *Annual Report*, 1962, p. 306.
11. 'Face to Face', BBC TV, 15 October 1961.

That was Cousins's style of telling Gaitskell, Wilson, Callaghan – and anyone else within earshot – that he would be ready to do a deal on wages so long as a Labour Government pursued strong socialist policies. Even so the 1962 Congress was neither the psychological nor the political moment for Harold Wilson or James Callaghan to start raising such questions. The TUC was busy trying to bury NIC – and all other proposals for intervention in the sacred field of free collective bargaining. James Callaghan had an uneasy feeling as he sat through that Congress that his own task at the Treasury, come a Labour Government, was going to be extraordinarily difficult. He was right. It was part of his grooming for the Premiership to come.

George Woodcock's speech, which launched the TUC on a new course of cooperation with the Macmillan Government, was possibly the most powerful, philosophical speech on economic planning and relations between the trade unions and the State to come from a TUC platform in post-war years. It was also one of the most intricate. Woodcock separated the TUC opposition to NIC from his support for NEDC, but acknowledged that there were sceptics as well as outright opponents in his audience who saw no distinction between the two sets of initials. His performance was one of sheer intellectual brilliance, in which he invoked Rousseau's General Will in aid of TUC support for NEDC and opposition to NIC :

> If you want a democracy – and this *is* a kind of democracy – to get restraint of any kind there is one thing you must seek to do; you must seek to create, to have accepted, what Rousseau called a General Will. If the Government of this country want their citizens to act reasonably their first object should be to create a mood, an attitude in which people will be readily disposed towards reason, towards responsibility and towards dignity. That is where you start in this country if you want people to act with reason and restraint and with a sense of responsibility. Create the mood, create the desire on the part of the people to do it. Do not seek to impose upon them some conception of restraint which is entirely your own, which is not related to their circumstances, which draws nothing from them, no response at all. You must get at the roots, get at the things which move people . . .

He ridiculed the Conservative philosophy of 'setting the people free' with an eloquence unusual for the speaker, as well for Trade Union Congresses :

> Private enterprise and competition, as advocated constantly by the Government, as the rule which determines all their policies, has never yet produced a decent citizen. All that it does is produce the spiv and sometimes the thug. The Government have consistently – not simply this Government but the Conservative Governments we have had since 1950 – boasted and made big speeches about their object being to set the people free. In general terms, that is a worthy subject, a very worthy objective indeed, and if you leave it

in general terms I can subscribe to it. But what are they to be free of? Are we to be free of all decency, all responsibility? Is that what setting the people free means . . . Set the people free and the weakest are the ones that go to the wall. Freedom for all really means restrictions for some and freedom for some.

Having dismissed the concept of NIC, and the whole notion of the unions accepting a limitation on their wage bargaining freedom in a society which Harold Wilson had earlier in the week described as the 'candyfloss economy', Woodcock then went on to lecture the Congress on the implications of planning with NEDC.

The NEDC proposal, he said, was 'a serious undertaking'; it was something the TUC had been asking for, at least in concept, for a long time. It was something which, when first presented to him by Selwyn Lloyd, had aroused his doubts and suspicions. But as discussions with the Government proceeded he realised that NEDC contained, or could be made to contain, the ingredients of a very important step forward in economic planning. Even so it was still 'a subject on which we cannot be certain'. Nobody could predict what might happen or how things might develop. But it would be absurd and self-defeating for the TUC to sidestep the opportunity. Woodcock did not flinch from the wages issue, either. In dismissing NIC he did not dismiss incomes policy as such.

'If everything comes in' (and by 'everything' he made it clear he meant the entire range of the nation's economic affairs and social priorities), he said,

we will not be afraid of discussing at NEDC what part wages can play in a plan for genuine progress. We make no commitment at all; we cannot do that. But nobody should run away with the idea that we are afraid of discussing wages if we can get the discussion in a comprehensive scheme in which we are all playing our part. What we object to is this singling out of wages, this idea that we are the only culprits in this country, that we have no legitimate objectives, that we are the ones at fault.

Woodcock referred to 'the gross injustices and inequalities there are in this country' which would have to be remedied by the Government if they wanted trade union support. Of course, even given that kind of approach by Government, the unions would still encounter great difficulties in trying to operate a wages policy.

He went on:

I know – and this Government do not seem to know – that it is not easy to move in this wages field, that trade unions quite rightly claim, in this matter ultimate sovereignty for themselves, and of course they must because a union in the last event is responsible to its members, it must do the things eventually – whatever may be done by argument and persuasion – that its members want it to do.

So, said Woodcock, there could be 'no formal control of wages', no pay pause, no guiding light, no precision or strict scientific measurement of what this or that union could or could not have. With a declaration of principle from which he never wavered throughout his period as TUC General Secretary, he told the Macmillan Government, as he later told the Wilson Government: 'You cannot have that kind of wages policy.' All that was possible in the best of all possible worlds was to do 'the best we can'. But that was to come later ...

By his eloquence, as much as by his pledges against wage restraint and the conformity expected by the Government, Woodcock commanded respect and support from Cousins, as well as from the great majority of the Congress delegates, though some disagreed with him on ideological grounds. Even his sternest opponents could not disguise their admiration for the quality, and the calibre of Woodcock's performance. From Frank Cousins it drew a firm commitment to his participation in NEDC – warning the Government that it must not be used as a backdoor to wage restraint. He echoed Woodcock in denouncing the kind of society the Conservative Government reflected and spoke for, the degree of social inequity which remained and which the unions were in business to combat.

But what of planning under the status quo? What was to be the role of a trade union, especially a militantly-led trade union, in a mixed economy under a Conservative Government which offered a new form of institutional planning mechanism? Woodcock's speech and Woodcock's influence beforehand were reflected in Cousins's reply, which only half-concealed his underlying doubts. He said:

As to NEDC, I have repeatedly said in public that my own union is now proud that we are associated with it. Whether it works is a different thing. Whether it is able to persuade employer interests that, for the good of the community, there should be a direction of labour into certain areas, whether we should try to direct industries where it is not thought profitable for themselves to go, whether they will take the guidance of the country's need, I am not sure. But one thing can be said: if the opportunity presents itself the British trade union movement as a whole will play its part in improving the lot of the people of this country as a whole.

One does not have to labour the significance of that commitment. At the same time Cousins drew his model for social and economic cooperation, which left a huge area for freedom of action by the unions:

But we are not going to accept that this means losing sovereignties, losing identities, losing power. While this system [the free enterprise system] maintains itself we also will maintain ourselves. In our approach to planning, in our request for co-ordinated effort on the part of the unions and the setting down of what the policies for expansion really are there should be no misunderstanding about why. We want a new system designed to create instead of 'free for all', a 'fair for all', and when this is there, we shall be with it.

It may not have been the most elegant way of stating the point, but no one misunderstood the message. It was the same as in 1956: 'While there is a free for all we will be part of "all".' Fundamentally nothing had changed except the date on the calendar; but *that* was important.

The day before the economic debate Cousins persuaded the Congress to support his union's motion calling for a Job Security Charter covering a wide range of 'fringe benefits'. These would include redundancy agreements, pensions, sick pay benefits and a national campaign, involving all unions and employers, to try to reduce factory accidents. He wanted the General Council to organise this united campaign to provide improved facilities and job security agreements throughout industry. No one, he thought, could object to the sentiments of this proposal – though some unions did so on the grounds that it was not a union's job to help employers negotiate redundancy agreements. It was, as someone suggested, like 'buying employment' or 'selling jobs'. Cousins retorted that the notion that every worker could stay put in his or her present job for all time was outmoded.

He knew, of course, that these views, alongside his acceptance of a seat on NEDC, would inevitably invite charges that he had 'gone soft'. He met that challenge forcefully in an article in the *Record* immediately after the Blackpool TUC. It was unusual for the General Secretary to present his own 'personal report' on the TUC in the union journal; the report on the TUC and the Labour Party conferences was normally written by a union official attending as a member of the TGWU delegation. But the 1962 TUC was a special occasion, which Cousins recognised in his commentary:

Trade unionists as a group are traditionally cautious people not given to rushing headlong into anything. Nevertheless the atmosphere of new ideas and imaginative proposals was unmistakable at this year's annual Congress of the TUC at Blackpool. Provided this is not lost in an effort to serve sectional interests or in sterile argument it could be the beginning of a very fruitful period in trade union history.

The theme of this must be militancy combined with responsibility, and not something designed with a view to weakening trade union strength or policy. On the contrary it is vital that the unions should stimulate economic expansion by keeping up their pressures. By leading the way to economic planning and showing a willingness to assess their own role in this, increased assistance can be given to the effort for greater output which will enable their demands to be met and other just calls upon the economy being also satisfied.[12]

He went on to defend his stand on redundancy agreements, as well as membership of NEDC, and his commitment to the experiment in planning. What he said in the article is less important than the fact that he felt it necessary to say it. As he observed, the issues which faced that TUC 'were momentous and remain so' and because of that he 'thought it desirable to report direct to the membership in this issue of the *Record*'.

In some ways the most remarkable feature of that Congress was something Frank Cousins did *not* do – he did not speak in the nuclear disarmament debate, on the last morning of the conference. John Horner of the Fire Brigades' Union moved the now traditional nuclear disarmament motion. It was supported by two other speakers, and opposed for the General Council by William (now Sir William) Webber, and lost on a show of hands. The TGWU voted for it, although Frank Cousins did not attempt to speak in the debate. Instead he seconded (an unusual order of precedence in itself) a motion calling for the ending of Polaris missile bases in Britain. This time, to the consternation of the majority on the General Council, the motion was carried on a show of hands. But it all seemed somewhat perfunctory: a last-minute, Friday morning romp through countless motions, many of them immensely controversial, but dealt with in a style which suggested casual indifference or an impatient acceptance of the unavoidable. This was all very different from previous years. Again it was symptomatic of the Woodcock 'new image' and the success of his determined attempt to defuse the defence issue which in his own words, had come so near to undermining the industrial work of the TUC.

Nor did Frank Cousins speak on the Common Market at that TUC though there were four motions on the subject, ranging from one which was specifically opposed to others which either supported, or opposed, British membership with qualifications. The TGWU remained faithful to the official TUC position – uncommitted pending further negotiations. In fact Cousins was saving his ammunition for the Labour Party conference, where he knew there would be a decisive debate. What he did *not* know in advance, was what would be said at that memorable Brighton conference, which was fated to be Gaitskell's last – at the very moment when a reconciliation with Frank Cousins had opened up.

In those weeks before the Brighton conference the Common Market became a focal point of national attention. The Government had convened a conference of Commonwealth Prime Ministers, held between the TUC and the

12. TGWU *Record*, October 1962, p. 32.

Labour Party conferences, at which Harold Macmillan sought to sell the idea of British membership of EEC to a sceptical, and in some instances an outrightly hostile, Commonwealth gathering. Before that, the TUC leaders had been bombarded by a series of persuasive meetings with Ministers as well as a 3,500 word memorandum from Edward Heath, who was then the British Minister in charge of the negotiations in Brussels. The emphasis of Ministerial persuasion with the TUC, as with the Commonwealth Prime Ministers, was that too much was being made of the economic disadvantages of British membership. The persuasion was as convincing to the majority of the TUC leadership as it was to the Commonwealth leaders. They remained sceptical and hostile. In fact, opinion inside the British trade unions had perceptibly shifted against entry. The Blackpool TUC already demonstrated the weakening in pro-Market feeling among the majority of unions and the deepening of anti-Market feeling among those unions who had always been hostile. Even more significant was the increasing confusion among unions who found it difficult to make up their minds one way or the other.

Hugh Gaitskell was unusually sensitive to this. He felt, as possibly he had never before felt with such keen precision, that the mood of the Labour Movement was against the Government's application, as was perhaps, even the mood of the British people as a whole. Nobody could be sure of that, especially at that early stage of the negotiations when the issues appeared even more complex than they became later. It was already clear that the Labour Party's policy of 'no commitment' and 'wait-and-see' would be confirmed by the Brighton conference, but beyond that there was doubt, speculation and great guessing as to what tone Hugh Gaitskell would adopt. The Party executive issued a long policy statement on the eve of the conference which laid down five specific conditions for British entry. These were:

1. Strong and binding safeguards for the trade and other interests of our friends and partners in the Commonwealth.

2. Freedom as at present to pursue our own foreign policy.

3. Fulfilment of the Goverment's pledge to our associates in the European Free Trade Area (EFTA).

4. The right to plan our own economy.

5. Guarantees to safeguard the position of British agriculture.

That statement spelled out in great details the arguments for and against membership. It concluded that if the five conditions were met by the EEC, then Britain should join, but if they were rejected then 'Britain should not enter and the present negotiations should be brought to a halt'. The orientation was strongly pro-Commonwealth, pro-World Community, questioning the inward-looking tendencies endemic within the Common Market – but it was not, in the last resort, wholly anti-Market. The door was left open. It was certainly a negotiable document – for the Labour Party. But *after* Hugh Gaitskell's remarkable speech in support of that document on the morning of Wednesday 3 October few people doubted that the Labour Party was in a clearly anti-market position.

Gaitskell's speech staggered the conference by its length (almost one and a half hours) as well as by the brilliance of its construction and delivery; it astonished and dismayed many of Gaitskell's friends inside and outside the Labour Party; it bewildered and enthralled his former critics (especially inside the Labour Movement); to this day it remains one of the great political puzzles of modern times.

With only a handful of exceptions Gaitskell's monumental assault on the Common Market was greeted by cries of astonished pain from most media commentators. The Press was almost universally behind the Government's application to join the EEC, and clearly did not expect the man they had previously hailed as a 'sensible moderate' Labour leader to turn so savagely on the conventional wisdom of the period. And no wonder. Gaitskell appeared to have behaved in a most uncharacteristic manner. He appealed to deep sentiment rather than to any statistical neutrality. He spoke of his attachment to the Commonwealth in tones almost of socialist blimpism:

> We are not just part of Europe – at least not yet. We have a different history. We have ties and links which run across the whole world, and for me at least the Commonwealth, the modern Commonwealth which owes its creation fundamentally to those vital historic decisions of the Labour Government [ie, the Attlee Government] is something I want to cherish.

He angered many of his friends by what they regarded as an overstretched call to British chauvinism, especially his reference to the British and Commonwealth contribution during the First World War and to the New Zealand, Australian and Canadian losses at Vimy Ridge and Gallipoli. He observed that while European culture and history had much to proclaim in names like Goethe, Leonardo, Voltaire and Picasso, there had also been Hitler and Mussolini. So it went on, and on. In his passionate peroration Gaitskell called for a test of public opinion before any binding decisions were taken: 'The only right and proper and democratic thing is to let the people decide the issue.' He said he was not closing the door on the Market, but:

> We must reject the terms so far negotiated for they are quite inadequate; they do not fulfil either our own conditions or the Government's pledges. But no final decision can be taken until we know the final terms and when that moment comes we shall judge it in the light of the conditions that we have laid down.

The man in the conference chair was Harold Wilson. He too was spell-bound and described Gaitskell's speech as 'this historic speech' – which it most certainly was. Wilson then proposed that the speech should be immediately printed and made available to every Party member in the country. Harold Wilson's suggestion was picked up at once by Frank Cousins, who offered TGWU funds to finance the printing and distribution of a million copies. A spontaneous gesture, or a premeditated ploy? Frank Cousins insists that it was 'absolutely spontaneous'. He did not know what Gaitskell was going to say before he rose to speak. In fact he says he had always had the feeling that Gaitskell was basically pro-Market. 'But,' he adds, 'as I sat and listened to that speech I felt it was the most committing anti-Common Market statement we had ever heard. Not just from a Labour leader but from anyone of authority.'

But even if Gaitskell had a General Election and not a referendum in mind, there is no doubt he was asking for a specific mandate on the issue of British entry into the Common Market.

As Gaitskell was drawing to the close Cousins turned to his union President, Len Forden, to say: 'Len, we must get this on the record. Will you back me if I urge that we finance the printing and distribution of the speech from union funds?' Forden agreed and began sounding out members of the TGWU executive before Gaitskell sat down. It was as spontaneous as that. But it was a gesture by Cousins which rippled out far beyond the Brighton waterfront. It led directly to the reconciliation with Gaitskell.

Cousins's enthusiasm for Gaitskell's speech was by no means shared by all his TUC General Council colleagues. Jack (later Lord) Cooper of the General and Municipal Workers' Union chastised Gaitskell for the speech and said very plainly that he regretted it. He also regretted the proposals to publicise it. 'I do not think Hugh Gaitskell's speech – and I have some ideas about the wisdom of publicising that speech: every man to his point of view – I do not think it was presented as well as it might have been,' said Cooper. Such a comment coming from the leader of the General and Municipal Workers, Gaitskell's own union, and in the past a cornerstone of his support, was somewhat more than a casual offhand remark. It was a savage rebuke.

Cousins told the conference, immediately after Cooper had spoken, that he regarded Gaitskell's speech as 'one of the best speeches on the subject I have ever heard, probably one of the finest you will ever hear on it . . .'

What an extraordinary turn of events it was. The right-wing traditional supporters of Gaitskell in the unions and the Parliamentary Party, were stunned into shock and horror; the Left were jubilant though amazed. As one member of the Campaign for Democratic Socialism said, 'The worst part about the whole thing are the people who are supporting Hugh!' At the end of that debate George Brown, remaining firm to his pro-Market convictions, danced along the tightrope in a speech which was as courageous and as candid as it could be without actually exploding into a blazing rejection of all Gaitskell had said. Brown, at the outset, appealed for sympathy in his impossible task of asking support for something everyone knew he disagreed with. Somehow he came through the ordeal, arguing with himself and Gaitskell in almost every passage, and ending up a rather dejected victor in a fight he would no doubt have preferred to have lost.

Frank Cousins recalls George Brown's reactions earlier that day, listening to Hugh Gaitskell. 'He sat there, on the platform, in a state of shock, constantly amending his own notes as Gaitskell spoke.' It was not surprising. George Brown in his memoirs discloses that he never saw – or was told about – the contents of Gaitskell's speech in advance, even though he was deputed to wind up the debate.

He describes his own reactions to the scenes of conference jubilation after Gaitskell's speech :

> Emotionally, intellectually and in the manner of its delivery this speech was most compelling. It was followed by a standing ovation led to my horror by Wilson and all the anti-Gaitskellites. Frank Cousins of the Transport Workers, who had been bitterly anti-Gaitskell announced that his union would pay for a million copies of 'this great speech' to be printed and circulated throughout the country. Sam Watson and I, who had led the fight in the National Executive to get the policy document, unsatisfactory as it was, into some sort of European context, looked at each other wondering what on earth we did next.

George Brown got a little satisfaction out of it all later when it was proposed, by Margaret Herbison, that the Cousins offer to finance the printing and distribution of the pamphlet should be gladly accepted, provided the official Party statement and George Brown's reply went with it. It was as bizarre as that.

What lay behind the remarkable switch in Gaitskell's position – always presuming that he *had* switched – a move regarded by so many as a wholly uncharacteristic U-turn. Perhaps there is a clue in a comment offered the following day by *The Times* political correspondent : 'Some delegates clearly thought it was only a matter of time before Mr Gaitskell openly set himself at the head of an anti-Market campaign and swept on to lead Labour to victory in a General Election.' Was it in fact the imminence of a General Election that was concentrating the minds of both Gaitskell and Cousins? The evidence suggests that it had a powerful influence, even if it was not wholly responsible.

From the authority of Baroness Gaitskell I have it that Hugh Gaitskell had reached the conclusion, long before the Brighton conference, that Britain had no real chance of securing membership of the EEC because of de Gaulle's opposition:

> Hugh knew we hadn't an earthly chance of getting in. He was convinced of that after talks with the French. He was not against the Common Market in principle, but he argued that the economic case was not proved and he was a great believer in the Commonwealth. He felt it was a factor for stability in the world.

During the months preceding the Brighton conference Gaitskell had become increasingly convinced that the French would string Macmillan along but, in the end, would block the British membership. He foresaw with a rare political prescience an almost endless and ultimately futile trail of negotiations in Brussels and through Paris that would eventually end in failure on Macmillan's doorstep. And he regarded any Labour Party involvement in such a process as politically damaging to the Party's electoral prospects, as well as wrong in itself. There was another aspect to this. Many of those who were closest to Gaitskell at the time suggest that he was haunted by the possibility of yet another outbreak of internal Party dissension. He was as exhausted by the nuclear disarmament controversy as Frank Cousins. He wanted to grasp at the opportunity of a new unity possibly more avidly than Cousins.

He knew that the Common Market could – and almost certainly would – split the Labour Party as deeply as nuclear disarmament. Moreover, unlike some other issues which could be superficially labelled as Left v. Right, the Common Market divided people of all political colours. Even the Conservative Party was already showing divisions on it; only the Liberals appeared to be united in favour of the EEC. Gaitskell is said to have reasoned that it would be wholly counter-productive to split the Labour Movement once again, after the bitter fights which had been going on almost non-stop since he assumed the leadership, in favour of something that was still so uncertain, unclear, and, in his opinion, unlikely to succeed. How far this reasoning influenced his rejection of the Common Market, on the terms then available, and how far he had an emotional opposition to it in any event can only be guessed at. There are those who claim that it tipped the scales.

If he knew that a pro-Market stance would certainly split the Labour Movement and provoke a renewed outbreak of strife which might again threaten his leadership; if he also felt that there was no chance of British membership in advance of the next General Election; if in addition he sensed that his own deep misgivings about the EEC were shared widely throughout the country: *then* Gaitskell would have been absurdly reckless to have taken any other course than the one he chose.

Those who accused him of 'selling out his principles' were those who were unquestioningly in favour of British membership of the Common Market and who regarded all opponents of their cause either as fools or knaves or both. Frank Cousins's own view of Gaitskell's 'transformation' is that it was based on impulse and instinct. Cousins rejects the view that Gaitskell deliberately 'used' the Market issue to reunite the Labour Movement and to make peace with his old enemies – like Cousins. In short, it was not a deliberate gesture of appeasement towards the Left, or any other group. This would have been totally out of character for Gaitskell, Cousins says – 'I believe Hugh Gaitskell was an honest man; I really do believe he was intellectually honest.' So Cousins rules out any narrow, tactical operation. On the other hand he is convinced that the most persuasive case against the Common Market, in Gaitskell's mind, was the economic rather than the political one. Cousins suggests that Gaitskell had genuinely reached the conclusion that the effect on Britain of membership of the EEC would either be economically neutral at best or at worst damaging, and that in these circumstances the political gains would be mostly negative. This led him to an instinctive feeling that on balance the British people would be hostile to the concept and that they would react strongly against any political party which forced Britain into the Market.

The evidence that the Labour Movement was in the grip of a pre-election mood for reconciliation, if not unity at all costs, was widely apparent at the Brighton conference. It certainly affected Frank Cousins. His most belligerent speech was one directed against the then head of British Railways, Dr. Richard (later Lord) Beeching who at the time was in the midst of a national dispute with the National Union of Railwaymen over the closure of railway workshops and the axing of 18,000 jobs spread over a five-year period. The NUR had called a one-day national rail strike in the middle of the Labour Party conference week in protest against the Beeching closure plan. Cousins was in trouble with his London busmen for refusing to sanction a busmen's strike in support of the one-day stoppage. He said it would only unnecessarily alienate public opinion – a claim which was met by bitter comments from the busmen. None the less, Cousins stuck to his argument and told the busmen not to strike (a few did, in fact), using the point that the NUR had specifically asked the TGWU not to call out their busmen. And in the transport debate Cousins lashed at Beeching as 'the instrument of an opinion which has been taken by a Government. He [Beeching] may be a supporter of the view held by the group who believe in Tory capitalism – he comes from that background. He believes in industry based on the profit motive.' He conceded that it wasn't only Beeching but also the Government who was responsible for the policy of tearing up the railways, and that it was using Beeching as its tool. On the other hand, Cousins described the Railways Board chairman 'as probably the most insolent man we have ever talked to'.

That apart, for Frank Cousins it was an unusual Labour Party conference, to say the least. In every area the dominant theme was of unity. Even the TGWU's own journal in commenting on the Brighton conference observed perhaps with a little asperity : 'It was clear that the Left wing of the Party had decided to gave up the internal struggle over policy and to face the electorate in unity.'[13] The same author was remarkably candid about Frank Cousins's handling of the debate on nuclear tests. Cousins moved the TGWU motion calling for a reaffirmation of the Labour Party's stand against nuclear tests by *any* country. By then such a motion was largely non-controversial, and Cousins was relaxed and confident in his speech. 'It was clear that he had no wish to do more than prevent any further retreat from the policy position taken up at last year's conference', said the *Record* reporter, adding that : 'He did not risk making a personal attack on the role of the Party leader in this affair, conspicuous though it was. In this debate Frank Cousins was at his logical best and had the conference enthusiastically with him.'

Evidently the TGWU's own observer found the occasion something of a strain on his own credulity. The TGWU motion on nuclear tests was passed with acclamation, accompanied by the applause of Hugh Gaitskell, as well as vocal support on the platform from Sam Watson, the Durham miners' leader and chairman of the Party's international committee. For the first time Frank Cousins found himself on the side of the gods in a defence debate.

The turn of events was almost too much for most delegates to grasp. Yet everyone pulled back from the brink of controversy. Gaitskell's speech, and the preceding statement on the Common Market which made so many concessions to the anti-Market view and to left-wing opinion, had set the tone for a whole series of compromises and even evasions. Symptomatic of this was the fate of a move by some right-wing members of the Party executive to expel Bertrand Russell and Canon Collins from the Labour Party. They were accused of 'associating with a Moscow-organised peace conference' the previous summer. The proposal to expel them had already caused a tremendous rumpus – not confined to the Left – and had left the proposers looking rather absurd. When the issue came before the Brighton conference, during a private session, it was defeated by 3,497,000 to 2,793,000 with Cousins speaking against the proposal. What was interesting about this debate was George Brown's almost sheepish and self-conscious advocacy of the original idea. Even in private session no one, not even the tempestuous Brown, was anxious to open up old wounds.

The climax to the Gaitskell-Cousins reconciliation came a few weeks after the Brighton conference when the Gaitskells invited the Cousinses to dinner

13. TGWU *Record*, November 1962, p. 17.

at their Hampstead home. Gaitskell had taken the precaution of sounding out Cousins in advance about the idea of a quiet private talk about 'the future'. The Cousinses had been to Frognal only once before, and that visit had been a disastrous failure. Baroness Gaitskell recalls the previous occasion as a party at which Frank and Nance Cousins appeared to be isolated, surrounded by the Gaitskellites camp: 'Frank didn't much like some of our friends. He didn't think they were working-class; he thought them a bit stuffy and intellectual . . .'So the dinner party on 12 November was a private foursome, Hugh and Dora Gaitskell, Frank and Nance Cousins. And it was a huge success. After a good meal, there was a long period of candid reminiscing over recent disagreements culminating in a joint conviction that they must now agree to work together in the wider interests of winning the next General Election. Neither man sought to disguise their differences; they did not pretend that Brighton had resolved their policy conflicts; neither did they minimise the risks of future conflict. But at that moment both recognised they must try to work together. Gaitskell reflected on the kind of people he would like in his Cabinet if Labour won the election. He mentioned Crossman and Barbara Castle. He told Cousins that he would like him to join the Government. As Cousins recalls the dialogue Gaitskell said: 'We are going to be very short of talent; will you come into a Government?' Cousins replied: 'Let's not rule it out.' He did not give a firm commitment because, as he put it to Gaitskell, his primary concern was to help get a Labour Government elected rather than to look for a Government post for himself.

Lady Gaitskell recalls that Hugh Gaitskell made it quite clear that he wanted Frank Cousins to join the Government – probably as Minister of Transport – and that Cousins 'seemed to accept the idea'.

Cousins said to Gaitskell that he was getting older (he was 58) and though he was not concerned to get a job for himself in Government he certainly wanted to work creatively for a Labour Government. Yet Cousins wanted to keep his options open about actually moving into politics. Even so Gaitskell had sown the seed which, two years later, Wilson harvested when he recruited Frank Cousins to his 1964 Cabinet. Whether a Gaitskell-Cousins relationship in a Labour Government would have been any more successful than the Wilson-Cousins relationship turned out to be, is in my view unlikely. For Cousins the political isolation he would have felt inside a Gaitskell Cabinet would have been as great, if not greater, than his experience in the Wilson Government. He would have found the same irritants inside the Cabinet room, and on the floor of the Commons, as he did under Harold Wilson. It is argued by some that Gaitskell would have made a more radical Prime Minister than Harold Wilson and that this radicalism, especially on social policies, might have been used to sustain his new relationship with Frank Cousins. That seems improbable to me. I agree with Margaret

Stewart's argument that 'If Harold Wilson with his superior political sense and capacity to handle awkward colleagues failed to keep Cousins in the fold it is unlikely that Gaitskell would have succeeded.'[14] At any rate it was not to be. Gaitskell's death in January 1963 changed everything; the entire Labour scene was once again transformed by a wholly unexpected death. Within a couple of months of the great reconciliation between Cousins and Gaitskell the Labour Party had a new leader, Harold Wilson. Death, once more, became a determinant in Cousins's life.

14. Margaret Stewart, *Frank Cousins: A Study* (Hutchinson, 1968), p. 115.

Chapter Nineteen

THE WHITE HEAT

Hugh Gaitskell died on the night of Friday 18 January 1963. As with Bevan the death struck the political life of the country, not just the Labour Party, a severe blow. With Gaitskell the poignancy was perhaps greater because of the nearness to his long-sought objective, leading a Labour Government. Most observers believed that Gaitskell was as near to that as it is possible to get to a political certainty. His death was swift, the result of a rare disease, and inevitably it left the Labour Party completely unprepared and bewildered. The thought of facing a leadership contest after so much strife and agony in the three or four preceding years filled many in the Labour hierarchy with a sense of utter dismay. Yet, brutal though it may appear, there were others who recognised that this was an unexpected opportunity for a completely new start to the task of rebuilding unity under a new leader of the Party. It offered a way out of the political trauma which had haunted and disrupted the Party for so long.

The fight for succession therefore became inextricably linked with a deep feeling that the new leader ought to be someone who would bandage wounds, who would help to heal the scars and who would put the unity of the Labour Movement at the top of his list of priorities. It was this therapeutic role more than any sense of ideology or even identifiable political programme which animated the cause of Harold Wilson. And whatever else his critics will say about him and his place in history it remains true that Wilson's outstanding contribution has been to hold the Labour Party together. In that sense he lived up to his original promise.

The contest for Gaitskell's succession was a bitterly fought affair, surpassing in animosity even the spiteful and malicious atmosphere pervasive at the time of Gaitskell's own election. Shortly before Gaitskell's death the deputy leader, George Brown, was on a tour of north-west England investigating the unemployment crisis which, that month, had reached a new post-war peak (apart from the 1947 fuel crisis) of 815,000. Brown was in Burnley when he was told that Gaitskell was dying. A howling blizzard blanketed north-west England, and indeed most of Britain was in the grip of one of the worst winters of the century. None the less, when Brown heard the news from London he insisted that the tour should be shelved. A police-escorted convoy of cars drove that night, through the blizzard, to Manchester where Brown had arranged for an RAF plane to fly him to London.

He was determined to get back before Gaitskell died and he left Douglas Jay, who had been accompanying him, to continue the tour. Quite apart from all other considerations George Brown knew that the fight for succession would be a brutal one. On the night Gaitskell died Brown was at the home of Herbert (later Lord) Morrison, where Morrison counselled him on the hard fight he would have to win the leadership.[1] Brown claims that he was unsure about whether he ought to stand but finally decided that since he had been acting leader during Gaitskell's illness 'it would be wrong to turn round now and say I didn't want it. My friends all said that of course I must stand for the election. So I did.'

On that same night of 18 January in the senior Common Room of Nuffield College, Oxford, a group of TUC leaders were relaxing after dinner when news reached them that Gaitskell had died. The group included George Woodcock, Bill Carron, William Webber, Jack Cooper and Frank Cousins. For a time the news stunned them. Then their solicitude for Gaitskell's family turned to contemplation of the event's political significance and speculation about the likely successor. George Brown's name was an obvious one, much favoured by one or two of the TUC gathering; Harold Wilson and James Callaghan were two others obviously on the list. Anthony Greenwood was another, though less obvious, candidate.[2] The three principal candidates, Brown, Wilson and Callaghan, all had their supporters and their critics among the TUC group. Then Woodcock turned to Cousins and, to the astonishment of the others, said: 'What about you, Frank?' A silence surrounded the group as Woodcock developed his case that if Cousins was as interested in politics as his behaviour in recent years had suggested then he ought seriously to consider entering Parliament with the aim, perhaps, of becoming leader of the Party. Moreover, Woodcock believed that if the TGWU leader was prepared to chuck his hat in the ring he would be a serious contender there and then. On the face of it Woodcock's proposal seemed (and perhaps was) an absurd idea. Yet he still holds to his original contention that he was making a serious proposal to Cousins.

Was it in fact such a fantasy on Woodcock's part?

The answer must be, yes, because it was inconceivable that the Parlia-

1. See Lord George Brown, *In My Way* (Gollancz, 1970), pp. 83–92.
2. *Ibid.*, p. 83.

mentary Labour Party would at that stage have chosen anyone from outside its own ranks for the leadership. For a trade union leader to be brought in at a high level following the election of a Labour Government is one thing, but to have a trade union leader who is not an MP, no matter how powerful he may be, thrust upon the Parliamentary Party as its leader is quite another matter. In a state of grave crisis with the possible disruption of the Labour Party it might be a possibility, though still unlikely; but in the conditions of 1963 it was hardly more than an impish suggestion of Woodcock's however seriously he might have meant it. Yet it was by no means the first time Cousins had been presented with such ideas. At least twice before, George Brown had muttered similar notions, only to be summarily dismissed by Cousins. During the height of the Gaitskell-Cousins fight over nuclear disarmament Brown had put forward the idea that Cousins ought to come into Parliamentary politics, and later, in a mood of despair about the way the Party leadership had fallen into middle-class hands Brown put to Cousins the idea of a joint Brown-Cousins leadership axis inside the Parliamentary Labour Party in an attempt to restore 'genuine working-class leadership'.

Nor was George Brown alone in these thoughts. Some time before Gaitskell's death Cousins was exposed to other pressures, genuine or not, from various quarters who claimed they were anxious to 'project' him into a position of much greater power and authority in the Labour Party. One such lobbyist was Cecil Harmsworth King, then chairman of the *Daily Mirror* group. Invited to dine with Mr and Mrs King at their Chelsea home Frank and Nance Cousins found themselves, separately, flattered by the King household. To Cousins himself Cecil King is said to have suggested that the time had come for Cousins to 'drop his rebellious policies' and his 'quite futile' campaign on nuclear disarmament and to turn his gifts toward the more positive role of trade union statesman, in the Ernest Bevin tradition. Such a switch in his public role, King is claimed to have proposed, would be supported by many newspapers, and certainly the *Daily Mirror*. With such backing, it was hinted, Cousins could be 'made': no post, however illustrious, would be beyond his reach. 'There was no doubt in my mind about the purpose of such musings and hints,' says Frank Cousins. He certainly took them to imply that King was prepared to back him for 'a leadership role'. After the dinner party Frank and Nance Cousins exchanged notes and discovered that they had separately been tested on the same theme. Both had reacted with immediate and instinctive resentment. They were never again invited to dine with the Kings.

Cousins repeated several times what he had told John Freeman in the famous TV interview in October 1961 – that he had no intention of abandoning his role in the trade union movement to enter Parliament. Yet the rumours persisted. Curiously, they were resurrected even *after* Wilson had been elected – partly, perhaps, because of the active role Cousins played in working for Wilson's election. In March Cousins turned up unexpectedly at a London busmen's conference to make it clear to his members that he had no personal political ambitions. The busmen were at the time involved in a renewed fight for higher wages and there was a danger of strike action. Some of the leaders took the view that they were getting insufficient backing from Cousins and suggested that his lack of enthusiasm might be due to his 'political ambitions'. It was all 'quite untrue', Cousins assured them. He and the union executive were solidly behind the bus crews' pay claim. Then he added that while it was a fact that he was a 'political' General Secretary of the union in the full sense of that phrase he had no personal ambitions to go into Parliamentary politics. He saw his role as helping Labour's cause through the TGWU, and its policies.

There was certainly no doubt about the role – possibly the key role – played by Cousins in the election of Harold Wilson. It was a role which George Brown, bearing an obvious grudge, fully acknowledges in his account of Wilson's victory over himself on 14 February 1963. Brown offers the studied understatement of the period by describing the contest as 'not a nice election'.[3] He refers to the Left being 'pretty solidly against me' and to Frank Cousins's policy of 'consolidating his position against the legacy which the old Bevin-Deakin hierarchy had left behind and I suffered in the process'. In fact there was no need for Cousins to 'consolidate' his position; by then it was firm.

The most important political question for Cousins was – which of the three main candidates would be most likely to give the Labour Party a leftward tilt? His experiences with George Brown during the H-bomb phase had left an indelible sourness. He had never felt any overwhelming attraction to Jim Callaghan, whom he regarded as being no less right-wing than Brown but without Brown's attractive features – features which always made it hard for Cousins to actively dislike him. The only question-mark against supporting Wilson – and it was not a strong one – was whether Anthony Greenwood, who was chairman of the Labour Party that year, might stand. Although he certainly considered doing so, he was persuaded not to stand in favour of Wilson. Greenwood (now Lord Greenwood of Rossendale) has told the author that he had no serious intention of contesting the leadership. He disputes Crossman's account of this. But he *was* approached to stand. His account of the events is that he was telephoned one Sunday morning shortly after Gaitskell's death by a right-wing MP who suggested that he should stand for the leadership. Greenwood claims that the caller was full of praise for his qualities and argued that he would stand a good chance of winning against Brown and Callaghan. 'Of course I recognised that this

3. *Loc. cit.*

MP, quite apart from anything else, was probably seeking to split the pro-Wilson vote,' Greenwood has told me. 'No, it was never in my mind to contest the leadership role. When I stood before, it was simply to put some fire into Harold.'

Cousins played a prominent part behind the scenes in clearing the decks so that Wilson could have a clear run as far as the Left was concerned. He had become quite convinced that Wilson was the man to support; the one man available to give the Labour Movement both a Leftward tilt and a new sense of unity; a man with whom he would be able to work and establish the kind of political and even personal relationship that would have been improbable with Hugh Gaitskell, even allowing for their reconciliation. This did not make Cousins a devotee of Wilson. Their previous contacts had been almost wholly on an official basis, through Labour Party and TUC committee work. This had at least one advantage : there was no history of distrust or mutual conflict, no legacy of serious political disagreement. Wilson had managed to convey the impression of always being on the side of the Left without in any way detaching himself from the centre of the Party. Through his panel of TGWU-sponsored MPs, through direct and indirect methods of making his views and opinions known, in the corridors of Parliament as well as Transport House, Cousins transmitted his message : he was fully behind Harold Wilson.

Shortly before the ballot took place for the leadership in February Cousins and Wilson met; they talked for nearly two hours in the privacy of Cousins's Austin saloon, parked outside the Commons. The TGWU leader made it clear that he would do everything he could to help Wilson win the leadership, even though he knew it would incur the everlasting wrath of George Brown. There was no 'social compact' between the two men, but there was an 'understanding'. It was an understanding, in Cousins's view, that Wilson would pursue radical, even left-wing policies and that if Labour won the next election the Wilson administration would work for the radical reform of British society. They exchanged views on housing, schools, transport, economic planning and industrial priorities; they even talked over the delicate field of wages policies. They discussed Britain's role and influence in international affairs and how this might be transformed under a Labour Government. Cousins was tolerably satisfied that Wilson was the man to lead the next Labour Government along such a crusading road although he would need a great deal of help – not least from the trade unions. There was no question, at that time, of Wilson even tempting Cousins with the thought of joining a Labour Government. The idea was probably lurking promisingly at the back of Wilson's mind, but it was not mentioned during that meeting in the Austin saloon.

This was the first time anything like a close relationship was established between Harold Wilson and Frank Cousins, but it clearly laid the foundation for an increasingly fruitful and developing contact during the 20 months which lay between Wilson's election as Labour Party leader and the General Election of October 1964.

It required two ballots to decide the leadership. In the first Wilson came top of the poll with 115 votes, to George Brown's 88 and Jim Callaghan's 41. Since there was no absolute majority a second ballot was necessary and this was held on 14 February 1963. Wilson won it by 144 to George Brown's 103.

Brown was embittered by the result and by Cousins's behaviour, although it is hard to understand why he expected the TGWU leader to support him after the experiences of 1959 to 1962. He never really forgave Cousins for what he regarded as an act of spite and 'treachery' towards an 'old union colleague'. Brown was, of course, hopelessly sentimentalising the situation. There had been no political accord between the two men even before the nuclear disarmament row. None the less, George Brown felt he had been 'let down' by Frank Cousins, and the resentment rankled on into the period when they sat in Cabinet together. It was the resentment of a man who believed he had been let down not so much by a person as by an ethos – the ethos of trade union and working-class solidarity. This was based on a belief that he, George Brown, as a solid son of the working class, was entitled to Cousins's support, entitled to the full backing of his 'own union', entitled to the loyalty of his 'own people', especially in a contest with a smart chap from the lower middle class who had all the advantages of a university education, Oxford to boot, and a professional background, while he, the son of an East End lorry driver, had had to fight every inch of the way. Brown saw it almost in terms of class betrayal, though this was a phrase he would himself disdain to use.

We learn from the diaries of Richard Crossman (February–March 1963) that there was a general feeling of elation among the Left and the Centre of the Labour Party in Parliament that the 'Gaitskell straitjacket has dropped off our shoulders and that the Labour Party is free to be itself again . . .'[4] Crossman himself disclosed that he was so frustrated and depressed by the style of Gaitskell's leadership that he considered retiring from politics, or possibly taking a life peerage if Gaitskell had lived – or if George Brown had beaten Wilson. He rejoiced in Wilson's victory, and a diary note describes Wilson's own reactions to his election as Party leader :

Of course he was exhilarated and excited but he was also extraordinarily professional and sensible. Though vain he is certainly not conceited. Though enormously intelligent he is certainly not an intellectual. He is a supremely professional politician – in this he resembles Kennedy. But he is also an agile

4. Richard Crossman, the unpublished diaries, 8 February 1963.

manœuvrer and something of a demagogue hence a wonderful listener who can pick the brains of skilful people, qualities he shares with Lloyd George I have a strong feeling that he will make a far better leader than Gaitskell.[5]

Crossman admitted that he was prejudiced in Wilson's favour and was now as 'close' to Wilson as he had once been to Gaitskell, and added:

Of course there will be moments of appalling disillusion and depression but it is my settled conviction that Harold Wilson will be a far better PM than Hugh Gaitskell would have been, far less autocratic and imperious, far less impulsive and above all open to ideas in a way Hugh was not.[6]

This last point about Wilson being prepared to listen to a wider band of ideas was certainly one of the features Cousins found most attractive in Wilson, compared with Gaitskell.

A sense of liberation ran through the whole left wing of the Labour Party at that time. The enthusiasms reflected by the Crossman diaries do not exaggerate this feeling. A completely new start could be made, it was felt, after years of bitterness, strife and divisions which had brought the Party to the very edge of the abyss, divisions which the Left believed had been made worse by tactless and insensitive right-wing leadership – not just Gaitskell, but, more particularly, those who surrounded him. There was, no doubt, a good deal of self-righteousness in this left-wing attitude, since it automatically assumed that all the flaws, politically as well as emotionally, lay with the Right. A few of the more introspective members of the Left were ready to admit to their own irrationalities as well, yet it was not a period of great ideological self-searching or reflective research into the changing condition of British society.

It seemed less urgent to consider the underlying political problems of our time, or to probe the intellectual dilemmas that had precipitated so much of the past conflict. The absolute priority was to ensure that the image the Labour Party presented to the country would, in future, be of a more united party. That was the self-evident role for Harold Wilson and he performed it with superb competence. He was also instinctively aware of the widespread impatience among a younger generation over the style and practices of the Macmillan administration. British life was changing too slowly for this generation. There were still far too many obstacles in the way, social economic, cultural, and far too many rigidities in Britain's institutions. Politics and politicians were being challenged with a remarkable new confidence and

5. *Loc. cit.*
6. *Loc cit.*

the heroes of TV and pop-culture invaded the old citadels of certainty and conformity. When the phrase 'new technology' was used, loosely and without much preciseness of direction – as Harold Wilson often did – it was frequently offered as an umbrella term to express a dissatisfaction with the crusted conventions, mannerisms and techniques of a world that appeared to be dying of anaemia. Deservedly or not, the Conservative Government of Macmillan was thought to typify this world. Macmillan himself possessed the grand Edwardian style. He had wit, wisdom and compassion. He presided over a team of great talent with the ease and perhaps the gullibility of a cultured master-politician. But, outside the well of Whitehall, people in the sidestreets of Britain's cities were suspicious of his fading flourishes. They felt, in their veins, that Britain was missing out, though they were not quite clear why, or what to do about it, or where it had all gone wrong. Was it the need for a social or political revolution? Were the 'rebels' correct when they attacked the deeply-rooted class structure of Britain, with its absurd inequalities? Was it a fact that we were appallingly inefficient industrially compared with the Germans and the Japanese? Was it that we had a particularly bloody-minded proletariat? There was great bewilderment in Britain in that springtime of 1963, especially after the General in Paris had contemptuously replied 'NON' to Britain's application to join the EEC. With that grand disdainful sweep of his imperious arm de Gaulle, on January 14, only a few days before Gaitskell died, vetoed British entry into the Common Market. With the same sweep de Gaulle also partly scuppered the Nassau agreement between Macmillan and John F. Kennedy, in which the Americans agreed to supply Polaris missiles to Britain and to set up a multilateral NATO nuclear force of Polaris submarines with a string of bases throughout Europe. De Gaulle wanted none of this. The price of American nuclear cover was too high for the General, especially if it meant having to put up with British membership of EEC. Here was more of the 'new technology': Polaris. A submarine with a deadly nuclear sardine in its belly, ready to destroy Russian cities whenever zero hour was signalled. The march of progress continued to tramp towards universal destruction. No wonder the new leader of the Labour Party felt he was entering a totally new political minefield, without any ready-made ideological maps to guide him and a still potentially divided Labour Party behind him. Towards the middle of March that year, less than a month after his election, Wilson went to a dinner party at Barbara Castle's home. It was a mini-convention of the Left, according to Crossman.[7] Michael Foot, George Wigg, Anthony Greenwood, Judith Hart as well as Crossman were in attendance to congratulate Wilson and ordain him as their chosen leader. The careful and cautious lad

---

7. Richard Crossman, the unpublished diaries, 12 March 1963.

from Huddersfield puffed away on his pipe and observed to his friends : 'You must understand that I am running a Bolshevik Revolution with a Czarist Shadow Cabinet.'[8]

The National Economic Development Council had already made its mark by the turn of 1962. In October the NEDC office produced its first report on an economic model designed to lift the British economy out of its gloom, stagnation and backwardness by the middle of the 1960s. A 75-page document demonstrated what a growth rate of 4 per cent per year would involve for the nation up till the end of 1966. The report set out an ambitious programme of requirements based on the fundamental assumptions that to get things on the correct track we needed a rate of investment of 6.2 per cent per year and an increase by 3.3 per cent a year in productivity per worker. There were vague hints about the need to restrain personal consumption and incomes, but such hints were inevitably shaded in a very pale outline of grey. In the light of this, 1963 was designated as National Productivity Year. Alas, it opened with a record level of unemployment and the spread of industrial despondency.

Unemployment moved up by 3.3 per cent in February to 932,939. Everything, including the frightful winter of ice and snow, was advanced as a possible reason for the depression, but the thought of coupling this situation with a drive for productivity and industrial modernisation struck the TGWU as a kind of sick joke. In the March issue of *Record*, the union journal, it was noted : 'The old fears are back, along with the determination not to work oneself or one's workmates out of a job while unemployment persists.' On 26 March the unions organised a mass demonstration at the House of Commons against the rise of unemployment. Well over 5,000 marched from Euston Station to Westminster to lobby their MPs. The scenes of protest were reminiscent of the 1930s. The huge increase in the number of jobless was in fact a passing economic aberration – or so it seemed. By the summer of 1963 the figure fell to below 500,000. In July it was down to 2 per cent. But the winter crisis had demonstrated to the country that the affluence of the early 1960s was indeed a fragile plant. The April Budget, the first produced by Reginald Maudling, was the signal for another change in Government policy, a turn back towards an expansionist policy which was to take the country through 1964, and which the Conservatives hoped would bring them a renewed mandate from the elecorate. They used it to pump money into the economy, concentrating on public work schemes in Scotland and the North East. That April also saw Dr Richard Beeching publish his famous report on the modernisation of the railways, a report which he had been ready and anxious to issue earlier in the year but had been held back by the

8. *Ibid.*

Government. The Cabinet had no wish to allow an already serious unemployment crisis to be aggravated politically by the publication of Beeching's plan for widespread cuts in railway services and redundancies for railwaymen.

The Government desperately needed to establish a closer and warmer relationship with the trade unions but could see no easy way of achieving this. The National Incomes Commission blotted its copybook with its very first report, in which it condemned an agreement reached in the Scottish building industry giving workers a 40 hour week. The Commission warned against the shorter working spreading through industry, and repeated the need for an incomes policy which would enable wage rises to be held within the guideline figures of 3 to $3\frac{1}{2}$ per cent set by the new Chancellor. The Treasury's Economic Adviser, Sir Alex Cairncross, was busily defending the old 'norm' of 2 to $2\frac{1}{2}$ per cent when he gave evidence to NIC, only to be repudiated a few weeks later by his Chancellor, who proclaimed the new 'guiding light' of 3 to $5\frac{1}{2}$ per cent. It didn't help to inspire confidence in the Treasury's handling of the economic affairs of the nation, even less in the Government's internal communications system.

Almost parallel with Maudling's first Budget, the NEDC produced its second and perhaps most important report: 'Conditions Favourable to Faster Growth'. This elaborated on the theme of the 4 per cent growth rate which the NEDC had already set for the nation. It exposed the obstacles to economic expansion, including the serious lag in industrial investment, managerial as well as trade union short-sightedness, technical difficulties, the abysmal attitude on all sides towards modernised methods, the lack of proper industrial training systems and, of course, the problem of wages: 'There will be a need for policies to ensure that money, incomes, wages, salaries, profits as a whole rise substantially less rapidly than in the past.' It was, indeed, all there: spelled out perhaps in more closely related detail than before, but essentially it was the same basic message about Britain having fallen behind and the need for a new effort of cooperative national endeavour. Since Maudling's economic advisers and the NEDC staff had clearly worked in harmony it was not surprising that the Chancellor's first Budget was an ambitiously, and even audaciously, expansionist one. Yet the truth is that it was already too late to rescue the economy in any significant way. The investment gap between Britain and her principal European competitors had already become too wide. The catching-up operation was too late. In retrospect it can be seen that the missed opportunities of the late 1950s and early 1960s left the British economy exposed to increasing industrial weaknesses from which it has still not recovered. The expansionist boom from mid-1963 until October 1964, when the Wilson Government came into office, certainly injected a fresh glow of optimism into industry, encouraging a return to growth. New jobs were created in Scotland, the North

East and other depressed areas. But there was little planned modernisation, an absurd absence of investment priorities, no substantial attempt at the reshaping of managerial attitudes – all of which were needed to give British industry the 'technological' edge it so desperately required to face the challenge of the next decade. In a curious way Macmillan himself seemed to sense the inadequacies of his own Government, possibly even of his own traditional values. He noted in May, as the economic picture brightened and unemployment fell that, although the country's spirits appeared to lift, there was still a strange mood over the land. It seemed to him that the British people were: 'Becoming more and more cynical and satirical'.[8] He went on :

> I read a most depressing account, based on question and answer, of what the young intelligentsia are supposed to be thinking. The number questioned was 7,000 or so, the questions were detailed and very well devised. Religion, morality, patriotism, honour, all these are at a discount. Envy (although concealed) is a strong emotion and a rather doleful highbrow concept of a good time. How to appeal to this type is not an easy problem to resolve.

It was in fact, beyond him and his Government, to resolve that problem – and many others. He was increasingly becoming the butt of a scintillating leader of the Opposition : Harold Wilson found that the more he sharpened his claws at Macmillan's expense, the more impact he made. With remarkable swiftness and confidence Wilson established himself in an unchallengeable position as the new leader of the Labour Party. Anthony Greenwood, commenting on the new mood in the Labour Party, wrote in the TGWU journal after listening to one of Wilson's early speeches :

> As I walked out across New Palace Yard that night I reflected on how little is left of the old defence controversy which racked the party for so long and how far we have travelled on the road our union [the TGWU] pioneered. The new leadership, if it seizes the opportunity and realises that Labour must be a broad-based party, can develop the new unity and mobilize all wings of our movement for a great victory at the polls.[9]

As early as March 1963 the Labour Party's national executive was inviting the TUC General Council to set up a joint group for an 'exchange of views on economic policy matters'. The TUC appointed its six NEDC representatives to work with the Party leaders and discuss the kind of planning machinery they would wish to see developed under a Labour Government. The initiative for this joint enterprise had come from the Party's home policy sub-committee chaired by George Brown. He was already working on the general concept of a separate Ministry for Economic Planning, a depart-

8. Harold Macmillan, *At the End of the Day* (Macmillan, 1973), p. 408.
9. TGWU *Record*, March 1963, p. 40.

ment that could be hived off from the Treasury. He, along with Harold Wilson, was insistent that the TUC leaders should be brought into the discussions at the earliest stage. So the TUC's NEDC six joined Labour's 'inner group' of planners, a group in which Frank Cousins played a key role.

. If one were to search for a clearly identifiable point in the embryonic growth of the Ministry of Technology as well as the Department of Economic Affairs the spotlight would come to rest on that 'inner group' of Labour Party and TUC leaders who began detailed work in April 1963. Moreover, it was in this group that there emerged the first rumblings of doubt about the role of the NEDC under a future Labour Government – whether it would be better to centralise the whole economic planning operation, including trade union participation, within a new Government department (as George Brown preferred), or whether the NEDC should retain broadly its existing form (which both Woodcock and Cousins preferred). Parallel with this group Wilson had also formed an informal working party on science and technology and had given Crossman the job of organising it and building up a programme of work. Wilson brought in the famous physicist Professor Patrick Blackett (later Lord Blackett) who, together with Crossman, set about creating panels of scientists, academics and technologists to work on a draft programme for Labour's science and technology policy – the programme which laid the basis for Wilson's famous speech to the Labour Party conference at Scarborough in 1963. In the earlier stages Frank Cousins was only on the fringes of this science and technology group. He was not so much intimately involved as 'interested'. Wilson knew of his personal interest in technology and of Cousins's concern to help the Party to draft a policy on the modernisation of British industry. So it followed that when Cousins joined the Labour Party-TUC working party he immediately became much more closely involved. And, true to form, he spent some time at the first meeting criticising the papers prepared up to that point. He regarded them as too academic, not practical enough. In any event he seemed determined to make the point that the Labour Party needed to listen much more attentively to the voice of experience and practicality as embodied in the trade union movement.

It might be recalled at this stage that Cousins, who had been a member of a strong team of TUC leaders visiting Sweden the previous autumn, was greatly impressed by the close and quite unique relationship between Sweden's TUC and the Social Democratic Government. He was not an uncritical admirer of the Swedish system – he had strong doubts about the highly centralised and closely regulated system of industrial relations – yet he *was* impressed by the liaison between the Government's social and economic planning policies and the functions of the trade unions. He did not have any clear idea of how such a system might be successfully developed in British conditions, but the Swedish experience did a good deal to relieve his doubts about the potential value of an organisation like the NEDC. He envisaged that it might be used as an important vehicle to develop an integrated relationship on planning social and economic priorities under a Labour Government. At that stage, and later when he began work with the Labour Party-TUC joint committee, a number of possibilities began to take shape in Cousins's mind. The one thing that did not occur to him then was that he himself would end up as Minister of Technology in Harold Wilson's first Cabinet.

This was a period full of paradox. The TUC was seen to be cooperating, albeit through the NEDC, with a Conservative Government which, in the eyes of many people not necessarily dedicated to Labour, was in its final phase. How far should this cooperation extend? How much could leaders afford to be seen, publicly, to be playing a game of political wait-and-see? It was a period of tightrope walking and careful evasion, a period when the union leadership collectively was being drawn more closely into the inner sanctum of Labour Party strategy in preparation for the General Election, which was now only a matter of months away. The strongest speculation at that time was that Macmillan would choose to go to the country in the spring of 1964. Harold Wilson was working to that timetable in the first half of 1963. All of this made the TUC's position in the NEDC prickly and uncertain.

At the same time the unions could not simply mark time in the NEDC. They had to be seen to be constructive. The trade union 'image' had already been diminished in the public eye because of the strike record and the increasing 'indiscipline' on the shop floor. Yet when the Government began a dialogue on the subject of 'incomes policy' the TUC found itself in a dilemma. Woodcock in particular was in difficulties. He had always accepted as a basic premise that it would be necessary to devise some kind of incomes policy if inflation was to be controlled or higher unemployment kept at bay. His one absolute condition was that it must be a voluntary policy, the unions should be asked to undertake a voluntary commitment. But to begin work on an incomes policy under a Conservative Government was, as every member of the TUC General Council knew, quite out of the question with an election in the offing.

The Chancelor, Reginald Maudling, an astute politician, understood the TUC's dilemma but that didn't prevent him from doing everything possible to try to seduce the union leaders into a commitment. It was a time when the very phrase 'incomes policy' had begun to develop its own special fashionable flavour and mythology. Wage restraint as such was an 'out-phrase'; incomes policy was the 'in-phrase'. In practice both phrases almost always meant the same thing or, at least the instrument in mind was intended to achieve the same end – to reduce the pressure of consumer demand by some form of wage regulations, voluntary if possible, by statute if necessary. The variety of formulae was countless. And the Chancellor plainly saw in the NEDC an ideal platform from which he could test reaction and advance his case. Maudling, of course, was chasing an illusion and almost certainly knew it. What he did succeed in achieving was to get the subject debated more widely than ever before. Incomes policy became virtually an obsessional topic within the national dialogue on inflation. What 'technology' had become to the scientist and the industrialist, 'incomes policy' became to the economist and the industrial relations specialist, at all levels.

Frank Cousins was far from insensitive to this explosion of interest. His instinct told him that it was a minefield to be avoided. He was quite determined not to be trapped into a firm commitment – not by Maudling, to be sure, nor even by Harold Wilson or George Woodcock if he could possibly avoid it. As far as he was concerned the unions had to preserve their freedom of action *outside* the developing relationship with the State. He understood the logic of those who wanted an incomes policy, he was prepared to accept that a complete wages policy was inevitable in a collectivised system, but he would not tangle with a phrase such as 'incomes policy' (which he simply reread as 'wage restraint') so long as the trade unions had to operate within a market economy. It was a view Cousins took very firmly in 1963 – indeed, a view he had always taken – and it was something he never shifted from, even when the price of his conviction meant resigning from the Cabinet.

Woodcock had already discovered that Cousins had the classic built-in contradiction of all trade union leaders – the desire to keep Government at arm's length while, at the same time, pressing to exert an ever-increasing influence on Government policies and behaviour. It was the best-of-both-worlds view, an intellectual paradox, familiar to every government and trade union movement outside the Communist world. The paradox has become the single most difficult problem to be solved in trade union relations with the State in a democratic society. Fully collectivised systems have no such paradox – at least not openly (what happens below the surface is altogether another question). But in liberal democratic societies the relationship between the State and organised labour, especially in a country such as Britain with a long tradition of a *political* labour movement, is a frictional situation which must become more abrasive so long as the unions insist on keeping their distance. How to resolve the conflict, outside the development of a more collectivised socialist system, is indeed the most critical question for the unions and the State in modern times. It is at the root of the wages problem – though it is not, at root, a wages problem. It is a question of the management, as well as the production, of total resources. Sometimes 'incomes policy' has been interpreted to mean precisely that, but most times it has been used as a euphemism for wage restraint. The main issues are still unresolved and indeed may not be capable of any absolute resolution; only a slow, painful, but constant shift towards a new social and economic structure within which cooperative actions become the 'norm' offers positive hope. Even then it will be essential to accept the limitations of what is possible, sensible and reasonable if tyranny is to be averted. For whatever the name given to the political system there will always be areas of non-cooperation. But how is it possible to resolve the basic conflict of interest within a mixed, and essentially a market, economy? From 1963 till 1966 the problem haunted not only Frank Cousins but the whole Wilson Cabinet. It still hovers over the entire political scene – today more powerfully than ever.

In the spring of 1963, with the TUC playing a larger role both with the Government and inside the Labour Party's policy-making bodies, Frank Cousins was more relaxed, though his workload had increased vastly. His position inside the TUC General Council was stronger than it had ever been. Woodcock's friendship, the trust he had generated, gave Cousins a new confidence and a heightened interest in TUC affairs. Wilson's leadership in Opposition also inspired Cousins with a new belief in the Party's potential. At last he felt some positive direction, a distinctive shift away from the negative, desultory oppressive politics and policies of the past. At the union's Bristol festival in May Cousins announced that the TGWU had given £75,000 to the Labour Party to help in developing a propaganda and information service in readiness for the coming General Election. He spoke with unusual passion about the urgent need to unseat the Conservative Government. 'We want, we need and we intend to have a Labour Government', he told the meeting.[10]

Meanwhile in British Guiana Dr Cheddi Jagan's left-wing Government had come into open conflict with the trade unions. A general strike and a state of emergency followed the British Guiana TUC's rejection of a Government Bill, the implications of which could have led to direct Government interference in the conduct and perhaps the organisation of unions. The Bill would effectively have enabled the Government to influence, if not select, which unions represented groups of workers. There was a deep and bitter cross-current of political hostility between the Prime Minister and those who led the main unions in Guiana, men like Forbes Burnham. The crisis was referred to the British TUC, which for a long time had taken a close interest in the affairs of the then colonial territory.

On 23 May the TUC's Commonwealth Advisory Committee discussed the critical situation; it was told that the general strike could lead to the collapse of Jagan's Government, the suspension of the constitution and the abandonment of Government by elected representatives – at least for a

10. TGWU *Record*, June 1963, p. 34. The Labour Party had appealed to the unions to help raise £500,000 for a General Election Campaign Fund.

period. The TUC leaders agreed to take immediate action by sending out a special envoy as their 'ambassador' to help the two sides to find a solution. The man they chose was Frank Cousins. This indeed showed a remarkable change in Cousins's standing with his TUC colleagues. Plainly it was George Woodcock's wish that someone of Cousins's authority and power should be sent to British Guiana as an indication of how seriously the British viewed the crisis. Yet it was a strange twist in the wheel of fortune for Cousins himself. Here was the leading left-wing trade union figure in Britain, for years embattled against his trade union and political colleagues, now being sent out as the 'TUC ambassador' to try to resolve a crisis between a left-wing Government and the unions in a British colony. The irony was indeed too much to hold true for long.

In the afternoon of 30 May Cousins was at his home at Epsom Downs, Surrey, preparing to depart for Guiana. He had completed his packing and had a few hours to spare before leaving home for the airport. What better place was there to spend a few waiting hours than in the garden, the haven where he could always find relaxation as nowhere else? He was bending over his favourite bed of gladioli when Nance Cousins heard him cry out with a shrill, piercing yell. She found him collapsed, stretched out by the flower bed. Frank Cousins had suffered a severe coronary. Cousins was then 58, at the peak of his powers. Since becoming General Secretary he had worked ceaselessly at a pace that would have been beyond even the unusually dedicated. He was rarely in bed before the early hours of the morning and it was even rarer for him to rise later than 6 a.m. Most mornings he was at his desk before 8 a.m. But more than the sheer physical effort he had put into the job, the emotional strain of the long battles inside the TUC and the Labour Party had taken its toll. The doctors had little doubt that this stress contributed considerably to his heart attack, which was more severe than they at first admitted. A huge tear had occurred in one of the arteries, and possibly his life was saved by Nance's quick decision not to try to move him from where he had collapsed by the flower bed. He was there when the ambulance arrived. Any previous disturbance might well have precipitated further damage. It was indeed several days before he was removed to hospital. Meanwhile the doctors played it low-key by saying that Frank Cousins needed 'a rest for a month'. In fact it was two and a half months before he returned to his desk. He remained in hospital throughout the union's biennial delegate conference held at Scarborough in July, though he kept very much in touch with affairs.

The TGWU's executive was in session the week that Cousins had his heart attack. Indeed, on that very morning he was actively engaged in preparing for what he knew would be a vitally important conference. Cousins proposed that they should depart from traditional practice and actually invite a politician to speak from the platform in July! It was without precedent, but he wanted the leader of the Labour Party, described as 'Brother J. H. Wilson MP', to address the conference, 'having regard to the declared policy of the union to do everything possible to secure the early return of a Labour Government'.

Months later it was speculated that the decision to create an entirely new post in the union's hierarchy, that of Assistant Executive Secretary, arose directly as a result of Cousins's heart attack. That seemed a logical enough explanation, yet it was not true. Plans to establish this new post, to ease the burdens falling on the General Secretary and his assistant, were being discussed informally as far back as the middle of 1962, and the first formal move to create the job was minuted at a meeting of the union's finance and general purposes committee on 7 February 1963.

The crucial thing to appreciate is that Frank Cousins had already begun to consider his succession months before his heart attack, and a long time before he moved into Government. The case for a further appointment at such a senior level was strong enough alone on the grounds of workload, the expanding responsibilities of both General Secretary and Assistant General Secretary, and the union's developing character (with a membership at the turn of 1962–3 of 1,369,718). There was a clear need to have a national official at headquarters responsible for membership organisation, someone with a deep knowledge of union organisation in a range of industries, but especially in the growth industries where the membership potential was greatest. The idea had been put in Frank Cousins's mind by Alf Chandler a long while before formal discussion began with the union executive. The name of James Larkin Jones had also been mentioned at an earlier stage. He was an outstanding – perhaps an obvious – choice as a potential successor to Cousins. After all he had come within one vote of becoming the Assistant General Secretary nearly fifteen years earlier when Jock Tiffin defeated him – that was when Deakin decided Jones was unacceptable on political grounds. His ability and his record of achievement for the TGWU were not questioned even by his staunchest political, or personal, critics, of whom there were quite a number in the union's hierarchy. For 16 years Jack Jones had remained in Coventry as District Secretary until, early in 1955, he was appointed trade group secretary to the engineering and chemical section in Region 5 (the Midlands). A year later he became Regional Secretary — the principal post in a key area.

In over six years Jack Jones's impact on trade union affairs in the Midlands had been almost as profound as Frank Cousins's impact at national level. The two men shared much common ground in their political thinking. They also shared the common experience of having been specifically selected by Arthur Deakin for disfavour. They shared the belief that the TGWU had languished for far too long under the old hierarchical structure and needed to give the rank and file much greater opportunities for self-expression. They were personal friends who had shared family holidays. When it became known that Cousins was proposing a new national post and that the eventual holder would be cast as a sort of 'Number Three' in the hierarchy, the gossip quickly spread that Cousins was grooming his successor. Nor was it surprising that this same gossip suggested – well ahead of any nominations – that his name would almost certainly be James Larkin Jones.

On 30 April, a month before Cousins's heart attack, nine names were short-listed, but it wasn't until 21 August, a week after Cousins returned to work, that the final stage was reached. Cousins wanted to be certain he was present when the final decisions were being taken and he had already been told that it would be August, at the earliest, before he was fit enough to return to the union. The original intention had been to make the appointment in June, so that the new man could be 'presented' to the biennial delegate conference in July. But that could not be, in view of Cousins's illness. None the less, very few observers or senior officials at that Scarborough conference seriously doubted that Jack Jones would be the chosen man for the role. And very few doubted that, once chosen, he would become heir apparent. Harry Nicholas, nearly the same age as Cousins, was unlikely to succeed – unless Cousins died some years before retirement, or, as it was sometimes mooted, he joined a Labour Government at some future date. The prophets were right. Jack Jones was appointed to start his duties as Assistant Executive Officer on 7 October.

It was an unfamiliar Transport Union conference without the figure of Frank Cousins stalking through the hall or commanding the delegates to march with him in a crusade. He had, in three previous delegate conferences, turned the TGWU into 'The Cousins union'. He resented and rejected that description, but it stuck. His absence from Scarborough in July 1963 was as much a talking point among delegates and observers as anything the conference itself debated. Would he return quickly? Would he be mellowed, or still an angry rebellious figure? Would he be tempted to join a Labour Government if Harold Wilson won the next election? If so, what would happen to Harry Nicholas – or the 'new man'? The speculation was endless and invariably wrong.

Cousins himself had planned to give the conference the theme of 'modernisation'. He viewed the rise in unemployment as something more fundamental than a routine cyclical recession. He believed it represented a deeper shift in the structure of British industry resulting from increasing technology and new patterns of social and economic demand. With these developments he was convinced there was an urgent need for the unions to rethink and reshape its own policies and practices. He was persuaded, partly as a result of his experience as a TUC representative on the council of the Department of Scientific and Industrial Research (DSIR), that the technological potential already available to industry was frighteningly large, and that the unions were in serious danger of being overtaken by events unless they matched their attitudes to the pace of industrial change – both real and potential.

The experience he had gained as a member of DSIR had a quite profound influence on Cousins's later thinking. Perhaps it was an inspired move by Lord Hailsham (Quintin Hogg MP) when, as the Minister for Science and Education (ironically, a kind of precursor of Cousins) he invited the TGWU leader to join the governing council of DSIR. The Hailsham invitation came at the end of 1960, a date of significance because it was shortly after Cousins's victory over Gaitskell at the Scarborough Party conference. Clearly it reflected the anxiety of the Macmillan Government that the H-bomb uproar might conceivably escalate beyond the customary proportions of public protest. The Hailsham offer was certainly more to do with that than with the Government's fondness for Frank Cousins. It seems highly probable that the Government was trying, indirectly, to woo Cousins to the DSIR. As Hailsham has told the author, it upset many of them – and even upset some Cabinet Ministers – that a rebellious, left-wing socialist who had given the Government so much trouble should now be invited to join such an important group as the DSIR which, apart from other things, handled secret material on defence. Indeed the DSIR was one of the most important public advisory committees available to the Government. But Hailsham insisted on going through with his choice. The DSIR already had one representative from the TUC – the right-wing leader of the Steelworkers' Union, Harry Douglass; what he required was a balancing view from the Left. That was another reason why he wanted Cousins. And he won the approval of Macmillan on the grounds that such an appointment would inevitably expose Cousins to the 'problems' facing the Government in the field of scientific and industrial development – in the area of defence as well as civil affairs.

Cousins's DSIR experience in the next two years became an increasing fascination to him. Science and technology had always held a compelling attraction for Cousins. It extended to his appetite for science fiction, to astronomy, and even, in some respects, to his sometimes wistful search for a quasi-mystical explanation of life. There were many ingredients in Cousins's interest in technology. Hailsham's invitation – always assuming it was *his* original idea – certainly bore fruit, though it did not seduce the TGWU leader from his convictions about nuclear disarmament. What it did do was to confirm his interest in scientific development and give this interest a new form. It certainly convinced Cousins of the need for widespread social and economic reforms to realise and to control the technological potential he now knew to be available to society if society chose to use it. The question for him was, how is society to cope with this challenge? More precisely, how should the trade unions react? He was planning to try to answer some of these questions at the biennial delegate conference in 1963.

That conference was not, however, given over entirely to the theme of how to modernise British Industry, let alone trade union attitudes. As with any other union conference the agenda read like a catalogue of everyday basic concerns : wages, jobs, houses, schools; what happens during sickness or after a factory injury; prices, living standards, pensions – the whole panoply of ordinary problems. Yet there was a difference. The theme of change, inescapable, widespread and far-reaching change, was dominant. It was presented as a kind of *'charter-for-change'* by Harry Nicholas on the second day, and he faithfully sought to reflect the views of Frank Cousins. 'The charter' was also a prospectus of hope and aspiration. More leisure, not just to be measured by shorter working hours or longer holidays but, as Cousins had suggested shortly before his heart attack, perhaps a shorter working year. The creation of new opportunities for working people to enrich their lives and experience by extending it a dimension beyond the assembly line, the factory and the work-machine. Nor was that all : industrial change, automation, technology, whatever the label given to the new uprooting process, would need altogether new social horizons : an integrated, national system of industrial training and retraining for new skills, no matter what the age of the displaced worker might be; the overhaul and modernisation (perhaps even the scrapping) of the old apprenticeship schemes; a new scheme for redundancy payments and job replacement, and a national plan to provide housing for workers who had to move because of industrial change. The charter was, in that sense, a new social and political design spelled out in the matter-of-fact terms of everyday life rather than the rhetoric of socialist theory. That was in fact how Cousins interpreted the image of the future he glimpsed in the crystal ball.

Nicholas offered it to the Transport Union conference in 1963 as a programme that could guide the union's industrial policy in the years ahead and, hopefully, form part of the foundation on which the trade unions would be able to build in cooperation with a Labour Government. It was imaginative enough. Perhaps Frank Cousins would have given the charter a larger charisma, perhaps someone, searching for the inevitable slogan might even have christened it 'The Cousins Charter'. It matters not. As it was, Harry Nicholas presented the scenario with sincerity, expertise and logic. There was nothing lacking in the argument.

It was all painted in against the background of Harold Wilson's speech to the conference on the opening day. He offered a 'partnership' between the trade unions and a future Labour Government based on an implicit deal – that the unions would work within the terms of some form of incomes restraint policy in exchange for an extensive programme of legislation for the radical reform of Britain. It is hard to tell whether the implicit message was clearly understood, perhaps it was. Certainly several delegates later repudiated the idea of wage restraint, whether it came from a Labour

Government or a Conservative Government. Yet, that speech contained all the main ingredients for the conflict which was to explode later in the 1960s. Wilson asked specifically for trade union cooperation in wage restraint – promising, at the same time, that a Labour Government would seek to restrain *all* incomes, not merely wages. He asked for a curb on unofficial strikes, a reduction in restrictive practices and an altogether new spirit of cooperation from the unions. In return, he pledged that a Labour Government would attack the profiteers, the tax avoiders, the property speculators. It was indeed, a social contract in premature form, long before the name had been extracted from Rousseau, and put in the context of 1974. In fact it was a speech regarded, even then, as possibly the most important Harold Wilson had delivered to the trade unions since he became leader of the Labour Party.

The omens were not picked out at the time. In any event, no one quite knew what was meant by an incomes policy, it meant so many different things to different people and different pressure groups. It certainly implied wage restraint. Yet in what form, and through what institutional machinery, was still unclear. The unions would certainly not tolerate any revamped NIC being introduced by a Labour Government. Harold Wilson knew that; he promised that the NIC would be abolished and that the NEDC would be used more actively as a kind of powerhouse for 'socialist economic planning'. Nor was there at that stage any thought of introducing the paraphernalia of statutory incomes control. It was all going to be done by brotherly negotiation; a common purpose was to inspire unity of action. There were sceptics who were dubious about these lofty ideals and – some silently reflected – naïve hopes, but they kept quiet. The harbingers of gloom were rarely to be heard, nor at this stage often to be seen.

Meanwhile Frank Cousins, recovering from his heart attack, was making it clear that he would attend the Trades Union Congress in September. And George Woodcock was busily preparing a 10,000 word document on economic planning which was to force the whole issue of pay restraint into the open in an unexpectedly dramatic manner. In a sense it was prompted, if not inspired, by the TUC's experience so far in the NEDC and particularly by the first NEDC report. The Woodcock document dealt with the entire spectrum of economic planning, its likely impact on the existing industrial structure and on trade union attitudes. It examined in great detail the implications of planning and industrial change, whatever Government was in power. And it discussed, carefully but courageously, the most sensitive area of all – the problem of prices and incomes policy. Woodcock's document in effect echoed the warnings of the original NEDC document: that wages could not possibly be separated from the processes of economic planning. That was an inescapable, but none the less unpopular truth.

The Woodcock document, officially known as the TUC Supplementary Report, was issued shortly before the Brighton Congress and, predictably, it caused a great stirring in trade union dovecotes. The Congress agenda already contained several motions flatly opposed to any form of wage restraint the most specific coming from the Boilermakers' Society. None the less Paragraph 40 of the Supplementary Report included this sentence :

> The General Council accept the view expressed in the NEDC report on Conditions Favourable to Faster Growth that it is necessary to ensure that money incomes as a whole [wages, salaries and profits] rise less rapidly than in the past and to find a solution of the difficult problems involved in a policy for prices and money incomes.

This was perhaps an unfortunate choice of phrase, though that was really beside the point. Paragraph 40 was condemned at many preliminary meetings of delegations as a piece of political stupidity. The argument was that it offered a golden opportunity to the Conservative Government to fasten wage restraint on the unions. The Paragraph led to a series of blazing rows (not all of them behind the scenes) between Cousins and Woodcock, rows which came nearer endangering their friendship and trust than anything before or afterwards.

Woodcock regarded Paragraph 40, as indeed he viewed the whole report, as a statement of the obvious. The report had been widely praised in the Press as one of the most impressive and constructive documents to emerge from the TUC since the war. But Frank Cousins was uncertain about his reaction. In general he was impressed by the report, but he was dubious over Paragraph 40, and he harassed Woodcock at the pre-Congress meetings of the General Council by demanding clarification. Was it tantamount to saying that the TUC was ready to cooperate with the Government in accepting wage restraint? If not, what *did* it imply? Cousins was anxious not to split the Congress on wages policy. Along with the rest of the TUC leadership he believed that this Brighton Conference would probably be the last before a General Election. They wanted to prepare the ground for a Labour Government, yet at the same time to avoid falling into an incomes policy trap that a Conservative Government could exploit.

At first Cousins opposed motions from other unions, such as the Boilermakers', calling for a clear and unqualified declaration against any form of wage restraint. Then the AEU decided to oppose the report because of the offending paragraph. Other delegations havered and hesitated; Cousins himself began to shift towards a more precise stand – in opposition to Woodcock. He had not wanted to be the first to precipitate a public demonstration of boat-rocking. Now this was becoming unavoidable. Indeed he was chided by his left-wing friends and allies on the TUC General Council, Robert Willis, and John Newton, for his hesitancy and his readiness, even eagerness they suspected, to compromise. Their view was clear from the start – outright opposition to even the mildest suggestion that the TUC would cooperate in any policy of wage restraint. During the weekend leading up to the Brighton Congress, as union delegations began to line up on either side of Paragraph 40, the gulf between Woodcock and Cousins widened perceptibly.

The Congress was scheduled to debate economic policy on Wednesday, and the fight against Paragraph 40 went on up till the eve of that debate. On the Tuesday night Woodcock, under increasing pressure from Cousins to amend it, yielded to a compromise; it was rewritten to replace the offending sentence on wage restraint by a soporific passage which neither satisfied, nor offended, anybody. It read:

> As the NEDC recognised a policy for prices and money incomes could succeed only if everybody concerned was convinced that it was a necessary part of a wider programme for the growth of real incomes, and that restraint by one section of the community would not merely result in a gain by other sections. One of the necessary factors in economic growth must, indeed, be an expansion of real purchasing power. To restrain real increases in wages and salaries could defeat such a programme. Equally to allow prices and profits to rise unchecked would undermine the foundations of a policy of planned growth. As a part of any such policy it would moreover be essential for the NEDC to re-examine the present inequitable distribution of the nation's wealth, with which it has so far dealt only inferentially when discussing the pattern of taxation.

Whatever the revised Paragraph 40 meant (and who could say?), it clearly did *not* accept wage restraint. In the lead-up to its revision Woodcock and Cousins clashed several times during that Tuesday, at one point openly in front of the TV cameras. It was primarily pressure from Cousins that persuaded Woodcock to retreat. It was unprecedented for a TUC report of that importance, already nominally approved by a vote of the General Council, to be amended before presentation to the Congress. Woodcock was rebuked by the right wing of the General Council for allowing himself to be (as they put it) 'browbeaten by Cousins', they described him, not without malicious intent, of being a 'prisoner of Cousins'. Woodcock shrugged philosophically. Inwardly he was disappointed and saddened by what had happened, but he was nevertheless determined not to make an enemy of Frank Cousins. It was more important to retain Cousins's support, Woodcock believed, than to score a victory on a point of principle that might have the TUC policies in ruins. It was Woodcock's conviction that unless he kept Cousins's trust the General Council would inevitably be thrust back into the negative, sullen postures that he faced when he became general secretary. It was worth an amendment to Paragraph 40 to prevent that.

For Woodcock, as for Cousins, the build-up to the debate on Wednesday had become a psychological problem, as much as anything else. Every delegate was tensed to witness the two giants in open fight. The TV cameras, now filming every minute of the Congress were poised for the impact. Woodcock's two speeches, one presenting his report and the second winding up the debate, were among the most emotional I ever heard him give. But emotion apart, his presentation of the case for economic planning and his lecture on the implications for the unions made his speeches rank alongside the best ever given from a Congress platform. How, he asked, are the unions to tackle the enormous problem of wage discipline? How are they to fit in with the requirements of contemporary planning? What can they do to help? These questions were posed with a candour and an honest search for truth – as they might well be posed again today. He said :

I am appalled not only at the practical difficulties of any attempt to move from generalities to practices. Believe me I am also as conscious as any of you of the fearful injustices of this society of ours, of the contrast between working people and people who get their living in other and easier ways. I am also, if I may say so, sometimes appalled at the injustices between different groups of workpeople as well . . .

Woodcock accepted that any interference in the sacred right of free wage bargaining was entirely foreign to the union way of thinking. Trade unions, he agreed, were in the business of wages. That was what they were there for; it was why they were created.

Yet, he suggested, perhaps the unions had 'concentrated too much on wages', too little on the wider implications of their changing role in a society that was itself going through considerable changes. In the conditions of 1963 they could not escape the fact that wages had to be considered an integral part of the whole economic planning process.

Do you think that this is a problem created by a Government of a political complexion; it is not. It is created by these circumstances, intensified, if I may say so, as a problem of wages by the fact that today in 1963, and for some time, the Government do assume the right to interfere in economic and industrial affairs and acept the responsibility for doing it. That is a very different thing from the situation before the war. And if the Government have responsibilities can we say to them that they have no right to the tools, to the means of fulfilling their responsibilities? Can we deny them a view? Well, I personally doubt it . . .

The message was repeated in various forms. If the unions wanted the Government to intervene in economic affairs, to introduce planning commitments, to have a view about social and economic priorities, then it was right that the Government (of whichever political party) should ask the unions for a matching commitment. That was Woodcock's logic. It never changed. It was a logic which he hammered at throughout his term of office and which, though it resulted in such limited responses, nevertheless laid a basis on which the central institution of British trade unionism is still trying hard to erect a meaningful structure.

For much of Woodcock's *tour de force* he seemed, often, to be arguing in the direction of one man – the General Secretary of the TGWU, who was sitting with his delegation in the body of the hall. 'Don't erect a prohibition', cried Woodcock, both fists clenched and thrust forward as he stared towards Frank Cousins. And, finally, rather in the style of Gaitskell's 'fight again' speech in 1960, Woodcock reflected on the likelihood that motions rejecting any form of pay restraint would be carried overwhelmingly :

> All I say today – I have said this before and I say it again – is that I am not, though the two things are related, very much concerned with votes. Whether you pass this Supplementary Report or not to me matters less han the impression I shall have at the end of today as to what we of the TUC should be doing in October, November and December of this year and in the months that follow ...

How did Frank Cousins react to this major – and it *was* a *major* – challenge from Woodcock? He did so by repudiating the concept of wage restraint so long as trade unions operated within a market economy. It was his most powerful and most illuminating warning to the Labour Government, which was to come into office a year later. A warning that he would not accept formalised restraints on the freedom of the unions – not even from a Labour Government. But what of the trade union role in planning, particularly in relation to the NEDC?

> There are people who think that planning for the use of the resources of the country can be done through the instrument which we are not attempt-to use, the NEDC, I think the NEDC has done useful work. I do not think it is the instrument which will determine trade union attitudes'.

He chided Woodcock's reference to the trade unions having 'left Trafalgar Square' for the committee rooms of Whitehall, and he reminded the Congress that he, for one, had not left Trafalgar Square. Had he not been there quite recently on another mission – against the Bomb? And then he went on to wages :

> I say again to you, from my union, they will not allow me – and I would not ask them – to be part of the same kind of procedure that we were under during the last Labour Government when we adopted a statement about

incomes, profits and prices and every one of us went our separate ways. When we have achieved a measure of planning and a Socialist Government and, if I have to say to my members, 'We must now excercise restraint' I will say it and when I say it I will mean it.

George says we want to influence Governments . . . I am not conceited enough to think that they are influenced by what I say. I think they are influenced by the power of the people I represent. When I talk to the Government about the London dockers, the country dockers, the country busmen, the factory workers and the road haulage workers they are much more influenced when I am saying the things my members want me to say. We will not have wage restraint, whoever brings it and wraps it up for us.

That final sentence, delivered with the vigour and vehemence of a Cousins apparently at the peak of his strength again became a classical reference in the months ahead. Even at the time it was interpreted far and wide as a warning not merely to Maudling and the Tory Government, but Harold Wilson as well. Cousins, however, insists that the warning was specific to the Conservative Government of the day. He claims he was reflecting an irritation at the way that Maudling had sought to ensnare the TUC members on the NEDC into an acceptance of an incomes policy which could well have damaged Labour's electoral prospects. Frank Cousins believed that if he had not taken the stand he did at the 1963 Congress, then many General Council members might have been prepared to do a deal with Maudling through NEDC. 'There was very much of a wish to have an incomes policy among some members of the TUC at that time,' Cousins claims. It was a wish by no means confined to Woodcock.

Yet Cousins's critique of incomes policy and wage restraint was clearly wider than that. Those who regarded his warning shot in September 1963 as a portent of things to come were not wrong. He was consistent. He had always opposed a 'wages trap'. He remembered his own bitter experiences in the late 1940s under Arthur Deakin, during the wages freeze of the Attlee Government. He sometimes wavered under the logical force of the case on economic planning. He *did* recognise the cogency of the argument that wages could not be excluded from the planning process. But unlike Woodcock he was essentially, perhaps primarily, a political animal. He was not a philosophical one, nor, for that matter, simply a trade union leader in pursuit of wage increases for their own sake to the exclusion of all else. He believed deeply that to compromise the freedom of the unions, within the present social system, was to diminish a fundamental political strength which working people had forged. Increasingly the paradox of absolute sovereignty for trade union collective bargaining within a process of expanding State intervention in economic affairs was to baffle, torment and confuse the logicians. It was to torture Frank Cousins in the years to come. As he always claimed to me : 'You cannot make incomes policy work outside a firm decision by

367

Government to make it work. And that involves virtually a dictatorial Government.' That was the view he consistently upheld when he became a member of Harold Wilson's Cabinet in the autumn of 1964. So, for all Cousins's qualifications about the meaning of his 1963 warning, it was certainly a signal to Harold Wilson as much as to Maudling and Macmillan.

The outcome of the Brighton Congress (and it was the most important and most self-searching TUC debate on wages policy since the Conservatives came back to power) was a vote to face both ways. The amended Woodcock report was approved by 7,474,000 to 629,000 (the Boilermakers, in consistency, voted against it), and the Boilermakers' own motion condemning 'any form' of wage restraint was passed by a wafer-thin majority – 4,283,000 to 3,903,000. The six largest unions split evenly on this vote, with Frank Cousins supporting the Boilermakers' motion as well as the Woodcock report. Cousins insisted that he supported the Boilermakers primarily because Ted Hill gave a pledge from the rostrum that his 'total opposition' referred only to the position under the Conservative Government. 'I don't trust the Tories', he growled, but he declared his readiness to support a plea for wage restraint from a Labour Government should Harold Wilson ask for it. That sanctified the issue for Frank Cousins. It failed to impress George Woodcock, who took the sceptics' view that the unions would almost certainly behave no differently under a Labour Government, no matter what they said in open Congress. He was to prove right.

Cousins had no illusions about the scepticism that was rife after the Brighton Congress. In his union journal the following month he offered a long explanation of the meaning that he attached to his phrase about rejecting wage restraint, 'whoever wrapped it up'. Again he insisted that the reference was specifically directed against the policies of the existing Government. Under other circumstances, he then asked, 'Will trade unionists be able to assert that everything else can be planned except wages? Our answer must obviously be "No". We would expect a Labour Government to raise this question with us in precisely this way.' He went on :

> Unfortunately the situation which faced the trade union movement at Brighton was far different from this. An atmosphere had been created in which it was being said that by accepting the General Council's document [ie the Woodcock report] the unions were accepting wage restraint under the present circumstances. Such a misconception had to be removed . . .

Under different conditions, with a Labour Government in power armed with a policy to alter the structure of society, things could be different. Even so, Cousins argued the problem of wage control was an exceptionally complex one :

There is a somewhat glib assumption that wages are easily controllable if workers are reasonable and the trade unions are 'statesmanlike' or 'responsible'. Anyone with an intimate knowledge of how wages are made up in industry knows this to be far from the truth.

The unions themselves and others who advise us how we should conduct our affairs must remember one important thing, frequently lost sight of, the source of our power, authority and influence is in the membership. If we do not fulfil the purposes for which members join unions, to protect and raise their real standard of living, then the unions will wither and finally die. We can give leadership, we can persuade, but basically we must serve trade union purposes.

The knowledge that every trade union leader must take his members with him gives final emphasis to one very important point. Methods of wage determination can only change drastically as the system does. If Governments want the unions to alter the style of wage bargaining they must prove to us – and to the members – that the new system will be fairer than the present one, that there is the intention and the means of establishing better results than at present. When that is made clear to us, there will be no hesitation on part of the trade unions for full participation – but such a situation does not exist now. That is attempts to control wages in the middle of an uncontrolled system in which the Government has sponsored the ideas of free enterprise and 'every man for himself' have been rejected and must fail.

That article was a carefully prepared statement of Cousins's views. It expressed all his misgivings and his doubts about *the feasibility of wage restraint, even under a Labour Government.* It remains just about as good a reflection of the inner-conflict within the Labour Movement as one can get. It illustrates the dilemma inherent in the trade union role and yet it begs all the questions. For even if it is possible for a censensus to be reached, and for the leadership, including all the varieties of socialist thinking, to accept a policy of wage restraint, it still remains for them to secure their members' acceptance, and to *maintain* that acceptance. To go beyond that point leads inevitably into restrictions on personal freedom and choice, and at once to amend the entire function of a trade union. The union becomes an instrument or an appendage of State (or community) policy. Its role changes, and its members are no longer people with a choice to join or not to join; that becomes almost irrelevant. Inescapably, the union is moulded into an arm of executive authority. This may be a perfectly logical and even legitimate role for it to play in a collectivist society, but it is not the same as the role of a representative democratic body, able at least to reflect the irrational as well as rational views of ordinary people. Here there is – and there has always been – a primary dilemma. Socialist theory has been able to avoid it – but not to resolve it – only by insisting that a fundamental conflict of interest between workers and their production relationships no longer exists once 'socialism' is established, and the means of production, distribution and exchange have been socialised. Experience has taught differently. There can be and there is conflict between labour and labour. It may or may not be 'fundamental', but it is there and it has to be resolved. It can be resolved by representative institutions operating within a different order of values, or it can be resolved by bayonets and prisons. It cannot be wished away. The conflict is as old as the hills and as fresh as the computer, it explains much of the failure of the Communist countries, and it burns at the root of much of the perpetual frustrated attempt of social democratic Governments to resolve the 'crisis of wages and inflation' within market (or mixed) economies. It is the heart of the matter. No one need be surprised that neither the TUC nor the Labour Government could produce a magic formula for ending their conflict in 1963, or 1964, or the years that followed. They continue to struggle for an answer.

For all this, the main focus of Harold Wilson's attention as he moved towards his first conference as Labour Party leader was not the abstractions of incomes policy. Other factors were exercising his fertile mind. He remained convinced that the 1963 annual conference would be the last before a General Election which, he still believed, would take place in March or April 1964. He did not think the Conservatives would risk waiting until later because of the uncertain state of the British economy (beginning to expand again, but on very shaky foundations) and because of the fatigue of the Macmillan administration – a fatigue that had become plain to the whole nation, especially to senior civil servants, who felt stultified by the inertia of the political scene.

Harold Wilson's major preoccupation from the middle of 1963 had been to prepare the ground for a Labour Government which, with increasing confidence, he believed could emerge from the soon-to-be-held election. Nothing could be left to chance. Much detailed planning work required to be done. The structure as well as the policies of his Government needed to be sketched out – and speedily. He asked Richard Crossman to take charge of a large area of this activity and in particular to start work on policies and ideas for completely new departments of science, higher education, and technology (although at first this was not specified as a new and independent department of state). Wilson himself had been chairman of the Labour Party's NEC sub-committee on science and industry before he became Party leader. He handed that job to Crossman. All this was well under way by mid-1963. In addition to Wilson's (and Crossman's) own programme the home policy committee of the Party's executive was also involved with the science, technology and economic planning syndrome. The Party's head of economic research, Peter Shore (not yet an MP) was busily preparing a paper on 'Labour and the Scientific Revolution'. I make these points simply to illustrate that the Wilson speech at Scarborough in 1963 was not something dreamed up in the few weeks between the TUC and the Labour Party conferences but a carefully prepared strategy. Gradually Wilson drew together the threads of all this work and began to shape it into a theme – the theme which he unveiled at Scarborough. It was against this backcloth that the Labour Party leadership then sketched in their policies for economic planning social priorities – and, ultimately, incomes. All other issues were to be slotted into the larger framework of a grand new design for the modernisation of Britain.

Behind the scenes in the private meetings of various groups, socialism itself was being given a new set of scientific skis. Or so they all believed. At a meeting of scientists organised by Crossman in June 1963 – with Wilson present – the talk concentrated on the role of the economic planning departments. The Department of Economic Affairs was already in embryo. Wilson mused that it might be necessary to downgrade the Treasury's role and the post of Chancellor,[11] Professor Blackett proposed a new department, a king of super-Ministry for Industry that would have the powers and functions of the wartime Ministry of Supply. He envisaged that it would be responsible for the development of science and technology throughout the private sector. Blackett's original memorandum to Wilson, 'The case for a Ministry of Technology', submitted in mid-1963, may well have been the founding paper for that new department of state. At that early stage, however, Wilson was uncertain about the functions to be allocated to the various new departments in embryo. Even so it was a combination of Blackett's promptings, his paper and the work of the Crossman group that laid the foundations for Wilson's Scarborough speech.

Since becoming leader of the Labour Party Wilson had seen a good deal of Frank Cousins, though their meetings had been interrupted by Cousins's illness. The two men established a 'close relationship' of sorts, though they were certainly not intimate friends. 'Close relationship' is a phrase that is difficult to assess in political life. Such alliances can spring up rapidly from sparse enough roots and disappear equally swiftly. In the case of Wilson and Cousins it was a relationship they both welcomed because they both needed it. Cousins desperately needed someone at the head of the Labour Party with whom he could work and in the relationship with whom there were no traces of old, even if forgiven, bitterness; Wilson, no less desperately, needed a reliable ally in the trade union movement, preferably an ally without commitments to union orthodoxy – who better than Frank Cousins? It does not lessen the quality of their relationship to underline their mutual need for it. Yet perhaps it encouraged both of them to assume too readily that a mutual commitment was implicit in the very nature of the relationship. Cousins saw in Wilson the basis for a completely new start in Labour

11. Richard Crossman, the unpublished diaries, 26 June 1963.

Party policy. There was a tendency for him to idealise the 'new era', much in the way that Wilson accepted Cousins's 'changed attitude' towards an incomes policy as a guarantee for the future. Cousins took Wilson seriously on the issue of science, technology and the industrial restructuring of Britain, he believed that a Labour Government under Harold Wilson *would* strive with muscle to achieve that grand design. For his part, Wilson saw the partnership with Cousins as a crucial talisman for trade union cooperation across a broad spectrum of policy – most of all, over incomes policy. Cousins did not encourage Wilson to believe he would be instrumental in supporting a policy of wage restraint, but he had a tendency to use phrases about the 'positive' aspects of incomes policy which gave Wilson some encouragement. On the eve of the Scarborough conference, for instance, the TGWU agreed to support a motion from the General and Municipal Workers which set out a six-point-programme on economic planning. It proposed a National Industrial Planning Board to guide development towards a planned economy, and Clause 4 (!) of that motion accepted the need for 'an incomes policy to include salaries, wages, dividends and profits (including speculative profits) and social security benefits'.

Cousins supported this – though there was much arguing and dissension behind the scenes before he did so – and commented to the Press on the eve of the conference: 'This resolution expresses general endorsement of the idea that an incomes policy is a social problem and not merely a wages issue.' There was great ambivalence toward any reference to the fateful phrase 'incomes policy'. It was an ambivalence by no means confined to Frank Cousins, though he was blamed then, and has often been blamed since, for his capacity to camouflage by his words what was really happening in his mind. Frank Cousins's mind was in fact quite clear and firm; he would *not* support a policy of wage restraint, whatever it was called and whoever wrapped it up. I recall his insistence to me at this same Scarborough conference that those journalists (including myself) who had been implying that he had accepted the implications of an incomes policy (in the then conventional meaning of that phrase) were quite wrong. He had not. Yet he was ambivalent and no doubt even selfdeluding in assuming that he could skim the surface of the wages swamp by talking, as he did during the economic debate at that conference, about his readiness to support 'a planned growth of wages' under a Labour Government. That was the phrase Cousins used to gloss over the controversy of incomes policy. It became a famous and much debated phrase in the months ahead. In support of the GMW motion moved by the General Secretary Jack Cooper Cousins made this important declaration of intent:

There is no difference in attitude in this conference about what we mean. We mean we want a planned economic rate of growth which will enable us to have improvements in our real standards of wages. And why do we mean this? Because it is attitudes and intentions again, I repeat, that we are talking about [shades of George Woodcock!] You cannot define the detail of a policy in a conference; everybody knows that. You can only define attitudes towards problems that exist. There is nobody here who can say what a level of wages is for an individual worker or the comparison between two groups of workers or the relative importance of a collective group of workers to the community. We do not determine *them* here, we determine them over board room tables, we determine them sitting opposite the employers; and we shall continue to do that until such time as the system changes to ensure that we do get a better rate of return for the labour that we put in, and nobody has any doubt about this.

Just to make sure that 'nobody' did have any doubts about what *he* meant (indeed, what he said was almost a repeat of his speech at the TUC) Cousins then spelled it out quite clearly in his peroration :

Harold Wilson knows this, Harold says this every time he gets the opportunity. He is wanting to be part of a team that is going to change the system, and the function of a trade union will change along with a change in political function; it is bound to do. I would suggest to you that one of the things we should always remember is that when we are putting a government in, as we are intending to do, to help us to plan the economy, we have the trust that it is the same kind of economy they are helping to create . . .

That became one of the principal problems when Cousins went into Cabinet, only to discover that *his* concept of a 'planned economy' was not 'the same kind of economy' as that of the majority of his colleagues. But in the halcyon days of autumn 1963 there was still trust. There was a conviction that general prespectives were sufficiently parallel. Cousins had doubts; of that there is no question. Yet he felt he was justified in offering hostages to fortune, even if the hostages were such dubious and deceptive labels as the 'planned growth of wages'.

Before the Scarborough conference, and after the Brighton TUC, Cousins and Wilson met to discuss the whole area of their thinking. Wilson explained his anxieties about wages policy; Cousins repeated his refusal to give any commitments he could not later redeem. Industrial restructuring loomed large in their discussions. Scientific and technological development mattered greatly to Cousins and he had already convinced Wilson of his profound interest in that area. One issue inevitably rolled into another. At one lunchtime meeting between Wilson and Cousins Richard Crossman noted in his diary that he was fascinated to study the relationship between the two. The main purpose of that lunch, Crossman wrote, was to 'discuss our science statement and ensure that Frank would give it his full support'.[12] This is a bit churlish of Crossman, since he failed to add that Cousins had already played a substantial role in helping to shape the final draft of the Party policy on science and technology – the draft which became the basis of Wilson's Scarborough speech. After all, Cousins was a member of the Party sub-committee from which most of the text emerged. It would be easy to claim on the basis of all this – the relationship between Cousins and Wilson, the concentration on science and technology and the relegation of wages policy to a role within the process of industrial change – that it was the period when the Ministry of Technology was born and when Cousins was being enticed to join a Wilson Cabinet. Yet this is not the case. It took many more meetings after Scarborough, much gentle pressure and persuasion and, most of all, agonising heart-searching by Cousins before he finally consented to enter Parliamentary politics. It would be absurd to suggest that the thought had never entered the heads of Wilson or Cousins by the autumn of 1963, when they were as close to each other as they were ever to become, yet the truth is that the idea was not specifically mentioned until the summer of 1964. By that time there had been a great deal more heart-searching by Cousins, his family and a few of his closest friends.

What an extraordinary contrast the scene presented at Scarborough 1963 compared with Scarborough 1960. It was hard to believe that only three years had passed since the Labour Party hovered on the verge of fratricide, or three years since Cousins and Gaitskell were locked in an unforgettable struggle over nuclear disarmament, a struggle that seemed to have immobilised the Labour Party as an electoral force. Who, then, could possibly have predicted such a transformation? Through 1960 and into 1962 Macmillan's Government appeared immovably strong. The de Gaulle veto on Macmillan's application to join the EEC seemed to signal the turn in the Conservative fortunes. Later in 1963 the Tories, already faltering, were rocked by a series of blows, including personal scandals like the Profumo affair, from which they never really recovered. By the end of the year Macmillan had gone, retired to his Sussex retreat, and Home was in the stop-gap role of spinning things out until he was sufficiently established to call a General Election. At that point very few would have offered high odds on a Conservative victory.

There was no precise turning-point. There rarely is, though politicians and journalists like to believe in them. Turning points are convenient dots on historians' charts but they are seldom accurately placed. The change in the affairs of the Labour Movement was a slow, and we have glimpsed, a largely fortuitous sequence of events. Some were predictable and quite

12. Richard Crossman, the unpublished diaries, 25 September 1963.

explicable in terms of political analysis, but many were guided far more by chance than by the formulation of political science.

None the less, the temptation to select a turning point, to place a dot on the history chart, is overwhelming. And it is overwhelming here because there is one obvious selection: Harold Wilson's speech about the 'white heat' of technology at the Scarborough Party conference. This was indeed the strongest and most confident voice to be heard from the Labour Party since it had begun to repair the damage of a decade. Everything in that famous speech reflected a Harold Wilson who was convinced – and was in the act of convincing the nation – that he would soon be leading a Labour Government. It took the nation by surprise after the stylised Edwardian languor of the fading Macmillan era. This was as much an emotional experience for the nation as a political signpost. But it worked almost as if by magic. Clearly it did the trick, if indeed tricking was the requirement or even the intention.

The country wanted, and needed, a message of hope. The British wanted, and needed, to be reminded that Britain still had a future in spite of the endless frustrations that seemed to haunt the post-war attempts to make the best of their uniquely talented though persistently maligned nation. At Scarborough Wilson offered hope to Britain in a new kind of mix; science, technology, and the new emotional impulses in modern society, blended together to form the yeast for a radical political programme. He displayed, brilliantly, the world map of technological change and development, the dangers as well as the opportunities. 'These facts', he told the conference, after reciting the vast catalogue of existing and potential change, 'these inescapable facts put the whole argument about industry and economics and Socialism in a new perspective.'

He also set out his programme for transforming the machinery of Government itself, for introducing new Ministries into Whitehall and injecting into the civil service the serum of technological change. The new departments of state would include a separate Ministry for Disarmament, one for Higher Education, yet another for Science. There was no specific reference to a new Ministry of Technology. But it was there already in spirit.

Frank Cousins knew it was there in spirit, but he did *not* know how the spirit would be translated into bones and marrow. He heard Wilson use a phrase that he himself had quoted to the Party leader some time before, an observation from Swift's *Gulliver's Travels*:

Whoever could make two ears of corn or two blades of grass to grow upon a spot of ground where only one grew before would deserve better of mankind and do more essential service to his country than the whole race of politicians put together.

The Wilson speech galvanised the Labour Movement, and also made a profound impact on national politics. It put Wilson on the road to Downing Street. Crossman noted in his diary that Wilson had scored a 'great triumph'. He added that Wilson 'had provided the revision of socialism, the application of socialism to modern times, which Gaitskell and Crossland tried to do and had completely failed. Harold had achieved it in *that* speech.'[13] Cousins's responses to *that* speech were in the same lyrical vein. He was fulsome not only in praise of Wilson but also of the theme Wilson had chosen to illustrate the message of modern socialism in Britain.

'I think it is a great thing that we are taking science as our main theme,' declared Cousins, speaking third in the general debate that followed Wilson's *tour de force*. Paying tribute to Wilson as well as to the subject, he then added the warning that it was not enough simply to pay lip service to the message of science. For, he asked, with a touch of rhetoric, what after all is science? He answered himself in this way:

> To many people it is different things. It can be the basis of those little thriller stories that you can buy in science fiction; it can be the background in which the terrible weapons of destructions are created; it can be many other things. To me it means this: it is a vision with its working clothes on, nothing more and nothing less. We know what can be done but whether we give effect to it depends whether we harness the thing, whether we make it applicable to the kind of world we want.

Cousins referred to his own experiences on DSIR, and the fascination the whole subject had for him:

> I went on DSIR with a great deal of trepidation, because it is a body in which scientists and chemists and technologists sit with us. It was thrilling; it was great to listen to these men talking about the possibilities. It was paralysing to see the limitation of opportunity that comes because the dead hand of monetary control comes over it . . .

He spoke like a schoolboy newly introduced to the mysteries of science; his enthusiasm was so manifest that it became infectious, as indeed Wilson's enthusing had infected him and many others. Cousins genuinely believed that the next Labour Government, equipped with this conception of the role of science, would be able, and certainly willing, to extend the frontiers of socialism across the land, and to play a significant role in similarly influencing world developments. He did not want to welcome the new technological age into Britain only to see it produce mass unemployment and fear, as had happened recently in the United States:

> We are not willing to be guided into a new world where half of the people do not even get the benefits of this world. We want a new world where

13. Richard Crossman, the unpublished diaries, 8 October 1963.

training and skill is done for the benefit of assisting any change into a new order. Therefore let us remember that along with the scientists there are the craftsmen, the non-craftsmen, who have to be trained to fit into this new world order. I am sure Harold made this quite clear. They were thinking, when they talked of applicability of science, that this covers a whole range of people, fitting them into a new social order with science as its background.

The cry of 'a new social order' was heard far and wide that week. It was echoed and re-echoed in the debates that followed, in the criticisms of the way that men like Dr Beeching had handled the modernisation of British Railways; in the way that a future Labour Government must tackle the problems of an integrated transport system; in discussion of a new concept for the social services, for housing, for education. The white heat was kindled, to be sure. Or so the delegates in Scarborough believed.

It was now only a matter of time till the General Election. Parliament would have to be dissolved by the autumn of 1964. But with Macmillan gone the chances of a rapid election earlier in the year, as Wilson expected, began to recede. Not that Frank Cousins was waiting with uncontrollable impatience for the election to begin. There were other things to do. And although he had quite recovered from his heart attack and had plunged with all his old vigour into both the TUC and Labour Party conference, he had not yet followed his doctors' advice to take a rest and a holiday. After his return to Transport House in August Cousins had worked non-stop. With the Labour Party conference behind him he went in early November to Yugoslavia with a TUC delegation, the first official TUC visit to a Communist country since the breakup in 1949 of the World Federation of Trade Unions (WFTU) and the formation of the International Confederation of Free Trade Unions (ICFTU). It was a visit Cousins was determined not to miss, so he postponed any thoughts of a rest or a holiday. The proposed trip had already come under fire from the American unions, especially from George Meany, the President of America's TUC (AF of L-CIO), who believed that the British trade union movement was breaking ranks and undermining the anti-communist work of the ICFTU. It was, moreover, general knowledge that George Woodcock wanted to use this visit as a 'pathfinder' mission to break the ice in the cold war of international trade union relations. Woodcock saw the Yugoslav trip not only as interesting in its own right (to study the Yugoslav system of workers' councils) but also as a possible prelude to visits to the more 'orthodox' Communist countries in Eastern Europe, and indeed to the Soviet Union. Cousins supported him completely; indeed he encouraged him. And although it was to take some years before the visits were extended, that mission to Yugoslavia broke the deadlock in East-West trade union relations.

When Cousins returned to report to his union executive meeting at the beginning of December, he was told that the finance and general purposes committee had recommended in his absence that he should take 'an extended period of leave of absence' so that he could recuperate 'entirely free from the cares of office'. Shortly before Christmas Frank and Nance left for a holiday in the West Indies. They returned in February 1964, in time for the union's executive meeting at the beginning of March. At the end of that meeting Cousins was seen to be back in absolute command as well as full health. After his first day he called a Press conference to announce that the union's membership had reached a new peak of 1,412,603 at the end of 1963, an increase of 42,885 in the year. It was, Cousins reported, the fourth successive year that the union had achieved a record membership. And this had been done at a time when trade union membership in general was *not* rising. The next day *The Times* reported that Frank Cousins was back to 'his old form as his buoyant, emphatic, confident self. Mr Cousins stepped sprightly on to the rostrum of Transport Hall with a confidence that would not have disgraced Cassius Clay. The impression he made was indisputably that here was Britain's most powerful trade union leader, strong and sun-tanned, and ready for another bout.'

The 'bout' was still more than seven months away. When it came it was in a most unusual, if not entirely unexpected, boxing ring, where the rules of the game were utterly different from anything Frank Cousins had previously encountered.

Chapter Twenty

TOWARDS THE NEW
SOCIAL ORDER

HAROLD WILSON : If there had never been a case for Socialism before, automation would have created it ...

FRANK COUSINS : We want a new world where training and skill is done for
the benefit of assisting any change into a new order ...

(Extracts from their speeches at the Labour Party conference, Scarborough
1963)

Thus spoke the hopefuls of yesteryear. However, it is not for anyone to sneer
at such observations. By most rational standards, certainly by any radical
ones, both statements can stand the test of time. To recall the age in which
they were spoken is to give added emphasis to the impulses behind them.
If we search for that magic dividing line between the recent past and the
modern present (which, to be sure, is a line that may even exist!) what
better place is there to draw it than at the moment Harold Macmillan left
the political stage with a reluctant wave and a superbly sad smile? Perhaps
he, too, sensed it was the end of an epoch. At any rate his illness and his
departure, however painful, probably came at the right historic moment.
He had become confused if not bewildered by the strange behaviour patterns
of a new age. It was not just the actions of colleagues who had been getting
involved in sordid sex intrigues or, worse, deliberately misleading the House
of Commons; it was the whole panoply of new-fangled nonsense which
bemused the old gentleman. Yet, in another sense, he tended to appreciate,
if not to understand, the emotional undertow rather better than most of his
Tory colleagues and, perhaps, some of his socialist critics. He recognised that
he, for one, was not 'with it', that 'change' was pervading the fabric of British
life with, as he viewed it, a certain tastelessness, a lack of style. What to do

about 'change' and, assuming one knew, how to go about doing it, appeared to him as a vast political conundrum.

Science, technology and modernisation – all of which were frequently lumped together under the convenient if inaccurate label of automation – comprised an obvious and appealing formula. It seemed the right thing for the British to get acquainted with. Yet there was so much mystique surrounding the clichés that common sense was often obscured. Neither Right nor Left in British politics had any clear notion of how to tackle these impulses for change. The Left was better attuned to what was bubbling beneath the surface; it was philosophically more equipped to interpret the signals of a quickening national pulse. But it had its blind spots, just as much as the Right. On the Left, as everywhere else, there was intellectual rigidity and emotional conservatism. The trade unions were no better than any other sector in responding quickly or with imagination. Intuition? Yes, there was that. Instinctive reaction to the shift of opinion, to the change in habits, to the smouldering fires of new expectations, to the questioning as well as the questings of young minds? Yes, there was often enough a surprisingly healthy instinctive response to all these impulses within some of the unions. They had been reflected in the 1950s, perhaps clumsily, sometimes falteringly, by a new generation of officials rising to the top – most of all, by Frank Cousins. And they were being reflected again in the 1960s, with more conviction and more organised power. After nearly a decade in office, a period dominated almost entirely by his struggle to disentangle trade union thinking from past myths and its own defensiveness, Cousins now began to feel that there was at last a remarkable opportunity for further advance.

He somehow felt that industrial modernisation, by its very nature, would compel fundamental changes in the organisation of British Society; that the changes already taking place in the struggles of industry, powered as they would be increasingly by scientific innovation and the need for capital resources beyond the means of conventional capitalism, would bring nearer the day of socialism in Britain. He was enough of a Marxist to believe that the growth of technology and the rise in working-class living standards and opportunities would not erode the 'need for socialism', as some claimed, but would, in fact, provide a necessary foundation for it. The vision was there, even if the blueprint was not. For neither Frank Cousins nor anyone else on the Left in the Labour Movement had sat down to work out a precise political and economic framework; nobody had faced up to the contradictions and complexities involved in trying to transform the system into a socialist one. They sensed that a 'new order' was arriving and that this must inevitably expedite progress towards socialism, but no one knew quite how this was to be achieved. To be sure, the old conventional methods and relationships were going, and few of the old rules applied. By the mid-sixties the 'great awakening' in shop-floor awareness had established strong roots, though the certainties of established thinking, established disciplines, established authority and social relationships were all in a state of flux. The epoch of the grand illusion seemed to close with Macmillan's good-bye wave. The entire social and political climate seemed to be poised beside a huge question mark. What had the future to say?

The attractions of vague terms such as 'technology', 'science', 'a new order', were therefore tempting and often overwhelming. The reality behind them was obliging politicians, industrialists and union leaders to think in broader political and social dimensions. And to socialists they appeared to offer a path towards real power – a path that had so far eluded them in the liberal democracies. The road to socialism seemed to be paved with computers. By some alchemy of electronic magic – it was even contemplated – capitalism itself, and its social mores, might be undermined not by class war or revolution but by the inevitabilities of science and the demands of industrial modernisation, forcing economic and political change on a hitherto unthinkable scale. Up went the slogan that 'we are all marxists now'. It was a beguiling thought. 'Socialism through technology' became the password. Perhaps it still is.

The British economy was already in a state of quite rapid change by 1964, a year which seems to have marked a particularly sharp increase in the trend towards industrial restructuring, mergers and rationalisation. The profit margins of the largest companies were under strain, partly because of the intense competition in foreign markets, the lack of capital to invest in modern equipment that could have helped them to match foreign competition, and the growth of militancy behind wage demands.[1] Yet much of the underlying economic sickness was concealed by the return of boom conditions. It seemed that the upswing was again likely to help the Conservatives, even though Maudling did not use his Budget overtly to inject a further transfusion of credit into the system. His actions were, in fact, quite restrained, though not restrained enough to correct the growing balance of payments deficit. Maudling's objective was one of Budget neutrality in a difficult and uncertain period of international trade. In any event it was calculated that it would be politically as well as economically unwise to indulge in financial gymnastics this side of the election announced for the autumn by Home, Macmillan's successor. At the same time Maudling (without much conviction) and the NEDC office (with much more dedication) sought to make headway toward a prices and incomes policy. But these efforts collapsed when a group of Britain's main employers' organisations rejected, as unworkable, any idea that a profits and prices policy could be traded off with the unions in exchange for a wages policy. It was the final blow to any

1. See Andrew Glyn and Bob Sutcliffe, *British Capitalism: Workers and the Profits Squeeze* (Harmondsworth: Penguin, 1972), pp. 54–64.

surviving hopes of achieving an agreed prices and incomes policy before polling day.

This collapse occurred in March, a month before Maudling's Budget. It was followed by increasing signs that the major employers were preparing their defences against the likelihood of a Labour Government just as strenuously as the trade unions were building up their aspirations. Maudling continued to harbour some hope that it might just be possible to get some sort of agreement with the TUC, but by midsummer he had given up. By then wage settlements were being made well in excess of the Government's $3\frac{1}{2}$ per cent directive. It was the London busmen who again snuffed out the 'guiding light'. After much pressure from the busmen a court of inquiry was appointed to arbitrate on their claim and the inquiry awarded substantial increases beyond the Government 'norm', paving the way for other big settlements in the public sector. Meanwhile the local elections, as well as the opinion polls, gave evidence that the country was swinging substantially to Labour.

Throughout this period Frank Cousins continued to make speeches against any policy of wage restraint under 'the existing system of society'. At the same time the twin themes of automation and new technology crept into every speech he made. At Oxford in June he said :

> It is not the intention of the trade union Movement to hold back its members' wage claims if they are justified. It is our purpose to sell our labour and our skill in open market to the best of our ability while we live under the present system.[2]

Occasionally, as at Oxford, Cousins would depart from the theme of industrial modernisation and wages policy to talk about international affairs. He referred specifically to apartheid in South Africa, not only condemning the regime – as he had done often before – but also announcing his readiness to support wider protest measures in Britain. The TGWU had recently contributed £1,000 to the South Africa Relief Fund (in November 1963) and, according to Canon John Collins, Cousins was the principal figure in the trade union movement seeking to help, and inspire others to help, the South Africa Defence and Aid Fund which Cannon Collins ran. During March Cousins was interviewed by the *Sunday Mirror*, which published a series of three articles in what must then have ranked as the most extensive coverage given to the views of a single trade union leader by a national newspaper.[3] In this series Cousins again explained his general philosophy and his attitude, not merely on wages policy but on the whole sphere of trade union relations with Government and industry :

2. TGWU *Record*, August 1964, pp. 32–4.
3. *Sunday Mirror*, 15, 22, 29 March 1964.

The unions are foraging in the world in which they live. If the world is going to change they will change with it. But they cannot change in order to change the world, particularly if one recognises the reactionary anti-trade union attitudes which still exist in some quarters.

Inevitably, of course, there will be a change in our functions as our status in relation to both Government and employers changes. If we become part of a central planning body we have to accept the responsibility of assisting in the determination of what an economy working at full pressure can stand – in addition to getting the economy up to full capacity. The unions can, and do, help to bring in the new measures which will create the scientific and industrial revolution.

At the end of these interviews Cousins reflected on his own personal future. Would he be tempted into a future Labour Government?

I made my choice a long time ago. Before the war when I was just starting as a trade union officer I was offered a Parliamentary seat which would have been safe through the worst setbacks which could have befallen the Labour Party. But Ernie Bevin's advice was that young men ought to stay with the union to follow his generation. I took that advice and have never regretted it.

There have been other opportunities since and I have still turned them down. As general secretary I have an important task in the political and trade union structure of this country. I think I am useful here and I have no wish to be Foreign Secretary, Minister of Defence, Chancellor of the Exchequer or anything like that. This is the only worthwhile job for me.

Why did Cousins change his mind?

There were many accounts at the time, and the explanations one hears even now are full of contradictory certainties. Cousins says he was not finally persuaded until the last minute at the end of the election campaign in October when he and Harold Wilson shared the same eve-of-poll platform at St George's Hall, Liverpool. It was fortuitous that he happened to be there, fortuitous that he stayed on with Wilson into the early hours of the morning of polling day, Thursday 15 October, when a tired but confident Wilson entertained him at the Adelphi Hotel. At half an hour past midnight Cousins went up to Wilson's room. That was where it was settled. I recall him leaving the hotel lounge where he was drinking with a group of journalists who had been covering Wilson's election tour, including myself. When he came down to rejoin us, perhaps an hour later, he knew he would be Minister of Technology if Labour secured a majority. Not Foreign Secretary, Minister of Defence or Chancellor – but the job that really attracted him, really persuaded him that he was doing the right thing.

We will return to the Adelphi in due course. Now we must, once again, turn back the clock a few months.

The truth is that by the time Cousins walked into Wilson's room in Liverpool in the early hours of that Thursday he had already been sufficiently pressured and persuaded. The lead up had began in the early summer. At first he resisted Wilson's promptings and proddings. He refused to give any commitment. But he was visibly arguing with himself as well as with his family and close friends (including Michael Foot and Jack Jones). He was arguing in particular with Nance. She was against the idea from the beginning, and she never wavered from that view. She was not simply against him joining a Labour Government; she believed most vehemently that his real role (an infinitely more important one in her view) was to remain General Secretary of the largest trade union in the country. To Nance Cousins *that* job was more important in the fight for socialist policies than a Ministerial seat in Harold Wilson's Cabinet.

The first precise invitation came to Frank Cousins early in July when he dined with Harold Wilson. The Labour Party leader suggested a variety of possible jobs including a brand new department he was proposing to set up – the Ministry of Technology. (According to Crossman's diary, Wilson told him that he was now committed to a seperate Ministry of Technology. He proposed to separate this new department from Education and Science and Economic Affairs.[4]) Cousins immediately showed his interest. The idea of starting this from scratch, charged with the sponsorship of helping to modernise British industry had an immense appeal to Cousins. Yet even at that early stage Wilson cautioned that it would be a difficult task to start such a department; he sought to dampen Cousins's enthusiasm, because he did not then favour Cousins for that particularly challenging role. Wilson urged him to think about it and they talked about other possibilities such as the Ministries of Transport, Housing, Labour, even the Board of Trade. Still, that was not the real issue from Wilson's point of view. He wanted to interest the TGWU leader in the concept. To Wilson the important thing was to involve Cousins in his Government, to secure a commitment from the leader of the country's largest union – a leader, and a union, that could be a serious embarrassment as a rogue elephant if Labour won the election. The Wilsonian techniques of flattery – by no means falsely offered – were on full display. Harold Wilson told Frank Cousins that he wanted him in the Cabinet as a 'man of strength'. He wasn't interested in any other trade union leader; it was Cousins he wanted and Cousins he was asking for.

The next month they met again, this time in the Scilly Isles, where the Wilson family were taking their traditional summer holiday. Frank and

4. Richard Crossman, the unpublished diaries, 19 December 1963.

Nance Cousins went there from their old farmhouse at Godolphin Cross, in Cornwall. They had bought the house cheaply after Frank's heart attack. The idea was that it would be a rest-home retreat, perhaps even a place to which they would both retire. In August the Wilsons invited the Cousins's to spend a day at their house in the Scillies: again the pressure was on for Frank to join a Wilson Cabinet. This time the Party leader frankly stated that it was essential, in his view, to have a senior trade union leader in the Government; he repeated that the man he wanted was Frank Cousins. But perhaps the hint was there that if Cousins refused, then Wilson might consider someone else. How could he refuse? Cousins pondered the problem. He had stated publicly that he would not leave the TGWU to enter politics. He had given private undertakings to friends within the union that, to him, the TGWU was his prime concern. How could he go back on such promises? It was not only against his character to do so; it was also against Nance's advice (and, he reflected, she was usually right). And yet – how could he refuse the tempting bait Wilson was offering? He was tormented and torn. He stalled.

Wilson understood Cousins's dilemma. He argued that the union would understand the need and the urgency of the call from a Labour Government. It had happened in Bevin's case. After all, Bevin also had always dismissed the idea of going into Parliamentary politics. He had always put the TGWU above all else. Yet, Wilson observed, when the call came during the war for Bevin to enter Churchill's war Cabinet Bevin changed *his* mind. The contemporary situation for the Labour Movement, Wilson claimed, was no less urgent. It was already clear that a Labour Government would probably inherit a serious economic crisis; no one outside the Cabinet and the senior civil service knew the extent of that crisis but, Wilson told Cousins, it was evident that it would be grave. Labour, even with a big majority, would face a very difficult task. It was essential in such circumstances to have people of strength like Frank Cousins in the Cabinet.

Who in the end could resist such blandishments? Nance Cousins tried to. She continued to urge Frank to turn down the offer, alluring though – as she conceded – it was. Family meetings took place at which John (by then a full-time official of the TGWU, since his appointment on 14 October 1963) sided with his father. During the weeks that followed the meeting at the Wilsons' Scilly home Cousins debated and argued with his family and a handful of friends (again including Michael Foot, who believed he was right to accept Wilson's invitation) – but most of all with himself. John Cousins recalls one critical moment in the family debate shortly before the election campaign began. His father summoned John and his then wife Joan to the family home at Pine Walk, Carshalton Beeches. 'He brought out a bottle of whisky, put it on the table and said: "Come on, we've got to decide now whether I accept Harold Wilson's invitation or not." I never remember him having done anything like that before. He and I thought he should go into the Government, but my mother and my wife thought he should not.'

Frank Cousins himself has told me about those pressurising weeks:

> I was persuaded perhaps against my better judgment that it was the thing to do. Along with almost everybody else [in the Labour Movement] I was firmly of the opinion that we were going to tackle things like the re-distribution of wealth, the extension of public ownership, and so forth. Of course, Nance was always against my going in, but I don't regret it. I don't think we would have had any justification for our later arguments against income policy if it could have been said, 'Well, we asked you to join but you refused. Now don't blame us because we didn't succeed.'

He was convinced that he might be able to exercise some decisive influence inside a Labour Cabinet. Inevitably he reflected on Bevin and Bevin's influence with Attlee. Could he, he wondered, be 'a Bevin' to Wilson? At any rate he believed he could do 'something useful' in a Labour Government. By the time the Trades Union Congress arrived, in September, Cousins was vir-tually – though not yet wholly – convinced that he ought to accept Wilson's invitation. George Woodcock recalls a conversation with Cousins even before Cousins's heart attack in 1963 in which he told the TUC General Secretary that Wilson would like both of them to join a Labour Government. Accord-ing to Woodcock, Cousins was inclined, in a rather casual manner, to accept the idea even at that early stage. Though again, Woodcock says that when Cousins returned from his recuperation holiday in the West Indies (February 1964) he seemed to 'have lost interest in the notion'. Certainly when the two men were in Yugoslavia in November 1963 I recall them discussing with each other the possibility of both going into a Labour Cabinet. It may have been casual, light-hearted, speculative ruminating, but there was an edge of seriousness about it – though Woodcock was adamant that he would not accept a post in a Labour Government. (The job of Chancellor had been vaguely canvassed as a possibility for him.)

Speculation about Frank Cousins emerged again at the Durham Miners' Gala on 18 July 1964 (which was *after* Cousins's dinner date with Wilson). According to George Woodcock's account (which he had from George Brown)[5] Cousins told Brown that Wilson wanted him (Cousins) in a Labour Government as 'the principal Economics Minister'. This may have been an impish remark designed as much to incite as to inform George Brown. It certainly succeeded in achieving the former. According to Woodcock, Brown was furious. Immediately after the Durham Gala he challenged

---

5. Frank Cousins's appearance at the Durham Miners' Gala of July 1964 was excep-tional. It was exceptional for the miners to invite the leader of another major trade union to speak at their 'Great Meet'. The platform usually was reserved for NUM leaders plus prominent Labour politicians.

Wilson on the Cousins story. It should be remembered that by this time Brown had been designated by Wilson for the job of Economics Minister of the proposed new Department of Economics Affairs. For a year Brown had worked with great diligence on plans for such a Department. The vision of all this disappearing because of a private Wilson-Cousins deal exasperated Brown beyond words, as well it might. But Wilson told him to calm down; Brown had misunderstood Cousins. Nothing of the sort had been offered to the TGWU leader.

Woodcock carries the story a stage further by suggesting that the guessing game continued up till the day after polling. At an election victory party in Transport House on 16 October the issue of who would do what again arose. Woodcock's account is that Cousins left Brown with the impression that they were to 'run in harness' as the two chief Economic Ministers. In effect they would share responsibility inside the Cabinet for the general sweep of economic strategy, thus demoting the role of the Chancellor, who was to be James Callaghan. Brown (according to Woodcock's version) told Cousins bluntly that he had no intention of 'sharing responsibility' with Cousins or anyone else. He saw the new Department of Economic Affairs as the principal vehicle for the Government's economic strategy. Again Brown went to Wilson to seek reassurance, and, apparently received it. In recalling these events George Woodcock's point is to underline his belief (at the time and now) that Cousins was being 'bought off' too cheaply and without proper guarantees. Woodcock also believes that Wilson's purpose was to disarm Cousins by bringing him into the Government. Once in, he was trapped. The TUC General Secretary says he warned Cousins this would happen and advised him not to accept Wilson's invitation. But when these matters were being discussed between Cousins and Woodcock, principally at the Blackpool TUC in September, it was almost certainly too late for Cousins to be dissuaded.

The Trades Union Congress in September was in fact little more than a preliminary canter to the General Election campaign although Woodcock was at no time over-enamoured of the idea that it would be turned into a pre-election rally. He feared this could have embarrassing side-effects on the politically 'neutral' white-collar unions and the civil service organisations in the TUC. He even objected – no doubt with tongue-in-cheek – to a motion on the agenda urging the unions to do 'everything possible to ensure an electoral victory for the Labour Party at the forthcoming general election'. The motion remained on the agenda, but it was left until the very last moments of the Congress, when it was moved, seconded and with only one further speaker carried by a shout. By then the 'non-political' unions had fled, anyway.

Harold Wilson had been invited to address the Congress, an invitation no one challenged. He spoke on the afternoon of the first day, setting the tone for the entire week. He re-echoed some of his themes from the technology speech of 1963 but, more specifically, he referred to the legal confusion that had arisen that year over trade union law following the Rookes v. Barnard judgment. He pledged that a Labour Government would clear away this confusion and restore to the unions the full protection of the 1906 Trade Disputes Act. The Rookes v. Barnard case had been trundling through the courts since May 1961 when Mr Douglas Rookes won £7,500 damages on the grounds that he was unfairly dismissed by British Overseas Airways Corporation under pressure from local officials of the Draughtsmen's Union (now named TASS and a part of the AUEW). The Barnard in this case was Mr Alfred James Barnard, a union official.

The case became a classic one involving the closed shop.[6] It went to the Appeals Court, which reversed the Rookes judgment, but on a further appeal to the House of Lords, Rookes was vindicated and in January 1964 the Lords ordered a new trial to decide the question of damages. The whole issue struck at the roots of the protection which trade union officials believed they had under the 1906 Act. The law appeared to be in utter confusion and the TUC, demanded Government action to clarify the position. The Government refused to act. An unsympathetic Minister of Labour (Joseph Godber) told the TUC that the Government believed the unions were exaggerating the implications of the Lords' ruling. The TUC didn't think so, nor did an unusually furious George Woodcock. So Wilson knew he was on firm ground when he pledged at the Congress that a Labour Government would 'legislate to put this matter of legal interpretation beyond all doubt', a comment that drew the strongest applause of any passage in the speech.

At the same time Wilson said he did not see any particular need for a Royal Commission on the Trade Unions (he was to change his mind later) – a solution 'which will take minutes and waste years'. What he did see was the need for a great partnership between the unions and the Government (the phrase he had first used at the TGWU conference in July 1963). 'We shall be partners in a great adventure,' he promised the Congress. 'We shall consult – and I mean consult, not present you with a diktat; we shall listen and we shall say what in our view the national interest demands.' Pointedly he then switched to incomes policy, recalling the decision at the 1963 Party conference to support such a policy. He reminded the Congress :

Every major organisation here today is on record as supporting a policy of planned expansion of incomes related to the country's rising productivity. A Labour Government will ask for this to be made a reality . . . We have the right to ask for an incomes policy because we are prepared to contribute the

---

6. It was not, in strict legal terms, a closed shop dispute but rather one involving charges of conspiracy against union officials and the right to threaten and organise strikes. It so happened that the central issue *was* 100 per cent union membership.

three necessary conditions. First an assurance of rising production and rising incomes so that the sacrifice, the restraint, for which we ask is matched by an assurance that it will result in increased production and increased rewards. Second, an assurance of equity and social justice in that our policies will be directed to the benefit of the nation as a whole and not to the advantage of a sectional interest. Third, an assurance that what we ask for in wages and salaries will apply equally to profits and dividends and rents.

It is hard to see what more Wilson could have done to spell out the need for an incomes policy, or to stress more precisely that a Labour Government would expect the unions to redeem their promises and resolutions. At the end of his speech he was given a standing ovation and the Congress sang 'For he's a jolly good fellow'. The election campaign of October 1964 had begun. So, too, had the next Government's problems.

One of the most significant features of the wages debate in the middle of that Congress week was the silence of the leaders of the major unions, except for the late Leslie Cannon of the Electrical Trades Union (EEPTU), who warned of the complexities involved in trying to work out an equitable incomes policy. His warning against complacency when faced with 'a task of this magnitude' was noted, though no one seriously took up his point. Pre-election euphoria was already taking over. The motion on economic policy, planning and wages ran to 392 words; it was an extraordinary omnibus motion which covered everything, but meant little. It embraced the acceptance of incomes policy but was hedged around with so many qualifications that it was hard for any union, however sceptical, to object to it. And it was brilliantly moved by James Mortimer of the Draughtsmens' Union, who offered the Congress a superb lecture on socialist economic priorities. Frank Cousins did not speak in that debate, nor did George Woodcock. Indeed Cousins's main speeches at that Congress were on industrial training (in which he urged the need for a completely new approach, with Government sponsored training centres), and on trade union structure. It was left to Woodcock, near the end of the Congress, to bring the proceedings to life by unexpectedly throwing out an invitation, to whichever Party came into office after the election, to hold an inquiry into the unions if it wished. 'We have nothing to hide. I am prepared to explain trade unionism to anyone in this country.' It was not only a bold challenge – it was, no doubt, also a shrewd political move, since the Conservative Party had already declared itself in favour of appointing a Royal Commission on the trade unions if it won the election. Woodcock's open invitation clearly helped the Labour Party. It is likely that Labour would have suffered from any trade union resistance to an inquiry at a time when there was a good deal of public alarm at the growing power of trade unionism and the growth of unofficial strikes. So it seemed that even Woodcock had been drawn into the political scene. Indeed, in his winding up speech at the close of the Congress the TUC General

Secretary actually committed himself publicly to suporting the return of a Labour Government:

> I am sure that you will have a Labour Government. I will not use Congress at any time for electoral purposes but I will say, speaking now as the general secretary of the TUC and not as a politician that I really hope there will be a Labour Government because I do think that if the present Government are returned this time they will be insufferable . . .

But Woodcock warned the Congress that the election of a Labour Government would involve a real challenge: the unions would be called on to respond to economic planning. It would, he said, no longer be a matter of 'shouting of slogans'. The pressure would be on; the pressure 'to get things done'. By that he meant incomes policy; he meant a trade union commitment to accepting social and economic priorities; he meant all the things that, as he recalled, were so immensely difficult for the unions when the Attlee Governments of 1945–51 grappled with crisis after crisis. Woodcock said he would be 'interested to hear the speeches next year' if a Labour Government was elected. He was rewarded for his insight and his scepticism; they were indeed interesting.

Yet that was no moment for philosophising. Woodcock was wasting his breath. The unions were eagerly awaiting the close of thirteen years of Tory rule: and who could blame them? In the TGWU *Record* that month Jack Jones wrote a panegyric on Harold Wilson in reviewing a new paperback on the Labour Party leader.[7] Jones referred to Wilson as a great leader not only with a 'brilliant mind but also a deep human understanding'. Of course there would be problems to face; Jones mentioned incomes policy and suggested:

> some of us may have reservations as to how such a policy could effectively be achieved in the short-term without strong socialist measures, but all of us will be with Harold when he says, 'We have got to have planning for expansion not just one year in every four but steady purposive planning year in and year out.'

The TGWU gave a further £25,000 to the Labour Party's election fund, bringing the union's total contribution up to £100,000. Nothing was spared by the union in its enthusiasm to secure the election of a Labour Government. Cousins had given a pledge that the TGWU would throw everything into the fight, and he was now redeeming that pledge. He joined with Harold Wilson in writing pre-election campaigning articles in the October issue of the *Record*. In fact Frank Cousins had planned a speaking tour for himself during the election campaign, scheduled to reach a climax in Liverpool at

7. TGWU *Record*, September 1964, pp. 3–5.

an eve-of-poll meeting on Wednesday 14 October. He kept that date, but a crisis in the docks upset his plans for a speaking tour.

Exactly two weeks before polling day Cousins was forced to intervene in a dispute over dockers' pay. The dispute was already threatening to become an explosive issue in the election campaign and, if allowed to develop, might well have had a devastating effect on Labour's prospects. A national claim for an extra £1 5s. a week had been submitted for the nation's 65,000 dockers, and the port employers had responded by offering precisely half the amount. Unofficial dockers' leaders were already active in demanding 'action' to fight the employers, election or not.

The whole issue was complicated, as always in docks disputes, by left-over problems from earlier unresolved disputes – the industry's wages structure (a jungle of differing rates), the lack of proper welfare amenities, the whole question of decasualisation, the irregularity of the industry and the deep malaise in industrial relations throughout the ports. Added to this was the old and seemingly intractable problem of those ports like Liverpool where thousands of dockers were either in a rival union, the Stevedores – an inheritance from the troubles of the 1950s – or were in no union at all. Thousands of still disgruntled, lapsed members of the TGWU were working in the Merseyside docks without a union card.

Cousins had another crack at this hard nut by going to Liverpool on the night of 5 October in the hope of being able to rally support for the TGWU and its policies in pursuit of better wages and conditions in the industry. He spoke to a meeting organised by his local officials in the Liverpool Stadium, but it was tough going all the way. His audience of around 2,500 Liverpool dockers – half the Stadium's capacity – gave him a rough ride, and at times he was jeered and booed as he outlined the advantages of being in the TGWU. It was hardly a happy augury for the days ahead. Two days later at a docks delegate conference in London Cousins's proposal for an interim settlement of the pay dispute was rejected. He wanted the conference to accept the port employers' offer, and then to pursue a full-scale inquiry into the wages structure and the question of decasualisation. The delegates wouldn't accept that, though they did agree to defer a final decision until after the election.

On the day of that delegate conference 16,500 dockers came out on unofficial strike for the day in London, Liverpool and Hull. It was a warning to their union delegates, and to their national leaders, not to accept the employers' offer but to press for the full 25s. a week extra. Cousins had gained time by getting the final decision postponed – but nothing else. It would not be wrong to say that, at that stage, Cousins was putting the interests of a Labour election victory above the immediate issue of a dockers' pay rise, or at least the pursuit of a rise that might have led to a confrontation with the port employers.

The question of what effect industrial trouble has on the Labour Party's prospects during an election campaign is much more debatable now than it was in 1964. The miners' crisis election of February 1974 would appear to have left the Conservatives no less vulnerable than the Labour Party to the scorn of the electorate over the handling of industrial conflict. But that was not how it seemed ten years earlier. Any strike was then held to be 'an embarrassment' to Labour's chances. It was readily assumed (perhaps too readily and on inadequate evidence) that the electorate automatically associated industrial trouble with the Labour Party, in so far as the unions had political links with Labour and not with the other parties. Because most people recognised that Labour had an obligation to the unions it was also assumed that Labour was therefore in a strong position to determine the unions' industrial policies even down to day-to-day tactical issues of strikes, official or unofficial. In 1964 it was certainly held to be true that strikes, almost regardless of merit, were a potent electoral liability for the Labour Party. So much so that at the start of the campaign Harold Wilson found himself in troubled waters over a strike of 300 workers at the Hardy Spicer motor component plant in the Midlands. Assuming that the stoppage might do serious harm to Labour Mr Wilson turned his fire on the Hardy Spicer management and, in effect, accused them of inciting the dispute to embarrass the Labour Party. That, at any rate, was the implication of Mr Wilson's case. For the first week of the campaign the Hardy Spicer row virtually dominated the headlines, so obsessed was everyone, the media people as well as the politicians, with the effects of industrial trouble on Labour's election prospects.

The election of February 1974 may have finally disproved that industrial conflict – even on such a grave national scale as the miners' strike of that year – necessarily operates to the Labour Party's disadvantage. The shift of radical thinking and radical action throughout British society between 1964 and 1974 has been so great that few people now retain the illusion that the Conservatives are in any way better equipped to handle industrial conflict – in fact, the contrary is probably the case. That was not so in 1964, however, so that Frank Cousins was deeply dismayed by the unresolved docks dispute. The opinion polls around the middle of the campaign showed that the Conservatives had not lost as much electoral sympathy as the Labour Party leaders had assumed – or, indeed, as the pundits had been predicting. This added to the sense of uncertainty and to the importance of such issues as industrial problems, which might have swayed marginal voters. Two days before polling – on Tuesday 13 October – Cousins led the TGWU dock negotiating team in yet another attempt to break the deadlock over the pay claim. The employers wouldn't budge. After all, there was no incentive for them to settle quickly. Cousins, on his side, knew perfectly well that if it had not been for the election he would have been facing a call for official strike action in the docks, a call he would no doubt have been disposed to support. All he could do now was to stall and play for time.

In the event the docks dispute was resolved after the election when the new Minister of Labour, Ray Gunter, appointed a court of inquiry under the chairmanship of Lord Devlin. This inquiry rapidly produced an interim wage settlement and followed this, in August 1965, with a final report on the modernisation of the docks industry. It was that Devlin Report which paved the way, eventually, for decasualisation. In fact it produced the kind of inquiry, and even the ultimate outcome, which Cousins had sought earlier, when he failed to persuade his docks degelates to accept his formula for an interim payment and then to pursue a wide-ranging inquiry. But that is another story. The fact is that the docks crisis effectively limited the active role Cousins could play in the election campaign. Still, it did not prevent him from keeping his promise to speak on Harold Wilson's eve-of-poll platform in Liverpool at St George's Hall. And that was indeed an extraordinary night.

St George's Hall was full to overflowing. Between 4,000 and 5,000 people somehow squeezed themselves into the hall, and at least another 2,000 were outside in the square. The speeches by Wilson and Cousins were relayed into the streets around the centre of Liverpool, and at the end of the meeting Harold and Mary Wilson walked back to the Adelphi Hotel, along with Frank Cousins, at the head of several thousand people chanting and singing a spiritual about a Labour victory. That was a remarkable meeting by any standards of election campaigning. During his speech Cousins, who was up immediately before Wilson, referred to his own and his union's attachment to the Party leader. 'One reason we are bound to the Labour Movement is because of the man who leads it,' said the TGWU leader, pointing to Harold Wilson. In his own speech Wilson praised Cousins's courage and his stamina in standing up to the persistent propaganda attacks on him, by which Wilson said, he had been placed 'in the position of No. 1 in Tory demonology'.

Back at the hotel Cousins waited for Wilson to call him to his room. When the call came, shortly after midnight, the final act of agreement was reached. Now the seal of office effectively only hinged on the poll. Cousins admits that the euphoric atmosphere in Liverpool on that eve-of-poll night did much to concentrate his mind and clinch his decision. 'I might never have gone into the Government had I not ended up in Liverpool that night.'

In the morning, Wilson returned to London on the 8.15 train, still uncertain as to whether he would be Prime Minister. The gap between Labour's early lead and the Tory recovery had narrowed in the early hours of Friday morning. It wasn't until mid-afternoon that the outcome became clear. Labour had the narrowest of wafer-thin majorities: 317 seats against the Conservatives' 303, with 9 Liberals. The aggregate votes showed the country neatly divided down the middle: Labour 12,205,576 (44.1%); Conservatives 12,02,407 (43.4%); Liberals 3,093,316 (11.2%); others 348,914 (1.3%).

So uncertain was the outcome that up till the last minute Wilson was hesitant about changing into formal morning dress to go to the Palace. He actually changed into a black jacket and striped trousers while I sat and talked with him in Room 113 at Transport House. He still had his wine-coloured election campaign braces dangling over his shoulders. His conversation, up until a few minutes earlier, had been punctuated by a repetitive 'if I am called to the Palace . . . if . . .' He left Transport House at 3.25 that Friday afternoon to become the youngest Prime Minister since Lord Roseberry in 1894. Wilson was 48 (Roseberry had been 47) – considerably below the average age of the Cabinet of twenty-three he assembled around him during that weekend. Their average age was 56.

From Buckingham Palace he went to Downing Street and the announcement of his first Cabinet that same evening: George Brown, First Secretary and Minister for Economic Affairs; Patrick Gordon Walker, Foreign Secretary; Herbert Bowden, Lord President and Leader of the Commons; Lord Gardiner, Lord Chancellor; James Callaghan, Chancellor of the Exchequer; Dennis Healey, Minister of Defence; and Edward Short, chief Whip. He spoke to Frank Cousins on the telephone and invited him to become Minister of Technology. Of course, Cousins was prepared, but he still demanded time to consult his executive before accepting the post. He immediately summoned a special meeting of the General Executive Council next morning. At 10.30 that Saturday Cousins reported to the thirty-eight members of the union's executive, plus Harry Nicholas and Jack Jones, that Wilson wanted him to join the Government. An extract from the official minute reads as follows:

> The decision which the Council was required to take was a serious one and he personally, with reluctance and regret, had found it necessary having had long and searching consultations with his Executive Officer colleagues, to revise his own desire frequently expressed publicly in the past, to remain actively working for the Union. He would feel the temporary parting most keenly, having regard to his long and active association at all levels. On the other hand the problems were so big, and the needs of the people of the country too urgent for anyone to stand back and it was in this spirit that he requested leave of absence from the General Secretaryship of the Union in order to permit of his acceptance of Office in the new Government.

Not every member of the executive was as enthusiastic as this unilluminating, dry official minute suggests. Privately Harry Nicholas advised Cousins against going into Government, though he knew that his mind had been made up. Cousins was not to be shifted at that late stage. In the executive

J. W. (Bill) Jones, the Vice President and the London busmen's leader, voted against Cousins joining the Government. His vote was the only one registered in opposition that morning. (This was an interesting and important portent for the future, since it was Bill Jones who, two years later, played a significant part in compelling Cousins to make up his mind to return to the union.) Jones's opposition was not based on any personal or political dislike of Frank Cousins – quite the opposite. He believed it was politically more important for the Left to have Cousins remain as General Secretary of the TGWU than for him to enter a Wilson Cabinet, where, like Woodcock, Jones believed Cousins would be trapped.

Bill Jones has told me that he felt Wilson would 'use him [Cousins] and cut him off and divorce him from the progressives within the Movement. I felt that political pressures within the Government might reduce him – he wouldn't have been the first.' The executive, notwithstanding Jones's opposition, gave Cousins leave of absence without pay, on the understanding that he could return to his post as General Secretary at any time, and agreed to continue his pension provided he paid both his own and the union's contribution to the pension fund, which was the union's established practice in all instances of leave of absence. The same executive meeting then promoted Harry Nicholas to acting General Secretary and Jack Jones to acting Assistant General Secretary. They completed the business by sending a message to the Prime Minister congratulating him on Labour's success and pledging the TGWU's 'goodwill and co-operation in a common desire to ensure the success of the new Government and for your future health and well-being'. Nor was that the only hostage to fortune held out by that memorable special executive session. The previous Minute registered the conviction that Labour's victory was not merely 'a splendid achievement' but envisaged 'a new era of social justice leading to a better civilisation'. Such were the hopes kindled in even the most hardened hearts on that bright morning in October 1964, as Frank Cousins left Transport House for Downing Street and his official appointment as Minister of Technology.

Such optimism was necessary, even if scarcely justifiable. Outside the hothouse atmosphere of Westminster and a Labour Movement basking in the sunshine of power, some ominous shadows were cast across the sunlit paths to the new Britain. On the very day of the polls Khrushchev was sacked in Moscow. The next day, practically at the moment when Harold Wilson was on his way from Transport House to Buckingham Palace to collect the Queen's commission to form a Government, China was exploding her first atomic bomb. The two events seemed to make international peace more precarious and uncertain than ever.

Morover, at home the balance of payments crisis was greater than anyone in the Labour leadership had imagined. Wilson had picked up hints during the election campaign. But they were too insubstantial for him to risk making allegations against the Tory Government's handling of the economic situation lest it precipitate a serious run on sterling. When Wilson opened the books he was genuinely shocked. So were the Ministers in whom he confided on his first evening in Downing Street. Hence the reference, albeit guarded, in Cousins's opening remarks to the TGWU executive on 17 October to the 'gravity of the situation'.

Cousins's appointment to the Wilson Cabinet was perhaps less of a surprise than his designation as Minister of Technology. The Press comment was almost unanimously hostile, at best patronising and sanctimonious. *The Times* pontificated:

> Whatever may be thought of Mr Cousins's qualifications even with Sir Charles Snow at his elbow to inspire British industry with technological revolution (and he if anybody should be able to sell the idea to trade unionists) a Labour Prime Minister can feel more comfortable having him in the Cabinet rather than leaving him outside as a potential focus of resistance.[8]

The paper's Labour Correspondent took up the theme that Wilson had appointed Cousins to make him a prisoner. 'The Prime Minister', he wrote, 'whether he thought of it in this way or not, has adopted the old trade union practice of dealing with the awkward man by promoting him.' Even so the Labour Correspondent suggested, with a touch of sentimentality, that 'the trade union movement will not seem the same without Mr Cousins, who has been a controversial figure in the leadership for the past 8 years.'

The second person Frank Cousins told that he had accepted a place in Wilson's Cabinet after he telephoned his family, was George Woodcock. The TUC General Secretary was dismayed, and said so in uncharacteristically strong language, Cousins tells me. Woodcock protested over the telephone that he was being left isolated on the TUC General Council. 'You're a fine one,' Woodcock told Cousins, 'leaving me with that bloody lot.' Woodcock's own account is somewhat less dramatic, though its import amounts to the same thing. He recalls telling Frank Cousins that he was making a 'great mistake', that he was extremely sorry to lose him from the TUC General Council, and that it would leave the Council seriously weakened. I have already mentioned Woodcock's assessment of Cousins's role as a member of the TUC General Council, in which he placed him as 'the most outstanding member' during Woodcock's time as TUC General Secretary. There was no greater compliment Woodcock could pay than to say that Cousins resembled Ernest Bevin, who was Woodcock's hero-figure in the trade union pantheon. Woodcock says:

> Frank was very much like Bevin, 'though of course Bevin was operating at a different time. Bevin was highly constructive whereas Frank was a critic.

8. *The Times*, 20 October 1964.

The difference was the context in which they were working. When Frank was on the TUC General Council the TUC were always under more pressure to take a positive stand in relations with Government. Bevin was there in pre-war years when the scene was very different, when the unions were fighting for recognition, acceptance, against resistance and Government indifference.

Woodcock did miss Cousins. But Cousins also left others behind on the General Council who regretted his departure – improbable names, perhaps, like the late Sir Tom O'Brien, a Falstaffian figure who was a much more serious political animal than he was given credit for being. O'Brien told me the story of one of Cousins's last gestures at the TUC before he went into the Government. This was in connection with the death of the *Daily Herald* in September 1964.[9] The TUC were in negotiations with the proprietors of the *Herald*, the International Publishing Corporation, for several months up till February 1964, when it was agreed that the TUC interest would be bought out in preparation for the launching of a new newspaper, owned by IPC and following much of the *Herald* tradition, to be called the *Sun*. Apart from the compensation paid to the TUC there was an offer of £1,000 personal payment to the TUC 'directors' on the *Daily Herald* Board, of which Frank Cousins and Sir Tom O'Brien were members. O'Brien impishly recalled that he decided to keep his £1,000, but Cousins refused to take it. He instructed that the money should be sent to Oxfam, which subsequently passed it on to President Kaunda of Zambia, where it was used for the medical protection of cattle.

The last edition of the *Daily Herald* appeared on Saturday 14 September 1964, a depressing day for the Labour Movement. Despite all the hope and professional idealism invested in its successor, the *Sun* (which started on 16 September, as the election campaign began to roll), nothing could effectively replace the *Herald* in the journalistic mythology of the Labour Movement. It had been nourished as part of the soul, the blood and the bone of the unions and the Labour Party since beginning as a strike sheet of the London Society of Compositors in 1911. Handed on to George Lansbury, its first editor who carried it through until the 1920s, revived and reorganised by Ernest Bevin and Lord Southwood for Odhams Press in 1929, the *Herald*, to everyone's amazement, became the first of the Fleet Street nationals to rise above the two million circulation figure in the 1930s. Now it was dead. The gap left by the *Herald* has never been filled and at the time Frank Cousins doubted whether it would be. He had already held a number of private discussions to test the possibility of helping to finance and launch

9. See TUC *Annual Report*, 1964, pp. 337–51, for a full account of the negotiations which brought the end of the *Daily Herald*. Talks on IPC proposals to close the *Daily Herald* began with the TUC in July 1963.

a new paper of the Left to take over from the *Herald* and, indeed, he obtained the informal approval of the TGWU executive to do so. But with the birth of the *Sun* his plan was shelved, on the reasonable grounds that it would be near to impossible to launch a new socialist daily newspaper in competition with the IPC-backed and financed *Sun*. None the less, Cousins's report to the TGWU executive on the disappearance of the *Herald* reflected his disappointment, and his conviction that sooner or later the Labour Movement would have to consider relaunching a socialist daily newspaper.

Frank Cousins had no more illusions about the Press than most of the newspapers appeared to have about him. At any rate the chorus of disapproval about his appointment continued for several days after the Wilson Government was completed. *The Times*, maintaining its sanctimonious attitude towards Cousins, returned to the theme on the Wednesday after the election. They objected to what seemed to be the Prime Minister's objective to give Frank Cousins much wider powers and authority that had been originally considered likely – giving him, as *The Times* saw it, a finger in every big pie from education and science to the 'automated production of nuts and bolts'. It went on : 'for a man who was until recently determined to stay outside the House of Commons this is a remarkable change of heart. It is also a remarkable declaration of faith in him by Mr. Wilson.'

It did not trouble Cousins or Wilson to see this kind of criticism. At that stage their relationship was understandably stronger than ever. Wilson had persuaded Cousins to change his mind, against the strongest counter-arguments of Nance Cousins (a remarkable enough achievement in itself), by convincing him that there was a major role for him in the Government. According to Cousins, Wilson invited him into the Government not simply as Minister of Technology, nor mainly (if at all) to try to trap him as a potential external threat to a Labour Government, but 'to help him fight against the right wing in the Cabinet' which Wilson recognised would be in a majority. He told Cousins, 'I want you to be close to me, Frank. There is no one else I can trust as I can trust you. That is because I know you are the one man who doesn't want my job.'

Perhaps *The Times*'s comment about Wilson's 'faith' in Cousins was nearer the truth than the writer realised. At any rate there *was* a mutual faith. There was also mutual hope at that moment that, despite its narrow majority, and despite the economic crisis, the new Government now had the opportunity to set about changing society. They believed that the blend of technology with socialist doctrine was an unbeatable combination, that radical change and new social horizons could emerge from the computer. Why did it all fail? Why does it now seem to have been such a naïve dream? The answer could be that it did not *fail*, but rather that it did not rise to the expected heights. Much in it succeeded, within the limitations of Government power, the qualifications of the democratic process, and the fallibility of human action.

Perhaps, as both Cousins and Wilson now think, the outcome might have been different, if they had behaved differently, if they had remained closer within the system of Government, if they had not made the errors of judgement to which both now admit to. More likely not. Wilson certainly believes he failed to give Cousins the help and the power he ought to have had at the newly-fledged Ministry of Technology. Wilson has told me that there were many administrative as well as political mistakes that he now accepts were his fault. Cousins equally acknowledges that he underestimated the problems of moving into the world of Government and Parliamentary politics. He believed that Government could get things done, that, given the will and the determination within a Cabinet, mountains could be moved. As a man of action, capable of using a powerful machine like a large trade union to get things done – albeit within narrower terms of reference – he was at first angered and shocked, then depressed and finally disillusioned to discover that Parliamentary Government and the Cabinet system had such serious limitations. There was no magic drawer in which the formula of effective power was kept. There was only the *mechanism* of power. The substance was much more illusory. It was this, perhaps above all else, which was to prove the biggest disillusionment to Frank Cousins in Government, this more than anything else that, ultimately, made his resignation a question more of time than of principle.

When he explained his reasons for changing his mind about going into Government to TGWU members in the union's journal Cousins confessed :

> This is a challenge to me personally in the new job – but it is also a responsibility for the whole Movement. We now have the opportunity to prove that *our* criticisms of ineffective Government were right, and we must now try to give the country the leadership it needs. That is why in the end the General Executive Council [of the TGWU] and myself had no option but to agree that I should play in the new Government.[10]

Having held such high hopes, it was all the more difficult and depressing to find the reality such a profound disappointment.

10. TGWU *Record*, December 1964, pp. 32–3.

Chapter Twenty-one

INSIDE THE WHALE

Give yourself over to the world-process, stop fighting against it or pretending that you control it; simply accept it, endure it, record it. Get inside the whale — or rather admit you are inside the whale (for you *are*, of course).

George Orwell, *Inside the Whale*

Frank Cousins's problem, in Government as much as outside, was invariably that he could never accept that he was inside the whale. It is hard for any man who is inspired, or perhaps even deluded, by a belief that he has a mission to change the 'world process' to which Orwell alludes, to accept that there are serious limitations to power of any kind. Cousins saw his invitation to join the Wilson Cabinet as an opportunity to realise at least some of his deep ambition to help change the established social and political pattern of English life in which he had been reared and had witnessed so much injustice. It is hard and profoundly disenchanting to come to terms with the knowledge that there are enormous obstacles in the path of such a vision and that there are inescapable limitations to what can be done even by the most dedicated of radical Governments. Yet to add to the frustration the Wilson Government of 1964 proved to be far less radical, far less imaginative, than even Cousins — with all his initial scepticism — believed possible.

Cousins realised that with a slender majority of five (to be reduced still further before long) the Government's difficulties were going to be immense. Yet he still reckoned these could be overcome, given the resolve and the will-power of his new colleagues. In a sense he saw 1964 as potentially another 1945, despite the obvious difference in circumstances, and an electorate that was, undoubtedly, more politically sceptical, if not already cynical. There is no doubt that he underestimated the complexities of Whitehall, within the civil service 'whale'; he overestimated the determination of his colleagues, all professional politicians with a keen sense of what is feasible within the limitations of Parliamentary Government; he also miscalculated the differences between the role of a powerful trade union leader and that of a Cabinet Minister working within a team of, in the main, highly motivated extroverts. The leader of an organisation as powerful as the TGWU, or any of the other major trade unions, is an emperor in his 'own' domain. He is neither an isolated nor an omnipotent potentate, but he is able, most of the time, to determine a line of action and pursue it. He can command men – even if it is never actually put that way – to stop work, though it is less easy to persuade them to restart. He administers a kind of independent province within the body of the State. Union leaders have sometimes been likened to feudal barons: the comparison is quite absurd, but it is not difficult to see why it has been made. Nor is it hard to understand why the friendly critics of Cousins's decision to enter the Wilson Government warned him that he was throwing away the substance of one sort of power for the mere shadow of a wider sort. Moreover, it is far from easy for a man who has reached 60, has led the biggest trade union in the country, and has been used to seeing his instructions carried out by a nationwide machine of officials suddenly to be plunged into the strange new world of Cabinet Government. Cousins now had to slot into a team of politicians, each of them furiously peddling his own departmental claims and ambitions yet, at the same time, dependent for mutual survival on an unwritten (and sometimes reluctantly accepted) pact of ideological identity. It was not in the least like the Transport and General Workers' Union, as Cousins frequently mused to Wilson in those early days.

It would be quite false, therefore, to suppose that Frank Cousins went into the Labour Government without illusions. That much was clear from his message to TGWU members explaining his change of mind about entering Parliamentary politics. Perhaps, indeed, he had too many illusions. He probably *did* believe that he could help to give the country 'the leadership it needs'. After all, he had been encouraged to think that Harold Wilson looked on him as a kind of latter-day Ernest Bevin. He clearly saw the possibility of a Wilson-Cousins relationship developing into something like the earlier Attlee-Bevin axis. This all helped to fortify his conviction that 'something' could be done, and also helped to cushion his own private anxieties, deep enough at the time, about how he might fit into the Parliamentary scene – a scene he was entering for the first time at an age when many trade union leaders might be already thinking of retirement. Yet he reflected that Bevin was almost precisely the same age – a few months younger, in fact – when he became Minister of Labour in May 1940. Till that time Bevin had never sat in Parliament, held any Ministerial post, or indeed sat on the Labour Party's National Executive Committee. At least Cousins had done the latter, albeit for a few brief months. The parallels were obvious, to be sure, though the political and social scenario was in fact completely different. The change from trade union leadership to the Cabinet room was difficult enough for Bevin, but at least he entered a war-time coalition under a national leader whose support, if not unanimous, was at least unique for any British politician in modern times. To that extent Bevin was protected from the excesses of Parliamentary, Press and even public criticism in a way that was unthinkable in Cousins's case. His appointment by Wilson was greeted by most of the newspapers with scarcely concealed derision, by the Parliamentary Opposition as a Wilsonian gimmick, and by many public voices as, at best, an oddity. When eventually Cousins took his Parliamentary seat (not until the end of January 1965) he was treated to an exceptionally rough ride by the Tories – unusual, that is, even allowing for the tempestuous childishness of so much of the routine Parliamentary knock-about.

Cousins's uncertainties, anxieties and mistakes in handling his early months as a Cabinet Minister and as Minister of Technology were no more glaring than Bevin's had been. Yet he was never accorded – and, to be fair, never expected – the tolerance or privileged protection in Parliament or anywhere else that Bevin's wartime role ensured. Nor, unlike Bevin, did he inherit an established department of Government with a ready-made hierarchy and staff of civil servants. There was nothing to inherit. And he was soon to learn what a huge disadvantage it is to begin a completely new Department of State without any Parliamentary channels or any strong footholds in the corridors of Whitehall power. In his biography of Ernest Bevin, Lord Bullock tells a good story of Bevin's first day at the war-time Ministry of Labour. Bevin's predecessor had gone, and the senior staff were introduced to the new Minister by the Parliamentary Secretary, Ralph Assheton, later to become Chairman of the Conservative Party.

> When the civilities were completed and the room empty again Bevin, fling-ing himself back in his chair and looking at Assheton, asked : 'Well, Ralph, what do I do next?'
> Taken aback by the question Assheton gave the conventional reply that he could rely on his officials to put any proposals into effect provided he [the Minister] knew what he wanted to do. This suited Bevin. He might be ignorant of procedure but he had arrived with plenty of ideas about what to do. 'Then if I were you,' Assheton advised him, 'I'd go off home and put them down on paper.'[1]

Frank Cousins was in an almost identical vacuum – though still worse. He lacked any institutional framework either to project his interest inside the Whitehall 'whale' or to protect his external political flanks. The entire White-hall scene was in a state of frantic departmental reorganisation, almost

1. Alan Bullock, *The Life and Times of Ernest Bevin* Vols II, (Heinemann, 1967), p. 12.

parallel, in that respect, with the scurrying changes of 1940. Moreover, the economic crisis that the Wilson Government inherited – but did not fully appreciate until they opened the books on arrival – meant that there was no time to spend on departmental delicacies. Priority had to be given – and was given – to those departments with an immediate and direct responsibility for handling the economic crisis – the Treasury, the Board of Trade and the newly created Department of Economic Affairs, George Brown's Ministry. From the moment that Wilson summoned his first Cabinet, on the Monday morning after the election, the focus of Government was fixed on a rapid staunching of the drain in the balance of payments. The logic behind this was irrefutable. At the same time it assisted the other major new department, George Brown's DEA, to steal a march on the Ministry of Technology. And, remembering Brown's sensitivity about his entitlement to priority, Wilson gave the DEA the pick of the available talent in Whitehall as well as a first claim on introducing 'outside' advisers into the Government machine. In retrospect it is hard to say whether this gave Brown's department any lasting or significant advantage, but it certainly made Cousins's early days more difficult and left him with a feeling of isolation which, in many ways, reminded him of his earliest moments as a member of the TUC General Council.

When the Ministry of Technology was born on Saturday 17 October 1964 there was nothing but a plan and a prayer. No headquarters, no staff, not even funds. Parliamentary approval had yet to be obtained for the financial provision of this new department. The plan was there, along with the concept. But until the election was won nothing could be done to provide a more material basis, nor had the civil service done any serious preparation. Before Cousins went to Downing Street that Saturday, to report to Wilson that he had been granted leave of absence by the TGWU, very little *could* be done. From that moment the hustle began. Cousins spent the weekend assembling a handful of key people who were to form the nucleus of his new Ministry.

One of the first men he called on the telephone at the Prime Minister's suggestion, was Sir Solly (now Lord) Zuckerman, the Government's chief scientific adviser, later to become Chairman of the Central Advisory Committee for Science and Technology. Zuckerman had been at the centre of affairs as an adviser since 1960, in the middle of the Macmillan period, and he knew a great deal about the inner workings of Whitehall, especially where they concerned the military-industrial complex. He also shared the conviction that a new department to concentrate on Technology and Science was essential, though he was less convinced that Harold Wilson or the Labour Party planners had thought it through in sufficient detail. Zuckerman was not involved in the planning build-up of 1963, although he had been invited along with Blackett to join the team of scientists working with the Labour

Party. But Zuckerman turned down the invitation, partly for personal reasons but also because he regarded such involvement as potentially politically embarrassing – especially since he held such a high Government post in an area of defence secrets where 'outside' party political contacts could be sensitive. None the less, Zuckerman supported the concept of a Ministry of Technology. That was why Wilson suggested that Cousins's first approach should be to the chief scientific adviser. The two men met on that same Saturday evening and, rather in the style of Bevin's question to Assheton in 1940, Cousins asked Zuckerman what *he* thought should be the first steps. Zuckerman was surprised at Cousins's frank admission that, though he had his own ideas, he was open to any proposals. Zuckerman himself had had a busy day. Summoned by Denis Healey, the new Minister of Defence, early that same morning he spent several hours briefing him. Then he saw George Brown, who wanted advice on how to tackle *his* problems at the new Department of Economic Affairs. By the time Zuckerman reached Frank Cousins that evening he was exhausted, though he was still able to provide the Minister of Technology with a set of ideas on how to get the new department off the ground. 'Frank Cousins didn't really seem to know what to do at that stage', is how Zuckerman now reflects on that discussion.

At that juncture Cousins had still not been allocated a Permanent Secretary; or at least he had not agreed one with the Prime Minister. He had been offered Sir Bruce Fraser from the Ministry of Health, but Fraser, a 53-year-old, tough-minded Scot, objected to the post (and to his prospective Minister) so a replacement had to be found quickly. Sir Maurice Dean, 58, was transferred from the Department of Education and Science, where he was replaced by Sir Bruce Fraser. Zuckerman played a part in suggesting Dean; for one thing they both shared the belief that the new Ministry of Technology ought to be, in effect, a Ministry for Industry. Certainly they both regarded the concept outlines by the Labour Party's planning group as too limited. In fact Zuckerman's view took an even wider sweep than Dean's. He believed the new Department, from the start, ought to embrace defence aspects of technology as well as civil industry. He based this belief on the inter-relationship between defence and civil industrial development. In 1964 the central Government was spending some £2,000 million (6.8 per cent of GNP) on defence contracts, most of which involved procurement and orders within British industry. This magnitude of spending naturally had a profound effect on the entire economic planning, industrial research and design, development and investment policies of large sectors of British industry. It was impossible in practice to separate the roles. Unless the new Ministry of Technology had an effective voice in determining the relationship between the two sectors, which formed this military-industrial complex, then there would inevitably be serious limitations to the influence and power of the new Department.

Cousins realised this clearly enough but in fact he was never given such powers over the defence complex nor, until very much later in his Ministerial career, was he given the extended powers over wider sections of civil industry that both he and Sir Maurice Dean proposed from the start. It is not easy to be clear about the reasons for this. As far as defence is concerned Cousins would clearly have found it politically embarrassing to have had a strong voice in Cabinet committee decisions concerning the details of Government defence programmes he disapproved of. Moreover, his presence in such counsels would have greatly added to Wilson's difficulties with other Cabinet members, most certainly with his Minister of Defence, Denis Healey. Indeed, one of the reasons why the Prime Minister delayed for so long before conceding the wider industrial powers promised to Cousins's Ministry was because of the strong objections that came from George Brown. He always feared that *his* new Department might be eroded, if not by Treasury malevolence then by the ambitions of his colleagues.

The appointment of the late Sir Maurice Dean was the first real foundation stone of the new Ministry. Cousins and Dean liked each other from the start and saw the role and functions of the new Ministry in the same light. Whether Sir Maurice carried sufficient force among the highest echelons of the civil service is another question. There are those who now suggest that if it was a Prime Ministerial error to put Frank Cousins in such an exposed post as a starting-off point, then it was an even bigger mistake to deprive him of a really powerful Permanent Secretary drawn from one of the senior departments in Whitehall. It is only fair to say that this view is not held by Frank Cousins himself. He does not believe that a more powerful mandarin would have substantially made much difference. The ultimate weaknesses of the Ministry of Technology were not due, he believes, to any intrinsic department inadequacies so much as the failure of overall Government policy – and perhaps even more, the absence of a radical vision in the Wilson Cabinet or the will to carry out such a vision, assuming it was there in the first place.

Once Sir Maurice Dean had been assigned, the Minister was given a private secretary, Christopher Herzig. Again, the two became firm friends, although not before the relationship had been through an inevitable apprenticeship of suspicion. At the outset, Cousins was deeply wary of the civil service. He was convinced that they would deliberately put obstacles in the way of his radical plans, not because they were maliciously reactionary but because that was their natural response to any Government which seriously set out to change the *status quo*. It took several months for the Cousins-Herzig relationship to overcome this tension. When finally it did Cousins found he had in Herzig a remarkably loyal and dedicated private secretary. The Cousins launch-team was completed by the appointment of Professor Patrick Blackett and C. P. Snow. Blackett's appointment was the most predictable of all. More than any other single individual he had a right to describe the new Ministry as his brainchild.

Blackett was one of the most distinguished physicists in Britain, indeed, in the world. He had already played a major role in drawing up the blueprint for a Ministry of Technology. It was on the basis of his original paper to Harold Wilson that the concept had been developed. And like Zuckerman and Dean, he saw the new department originally as an all-embracing Ministry for Industry. We know that Wilson, at the earlier stages in 1963 and 1964, was toying with the notion of creating three separate departments : one for economic planning (which eventually became the DEA); another for industry and technology; and a third for science and education. According to Crossman's diaries, Wilson actually earmarked Blackett for a Ministerial post in the new science department. The original idea was to appoint a Crossman-Blackett Ministerial team for science and higher education. But according to Crossman this was dropped following a Press campaign against Blackett towards the end of 1963.[2] Several newspapers, including the *Observer* and the *Daily Express*, alleged that the Professor was regarded by Whitehall as a 'security risk'. Whatever the reason, Wilson never made any subsequent suggestion that the Professor should enter a Labour Government as a Minister.

I have been unable to trace any convincing evidence to support Crossman's view, but that is to not say there is no substance to the story. What does appear to be the case is that Blackett had both professional and political enemies in Whitehall, some of whom may have been only too ready to exploit and exaggerate his well known left-wing views. Blackett never concealed his socialist convictions, nor did he hesitate to speak out against the British development of the H-bomb. He supported nuclear disarmament, though he did not involve himself in the general political campaign. For all these reasons it is not improbable that this distinguished man and outstanding scientist was labelled as a 'security risk'. At all events this did not prevent Harold Wilson appointing him as chief adviser to Frank Cousins at the Ministry of Technology, where he became a kind of chief-of-staff. His formal title was that of Deputy Chairman of the Advisory Council to the Minister (Cousins being Chairman), a post for which he was given leave of absence by Imperial College. Blackett was then 67.

Sir Charles Snow (C. P. Snow) was made Parliamentary Secretary to Cousins and given a life peerage to take him into Parliament for the first time, at the age of 59. Snow was at a still greater disadvantage than Frank Cousins, so far as Parliament was concerned. Despite an earlier spell in the civil service during World War II (when he was engaged in selecting scientific personnel), Snow's practical experience in active politics was extremely

2. Richard Crossman, the unpublished diaries, 17 July and 7 November 1963.

limited. He proved, indeed, to be one of the major weaknesses in that founding team and did not long remain as a Minister. Yet by the time Snow was replaced, the Ministry of Techology had already suffered both in Parliament and in Whitehall from a lack of force and expertise.

It was seen as a new Department with a powerful figurehead as Minister, but ill served by some of his closest lieutenants and insufficiently supported by his Prime Minister. Nothing is now more enlightening than an admission made to me by Harold Wilson in later years that he accepts responsibility for failing to give Frank Cousins stronger support both in terms of personnel as well as policy-making, from the very start of the Ministry of Technology. Having brought Cousins into the Government with tempting, not to say glowing, visions of what might be achieved, the Prime Minister, finding himself swamped by the magnitude of the economic crisis, allowed his Minister of Technology to steer a lonely and inadequately aided course towards the reefs of Whitehall among turbulent events which almost sank the Labour Government in those late months of 1964. It is arguable that Frank Cousins's career as a Minister might have been very different had his Prime Minister devoted more care to ensuring he had the right support in those earliest moments of the Ministry of Technology. But Cousins had to fend for himself; he even had to go in search of a home for his new Ministry while his new Permanent Secretary was struggling to recruit typists and his private secretary was out borrowing paper clips! Harold Wilson meanwhile was fighting for the survival of his Government, the fate of which was stilll very much in the balance.[3]

The 'first five' men of the Ministry of Technology met together for an inaugural session on Monday, 19 October in the office of the Paymaster General at 72 Whitehall. It was an astonishing start for a new and radically disposed Department of State. Christopher Herzig recalls that day when he first met his new Minister on the doorstep of No. 72. He greeted Frank Cousins and the two men faced each other, uneasily, in a moment of awkward silence as they moved towards *the* room – the room which, at the time, *was* the new Ministry. Its previous occupant was William Deedes, MP (now editor-in-chief of the *Daily Telegraph*), who had worked there as Minister in charge of the Tory Government's information services. When Deedes came back to collect his belongings he greeted Cousins with a friendly assurance that since he now had to vacate his old room, he preferred to hand over to a political opponent rather than be displaced by a fellow Conservative. Sir Maurice Dean recalled to me the 'one-room Ministry' of those first few days with a wry smile and perhaps not without a trace of pain. He had the task of building up a staff by scratching around Whitehall departments as best he could. The change of Government, and with it all the signs of a

3. See Harold Wilson, *The Labour Government, 1964–1970* (Wiedenfeld & Nicholson, 1971), pp. 19–37.

considerable change in the style of Government, as well as the creation of four brand-new departments, had stirred Whitehall into a feverish game of musical chairs. The new departments were in competition with each other in the search for staff (of all grades) as well as premises. Elbows were often used in a most un-Whitehall manner.

In all cases, perhaps apart from one, the new departments had powerful Ministers determined to try to get their own way and their own choice of civil servants as well as buildings. George Brown, at the DEA, was matched by the feminine vigour of Barbara Castle at the new Ministry for Overseas Aid and Development. Both were deploying their natural talents for fishing in the Whitehall waters and trawling for the best. Then there was Fred Willey at the newly created Ministry of Land and Natural Resources, a curious hybrid drawn together from various departments such as Town and Country Planning, Housing and Local Government. Mr Willey may not have been cast in the same competitive mould as George Brown or Barbara Castle, but he too had to build up his staff. The Whitehall clamour was so intense that Sir Maurice Dean was obliged to recruit some secretarial and shorthand-typist staff from outside employment agencies. To add to the general confusion, the Government in its early enthusiasm for a radical reform in the 'machinery of Government' overran the ration of Ministerial portfolios. The upshot was that Frank Cousins could not be paid as a Minister until Parliament passed a new Bill, to increase the number of permitted Ministers. Since Cousins did not, at that time, even have a Parliamentary seat (he did not enter the House of Commons as MP for Nuneaton until the end of January 1965) he was not paid for his duties as Minister of Technology for some five months. During that time he lived on his private savings. He received no payment from the TGWU, having ceased to be on the union's payroll as soon as its executive granted him leave of absence. It must be one of the few instances in modern political times where a Cabinet Minister has actually subsidised the Government, and the taxpayer, for the privilege of being a Minister of the Crown.

The search for a suitable home for the new Ministry of Technology had some equally bizarre touches to it. At first Cousins was offered an office in the Privy Council building or Shell Mex House in the Strand, home of the former Ministry of Supply. He rejected both. He had particular reason to reject the Shell Mex building: it was the place he remembered vividly from his days as a national officer in the union's road haulage section, when he fought to improve his members' wages and conditions. He didn't like the place in those days, and he had no reason to change his mind now. He regarded the building as old-fashioned and fusty. He told the Ministry of Works' senior civil servant that he required a completely new type of building for the Ministry of Technology.

'I want something made of modern glass and steel construction', Cousins instructed him, 'a building with a flat roof on which a helicopter could land.'

The man from the Ministry looked bewildered. 'But Minister', he protested, 'we have no buildings like that'.

'Then,' Cousins replied, 'you'll have to build one' – as if he was asking the Ministry of Works to provide him with a new desk. The civil servant had not detected the mischievous glint in Cousins's eyes. He coughed in astonishment. 'But Minister,' he protested, 'that would take *years*.'

'Look', Cousins said seriously, 'I pass one such building every morning on my way in – Millbank Towers, the Vickers building. What's wrong with that?'

The man from the Ministry of Works looked amazed and even hurt. There was no space available in Millbank Towers, he said. Cousins waved aside the protest. 'Of course there's space. I know there is. You'd better go and find out for yourself, but I promise you, I know there's floor space to spare. And if not, then please let the Prime Minister know that I will work from my old union headquarters at Transport House until you can find suitable premises.'

Within days the Ministry of Technology was installed in Millbank Towers.

The same kind of straight from the shoulder response had greeted the Cabinet Secretary Sir Burke (now Lord) Trend when Frank Cousins was offered Sir Bruce Fraser as his Permanent Secretary. 'No,' said Cousins. 'Why?' asked Sir Burke. 'Two reasons,' replied Cousins with all the arrogant brusqueness he could muster. 'One, he doesn't like me. Two, I don't like him.' And that was that.

The scenario seems even more bizarre when one considers the Prime Minister's first injunction to his new Minister of Technology on the Saturday morning of his appointment. Cousins asked Wilson what, in the Prime Minister's view, was the first priority. 'You have between four and six weeks to save the computer industry,' Wilson told him. There was no doubt in Wilson's mind that the British computer industry would be overwhelmed by foreign – especially American – competition unless Cousins could mount a major rescue operation. And against all the odds that is, in fact, what the new Minister actually succeeded in doing – though in rather more than six weeks.

In that frantic and heady time – the famous first hundred days of the Wilson Government – the administration was almost overwhelmed by the economic crisis. The huge balance of payments deficit had a shattering impact on the first Cabinet meetings and, even more so, on the informal gatherings of a handful of economic Ministers who met with the Prime Minister and senior civil servants. The record of those first few weeks is still unclear, despite the Crossman diaries and books by Harold Wilson and George Brown. Yet there is little doubt that the decision made personally by Harold Wilson not to devalue sterling was to become a decision of enormous significance for the entire lifetime of the Labour Government through to 1970. It is still arguable that if devaluation had taken place at the outset, as George Brown was urging (though he finally agreed to accept the Wilson view) then the whole record of the Wilson Government might have been more successful. Delaying devaluation until November 1967, it may be said, merely delayed the inevitable and made it much more difficult for the Government to mount a convincing recovery by 1970.

At any rate this crucial decision had to be taken and was taken, within a few days of the election by a small group of Ministers from which Cousins, like Crossman, was excluded. This is not to say that Cousins was either unaware or remained unconsulted. He was still close to Wilson and there is no suggestion that he was opposed to Wilson's view that the pound should be defended. Crossman records that it was

> quite clear that the preparations for dealing with the economic crisis . . . had been entirely done by Harold Wilson himself with the help of James Callaghan, George Brown and – I imagine – Douglas Jay at the Board of Trade.
>
> The crisis programme was just imposed on the rest of us. I didn't much like that. We were given the draft of the statement due next Monday (October 26) on the crisis and the measures to meet it. Personally I didn't think very highly of the draft but Cabinet as a whole had no advance notice so we simply had to accept the *fait accompli* or resign.[4]

Crossman's view, based on the first two Cabinet meetings, was that in a crisis the Prime Minister could consult whoever he wanted (and leave out anyone he did not wish to consult) and that 'once he has consulted, Cabinet must really go along'.

This is not quite how Cousins experienced those first few Cabinet meetings, nor does he agree with Crossman's assessment of Wilson's secrecy over the crisis measures of October/November 1964.

Cousins was a member of PESC, the public expenditure sub-committee of the Cabinet, and he was one of half a dozen Ministers whom Wilson *did* take into his confidence. As to the crisis measures, Cousins was not directly involved in working out the details of the measures – nor did he expect to be, since he was not immediately concerned, as was the Chancellor, or the Secretary of State of Economic Affairs. 'As a matter of fact we all knew the general area of discussion over the package of measures required to tackle the crisis', he had told me. 'We all knew the range, the options and the points being considered by the Ministers responsible. Obviously only a few could actually draw up the details. I didn't see anything wrong in that'. On the other hand Cousins does criticise the Cabinet's failure in those early days to stand up with sufficient firmness to the City and to other financial

4. Richard Crossman, *Diaries of a Cabinet Minister*, Vol. I, p. 28.

pressure. Harold Wilson has commented in his own record on those exerted by the Governor of the Bank of England, Lord Cromer, and the challenge that they represented to a Labour Government.[5] Cousins believes that in many ways the battle between the Government and the City began to be lost in those first few months, despite the fact that Wilson stood up to Cromer. 'It was then, in those first few months, that we really ought to have stood up to the financiers,' Cousins say now. 'But we didn't'. In saying that, he is not seeking to exonerate himself. He accepts his own share of that responsibility. But he would not necessarily share Crossman's view that Ministers were shielded and deliberately foxed by the tactics or the language of the civil service. In Cousin's view there simply was not the resolve among the Cabinet Ministers themselves to fight the City – or perhaps the full appreciation of what they might do, or should do, to fight it.

The crisis measures announced on 26 October were aimed at reducing imports and boosting exports. There was a surcharge of 15 per cent on all imports except food, tobacco and basic raw materials; a system of export rebates under which exporters could recover part of the taxes paid by them in the process of production; the establishment of a Commonwealth Exports Council. There was to be a review of Government expenditure, with particular emphasis on scrapping 'prestige projects' (incidentally this included a reference to the fact that the French Government had already been told of the British wish to 're-examine' the whole Concord project, though it was later discovered that there was a firm agreement with the French which could not be broken). There was a reference to talks already under way with the International Monetary Fund (IMF) over the use by Britain of her drawing rights – that is, international loans. The announcement also spoke of the Government's plan to consult both sides of industry on a plan to deal with productivity prices and incomes and a proposal to set up a Price Review Body. A White Paper published after the Government statement made the first specific reference to incomes policy. The White Paper promised:

> The Government will consult immediately with both sides of industry on the outline of a plan to increase productivity and to ensure that an incomes policy which covers all forms of income and is related to productivity becomes effective. A Price Review Body will be established. The Prime Minister, the First Secretary of State [George Brown] and the Chancellor of the Exchequer will be starting discussions, today, with the Trades Union Congress, the Federation of British Industry [predecessor of the Confederation of British Industry] and other organisations.

Two weeks later the emergency package was followed by an emergency Budget. On 11 November James Callaghan, the Chancellor, added fresh

5. Harold Wilson, *The Labour Government*, pp. 33–8.

measures to the restrictions announced on 26 October. Income tax was increased by 6d. in the £ (to a standard rate of 8s. 3d. in the £ from 6 April 1965). The Chancellor also gave the first hint of his tax reform proposals to be introduced in 1965, including a new corporation tax to replace the old profits tax and income tax on companies, and the Government's intention to operate a new capital gains tax from the spring Budget of 1965. This was announced at the same time that Mr Callaghan promised an increase in old age pensions.

It was becoming increasingly evident that the Labour Government would be clinging on to office with a minute majority in Parliament and uncertain support from international finance. Much depended on the degree of American aid. As George Brown has commented: 'It looked as if with American help we could build up the economy within a reasonably short period of time.'[6] What Brown does not say, but what was none the less emphatically the case, is that American support for sterling was secured at the price of tacit British acceptance of (if not overt support for) American action in Vietnam. There was, at least, a self-denying ordnance by the British Government not to raise any public questioning of United States foreign policy in South-East Asia and, more positively, to discourage and even rebuke any protest movement within the Labour Movement. This support for sterling was bought at an incredibly high price. On the domestic economic front it led, inescapably, to increased pressure from the IMF for a stronger incomes policy – much stronger than even George Brown had imagined necessary or indeed had wanted. Frank Cousins was not unaware of the possible longer-term significance of this crisis. At the same time he was, perhaps, too deeply engrossed in his own problems at the Ministry of Technology to be diverted at that stage. The whole task of setting it up was continuing to prove formidable.

Sir Maurice Dean described that period of gestation to me as 'rougher and colder than I had feared'. He quickly reached the conclusion that the Government machine simply couldn't cope, at short notice, with the problems of forming a new department of that magnitude under peace-time conditions. It was almost impossible to recruit the kind of people required: even the transfer of staff from one department in Whitehall to another was a matter of the most intricate and protracted negotiation. Even worse, the Treasury (then in direct control of civil service affairs) had no power to hand over named persons, or so they claimed. 'The resultant delays very nearly wrecked us,' Sir Maurice claims.

Nor was this hiatus confined merely to the first few months of the new Government. It continued through most of the first full year of Cousins's period at the Ministry and reached its most difficult moment in the mid-

---

6. George Brown, *In My Way* (Gollancz, 1970), p. 100.

summer of 1965. By then an Advisory Council was operating, a Budget approved, some fundamental decisions taken and, indeed, the computer industry rescued from what had seemed certain death. Yet the absence of 'dramatic' results and, no doubt more important in days of 'image consciousness', the deep reluctance of the Minister himself to indulge in publicity fanfares of even the most modest kind, left most observers with the impression that the new department was a white elephant snoozing away quietly while the Minister himself fumbled his way through an unfamiliar jungle. This was quite the wrong impression, but most people undoubtedly held it.

There were a number of significant exceptions to those who regarded Cousins's Parliamentary and Ministerial performance as a catalogue of failures – noteably Lord Hailsham, then the Tory Opposition spokesman for Science and Technology. As Quintin Hogg MP he responded to Frank Cousins's maiden speech on 18 February 1965 and pointed out that the new Minister was one of the very few people who had made their first speech to the Commons from the dispatch box. It was a distinction, said Hogg, that Cousins shared with his father. This distinction helped to draw the two men together in an improbable relationship which outlasted Cousins's Parliamentary career.

Lord Hailsham has since told me that while he was no admirer of Frank Cousins's politics his training as a barrister had taught him that it was important to 'get on with your opponent as one man to another' in the wider interests of public service. 'I thought Frank was treated ungenerously by our people. But the truth is that the House of Commons is a strange place. It simply doesn't like somebody with an outside reputation; someone who has already made a name for themselves before they enter the House. The House' Hailsham added 'will never forgive an outside reputation until they have broken it down. Then they will allow the person to try to make a new reputation for themselves in the House. It was the same with Bevin (albeit in different, war-time circumstances). The House tried to make him look silly. And they did the same with Frank Cousins'.

There is little question now that Harold Wilson himself greatly underestimated the difficulties Frank Cousins faced in setting up the Ministry of Technology. Nor was this simply an underestimate of the sheer physical problems involved, and the limitations of the Whitehall machine to respond to such a challenge. It was also a serious underestimate of Cousins's *personal* difficulties. In committee work his application to detail was brilliant; his sharp mind moved to the core of a problem as if drawn by magnetic impulse; his capacity to see things in the framework of historic development was unmatched in the trade union movement of his time. But he was not a good administrator. His friends as well as his critics inside the TGWU had in the past complained about his lack of attention to administrative detail. It was somehow not in his character to warm to the routine disciplines of organisation. Perhaps in the broader sense this did not matter when he was Minister of Technology. But it did tend, inevitably, to leave many of the basic organisational decisions to the civil servants, and they, in turn, had to contend with the inertia, even the hostility, of Whitehall. The civil service has a certain effortless capacity to demonstrate its disdain for the 'outsider' – especially when he is a man like Frank Cousins distinguished in another sphere of national affairs. The 'whale' is anxious to swallow its victim, although it sets out to do so, often enough, with kindness, decorum and an old world courtesy that can disarm even the roughest warrior from other battlefields. Frank Cousins was without doubt exposed not only to the disdain but to the swallowing technique, and though he sensed it all, and bridled, it was none the less a seriously impeding factor – particularly in that first, extremely difficult year.

The first task was to bring together under one administrative roof a broad band of institutions and activities already dealing with Government-sponsored scientific and technological research. Some had a history stretching back to the First World War, such as the Department of Scientific and Industrial Research (DSIR) or to the end of the Second World War, like the National Research Development Corporation (NRDC) set up by Sir Stafford Cripps in 1949. Indeed it was Cripps's idea to set up the NRDC in order to bring Government influence and encouragement to scientific invention in the hope of modernising British industry after the war – itself an early concept of the Ministry of Technology. There was also a collection of other research organisations for military and civil purposes to be brought under the Ministry's umbrella as well as the Atomic Energy Authority, the Ministry of Aviation (as it then was) and the universities – all of them with some bearing on the research and development functions allocated to the new Ministry.

These functions of the Ministry were described in an announcement by the Prime Minister, Harold Wilson, on 26 November 1964 :

The minister of Technology has the general responsibility of guiding and stimulating a major national effort to bring advanced technology and new processes into British industry. The methods employed will include an intensified use of the appropriate Research Stations and of the NRDC, civil development contracts and studies to identify particular industries or parts of industries suitable for action. The Minister will consider what changes might be made in the arrangements for procurement financed by public funds in order to contribute to the aim of promoting technological advance. He will initiate studies of the status of the engineering profession.

All these tasks will be undertaken in close consultation with the other departments concerned. As already announced the Minister will be responsible for the Atomic Energy Authority and the National Research Development Corporation and will take over the elements of the DSIR headquarters which have been concerned with research and technical development in industry. The Ministry of Technology will in future be the sponsor department for the machine tools, electronics, telecommunications and computer industries. The Ministry will also establish close relations with the British Standards Institution and will support their work in the engineering field. The Science and Technology Bill now before Parliament proposes that the powers of the Atomic Energy Authority shall be extended to permit the Authority to undertake research and development outside the atomic field. Legislative action will also be taken to increase the powers and resources of the NRDC.

The blueprint was not exactly a memorable text for a Ministry that would preside over Britain's technological revolution. True, it contained a good deal of substance, especially the sponsorship of some important industries, yet it was still some distance from the original concept of an all-powerful Ministry for Industry envisaged by Zuckerman and others. Sir Maurice Dean has modestly described the Prime Minister's remit as being 'not all that we had hoped for – but it was better than it might have been. Naturally we hoped that later on something more meaty would come along.'[7]

In fact the 'more meaty' bits did not come along until after both Cousins and Dean had gone, despite twenty months of fighting by both of them to expand the frontiers and powers of the Ministry. It was not until 1967–68 that Frank Cousins's successor, Tony Wedgwood Benn, could properly describe the Ministry of Technology as a 'Ministry for Industry'. But the original objective was achieved chiefly as a result of what Cousins had done or at least prepared in those first twenty months. What he did was to lay the foundation for the most powerful instrument for Government intervention in industry that Britain had ever known in peace-time. That was his legacy.

At the beginning he did not have to contend with the pressures of the House of Commons which, later, was to become for him such a time-consuming and frustrating experience. But he had to learn to fit into the machinery of Government, which he found no less frustrating than Parliament, and of course into the corporate Cabinet pattern. None of this was especially agreeable. The one thing which consistently rivetted his interest was the practical work of the fledgling Ministry, trying to put into operational effect the glib phrases of the technological revolution, seeking at all levels to put flesh on to the bones of political slogans. That is why he found saving the British computer industry so rewarding. It was one of these rare events in politics – a slogan quickly translated into practical action. At the same time

7. The late Sir Maurice Dean to the author.

he began his work, so to speak, at the level of first principles – when in doubt go to the people who have spent their lives trying to find out. One of Cousins's very first acts as Minister of Technology was to set about building around himself a team of advisers whose qualifications as industrialists, scientists, and men of practical achievement quickly established the team as one of the outstanding groups of 'outside' advisers ever to have sat in Whitehall during peace-time – a factor to which the critics of the new Ministry hardly ever referred.

In an interview that December with the science correspondent of the *Observer*, he was asked about the far horizons of his job. Was he attracted, perhaps most of all, to the emotional prospect of turning swords into ploughshares at the Atomic Energy Authority, of using the AEA's accumulated skills for peaceful purposes? 'The old Aldermaston marcher peeped out for a moment when he said : "That's what I would like to be remembered for." '

The search for a safe Parliamentary seat for the Minister of Technology was complicated by a variety of factors, not least by the Government's wafer-thin majority in the Commons. Another delicate problem was the position of Patrick Gordon Walker, the Foreign Secretary, who had been defeated at his Smethwick constituency in the General Election. A seat had to be found for him as well. Mr Gordon Walker was finally chosen to contest a by-election in Leyton, while to make room for Frank Cousins the Member for Nuneaton, Frank Bowles, was persuaded to accept a life peerage. The persuasion was not entirely painless. Frank Bowles later described the process as one that had left him 'shocked, tremendously worried and ill . . .' He spoke of the 'dramatic 24 hours' he was given to consider leaving the Commons for a life peerage. He openly confessed that his first reaction to the request from the Prime Minister was to reject it, but finally decided it was in the best interests of the Party, adding 'It is the biggest sacrifice I can make'[8] Frank Cousins attended the annual dinner of the Nuneaton constituency Labour Party on the night of 20 November 1964. 'I am deeply honoured and indebted to you,' he said, motioning towards Frank Bowles. 'Frankly, I didn't think you would take the peerage, because I know the dedication you have shown in your Parliamentary work'.[9] Frank Bowles denied that there was any ill feeling, personally towards Cousins, but there is no doubt that he felt a strong sense of injustice about the method of 'placing' distinguished outsiders in safe Parliamentary seats – and indeed there was something of a similar feeling in Leyton, where the long-serving much admired and deeply entrenched veteran Reginald Sorensen had been persuaded to take a life peerage to make way for Patrick Gordon Walker.

There was no great haste to hold the by-elections before the turn of the

8. *Daily Sketch*, 21 November 1964.
9. *Ibid.*

new year. Polling day at both Nuneaton and Leyton was fixed for 21 January 1965. Cousins was adopted on 5 January and began his campaign the next day. Nuneaton, at the very heart of England, was a constituency of nearly 62,000 with mining, engineering and textiles as its main industries, including many voters who worked in the motor car and aircraft factories of Coventry. Throughout the campaign Frank Cousins commuted regularly to the Ministry of Technology. He would leave Nuneaton at 7.30 a.m., go to Millbank, perhaps attend a Cabinet committee meeting, return to the Ministry and be back in Nuneaton for early afternoon to resume his campaign. One of the taunts thrown at him by his opponents – particularly the Conservative candidate, David Marland – was that if they elected him the voters of Nuneaton would see very little of their new member.

This message produced one of the best remembered incidents of that by-election. When Frank and Nance Cousins were campaigning in the town's shopping centre one morning a woman with a youngster pointed to Frank and exclaimed, loudly: 'Look, that's Frank Cousins. He will soon be our new MP. You'd better take a good look at him now because you're not likely to see him in this area again, once he gets into Parliament . . .' Nance Cousins reacted like a laser beam. She let fly with a stream of basic language which immortalised her in Nuneaton ears as a woman who was ready to speak her mind regardless of the political or social consequences. There was another squall when the Conservative candidate highlighted a complaint by some London bus delegates who were calling for Cousins to resign completely from the TGWU (where he remained nominally General Secretary). Mr Marland accused the Minister of Technology of 'having a temporary flirtation with parliamentary politics, keeping his successor [Harry Nicholas] out of a top job, and showing little confidence in the Government'. Frank Cousins dismissed it all as 'childish nonsense' though perhaps Mr Marland had been unwittingly near the bone. The Labour majority in Nuneaton fell from 11,702 to 5,241. The result was:

Frank Cousins (Labour)	18,325
David Marland (Conservative)	13,084
John Campbell (Liberal)	6,047

The swing from Labour to Conservative was 4.8 per cent, compared with the General Election swing of 1.8 per cent from Tory to Labour. But the total poll had fallen from 81.5 per cent to 60.8 per cent. The probability is that most of that large fall in the poll consisted of Labour voters. Frank Cousins's vote of 18,325 was down by 7,734 compared with Frank Bowles's vote, while the Conservative vote fell by only just over 1,000. A substantial number of Labour voters no doubt felt there was 'no need' for them to bother polling since it was a foregone conclusion, or some may have felt a personal loyalty to Bowles which they did not have to Cousins. Yet the Nuneaton poll was a roaring success compared with the parallel by-election at Leyton where Patrick Gordon Walker, the Foreign Secretary, was defeated in one of the most surprising results in modern British politics. Defending a General Election majority of 7,926 he was defeated by his Tory opponent with a majority of 205. Gordon Walker resigned from the Government, his post as Foreign Secretary taken by Michael Stewart.

The Leyton result was a severe blow for the Government. By reducing their majority from five to three it intensified the pressure on the entire Parliamentary Labour Party. Press comment speculated on a spring election, which clearly seemed to be on the cards. It only required a few Labour MPs to be ill or a Minister to be away from Britain at the moment of a crucial vote and the Government could have been defeated. But even without an election it meant that the Government had virtually no room was manœuvre. The pressure on Ministers was enormous, most of all on the unseasoned and unorthodox newcomers like Frank Cousins. Harold Wilson has written that after the Nuneaton and Leyton by-elections he told the Cabinet that while he wanted no changes of policy, 'no softening on the tough decisions we had to take to get the country right, we might perhaps go in for fewer self-inflicted wounds, such as certain ill-considered, ill-timed or provocative Parliamentary statements, less "ministerialitis" and, above all, an end to the persistent leaks which cast doubt on the unity or even the sense of purpose of the Government.'[10]

Perhaps implicit in this Wilsonian warning was a message to Frank Cousins, among others, in that Cabinet. Cousins had already demonstrated that he could be as difficult, stubborn and unyielding in the Cabinet as in the TUC General Council. He had respect neither for convention nor political platitude. He entered the Cabinet rather in the style with which he had started inside the TUC General Council – to do a job of work and not to submit easily to a hostile majority. The scenario was different, and the man himself had grown in stature as well as political maturity and sophistication. Even so the basic chemistry remained unchanged. His clashes with Cabinet colleagues who did not see things his way soon became common knowledge in the gossipy corridors of Westminster, giving rise to 'leaks' about squalls between Frank Cousins and George Brown, between Frank Cousins and Ray Gunter, and between Frank Cousins and Tom Fraser.

Among the Cabinet's difficulties in the first few months was the question of MP's pay. The issue came to a head early in November. The report by the Lawrence Committee established under the previous Government proposed that salaries should be raised from £1,750 to £3,250 a year, with corresponding increases for Ministers. About half the Cabinet, led by the

10. Harold Wilson, *The Labour Government*, p. 68.

Prime Minister, wanted the report accepted with the increased MP's salaries backdated to the beginning of the session. But Harold Wilson proposed that the Government should halve the recommended increase for Cabinet Ministers, and he volunteered to take no rise for himself. He was supported by a substantial section of the Cabinet including the Chancellor, James Callaghan. But George Brown opposed Wilson by arguing that if MPs got their rise then Ministers should also receive theirs. Cousins supported Brown, arguing the 'rate for the job' principle and claiming that a rise for MPs and Ministers would not jeopardise the incomes policy talks that had already begun between the Government and both sides of industry. Harold Wilson was defeated on the issue, largely as a result of the combined support for George Brown's view from Frank Cousins and Richard Crossman.[11]

Meanwhile George Brown, at the Department of Economic Affairs, was already marching towards his famous Declaration of Intent on a voluntary prices and incomes policy. And he was doing so against the advice of Frank Cousins, who persistently warned Brown – much to the profound irritation and even fury of the First Secretary – that his policy would not succeed, no matter what promises were made to him by the TUC and the employers' organisations. Repeatedly this led to open clashes between Cousins and Brown at Cabinet committees. The Declaration of Intent was signed on 16 December 1964 by the Government, the TUC and the employers' organisations. But even before the Joint Statement was published George Brown knew that he would have great difficulty in persuading his old union, the TGWU, to support it because of the implicit requirements that unions should subscribe to wage restraint.

This was the beginning of a long and hard road for the Labour Government. Ultimately, it led not only to Frank Cousins's resignation but, beyond that, to the policies of 1969, to Barbara Castle's equally contentious White Paper, 'In Place of Strife', then to the retreat from that policy in June 1969 and, almost certainly, to the Labour Government defeat in June 1970. The failure to find a satisfactory policy for incomes, and therefore the whole field of industrial relations, and the inability to reach an effective working relationship with the trade union movement, demoralised the Labour Movement and left the Government looking shattered in the eyes of the electorate. To allocate blame for such a failure would be to oversimplify the dilemma. For the problem lies at the root of an entire range of fundamental difficulties facing all modern industrial societies. Governments will go on struggling to find an acceptable working solution to the problem, but few will now claim, as the Labour Government of 1964 was tempted to, that a wages policy as such lies at the heart of the matter. It is only one part, though a crucial part,

11. See references to this in Richard Crossman, *The Diaries of a Cabinet Minister*, Vol. I (Hamish Hamilton and Jonathan Cape, 1975), 12 November 1964, pp. 53–4.

of the whole package of policies needed to guide a modern society through social and economic change and conflict.

The real criticism of the George Brown policy in 1964 is that it tended, or perhaps was in the end compelled, to put incomes policy at the very centre of economic policy, rather than to treat it as one important part of a complex political jigsaw. Frank Cousins instinctively felt this at the time – one says 'instinctively' because in December 1964 there was no certainty that the Labour Government *would* fail to see the picture in a broader context. Despite the frantic pressures the Government was still young enough, enthusiastic enough, hopeful enough, to have fought through those early uncertainties. Yet Cousins, already, felt instinctive doubts. Even at that stage he was beginning to harbour suspicions about the resolve of his colleagues.

Perhaps it was partly because he had been alerted by an old, almost forgotten, superstition about the number nineteen. This was his place in Cabinet seniority out of a total of twenty-three, behind Ray Gunter (Labour) and ahead only of Fred Peart (Agriculture), Fred Lee (Power), Tom Fraser (Transport) and Barbara Castle (Overseas Development). Cousins recalled that nineteen had been an unlucky number for him earlier in his life. It was pit stall 19 at Brodsworth colliery where he had his accident. Since then he always tried to avoid any connection with number nineteen! But he couldn't avoid his Cabinet slot.

More seriously, other contentious issues emerging in the Cabinet began to arouse Cousins's doubts. Already finding it difficult to fight for his corner in the field of Whitehall gamesmanship, he felt that the Cabinet decision to continue with Concorde was utterly mistaken. He wanted to scrap Concorde, regardless of the fact that this would have led to the French accusing Britain of violating a treaty obligation. Cousins wanted Concorde scrapped on the grounds that it was wrong to concentrate all Britain's technological resources on the aircraft industry and indeed virtually on this one particular aircraft. He saw this as a distortion of Britain's industrial potential, all the more dangerous because it was precisely from the more advanced, electronically based industries that the new thrust of a wider technology would have to emerge. He saw all too clearly and vividly that the concentration of resources on Concorde would still further imperil his own plans for the Ministry of Technology.

But he lost that battle, too. It is interesting to set this opposition to Concorde against Cousins's support for the British military plane TSR-2, which was another highly advanced piece of aviation technology, or at least his preference for this British plane against its American counterpart, the F-111A. The relative merits of the two planes, in terms of military performance, had been debated inside Whitehall for months – going back in fact to Home's Conservative Government. Indeed the TSR-2 story is a fascinating one, because it illustrates perhaps more vividly than any other single incident of that time precisely how difficult were the decisions which the 1964 Government *had* to make (quite apart from those they *wished* to make), and just how inter-locked they were with wider international considerations. For that reason it is worth spending a little time looking more closely at the question and the way Frank Cousins approached it.

In a sense the British Aircraft Corporation's TSR-2, a most advanced long-range reconnaissance bomber, was as important as Concorde to British aviation development. A whole new world of electronic aviation equipment was connected with the experimental work on the plane. But as it was excessively costly the TSR-2 was an obvious candidate for the axe, under the programme of severe economies forced on the Government. At the very moment when the Cabinet was deciding to retain the Concorde and honour the contract with the French (Ministers were especially anxious about the uproar that might have erupted throughout Europe if Britain had unilaterally reneged on that deal) the TSR-2 issue moved up to the front of queue for a decision. Unlike the case with the Concorde, there was an acceptable alternative – the American F-111A. The defence chiefs in London had become persuaded by the Americans that on balance the F-111A was a better (and cheaper) bet than the British plane. The argument presented to Ministers by the air staff was that the US swing-wing aircraft was preferable in defence terms, not simply on economic grounds, although the Americans were offering it on extremely favourable terms.

One must picture the political scene: the British economy was in serious difficulties, and, some would argue, more in need of American support (for sterling) than ever. The new Labour Government had still not publicly associated itself with President Johnson's Vietnam policy, but there was intense pressure (not least from the Foreign Office) so to do, even if in a modest form. With an almost non-existent majority Wilson could have chosen the line of blood, sweat, toil and tears. But even if that had been his style he believed that the country would not have supported such a policy of self-denial. No one can say whether that was a correct judgement. At any rate the full facts are not known about what really took place between the British and American defence staffs or, for that matter, within a small group of Cabinet Ministers where the decisions were finally taken. But it did become clear to Cousins that Denis Healey, the Minister of Defence, was completely sold on the F-111A and was equally convinced that the British plane should be abandoned. It was also clear to the Minister of Technology that some defence advisers, of whom Sir Solly Zuckerman was the most distinguished, were persuaded that the TSR-2 was a costly piece of British self-indulgence and should be dropped. What people like Zuckerman were *not* yet convinced about was the logic of purchasing the American plane. Cousins's own position was similarly uncertain. In principle he was against *both* planes. Yet he acknowledged that a defence case could be made out for having an aircraft of this range and capacity, and if this case could be sustained in the light of the country's economic problems, he would prefer to buy British rather than American.

On the other hand, Cousins challenged the defence chiefs on their own ground. At one Cabinet committee meeting with the service chiefs-of-staff Cousins demonstrated, perhaps too plainly, his profound disagreement with their reasoning, both on grounds of defence tactics and the need for either aircraft, and, again, on their preference for an American as against a British aircraft. The atmosphere at the meeting became so tense that Harold Wilson slipped a note across the table to Cousins (a normal enough Cabinet-room practice) urging him to be patient. Cousins was in the middle of an outburst against the military pundits, declaring that while he hadn't much faith in politicians he had still less in generals. Wilson's note urged: 'Play it cool, we can win our point by other methods.'[12] Cousins cooled. The service chiefs went on pressing for the F-111A. At that stage they wanted a firm Cabinet commitment to purchase at least 50 of the aircraft, though the precise numbers fluctuated up to about 150.

The issue straddled many Cabinet meetings and even more Cabinet committee meetings, before the decision was taken to abandon the TSR-2. But to quell the opposition the Prime Minister agreed to separate the two sides of the problem – cancelling the British plane and ordering the American alternative. Decision one, to scrap the TSR-2, was taken first, in the early spring of 1965. The next step, to buy the American plane, was delayed deliberately to soften the impact and minimise division inside the Cabinet. Between the two decisions there was a totally unpredicted 'happening' which further embarrassed Ministers and complicated the whole affair. Early in February 1965, not long after the Nuneaton by-election, Hawker-Siddeley, whose strong production zone was in the Coventry-Nuneaton area, replied to a challenge put to them by the Ministry of Aviation. Hawker's came forward with the design for a plane which contained the qualities of both – a kind of hybrid of the TSR-2 and the F-111A. This design, moreover, was cheaper to produce than the TSR-2, production time was cut and their prospectus was strongly competitive with that of the American plan. In fact the choice was so fine that the Aviation Minister, Roy Jenkins, reported to the Cabinet (of which he was not then a full member) that the Hawker-Siddeley proposal was 'embarrassingly good'.

It was only because the Hawker delivery date was two years later than

---

12. The precise wording of the note remains in some doubt. It could have read: 'Don't push your point now; leave it because we can win another way.' But the implication remains the same. Cousins believed that Wilson intended to let the defence chiefs have their say and exhaust their case, and then take a firm decision *against* their advice. Cousins insists that this was the only interpretation he could place on the Cabinet message.

the then promised American delivery date that Jenkins recommended the rejection of the British design. Jenkins, who had originally supported the TSR-2 against the F-111A, had (according to Frank Cousins) been converted by Denis Healey and the defence argument. Now, in a new and embarrassing situation, he was again persuaded by the defence staff argument and the combined pressures of a small group of Cabinet Ministers including the Prime Minister, the Chancellor and Denis Healey. In the end it was only Cousins and Crossman (both local MPs for Hawker-Siddeley workers and therefore regarded as 'special pleaders' who urged that the new British design should be seriously considered. It was a forlorn final gesture of defiance.

Cousins was bitterly critical of the decision, the more so because he had been led to believe that Harold Wilson had agreed with him originally and had then backed off under pressure – pressure never satisfactorily explained to the Cabinet in Cousins's presence. Relations, he says, were never quite the same between Cousins and Wilson after the TSR-2 episode. It is impossible to offer an absolute assessment of the scar it left on their relationship because so much else happened in the subsequent year to damage the mutual confidence and the euphoric sense of community that existed in October 1964. But after the TSR-2 controversy Cousins became convinced that his Prime Minister was not a wholly dependable ally. It also cast a long shadow over the difficulties he was having, in other spheres, trying to get the Ministry of Technology off the ground and over the nationalisation of steel which some Ministers wanted delaying or dropped altogether. But, perhaps most of all, it illustrated vividly to Frank Cousins just how extraordinarily difficult it was going to be to carry out policies without regard to American opinion and White House policies. To him the TSR-2 and the Hawker-Siddeley cases were classical examples of the limitations. Cousins saw the aircraft as important for British technological development, especially for its spin-off effects. There was also the question of jobs in the aircraft industry, already in decline, and the powerful psychological factor with its immediate negative impact on management as well as workers, skilled as well as unskilled. It was another example of the British losing out. At least that is how it seemed to Frank Cousins.

Zuckerman however puts a different gloss on the whole affair. He has suggested to the author that even the Cabinet did not know the full story. They opted for the F-111A purely on grounds of defence priorities. The American plane had a far better range than the TSR-2 and was operationally more effective. Moreover, the two year delay before any British alternative could be developed would have left a serious gap in Britain's air defence system. Only a handful of Ministers, Lord Zuckerman claims, knew the full story – and they did not include Cousins or Crossman. Indeed, the truth seems to be that the weight of opinion against the TSR-2 was already cast during the period of the previous Government, when a number of key

Ministers in the Home administration came down in favour of scrapping the British plane – something perhaps even the Wilson Government may not have realised. The ultimate irony was that although 142 F-111As were ordered the aircraft proved to be a fiasco, a disastrous flop, and not one was delivered. But the saga left a permanent scar on Cousins's mind and added perhaps decisively to his disenchantment. Crossman wrote in his diary:

> The tremendous decision to buy American and cut back the British aircraft contribution which Harold forced through or at least half forced through (everything still depends on whether the TSR2 is dropped or isn't dropped) has put us temporarily completely in the power of the Americans. I am not so much alarmed about this politically. It is perfectly possible even in Coventry to win respect for this policy and even to get votes. But I am alarmed at the feeling that we have put ourselves in the hands of the American politicians – an uneasy feeling which I share with Frank Cousins.
>
> Harold has shown a solid determination to re-create the Anglo-American axis, the special relationship between Britain and America very much along Bevinite lines. The more I think of this gamble the more I dislike it. We are cutting back the British aircraft industry in order to concentrate on maintaining our imperial position East of Suez. And we are doing that not because we need these bases ourselves but because the Americans can't defend the Far East on their own and need us there.[13]

Of course the TSR-2 issue was only one aspect of this dependence on the United States. Running parallel, and almost at the same time as the aircraft controversy, was the question of the Polaris submarines, the 'ultimate deterrent'. Nothing could have been more politically sensitive, from Frank Cousins's point of view. When Labour came into office two Polaris submarines were already on the stocks and there were plans for an additional three. Then the entire defence strategy came under review, partly because Labour promised in their election manifesto to review the Nassau Agreement of December 1962 at which Harold Macmillan secured President Kennedy's agreement for the British to build Polaris submarines together with the missiles to stock them. This was supposed to be Britain's 'independent' nuclear deterrent to replace the defunct Skybolt. Labour said that all this would be reviewed and the pretence of an independent deterrent stripped away. The TSR-2 came under the same review. But when it was decided not only to keep the existing Polaris programme but also to go ahead with building another two (instead of three) it was evident that the balance was weighed against continuing with TSR-2.[14]

Cousins was against building any more Polaris submarines and, to his

13. Richard Crossman, *Diaries of a Cabinet Minister*, Vol. I, 11 February 1965 (Hamish Hamilton and Jonathan Cape, 1975), p. 156.
14. See Harold Wilson, *The Labour Government*, pp. 40–5.

surprise, so too was George Brown. The First Secretary preferred to pool our deterrent force with the Europeans, especially the French, in a hopeful gesture for closer European cooperation and greater independence from the United States. But Harold Wilson and Denis Healey were strongly opposed to that. *Their* proposition was to establish an Atlantic Nuclear Force (ANF) as a counter-proposal to the American idea of a multilateral force (MLF) for which the United States had been pressing for some time and to which the British defence chiefs were opposed. A great deal of complicated defence politics on both sides of the Atlantic was involved in this argument and Harold Wilson, with Denis Healey, conceived the ANF idea as an alternative plan that would 'internationalise the British deterrent through NATO while avoiding the insoluble problems of mixed-manning (the American idea) and the political objections of appearing to give the Germans a finger on the nuclear "trigger" '.[15]

All of this tends to support the Zuckerman argument that the whole story of TSR-2, and much else, was part of a wider, more complex and elaborate defence saga, the details of which were known to very few Cabinet Ministers – and, perhaps the whole picture was known to none.

For the most part Cousins reacted by instinct, the instinctive belief that Britain's defence policy was wrong and that our apparently increasing reliance on the Americans seriously weakened any policy the Labour Government could have for effective political and economic independence of action.

About this time Crossman was observing Frank Cousins and assessing his impact inside the Cabinet. It is worth repeating the views he then wrote down in his diary. He saw Cousins as a curious mixture :

> He talked a great deal of nonsense on this occasion [it was a debate about postal rates]. Indeed I feel he is rapidly developing a standing in the Cabinet not unlike a cross between Nye Bevan and Manny Shinwell in the Attlee Cabinet. However, having said that, I must add that we need people like Frank Cousins in Cabinet, we need more of them. He is on the side of the angels. He is a very rare kind of man – one who still has a combination of real idealism and vitality and experience of practical power . . .[16]

Crossman himself was ambivalent towards Cousins. He began with something akin to adulation and admits that he would have 'adored working with him'.[17] Crossman says he regrets going to the Ministery of Housing in October 1964 instead of the job he *thought* he was going to get – the Department of Education and Science. The reason was that Education and Science

15. *Ibid.*, p. 44.
16. Richard Crossman, *The Diaries of a Cabinet Minister*, Vol. I, 14 January 1965, pp. 128–9.
17. *Ibid.*, p. 43.

in his view would need to work in the closest possible harness with the new Ministry of Technology, precisely what he would have liked to have done with Cousins there. Such was his admiration and respect for Frank Cousins at that stage. Eventually this enthusiasm distintegrated because of the Cabinet conflict over incomes policy in which Cousins and Crossman took opposite sides. Still later, the respect (if not the regard) returned when Crossman confessed that Cousins had been right all the time. But that is leaping a stage.

In fact those early months in the Cabinet did not consist entirely of defeats for Frank Cousins. There was one major and notable success quite early on when his pressure, more than that of any other member of the Wilson team, led to the resignation of the Railways Board chairman, Dr Richard Beeching.

The Beeching story exploded in mid-December 1964, after the Railways Board chairman had arranged with the Minister of Transport, Tom Fraser, that he would leave the Railways Board on 1 January. Beeching's report on the need to cut back drastically Britain's railway system had been published in the spring of 1963 and he was subsequently appointed chairman of British Railways. In the run-up to the election the Labour Party made it clear that they would stop the Beeching cuts and re-assess the entire situation. Beeching – who had publicly declared that he had no sympathy with Labour's views on this, or on most other things – announced his intention of leaving the Railways and returning to his old company, ICI, in 1965. Meanwhile he had agreed with Tom Fraser to spend several months after leaving his chair in preparing a new report on the co-ordination of all transport, which he would produce for the Minister by 31 May 1965. When this arrangement was reported to the Cabinet on 14 December, Tom Fraser offered it as a *fait accompli*, signed and sealed with the Prime Minister's approval. That was the isue which touched off a revolt by Frank Cousins, supported by Dick Crossman. They objected to the whole concept. Both made it clear that they wouldn't have it. Crossman's account takes up the story :

> Frank Cousins and I both blew our tops. Frank Cousins talked about it in the kind of way an ordinary rank and file Labour person would. He said : 'Here's a man we have denounced up hill and down dale, a man who is a bureaucratic enemy of public transport. Why should we give him this job? Any idea Beeching proposed would be discredited among the trade unions by the very fact that he proposed it.[18]

Between them Cousins and Crossman, who then seemed to be working as a close partnership in Cabinet, forced the Prime Minister to reconsider the

18. *Ibid.*, 14–15 December 1964, pp. 101–3.

entire scheme. They were, in fact, the only two prepared to take on Harold Wilson and press him strongly to accept the idea of having two independent assessors to sit alongside Beeching on the transport inquiry. Crossman went still further, demanding that the assessors should have 'a genuinely independent position'. At this point a Cabinet voice remarked, 'Well, the effect of that will be to keep Beeching out' – at which Frank Cousins snorted 'That would be a damned good thing'.

Tom Fraser told Beeching about the Cabinet decision to appoint assessors. Beeching immediately sought a meeting with Harold Wilson and demanded to know precisely what had happened, and why. He was told. From Downing Street Beeching went straight to the Ministry of Transport to hand in his resignation to Fraser. Someone close to Beeching, who was with him at the time, has described his deep anger – most of all against Frank Cousins. The two men did not know each other very well, but what little they did know they didn't like. Perhaps one reason for their mutual antipathy – politics apart – was the interesting similarity in some of their qualities. Both had a strong vein of authoritarianism; both were impatient with the civil service mentality; both saw the need to take big decisions about industry and carry them through with resolve. But there the matching elements must end. Beeching was intolerant of the human fallibility. At the Railways Board he had acquired a reputation for being a brilliant administrator but somewhat short on humanitarian feelings.

One of Cousins's main problems when he came into the Cabinet was to forget he was no longer actively the General Secretary of the Transport and General Workers' Union. It was an exceptionally difficult challenge for him, emotionally as well as practically (as it had been with Ernest Bevin during the war). Almost immediately after the Wilson Government was formed Cousins was put to the test – and, by standards of Government behaviour, failed. When the threat of a dock strike, hanging over the industrial landscape during the election campaign, was revived, the Minister of Labour, the late Ray Gunter, made a few Gunter-like remarks to rebuke the dockers and warn them about the consequences of a strike. It was understandable enough in the circumstances. But Cousins found such 'interference' quite intolerable. Before the next Cabinet meeting, while Ministers gathered in the hall of Downing Street outside the Cabinet room, Cousins buttonholed Gunter. Towering above the Minister of Labour he thrust his index finger at Gunter and warned him that any repetition of an attack of this kind on 'my members in the docks' would lead to an open showdown. 'You keep to your railwaymen', he demanded of the former president of the railway clerks' union, the Transport Salaried Staffs Association, 'and keep away from my members.' And to another Cabinet Minister he scathingly referred to Gunter as a 'jumped-up railway clerk'. Gunter, understandably incensed, took the matter to Wilson, who drew Frank Cousins aside to remind him

'You know, Frank, this is not the TGWU . . .' To which Cousins replied, without pausing to reflect, 'I am under no illusions about *that*!'

Still, there were amusing moments too. And probably none more so than the day Frank Cousins was called to Sandringham to be sworn in as a Privy Councillor (it was on the morning of Churchill's death, 24 January 1965). Cousins was still in his constituency when he was summoned to Sandringham. It meant meeting several other Ministers at Liverpool Street Station shortly after 8 a.m. on Sunday morning and it was certainly not his idea of a day out after such a fatiguing period. When he arrived at the station he spotted some of his colleagues, including Anthony Crosland, and without a blush inquired: 'Whose f—— idea was it that we should be here on this job, this morning?' Someone nodded in the direction of a spruce and elegant gentleman standing within earshot. It was the Queen's private secretary, Sir Michael Adeane. Sir Michael had plainly heard Cousins's explosion and it did not appear to endear the Minister of Technology to him. He made it plain that this was not the sort of language he expected from a Cabinet Minister on a Sunday morning, especially *en route* for a Privy Council. Cousins simply stalked off to find an empty compartment on the train. He was joined by the late Tony Crosland, who was always ready to have a kick at pomp. However, at Sandringham Cousins actually enjoyed himself. He established an immediate rapport with the Queen and within minutes was discussing the gardens in great technical detail. He walked round the flower beds with Her Majesty, who was amazed at his knowledge of the subject. He carried Prince Andrew in his arms, making clucking noises for the Royal child. He appeared at peace with all mankind . . .

To him all children were equal – equally interesting and attractive.

Chapter Twenty-two

THE MAN IN THE MINISTRY

When Frank Cousins began at Millbank Tower, his adopted Ministerial base, he asked his principal adviser, Professor Patrick Blackett, for some personal advice. With disarming candour Cousins said he would like the Professor to help him to understand more about science and technology. Cousins is not a modest man, but at times he injected into his style of leadership a galvanising demureness which compelled both respect and attention. This was preciscely the effect his request for knowledge had on Blackett.

After all, Cousins reminded Blackett, here he was, just an ordinary chap with a background of little formal schooling. His adult life, since leaving school at 14 and working in the pits, had been spent driving trucks and then as an official in the trade union movement. His 'universities', he observed, echoing Gorky, had been the long hours of working life and the hard experience of fighting for his members' living standards. He had never found it easy to discipline his mind to sustained reading of political theory. Yet he was captivated by science and technology, absorbed a great deal of surface knowledge about the subject and explored scientific theories. What he did read he remembered and frequently recalled it vividly. He was no bookworm, although he found himself increasingly drawn to science fiction, which had an unusually compelling force for him. But he recognised that he would require a great deal of grounding in the technicalities which underpinned many of the issues his new Ministry would be tackling. He also observed to Blackett that he would certainly be called on to mix with many of the top scientific brains both in Britain and overseas. This demanded he should have some professional tutoring in what it might be necessary to know. Blackett warmed to such an open, honest admission and such a humble request for knowledge. Cousins was a proud man as a trade union official, as a TUC 'statesman' and as a Cabinet Minister. He did not easily yield his confidences even to his closest associates. He needed to be sure of his relationships before he opened up. In this he was characteristic of his generation of working-class leaders; like them, he was guarded about some remoter corners of his earlier life. This was partly due to a profound conviction that such information was no business of the 'outside world' (since it might look like special pleading), but it was also due to a defensiveness about his experience in a working-class culture. Part of the arrogance, the prickly volatility of many working-class leaders stems from this same cultural defensiveness. It is a 'chippiness' seen in the personalities of men like George Brown, it was reflected in Aneurin Bevan's sometimes arrogant air of superiority and his conviction that working-class leaders had nothing to be defensive about, certainly nothing to apologise for – they had everything to feel superior about. Frank Cousins had very much more of Bevan than Brown in his make-up, but that did not prevent him from donning a protective armour.

When he declared himself to Professor Blackett it was a signal that he felt at ease with the man. There was also political rapport. Blackett found in Cousins a remarkably talented adult pupil, a man of unusual honesty and political integrity. The two men formed a formidable partnership. The Professor suggested a list of reading material which Cousins could study, and together with Sir William (now Lord Penney), then chairman of the Atomic Energy Authority, provided the Minister of Technology with books and papers to study. For months Cousins diligently read through them, in addition to his normal Cabinet papers. He set aside his favourite bedside reading of thrillers and science fiction to concentrate on the scarcely less remarkable material of real-life science. He studied the intricacies of nuclear physics, computer mathematics and electronic engineering. He learned rapidly, greatly impressing the academic minds who formed his advisory cordon.

Blackett had known Cousins slightly before he became Minister of Technology. The two had first met during Cousins's spell as a TUC representative on the National Research Development Council. But it was a casual acquaintance. There had been some contact during the preparations for Harold Wilson's technology speech at Scarborough in 1963. Yet it wasn't until the two men worked together that their friendship and mutual respect became fully developed. Blackett has told me that he found Cousins : 'an attractive and able man. He did not know an awful lot about manufacturing industry but he could handle things very well. He read a great deal about science and technology and was always ready to listen and to learn.' Even at the outset, before Blackett and Penney gave him the reading list, Blackett recalled that Cousins was 'quite reasonably well informed' on science and technology. On the other hand the Professor was not uncritical. He felt that Cousins was not the best choice for the difficult task of starting off a brand new department like the Ministry of Technology. In his view Harold Wilson ought to have appointed an experienced Minister with senior civil servants who knew their way through the Whitehall minefield. Blackett was critical of the Prime Minister for allowing Cousins to be pitched into such a situation without effective support:

> The Ministry of Technology started off on too small a scale. We should have started by being bigger and with more of the older departments drawn in. It ought to have been a Ministry for Industry from the start and we should have been linked more closely with the Department of Economic Affairs. Nevertheless we were on the right lines.

Blackett's is not the only voice critical of the way that Cousins was thrown in at the deep end. Others, including some civil servants who worked closely with Cousins, have said that it was an error of judgement by Wilson to have given Cousins that particular post. It needed someone who knew how to bully his way through the formidable civil service network; but in that respect Wilson's choice was limited, since very few of his 1964 Cabinet had had previous Ministerial experience.

As one of the principal architects of the concept Blackett was naturally convinced that the Ministry, despite all teething troubles, was an essential part of the new fabric of government. He saw it as the sponsoring department for a radical restructuring of British industry, which the Professor believed had been left behind by technological developments in Germany, Japan and the United States. Blackett believed passionately that the only hope for British industry lay in a combination of technological reorganisation and concentration on industrial priorities. He regarded the multiplicity of production units, under-financed and often ineffectually managed, as 'a disastrous feature of British industry'. It followed that he saw the new Ministry as a major instrument for correcting this weakness, and he saw his Minister as the most important single personality in working to that end.

> Our object was better management, a better industrial structure for the whole country and the better use of technology. All of these are fairly obvious things which needed to be done. Frank put a lot of energy into doing that job. He worked very hard – but he didn't get the support he ought to have had.

Yet the fact remains that very few people recognised the significance of the Ministry of Technology at the time; a decade later the arguments about technology, lack of investment, Britain's industrial backwardness – all the same issues – still remain at the heart of political and economic debate. But in 1964 the very phrase 'technology' was both over-used and under-explained at the same time. It became a politician's catchphrase. It had a certain dazzle. It seemed both to offer an engaging short-cut to the future, and a scientific switch-gear for national prosperity. Yet it was easier to convey the allure than to produce the effects. On the other hand Cousins was hostile to any simplistic public relations. He was impatient, even contemptuous, of the 'image-making' process. So the paradox was that while the word 'technology' cast its own special spell across the land Frank Cousins, in the new Ministry, retreated into a quiet, sober, inner shell underneath which his team sought to establish firm foundations, build carefully, even over-cautiously, away from the floodlights of publicity. They knew it would be a long haul, yet, outside, the world waited impatiently for quick results.

Even Cousins's Cabinet colleagues were somewhat mystified about what, precisely, was going on in the 'big tower' along the road from the Palace of Westminster. Cousins was no better at communicating to his Cabinet colleagues than to the outside world. He preferred to spend his time getting things moving, actually 'doing things', rather than in the endless proliferation of Ministerial meetings or Press conferences. Many of his colleagues – even those most sympathetic to him – have testified to his long silences and his awkwardness at Cabinet meetings. To those who did not know him well, or were inclined all too readily to recall past political conflicts, he was quickly set down as 'a failure' in Cabinet, if not as a Minister. His absence from the House of Commons for the first three months of his Ministry was a serious handicap in this respect, as in many others. It prevented Cousins from experiencing the political ambience needed for effective Cabinet dialogue. Cabinet colleagues in the 1964–6 Government explained their reaction to Frank Cousins simply by claiming that they never really knew what was 'going on' at the Ministry of Technology. Yet expectations were built too loftily, too soon. So much had been said on the technology theme that most people, including some of these Cabinet colleagues, expected to see dramatic results rather too quickly. As Margaret Stewart suggests, 'The Ministry of Technology was undoubtedly 'oversold' at the beginning and the public expected spectacular, almost science-fiction results.[1] That in itself was an incipient handicap to Frank Cousins – a handicap which he fully recognised and which persuaded him (if he needed persuading) that it would have been imprudent to respond to the popular demand for fanfares. Moreover, until he became an MP he could not effectively respond in Parliament to the prolonged and ruthless attacks on his Ministry and himself. His Parliamentary questions were answered for him in the Commons by a junior Minister from Michael Stewart's Department of Education and Science, while in the Upper House Lord Snow did his best to bat on a series of unfamiliar and tricky wickets. It was scarcely the most propitious opening for the technological revolution.

Frank Cousins would have liked to have appointed Michael Foot as his Parliamentary Secretary, but nothing came of this – nothing, that is, except

---

1. Margaret Stewart, *Frank Cousins: A Study* (Hutchinson, 1968), p. 122.

a great deal of doubt in Frank Cousins's mind as to whether the Prime Minister, who knew of his wish, ever approached Foot. Foot was indeed never approached by Harold Wilson; he was never directly offered any job in the 1964 Government. At the time it was suggested that the Prime Minister made 'certain soundings' through Michael Foot's brother the late Sir Dingle. There was no truth in these rumours. Cousins did ask Wilson about Michael Foot but was informed that, according to the information reaching the Prime Minister, Foot did not wish to have a Government post. Precisely how the Prime Minister knew this remains a mystery. My own personal recollection is that Frank Cousins wanted to have Michael Foot, but did not feel it was his role to make a personal approach to someone who was already a close personal as well as political friend without first securing the Prime Minister's approval. Perhaps he expected Foot to make the first move, but that was not in his character. The episode is important for two reasons: for what was and for what might have been. A Cousins-Foot team at the Ministry of Technology could well have transformed the public image of what was seen by the world outside as a rather grey and unimaginative new department of State.

There is nothing more to add to the account, according to Michael Foot. But there was a sequel. In the weeks before the General Election of 1966, Foot was approached by Ernest Fernyhough, MP (then Harold Wilson's PPS) and asked if he would like to consider taking over the Ministry of Technology from Frank Cousins. Fernyhough told Foot that the Prime Minister believed Cousins was then on the verge of resignation. The idea evidently was that Foot would become Minister of Technology with a seat in the Cabinet. Not surprisingly, Foot would have nothing to do with such a scheme. He told Fernyhough to inform Harold Wilson that he could hardly be expected to take over a Government post from a personal and political friend with whose criticisms of Government policy he agreed. He would never dream of doing such a thing. Didn't the Prime Minister know, Foot inquired of Fernyhough, about his (Foot's) views on Vietnam, incomes policy, and so on, all of which coincided with Frank Cousins's views? Fernyhough was sent away with a categorical rejection of the feeler. But it was evident from Fernyhough's attitude that the Prime Minister was anticipating Cousins's imminent resignation.

A Cousins-Foot combination at the fledgling Ministry would probably have attracted more, not less, political criticism, there would certainly have been no lack of publicity, most of it no doubt at least as adverse as, in the event, it turned out to be without Foot. Yet on the positive side Frank Cousins would have had, in the House of Commons, an outstanding ally. Michael Foot, had already established himself as the most brilliant debater in the Commons, and what he may have lacked in administrative experience he would have more than made up for in defending both his Minister and the political philosophy behind the new Department. That is 'what might have been'. What happened was somewhat less inspiring. Cousins soldiered on with a makeshift arrangement in the Commons and Lord Snow in the Lords until his own entry into Parliament in February 1965. Snow was kept on until the autumn when, in his first reshuffle, Harold Wilson finally strengthened the Technology team by transferring Richard Marsh, then a junior Minister at the Ministry of Labour under Ray Gunter, to become joint Parliamentary Secretary to Frank Cousins. It was a surprisingly effective appointment; Cousins and Marsh worked exceptionally well together. They fitted each other's style and later, when Marsh was a Cabinet Minister in his own right, they formed an alliance in opposition to the Government's prices and incomes policy that gave Cousins some solace in what was for him a period of intense strain and depressing isolation.

The criticism of the new department which came from the Press, and the often malicious sniping from the Opposition in Parliament, was not echoed in the senior board rooms of industry. Quite the opposite. Many of the country's top industrialists regarded the new Department as an extremely hopeful sign that Whitehall was, at last, beginning to recognise the longer-term nature of Britain's industrial problems. Cousins knew that there was great potential goodwill for his new Ministry among many leading tycoons, and he also recognised the need to bring some of them into a close working relationship with the Ministry. With Blackett and Sir Maurice Dean the Minister drew up a formidable list of people whom they would wish to have as a regular Advisory Council on Technology. Perhaps the most revealing feature of all, in those early months, was that not one 'top name' on the original list turned down the invitation. Each was an exceptionally busy and important figure in his own field. Cousins's view was that it was pointless to approach people who were *not* already exceptionally stretched, since *they* were the men to have. Today the list reads like the Cabinet of 'Great Britain Ltd. Government' – a concept which tycoons in the mid-sixties are said to have spent their Sundays evenings endlessly debating not always as a mere innocuous after-dinner parlour game.

Cousins, as chairman of his Advisory Council, urged Blackett to accept the role of deputy chairman and the list included: Sir Leon Bagrit (then chairman of Elliot-Automation); Lord Brown (former chairman of Glacier Metal and also a former Minister in the Wilson Government); Sir Arnold Hall (boss of Hawker-Siddeley); Lord Kearton (then chairman of Court-aulds, now head of the BNOC); Sir Willliam (later Lord) Caron (President of the Amalgamated Union of Engineering Workers, then the AEU); Lord Nelson of Stafford (chairman of English Electric, later merged with AEI into GEC); Sir Hugh Tett (then chairman of Esso Oil); Professor M. J. Lighthill (Imperial College, London); the Vice Chancellors of the Universities of Strathclyde and of Lancaster; and later Professor Bruce Williams, Dean of the School of Economics at Manchester University, who joined the Advisory Council as an economic adviser.

One of the biggest and most distinguished of the fishes enticed into the Technology net was Dr John Adams, a brilliant nuclear physicist, who was persuaded to join the department by Patrick Blackett. Adams came in July 1965 when the Ministry's fortunes and prestige appeared to be at the lowest point, and when Cousins himself had already begun to have serious doubts about how long he could stand the frustrations of the Government machine. Adams seemed to inject new hope and fresh energy into a dispirited team. He joined as Controller, which meant that he organised the Ministry's practical work. He was (and is) an outstanding nuclear engineer, and his organisational ability combined with his scientific knowledge quickly began to transform the atmosphere of Millbank Tower. From that moment there was a revival of drive. With the gradual influx of reinforcements and adhesions from other departments the Ministry of Technology was rejuvenated. Cousins felt fortified – though by then he retained fewer and fewer illusions.

In Parliament he had to withstand an unremitting barrage of questioning designed not to elicit information but to maximise opportunities for ridicule and exploit every conceivable political advantage. No doubt a more skilled Parliamentary performer would have dismissed much of it as irrelevant drivel. But the sensitive, introspective, perhaps even occasionally credulous Cousins found the experience distracting and extremely disenchanting. Hansard is full of examples of the taunts and jibes he constantly encountered. He had scarcely touched down in the House of Commons before the hounds were snapping at his heels. Take, for instance, Question Time on 2 March. Mr Dudley Smith, MP attacked him for something he had written long before on public ownership for *Tribune*; Mr Eldon Griffiths, MP jibed at the Minister of Technology for having his hand in his pocket as he addressed the House; Mr Neil Marten, MP goaded Cousins with references to his past 'antics' with CND and the Aldermaston marchers. Commander Courtney MP took up a similar theme with a few added implied insults, and when Cousins roared back and, with a jabbing finger, shouted the un-Parliamentary 'You——' at the Commander (instead of 'the Honourable Member for . . .') there were shrill cries of 'Order' from the Opposition and the Minister was forced to apologise to the Speaker. 'You will have to accept that I think of "you" in that way', Cousins explained, plaintively. Then he apologised : 'No offence is intended, Mr. Speaker. My experience in the past has been directing thoughts to people who did not mind.' It was a completely new world to Frank Cousins.

Even in 1966 Cousins was still having difficulty in reconciling himself to the Parliamentary processes. During his Department's Question Time session of Tuesday 15 February that year he came under strong pressure across a range of issues from computer manufacture, advanced gas-cooled reactors, sea water desalination, and numerically controlled machine tools, to Hovercraft and mono-wheel-drive tractors. He and Richard Marsh took it in turn to answer the barrage of questions. Toward the end Hector Hughes, MP pursued the Minister about his plans for the new prototype reactor near Dounreay in Scotland. This was in fact one of Cousins's achievements and Hector Hughes's question had in a sense been designed to evoke a Parliamentary appreciation. It did – on the Labour benches – but it also delayed the proceedings, and the Speaker, Horace (now Lord) King, chastised Cousins for appearing to delay his reply. An angry Cousins showed his irritation with the Speaker in unmistakable form. And the incident brought a note of apology from the Speaker :

Dear Frank,
   You were right to protest when I complained about a long answer and justify it. Don't ever hesitate if you think I have been too sharp.
   But I am trying steadily, minute by minute, to speed up questions – and they dragged a little today. Do remember that when I jump in it is never personal but always with the goal in view, that is something like 50 questions a day, with more supplementaries than ever before – but everything more concise.
   I realise that some answers, and some questions, must in the nature of things and because of their complexity, be long. No doubt yours was one such.
                                        Warmest regards
                                        Horace King.[2]

It was a headmasterly note from the Speaker to a friendly member of the class, but a member who from time to time showed quite clearly his contempt and irritation for the rules of the classroom. Much of this prep school behaviour pattern was no doubt light-hearted and innocuous enough. It was all part of the Parliamentary game. But Cousins did not regard it as 'a game'. He took his job seriously, and he felt that the House of Commons had an obligation to do the same. He discovered, to his distress, that he had been wrong in that assessment; he quickly found that the majority of the Opposition were less interested in using Question Time as a vital mechanism by which to lever information out of the Government than to ridicule and poke fun at Ministers and their policies. Cousins looked upon this as a waste of the democratic process and a cynical misuse of his (and Government) time. He learned, slowly and painfully.

2. Letter from Horace King to Frank Cousins, 15 February 1966. The extracts from Hansard are from the same date.

Yet, by the time he left the House he had developed a style and a much more relaxed manner which suggested he would have become an attractive, and a highly effective, Parliamentary debater. Even the humour of technology was beginning to show through in his later answers at Question Time. The late Tom Driberg, once asked him (perhaps he was even encouraged to do so!) to explain the Ministry's relationship with the Gribble (a wood-boring insect). Was the Minister, Mr Driberg inquired, watching the activities of these parasites? With a swift glance at the Opposition benches Cousins replied: 'Yes, I am getting quite used to the activities of boring pests.'

Sir Maurice Dean has observed that much in Cousins reminded him of Ernest Bevin, with whom he had worked shortly after the war. 'Many of the qualities were the same,' says Dean. 'Of course, politically, they were very different men. But there was the same love of humanity, the same type of humour, the same irritation and even fury with the kind of people who were taunting Cousins in his first year in Parliament.' Somehow Cousins weathered the ridicule. He weathered it primarily because he was absorbed in his task as Minister, building up the department, assembling a team around him, convinced that regardless of the critics he was actually *doing something* that mattered to the country. The criticism, in fact, seemed to strengthen his resolve and fortify his determination to prove the worth of the new Department.

The British computer industry—as Harold Wilson had told Cousins at his appointment – was in urgent need of salvation. International competition had driven it to the brink of collapse. Much of this competition was dominated by the American electronics industry, which had established a commanding position in the markets of Europe. Against such opposition it had become virtually impossible to sell British equipment to the United States, even where it was genuinely technically competitive (as it frequently was), because of the high tariff wall. If the British computer industry succeeded in persuading any American federal authority to consider a British purchase, the home-based competitors in the US were given a price advantage of up to 50 per cent under the Buy American Act.[3]

There was nothing basically wrong with the design or workmanship of British computers. But against the strength of the American competition and protected markets the only thing that could save the British industry was the guarantee of some stability and orders especially in the home market. This is what the Ministry of Technology rescue programme set out to achieve. Cousins developed a policy for the purchase of computers in the public sector, and in cooperation with other Ministries set out to make sure that British computers were bought – and that the industry tailored its product to the requirements of the public sector. Cousins had to fight hard.

3. See Sir Maurice Dean's lecture to Strathclyde University, 19 May 1967.

Despite the Prime Minister's injunction that he must save the industry – in six weeks! – there was frequently strong opposition to the Buy-British campaign. A typical problem emerged over defence equipment. The Ministry of Defence had ordered an American computer for naval use. Cousins put pressure on the Department to switch to a British model and sought Harold Wilson's support for the switch. But the defence chiefs insisted on the American model – because, they claimed, they had been forced to dovetail their entire programming work into the NATO system, and that meant using American equipment. No British counterpart existed. Cousins viewed this as a classical example of how the system of international defence planning helped to condition the development (or non-development) of certain key industries and hampered British interests.

Cousins also established a Computer Advisory Service within the Ministry; a review was started to measure the computer requirements in the universities and research councils (something that had gone by default previously); and development contracts were issued for computer research in the universities. A National Computing Centre was set up at Manchester to provide a programme library, to sponsor a schedule of 'software' and to train people in computer programming and systems analysis. All this had to be started from scratch; astonishing though it may now seem, none of this had been done before the Cousins initiative. Perhaps most crucial of all at the time was Cousins's instruction to the National Research Development Corporation (NRDC) to invest £5 million in ICT (later merged with English Electric Computers to form ICL) and another £2 millions were invested in Elliot-Automation to help in developing computer-based automation systems. None of this could possibly transform the situation overnight. The work was started and the monies approved; teams of experts were assembled and enthusiasm was injected – but results took a little longer. It was not possible for Cousins to report to Parliament during 1965 that the computer industry had been saved. Yet the effect of his actions was precisely that.

Lord Penney, who worked under Cousins as chairman of the Atomic Energy Authority, subscribes to this view, but claims that the rescue operation was an inadequate one. To have made a lasting impact, he says, at least twenty computers, each costing about £1 million (in 1965 prices) should have been ordered. Nothing like that was achieved, though Penney along with the rest of the senior team at the Ministry went round the country trying to persuade various institutions and companies to make more use of the computer. Mostly they were greeted with scepticism and a complacent 'but what do *we* need a computer for?' Occasionally the 'hard sell' approach was necessary and was used successfully, as in the case of the Ministry of Pensions. It wanted to buy American but Cousins put the squeeze on the Ministry, and with the help of the Prime Minister, the Pensions Department was 'persuaded' to buy a British computer to handle its social service accounting. But persuasion failed when applied to the nationalised British European Airways; they were committed to buying an American computer because they had adopted the American system for the automation of airline bookings. Compared with the United States the use and application of computer technology in Britain was already five years behind in 1965, and Cousins found it hard to bridge that gap, given the meagre resources at his disposal and lack of political will at the top.

Meanwhile Cousins was working on an almost equally difficult exercise – to absorb into the Ministry of Technology the outposts of scientific and technological research which had proliferated without overall direction or design, during the previous twenty years. Cousins's Ministry became responsible, at least in name, for the Atomic Energy Authority in January 1965, for NRDC the following month, and for the DSIR in April. In Sir Maurice Dean's view it was not until the DSIR was absorbed that the Ministry of Technology could effectively get down to its job of rationalising the work of Government-sponsored research establishments. Incredibly, there were ten separate DSIR research units and laboratories, covering practically every type of research. The entire network had to be reorganised and fitted into a wider programme of research and development.

'Absorbing' the Atomic Energy Authority, then under the chairmanship of Sir William (later Lord) Penney, presented a special problem to Frank Cousins. For the first time in Government he could not escape taking direct responsibility for an area of activity which might challenge one of his deepest political and moral commitments – his opposition to nuclear weapons. The AEA was responsible not only for the civil development of nuclear energy but also for the military wing, and Penney was the 'father' of the British H-bomb. But Cousins could not decline responsibility for this critical area of technology, especially since he, as well as most of his advisers, was convinced that the new Ministry, to be effective, must have a much wider industrial catchment area. Cousins resolved his dilemma by deciding to distance himself deliberately from defence affairs – at least, wherever it was possible for him to do so. When Wilson invited him to join the Cabinet's defence and overseas policy committee Cousins refused. The Prime Minister pressed him to reconsider this decision. He reminded Cousins that the DOP Cabinet committee was, in a sense, the 'inner ring' of Government policy-makers, since it included all the senior Cabinet Ministers like George Brown, James Callaghan and Denis Healey. But Cousins was adamant in his refusal. He did not want to be committed to a defence policy which he knew, from the outset, he would find repellent. From Wilson's point of view it would have been valuable to contain Cousins within the small policy-making 'inner Cabinet', but Cousins insisted on remaining aloof.

His rationalisation of this apparently equivocal attitude was, essentially, that if he was to fight successfully for a specific policy it would be better to concentrate on areas in which he might be able to exercise some significant influence – such as domestic economic and social policy. He felt he would be powerless to change the fundamentals of the Government's foreign and defence policies. And in that event he did not wish to be a party to the commitments made by the 'inner ring' of Ministers. Some of Cousins's left-wing colleagues in Cabinet regarded this attitude as uncharacteristically weak and illogical. After all, they reasoned, Cousins *was* a member of the Cabinet and was bound by its collective decisions, so his argument about not being committed to defence policy appeared to them to be of dubious weight. They also argued that much the same kind of case could be presented against joining any Cabinet committee – certainly the economic policy committee, of which Cousins *was* a member. None the less Cousins would not be shifted. He later explained his resistance to membership of the DOP committee in terms similar to those he used to explain his general disenchantment with the Wilson Government of 1964–6. He quickly discovered, he says, that Wilson had adopted a 'completely Gaitskellite foreign policy' and was largely impervious to argument from the Left.

The East of Suez policy was still a paramount feature of Government thinking – partly, in Cousins's view, to compensate the Americans for the British refusal to send troops to Vietnam and partly to try to sustain the pretence that Britain remained a world military power. Cousins claims that Wilson was quite immovable on this, despite constant criticism from himself and other Ministers, and despite the increasing economic illogicality of trying to maintain such a world posture. For these and other reasons – such as the occasion when Cousins attacked the Foreign Secretary, Michael Stewart, in Cabinet for supporting the US mass bombing of Vietnam, and was then rebuked for it by Wilson[4] – the Minister of Technology took the view that he ought to concentrate on trying to get his new department functioning effectively, rather than become drawn into a fierce internal fight over foreign policy.

The result was that when the Atomic Energy Authority was brought under his umbrella Cousins told Penney that he did not wish to become involved in the defence side of its operations : that responsibility would rest with the Minister of Defence. As with foreign policy, so with defence matters : Cousins sought to avoid any direct conflict. Penney was surprised as well as curious about this. He had had no previous contact with Cousins beforehand and had known only of Cousins's reputation – as a trade union militant, a nuclear disarmer, a tough and difficult left-winger. He feared the worst in the new relationship, but was again surprised by what he found. Cousins

4. The United States began mass bombing tactics in Vietnam on 7 February. Michael Stewart publicly declared the British Government's support for this, and the following month, after a visit to Washington, declared : 'Britain wholly supports American action in Vietnam' – *The Times*, 25 March 1965.

told him frankly that he would not wish to become involved in the nuclear weapons branch of the AEA. When Penney pressed him for reasons, Cousins said that he accepted the majority view and must continue to do so while remaining a member of the Government. But, he added, he remained opposed to the manufacture of nuclear weapons, so he did not wish personally to play any direct role in that sphere. 'After that we never discussed nuclear weapons,' Lord Penney has told me. He saw Cousins as an immensely honest man, a quite unusual politician, but, in a sense, 'too simple and straight. It's an endearing quality, but perhaps it's not quite the best recipe for a Minister'. Realism or cynicism? It was the scientist speaking of the politician as a breed and a specie.

Lord Penney sums up Cousins in this way:

> Frank had a very good mind. He picked up and absorbed complicated material very quickly. He would listen for hours to us [Penney, Blackett, John Adams, etc.] talking. Then he would go into the field and see the people doing the work and ask them the most penetrating questions.
>
> He would often judge things on the basis of what he thought of the person. He was a good judge of people – although this measure of judgment doesn't always appeal to the scientist.

Cousins was, however, greatly concerned about the general development of nuclear energy for civil use. In the mid-sixties optimism about the potential of nuclear power was still heady. There were doubts about the time scale of development, about costs, and about some of the technology. The first glow of nuclear euphoria had passed. But it was still seen as a vital fuel for the future and, in theory, Britain remained ahead of the world, though others were catching up rapidly. Penney at the AEA was cautious – sometimes too cautious for Blackett. Penney believed that nothing should be done hastily, the risks were too great and the yield too uncertain. His reasoning was: a nuclear power station takes six years to build, then possibly another four or five years to iron out the snags and run it in to operational effectiveness. Nor is that the end of the trial period. Penney took the view that it would require a further four or five years to decide, on the basis of experience, what would be the best design and technique to order for the second generation of nuclear power stations. Nobody realised, in the earliest stages, that a nuclear power programme would involve such a long-drawn-out time scale, indeed, the full implications of the problems involved have only recently become clearer. Fifteen years of development is a long time for a power station programme – especially when the lives of Governments are limited to a maximum of five years at a time. The time scales of modern technology have indeed outpaced those of contemporary politics, making modern Government much more complex. For the more advanced forms of nuclear power development, like the Advanced Gas Cooled Reactor, the prototype of which was based at Dounreay by Cousins, the time-scale estimate is about twenty years. So there was little prospect of dramatic and speedy achievement in this sphere. Most of the projects that Cousins was handling had long time-leads, and each one was inescapably an invitation to the taunts of his political opponents.

In a full-scale debate on the Ministry of Technology in the Commons in July 1965 the Conservative Opposition derided the record of the Minister and his department. The Shadow Minister of Technology, the late Ernest Marples, jeered and joked. But he also made many telling points about the difficulties of a country of Britain's size competing with the international market in modern technology. Marples knew where to place his barbs. He argued that the Minister ought to have had the power to co-ordinate and maybe control all the computers in Government departments – indeed, that the Ministry ought to have had a broader co-ordinating role over a wide area of industry to help in the modernisation of Britain. Cousins knew that Marples was talking a great deal of sense, even if his speech was laced with predictable political jibes. In his reply he plaintively declared that many of the Opposition's complaints had been 'directed toward trying to establish that I have not in a short time resolved the economic mess in which we found ourselves'.[5]

Behind the scenes Cousins continued to throw all his energies into his work, drawing great strength and comfort from his unpublicised successes. Installing the prototype advanced reactor station in the north of Scotland was one such success. The majority of his advisers, and quite a few of his fellow Ministers, argued that to site it at Dounreay was absurdly uneconomic and physically unrealistic. Cousins, however, fought for the 'social factors' to be considered; there was high unemployment in the area and little hope. Building a nuclear power plant would help to generate new hope as well as jobs in the north of Scotland – so long a neglected and depopulated zone. Another consideration was its remoteness from the large industrial conurbations which, he argued, was an advantage in terms of nuclear safety, as well as waste disposal. He won his fight, much to the delight of the local population. The local Caithness and Sutherland Labour Party regarded the triumph with particular satisfaction, since they had lobbied Cousins personally during an early fact-finding visit to the area. One of its officials takes up the story :

> I wrote and asked to meet the Minister to try and put more pressure on him to have this project in Caithness owing to the high unemployment in the area (we didn't then have a Labour MP). I received word that Mr. Cousins would see me for five minutes that evening; this turned into a 15 minute session and when I told him that the local Labour Party were meeting that night and it would do morale a power of good if he could come for 5

5. *The Times*, Parliamentary Report, 15 July 1965.

minutes and meet them, this he did; but the meeting lasted for twenty minutes. It was marvellous that a Government Minister could find time during a ministerial visit to come and talk to a small Labour Party branch.[6]

This was not in fact an unusual gesture for Frank Cousins to make. His own constituents found him similarly disposed to help, always in the least formal manner and with the usual overwhelming preference for no publicity. Officials in his constituency have told me of 'the countless small things Frank has done to help nameless people; he was always helping people and never advertising it. He would never mention these things to anyone, they leaked out afterwards – though not always. He preferred to keep things quiet. No fuss, that was Frank.'

Despite growing disenchantment with his new role, the frustrations of Whitehall, the internal combat of Cabinet, Cousins found rewards not only in his inner conviction that the Technology job really was worth while but also in the practical help, often in the smallest and humblest ways, that he was able to offer people. It was, perhaps, a typical reflex of the trade union official who had strayed into Parliamentary politics.

In June 1965 Frank Cousins launched yet another initiative – to help the ailing machine tool industry, an industry almost as deeply in distress as British computers. Ministerial intervention was on a more modest scale here, but it had a similar objective. Cousins offered the industry a Government guarantee to purchase 'pre-production models' of new machine tools – that is, basically, experimental work – as well as Government-financed research and development contracts. He also introduced a policy of 'sale or return' for modern, highly sophisticated (and therefore expensive) machine tools, enabling firms to experiment with advanced prototypes without too much risk to their own hard-pressed resources. The combination of these moves provided a very significant crutch for the long-troubled machine tool industry, though the help was still insufficient to meet all its needs.

Inevitably the results of such initiatives were painfully slow in appearing, as in other aspects of Cousins's work. The complexity of the problem deepened with each individual case. This would have been an immensely demanding task for a long-established Ministry: it was much more of a challenge to a brand-new Department. As William Plowden noted some years later, in a review of the Ministry's progress:

Modernising British industry does not show results overnight; even the arrangements to allow industry to try out numerically controlled machine tools on a 'sale or return' basis necessarily allows a trial period of up to 2 years.[7]

6. Letter to the author from Mr Neil J. Treasurer of Thurso, Caithness.
7. *New Society*, 12 January 1967, p. 51.

Time was of the essence. Cousins knew that it would take three, four, perhaps five years before the Ministry's impact could begin to be publicly demonstrated. He had not got that amount of time. At first the Ministry of Technology believed that a central part of its role would be to try to influence the way of Government went about its public procurement policy. A huge amount of public spending was involved each year (£6,000 million at 1965 prices) in Government purchasing direct or indirect, of both military and civil equipment. This was an obvious area in which the State could try to encourage better industrial organisation, more effective scientific and technological progress and greater co-ordination. Yet the problem proved too much for the new Ministry. The difficulty was that the chief criterion in Government purchasing policy – reasonably enough – has always been to go for the lowest tender offering the most effective proposition. This did not always imply that such a tender was in the best long-term interests of the industry or the country's industrial development. And connecting the 'lowest tender' policy with a new criterion of modernisation proved too elusive a task, which could not be carried out by the Ministry of Technology alone. It was only on the narrower, more specific fronts, such as computers and machine tools, that progress was made.

No 'outsider' had a more advantageous ringside view of all this than the chairman of Courtaulds, Lord Kearton (now head of BNOC). He was a member of the original Advisory Council and later became the first chairman of the Industrial Re-organisation Corporation (IRC), which was in fact born inside the Ministry of Technology. Kearton was – and remains – a great admirer of Frank Cousins. He has told me that he saw Cousins as 'an outstanding and commanding man . . . a first class Minister . . . one of the very few in politics who could also talk to leaders of industry in *their* language'. But he also saw Cousins as a Minister who was 'hobbled more by the civil service than any other Minister in the Wilson Government. The civil service thought they could put him into a difficult corner. After all, he had no previous experience of Westminster politics; he had a brand new department to start from scratch and he had insufficient backing in his fight against the mandarins of Whitehall. Wilson gave him an almost impossible job in starting a completely new Ministry without the right kind of backing.'

Kearton recalls his first visit to see Frank Cousins at the newly-formed Ministry:

He had only a few people around him, and a girl secretary. He was sitting behind a large desk, dressed in an old cardigan with holes in the elbow. Most unlike a Cabinet Minister. There he was, grappling with the problem of getting the Ministry off the ground. He fought the civil service constantly, but I don't think he had all that much help from his colleagues, not even from Harold Wilson. Still it was an enormous achievement for Frank to have got the Ministry off the ground at all. After all no matter what the Heath Government, may now say it was the Ministry of Technology that formed the basis for the Department of Trade and Industry.

(Lord Kearton told me this in June 1973 when the Conservative Government under Edward Heath were in office and had changed the name from the Ministry of Technology to the Department of Trade and Industry. This was divided up into two separate departments by the Wilson Governments of 1974.)

Kearton had his own criticisms of Cousins's style of Ministerial control. His main one is that Cousins was *not bold enough*. Kearton, who described himself to me as 'a Tory-minded person', felt that Cousins was not 'socialist enough' as Minister of Technology. He was, in Kearton's view, too timid in his approach to Britain's industrial problems. Kearton himself, perhaps *because* of his industrial experience, saw the potential for Government intervention and believed that the Labour victory of 1964 offered the Wilson administration a tremendous opportunity to begin the reshaping of British industry and to establish a new partnership with the State. He regarded the Cousins Ministry – and especially its unorthodox Minister – as an ideal instrument for such change: 'I urged Frank Cousins to be much tougher. He ought to have been much bolder both with the machine tool industry and the computer industry. I told him so at the time. As a matter of fact Frank thought I was a bit wild.'

Lord Kearton now takes the view that it was a great mistake for Cousins to have resigned from the Government: 'He was just beginning to make an impact in national politics, and even in Parliament. In my view, it was a blow from which the Wilson Government did not recover. There were very few men in that Wilson Government who really understood ordinary people in the way Frank Cousins did.' Kearton believes that the absence of a man like Cousins, especially in 1969, left the Wilson Cabinet exposed to errors of judgement and policies which led to their defeat in 1970.

What of the men who worked most closely with Cousins at the Ministry of Technology? – Sir Maurice Dean, his Permanent Secretary, and Christopher Herzig, his private secretary. Both admired him enormously, though their praise is less fulsome than Lord Kearton's. Dean and Herzig regarded Frank Cousins principally as a man of outstanding courage and unstained principle. They are less sure than Kearton that he was an effective Minister. Herzig was personally devoted to his Minister, to an extent quite unusual in any civil servant. Yet he believes that it was Cousins's failure to come to terms with the Parliamentary process and the machinery of Government that exposed him to many of the problems he encountered, both inside the Cabinet and the House of Commons. In Herzig's view it also led to

Cousins's deep disillusionment with Parliamentary politics as such. He told me : 'Frank was surprised to find that political life, at Cabinet level, can be so frustrating. He had expected something else – and I was surprised at that. It led to his growing disenchantment.'

According to Herzig the deepest shocks to Cousins came not so much through such emotional issues of foreign policy at Vietnam; Cousins was *not* surprised to discover his colleagues in Cabinet pursuing a strongly pro-American policy in the Far East. What really shocked and disappointed him was his discovery of just how conservative a Labour Government could be, especially in its handling of domestic economic policy and its failure to challenge the accepted wisdom of the Treasury. The Government's timidity over steel nationalisation (during the 1964–6 period) enraged Frank Cousins. The flaccid way it dealt with defence decisions, especially on issues like Polaris and TSR-2, astonished the newcomer to Cabinet policy-making. Cousins felt 'let down' (a phrase he has frequently used about his experiences in that period) by his colleagues, who, it seemed, had made all the gestures and noises of support for one policy and then turned round to support different ones.

Herzig observes :

> Perhaps Frank Cousins hadn't realised the terrible difficulties involved in cuts in defence expenditure until he was exposed to this experience. Perhaps he hadn't fully appreciated the problems involved in finding alternative work for factories engaged in defence production.

Cousins rejects this. Of course, he claims, he recognised the difficulties and the problems. But he insists that the real difficulty was the absence of resolve among his Cabinet colleagues. Curiously, however, some of the civil servants who worked with Cousins at the time claim that he was un-characteristically diffident about arguing out his case in full Cabinet. He was inclined to wait until he thought he had the Prime Minister's support before moving strongly on any departmental issue, especially one that might be particularly controversial in Whitehall. But then this is not an entirely novel approach for any Cabinet Minister.

From others who worked closely with Cousins the impression comes through of a frequently moody man, sometimes reflecting a strong sensitivity about his lack of Whitehall experience and know-how. 'He tended to work too much through his top people and neglect those lower down,' is the view of one senior civil servant in the Ministry at the time. 'Yet,' the same man adds, 'he was a very good judge of people, really excellent. Perhaps his biggest handicap in terms of working method was that he lacked a systematic way of approaching intellectual problems. No doubt this was because he had never been trained to work that way. On the other hand he was very good at getting to the heart of any problem, quickly and shrewdly.'

Sir Maurice Dean observes that many of these qualities were precisely those he had noted in Ernest Bevin when Bevin was Foreign Secretary. They are indeed the instinctive qualities of men who had no really formal education but whose minds were sharpened, perhaps to a degree of excessive sensitivity, by the harsh experiences they encountered in their earlier fight for survival. Such experiences are sometimes regarded as 'an education in itself', but that is an over-simple view. The imbalance inherent in such a schooling can produce irrational behaviour and lopsided development no less conspicuous than that of the upper-class intellectual who has no real conception of the life style and problems of lesser mortals lower down the social scale.

Cousins's work style at the Ministry of Technology was largely patterned on the habits of a lifetime as a trade union official. He worked long hours in bursts of strenuous, concentrated activity. He was invariably at his desk before 8 a.m. (as he had been as General Secretary of the TGWU), and this made life difficult for his civil servants, since he always liked to start with a session of reading Cabinet papers for that day's work – with his civil servants' comments appended. He would frequently work late into the evening if he wasn't attending any official functions, which he disliked, anyway. His pace and his working capacity set an exceptionally exacting standard for all around him. Richard Marsh, who was a Parliamentary secretary with Frank Cousins for a critical period up until his resignation from the Government, was a great admirer of Cousins both as a man and as a Minister, but he remarks that Cousins had 'very peculiar' method of running a large department. 'He used the phone call technique and also often wandered in and out of people's offices. He liked the personal contact method rather than the customary Civil Service routine.' In Parliament the Cousins approach was equally informal according to Marsh :

You saw so much of him all the time that you were constantly chatting to him. We would frequently lunch in the House of Commons cafeteria. It was a free and easy atmosphere to work in and often we used to walk in and out of each other's offices. Of course Frank was a figurehead but he managed to get an amazing number of people prepared to work for him and to work sincerely. Mintech started off as a bit of a joke but in the end it became a major Ministry.

Cousins's work style meant that he needed facilities at hand for changing his clothes, bathing, even a quiet restroom. Most of the main Government departments have such amenities available for Ministers, as a matter of course. But because Cousins was housed in a non-traditional building – Millbank Tower – they were not readily available. Cousins therefore asked the Ministry of Works to build additional toilet facilities adjoining his eleventh-floor Ministerial suite, a request which produced one of the more bizarre experiences in Cousins's career as a Minister. When the news leaked out before work commenced, the issue was raised in Parliament by the Liberal MP for Orpington, Eric Lubbock (now Lord Avebury). Lubbock chided the Government for renting floor space in Millbank Tower in the first place, then asked 'what recent plumbing facilities have been authorised on the 11th floor of the Ministry of Technology's offices at Millbank Tower; what they have cost and under which Vote they were authorised.'

The Minister of Works, Charles Pannell (now Lord) replied that no work had commenced or had been authorised so far, but estimates had been sought for a separate lavatory and washing facilities for the Minister and senior officials.

It is normal practice for a senior Minister to have a separate lavatory both under this and the previous Government. There are 28 Ministers who have this facility. Ten have a separate bathroom, including the Minister of Public Building and Works [that is, himself] whose bathroom was installed of course over 20 years ago. I could give a list of them but cleanliness was not unknown of course to the previous administration and I hope it will be practised by this one.[8]

The Minister of Works explained later that it might have cost about £1,000, but that was not the point. Cousins was so incensed at the Parliamentary fuss about what he regarded as purely as a matter of internal organisation that he refused to have any of the work done. Instead, he went on changing in a communal washroom.

Not that Frank Cousins was particularly fastidious in his style of dress. He didn't like wearing evening dress and was not punctilious in ensuring that the match of clothing was traditionally exact. On one occasion at Lancaster House, when he was one of the host Ministers at a Government reception to foreign guests, Cousins's wardrobe gave his civil servants a few anxious moments. As he prepared to leave Millbank Tower with Christopher Herzig, the private secretary noticed that Cousins was wearing a pair of brown suede 'hush puppy' shoes with his black evenings clothes. 'Minister', Herzig began hesitantly, 'forgive me for pointing this out, but you are wearing brown suede shoes. Would you like me to bring you a pair of black shoes?' 'No,' Cousins replied, 'I'm alright as I am. They're comfortable, and remember we have a lot of standing up to do . . .' Herzig pressed his case in the most delicate and diplomatic manner. It wasn't quite the 'done thing' for a Cabinet Minister to turn up at Lancaster House in evening dress wearing brown 'hush puppy' shoes. Perhaps not, said Cousins, 'but that's the way I'm going'. He made it clear that the final word on the issue had been spoken. Herzig disappeared for a while, returning with a pair of

8. Hansard, 15 March 1965, Cols. 863/4.

brown suede 'hush puppy' shoes which he put on with *his* black evening clothes. He preferred to join the irregularity of his non-conformist Minister rather than let the side down with a show of disunity. That was civil servant gallantry at its British best.

Sometimes Cousins's unorthodoxy led him into more turbulent waters, as on the occasion when the DSIR was being absorbed into the Ministry of Technology. A gap in the payment of salaries to the DSIR staff occurred as they were being brought under the Technology umbrella. Frank Cousins was thereupon called to authorise a special grant of £180,000 to cover this hiatus. He instructed his civil servants to pay the £180,000 in order that the DSIR staff could receive their cheques without any break. But he was then told that this could not be done without prior approval from the Treasury. As the Ministry of Technology did not have its own Vote to pay such an amount, the Treasury had to provide formal approval. That is the nature of things in the Government machine. Cousins was told, as was proper for him to be told, that he could not authorise the payment without the Treasury agreement. 'Never mind about that,' Cousins ordered his officials. 'I am instructing you to pay the money.'

'With respect, Minister,' one of the advisers began, 'you simply cannot do that without Treasury approval.'

'But', Cousins snapped back, 'I am instructing you to pay.'

'But, Minister,' the official protest continued, 'do you realise what you are doing? If you don't have Treasury authority you yourself will become personally responsible for finding the money.'

Cousins was not appeased. 'Well,' he said, 'if the worst comes to the worst the Transport and General Workers' Union will pay the salaries of these people.' He sent his officials away with specific instructions to pay the DSIR staff. This was, no doubt, a characteristic trade union attitude: the people must be paid, go out and find the money. But it caused a rumpus in Cabinet. At the next meeting of the Public Expenditure Committee Cousins was cross-examined about the unauthorised payment. He stood his ground and angrily rebuked some of his colleagues for their bureaucratic approach. None the less Cousins was read a lecture by the Prime Minister, who told him that was not the way Ministerial Government was conducted and appealed to him not to do it again. After the meeting Cousins drew Wilson aside, and with that, by then, well-known directness of approach told the Prime Minister: 'Harold, do you want this job done or not? If you do, all right; the money has to be found. If not, just say so; and in that case you don't need me here.'

To the civil service mind, and even to his colleagues, Cousins's behaviour was quite unreasonable, and in the context of Ministerial responsibility and Treasury accountability he was breaking all the rules of the game. Yet it was symptomatic of his developing frustration with the processes of Government, which he found devious and unnecessarily bureaucratic, and possibly even more with what he saw as an over-addiction to convention on the part of his Cabinet colleagues.

There was another aspect to his irritation. The timing of these incidents coincided with the beginning of the Government's drive for a prices and incomes policy and the setting up of the Prices and Incomes Board under the former Conservative MP and Minister Aubrey Jones. Cousins was hostile to the entire policy and had clashed persistently over this with George Brown. But the policy went ahead in spite of his strong opposition. It was launched on 8 April 1965 with a White Paper,[9] which set out to keep prices stable and incomes within a national average of 3 to $3\frac{1}{2}$ per cent increases a year.

The Aubrey Jones Board was not provided with any independent 'teeth'; it was not asked to enforce its own findings. Its role was primarily to influence public opinion, helping to create a new awareness of the role of wages and prices in the nation's fight against inflation and for economic growth. It was an exercise in trying to live with full employment, growth, and the Welfare State.

The White Paper laid down the guidelines for the 3 to $3\frac{1}{2}$ per cent 'norm', outlining the inevitable 'exceptions'. As in so many similar subsequent White Papers on incomes policy, the exceptions left sufficient scope for widespread breaches of the 'norm'. Almost every firm, like almost every union, could make a case for special consideration. Even where companies or industries failed to make out a sufficiently strong case for increasing prices (or a union for a wage claim) there was nothing ultimately to prevent a group using its market position or bargaining strength to get what it wanted. Even so George Brown saw that White Paper of April 1965 as the starting point on the road to a more just and equitable prices and incomes policy. In one sense he was surely correct; no Government since has been able to be without some form of incomes policy, whatever the name applied to the precise economic doctrine. The Heath Government of 1970 began by abolishing the Aubrey Jones Board, but lived (and died) to regret it.

This was, at the time, the most comprehensive attempt made by any Government to achieve a voluntary prices and incomes policy and George Brown, as well as Harold Wilson, placed great faith in it. They saw the new Board as a unique and important innovation. They believed the appointment of a former Tory Minister was a major political 'catch' (as indeed it was). Certainly it caused surprise and consternation inside the Conservative Party. George Brown recognised that the policy was based on a fragile foundation : it depended absolutely on the support of the trade unions and the employers. And he worked especially hard, and successfully,

9. See the White Papers, 'Machinery of Prices and Incomes Policy', Cmnd. 2577, 1965, and 'Prices and Incomes Policy', Cmnd. 2639, 1965.

to secure the suport of Cousins's old ally, George Woodcock. But inside and outside the Cabinet the Secretary of State for Economic Affairs was assailed by Frank Cousins, who warned him that the policy would *not* work. What disturbed him was that the Government had begun to play a direct interventionist role in wage bargainings. The old bogey was raising its head again – this time within his own Government. He reflected bitterly on his earlier battles against wage restraint and he felt himself being trapped by the very forces he had fought against for so long and, in a sense, by the issues that had brought him to the top of the trade union movement. It was a cruel dilemma.

When George Brown himself spoke at the special conference of the TUC on 30 April he made a strong plea for incomes policy on the grounds that it was an essential part of a wider Government economic strategy and would be closely linked to the National Plan (then being prepared). The trade union movement, he told that conference, had to choose between 'order or chaos, planning or anarchy'. And throughout the conference the strongest possible feeling was expressed by supporters of the incomes policy that the Government's continuation in power would depend on the policy's success.

On paper there was a massive victory for George Brown and the Government – 6,649,000 to 1,811,000. But nearly 1,500,000 of the minority vote came from the TGWU, the country's largest union, and the union whose opposition could effectively wreck the ultimate success of the whole policy. Harry Nicholas denied that Frank Cousins's opposition to the policy had made any difference. He insisted that the TGWU executive had reached its decision quite independent of Cousins's views. Perhaps this was so. But there can be little doubt that the knowledge of Cousins's fierce fight inside the Government had its effect in determining which way the TGWU vote went that day.

George Brown was incensed. He telephoned Harry Nicholas immediately the vote was known and blasted the TGWU's acting General Secretary in blistering Brown-like terms. Later that evening the Economics Minister told me that he would fight the opposition of his old union – and Frank Cousins. 'I am going to fight and I am going through with the policy in the interest of my fellow members of the TGWU. If I am obstructed I will have to fight.'[10] It was indeed an extraordinary situation that the largest union of all, whose general secretary was now sitting in the Cabinet, had ostentatiously opposed a central feature of the Government's economic policy – and it was of course a situation taken up by all the Press. Few newspapers failed to draw the obvious conclusion about deep divisions inside the Government and the curious role of Frank Cousins.

The prospectus presented by George Brown as the justification of his policy at the time remains the central objective of all incomes policies – the need

10. The *Sun*, 1 May 1965.

to inject a greater degree of social and economic justice into collective bargaining and the need to relate wages to all other resources in any framework of economic planning. The weakness of that policy, as with so many since, was that too much weight and dependence was placed on the function of an incomes policy as a critical base for the wider economic strategy. Incomes policy was seen as a possible panacea for many economic ills; and it had different meanings for different people. To some it was an obsession, as if no other element of economic policy existed. It was regarded as a crucial instrument in the fight to curb domestic inflation, to protect sterling and to cure the chronic balance of payments problem. It was not at that stage seen as simply one element in a much broader package of economic policies. Too much was demanded of the policy, and even without the opposition of Frank Cousins it could not have stood the strain of such pressures and ambitions. With Cousins's opposition inside the Government, and the TGWU outside, its fate seemed sealed.

It is too much of a simplification to say that Cousins's own fate as a member of the Wilson Government was also sealed at that moment – it was nothing quite as final as that. There was another year of internal battles, another year of fighting to try to expand the powers of the Ministry of Technology, another year of increasing tension with the Whitehall machine – before the final explosion of resignation in July 1966. Yet by mid-1965 the pitch had been marked out. Cousins had few illusions then that he could succeed in persuading the Prime Minister or the majority of his Cabinet colleagues to steer away from a policy dominated, as he saw it, by wage restriction. They had embarked on a journey from which there was no logical return. Once the foundations for an income policy had been laid it was inconceivable that it could be easily abandoned. Equally it was predictable that, once installed as a centrepice of economic policy, it would need to be strengthened and would eventually develop some form of statutory system. This was what Frank Cousins feared. From that moment he began to see with greater clarity the road ahead for the Government – and for himself.

In spite of all the political pressures and Cabinet conflicts Cousins remained devoted to his task of building up the Ministry of Technology. At Millbank Tower he felt he could escape from the absurdities of Parliamentary Question Time, from the eternal wrangle with his Cabinet colleagues, from the shallows of politics: he could immerse himself in trying to do 'a real job', as he described it. After he had been Minister for six months I went to see him and found him privately as rebellious as ever about what the Government was *not* doing and some of the things it *was* doing – especially giving support to the United States in Vietnam and delaying over steel nationalisation. Yet he remained as fervent as ever in the belief that his job at the new

Ministry was a job worth doing, and just as convinced that its value to the nation would be proved in time, whether he was there or not.

At the heart of the Ministry was the concept of interventionism. British industry for a variety of reasons had failed to keep pace with its foreign competitors. Some major industries were behind their foreign counterparts in the field of research, scientific and technological innovation and, perhaps even more serious, the application and development of knowledge available in Britain – knowledge that was frequently well ahead of that of most other countries but not yet effectively applied to the motive power of British industry. This was the widening gap that Cousins wanted to bridge. The impulse behind the new Department was the conviction that British industrial methods and organisation were in need of radical overhaul and a new drive – not only at the top, but at shop-floor level, even in the structure of trade unionism itself. That was the diagnosis. Precisely what was to be done about it was another question. The Ministry was becoming a kind of umbrella organisation for research and development, but what was needed was a more direct instrument that could influence the detailed development of industrial change and at the same time be free from Whitehall bureaucracy, or at least keep it at arm's length.

Well before the birth of the Ministry it was clear that engineering was one of the crucial areas in which Britain's industrial base had deteriorated compared with Germany, Japan and the United States. British engineering firms were, on the whole, too small, under-financed, lacking in research and technological expertise. The growth of mergers in the early 1960s had not been satisfactorily tailored to meet the nation's needs. Short-term financial considerations had tended to be more compelling than British industrial priorities. Something much more imaginative and much more radical was required. This is what the IRC (Industrial Reorganisation Corporation) was designed to achieve.

There is still a commonly held belief that the IRC was the brainchild of George Brown – or, at least, that it was conceived within the Department of Economic Affairs. That is not the case. It was born inside the Ministry of Technology and nurtured by Cousins and Blackett until it was strong enough in sinew to be handed over to the DEA. The idea itself owed a good deal to the Italian IRI (Industrial Reconstruction Institution) which had its origins in the early 1930s under Mussolini. Such parentage might have doomed its prospects in Britain from the outset, had it not been for the fact that in post-fascist Italy a reorganised IRI had achieved remarkable successes in helping to revive and reshape the economy. (Richard Marsh has told me that soon after he joined the Ministry as Frank Cousins's Parliamentary secretary Cousins sent him off to Italy to study the Italian IRI and report back on how it operated.) In any event the version taken up by the Wilson Government in 1965 was very much a British adaptation.

Its origins go back to October 1964, shortly after the election of the Labour Government. Mr Ben Cant, head of Hamworthy Engineering Company in Poole, Dorset, wrote to the chairman of his parent company, Sir Henry Wilson Smith of the Powell Duffryn group, suggesting a plan for regenerating British industry. It was a brilliant analysis of the deep malaise in British industry and Sir Henry, much impressed by Cant's paper, sent it on to Sir Maurice Dean at the Ministry of Technology, whom he knew.

In January 1965 Dean began discussions with Cant about a possible seconding to the Ministry. Cant's paper, 'Attrition or Breakthrough? Some Notes on Britain's Industrial Future', did not specifically refer to an IRC, but he spelled out the need for such an institution which with State aid could trigger off the realignment of companies necessary, in his view, for industrial regeneration. In April arrangements were completed for Cant to be assigned to the Ministry for two days a week at a fee of £3,000 a year – to be paid into his company, Hamworthy Engineering, and not to him personally. This arrangement was scheduled to last for twelve months. The project was as exciting for Cant as for the Ministry, and he recorded that 'The Ministry was new and small, the elan was magnificent and infectious, power groups and inter-divisional jealousies were totally absent.'[11]

On 5 July Cousins submitted a memorandum to his Advisory Council, urging them to consider Cant's proposals. But he did not mimimise his doubts that such a fundamental reorganisation of British industry could be achieved without strong Government intervention, which 'would create controversy'.

Cant's paper emphasised the 'urgent need for Government to make it clear beyond doubt that purposeful concentration of resources is a vital national need not an equivocal state likely to be frustrated by monopolies and restrictive practices legislation.' Cant was throwing an absolute commitment into his fight for a thoroughgoing and radical overhaul of British industry, and doing so in a manner which attracted expression of both admiration and caution from Cousins and his senior advisers.

Through the summer months of 1965, while George Brown was putting the finishing touches to his National Plan, the Ministry of Technology team worked hard on the Cant plan. Blackett and Sir Maurice Dean gave every support. By August there was a draft outline for a new public corporation which then had the title of NATCORD – National Corporation for Company Reconstruction and Development. By September early drafts of the plan were being fed into the official machine for processing to Cabinet and Departmental committees. At this point George Brown made it clear that any such corporation must come under his own umbrella. Fervour over the National Plan, published that month, was at its peak at the very

11. This information is based on access to the private papers on IRC made available to the author by the generosity of its first chairman, Lord Kearton.

time when Cousins was pushing the concept of a new public corporation to help streamline British industry. Inevitably a conflict arose as to which department should be the sponsoring Ministry. Cousins and Dean had fought a long battle to enlarge their powers over and responsibility for industry. George Brown, fighting for his own corner against Treasury claims as the principal economic department, was determined not to have his territory trespassed on and perhaps reduced by the enlargement of Cousins's Ministry.

Let us digress for a moment and recall the overall scene in the summer and early autumn of 1965. The pressure on sterling continued throughout the summer. Despite the TUC's acceptance in April of a voluntary incomes policy there was little respite from the rising curve of domestic inflation. By July the balance of payments situation had become critical again. A further 'crisis Budget' included tighter exchange controls, reduced finance for imports and a string of measures to deflate the home economy, with some cuts in public services. Support for sterling was sought through the IMF and from the United States. In August there was a private meeting between the Chancellor James Callaghan, George Brown and the US Treasury Secretary Henry Fowler, at which the British Government was said to have given certain assurances about the conduct of economic policy in exchange for continuing international support for sterling. These 'assurances' were later to become the basis of a major conflict between Frank Cousins and Harold Wilson. At the time, Cousins was given the impression that the UK's economic situation was so critical that a further strengthening in the prices and incomes policy had become inescapable. He was dubious about the rationale behind this argument and again voiced the strongest opposition – but accepted the situation, with the greatest reluctance.

Meanwhile George Brown went to the 1965 Trades Union Congress at Brighton to persuade the General Council to accept a tougher wages policy, without parallel in Government-TUC relations. The First Secretary of State (as he then was) remained in Brighton until the General Council accepted its new role, as a preliminary to a statutory system of 'early warning' on all price increases and pay claims which the Government was proposing to introduce at a later stage. The basis of George Brown's proposed new legislation was to provide the Prices and Incomes Board with stronger powers to inquire into, and delay, the settlement of price increases and pay settlements. As an interim measure, to act as a preliminary brake on pay demands, Brown asked the TUC to set up its own vetting committee, to control the claims of all affiliated unions. He succeeded in persuading the majority to back this and the General Council voted twice on that memorable day to support the Government's wishes by 23 to 6 and by 22 to 6.

The three members of the TGWU opposed that decision, and later when the Congress itself voted to accept this historic regulation the TGWU again went in opposition. This time they had a great deal more support than at the special conference in April. The majority in favour of support for the Government was seriously reduced to 1,939,000. If the AEU had joined the TGWU the vote would have been lost. Two weeks later the TGWU executive came out in full blast against the Government's new proposals and the TUC's plan to vet all pay claims. The TUC leaders had already appointed their vetting committee, which paradoxically included the name of Harry Nicholas, the TGWU's acting General Secretary. None the less the union executive declared that it would oppose the entire operation. The vetting scheme, they said, 'will not be allowed to interfere with the normal process of collective bargaining or cause delay in the prosecution of wage claims so far as this union is concerned'.

All this was happening while Cousins battled on inside the Cabinet to try to win wider powers for his Ministry and to protect it from erosion. At times it seemed to Cousins that the task was an impossible one. He found relief in the periodic apearances he made at regional festivals of the TGWU as 'guest' of the union. At Bristol and Leicester that year he made speeches which, for those who could read between the lines, demonstrated his uneasiness inside the Government. But it was at the union's biennial delegate conference at Portsmouth that the signs of a real rift inside the Government became unmistakable. The conference had already spent a week passing motions critical of the Government – on wages policy, Vietnam, the need for a much more rapid extension of public ownership. Then, on the final day, a Friday, Cousins arrived in Portsmouth quite unexpectedly. At the last moment he decided to attend the conference – and to speak. His speech, full of scarcely veiled hints about his views on wages policy, Vietnam and other issues, was clearly designed to demonstrate to the union's delegates (and to his Cabinet colleagues) that he had much more in common with their views and their resolutions than with Government policy. At the end of his speech he said with plainly intended significance: 'I know, as I have always known, where the strength of any man in my kind of job lies. It lies with the people who put him there.'

The Portsmouth incident was picked on by the Press to criticise Cousins. Some newspapers were already beginning to urge Wilson to sack him for disloyalty. And the Prime Minister was undoubtedly upset and angered by the Minister of Technology's decision to attend his union conference and speak in the way he did – without having informed Downing Street of his intention to do so. No one could possibly misunderstand the effect of Cousins's message to the Portsmouth conference of the TGWU. Stated baldly it was simply: 'I am with you – and not with the Government.' As Parliament rose for the summer recess the *Spectator* noted: 'The political columnists have made up their end-of-term reports and have switched from speculating about the Tory leadership to the fascinating game of forecasting

Cabinet reshuffles. All of them list Frank Cousins for the chopper . . .' It did not seem improbable.

The bitterness came to the boil that summer. Cousins's opposition to George Brown's proposals overlapped into his fight to extend the powers of his Ministry, and the issue of IRC interlocked with both. It was becoming increasingly clear to Cousins that he would not win on incomes policy, nor would he be able to retain the sponsorship of IRC. He might conceivably secure extended powers for the Ministry of Technology, but even this concession, he felt, would be limited because of the Prime Minister's anxiety to ensure that neither George Brown at the DEA nor James Callaghan at the Treasury was too outraged by any increase in Frank Cousins's status and authority. By the autumn it was plain that IRC, which had secured substantial support among Ministers and senior Whitehall officials, would be approved and come into operation early in 1966. It was equally clear that it had slipped away from Cousins into the orbit of the DEA. The final decisions were not taken until the end of the year, but by October it was clear that Cousins had lost that battle. It was without question another cause for Cousins to reflect, bitterly, that Wilson's tempting bait which attracted him to join the Government – the bait of a close personal and political relationship with the Prime Minister – had by all appearances withered into insignificance. At least that is how Cousins viewed the situation. It was not how Harold Wilson or other Cabinet members saw it. They regarded Cousins's attitude as inflexible, unreasonable, stubborn and even arrogant.

It is perhaps useful, at this stage, to ask why they should have judged Cousins in this way. After all, stubbornness, arrogance, unreasonableness and inflexibility are traits not entirely unknown in Cabinet Ministers and Prime Ministers. They are part of the very weave of politics. Possibly the real clue to the feeling against Cousins was the belief that he was playing a dual role; that he was never wholly 'with them' in Government, but instead, firmly attached to his role as General Secretary of the Transport and General Workers' Union. For politicians to observe one of their colleagues maintaining a power base *outside* their own political dimension clearly can be a source of immense irritation. The dichotomy which they accurately sensed in Cousins's loyalties infuriated some of his Cabinet colleagues and fed their temptation to dismiss him as a serious politician. For Cousins it was also a classical dilemma, and one which is bound to face the 'outsider' drawn into the Government from the trade union hierachy or the top ranks of industry. It was also a question of age.

Sir Richard Marsh's observation on this point is interesting because Marsh – a much younger man – was himself a trade union official before becoming an MP. He believes that part of Cousins's problem was the abrupt change from the trade union sphere to politics without any period of acclimatisation.

Politics was a new world with completely different methods of behaviour. He suggested to me:

> No trade union general secretary can exert the same power and influence within a Labour Cabinet as he can within his own union. A general secretary of a trade union is in a position to make and take decisions on his own in a way that is not possible in Government . . . Frank Cousins was also an incredibly honest man, almost to the point sometimes of naïvety. Standards of honesty in politics are generally high – but they are standards largely peculiar to politics. At one extreme any Chancellor proposing to devalue will deny that the thought has ever entered his head. Similarly no politician will feel himself bound by a speech made at a Party conference two years earlier when the facts are clearly against the policy.

For Frank Cousins, with his thrustful, trade-union-type candour and his practicality as a man who wanted to get things done rather than intellectualise around a Whitehall table, it became intolerable to endure the conflict between what is politically feasible for Cabinet Government and what is industrially desirable for a trade union leader. The result, however long delayed, was as unavoidable as it was explosive.

Marsh, who was probably as close to Cousins as any member of the Parliamentary Labour Party at the time of his resignation, believed then – and still does – that Cousins was wrong to go. He does not think Cousins was wrong to accept the original invitation to join the Government, and once there he should, in Marsh's view, have stayed to fight it out. He left a yawning gap in the Cabinet because there was no experienced trade union leader there to pick up the challenge; no one who could have replaced him as a man with the 'common touch'. Yet by the time Cousins left it was already too late to correct the disenchantment. The road to resignation had begun a long time before July 1966.

Chapter Twenty-three

BREAKING OUT OF GOVERNMENT

It is probable that Labour's election victory of 1964 will eventually be seen as the great watershed in post-war British politics as far as the traditional two-party system is concerned. The Conservatives had by then run out of steam, of ideas and of political panache after their thirteen years in office, in which they had governed under four Prime Ministers, Churchill, Eden, Macmillan and Douglas Home. An aura of weariness covered the Tories. Labour, under Harold Wilson in his first election campaign, seemed fresh, vigorously on the offensive, and in an exceptionally strong position. It seemed axiomatic that they were capable of harnessing a new generation of voters to supporting the 'white heat' of technology as the motive force that was necessary to drive Britain forward into a new and exciting age of industrial modernisation allied to social justice. That was the jewel held aloft by the Labour Party under Wilson. It compared strongly with the ageing, lethargic privileged anachronisms of a Conservative Government led by a 14th Earl. In retrospect the extraordinary feature of that General Election is that Douglas Home was able to run Wilson to such a wafer-thin result. To account for that one would need to consider the mood of national self-indulgence and self-delusion that was rife in (and encouraged by) the Macmillan years, and the continuing doubts in the middle ground of British politics that Labour did not have the capacity nor the men of experience to govern the country.

Labour had certainly aroused a younger generation of voters but they had not convinced the older middle classes. The country seemed divided, in a sense, between the younger, idealistic, hopeful generations who, if they had a foot on the ladder at all, were all on the lower rungs, and the older generations, among whom there were many working-class as well as middle-class people who had tasted real affluence under the Conservatives and like what they had experienced. The cynicism about politics in general that spread between 1964 and 1970 came in large measure from the younger hopefuls of 1964. It was a cynicism that was not sufficiently recognised or understood by the Labour Party leaders in 1970 and certainly not by Harold Wilson. Yet it would be absurd to suggest that this cynicism, now such a common feature of the 'public mind', was due primarily to the failures of the Labour Governments from 1964 to 1970. Of course it had taken deep root long before.

Great social and economic changes had been taking place in the decade from 1955 to 1965, changes that affected the attitudes and psychology of the British. The nation was forced to come to terms with the fact that it was no longer a major military and economic power in the world. Suez left deep scars; there was scarcely any scope for mistaking the real significance of that débâcle. The British, the proud imperious British, were understandably reluctant to accept the verdict of history. No nation likes accepting that, least of all a nation with such a tradition of power, dominance and self-confidence. The truth was that the price Britain had been forced to pay for victory in the Second World War was one which she found increasingly difficult to meet, in both psychological as well as industrial terms, in the two decades that followed 1945. The balance of world power had turned against the British. That had been the message implicit in Mr Ben Cant's original paper which led to the birth of the Industrial Reorganisation Corporation. It may also have been the dominant message behind a new dimension of industrial and social turbulence – even violence – that erupted across the political paths from the mid-sixties onwards. To be sure the sixties need to be seen as an unusual decade. New social values mushroomed amid the perceived or assumed affluence. Political commitment weakened. An international permissiveness flourished, parallel almost with the growth and influence of the multi-national companies. Domestic planning for secondary powers like Britain began to assume complexities that had not previously been considered – perhaps akin to some of the new pressures on individual families as they grappled with new sets of social and economic values. The entire scene raised quite new questions and problems.

The problems impinged on hitherto sovereign Governments as much as on shop-stewards and managements of industries. The international and the national scene were experiencing a metamorphosis at a tempo that surprised most and confounded everyone. It was indeed a decade of white heat and change, though not quite as Harold Wilson had imagined at Scarborough in 1963.

To allocate to the Wilson Governments of 1964–70 a major share of the blame for an almost complete failure by Britain to meet these new challenges would be, to say the least, politically and intellectually idiosyncratic. None the less there *was* a deep failure. It is a failure already noted in the day-today events of the Crossman diaries as well as in Harold Wilson's own record of his stewardship. Why did those Governments fail? How does one genuinely measure success? Or is it, as so often in history, that success is merely the occasional lapse from the normal routine of human aspiration being overwhelmed by failure?

Several distinguished economists lay the blame for Labour's failure on the Government's chronic inability to meet the challenge of the balance of payments crisis – which it inherited in 1964. The critics include in their armoury of attack the decision not to devalue the pound in 1964 or at the second most opportune time, July 1966 (by which time the Government had an overall majority of nearly 100.) It is argued also that the Welfare State and full employment had between them become an intolerable burden for an impoverished and industrially enfeebled country like Britain to sustain, and that the Government therefore ought to have allowed the exchange rate to find its 'proper international level' – all of which, some of the experts claim, would have helped to restore economic growth, modernisation and national self-esteem. That is a right-wing view. The left wing would argue just as strenuously that it was a collapse in socialist conviction that wrecked the 1964–70 Governments – a failure of political nerve, an absence of resolve and determination to put into operation plans for a radical regeneration of Britain and to evoke a quite new spirit of response from the British people on the basis of sacrifice – for a collective, socialist, purpose. That is the view taken by Frank Cousins.

There are those who believe that the failure had a much narrower base. In his review of the Labour Governments, 1964–70 Professor Wilfred Beckerman suggests : 'It is in the field of labour relations and income policy, perhaps, that one can identify the greatest – and also the most excusable – failure of the Labour Government.'[1] Beckerman appears to be repeating the mistake made by George Brown, and others, at the time. They believed that an effective prices and incomes policy could play a central role in containing demand inflation, and could be used as a main instrument of economic strategy. It was this which brought Brown and the Government into conflict not only with Cousins but eventually with most of the trade union movement and indeed in the end with the majority in the Parliamentary Labour Party. In that sense Beckerman is correct; it *was* a central feature in the failure of the Government. The 1969 retreat by almost the entire Wilson Cabinet over Barbara Castle's 'In Place of Strife' policy was only a belated recognition of what Cousins had been arguing in Cabinet from the start – that no Labour Government (and indeed possibly no Government) can govern in the teeth of trade union opposition. That is a lesson which is still being learned and which is of course still being challenged. But while Frank

---

1. Wilfred Beckerman (Ed.), *The Labour Government's Economic Record, 1964–1970* (Duckworth, 1972), p. 69.

Cousins did not refine his case in terms of a wider development of political and industrial democracy – the nub of the whole debate – that was the essence of his disagreement with the Wilson Government.

Of course there is another side to the difficulty of recognising the growth of popular democracy. If no Labour Government can govern effectively without trade union support then it must follow that such a Government, given that it is pursuing a tolerably socialist policy, must have trade union support for some form of incomes discipline, that is to say, a wages policy. The alternative to this would be for British socialists to take the extreme view that nothing can or should be done constructively until the millenium arrives, to assume a strategy based on trying to turn the unions into the vanguard of a revolutionary army whose function would be to smash the State. Only then, the extreme view might argue, will it be possible to develop an effective socialist policy in which wages, like all else, would be subject to a system of controls. One has only to outline the strategy to observe its basic flaws and contradictions. As always it is a question of degree.

As early as March 1965 Cousins was already expressing inner doubts about his decision to become a Minister. He felt frustrated at not being able to attack the Government, publicly, over its Vietnam policy; over the delay in renationalising the steel industry, and, indeed, over George Brown's policies with the trade unions. Inside the Cabinet he quickly found himself isolated in a minority protesting about Vietnam, steel, defence policy and the cancellation of TSR-2. True, his views on some issues were sometimes supported by Fred Peart, Barbara Castle, Edward Short, Fred Lee, Anthony Greenwood and especially Richard Crossman, with whom Cousins had established a strong rapport. Yet on the whole Cousins found himself in a situation somewhat similar to that he had experienced when he first joined the TUC General Council. Somehow he didn't 'fit in' to the pattern. He always sensed a tension between himself and the 'professional politicians' in the Cabinet. He had felt much the same about the 'professional trade union general secretaries' of the TUC hierarchy in the mid-1950s.

By the spring of 1965, after less than six months in Government, Cousins was already talking about resignation. Richard Crossman notes that on 10 May Frank Cousins told him that 'he had been thinking of resigning for some time owing to his dissatisfaction with his job'.[2] But Cousins was not dissatisfied with his own job so much as with the behaviour and policies of some of his colleagues. For example, George Brown, with whom Cousins had a persistent love-hate relationship, had infuriated him by making a public statement which seemed designed to force the Government to retreat from its election pledge of outright public ownership of the steel industry.

2. Richard Crossman, *The Diaries of a Cabinet Minister*, Vol. I (Hamish Hamilton and Jonathan Cape, 1975), 10 May 1965, p. 213.

The Cabinet was in some disarray over steel policy. Certainly Crossman (also angered by George Brown's outburst) suggests that he was alarmed at the prospect of Cousins quitting the Government. At that time Crossman had a closer relationship than any other Cabinet colleague succeeded in establishing with Frank Cousins. Crossman's early evaluations of Cousins in Government are mostly complimentary. He changed his views before July 1966, though to be fair he never actually went back on his original assessment which was noted in his diary in April 1965. Crossman was observing his Cabinet colleagues with characteristic indelicacy, and came finally to Frank Cousins :

> I have left Frank Cousins to the last because he's a real mystery man, still. He sounds like a terrible old blatherer talking on every subject and usually saying the obvious thing. But he does say it in a working class way and that's important because nobody else talks in that way in this Cabinet and we ought to be reminded of what sensible people think in the Labour Movement. This he reflects very faithfully and he also displays every now and then the kind of expertise which the General Secretary of the TGWU should show on a subject such as the docks.
>
> What kind of a Ministry he is building in Vickers House on the Embankment I have no idea. All I know is that he is occupying more and more floors and getting tremendous backing from Harold Wilson who believes passionately that his new Ministry of Technology has got to succeed if he is going to keep his promise to modernise British industry. And of course there is one other thing to say about Frank, he is the only trade union leader introduced by Harold Wilson into his Cabinet. As such he exerts at minimum a very powerful veto.[3]

This is, to be sure, an outrageously patronising comment, though not surprising from Crossman, who was finding it difficult to get his own housing plans through Cabinet.

Crossman's comment on George Brown's performance up till then was full of superlatives. Brown had emerged 'as complete king in incomes policy and he has run it on his own, brilliantly successfully'.[4] It was not the view taken by Cousins. The tension between Brown and Cousins was particularly high in the spring of 1965. Brown, pushing ahead zealously with his prices and incomes policy and preparing his National Plan, was a dominant figure in the Cabinet and, on his day, could overshadow any of his colleagues. From the start Cousins regarded Brown's wages policy as unacceptable; he also believed that Brown had a disturbingly strong influence on the Prime Minister. Moreover, the TGWU General Secretary was especially irked by the arrogant manner with which George Brown claimed to be a 'trade union

3. *Ibid.*, 18 April 1965, p. 204.
4. *Ibid.*, 18 April 1965, p. 203.

spokesman' in the Cabinet. Cousins reflected frequently that Brown had been a very junior and minor official of the TGWU before he became an MP in 1945. The two men squared up to each other like a pair of prime peacocks, spitting and clawing. When Brown wrote an article for the TGWU journal the *Record*, defending his prices and incomes policy as 'a landmark in British history',[5] Cousins was furious.

Throughout the whole of that period the TGWU maintained its opposition to the Government's wages policy. The most vigorous opponent of it, apart from Frank Cousins himself, was Jack Jones, who was then acting Assistant General Secretary. Ominously in the July 1965 issue of the *Record* came this concluding paragraph to a long attack on Government policy by Jack Jones :

> The Government should remember (too) that in the last resort their strength in the country depends upon the support of the working people and of their organisations the trade unions. Any policy which undermines the trade unions by creating stresses between the leadership and the members will weaken not only the trade unions but the Labour Government itself.

Towards the end of July there came one of those extraordinary squalls across the international monetary scene which have since become familiar as a form of summertime 'monetary madness', when speculators take advantage of politicians who are about to snooze in the sun. In 1965 it was still a comparatively novel experience, certainly for Harold Wilson's Government. At first the British Prime Minister adopted a solidly Walter Raleigh-like attitude towards the whole scare, as he disclosed in his book *The Labour Government, 1964–1970*. He refused to allow the alarmist demands of the Governor of the Bank of England to disturb his plans to holiday in the Scilly Isles and refused to be panicked into flying to Washington for urgent consultations with the President and his advisers. None the less the telephone line between the Prime Minister's Scilly base and the Cabinet Office was kept very busy throughout early August as the pressure mounted for some action to protect sterling from what the Governor of the Bank described as a possible 'collapse of the world monetary system'.

George Brown, holidaying in the South of France, and the Chancellor James Callaghan, on the Isle of Wight, were kept in touch with the Prime Minister by a telephonic 'hook-up' system, and the Cabinet secretary kept Harold Wilson informed of the views of Joe Fowler, American Secretary of the Treasury, who was particularly worried about the fate of sterling. He was also, not surprisingly, concerned about the impact any financial crisis would have on the dollar. Wilson records that Fowler was 'afraid of an

5. TGWU *Record*, May 1965, pp. 16–18.

inflationary situation developing'[6] and the American Treasury Minister expressed particular doubts about the voluntary prices and incomes policy which the British Government were operating. Mr Wilson's record of this period goes on to explain :

> While he [Fowler] did not attempt in any way to make terms or give us orders he was apprehensive that if further central bank aid were required it would be difficult to mount if we had no better safeguard against inflation than the voluntary service. It was in these circumstances that we began first to think in terms of statutory powers.[7]

In fact Joe Fowler was rather more specific than the Wilson record suggests. He told Callaghan that in his view it would be difficult for Britain to get the required borrowing without some form of legally controlled wage restraint.

Wilson had by now become alerted to a worsening situation in the international markets and intense pressure on sterling. He knew however that a statutory wages policy would cause a grave split in the Cabinet, especially with Frank Cousins. So in mid-August he decided to pay a visit to the Cousins family, who were holidaying at their farmhouse in Cornwall. The Prime Minister crossed to the mainland on Sunday 15 August to hold a series of talks with various Ministers, chiefly about the crisis that had blown up over Singapore and the Malaysian Federation. Then he visited Frank Cousins. To Wilson's surprise Cousins appeared to take the news of an impending wages policy crisis with a calmness which, Wilson claims, led him to believe that there might not be such a rumpus in Cabinet after all.

A special Cabinet meeting was called for Wednesday 1 September to thrash out the future prices and incomes policies. It was then that the Chancellor, James Callaghan, explained the necessity for statutory powers. George Brown said he would go to Brighton to hold talks with the TUC leaders on the eve of their 97th Congress. He had already been in private consultation with George Woodcock. Frank Cousins exploded with indignation at the proposal to turn a voluntary incomes policy, which he had always distrusted and disapproved of, into a legally controlled policy, which he utterly rejected. That was the first time Cousins challenged Callaghan by demanding to know whether it was true that the Americans were bringing pressure on the British Government for a statutory wages policy in exchange for their agreement to support sterling. Callaghan denied Cousins's implied charge, but what the Chancellor did not say was that Britain would not have been able to borrow unless the Cabinet agreed to some form of legal

---

6. Harold Wilson, *The Labour Government, 1964–70* (Weidenfeld and Nicholson, 1971), pp. 131–2.
7. *Ibid.*, pp. 131–2.

restraint on pay. It was the first of many Cabinet sessions on the subject, and the first of many at which Cousins would find himself in an increasingly dwindling minority reduced ultimately to one.

Later in September there was a special all-day meeting of the Cabinet at Chequers to discuss the economic crisis in general, and the proposed wages legislation in particular. The question of Callaghan's alleged 'pledge' to the Americans came up again – and again it was hedged around. Nevertheless Cousins then registered for the first time at a Cabinet meeting that he was considering resignation. The Crossman diaries note Cousins turning to his colleagues in exasperation and exclaiming : 'Every time I am asked what I am doing here in Cabinet I keep on saying to myself that I should do more good outside, getting production going in the unions than sitting here. I think it's time I resigned.'[8]

Crossman also notes that Frank Cousins broke into the economic debate with 'outraged indignation', at Callaghan, declaring : 'How hypocritical can we get? The trade unions really hate your incomes policy. I myself disagree with it so utterly that I can no longer make a political speech. I can only speak on technological problems. Why can't you swing our policy away from incomes control towards productivity, following the lead which Harold Wilson gave us at Bristol last Saturday?'[9] (The Prime Minister had made a speech at Bristol on 4 September calling for the setting up of factory production committees – a Cousins idea.) By the time of the Chequers meeting the Trades Union Congress had already agreed to support the Government's new proposals – or at least to take powers themselves to stiffen the policy of voluntary wage restraint by setting up their own committee for 'vetting' pay claims from member unions. This was a unique step for the TUC General Council, taken only after a series of extraordinary pre-Congress sessions with George Brown who went to Brighton specifically to lobby them.

The Chequers Cabinet meeting was poised midway between the Congress and the Labour Party conference. Even before Frank Cousins's resignation threat and outburst at Chequers his opposition to any statutory policy was already widely known, and his views were being echoed by the TGWU in opposing both the Government's proposals and the TUC's halfway house plan to 'vet' all future pay claims. But the TGWU was now to find itself in the unusual position of leading a rebellious minority fighting a Labour Government of which their own General Secretary was a leading member.

The First Secretary of State devoted an entire day, the Friday before Congress opened, to persuading the TUC General Council to accept a system of voluntary 'policing' of pay claims. He forayed in and out of the General

8. Richard Crossman, *The Diaries of a Cabinet Minister*, Vol. I, 12 September 1965, p. 321.
  9. *Ibid.*

Council meeting at the Metropole Hotel, arguing, explaining, sometimes shouting and banging the table, to drive home his case that the British economy (and indeed the Labour Government's fate) hinged on the degree of responsibility the TUC were prepared to accept to restrain pay demands. George Woodcock was doubtful about Brown's harrying tactics, though sympathetic to the philosophy of restraint. The truth was that Woodcock was unsure of his ability to secure a Congress majority for what amounted to a new departure for the TUC, a measure of centralised authority over the wages policies and practices of member unions. It was no less than that. In the event the Congress agreed, narrowly, to give the General Council powers to 'vet' all major pay claims. The vote of 5,251,000 to 3,312,000 (a majority of 1,939,000) was close enough to reflect the deep divisions inside the trade union movement and, of course, the huge vote of the TGWU in opposition to the Government.

The fight then shifted to the floor of the Labour Party conference at Blackpool. Cousins had not been at the Brighton TUC. There was no reason for him to attend. And he was doubtful, up till the last moment, whether to attend the Blackpool conference. Before it began several newspapers played around with the guessing game 'Will he, or won't he, come to Blackpool? If he comes, what will he be up to? Will he make a public declaration of sympathy with his union's opposition to Government policies? Or will he sit as a silent and sullen onlooker?' Cousins became the talking point of the weekend Press on the eve of the conference, and of the morning papers on the day the conference opened. Almost everyone assumed that there would have to be another General Election before the next season of Party conferences. Blackpool 1965 was therefore seen as an occasion for the minimum amount of boat-rocking. But that did not deter Cousins from demonstrating his distaste for the Government's policies.

When he arrived at Blackpool on the Monday he asked for a ticket to sit on the platform, with other Ministers who were not members of the Labour Party's National Executive. But by then the conference officials had distributed all available platform tickets so Cousins was obliged to sit in the body of the hall. He was invited to sit with the TGWU delegation and he naturally chose to do so. But this precipitated an uproar in the next morning's newspapers, especially the *Daily Mail*. That newspaper's political correspondent suggested that Cousins, in the midst of a major split with his Cabinet colleagues, had 'no status' at the conference. The *Mail* also taunted him for his silence, and declared that even his mere appearance at the conferences could be interpreted as a demonstration of dissent from Government policy. Either way he could do no right.

Cousins spent a miserable and an angry week at Blackpool. The centre-piece of the conference was George Brown's National Plan. Harold Wilson, offering a keynote to the National Plan debate, told the conference that it was 'a breakthrough in the whole history of economic Government by consent and consensus'. And in Brown's speech – a superbly organised conference performance – the deputy leader sought to weld the concept of national economic planning with the necessity for a wages (and prices) policy. Cousins sat with the TGWU delegation seething and burning like a volcano about to erupt. At the end of the debate the vast majority of the conference rose to its feet cheering and clapping Brown. But Cousins sat with the rest of the TGWU delegation rooted to their seats, unsmiling, staring into the middle distance with that look of stony resolution for which he had become famous. From the platform, on his feet, beetroot-red, George Brown glowered down at his Cabinet colleague and the entire seated delegation of the country's largest union. Brown's *own* union. Tense and dramatic as the scene was, there was also almost a touch of pathos in the sight of these two leaders publicly demonstrating their love-hate.

That entire debate produced a great deal of confusion, bitterness and anguish. But it did little to point the way towards a solution of the major problems facing the Government. The vote on incomes policy produced a narrower majority than at the TUC – 3,635,000 to 2,540,000 – largely because the engineers (AUEW) switched from support for the policy, as at the TUC, to join the TGWU in opposition. This was based on a somewhat obscurantist interpretation of being in favour of a voluntary wages policy (operated by the TUC) but opposing any compulsory policy that might be introduced by the Government. Yet George Brown promised the conference that the Government would *not* use the powers he was proposing to introduce to strengthen the prices and wages policy. It was all extremely dialectical and no doubt baffling to the neutral observer.

What was George Brown proposing? He wanted powers that would give the Prices and Incomes Board the right to call witnesses and to produce evidence in any inquiry held into a particular wage or price issue. Another section of the legislation would seek powers to enforce an 'early warning' system for all price increases and pay claims. And what Brown promised was that these powers would not be used until the voluntary scheme, proposed by the TUC to 'vet' all pay claims, had been given a fair chance to work. For George Brown the success of the National Plan depended on achieving an effective incomes policy. Since the beginning of 1964, he told the conference, the 'rate at which wage and salary increases are now being achieved' had more than doubled. 'Do not let us pretend to ourselves that we can stand an inflation of that order and yet remain competitive and keep up our real living standards here at home.'

'What I want,' he went on, 'is the planned and orderly growth of incomes related to the planned and orderly growth of production.' That is now a well-trodden path of political hope: in 1965 the battle to convince the unions that wages had a crucial role in economic planning was still greeted with great scepticism, not only because many union leaders doubted the effectiveness of planning in a mixed economy but also because some of them were fundamentally opposed to the idea of trading away their freedom to bargain in the market-place.

One particular passage in Brown's speech profoundly irritated the TGWU delegation. 'May I say to you as a trade union official, speaking for my own union, as well as for others, you can have it jolly unfair between groups of workers in the same trade union. We have been operating the law of the jungle ourselves while condemning it for every other purpose.'

It was an altogether characteristically tough, unapologetic Brown speech: brilliant by conference standards. It was also a desperate speech, because although the actual result was guaranteed the size of the majority was far from certain. It was indeed a desperate attempt to convince the conference that the sceptics were wrong, that the Government *was* serious about its planning mechanism, that the critics (like the un-named Frank Cousins) were wildly mistaken.

'We are now planning the economy', said George Brown, 'we are now choosing the social priorities – and operating these. We are now doing all the things our movement has always said were essential pre-requisites for a prices and incomes policy. There is a financial and economic and social revolution going on . . .' That was the language of the hour. Yet it did little to persuade the doubters and the dissenters.

The TGWU opposition was voiced by Harry Nicholas. His appeal was for the Government to turn away from its 'restrictive wages policy' to a more positive one based on expansion, productivity and industrial efficiency (a reflection of what Cousins had been arguing inside the Cabinet). Nicholas did not argue outright against any form of wages policy, as did Clive Jenkins, who accused George Brown of seeking to 'hobble the unions'. Jenkins's case was that while he was not against a planned incomes policy in principle he was opposed to 'a planned incomes policy in an unplanned society . . .'

The Chancellor, James Callaghan, pleaded with the conference to face the economic realities. A successful wages policy was essential to resolving Britain's balance of payments deficit, he argued. He also assured the conference that there was no 'secret pledge' to the International Monetary Fund (IMF) offering a statutory incomes policy in exchange for an IMF guarantee to sterling.[10] This was something that had already caused great conflict

10. In his diaries Crossman relates at length the details of a special all-day meeting of the Cabinet at Chequers which was held between the TUC and Labour Party conferences (on 12 September 1965). The economic crisis was the main item on the agenda. It is clear from Crossman's account that the main pressure for a tougher wages policy was coming from the foreign bankers. In fact both Callaghan and Brown tacitly admitted this. Crossman then notes: 'Douglas Jay [President of the Board of Trade] made

(continued overleaf)

between Wilson, Callaghan and Cousins. Cousins had become convinced that such a pledge existed (and indeed he had been encouraged to believe it by George Brown himself). But in Cabinet, and informally, the Prime Minister and the Chancellor had denied that any such undertaking existed. Callaghan pointedly told the Blackpool conference:

> Let me say in passing that so far as pledges are concerned in respect of the loan from the IMF that I have given only one pledge and that pledge has been made public. It is that we should get ourselves into balance by the end of 1966; it is not an unfair pledge to ask for if you are being given a substantial international loan. I gave that pledge and the whole Cabinet is of course responsible for the pledge too – and it is essential that we should bend and adjust our policies to achieve this end . . .

Callaghan also taunted Harry Nicholas (and indeed the TGWU as such) with adopting a posture akin to Enoch Powell's on wages policy: 'He believes in the market economy, he believes in unemployment to solve this particular problem . . .' There were only two ways of solving the economic problem, the Chancellor said – looking hard at Frank Cousins sitting beside Harry Nicholas, as he emphasised his words – 'it will be solved by unemployment by substantial deflation, or it will be solved by a prices and incomes policy.'

Cousins was furious at this comparison with Powell, and it clearly influenced a counter-attack which later appeared in the TGWU journal's review of the conference, containing the following passage:

> James Callaghan made great play about what he called the curious parallel of thinking between the opponents of the Government's incomes policy and Mr. Enoch Powell . . . Enoch Powell argued that there were limits to which controls can be applied in a competitive private enterprise system. But this is what socialists have always argued; you can't plan capitalism. Why should we apologise because Enoch Powell has happened to glimpse this truth? After all Louis XV forecast the French Revolution. The reactionary and degenerate qualities of the observer did not make it any the less true.[11]

---

one point which blew the gaff about Callaghan's dealings in the USA [Callaghan had recently returned from Washington]. He pointed out to George Brown that we can't reflate this autumn without breaking the pledges which James Callaghan made to Fowler in Washington. I wasn't surprised when Callaghan solemnly intervened and said there was some misunderstanding since we had made no pledges at all to Fowler, there could be no question of this. If a denial ever completely confirmed a statement it was Callaghan's on that occasion.' Richard Crossman, *The Diaries of a Cabinet Minister*, Vol. I, 12 September 1965, pp. 317–23 (Hamish Hamilton & Jonathan Cape, 1975).

11. TGWU *Record*, November 1965. pp. 20–1.

Relations between Frank Cousins and the majority of his Cabinet colleagues now appeared to be moving towards something of a climax. This was specially true of George Brown. On the night following the incomes policy debate Cousins and Brown had a stand-up row in a room of the headquarters hotel at Blackpool. Brown, himself infuriated by the way Cousins had snubbed him earlier in the day in the conference hall, accused Cousins of being 'dictator'. If he were Prime Minister, Brown declared, Cousins would be sacked from the Government, on the spot. He accused Cousins of disloyalty to the Government and with influencing the TGWU by remote control, despite being in the Government. Cousins did not pull back from the encounter. He told George Brown that if he had to put up with 'any more of this kind of behaviour from you . . .' then he would see Harold Wilson and demand Brown's removal from the Cabinet. He would no longer tolerate Brown's 'irrational rantings and ravings'. The row between the two men followed them back to London and into a meeting of the National Economic Development Council the following week. George Brown was there defending his policy in the face of criticism from the CBI, which was caustic about the National Plan, among other things. Afterwards he rounded on Cousins in a stream of highly undiplomatic language for remaining silent while the employers attacked Government policy. Cousins warned him to hold his tongue, and again threatened to go to Wilson with a 'him or me' ultimatum.

Throughout this period Brown was receiving a good deal of support from the Press for his broadsides on Cousins. After the Party conference the national newspapers again turned on the Minister of Technology, this time in an even sterner tone. William Rees-Mogg in the *Sunday Times* concluded that by joining the Wilson Cabinet Frank Cousins had become a hostage to the Prime Minister. Yet, he observed, 'because he cannot bring himself to be a normal member of the Cabinet he is also a hostage to the Opposition'.[12] (Heath, the Conservative leader, had frequently attacked Cousins for his silence on incomes policy.) He went on :

> So long as the present ambiguous position continues, Mr. Cousins will always, and rightly, be subject to similar attacks. The choice does therefore lie with him. He can go back to his union or he can give up the union and support the Cabinet in which he sits. In particular he must if he is to remain in the Cabinet give public support to the Cabinet's wages policy. He cannot remain in the Cabinet but not of it.[13]

This was a perceptive observation. Indeed it may well have been encouraged, if not actively inspired, by members of the Cabinet not averse to seeking Press support for their campaign to drive Cousins out of the Government.

12. *Sunday Times*, 3 October 1965.
13. *Sunday Times*, 3 October 1965.

Cousins's bitter and sustained opposition to the Government's wages policy was by no means confined to his conflict with George Brown. It was ranged also against the Chancellor, James Callaghan, and the Minister of Labour, Ray Gunter. It was even levelled against some of his Cabinet colleagues on the Left, including Barbara Castle, all of whom supported the Brown policy, albeit for different reasons. Frequently Frank Cousins found himself involved in disputes with Mrs Castle that were just as volatile (he once reduced her to tears at a meeting of Ministers) as any he was having with the Right wing of the Cabinet. The rest of the Left in the Cabinet certainly believed in the need for an incomes policy if there was to be any serious economic planning. Their criticism of their colleagues was directed at the absence of a convincing programme of economic planning across the broad sweep of industry and measures to curb the wealthier sections of British society. But they did not accept Frank Cousins's argument against *any* interference in the freedom of wage bargaining. In that stance he was in a minority of one.

Still, the tension inside the Wilson Government was not confined to a battle between Frank Cousins and the rest. There were numerous other deep, long-simmering conflicts between several of the senior Ministers. Among the most notable of these was the struggle between James Callaghan and George Brown. The overlap in their departmental functions as well as the contrast of their personalities fed their animosities. Indeed the Chancellor (himself under heavy pressures from Britain's international creditors) was if anything more of a hawk on incomes policy than Brown. Callaghan would have preferred a full-scale wage freeze rather than Brown's 'compromise' plan for an early warning system which, incidentally, was described to be by another Cabinet Minister at the time as 'tinkering around' with the problem.

Most of the Cabinet, however, were satisfied that 'something' had to be done to strengthen the curb on pay claims. Most of them were also anxious, of course, to give the TUC 'vetting' scheme the maximum opportunity to prove itself. Yet they believed that legislation would be necessary to provide, at the minimum, a 'backstop' in case the voluntary discipline failed. Cousins continued to fight against both routes to tighter wage control. And he continued to sound warnings of imminent resignation throughout the months following his September threat at Chequers.

While a Cabinet committee struggled on through November and December, grappling with the complexities of drafting the new legislation on wages (the early warning plan), Harold Wilson decided to make one final attempt to reconcile Frank Cousins to the Government's general policy. He accepted many of Cousins's earlier proposals outlining a plan to extend the authority of the Ministry of Technology. The effect of the original proposals would have been to transform Mintech into a 'super department' for Industry and Production. That was not quite what Mr Wilson had in mind, but he did see political advantages in substantially extending Frank Cousins's Ministerial remit. It might, the Prime Minister thought, help to bring Cousins more into line with general Government policies, if not with the incomes policy as such. It would certainly demonstrate Government confidence in the technology syndrome and help to give the Ministry (and its Minister) greater political muscle inside, and outside, the Cabinet. And, by the same token, it would help to bring Cousins more into balance with George Brown. Wilson recognised that the imbalance between the two departments, Brown's DEA and Cousins's Technology, contributed to the friction between the two men. Another aspect appealed to Harold Wilson's sense of political occasion : giving Frank Cousins extra powers would demonstrate that the Prime Minister was not to be intimidated by the Press's 'Cousins Must Go' campaign.[14]

What happened in practice, however, was very different. The news of the plan to promote Cousins leaked out prematurely, and this was used by Wilson as a reason to delay the announcement and, as it turned out, to water down the original concept. The full scale of the wider powers for Technology did not come into operation until the following June. By then the die had been cast for Frank Cousins. But there is nothing to suggest that even if he had secured those extra powers at the end of 1965 it would have made any significant difference to his basic attitude towards remaining in the Government.

George Brown was uncontrollably angry when he learned of Wilson's plan to promote Cousins and the Ministry of Technology. Once again he threatened to resign. Brown saw the Wilson-Cousins deal as a move against his own Department. He also objected, with even greater vigour, to the Prime Minister offering still more power to the one man in the Cabinet who, as he saw it, had displayed open disloyalty to the Government's incomes policy. Wilson did not entirely bow to Brown. He continued to offer Cousins control over the iron and steel industry (which was about to be nationalised) and over a wide sector of administration then under the control of Douglas Jay at the Board of Trade. The general idea was for the enlarged Ministry of Technology to absorb responsibility for the Development Areas from the Board of Trade, along with sponsorship for the engineering and shipbuilding industries. This would have left the Board of Trade as a pure Ministry

14. In his book *The Cecil King Diary, 1965–70* by Cecil Harmsworth King (Cape 1972), King notes, on Thursday, 14 October 1965 (p. 38): 'It appears that in spite of Cousins's disloyalty he is very close to Wilson, who promised him that engineering should be detached from the Board of Trade and added to Technology. This was published in The *Sun*, whereupon George Brown rushed round to point out that this could not possibly work – what would happen to all the little Neddies, etc. etc.? So this plan too, is postponed.'

for Exports. Yet this was not really what Cousins had in mind. He told the Prime Minister that he didn't want to become 'a glorified President of the Board of Trade'. He wanted the Ministry of Technology to have the authority it needed to modernise British industry. The Ministry was too constricted, as it stood; its effective powers over industry were virtually nil and its creative enterprises then at an embryonic stage were inevitably taking a long time to develop. Cousins proposed that his department should become a Ministry for Industry and he envisaged taking over the existing plans for productivity – then under George Brown's DEA. Wilson tried to balance what he recognised as the real merit in Cousins's argument with the fury that was coming from George Brown. Then his attention was diverted; at that moment the crisis in Rhodesia exploded and the row over the future of Ministry of Technology temporarily stalled if not shelved.

In the event, the Ministry's powers were enlarged at the end of 1965, but it was mainly a cosmetic, half-hearted operation. The mechanical and electrical engineering industries were added to the half dozen industries already under Mintech 'sponsorship' and Cousins was also made responsible for engineering standards and weights and measures. This was dramatised as putting Cousins in charge of a major production drive in the engineering industry, but it was, in fact, mostly window-dressing. And to balance even this modest boost to Cousins's Ministry the Prime Minister stressed, in his official statement, that George Brown would retain 'the central co-ordination of measures to promote the growth of industrial productivity'. That was precisely what Cousins wished to have under *his* direction.

Frank Cousins always saw the individual roles of the Treasury, the DEA and his own Ministry as ones which ought to be slotted into a broader, more co-ordinated system of industrial and economic policy. He saw the three departments as parts of an integrated whole and believed they ought to be run in the closest possible harness, possibly even under an 'overlord' type of Minister. Obviously there was an element of personal ambition in this. Yet in Cousins personal ambition could never be separated from his overall political concept; to him political power was not about personal status, certainly not about personal gain. To be sure there was a substantial stratum of vanity in the man. It had always been there, as we have seen, and it had not diminished with his move into Government. Yet his pressure to secure wider powers for his Ministry had not grown from any personal power-lust but rather from compelling arguments put to Cousins by a combination of forces, including Sir Maurice Dean, Professor Blackett and Ben Cant. Cousins was not propelled by any primal instinct to become an Industrial Emperor, he was impressed by the logic of the case put to him by his advisers and, not least, by the muddle, confusion and conservatism he found as he tried to plot his course through the Whitehall minefield.

The announcement that Frank Cousins was to have wider powers came finally from an almost casual statement by the Minister himself at the end of a Parliamentary debate on technology on 16 November 1965. That, too, was yet another bizarre episode.

The Conservatives were censuring Cousins and his Ministry and they chose the theme of the masterly inactivity of Wilson's brainchild. But the debate was for the most part reduced to farce. Quintin Hogg, who wound up for the Tories, adopted a 'music hall' style that depressed an already pathetic debate to the level of trivialised banality. Cousins's own mental state and his general morale were at an extremely low ebb. Few could have realised just how despondent he felt before he rose to speak. His fight inside the Cabinet had reached a climax. He felt friendless and deserted by his Cabinet colleagues and yet unable to reveal anything of his political torment. He had nothing new to tell the Commons and certainly no fresh initiatives to announce. He felt stifled, frustrated and, most of all, muted. Then came anticlimax. As Cousins was about to rise to reply to Quintin Hogg Wilson towards him and whispered: 'Tell them you're getting more powers'. Cousins, nonplussed, asked mechanically 'When?'. 'Just tell them that your powers are to be extended,' replied Wilson. Cousins was taken aback. He had no further opportunity to check the details before he was on his feet, poised in a misty uncertainty. His performance that night, winding up for the Government, was probably his worst Parliamentary occasion. It embarrassed his colleagues as much as it dismayed himself. Cries of 'resign' punctuated his speech as the Tories hounded his every sentence. Hogg had suggested that the best thing that could happen would be for the Ministry of Technology to be wound up. Cousins's reply came almost lamely and without conviction: 'I am sure he [Hogg] will be pleased to know that far from it being abolished there is an intention to strengthen it.' But it was a dismal end to a sad debate. The Press comment was universally condemning. Robin Page, Parliamentary correspondent of the pro-Government newspaper the *Sun*, wrote:

I have never heard the closing hour of a debate so completely unreportable . . . Mr Hogg made a speech which was hilarious – and almost irrelevant. Mr. Frank Cousins followed with a speech that caused suffering among Government supporters. Mr. Wilson sat listening to it, chewing his tie in anguish. Was this a serious debate? From the laughter it sounded more like a night at the London Palladium.

Of course no one, least of all the Press gallery, knew anything of Wilson's whispered assurances to Cousins as he was about to speak. But inevitably the fiasco of that debate led to renewed demands for Cousins's resignation. There was one significant exception to this clamour from the Press – the political correspondent of *The Times*, David Wood, who in two carefully considered pieces written early in 1966 came strongly to Cousins's defence with a surprising vigour and courage.

In the first on 14 February 1966 he wrote that Cousins was:

> one of a small number of working class leaders who have the influence to give the working class confidence in the upheaval that must be involved for them [in industrial change] but there is no sign that the thought ever enters the heads of Conservative backbenchers. For them Mr. Cousins is a parliamentary apprentice against whom any lightweight can score an easy debating point . . . In the Commons the Opposition try to treat him as their heaven-sent butt. It is not only too late in life for him to learn parliamentary gamesmanship, he has tasted enough real power and influence in other branches of politics to be sure that such gamesmanship is an irrelevant sham. He thinks the problems facing Britain today are much more serious than that.

In the second piece, a week later, he explained:

> Through technology Mr. Cousins sees a vision of a British industrial expansion akin to that of Victorian times – with the difference that in this industrial revolution the workers will share directly in the benefit.

But such unusually sympathetic Press treatment was of little real consolation to Frank Cousins by the early months of 1966. All the forebodings he ever had about political life seemed to come together with a combined impact. He was utterly disenchanted and quite convinced that the Government was losing its way after a mere year and a half in office. He regarded the George Brown National Plan as little more than superficial political gloss, lacking in any real conviction that the Government would be strong enough to ensure that the priorities, in socialist terms, were sustained. He felt himself isolated in Cabinet. It was an atmosphere in which he could now find no natural allies. He later told me that this was a period when he was coming to the conclusion that 'I had views that were quite incompatible with the views of many in that Cabinet.' True, there were Ministers with whom he could agree from time to time, but rarely on the fundamentals of political principle. His critics, of course, suggested that 'everyone is out of step except for Frank'. That was the view frequently voiced by his left-wing colleagues, particularly by Barbara Castle.

Anthony Greenwood, then Secretary of State for the Colonies, had been a long-standing ally and friend of Cousins. He had been with Cousins in the CND movement. Greenwood was also a member of the TGWU's parliamentary panel. There was every reason for presuming that the close relationship would have continued inside the Wilson Cabinet. But it didn't. Greenwood now concedes that some of the left-wing members of the Cabinet, himself included, must have been 'something of a disappointment to Frank. He probably expected more from a number of us, including myself and Barbara. I got the impression that when Frank came into the House of Commons he looked to us, especially, for support. He expected to be treated as a Left wing leader. Perhaps he expected a deference from some of us that we did not give.' It is clear the left-wing members of that Cabinet were singularly unimpressed by Frank Cousins's performance in Cabinet, as well as by his – to them – obsessional opposition to the incomes policy. Several of them subscribe to the assessment that Cousins was unpredictable (except on wages policy), prickly and stubbornly resistant to compromise, and they therefore tend to blame these characteristics rather than political principle for the loss of harmony between themselves and the TGWU leader. Even Crossman, who was still strongly sympathetic towards Cousins, noted in mid-1965 that he was beginning to feel that the Minister of Technology was 'being exceptionally favoured by the Prime Minister in discussions on computer policy, and I regretted while I respected his intransigent stand against a firm prices and incomes policy. This perhaps explains my inconsistent attitude towards him.'[15]

Crossman was certainly not alone in this ambivalence towards Frank Cousins. The Minister of Technology inevitably attracted strong support and equally aggressive hostility, sometimes elements of both from the same individual. The Prime Minister was one of them. Several times in the latter half of 1965 Cousins asked Wilson to 'release' him from the Government. The Prime Minister tried to soothe him, to persuade him that he *was* doing a vital job and that the tensions would ease. He had some success in this tactic because Cousins remained absorbed in his task at the Ministry of Technology, despite all his problems elsewhere. In October he visited the United States for a tour of the main American computer centres, in particular the MIT in Boston. He was immensely impressed by the speed and effectiveness with which the Americans were able to apply research to production methods in the factories. It made him all the more resentful of the obstacles he had been encountering at home. He was more certain than ever that, given the authority and the muscle, the British technological potential could be developed along similar lines. But that was not to be.

Oddly enough, almost right up till the General Election of March 1966, Cousins appeared to acquire fresh enthusiasm for his task at Mintech. Even in February, for example, he was still insisting that 'The Ministry of Technology (or its concept) will in the end make or break us. He saw it as a department with enormous potential. But it depends on how much it is used, for what and by whom . . .' That is how Frank Cousins put it to me.

15. Richard Crossman, *Diaries of a Cabinet Minister*, Vol. I, August 1965, p. 301.

Chapter Twenty-four

RESIGNATION

Frank Cousins was not opposed to a wages policy in the absolute sense. Given a form of Scandinavian socialist democracy – which he assumed would be the direction for a British Government after 1964 – he would have been prepared to accept an incomes policy as part of a broader political package of economic equity. But he saw no evidence that this was likely to happen under Harold Wilson. He saw only weakness and vacillation in the face of the economic storm, with policies determined by orthodox Treasury conventions. He saw the unions being asked to accept limitations which he did not consider were demanded of other major institutions in industry or the financial world. He also felt that the Ministers around him did not fully realise the sheer practical difficulties of operating an incomes policy in a market economy. He harked back again to his old cry : 'In a free for all, we must be part of the all.' Given different political priorities, a different stance and a more convincing style of leadership Cousins might conceivably have gone along with an incomes policy of some form. What he could not accept was what, in the end, he regarded as outright deception by his Cabinet colleagues, including the Prime Minister, though this amounted to little more than routine Ministerial political gamesmanship. Cousins's honesty, his simple, straightforward *naïveté* (qualities noted by Lord Penney and Sir Richard Marsh); his belief that a promise was a promise and a conviction was a conviction – these were attributes ingrained into his character. He could not bring himself to trivialise qualities he himself held in such respect. But in politics, as it was frequently put to him, a thick skin counts for more than purity of conscience.

Yet it was *not* Cousins's disagreement over incomes policy which finally determined his resignation in July 1966. It was his deep-seated fear that if he did not return soon to his post as TGWU General Secretary he would no longer be able to straddle the two worlds. And if he could no longer return to the union, then Cousins feared the TGWU would swing back again to the Right, under Harry Nicholas's leadership.

Frank Cousins wanted Jack Jones to succeed him as General Secretary. He had this in mind from the beginning of his own career in that post. He helped to bring Jones out of his district secretary's job in Coventry and appoint him first as secretary to the engineering and chemical trades group in the powerful Midland Region of the union and, shortly afterwards, to secretary of the Midlands Region – No. 5 region, which after London is the most influential in the TGWU. Then, early in 1963, Cousins (inspired by Alf Chandler) began to plan a new post of Assistant Executive Secretary at the union's headquarters which would effectively amount to No. 3 in the hierarchy. This was done largely in order to create a senior executive post for Jack Jones – and to put him in a springboard position from which in due time as a palpable heir-apparent he could succeed to general secretaryship of the TGWU. Jones was appointed to that post in August 1963.

There had never been any serious doubt in Cousins's mind that the man best suited, politically and industrially, to succeed him when he retired was James Larkin Jones. Yet in the spring of 1966 with Cousins in the Government it began to look somewhat less certain that Jones would be his successor. Cousins had an affection for Harry Nicholas as a man and as a loyal servant of the union. But he did not regard him as the man best fitted to keep the TGWU to a radical left-wing policy. None the less, Nicholas was growing in status and stature as acting General Secretary. He had a strong base and following in the union and it became increasingly clear to Cousins, and others in the union, that if Nicholas were to be formally confirmed as General Secretary – which would inevitably happen if Cousins decided to remain permanently in politics – then Jack Jones might never follow him in the job.

The reasoning behind this was that Nicholas would move the union back towards the Right, perhaps not as far as it had been under Deakin, but certainly in that direction. In that event the machine would swing behind Nicholas and when it came to electing a successor, Jack Jones would plainly be at a real, perhaps a decisive, disadvantage. This is now mere speculation. Yet there was sufficient prima facie evidence to convince Cousins that the future political course of the TGWU hinged on his return to the General Secretary's chair.

Inside the TGWU there were very strong pressures from many full-time officials – especially the older, longer-serving Deakin-appointed officials – to secure Nicholas's confirmation as General Secretary and, by the same token, to ensure that Cousins did not return to the union. Some of these officials were outspokenly hostile to both Cousins and Jack Jones, and certainly it was their determination, if not their specific plan, to make sure that Jones did not succeed, or, at least, to minimise his chances. The issue of succession therefore became an inextricable part of the whole background of ideas and debate against which Frank Cousins was trying to make up his mind whether to continue his fight inside the Cabinet or return to the TGWU.

Cousins did not become fully aware of the risk that existed to Jack Jones's ultimate succession until early in 1966, shortly before the General Election of 31 March. It was then that he really made up his mind to leave the Government, although the final phases of his resignation drama were to be played out like a slow, tantalising minuet over the following three months. A decisive moment in all this was the evening of Saturday 19 February, at the Cousins's home at Charshalton Beeches. It was then that he conclusively decided he would have to return to the TGWU at a suitable moment *after* the election. That decision was taken in the presence of a small family circle after he had discussed his future and argued the implications of resignation with Nance and his son, John, then a full-time official of the TGWU. John told his father that, in his view, it was essential for the union's future that Frank should return to the general secretaryship as soon as possible. John alarmed his father by his description of the internal state of affairs in the TGWU. The gist of his account was that the union would swing back to the Right unless Cousins returned to the helm.

Frank Cousins faced a fearful choice. Here was the Labour Party on the brink of a General Election; if he resigned from the Government immediately, the political consequences could be immense. By publicising the deep conflicts within the Wilson Cabinet it would quite clearly risk exposing the Government to defeat at the polls. Yet, he reflected, if indeed he had already made up his mind to return to his union, would it not be dishonest to go into the election campaign knowing that his period in Government was about to end? Would it not be deceiving his Cabinet colleagues, his Parliamentary colleagues, his constituents at Nuneaton, everyone to whom Cousins owed allegiance? Staring him in the face now was precisely the kind of action, that all his life he had sought to avoid – doing one thing and meaning another. It was wholly out of character with the personality and the chemistry of Frank Cousins. That was the cruelty of his dilemma. Of course, it was insoluble. He tried to avoid thinking about it too much; to some extent he no doubt deluded himself that some third option might, just conceivably, arise. He even mused over the possibility that he might be able to combine returning to the union with remaining as MP for Nuneaton – after his resignation from the Cabinet. In fact this is what he attempted to do, but the union's executive refused to accept his proposal. It had been long-standing practice in the TGWU that the union's General Secretary should not be a member of Parliament – a rule which the TGWU shares with a number of other major trade unions. In the end his parting with Nuneaton was the most bitter disappointment of Cousins's Parliamentary experience.

A few days before the decisive family conclave at Carshalton Beeches Cousins had been to see Harry Nicholas and Jack Jones at Transport House. He wanted to test their reactions to his plan to quit the Government and return to the union. The suggestion shocked and dismayed Nicholas but delighted and refreshed Jones. Nicholas expressed strong doubts about the wisdom of Cousins's decision. In particular he raised the question of the impact it would have on the Nuneaton Labour Party. He knew this was an extremely sensitive point for Cousins. But it became clear at that meeting that it was now only a question of time. Cousins's mind was hardening to the point where second thoughts could almost be ruled out. The process of disillusionment had taken control and it required only the confirmation of his family circle to convince him that there was no sensible alternative to a return to the trade union world where, he knew, he could tread firm and familiar ground once again, where he would be 'at home' among his 'own type of people'. Perhaps, he reflected, it had all been a mistake from the start. Yet, curiously, on that night of 19 February Nance was far less convinced than anyone else in the circle that it was right for Frank to resign, although she had been strongest of all in her doubts about the wisdom of his going into the Government.

That same day the news had come of the resignation from the Government of Christopher Mayhew, Minister for the Navy. Mayhew had been involved in a long fight to preserve the role of the Navy and to oppose the cuts proposed in the defence review. In particular he had opposed Denis Healey's plan (Healey was then Minister of Defence) to phase out the existing aircraft carriers which it was claimed would becoma obsolete by the 1970s and to place no new orders for carriers. Long-range, shore-based aircraft were to do their job. That, indeed, had been one of the principal roles originally planned for TSR-2 – the role now to be taken over by the American F-111A. The Mayhew resignation, coming just nine days before Harold Wilson announced the March election and on the eve of his departure (with Frank Cousins) for talks in Moscow, seemed, at the time, to be a serious boat-rocking exercise. It turned out to be an exceedingly minor squall, but that was not how Ministers reacted to it at the time, or indeed the Press and the Tory Opposition. And when the First Sea Lord, Sir David Luce, followed Mayhew within a few days, the Conservative leaders whipped up the defence controversy as a heaven-sent (as it seemed) opportunity to hit the Government on the brink of what most observers felt to be an imminent General Election. Defence is always an Achilles heel for a Labour Government and political sensitivities were acute. From Frank Cousins's point of view it cast a darker shadow across his plans for the timing of any resignation.

The thought of resignation had been constantly present in Frank Cousins's mind since the turn of the year. On virtually every major issue of controversy

Cousins was finding himself in a minority in the Cabinet sometimes of two or three, often of only one. On defence policy as well as domestic economic affairs Cousins had become labelled 'the odd man out'. At a Cabinet meeting in January Ministers had taken a final decision on the Defence White Paper and, in particular, on the purchase of the F-111A and the phasing out of aircraft carriers. Cousins had argued against these policies at earlier meetings, but his objections were brushed aside. He knew by then it was pointless to continue his fight, so he refused to attend that Cabinet meeting at which these final decisions were to be reached. It was an action not entirely without precedent in political affairs, but there were very few parallels. Curiously, it was never discovered by the Press.

At the beginning of February Cousins again mentioned resignation to Harold Wilson. He warned the Prime Minister that if the Cabinet persisted with its proposed legislation on incomes policy, then he would definitely resign. Wilson again sought to persuade him that the legislation was largely 'window dressing' designed, chiefly, to impress foreign opinion that Britain was serious in her determination to 'do something' about inflation. It was imperative that the Government should produce a policy of this nature to protect sterling – and the future of the Government. Cousins waved all this aside by insisting that the policy was wrong *in principle* and, in any event, simply wouldn't work in practice. He pointed out that what the Government was proposing would cause havoc in wage negotiations and probably do more damage to industrial relations than not having a statutory policy. In that event, he observed sardonically, it would hardly help to appease foreign opinion. Moreover, he warned the Prime Minister that he could not, and would not, speak in support of the legislation. He would vote against it, and when the General Election came (the date had not then been announced) he would speak publicly against it.

Angrily Harold Wilson told Cousins he could not do that. As a member of the Cabinet he was bound by the principle of collective responsibility. But Cousins was not impressed by such admonitions. He told the Prime Minister that *his* main responsibility was to his union members and to the wider Labour and trade union movement. His first loyalties were to the principles he had accepted from the moment he became a trade union official, the principles of socialism. What the Government was now proposing had nothing to do with socialism.

The Prime Minister countered with a severe and telling argument. All right, he told Cousins, but remember what you would be doing. You would destroy the Labour Government, perhaps even the Labour Party. We would be out in the political wilderness for years. What, asked Wilson, would that achieve? Would Cousins prefer to see a Conservative Government in office? The argument became fiercer. Wilson and Cousins had of course clashed increasingly since the summer of 1965 but not before with the passion and intensity of that February encounter. Wilson demanded to know Cousins's alternatives to the income policy proposals. How was he supposed to deal with George Brown if the 'early warning' Bill were to scrapped? That was not his problem, Cousins replied. Wilson must choose between himself and George Brown.

The Prime Minister pleaded with his Minister of Technology to think again. He urged him to reflect that politically they both wanted the same things. But with a majority of three he was trapped. It would be different, he assured Cousins, if they were returned with a larger majority. Wilson pleaded for time. Cousins must not walk out now. The damage to the Government and the entire Labour Movement would be immense. If in the end he was determined to resign, Wilson advised, he should wait for a few months after the election and then resign on some pretext of health or a desire to return to the TGWU. But not now.

Cousins's relations with Wilson had become so tense and difficult that he threatened to cancel an arrangement to accompany the Prime Minister to Moscow from 21 to 24 February. When it became known that the Bill outlining the proposed incomes policy was to be published on the 24 February, Cousins declared that he must be in London when the infamous measure was issued. The Prime Minister, on the other hand, was determined to have Cousins out of harm's way. Harold Wilson says he took Cousins to Moscow because 'a large part of our discussions were to be about trade and technological exchanges'.[1] That was true. But there was no necessity for Cousins to be personally present at the meetings. The Prime Minister's talks with Kosygin could have embraced all the relevant trade matters, without Cousins having separate negotiations at that particular time with his Soviet counterpart Kirillin. The truth is that Wilson wanted Cousins in Moscow to keep him away from Westminster. Civil servants who were close to both 10 Downing Street and the Ministry of Technology were convinced that the Prime Minister's motive for taking Frank Cousins was to ensure that the Minister of Technology did not resign while he was absent in Moscow. Harold Wilson certainly reckoned that this was a possibility at that time. And, although Cousins threatened to stay at home, in fact, he went to Moscow as directed.

By now the Prime Minister was thoroughly fed up with Cousins and his conscience. Indeed, Cousins had few illusions about this. He knew that Wilson would be glad to see him go, though in fact the Prime Minister was deeply ambivalent about his Minister of Technology. He found Cousins an irritating and furiously difficult man to handle. None the less he respected the TGWU leader and secretly admired his courage, tenacity and quite remarkable combination of determination and stubbornness. Wilson may

1. Harold Wilson, *The Labour Government, 1964–1970*, p. 213.

even have subconsciously envied Cousins's capacity for bloody-mindedness. He recognised the value of having such a commanding trade union figure in his Cabinet. Cousins was also beginning to make a real impression as Minister of Technology. The Ministry was at last becoming an important sector of Government and, despite its vociferous critics, its role was more clearly defined and its contribution increasingly worthwhile. Cousins was as conscious of his capacity to irritate the Prime Minister as Wilson was aware of the shadow that Cousins's attitude was now throwing across the business of Government. In those early weeks of 1966 when Cousins was an almost daily visitor to 10 Downing Street (repeatedly hammering away at the theme of the incomes policy legislation), Cousins said to Harold Wilson, in the friendliest possible way: 'Look, Harold you must be fed up with my coming in every day, like this. Let's stop kidding ourselves. You might as well agree to let me resign . . .' But Wilson wouldn't agree to any such thing.

Cousins recalls some amusing occasions during that most unamusing and querulous period. At one of his daily visits he was arguing with the Prime Minister when Wilson got up to walk round the room, puffing hard on his pipe, characteristic practice when he was troubled, or thinking hard about some intractable problem. As Wilson paced up and down Cousins, infuriated by his agitated and fidgety Prime Minister, suddenly shouted: 'Look, Harold, if you don't stop walking up and down like this you'll have me doing it – and then we'll only see each other as we pass.' It helped to relieve the tension . . .

The General Election was announced on 28 February. Parliament was dissolved on 10 March, and the campaign began the next day. George Brown's early warning legislation was now in suspension and, provided Labour won, would require to be reintroduced after the election. In that sense all bets were off, and Cousins could technically regard the campaign as an opportunity to wipe the slate clean. In theory it was possible to argue that a new Labour Government could start afresh. And indeed this is precisely what the Prime Minister is said to have told Cousins shortly before polling day. There is still much controversy about what was meant and what was said. But it cannot be seriously questioned that something of significance was *implied* during a telephone conversation between Wilson and Cousins in the middle of that election campaign.

Cousins had set up his personal base at the Newdigate Hotel, Nuneaton. About the middle of the campaign he was told by his agent, Alfred Allen, that his main election address was ready for the printer. All that was required was a new photograph. Cousins suddenly instructed Allen to hold everything. Casually he mentioned to his astonished agent that it was just possible that he might not be standing after all. He was waiting for a telephone call from the Prime Minister, who was in Liverpool. Cousins had been trying to contact Harold Wilson to obtain from him an undertaking that the incomes policy legislation would be scrapped or perhaps completely reconsidered. About a week before the election Wilson phoned Cousins from the Adelphi Hotel, Liverpool. They discussed the legislation. What, asked Cousins, would be the situation after the election, assuming Labour won? Would the incomes policy be dropped? Wilson hedged until Cousins hinted that he could still withdraw from the campaign. Wilson, plainly angered, warned again of the consequences of such an action and then, referring to the incomes policy legislation, told Cousins: 'There are many things that can be consigned to the incinerator – that included.' This, at any rate, is the phrase which Cousins insists was used by Wilson. Wilson believes it was much less specific. When he was later challenged by Cousins to explain why he had gone back on the promise, the Prime Minister denied ever making such a statement – certainly in the clear terms Cousins assumed.

Cousins himself admits that his interpretation of precisely what Harold Wilson said that afternoon may not be the right one. *He* believes it is; and he certainly believed (or wanted to believe) it was the correct interpretation in March 1966. On the other hand he agrees that the Prime Minister may not have regarded his statement as a promise, a commitment or anything more than an indication of what was *possible* in the event of a Labour victory. To be sure, it is hard to imagine how Wilson could ever have offered a categorical promise of the kind that Frank Cousins assumed.

That the prices and incomes policy should be *toughened* not *dropped*, was implicit, perhaps even explicit, in the election manifesto of the Labour Party. Nevertheless the Liverpool-Nuneaton telephone talk was to rankle with Frank Cousins as a final violation of the trust that had once existed between himself and the Prime Minister.

Cousins fought the election campaign against an unremitting barrage of Press criticism and, in some cases, open abuse if not libel. It was all meant to wound deeply. It did. Yet Cousins did not hit back at the Press as he might have been justified in doing. Perhaps the most wounding of all the attacks (because it was the most penetrating) came from the *Daily Mirror*, one of only two national newspapers supporting the Labour Party (the other was the pre-Murdoch *Sun*). At the very start of the campaign the *Mirror* launched a massive broadside against Cousins under a front-page headline: 'MR. COUSINS: SOMEONE HAS TO SAY IT'.[2] 'His presence in a Cabinet which believes in a prices and incomes policy', said the *Mirror*, was a 'cynical force' that had gone on for too long. 'The Prime Minister won't accept Mr. Cousins's resignation – and for some curious reason is frightened to sack him. The situation reflects no credit upon Mr. Cousins or Mr. Wilson . . . How long can this nonsense go on? Mr. Cousins does not look as if he is

2. The *Daily Mirror*, 10 March 1966.

enjoying it. Why should Mr Wilson allow him to endure it?' The *Mirror* ridiculed the TGWU for handing over £50,000 to help Labour fight the election and then attacking the very foundations of the policy on which the Government were fighting the election. Then came a few histrionic absurdities to pepper the dish : 'Frank Cousins will go down in history as the first – and the *Mirror* hopes the last – Minister to be a permanent and feared member of a Cabinet with which he totally disagrees. He is Ernie Bevin in reverse. He's Arthur Deakin upside down.' So, the *Mirror* concluded its message to Harold Wilson, pack up the double talk, the pretence, the public evasion, etc. – and sack Frank Cousins.

Inescapably this *Mirror* attack had its effect. It further embittered Cousins; it delighted George Brown; and it left Harold Wilson feeling awkward and embarrassed. But it had absolutely no impact on the election result, which produced a landslide win for Labour by a majority that surprised as well as elated Wilson. It was indeed a remarkable electoral victory. In the early hours of 1 April I was in Liverpool with Harold Wilson when the magnitude of the result was already becoming clear. He told the Huyton Labour Party gathering that the result was the 'biggest single peacetime victory since the election of 1906'. So it was. And it seemed at the time that this second successive Labour win might usher in a unique period in British political affairs. The question uppermost in the minds of many political observers was whether Labour could now govern the country with the conviction of a ruling party – the advantage the Conservatives had possessed for nearly a century. Many people saw the 1966 victory as an epoch-making event that would probably change the Labour Party as much as it might change the direction of the country – and, indeed, the role of the Conservative Party as well. With an overall majority of 97 Labour appeared set for a generation of power, given intelligent and courageous leadership – and a fair slice of luck.

In the first few months of the new Government, however, there was scarcely a moment without some kind of major crisis. Internationally the scene was clouded and confused by de Gaulle's melodramatic announcement in March that France would withdraw from NATO; Leonid Brezhnev became Secretary General of the Soviet Communist Party on March 29; in April the Cultural Revolution began in China. But it was the domestic economic front which confronted the Government with a mountain of problems. And it was on this front that its will seemed to collapse. It pursued neither an orthodox policy of monetary restraint, which would have involved a devaluation (or a floating pound) as most economists were urging (inside and outside Whitehall); nor would the majority of the Cabinet even begin to contemplate a more formidable left-wing policy of greater intervention in the affairs of private enterprise, coupled with an industrial strategy designed to steer the economy towards more collectivist solutions. Supported by some

486

if not all of their civil service advisers, they gave priority instead to a prices and incomes policy to curb an inflation already eroding many of their social and economic plans. It is now generally accepted that the Labour Government's major error of judgement was not to devalue after the 1966 election, or to allow the pound to float against other currencies. That would have brought some unemployment, but the failure to change the parity of the pound simply delayed the rise in unemployment until after the devaluation which was eventually forced on Britain in the following year.[3]

Both Harold Wilson and James Callaghan were determined to hold to their pledges not to devalue sterling. George Brown was in favour of doing so – not least because he recognised it was probably the only way to save his National Plan. Frank Cousins would not have opposed devaluation provided that a new economic policy was developed around the new parity and the statutory incomes policy abandoned. The catalogue of failure from July 1966 is now a well chronicled dirge. All the great hopes for economic growth, soaring productivity, planned expansion and regeneration of the social services fell at that formidable fence. So too, in another sense, did the chances of a completely new form of social contract with the trade unions – a contract that had to await the development of a new political and economic situation in 1974. It was an extraordinary sequel to what appeared in April 1966.

In the wake of his victory Harold Wilson made a number of changes in his Cabinet and in the remits handed to Ministers. Richard Marsh was brought into the Cabinet as Minister of Power, and was given the priority task of steering the steel nationalisation Bill through Parliament. His place as a Parliamentary Secretary at Technology was filled by Peter Shore, who had been working as Harold Wilson's PPS, more specifically as the unofficial head of a team of research advisers to the Prime Minister. Cousins's Ministry was also strengthened by Edmund Dell, who with Peter Shore shared joint Parliamentary Secretaryship to Frank Cousins. Both appointments were designed by Wilson to convince Cousins that his Department would get more support now that the Government's Parliamentary base was so much stronger. But it was also meant to compensate for the fact that Wilson was firmly committed to going ahead with the new legislation on prices and incomes, despite the known threat of Cousins's resignation. There was no delay, no second thoughts; no incinerator was in sight. From the first post-election Cabinet meeting on Maundy Thursday Cousins re-opened the fight

3. In his book *The Labour Government's Economic Record, 1964–70* (Duckworth, 1972), pp. 61–3, Professor Wilfred Beckerman suggests that 'There is little doubt that the decision to give absolute priority to the maintenance of the exchange rate (after the 1966 election) was the one great mistake of economic policy . . . there was further excuse for not devaluing the pound . . .'

to stop the legislation, but he knew then that his bid was doomed to fail. Wilson saw no way of reconciling Cousins's views with the pressures building up around him from his Cabinet colleagues and from external influences. Without doubt Callaghan's concern for a tougher wages policy accurately reflected the views of Britain's creditors. The Treasury view was that a serious wage and cost inflation was already building up in the pipeline. Chancellor Callaghan echoed this view repeatedly to his colleagues as he pushed and prodded George Brown into accepting a tougher incomes policy.

Within a few weeks of the General Election came the strike of the National Union of Seamen, which stretched on for 47 days[4], and this was laid at the door of a Communist Party conspiracy to overthrow the Government's wages policy. That was the essence of the famous speech made by Harold Wilson in the House of Commons on 20 June. He attacked the 'tightly knit group of politically motivated men' who were 'endangering the security of the industry and the economic welfare of the nation'. There was some substance in what the Prime Minister said, based on intelligence reports given to him by the Special Branch. He did his utmost to persuade the TUC and Fleet Street editors to take his charges seriously. Some of them did. Yet it was a superficial judgement, and certainly an oversimplified gloss on the reality of the seamen's situation. It did not convince Frank Cousins (who believed the seamen had an exceptionally strong case) nor George Woodcock, who simply refused to accept the implications of the Prime Minister's charges. Woodcock played a significant, perhaps in the end crucial, role in persuading the National Union of Seamen's executive to accept a formula for the ending of the strike, although Harold Wilson would still argue that it was his attack on the Communist conspirators that broke the back of their resistance. Whatever the Communist motives may have been, the handling of that strike both by the Government and the shipping companies did nothing to assist an early settlement. If anything, it played into the hands of potential conspirators. It was only much later when the strike had become an entrenched battle, that political influences played a part in prolonging the stoppage. But the root cause remained the long tradition of weak, compliant, and some would claim, corrupt, NUS leadership in the union's dealings with the shipping companies.

Both the industry and the Government completely failed to recognise the frustrations that were building up among rank-and-file seamen. Their deep and genuine discontent was directed as much, if not more, against their own union officials. The Prime Minister, in his later account of the strike, recognised this. Cousins was criticised at the time by his Cabinet colleagues for his failure to support their attack on the Seamen's Union. Yet he

4. 16 May to 1 July 1966.

believed that the strike – regardless of the way in which the Communist Party later exploited the situation – was used by the Government to justify its wages policy and, subsequently, as an excuse when the crisis broke in July that year. And he also believed that the Ministers' handling of the strike (he was especially critical of Ray Gunter, Minister of Labour) demonstrated the correctness of his view that the Government was incapable of understanding the feelings, motivations and frustrations of the shop floor or the ship's deck.

It would, of course, be idle to claim that the seamen's strike had no effect on Britain's precarious economic position in that summer of 1966, when the balance of payments deficit exposed the whole fabric of the British economy to the widest international speculation and political pressures. Even the slightest squall could precipitate a dramatic storm. But far too much has been made of the strike's effects. The sterling situation was critical before it started. The election result itself made Britain's situation more sensitive. Foreign bankers were scared when Labour was re-elected with such a huge majority pledged to a programme of social reform and public spending on a more substantial scale. The device of using statutory control of incomes was adopted by the Cabinet at least partly to persuade these bankers that the Government was determined to operate on orthodox nostrums of economic management. Indeed Wilson told his Cabinet colleagues immediately after the election – as he had told Cousins, in effect, before it – that if they were to go ahead with steel nationalisation (which he certainly favoured) then the new incomes policy legislation would be necessary as a form of 'offset' factor to demonstrate to the foreign bankers that the Labour Government was not going wildly socialist.[5]

There was certainly no unanimity in the Cabinet over the decision to fight the Seamen's Union. The newcomer, Dick Marsh, supported Frank Cousins. So did Barbara Castle. Richard Crossman observed in his diary that in his view the Cabinet was embarking on this course of action to defend an incomes policy which was already in ruins.[6] Outside the Government the TUC tried desperately to find a formula for a settlement. George Woodcock refused to be deterred by the Prime Minister's private as well as public blandishments about a Communist conspiracy or even by the more persuasive (to him) case for trying to preserve the incomes policy. Woodcock wanted to prevent the incomes policy from collapsing and to patch up the damage done by the recent settlements for higher salaried professional groups. But, like Crossman, he saw no sense in using the Seamen's Union as a scapegoat when the doctors, judges and civil servants had been let

5. Richard Crossman, *Diaries of a Cabinet Minister*, Vol. I (Hamish Hamilton and Jonathan Cape, 1975), 4 May 1966, p. 511.
6. *Ibid.*, 19 May 1966, p. 524.

through the net. To Frank Cousins the entire scene seemed farcical. It simply confirmed his irritation with the majority of his Cabinet colleagues and strengthened his conviction that it was time to depart. (When a committee of inquiry under Lord Pearson produced a formula for settling the strike Cousins was the only one of the 20 Cabinet Ministers present to vote against the Pearson formula. The Seamen's Union rejected it at first, but later the Pearson Report was used as the basis for ending the strike.)

A month after the strike started Wilson announced that Cousins was getting wider powers at the Ministry of Technology. On 16 June it was revealed that Mintech was to be made responsible for the shipbuilding (as well as the engineering) industry and eventually also for the production side of the Ministry of Aviation. It was the Prime Minister's belated response to the pressure Cousins and his Department had been exerting for almost a year, but he knew, then, that it was too late to have any real influence over Cousins's decision to leave. Ironically, however, the Ministry of Technology was at last becoming the Ministry for Industry that Cousins had urged from the start. He was naturally delighted with what was finally happening to his Department. But he had already begun to make practical arrangements for his return to the TGWU. Cousins told the union's executive in March that he wished them to confirm his status as General Secretary and to reaffirm, publicly, that he was merely on leave of absence.

Some members of the TGWU executive had long been restive about Cousins's dual role and wanted his position clarified. Several of them felt that it was unfair and unjust to leave Nicholas in a position of continuing uncertainty. The time had come, they believed, for a clear decision on the future of the general secretaryship: to force the issue to a head, one way or the other. Nor did these noises come only from the close friends and supporters of Harry Nicholas. *Their* motives were plain enough. The Left wing, too, was vocal on the issue. One of the most senior left-wing members of the executive was Bill Jones, the London busman, and he was prominent in demanding that a decision should be made quickly; he wanted Frank Cousins back in the General Secretary's chair. Indeed he was opposed to Cousins joining the Government in the first place. Jack Jones was also anxious to clear up the uncertainty. So it was arranged that Frank Cousins call in to see Harry Nicholas at Transport House early in June, when the union's executive was in session holding its quarterly meeting. Nicholas privately explained that he had asked Cousins to call in because some members of the executive 'were beginning to ask what was going to happen about Frank and the general secretaryship'.

'What do you mean, what's going to happen?' Cousins demanded with his customary sharpness. 'I'm on leave of absence, and you are acting general secretary.'

That was not satisfactory, Nicholas insisted with some courage. The executive now wanted to know what was going to happen on a more permanent basis.

'Oh, I see,' Cousins replied with a voice full of scorn. 'They want to know whether I am prepared to come back and cancel my leave of absence. All right, let's go down and meet the executive now and I will tell them myself that if they want to rescind my leave of absence, well, that's all right by me . . .' In Cousins's view, this was not what Nicholas had expected him to say, certainly not with such promptness. They went into the executive room and Cousins automatically sat beside the chairman, in the General Secretary's traditional chair. Nicholas announced, 'Brother Cousins, Minister of Technology, wants to say a few things to you . . .'

'No, I don't,' Cousins snapped in. 'I thought, according to what Harry has just been telling me, that *you* wanted to say something to *me* – or at least to ask me some questions.'

There was an awkward silence for some seconds, until an executive member from Merseyside broke the tension with a question. He wanted to know what Frank Cousins's position was – did he intend to return to the union or not? It was the moment Cousins had waited for and he pounced. Return to the union? Why, of course, straight away, if that was the wish of the executive. All they had to do was to rescind his leave of absence and he would return immediately. Indeed, Cousins persisted, as if determined to tease his critics, if the executive so wished he could arrange to be back at his union post by Monday (it was then Thursday).

'Do you mean,' asked Bill Jones, 'that if we now cancel your leave of absence you'll agree to come back?'

'Yes,' replied Cousins.

'Then I move that we rescind your leave of absence.'

That was not quite what the supporters of Harry Nicholas had hoped or expected. There was another awkward pause before someone else moved an amendment proposing that the existing situation should continue until Frank Cousins himself felt it was appropriate to end his term with the Government. The mover of this amendment (M. B. Blair) suggested that it was improper to make hasty decisions on such a critical issue. More time was needed to consider all the implications. The amendment was carried. Harry Nicholas played no further part in the proceedings, but he was plainly a dismayed man at the end of the session.

Hardly anything was disclosed to the Press after that meeting. The Labour correspondent of *The Times* noted that the proceedings 'were shrouded in the mystery characteristic of the union and in some circumstances of Mr. Cousins'. It was Jack Jones who met the Press afterwards to read an official statement which was as opaque as it was unrewarding. 'Frank Cousins, Minister of Technology,' the statement said, 'today met the Executive Council and discussed relationships within the union. The discussion took place

491

in a very friendly atmosphere and the Council expressed gratitude to Frank Cousins for calling on them and participating in a full and free exchange of views.' Surprisingly that statement produced no fresh burst of speculation about the imminent return of Cousins to the union, although a little careful in-depth inquiry work would certainly have led a newspaperman in that direction.

Cousins had only recently returned from another visit to the Soviet Union, his second in four months. The first, with Harold Wilson shortly before the election, led to a series of discussions on the exchange of technological know-how between the two countries and an invitation for Cousins to return for more detailed talks with his Russian counterpart and to visit the Soviet 'Science City' of Novosibirsk, in Siberia. The second visit strengthened Cousins's conviction that it was imperative for Britain to modernise her industries as an absolute priority. He had seen what was happening in the United States and the Soviet Union. Only a mere glimpse it is true, but enough to fortify his belief that British industry was falling seriously behind in the application of new technology – not in the invention or possession of the necessary knowledge, but in the direct application of that knowledge. Cousins also believed there was a considerable potential for expanding Anglo-Soviet trade and for mutual agreements covering the exchange of information about the development of new industrial techniques. One must remember that these two visits (in February and May of 1966) came long before the Russians established trade and technology deals with West Germany, France, Italy, Japan, and other countries – deals which Britain might have pioneered in 1966, given the political will. But Frank Cousins was no longer in a position to influence seriously the Prime Minister or the direction of Cabinet thinking on such issues.

Indeed, when he returned from Moscow in May Cousins had another series of clashes with Wilson over the general direction of British foreign policy as well as incomes policy. For a long time he had been trying to urge Harold Wilson to re-think the entire East-of-Suez commitment and to abandon what Cousins, and several others in the Cabinet by no means on the Left, regarded as a vainglorious attempt to preserve an international image of military power which could no longer be justified either by fact or fiction. Sheer economic prudence was also a determinant, Cousins argued. Wilson at that time was still clinging to the view that Britain must not relinquish her role as a world power. During one of his frequent clashes with Wilson at No. 10 Cousins specifically related the East of Suez obsession to the Government's attitude towards wages and domestic economic policy. Unless the Government abandoned its illusion about Britain's global role, Cousins declaimed, it would never be able to escape from the ignominious position of a permanent international debtor-nation, especially beholden to the United States. Vietnam, Cousins argued, was a typical example of

this. Why hadn't we taken a firm stand against US policy there, he demanded to know. The Prime Minister's reply was as inelegant as it was furious
– 'Because we can't kick our creditors in the balls.' To which Cousins retorted, quite simply, 'Why not?'

On 22 June, *en route* for Torquay to speak to the annual conference of
the Confederation of Shipbuilding and Engineering Unions, Cousins turned
to Christopher Herzig and quietly asked: 'When should I resign?' Herzig,
like a good civil servant, was supposed to know all the nuances behind that
question without betraying the slightest trace of surprise or consternation.
In any event he knew it was pointless, by then, to try to persuade Cousins
to change his mind. Herzig's cool and tactful reply was that if the Minister
had really made up his mind to go, then the appropriate moment in Parliamentary terms would be when the incomes policy Bill was published. It
was scheduled for early July. Herzig knew that the final break was now very
close indeed and he regretted it deeply because, apart from his personal
attachment to Frank Cousins, he believed that the Ministry was at last finding its feet. Having acquired wider powers and an altogether stronger status
in Whitehall, it could provide its Minister with a platform of much greater
potential influence.

Cousins's speech in Torquay was made to an audience wholly unaware of
the impending drama. Yet it is worth recalling if only because it was one of
the most impressive and indeed most important speeches Cousins delivered
as a Minister. He spoke as a socialist and a union leader rather than a
Cabinet Minister to a union audience of hardened professional bargainers.
'Today,' Cousins said, 'we are letting ourselves accept limitations and shortage in the midst of the greatest revelation of potential wealth and wellbeing
in the whole of humanity's history. If the knowledge and skill already available were fully applied we could multiply our available resources ten times
over . . .' Even on the eve of his departure from Government he was still
arguing the case for technology as the motive force for widespread political
change and social improvement. To him this remained central to the socialist
objective – much more than the sterility of purely ideological formulae. 'We
could increase our leisure and enrich our lives as far beyond the standards
of today as these are beyond the lives of working people in the wretched
early days of the industrial revolution. Our trouble is that our actions are
enfeebled and our progress shackled because we keep our sights too low . . .'

Few could have sensed the force and the passion with which he was trying
to speak to an audience beyond the Torquay conference, to an audience of
his colleagues in the Cabinet room, an audience that had long ceased to
listen to him, an audience which, perhaps, had never really understood his
motivations from the very beginning. His Torquay speech, the last he made
in public before resigning, was much praised, not least by some of his old
critics in the Press. The paradox was that the Press saw the Cousins perform-

ance as evidence of the growing stature of the Minister of Technology, who was, some of them considered, one of the commanding figures in the Wilson Cabinet.

In a powerful editorial comment *The Times* praised Cousins for putting the issues so forcibly to a trade union audience :

> Perhaps more than any other single person Mr. Frank Cousins could persuade the unions to abandon their remaining Luddite traditions and to stake their fortune on the increase in the national wealth that advancing technology and greater productivity can bring . . . If Mr. Cousins continues on the road he started yesterday, encouraging the unions to take their part in promoting the pursuit of productivity both Minister and Ministry could make a first-class contribution to Britain.

Cousins read that with a wry and sad smile. He reflected that it is all too often the case in political life that recognition invariably comes when it is too late to be of practical value – to the individual or the community he is seeking to serve.

Frank Cousins resigned on Sunday 3 July 1966. Few people could have been amazed by the announcement, but nevertheless it left the Labour Movement suffering from a sense of shock. The tone and style of Cousins's departure brought a cloud of anxiety over the Government for, as an editorial in *The Times* observed the next day :

> Two circumstances make the resignation the most politically significant since Aneurin Bevan's in 1951. As general secretary of the TGWU Mr. Cousins withdraws to a position of strength both in the party and the country; he is not confined to the relative obscurity of the backbenches. He also resigns on an issue and with a record before he accepted office that puts him in the forefront of a chronically dissident section of the Labour Party. It remains to be seen what use he makes of that opportunity. But it will be out of keeping with his past and with the tone of his letter of resignation if he does not exploit it for the purpose of forcing changes in the Government's policies.

The Times, with others, viewed Cousins's resignation as 'a heavy blow to Mr. Wilson and his Government', indeed a potential threat to the stability of the administration. With many others the paper saw the possibility of Cousins moving to the head of a left-wing rebellion, not merely on wages policy, but across a broad spectrum of socialist policies. The Left wing of the Labour Party had lacked a 'natural leader' since the death of Nye Bevan; now there was a possibility (a hope, in some people's minds, a grave danger, in the minds of others) that Frank Cousins might be persuaded to step into that breach. As *The Times* warned : 'All the time it [the Left] has lacked a substantial political figure with which it could be identified. It would now seem to have found one in Mr. Cousins, provided he is prepared to play.'

But he *wasn't* prepared 'to play'. Perhaps the disenchantment with the entire fabric of Parliamentary life had gone too far; age, too, played a significant influence. He was then approaching 62. The experiences of the previous twenty months had damped the fires.

Yet no one could be certain of this on the day of resignation. The fiery letter he addressed to Harold Wilson seemed to presage a continuing, even rougher battle. The exchange of correspondence lacked the usual routine bromides. Cousins's letter, which he handed personally to Wilson when he went to Downing Street at 11 a.m. on Sunday 3 July, was brutally candid – and completely in character with its author. In it he described the Prices and Incomes Bill – which was officially published the next day – as 'meaningless' and the whole concept of the Government's wages policy as 'fundamentally wrong in its conception and approach'. He also referred darkly to the fact that 'just before the general election you gave me to understand that you would help to break down the shibboleth of a belief that what we needed to secure economic recovery was sufficient power in the hands of the Government to compel the unions to accept, without question, the decisions of the National Board for Prices and Incomes. Unfortunately you did not maintain that view and so our present policy has taken us into a position where disputes such as the recent strike of the seamen have been inevitable.' This was a sharp reminder to the Prime Minister of their telephone conversation during the election campaign. The Cousins letter ran to nearly 1,000 words; it was the letter of an exceptionally angry, as well as disappointed, man.

Nor was the correspondence the only abrasive feature of that warm July morning. The meeting in Downing Street between the two men lasted only half an hour, but it was filled with a blistering crossfire of accusation and defence. Cousins's account suggests that even at that late stage Harold Wilson was still making a strenuous attempt to keep him in the Government. Other observers close to Wilson claim that he had long since abandoned any serious hope of that. Cousins charged Wilson with a failure to 'stand up' to his two principal economic Ministers, George Brown and Jim Callaghan; he told the Prime Minister that he felt 'let down' by the Government's actions since the election. He had been invited into the Government, Cousins recalled, because Wilson had told him that the Cabinet would require somebody of the Left, someone of his stature, to help balance the pronounced right-wing flavour. Moreover, Cousins complained that Wilson himself had given him the impression in 1964 that a Wilson-Cousins partnership would be a major characteristic of the Government. Yet the opposite had happened. Cousins accused Wilson of consistently 'siding with the Right wing of the Cabinet', while he had invariably found himself isolated, sometimes in a minority of one.

Central to the whole case against Wilson was Cousins's grievance against George Brown's incomes policy and Callaghan's echoing of international financial pressures. The Prime Minister asked him what alternative policy he had to offer. 'I'm always offering you alternative policies,' Cousins retorted, 'but you take no notice.' He then repeated a four-point programme which he claimed to have put before Wilson on several earlier occasions. Cousins proposed:

1. All wage increases should be linked to increased productivity.
2. There should be a price freeze.
3. Import quota restrictions should be introduced.
4. The Government should launch a major campaign for industrial modernisation, and the Prime Minister should himself take the initiative by calling a national productivity conference as soon as possible. (Which in fact Harold Wilson did, through NEDC, the following year.)

Wilson pointed out that these proposals, if carried out, could produce an even tougher incomes policy than the one planned by George Brown. Cousins agreed that they were tough, but he was not opposed to 'toughness'. His objection, he emphasized, was to the incomes policy currently advocated which would not work, would make the Government look ridiculous and would certainly not help to resolve the nation's economic problems. Wilson was not averse to considering these alternative proposals, even at that late stage; he offered to do so, provided that Cousins withdrew his resignation. But Cousins made it clear that his price for remaining in the Government would be the instant dropping of George Brown's Prices and Incomes Bill – and this Wilson could not, and would not, accept. He explained patiently that he simply could not go back on a Cabinet decision even if he wished to. It would make his position an intolerable one. Harold Wilson refers to Cousins's counter-proposals in his own description of the events of July, and notes that it was not that Frank Cousins was opposed to any form of incomes policy:

> On the contrary he was ready to advocate a very simple approach under which we would impose a strict control of all significant prices. Given this the employers would be very tough on wage claims . . . The practical problem was how to maintain an effective control of prices.[7]

Wilson goes on to point out the immense difficulties in operating a system of administered prices and concludes that 'the view of my colleagues responsible

7. Harold Wilson, *The Labour Government, 1964–1970*, p. 245.

for these matters confirmed my view of the impracticability of the idea'. This supports the view that Wilson had already given consideration to the Cousins Plan long before the resignation day and had come to the firm conclusion that it was inoperable. Even so, there seems no justification at all for Wilson's claim in the same context that 'I had given him the chance gracefully to withdraw at the time of the election'. The truth was quite the opposite.

Press comment on Cousins's departure was not all as complimentary as that of *The Times*. Most papers saw it not as a serious blow for the Government but as a relief for Wilson and his Cabinet colleagues. 'The Government will be stronger without him', concluded the *Guardian*. Almost all the Press took him to task for his attitude on incomes policy. 'Would Mr Cousins really go back to a "free for all" on wages and prices?' the *Guardian* asked. It continued :

> What Mr. Cousins offers in its place is a return to jungle warfare. He clothes it more discreetly. But that is the meaning of his insistence on 'the rights of trade unions to present claims freely on behalf of their members and to pursue such claims at any level to the best of their ability.' This is the right of the strong to try to get their own way regardless of the cost to fellow trade unionists or to the economy . . . It has little to do with the sense of voluntary co-operation between both sides of industry that Mr. Cousins mentions at the end of his resignation letter. But then his heart never was in the incomes policy. For months he has studiously avoided giving it his public backing . . .[8]

Frank Cousins knew that his arguments against the incomes policy sounded unconvincing to many people outside, and inside, the Labour Movement. He also found it genuinely difficult to express his own conflict of ideas on the subject. He understood perfectly well the logic of those who argued that an incomes policy, covering all incomes, was an inescapable part of socialist planning. He countered that by pointing out that no genuinely socialist plan was operating nor was any such model a serious prospect. In the meantime he would not support a policy which prevented the trade unions from functioning freely as part of a capitalist system, albeit a democratic liberal capitalist system. Under a Conservative Government such an argument is not nearly as difficult to sustain as it is under a Labour Government pledged to extending the frontiers of economic planning and social equity. What he was really arguing against was a much wider matter – the whole political style of the Wilson Government. But he could not do that publicly without endangering his entire relationship with Government both as a Minister and, subsequently, as the leader of the country's largest trade union. Indeed

8. The *Guardian*, 4 July 1966.

that is something he always shrank from doing – although he came near to it on several occasions befort his retirement from the TGWU.

Still, he was conscious of the gap between his public explanations and the general understanding and acceptance of his position. He therefore did an unusual thing a few days after his resignation – he agreed to give a major interview to a national newspaper to explain his position in much greater detail. He chose for the exercise the Conservative *Daily Mail*, in a signed interview. 'Why,' he asked, 'why should a trade unionist like me – dedicated by a lifetime's work and ideas to strive for a Labour Government in White-hall – walk out in its first really secure year of office?' Why, indeed. In nearly three thousand words Cousins spelled out his case for a completely new, modern approach to production; the need to link wages to such a production drive by providing incentives for workers to change their attitudes and jobs; a new system for settling industrial disputes by establishing local arbitration tribunals in the regions, empowered to conduct 'on the spot' industrial judgments; and a Government-sponsored drive to encourage industry to become more efficient. This was his prescription for the regeneration of British industry : a 'planned growth of the economy', as he described it. But he confessed that he could not envisage such a programme being introduced. He concluded in this way :

I mean no disrespect to my former Cabinet colleagues, many of them old friends, when I say I now firmly believe that our system of Government is not at present capable of planning the economy's growth. If ever there was a need for management study it is into the system of British Government.

This is, I know, not a new thought. But I have experienced it at first hand and have been able to see older entrenched Whitehall departments at work. And to see the freshness and spirit of adventure with which a completely new department like Technology has been able to set about its task. The Cabinet system itself may well have magnificent traditions going back to Walpole but, is it suited to a technological age when a man can encompass the earth in a few hours?

I believe there is a need for an inner Cabinet of key men with time and power to study our national problems in depth and to reach decisions in principle rather than in detail.

There, indeed, was a major critique of Government style and not just the Wilson Government. It reflected Cousins's profound disenchantment with the Parliamentary system as it operated, with the limitations of government machinery in the conduct of policy. As a socialist Cousins was committed to the view that Government mattered, that, given the political will, Government decisions could and should be made to function effectively. It was partly because he discovered the limitations of such power, or more particularly, the limitations of men in seeking to operate such potential power and influence, that he became disillusioned wth *his* Government and *his* colleagues. Of course he also gracefully recognised that they had become disenchanted with *his* impatience and *his* stubborn reluctance to work within '*their*' system of constraints.

Some years later I asked Frank Cousins why he had become disenchanted with the functioning of government – was that also a disenchantment with democracy itself? 'No', he replied, 'not with government as such, certainly not with democracy. Only with the limitations of the *people* in government, with their refusal, their reluctance, call it what you like, to use the instruments of change at their disposal.' He compared politicians unfavourably with trade union leaders. He came to appreciate, somewhat bitterly, that the language of politics and the actions of political leaders are by no means the same. He found that words did not have quite the same meaning or the same value as in the climate of trade union bargaining. He did not like what he discovered. There is a story Sir Richard Marsh tells about Cousins on the day he actually decided on the timing of his resignation. Marsh was travelling to a Cabinet meeting in the same car when the Minister of Technology disclosed his intention. 'He was quite euphoric once he had made up his mind to quit. He was delighted to be out of the Government. I was deeply critical of him going and somewhat depressed. I felt that we were losing one of the few members of the Cabinet with real, direct experience of the industrial worker. After all, there were no experienced trade union leaders left in the Government . . .'

Marsh makes an interesting observation about the power relationship between Cousins and Harold Wilson which helps to explain why Wilson, in the end, was less determined than might have been expected to persuade Cousins to remain in the Government. 'Here was a man,' Marsh observed, 'who had his own power base outside the Government. He was *not* politically ambitious. He did not want the Prime Minister's job. He was not interested in money. He was scrupulously honest. He was not frightened to speak his mind. That sort of man can be a very dangerous fellow to have in any Cabinet – and a very difficult one.'

To be sure, Cousins was a difficult man to work with, for the reasons listed by Marsh. But he was also difficult because he found the transition from trade union to political leadership so unattractive. Others like Cousins from both sides of industry have found the move into politics, in their mature years, similarly difficult. Ernest Bevin is the exception, only because the special circumstances of his membership of Churchill's War Cabinet enabled him to enjoy not only a unique political protection but, more important, to continue his style of trade union leadership and carry it with him into the functioning of a wartime Ministry of Labour. The brand of authoritarian, tycoonish, practical, down-to-earth qualities often associated with the leadership of great trade unions (perhaps especially the TGWU) was certainly no obstacle to Bevin at the wartime Ministry of Labour. Indeed it helped to cement the special relationship he had with Churchill. Such qualities in Cousins – albeit in a milder form than in Bevin – were a handicap to his relationships with Harold Wilson and most of his Cabinet colleagues. For Cousins the difficulty was not that the transfer to politics came too late in life. It was rather that the political context into which he was thrust required different qualities of persistence to those he had sharpened and developed in the world of trade unionism. It was said of Cousins that he would have made an outstanding industrial tycoon, especially at the head of one of the great State industries. This is probably true.

In his private summing up of Cousins as Minister of Technology talking to the author, Harold Wilson, has been generous in his praise and assessment. 'Frank created the modern Department of Industry, as we know it today. He was the first really interventionist Minister.' Wilson's principal complaint against Cousins was not his prickly behaviour but his failure to convey to the public, and sometimes to his colleagues, precisely what he was achieving at the infant Mintech. He simply wanted to get on with the job without being deflected into publicity stunts. Wilson sees this as a great mistake. But he also accepts that it was his own great error not to have agreed earlier with Cousins's request to turn the Ministry of Technology into an all-embracing Ministry for Industry.

Anthony Wedgwood Benn, who succeeded Frank Cousins at Technology, admits that he inherited an impressive empire of 'things that were happening'. Wilson told him to use his talents as a communicator to tell the country about the Department and repair the omissions of his predecessor. This was part of Benn's success at Technology. The fact, for instance, that Harwell scientists had been set to work to design artificial limbs for the child victims of thalidomide was kept secret by Frank Cousins, who saw no virtue in publicising what he considered to be an essential function of his role as Technology Minister. His motto was always – do the job rather than talk about it. Such self-abnegation carries its own rich rewards, but rarely in politics.

One of his final acts as a Minister was to tender his seals of office to the Queen. He had already had several meetings with Her Majesty, and had developed an unexpected (to him) warmth towards her. He found her always well informed and interested in his work, and keen to discuss the problems of modern industry and technology. The Queen asked Cousins why he was resigning and pressed him for his real reasons. 'Because,' he replied, 'the Government no longer believe in the policies for which they were elected, Ma'am.' They discussed the economic situation, wages, productivity, import controls and Cousins suddenly inquired : 'With permission, may I ask, is that dress you are wearing and your shoes, made in Britain, Ma'am ?' No, she told him, the dress was not. She was sorry to say it was not because she had been advised she could not get the same quality and style of material in Britain. Cousins was horrified and courteously told her so, going on to offer the Queen a little homily on the importance of buying British. She smiled a tolerant, very friendly smile as the ex-Minister of Technology backed out of the room. Not all his Cabinet colleagues were smiling so benevolently as he backed out of Government.

Chapter Twenty-five

THE RETURN OF THE NATIVE

The relief he felt at being out of captivity and back in his old room on the 4th floor of Transport House infected Frank Cousins with a feeling of euphoria. I talked with him in that room the day after the TGWU executive confirmed his return to the General Secretary's chair. 'I feel free. I feel as if I had never been away from the place for more than a week. I feel at home here. I wasn't, there . . .' He nodded in the direction of Whitehall as if it were an alien land. He sat in his leather-upholstered swivel-chair wearing a maroon-coloured TGWU tie under an old blue cardigan, smiling, at ease, his keen eyes twinkling merrily behind the lenses. The native had returned.

Yet the transition was not quite as smooth as his mood suggested. The emperor returning to the palace after a longish interval inevitably awakens anxieties and uncertainties as well as some resentment. Caesar's consuls had foreseen the return for some time, some with less confidence than others. In any event their preparedness was less obvious than their reluctant welcome. Harry Nicholas came into the General Secretary's room, which had been his own for nearly two years, on the Monday morning after Cousins's resignation to find the former Minister of Technology sitting snugly in his old chair, ready to greet his lieutenant. Nicholas was shaken and revealed his astonishment. True, Cousins had phoned him on Sunday morning to inform him of the resignation but Nicholas had no idea that he would be out of the General Secretary's role so speedily. He had assumed that Cousins would delay his return to active trade union leadership at least until the executive meeting. It was a substantial miscalculation. Surprisingly Nicholas had not assumed that Cousins would return to the union at all. He knew that the warrior was unhappy in the Parliamentary scene, but believed that the satis-

502

faction Cousins derived from his work at Technology would override his distaste for other features of political life. There was certainly no carefully laid plan to dissuade Frank Cousins from returning. Nor did Nicholas feel himself strong enough to challenge Cousins's decision to reinstate himself in the seat of TGWU power. The comparison with Arthur Deakin and Ernest Bevin, which some were inclined to make, was not an exact one. Deakin's resentment when Bevin returned after the end of the wartime Coalition Government in 1945 was stronger based and altogether more effective because Deakin had been acting General Secretary throughout the war years while Bevin was Minister of Labour in Churchill's Government. Moreover, Bevin had decided to stand again for Parliament in the 1945 election. So Nicholas made no attempt to emulate Deakin's claim to the job. He accepted, albeit grudgingly, Cousins's right to reclaim the general secretaryship. Nevertheless on that first morning after the resignation he told Cousins that while he was prepared to step back into the position of Assistant General Secretary he was not willing to do so at any loss of pay – a good trade union principle which Cousins acknowledged.

In order to satisfy Nicholas, and retain the £500 a year differential between the No. 1 and No. 2 posts in the union, it was necessary for Cousins to recommend to the executive that his own salary should be increased while leaving the existing pay of Nicholas and Jack Jones (who had been acting Assistant General Secretary on the assistant's pay scale) as they were. Of course this still left Cousins much poorer than before because he had forfeited his Minister's pay of £9,750 for a new pay scale of £3,750 as General Secretary of the TGWU. And while he remained MP for Nuneaton he agreed to pay his basic Parliamentary salary (then £3,250) into union funds. All these problems were put to a special meeting of the TGWU executive on 6 July. They met for five-and-a-half hours to decide the formal conditions under which Cousins would resume as General Secretary. First came a long statement by Cousins explaining why he had resigned and, in particular, emphasising the 'quite unacceptable restrictions upon independent trade union action' which the new legislation proposed. Each member of the executive was handed a copy of the exchange of letters between Harold Wilson and Frank Cousins as well as a copy of the Prices and Incomes Bill. A unanimous vote of confidence was passed in support of Cousins's action. Then came the delicate problem of his remaining MP for Nuneaton, which he strongly wished to do.

This time the executive demurred. They told him quite firmly that this would be quite impossible. They did not see how he could successfully do the two jobs, and he was instructed to resign his Parliamentary seat 'at the earliest possible moment', although they accepted that he should remain in Parliament in the meantime and, in particular, lead the fight against the Prices and Incomes Bill. Cousins was dismayed and greatly disappointed.

This decision also upset the Nuneaton Labour Party who, apart from other considerations, now faced their fourth Parliamentary election in two years. Moreover, Nuneaton had become attached to Frank Cousins, they very much wanted to keep him as their Member, and their insistence on this led to a most unusual 'concession' from the TGWU. Under pressure the executive agreed to meet an official delegation from the Nuneaton Labour Party. A three-man team from Nuneaton duly arrived, but it was made clear to them that the TGWU would not be shifted. The Nuneaton party continued to harass the union executive, but to no avail. The issue was also raised as a question of Parliamentary privilege by Eric Lubbock (now Lord Avebury), Liberal MP for Orpington, who wanted to know whether it was in order for an 'outside body' (ie, the TGWU executive) to dictate in this way to an MP. But the question was never pressed. According to Yvonne and Robert Ready (who at the time of the Cousins resignation were members of the Nuneaton Labour Party GMC), when he first told the Nuneaton Labour Party that he would have to resign his Parliamentary seat Frank Cousins explained that he 'could not have lived with his conscience had he stayed in the Cabinet'. This was accepted by the Nuneaton Party, who gave him their full confidence, but the more penetrating members believed that while the wages issue was paramount in Frank Cousins's mind he was also seriously concerned about the future of the TGWU – and feared that if he had not returned as general secretary the succession would not eventually pass to Jack Jones, Cousins's chosen heir apparent.

Indeed there was some evidence that this was more than a vague fear at the back of Cousins's mind, fed, to be sure, by information he had been given of what was happening inside the union during his absence. At the June meeting of the union's executive preparations had already begun to seek a new Assistant Executive Secretary to fill the gap left when Jack Jones was elevated to acting Assistant General Secretary. In fact the June meeting had resurrected an executive minute from March 1965 and on the suggestion of Harry Nicholas they were preparing to find a new No.3 for the union. There is little doubt that this encouraged Cousins's belief that Jones's position in the hierarchy might be weakened if Nicholas was to be confirmed as the General Secretary. At any rate, Cousins's return scotched all such moves and since Nicholas was approximately the same age as himself the return virtually guaranteed that Jack Jones would become the next General Secretary of the TGWU. Whatever weight one gives to the importance of this in Cousins's motivation for resigning from the Government there is certainly no question that it was primarily due to Cousins's leaving the Government that Jones was assured of the succession.

Cousins has since told me that he regrets not having fought harder to persuade the TGWU executive to let him remain as MP for Nuneaton *and* return as the union's General Secretary. He believes he could have succeeded, even though this would have meant a change of rule and a basic departure from previous policy. Others in the TGWU hierarchy (including Jack Jones) insist that this would not have been possible. Cousins admits that the strain of doing the two jobs would have been enormous. The all-night Parliamentary sitting during the committee stage of the Prices and Incomes Bill were immensely demanding. Several times in that period he came close to physical collapse. He was determined to lead the opposition to the legislation, line by line, comma by comma. He forced divisions in the early hours of the morning and compelled George Brown to sleep in his Ministerial room, sometimes coming down to the vote with his jacket and trousers over his pyjamas. Cousins would not yield an inch in that fight. But he now concedes that it 'almost killed me'. So it remains doubtful whether he would have been able to sustain such activities in the Commons and do his job as TGWU general secretary.

Where did the return to the TGWU leave Frank Cousins? What could he expect to achieve in the three years remaining to him as the leader of the largest union in the country? What influence did he expect to exert through that power on the TUC and the wider Labour Movement, if not the Government? Certainly he was convinced that his potential influence on affairs would be greater than it had been as a member of the Wilson Cabinet. He was satisfied that the trade union movement could be mobilised to push and prod the Government, and that he and his union could play a key role in this process. He saw possibilities for a more co-ordinated approach by the major trade unions, within the framework of an agreed TUC policy; he believed it might even be possible to move towards a Swedish-type system of combined national bargaining between the central institutions of the TUC and the newly formed Confederation of British Industry (CBI). Above all, he was convinced that the strength of the TGWU could be exerted to achieve a charter of industrial reforms and wage improvements – including a new £15 a week minimum wage which he was shortly to campaign for – that would raise the status and objectives of collective bargaining. Beside him as a principal lieutenant stood Jack Jones, and this, too, gave Cousins great satisfaction as well as support from an outstanding organiser. With only three years to go, Cousins could at least reflect he had ensured that the succession would pass to someone in his own mould of left-wing thinking, someone who was pledged to maintain the TGWU along the path set for it when Cousins took over ten years earlier.

Yet Cousins's elation at returning to the union was only part of the story. He was keenly aware that he was now entering the final phase of his public career. Three years is a brief span in which to try to compensate for some of the disappointments that he felt so sharply at that moment. All his life he had wanted to see a Labour Government in power, poised to take the country in the direction of the promised land. Having now backed out of a Labour Government because he believed it was *not* poised to do that, Cousins brooded over a profound sense of failure, partly perhaps his own failure, but more disturbingly, the failure of his hopes. Yet he also recognised that this was not quite the case. There had been enormous advances since he came to office as general secretary. In that decade the Labour Movement had travelled through several major convulsions. He had seen a shift from what had seemed a hopeless Parliamentary position, with the Labour Party deeply split, to one in which there was now a commanding majority which gave the Government an opportunity to introduce, and plan for, changes on a scale that had not seemed possible in 1955. The irony was that he had found it impossible to work within such a Government.

In those ten years the social and cultural scene in Britain had shifted considerably. The country was still struggling with immense problems in trying to discover a new role in a world that was changing with exceptional rapidity. The British people were by no means as prosperous as the glossy magazines and the advertising copywriters wished their readers to believe. Aneurin Bevan in his later years used to reflect with a certain fatalistic gravity that 'history had passed by the British working classes'. By that he meant that the British Labour Movement had changed from a force with a considerable influence on world events to one that had perforce to grapple with the implications of those events. The social changes that had once seemed to be within the grasp of the British Labour movement appeared to be slipping away while political leaders squabbled over diminished perspectives. That was the feeling Cousins had sought to convey in his Torquay speech; the impulse for the 'grand design' seemed weakened, or at least blurred. Cousins did not generally share the kind of doubts that afflict some intellectual socialists about material gains having no substance in social progress. Quite the contrary. He believed there was a readiness in the unions and the Labour Party to be too easily satisfied with the range of material gains so far achieved. Yet he also knew that it was not possible to measure progress by the supply of TV sets and deep freezers. A society can sense when it is flourishing and when it is stunted; when horizons are clouded and when they are clear; when it is in a condition of spiritual fatigue or when it is being carried forward by surges of hope and by dreams, however distant. It was these latter qualities which, he felt, were demonstrably lacking in the political leadership of the Labour Movement, indeed in Britain as a whole, in the midsixties. The failure of the 1966 Government was to his mind a failure of political will : it was a Government trapped by economic forces it did not adequately comprehend, and therefore had little chance of controlling.

If 1966 was the 'crunch year' (as so many observers now agree it was) then 1967, 1968, and 1969 were years in which the errors were compounded. The problems multiplied. A chronic balance of payments crisis, low growth, increasing unemployment, mounting industrial tensions, and a paralysis of investment left the Government, and the country, floundering in the grip of what seemed to be inexorable decline. This happened to coincide with a period of widespread change in social habits and moral values, the growth of sexual permissiveness corresponded with a rise in widespread industrial conflict, and perhaps both processes stemmed from common origins – an impulse for liberation from the disciplines of the past.

Cousins saw it partly in terms of Britain's diminished role in world affairs, determined by a political failure to readjust. The refusal (until late in the day) to recognise the economic and political absurdities involved in maintaining an East-of-Suez role was matched by the Government's refusal to devalue or float the pound. He believed that Britain's revival depended on recognising her new and more compact role. But all around him were the institutional fetters and blinkers of the past, cramping the vision and behaviour of his own political allies as well as supporting the prejudices of his political foes.

If we are to believe what Ministers subsequently said, the great economic crisis of July 1966 swept upon an unsuspecting Government like a typhoon from nowhere. It caught them when they were off balance, having just survived a long seaman's strike and what was thought at first to be a passing gale. Throughout June the pound had been rocky and under increasing pressure but the situation was not regarded as disastrous. When Frank Cousins resigned he was not aware of any new and still larger crisis that would, eventually, force the Government to impose a full-scale wages and prices freeze. But by the time Cousins made what amounted to his 'resignation speech' on 14 July it had become clear that something quite exceptional was about to burst upon the political scene. That was six days before the 'July measures' were announced. On that day the Prime Minister chose to preface the debate on the Prices and Incomes Bill by announcing that the Government would shortly be coming to Parliament with a new packet of measures to maintain the strength of sterling and protect the economy. The statement, vague though it was, clearly added fresh urgency to George Brown's proposals, though it did nothing to dampen Cousins's attack. He suspected that an elaborate operation was being mounted to fortify the Government's case for an even stronger incomes policy.

It is still difficult to be clear as to why the crisis developed so rapidly, or, to put it differently, why when it did break Ministers appear to have been surprised. A senior Minister has since told me that when the Chancellor was asked about the state of sterling early in July he responded: 'There isn't a cloud in the sky.' George Brown was told that the situation had rarely been better for July, always a notoriously difficult month on foreign exchange markets. Yet he has claimed that papers were circulating among some Ministers as early as June. If they were, then Cousins didn't see them, which was not an unusual experience even for the most senior Cabinet

Minister, as the Crossman diaries testify. Indeed there are certain Cabinet committees (nuclear security being one) for which no formal minutes or papers are ever circulated. They are kept locked up in the Prime Minister's room. The subject of devaluation – even the general fluctuations of sterling – is among the items treated with similar prudence.

On the other hand, adding to the mystery, when Cecil King lunched with the Prime Minister at Downing Street on 5 July (two days after Cousins's resignation) Wilson referred to an impending wage freeze,[1] and Crossman reports that in the Cabinet as early as 21 June Callaghan was urging 'a complete freeze' on wages. All told, the evidence suggests that the Government was in some disarray as it struggled to find a path between two opposing schools – one led by George Brown, who wanted to make industrial expansion a priority and gamble on a sterling devaluation, and the rest, led by Wilson and Callaghan, who were determined to cling to the sterling parity rate even if this involved a wage freeze, unemployment and cuts in Government spending. Brown was even prepared to drop his incomes policy bill if he could have got his way on devaluation. But it was not to be.

The sequence of events in July after Cousins's resignation was quite extraordinary. First came a barrage of 'sunshine' talk eminating from Ministers, principally the Treasury. This was followed by rumour after rumour about an impending crisis. Finally on 14 July there was Harold Wilson's grim foretaste of things to come which, by all accounts, followed a three-hour Cabinet meeting at which Callaghan presented his colleagues with a list of swingeing cuts and proposals for a price and wage freeze and George Brown, seeing his National Plan collapsing before his eyes, began to make resignation noises.

The debate on the Prices and Incomes Bill did not appear to be an anticlimax at the time, though it plainly was. George Brown defended it with his usual courage and vigour. The objectionable Part IV (with its penal sanctions) which was added later after the freeze was announced, was not then hinted at. Cousins's speech in the debate was generally acknowledged even by his most prejudiced critics as an outstanding Parliamentary performance by what was seen to be a liberated man. He followed Brown's introduction and Reginald Maudling who spoke, ineffectively, for the Tories. At 6.40 p.m. Cousins rose. He was at ease, self-composed, confident. The mantle of the Ministerial brief no longer impeded and confused him. He congratulated three maiden speakers before him and, with a smile, explained that he too was now making his maiden speech from the back benches. He assured the House that this was not designed as a 'resignation' speech. But he knew it would be taken as such.

He then embarked on an explanation of why he believed that the

1. Cecil King, *The Cecil King Diary, 1965–1970* (Cape, 1972), p. 75.

Government from which he had just resigned was pursuing the wrong policies: 'I have a deep conviction that we are going the wrong way, that we are tackling the wrong problem. Therefore we are bound to be using the wrong methods and finding the wrong solutions.' He was wearing his TGWU tie, which he unconsciously fingered from time to time. Beside him sat Manny (now Lord) Shinwell, father of the House of Commons and chairman of the Parliamentary Labour Party. Cousins spoke from notes, though he rarely glanced at them. Nance sat in the visitors' gallery, eyes glued as she stared down at a crowded House with every seat packed. Harold Wilson was not in the Chamber.

At times it seemed that Cousins was addressing a trade union gathering. He made it clear that he regarded industry, on both sides, as the more important part of his political life. Then to wage restraint: 'I am on record in many places as saying that I will not have wage restraint whoever wraps it up and brings it to me in whatever kind of parcel. I have said this publicly and I re-affirm my intention of resisting a wage restraint policy . . .' That was a clear warning that he would lead the TGWU in a frontal attack on the Government's policy from then on, that he would carry the attack to the TUC and, if necessary, onto the floor of the Labour Party conference. It was a formidable challenge to the Government. Cousins praised George Brown; he admired his courage, his fighting spirit, his ability. But, he lamented, George Brown had been misled: 'Influences that have been brought to bear are not the ones he originally anticipated' – an allusion to the international pressures applied to the Economics Secretary by way of the Treasury and the Chancellor. Brown, sitting next to Callaghan on the front bench, sat twiddling a pencil. He looked dark and tense. The Conservatives constantly punctuated Cousins's speech with applause, with nods and grunts of approval. But Cousins rounded on them too and warned that he would not vote for *their* amendment against the Bill. He had his own motion, signed by himself and six other members of the union's Parliamentary group. It read as follows:

That this House recognises that it is the intention of HM Government to solve the economic problems inherited from its Tory predecessors by expanding production, increasing exports and overcoming the balance of payments deficit; regards a planned growth of incomes as essential to the carrying out of a socialist economic policy and of the Government's social programme; accordingly considers that the present prices and incomes Bill containing penal legislation against trade unions should be rejected and that instead measures should be introduced to improve the incomes of the lower paid workers to launch a major drive to increase productivity linked with higher wages, to control dividends more effectively and to set up a system of price controls, and further urges HM Government to take action along the following lines, namely the introduction of a system of strict import controls, a strengthening of the controls over overseas capital investment, a drastic reduction of defence expenditure, in particular of British commitments east of Suez, and the extension of public ownership in the basic industries.[2]

This was in fact a substantial political platform in itself, which was to form the basis of all subsequent attacks on the Government from the TGWU in the years ahead. Indeed it is interesting, in retrospect, to compare the catalogue of proposals with what has subsequently developed as a left-wing platform, both within the trade union movement and the Parliamentary Labour Party (ie, the *Tribune* group).

At the heart of the speech came, once again, the great paradox for the socialist, the near-Marxist, but perhaps above all the democrat who saw in the trade unions the natural arm of popular dissent, the vehicle of the ordinary people, the increasingly important mechanism through which working people could express their grievances against social and economic injustices and contest the still more powerful mechanisms of established authority. How, asked Cousins, was *this* democracy to be advanced if the trade unions became shackled by State legislation of the kind the Government were now proposing?

> Our society is set, thank heavens, primarily on the voluntary basis. I say this as, I hope, a real social democrat. I know that I have been accused of all sorts of things, including totalitarian instincts. But basically I think that all people are entitled to assume that the power of the State will not be used to make them do things that collectively they disagree with.

Yet there was no reply in that declaration of faith in democracy to the challenge so often put to him: how did he reconcile his socialist beliefs with freedom for collective bargaining? Is there not a limit to the extent of such freedom in any serious system of economic planning? He did not discuss these basic problems in his speech. He echoed and re-echoed his conviction that the trade unions were instruments to be used by working people to improve their living standards and that any interference with their freedom to fulfil that function was a dangerous step along the road to authoritarianism.

The Press was generally flattering the next day. Every parliamentary writer agreed that it was Frank Cousins's best speech in the Commons. The *Daily Mail* reported: 'Mr. Cousins was loudly cheered by a section of his own party and by the Tory benches generally. Both were applauding for very different reasons.' The *Guardian* said: 'There had been several rude suggestions lately about who is the effective leader of the Opposition. Last

2. Hansard, 14 July 1966. Cor. 1792.

night it looked like Frank Cousins.' The *Guardian* writer went on to faintly praise Cousins's performance :

> This was an articulate, relaxed Mr. Cousins very different from that halting and maladroit figure who used to sit on the front bench failing to learn the elaborations of parliamentary custom and generally behaving like a round peg in a square hole.

Within a week of the debate and the Bill going to committee stage the Government announced the package of crisis measures. This included a six months freeze on prices and wages, to be followed by a further six months of 'severe restraint'. It also announced that the Prices and Incomes Bill would be used to operate the freeze by the device of adding new clauses – especially a Part IV, which would empower the Government to impose fines of up to £500 on any organisation in breach of the standstill. The proposed sanctions were by far the most severe ever taken by a British Government, as Harold Wilson himself admitted in a speech in Washington later in the month.

In the ensuing drama there came George Brown's resignation as Secretary of State at the Department of Economic Affairs. Nine hours later, under persuasive pressure from his friends, he withdrew his resignation. But he didn't remain at the DEA for much longer. On 10 August Brown was moved to the Foreign Office in a straight exchange of posts with Michael Stewart. It was the end of the National Plan; and effectively the end, too, of the DEA as a potent force in Whitehall.

The George Brown 'sensation' continued for a fortnight, but the public were treated only to the tip of the iceberg. Inside the Cabinet there were ructions, not least because of Part IV of the Prices and Incomes Bill. Crossman's record of the events reveals the depth of the Cabinet split over the implementation of the wages freeze. About a third of the Cabinet held genuine fears that the measures proposed by George Brown and his advisers were so draconian that they would not get through either the Trades Union Congress or the Labour Party conference. And Crossman has described George Brown's original draft for Part IV as something that would have given him 'complete economic dictatorial powers'.[3] In fact it was Crossman who successfully moved an amendment in Cabinet that had the effect of curtailing these extreme powers, which were made subject to the delaying device of a 28-day Parliamentary Order. Clearly there was substance in Cousin's claim that the Government had gone wild over its wages policy. Crossman himself had been highly critical of Frank Cousins up till this point. From an almost obsequious admiration in the early stages of the 1964 Government he had shifted his opinion to the point of open abuse. When

---

3. Crossman, Vol. I, 28 July 1966, p. 591.

Cousins finally resigned Crossman evinced no regret, quite the contrary. He wrote in his diary that he thought the Prime Minister had timed the whole operation perfectly: 'The resignation could not have come at a less inconvenient time for Harold Wilson.'[4] Crossman also dismissed the effect that Cousins's resignation would have on the Parliamentary Labour Party. He saw no likelihood of Cousins becoming a threat from the back benches, and certainly not a potential leader of the left-wing MPs. In the unpublished version of his diary Crossman was even stronger. Cousins's resignation, he wrote, was

> timed about right for Harold Wilson. It's true that it coincided with a crisis about Vietnam but on the whole it would have been far worse to have it in the spring before the election and I think Harold would have found it difficult to force it on Frank just after the election. I think Harold had to do everything he could to keep Frank in the Cabinet and so did George Brown and so did Jim Callaghan – because they were all frightened about the effects outside. Not the effect on Parliament, but probably entirely one of our relationships with the conference [Labour Party conference] and the trade union movement.[5]

In that same unpublished section Crossman talks of the blow to Nuneaton arising from Cousins's resignation: 'They of course were sick to death about it, they like him very much as a member, they have got to like him, he was a good member, a nice man, and they had just got used to him; they didn't want another by-election in the least.'

There appeared to be no sympathy of any kind coming from Crossman, whose only concern (a concern he evidently shared with most members of the Cabinet) was what Cousins might do now that he was back at the TGWU and on the rampage. Two years later, almost to the day, Crossman was taking a very different line in his diary. He came to the conclusion that Cousins had been right after all.

> One has to say, looking back . . . he [Frank Cousins] was probably right in warning the Cabinet of the unworkability of the whole thing we tried to do. The unworkability of the kind of legal mumbo-jumbo we got into with the new Incomes and Prices Bill. I am certainly now wise after the event, more impressed by what he said . . . than I was before.[6]

Before his death Dick Crossman had come almost full circle on the subject of Frank Cousins, although he still felt Cousins had been a failure as a

---

4. Crossman, Vol. I, 3 July 1966, p. 558.
5. Unpublished sections of the Crossman diary, drawn from his original transcript, 4 July 1968, notesheet No. 97.
6. Crossman diaries, Vol. I, p. 593.

Cabinet Minister. But by then he accepted the force of Cousins's case against a legally controlled wages policy and in retrospect saw the events of 1966 as a disastrous turning-point in the fortunes of Harold Wilson's 1966–70 Government. Even at the time Crossman became increasingly appalled at the prospect opening up as a result of George Brown's Bill, especially Part IV, under which the First Secretary and Secretary of State for Economic Affairs could : as he noted in his diary : 'penalise any employer or trade union that raises prices or raises wages. He can make every strike illegal and he can gaol any trade unionist who stands against his policy. This is economic dictatorship.'[7]

The Prices and Incomes Bill became law on 12 August, although the ultra-controversial Part IV did not become active until 5 October. The Cabinet, meeting in emergency session at the Grand Hotel Brighton, were then compelled to implement it, following a defiant refusal by the Newspaper Proprietors' Association to hold back a cost of living increase to print workers. Yet there was never any doubt that the Government would be forced to operate the legal provisions of the Act before long. The Order was laid before Parliament on 25 October, when 28 Labour MPs abstained in defiance of a three-line Whip. Frank Cousins was one of them. Twelve days later, on 6 November, Cousins announced his resignation as MP for Nuneaton. His last farewells were offered to the local party's general management committee at a two-and-a-half-hour meeting, in which Cousins expressed his deep regret at not being able to continue. As he left that meeting he told reporters : 'This is probably the saddest moment I have had for a long time, to have to say goodbye to a constituency party who have become very fond of me and I of them ...'[7]

The curtain on his brief Parliamentary career had, however, fallen on 15 October, when he made his last major speech to the Commons – in opposing the legislation on Part IV. By then Michael Stewart had taken over from George Brown at the Department of Economic Affairs, and introduced the motion to approve the Order of 5 October. It was a long and often tedious debate which raked again over the need for such powers, their likely effect and workability, and indeed the entire range of the Government's crisis measures and handling of the economic situation. It was 8.31 that evening before Frank Cousins rose to make his valedictory. The House was almost empty when he began. It was in the middle of normal feeding time for MPs. However, within minutes of Cousins rising the Chamber was packed with members crowding below the bar, squatting on the aisles and an atmosphere of excitement gradually spreading over a hitherto rather arid scene. Nance Cousins and their daughter Frances were in the gallery.

Cousins spoke again with that new authority and freedom which resig-

7. *The Times*, 7 November 1966.

nation had seemed to bestow. His manner was relaxed and almost conversational. He clutched a few notes but, as in July, he rarely consulted them. Again he found as much support from the Conservative benches as from the Left wing in his own party. But he disdained Tory approval, chiding them with having no really effective alternative policy. As to his own Government's policy Cousins dismissed it as wholly inoperable. Did the Government assume that everyone would simply accept Ministerial edicts as if they were laws of the Medes and the Persians? he asked. 'I will not accept that from any Government. This is what democracy is about.' He continued :

> The Government cannot control industry and the trade unions. All that they can do is to give guidance and help. One is not seeking a free-for-all by saying this. One ought to be in a position to say to both sides of industry, 'Production levels in this country are not good enough.' Modernisation is not just a theme. The Government ought to tell both sides to get together to solve the problems facing us . . .

None of this was fiery socialist doctrine. Cousins was accepting the limitations of the existing economic system but offering to try to make it work better by a much greater degree of industrial cooperation. It was a theme he was to develop later when he returned to the TUC General Council. He told the Government that if a Conservative administration had attempted to introduce the kind of legislation now before Parliament there would have been 'an industrial dispute of the type not seen since 1926'.

Cousins was perhaps more constructive in that speech than he had been in any of his earlier ones. He went beyond an attack on the Government's incomes policy by suggesting that the nation was ready to respond to a really dynamic lead from the Government. He did not deny that there was an economic crisis, but he insisted that the nation was not as 'industrially down' as some critics claimed.

> We must and could have some form of effective price control. We must have selective import restrictions whether or not our partners in various parts of the world like it. It is difficult to see how anyone can justify, the importation of things like fruit machines. I cannot understand why one should be told : 'There is no such thing as a good English camera. We can show you seven different types of foreign camera, but the English do not make decent cameras these days.' This state of affairs must be looked at if we are really facing the sort of economic problems which we are told we are facing.
>
> There must at the same time be another important review of our world role as a currency. It seems to depend on what sort of mood the Chancellor of the Exchequer is in as to whether he justifies it or tells us that we are at the mercy of the vagaries of the bankers here and abroad and whether they make a run on our currency.

This House should know that if our economic ills are to be faced, if we are to get out of our present problems, one thing has to be remembered. The trade unions, representing the workers, and the employers, must have a mutual confidence in several things. One is confidence in the future of the economy. Another is confidence in the Government – they must have confidence in the Government. There must be confidence in the trade unions. And we all have to recognise that the problem of efficiency will not be dealt with in this House . . .

I am a representative of a very large union and of a large number of workers who want to help this country out of its economic difficulties. But those workers are not satisfied that the way to get them to do that is to tell-them that they have no place in his except to be told by the Government. They are willing to be partners, but partners whose voice is heard, understood and respected and a voice to which regard is given.

Cousins's speech was hailed almost unanimously – except by his former Ministerial colleagues, as a triumphant success. The Tories cheered him, quite forgetting how they used to mock him a few months earlier; the left-wing MPs were fascinated and wholly impressed by his transformation as a Parliamentary speaker. Already there were mutterings about the possibility that Cousins might emerge as a new leader of the Left in the Parliamentary Labour Party. Indeed after that speech he was approached by a number of Labour MPs – as he was to be later, after he had left the Commons – who urged him to consider remaining in Parliament to lead the Left and even to challenge Harold Wilson, at a subsequent moment, for leadership of the Labour Party. But Cousins declined. In any event he could *not* remain MP for Nuneaton *and* general secretary of the TGWU. That had become clear.

The political correspondent of *The Times* paid Cousins a remarkable tribute on the day of his resignation from Nuneaton. 'It will be Westminster's loss, certainly in the sense that Governments will go on looking to the CBI and TUC for industry's voice rather than to anybody in Parliament', he wrote. 'Mr. Cousins's decision to resign as MP to concentrate on leading his big union means the final failure of a governmental and political experiment that had some importance.' He went on :

Mr. Cousins leaves Westminster a deeply disappointed man, far gone in cynicism about its archaic practices, its inadequacy for coping with the country's really big problems and its perverse genius for wasting the time and energies of practical men who want action. Some time ago I took a liking to Mr. Cousins as a man and those who like him must say that he had some doubtful notions about Parliament. He never understood Westminster politics. When I discussed the subject with him he seemed to show a dangerous impatience with British democratic methods so far as they consist of checks and delays on the executive. Then it came out that he preferred the American democratic system, where a President gathers round him as a Cabinet powerful, practical men not necessarily with a party or political commitment and gives them jobs.

His imminent resignation then should cause Westminster to spend as much time in critical self-examination as in mocking his Parliamentary failure. The faults are on both sides. Why is the Commons such a place where lawyers, teachers, journalists, PR men and rank and file trade unionists in abundance can make a contented career while the occasional tycoon from either side of the industry is a sad, frustrated misfit who quickly returns to the world he knows?

The Times man had detected the Cromwellian characteristics in Cousins – his impatience with questioning, his resentment toward the brakes that Parliament imposed on his impulses, his belligerent certainties, the exasperation with what he saw as trivial but what others would regard as important detail. Yet Cousins was actually mellowing in his anti-Parliamentarianism. Perhaps those last few months as a liberated back-bencher enabled him to taste the opportunities and the functions of a Parliamentary debating system that he had not previously considered, since he had not been a back-bencher before becoming a Minister. Perhaps if he had stayed he would have become, as many felt likely, a considerable Parliamentary figure. Yet the odds were against it, for the same reasons that he found it hard to tolerate the political behaviour of his Cabinet colleagues. His overwhelming conviction remained untarnished by Parliamentary sophistication that it was necessary to have specific political objectives, socialist objectives, and that he had to resist attempts to deflect him from such a goal.

These events all followed the battles at the Trades Union Congress and the Labour Party Conference, at both of which the 'Cousins row' (as the Press by then labelled the wages conflict) was the dominant feature. Harold Wilson sensed that there would be trouble at the TUC so he decided to get himself invited to address the Congress. On the opening day he delivered a speech that warned of the dangers of two million unemployed unless the unions cooperated with the Government's measures to beat the crisis. Wilson had made many speeches to the TUC before and he has made even more since the 1966 Congress, yet it is doubtful whether any have been as critical or as difficult as on that occasion. It was probably the most uncompromising speech a Labour leader has delivered to a Trades Union Congress. In essence the theme, repeated in a variety of ways, was that the days of completely free collective bargaining were over. If the post-war commitment to full employment was to be maintained, he said, in effect, then the unions would have to yield some of their traditional freedoms. The Prime Minister told the TUC that Britain was on an economic knife-edge:

One false careless step, particularly by the custodians of a major trading currency [sterling] could push the world into conditions not unlike those of the early 'thirties . . . and if that were to happen we as a nation more dependent than almost any other on overseas trade could well be plunged into a depression such as we have not seen in this generation, into a world depression where the workless might be numbered not as one and a half to two percent but at one and a half to two million.

Wilson knew he was asking for a great deal from his supporters. He was fully informed about the state of uncertainty, confusion and self-doubt among the TUC leadership. The union delegations almost without exception were deeply divided.

I know what we are asking. I know the loyalties as well as the pressures, the deep ingrained traditions inherited from the defensive days of this Movement. It is hard to say it, but we cannot fight the problems of tomorrow with the rusty weapons of the past. We face now a new challenge – the greatest I believe in our peace time history.

Wilson was given a standing ovation at the end. The great majority of delegates stood and clapped for almost a minute. But not the TGWU – at least not all of them. Frank Cousins and some two thirds of his delegation remained stonily in their seats : the rest stood and clapped. For some of them it was as much a demonstration of defiance against Frank Cousins and his views as an approval of Harold Wilson's speech. At least Cousins's return had not imposed any diktat on his delegation. Such a mixed response, not to say open defiance, would have been unthinkable from the TGWU team in Arthur Deakin's day.

George Woodcock was absent from that 1966 Congress. He had suffered a heart attack shortly before and his role was taken up, at very short notice, by his deputy Victor Feather. It was a ferociously daunting task for Feather, but he came through it bravely. Yet he was quite unable, perhaps even unwilling, to persuade Cousins or to offer any cautioning advice – as Woodcock would most certainly have tried. Not that even Woodcock's presence would have done much to blunt the edge of Frank Cousins's anger and bitterness that autumn. Cousins was not a popular figure at that Congress, though unpopularity, even hostility, among his General Council colleagues was by no means a novel experience for him. The resentment against him at that 1966 TUC was particularly strong. As in earlier years, it stemmed from a mixture of motives. There was a good deal of general hostility shown by those who were quick to recall old scores. There was renewed talk of his 'difficult personality', remarks about 'that man Cousins again'. There was resentment from some who regarded his resignation from the Government as an act of political treachery, or at least, of irresponsibility. Others feared that he would again stir up rank and file militancy in their own unions or that the TGWU, because of its membership spread and industrial influence, would simply make their life and their jobs more difficult. At any rate, the anti-Cousins undercurrent became a feature of the 1966 TUC, and it was reflected in a most tangible form in the vote Cousins received returning him to the TUC General Council. He attracted less support than his two other TGWU colleagues, Harry Nicholas and Mrs Marie Patterson. Cousins poled 7,514,000 compared with Nicholas's 8,712,000 and Mrs Patterson's 8,351,000. A small indicator, perhaps, but it was the Congress's own distinctive way of snubbing Cousins without having the power to humiliate him.

On the central issue of the pay freeze and the proposed 'reluctant acquiescence' Congress voted by an exceptionally narrow majority to go along with the Government. The vote was 4,567,000 to 4,223,000. No one could misinterpret that message; it was a moral defeat for the Government and certainly an insufficient majority to convince Ministers that they could rely on the trade unions' voluntary acceptance of the freeze. The new laws would have to be brought into operation. Despite Wilson's pleas the Congress split down the middle, with Frank Cousins leading the rebellion against the pay policy. Cousins's own motion was defeated by a more substantial majority of 1,134,000, but that again was more of a personal rebuke to him and to the TGWU than an accurate mirror of union opinion about the pay freeze.

Cousins's speech in the wages debate was a disappointment. It was almost as if he was nervous and over-tense. He lacked altogether the commanding effectiveness of his recent Parliamentary successes and appeared overtly self-conscious about the personal barrier that seemed to lie between him and the majority of the General Council. When he protested that his opposition to the Government's wages policy was not a personality conflict between himself and Harold Wilson there was a disbelieving rumble of 'Oh' from delegates. And as if recalling his earlier battles with Hugh Gaitskell, Cousins lapsed into the use of the third person, declaring that:

> It would be a tragedy if it [the conflict over pay policy] came down to one of personalities, if it came down to a question of whether it was the Labour Party versus the TUC or Harold Wilson versus Frank Cousins. It is nothing of the sort.
>
> It is in fact the continuation of a policy which in my union put forward in the days of Ernest Bevin and Arthur Deakin – that you cannot control by legislation the activities of the trade union movement.

It was unusual, even quaint, for Frank Cousins to invoke publicly the name of Arthur Deakin in support of any cause he was arguing. But what he said was absolutely correct. His attitude towards the Government's wages policy was in the true tradition of his predecessors. And he believed with total conviction that he was being consistent not only with Bevin and Deakin but also with his own faith in trade union freedom. The inconsistencies in his case did not appear to him to be of significance. 'Our opposition', he tried to explain to that TUC, 'is based on the belief that we have always held that you cannot have a social democracy and at the same time control by legislation the activity of a free trade union movement which is an essential part of that social democracy.' He recalled that it was exactly ten years earlier that he had made his memorable début at a TUC as General Secretary of the TGWU, and that had been to oppose a Conservative Government's pay restraint policy. Now there was a Labour Government in power – 'a Government of our choosing and one which we support, all of us . . .' But he added with great emphasis, there had been no change 'in the social order'.

It was a speech of contradictions as well as passion and resentments; a speech not remembered for its clarity so much as its brave attempt to put an ideological gloss on what had become a profound battle of wills between Frank Cousins and his former Cabinet colleagues. He dismissed Harold Wilson's speech and especially the warning of two million unemployed as scare-mongering. He was not at all convinced that the Prime Minister was being more than deliberately alarmist.

But let us leave that aside. What *was* the ideological basis for Cousins's absolutist case against any Government intervention in wages bargaining? Why did he, as a near-Marxist, repeatedly emphasise phrases such as 'social democracy'? The answer is not that he was being opportunist or intellectually dishonest, as some of his critics would claim. He had always held that it was possible to contain both strands of thought within the same socialist conviction. He saw no irreconcilable conflict between trade union freedom and genuine socialist planning. Indeed he regarded the first as a pre-condition of the second. He accepted that working-class institutions would be changed under a socialist system. But he had no time for those who believed that socialism would inescapably lead to the 'enslavement' of the unions within an all-powerful State apparatus. That was why he had always been critical of the Soviet Union. Once, in 1960, during a particularly difficult set of negotiations with the Ford Motor Company, he had been charged with ideological inconsistency by the Ford management, which was comparing Cousins with his right-wing colleagues in the TUC. Afterwards he remarked : 'Somehow they don't seem to accept that one can be militant and still remain pro-Labour, and social democrat.'[8]

Cousins carried his fight from the Blackpool TUC to the Labour Party conference at Brighton, where the tensions were even greater. For one thing

8. From Cousins's own private diary, 16 April 1960.

the unemployment and redundancy crisis had intensified even in the short time between the two conferences. This added a further dimension to the wages conflict. The British Motor Corporation (as British Leyland then was) had put 50,000 workers – about a third of their workforce – on to short time. Virtually every major industry was being forced to cut back, as the economic squeeze bit quickly into the home market. The car industry lay-offs came halfway between the TUC and Labour Party conferences, and this led to extraordinary scenes of protest outside the Party headquarters hotel in Brighton, where Harold Wilson found himself blockaded in by hundreds of protesting car workers. Trainloads of BMC shop stewards and workers journeyed from the Midlands to lobby the Labour Party conference. Their anger penetrated the conference debates and was picked up by speakers from the rostrum and used as yet another stick with which to beat the Government. Unemployment was rising fast in most consumer industries; it was the inevitable consequence of the July measures. The unions now began to see more vividly the fearful prospect of being trapped between a pay freeze *and* rising unemployment.

Perhaps this accounts for the fact that Cousins was loudly cheered when he took the rostrum at the Labour Party conference. The icy coolness, the open disdain that he had felt at the TUC was not repeated at the Brighton conference, although the voting result was more favourable to the Government. The pay freeze and the Government's economic policy were approved by a bigger majority than at the TUC – 3,836,000 to 2,515,000 – and the TGWU's own motion condemning the freeze and the Government's 'anti-trade union legislation' was defeated by an even larger margin, 3,925,000 to 2,471,000. The union voting had this time managed to secure an unexpectedly substantial proportion of support from the local constituency Labour parties.

Cousins knew he would be defeated in the voting. That was plain enough. But in his speech he declared that the voting mattered less than what happen on the workshop floor. He assumed, and predicted, that there would be a mass revolt against the policy – but he was proved wrong. However, he did have some voting successes. In the face of strong opposition from the Party leadership two important TGWU motions were forced through. One was an emergency resolution demanding that rising unemployment and short-time working should be cushioned by the systematic use of work-sharing and not by dismissals and redundancies. This only scraped through by a majority of 152,000, but it was received with triumphant whoops around the conference hall. Cousins's second success was on a foreign policy resolution calling on the Government to abandon its East-of-Suez policy and cut down on defence spending. Cousins himself moved this motion, which was seconded by Christopher Mayhew. It was carried by a majority of 538,000.

Yet the real success for Frank Cousins at that conference lay in an event outside – the traditional mid-week 'Tribune' rally, held that year in a crowded Corn Exchange.

When Aneurin Bevan was alive the 'Tribune' meetings, on the Wednesday night of Labour Party conference week, had become almost the major political event of the week. From the 'Tribune' platform Nye would declaim against the absurdities of official Party policy, ridicule the absence of socialist zeal, among his colleagues; taunt the Establishment of the Party and trade union hierarchy and deliver a catechism of socialist doctrine. From the 'Tribune' platform Bevan offered Labour's Left wing the inspiration which it invariably failed to get inside the conference itself. And sometimes his declarations became the political talking point of the entire season. No political writer or commentator could afford to miss the Bevan night at 'Tribune'. But after his death in 1960 'Tribune' rallies tended to become much tamer occasions in spite of Michael Foot's crescendoes on a Bevanite theme. The glamour of the occasion began to fade.

On the night of 5 October – the same night that the Cabinet met to implement Part IV of the Prices and Incomes legislation – Frank Cousins rekindled much of the old magic of those 'Tribune' occasions in a speech which many regarded at the time as his best public performance. It was Cousins's first appearance at a 'Tribune' rally – indeed the first time a general secretary of the TGWU had ever graced a 'Tribune' platform. How times had changed since Deakin denounced Bevan and regarded a 'Tribune' meeting as something worse than Hell. Tom Driberg was in the chair that night; Michael Foot was a fellow speaker. In the audience were MPs, many other trade union leaders and even a sprinkling of Cabinet Ministers, including Mrs Barbara Castle. They had been drawn to the meeting to hear Frank Cousins restate his reasons for resigning from the Government and they were not disappointed. Cousins confessed that he arrived in Brighton in a mood of 'black despair'. He did not, he emphasised, 'enjoy' the conflict into which he was now plunged, because 'loyalty means as much to me as it does to other people. We wonder sometimes whether we are always going to tear ourselves apart.'

Why did he resign? 'Because I believed that what was being done was wrong – absolutely and utterly wrong. A man is only as big as his own integrity', he added softly, his voice breaking slightly. But what about his oft-professed loyalties to his Government colleagues? he asked himself aloud. 'Well,' he told that huge audience, 'I haven't much uncritical loyalty. I have got a lot of loyalty but not uncritical . . .' And as if thinking inwardly of the Prime Minister, he added, mentioning no names, 'I don't think any man is entitled to ask for that.'

In the course of that speech Cousins openly criticised two of his former Cabinet colleagues – Jim Callaghan, for his policies and his attitude towards wages and the unions, and Ray Gunter, whom he had always scorned. An earlier speaker (David Pitt) had criticised the fact that none of Cousins's left-wing colleagues in Cabinet had resigned with him. Yet Cousins rejected this criticism. They had every right to remain in Government, he said, because they didn't agree with his views and they had as much right to their views as he had to his. No, he pleaded with the 'Tribune' audience, it was wrong to be intolerant towards the views of others who disagreed with him.

What of the Prime Minister himself? Cousins mused. Well, someone had already referred to the Prime Minister's comment after the Government's defeat (or rather, the Party leadership's defeat) on the TGWU motion about unemployment and short-time working. Harold Wilson had been asked by the BBC what he was going to do in the light of that defeat.

'Govern,' Wilson had replied with Attlee-like monosyllabism.

'Govern?' Cousins repeated, with rhetorical pausing and slight shaking of the head 'Nobody suggested that they shouldn't. In fact that is what we are asking them to do.' He said he was particularly irritated by Wilson's retort because he regarded the motion on unemployment as 'an important victory'. Cousins implied that he looked upon that voting success as a form of poetic compensation for having been defeated on the wages issue. He wound up in the grand style by proclaiming his faith in socialism, in the rank and file of the Labour Movement, in the ultimate vision replacing the squalid compromises in which they all then found themselves. He was given a rapturous ovation and left the 'Tribune' meeting buoyed by the experience. The mood of 'black despair' had lifted, at least temporarily.

Toward the end of 1966, and increasingly in 1967, Cousins criticised the Government in general and Harold Wilson in particular for 'drifting', for allowing themselves to be carried rudderless, as he saw it, by the tidal flow of events at home and abroad. When challenged to produce an alternative economic policy to the one he persistently attacked Cousins would say, 'We are not planning at all. We are simply dealing with problems as they come up.' This was a view shared by others, most of whom would not agree with Cousins's views on other matters. It was certainly a view held by several members of the Cabinet, on the Right as well as the Left. Richard Crossman told me at the end of October 1966 that in his view there was no real strategy behind Government policy. For two years, he added, Harold Wilson had been 'floundering' in both domestic and foreign policy. Crossman then protested that on foreign policy there was 'no real sense of purpose [in Government] except to tag on to Washington's coattails'. It was at that time that Crossman, who had previously been anti-Common Market, began to feel that the only salvation from continuing drift and decline would be to try again to join the EEC. In Crossman's view, reluctant though he was to accept the verdict, the prospect might just provide the impetus that he felt was desperately needed to galvanise the country and his Government colleagues. It transpired (it was not clear at the time) that my conversation with Crossman took place nine days after an all-day meeting of the Cabinet at Chequers when Ministers first discussed in detail proposals for a new British initiative on Common Market membership. This was revealed the following month, when Wilson told Parliament that he and George Brown would tour the six countries of the EEC for talks with their respective heads of Government. The Government, Wilson declared, would come to a final decision about re-opening formal negotiations in the light of these discussions, especially the talks with de Gaulle. But of course the decision to go into the EEC (providing the French were agreeable) had already been taken in principle at the Chequers meeting. Perhaps that decision was easier for some to take because they felt convinced that there was virtually no chance of being able to persuade the General in Paris to endorse the British application. To that extent the Wilson-Brown initiative was almost certainly a diversionary exercise, taken partly in desperation and partly in the hope that it might persuade foreign (and domestic) opinion that the British were making a really serious attempt to cure their persistent economic sickness.

Towards the end of 1966 the seriousness of Britain's economic condition and the awareness of industrial decline pervaded all political debate. True, there was not the acceptance or understanding of the problem that was to become such an important feature of the public mood a decade later – under the same Prime Minister. Yet there was a feeling that the best of the 'never-had-it-so-good' days were over. Frustration, even despair, began to creep across the country, reflecting two quite separate attitudes. There was a feeling among the working class, predominantly held by active trade unionists, that the wider horizons of a new Britain had already been abandoned, partly because of economic pressures and partly because the Labour leaders lacked conviction, courage and the epic-like qualities for which the rank and file so often yearn, even if misguidedly. Against that left-wing concensus there was an equally powerful feeling among the middle class, professional and business community that enterprise, initiative and reward were being crushed beneath a largely negative and restrictive set of Government policies.

The Left invariably complained because they believed that the policies pursued by the Government were not leading – and could not lead – to a developing socialism. The Right complained that the contrary was the case; that the restrictive policies were in fact reflecting the growth of socialism. Meanwhile the economic situation slid further into depression. Between July and October unemployment rose by over 170,000 to a level of 437,000. The unions were trapped between rising unemployment *and* a wage freeze. Growth was not only abandoned, it was effectively being murdered. Frustrations in British boardrooms encouraged overseas investment, despite the urgent need for domestic investment. There was no more talk of the Great Plan. The whole climate of hope, so vivid and alive earlier in 1966, was fast disappearing by the autumn of the same year. The trade union leaders knew what was wrong, not least Frank Cousins and George Woodcock. But what was to be done? How could the trade unions help the country toward an industrial revival without simply accepting the diktats of Whitehall – or without the social revolution which Cousins increasingly regarded as a prerequisite? Was there a form of 'middle way', to use a Macmillanesque phrase, between a continuing and damaging battle against the Government's policies and one which meekly accepted a declining role for the trade union movement alongside a decline in living standards? Cousins believed there was, and that it was worth attempting to follow. That autumn he astonished most of his General Council colleagues by proposing a completely new approach to national wage bargaining. By its very nature it involved member unions handing over some of their precious and coveted sovereignty to the TUC itself. This was the Cousins Plan.

The Cousins Plan was, in fact, based on a blueprint carefully prepared, in detail, by Jack Jones and later accepted by Cousins. It contained two main themes. First, to offer a constructive alternative to the total interventionism of Government and the prospect (so strongly outlined in Wilson's speech to the TUC) of an endless continuation of State intervention in wage bargaining. Secondly, to try to build up sufficient organised strength behind a system of voluntary wage bargaining discipline to pursuade the Government to withdraw, if not entirely then behind agreed lines of interest.

Cousins recognised that it was futile to continue with a policy which appeared (even if he didn't consider it to be so) negative and destructive. The only realistic alternative seemed to be to develop something on the lines of the Swedish Labour Market system, with a centralised employers organisation working in cooperation with the TUC to operate a voluntary, albeit controlled, system of collective bargaining within a wider economic strategy agreed with the Government. The concept was helped by the setting up that year of the Confederation of British Industry, a central body drawn together from the old Federation of British Industries, British Employers Confederation and the National Union of Manufacturers, Cousins in his plan saw the CBI potentially as the equivalent of the powerful Swedish Employers Federation, and he also envisaged the TUC gradually acquiring some of the power and influence of its Swedish equivalent, the LO. Combined with all this Cousins and Jones worked out a sub-scheme which might give the broader wages plan some immediate drama – a plan to campaign for a £15 a week minimum wage throughout industry.

It was a combination of these ideas that Cousins submitted in a document to the TUC early in October which was subsequently to form the basis for a campaign lasting till the autumn of the following year. Woodcock, back at the TUC after a convalescence, picked up the concept immediately (though he had strong reservations about its practicability). He summoned a special meeting of the TUC economic committee for 30 October – an all-day meeting on Sunday at Congress House. This was unique in itself, and a measure of the importance and urgency Woodcock and Cousins wanted to give the concept. Before that meeting Cousins launched a campaign for a £15 minimum weekly wage at a London Region rally of the TGWU, when he lifted a corner of the curtain on his proposals for a completely new style of centralised wage bargaining for British industry :

> We have set our sights too low on both sides of industry and have not produced either the prosperity or the efficiency of which Britain is capable. Some of our critics say that you cannot have social justice and our kind of free collective bargaining. We say we must now have a new initiative that puts flesh on the slogan [his old slogan] – 'Planned Growth of Wages'.

Again Cousins was engaged in the dialogue – with himself as much as with others – as to whether, and if so how, it was possible to combine 'free' trade unionism with socialist planning and greater economic justice. He accepted that this 'must involve of course the closest possible co-operation between the unions, management and the Government to raise output and efficiency through incentive and productivity bargaining.' Then he went on to develop his case for a new centralised system based on consent, without State or legal intervention :

> The creation of this new central employers body (the CBI) has made it quite practical to talk about central negotiations with the TUC on basic minimum wages, normal hours of employment, holidays, sick pay, etc. This is a great task for this central body.

But it was no use evading the issue of naming a figure for that minimum wage, he added, and then produced his demand for £15 a week :

> This figure is reasonable and urgent and it can and must be established. It is no more than you can get from some State benefits and it is certainly no more than a family needs today.

The average earnings for manual workers that October were £20 6s. 1d. for men and £10 1s. 4d. for women. It is difficult from official figures to calculate exactly how many workers were getting less than £15 a week, but estimates from the Department of Employment suggest that there were nearly two million men and four million women under that level. The proportions, of course, differed widely according to the industry. In distribution, for example, about half were earning less than £15 a week.

In that speech to his London region Cousins also began to develop, more specifically the theme of shop-floor power which was to become the dominant chord in industrial relations within a few years.

> More and more authority is moving to the work-shop level. Some people regret this feeling that power ought to be in the hands of those at the top. I do not agree. Of course there is a role of leadership and co-ordination but the day-to-day job must be directed to the place of work.

Changes had to be made, he insisted, to accommodate these developments and managements must be prepared to give more information : 'The secrecy of private enterprise about its industrial intentions is one of the most harmful of today's restrictive practices.'

Cousins was conscious of the force of his critics' case when they accused him of adopting a totally negative attitude. He told the London conference :

> People have said they do not want to go back to where we were before the freeze. For very different reasons neither do I. We have got to develop the theme of higher wages and the Government must be ready to play its part in backing us up on productivity and efficiency.
>
> I am not prepared just to make negative noises until the freeze is off about what we would have done if it weren't for the Government. We have got to do our job and that means paving the way for a big forward movement in wages. This is something we can work for – it will involve an effort for us all, but it is only through these positive efforts that the producers of wealth will get the standards they are entitled to.

Now that he was out of Government he felt free to pick up an entirely new initiative and, with the backing of his powerful union, try to harness the wider influence of the TUC. If he could succeed, he would indeed put the Government in some difficulty. But, of course, the odds were always against his success.

At the special meeting of the TUC economic committee on 30 October Cousins presented his case for what was, in effect, a 'takeover bid' for the nation's wage bargaining system. It was a bold, almost cheeky, enterprise – which, inevitably, again irritated some of his traditional critics inside the TUC General Council. Again it was a matter of obsessions; almost anything that Cousins did was, in their eyes, by definition, either wrong or eccentric. The main points of the Cousins document were :

1. To replace the time-consuming annual scramble in national wage bargaining by a more centralised system that would decide, by negotiation, the general structure of that year's pay policy.

2. This would free many union officials (and employers) from detailed work on wage negotiating bodies and enable them to play a more active role

in the drive for greater productivity and the overall improvement in industrial relations.

3. The centralised bargaining system would help the negotiators on both sides to identify and try to deal with special problems – of women workers and other lower paid citizens (this was before equal pay legislation).

4. It would – at least in theory – strengthen the role and influence of the TUC by putting it at the centre of activity.

The latter point quite naturally attracted George Woodcock, who, no less than Cousins, wanted to keep the Government at arm's length in the details of wage bargaining although he never shared Cousins's view that the Government could be kept out of overall wages strategy. Some of Cousins's critics regarded the whole concept as a 'bit of a publicity stunt', or, at best, Cousins's bid to score a point against the Government. It may have been the latter, but it was certainly never the former.

Agreement in principle was reached, uneasily no doubt. Then followed a hustle to improve and tighten the policy in readiness for endorsement by the November General Council. The hustle was not, of course, without immediate political motive. In Whitehall the Government was also hustling to prepare yet another White Paper to outline the policy for the period of 'severe restraint' – after the six months of total freeze. Enough had leaked out, often by courtesy of Ministers, to make it clear that this period would simply amount to a continuation of the freeze except for a few exceptional cases, still to be precisely defined. But it was also becoming apparent that the Government firmly intended to continue a strong, interventionist wages policy even after the full twelve months had elapsed. There was, in fact, no end in sight to a continuing Government role.

The knowledge that they might be hanged tomorrow certainly helped to concentrate TUC minds and even overrode objections to the author of the Cousins Plan. Early in November the TUC leaders met again to approve the new strategy, adding to it a proposal to call annual meetings of union executives early in the year to discuss suggestions on 'the general level of increase in wages and salaries that would be appropriate in the ensuing year'. These annual conferences of executives were to be quite separate from the normal annual Trades Union Congress in September.

The TUC's plan already began to assume the dimensions of an alternative TUC 'White Paper' – an alternative to the Government's – and behind it was the alliance of Woodcock and Cousins. The race was on. And it was made all the more urgent following a TV appearance by Aubrey Jones, chairman of the Prices and Incomes Board, who on 11 November appeared in a panel with Frank Cousins and Lord Robens (chairman of the Coal Board). Mr Jones advocated the need for Government to continue its emergency powers over both prices and incomes even when the freeze and period of 'severe restraint' was over. Cousins, overcome with fury, exploded

'That is just about the most extraordinary comment I have ever heard.' But Aubrey Jones (like Lord Robens) had become convinced of the need to curb the power of the trade union 'barons'. When the White Paper was published by the Government, shortly before the TUC General Council met (on 23 November), it spelled out not only a need for further severe restraint but laid down a 'zero norm' for 1967 with exceptions only for the very lowly paid or for whose workers who were able to establish genuine productivity agreements – all of which would have to be referred to the Aubrey Jones Board for approval.

The measure of the TUC's haste to launch its own counter-offensive can be assessed from the fact that no mention of its far-reaching reforms was included in the TUC's evidence to the Royal Commission on Trade Unions, then sitting under Lord Donovan. Yet the evidence was submitted early in November, at the very time the TUC leaders were busily drafting and re-drafting the Cousins Plan.

Once the plan was approved by the General Council preparations were made to hold a special conference of executives early in 1967. This was fixed for 2 March. In the meantime the TUC leaders kept up a ceaseless barrage of criticism, in private as well as in public, against the Government's proposals. Not all union leaders, of course, were opposed to Government intervention, although they may have given public lip-service to such opposition. Some leaders were in fact favourably disposed to legislative support for wage bargaining, since they expected from it a degree of strength which they could not otherwise expect to command by their own industrial muscle. In saying that, one is not denigrating their motives. Some unions, especially those in poorly organised industries where trade unionism was traditionally weak, were often at the mercy of unscrupulous employers and apathetic or fearful workers. That is why wages councils were still an important part of the wage negotiating system. To that extent state intervention – albeit in a more positive and generous form than was then the case – could be and often was an advantage for some unions.

At the private meetings between the Government and the TUC in the weeks leading to the special conference in March there was not the slightest encouragement to believe that the Cousins Plan would get far. The Government was sceptical and sometimes, in private, openly hostile. Shortly before the March conference the TUC leaders went to Downing Street to discuss the whole question with Harold Wilson, Michael Stewart and Ray Gunter, the trio principally concerned with incomes policy. Earlier the TUC had held a number of separate meetings with Stewart, who made it clear that he envisaged a continuing, even a permanent, incomes policy. It was not the happiest prospect for the union leaders, especially against a background of over 600,000 unemployed. Tension between Government and TUC leadership was rising, and was no longer confined to outbursts by Frank

Cousins. Indeed Cousins was at last beginning to find that his critique of Government policy was not received with such disdain by his TUC colleagues. At the Downing Street meeting, for instance, Stewart repeated his belief that 'We are still trying to bring into being a permanent incomes policy' – vindicating Cousins's repeated warnings to his TUC colleagues.[9] Wilson spoke of the Government's fearful dilemma over prices. What *could* the Government do, short of taking administrative control over all prices movements, which he regarded as out of the question except in wartime. He and Michael Stewart poured cold water on the TUC–CBI plan for a purely voluntary policy.

Gunter was altogether more inclined than Wilson or Stewart to look for virtue and potential value in the TUC's ideas. He actually referred, at that meeting, to the TUC proposals as a 'potentially historic document' which might set a new pattern for collective bargaining once the country was in an economic condition to return to 'free wage negotiations'. But that moment had not been reached, Gunter warned. For the time being there had to be some kind of Government legislative barrier. George Woodcock resisted all this argument. His indictment of the Government's allegiance to statutory control was total, especially in relation to Part IV of the Act. Like an inquisitorial counsel he cross-examined the Prime Minister on the value and effectiveness of Government powers. It was not, he told Harold Wilson, a question of what the Government wished to do, but rather a simple matter of what was practicable. What *could* the Government do with trade union recalcitrants? Drag them through the courts and put them in jail? What if the recalcitrants were 70,000 dockers? Woodcock asked with almost a malicious pleasure. (One might recall that this was five years before the five London dockers were jailed under the Industrial Relations Act of the Heath Government – a jailing which effectively killed that Act.)

Woodcock was not a popular figure in the Cabinet room. His authority, his arrogant command of his case, his brilliance as a dialectician and his casual indifference to the dignity of politicians, regardless of their rank, did not endear him to Cabinet Ministers, Labour or Conservative. That day he was in particularly good form. He lectured Wilson, Stewart and Gunter and reminded them (as they did not wish to be reminded) of the basic weakness of their case. The TUC General Secretary told them he had no faith in Government promises to abandon the more restrictive parts of the legislation at the end of twelve months. But in any event, whatever the Government chose to do, said Woodcock, the controls it proposed would simply break down and crack under the strain. 'They will die in your hands,' he declared, his voice rising to an unusual pitch of resonance. Woodcock, a man of many suppressed emotions, rarely permitted himself such outbursts. He reminded

9. These dialogues are based on notes taken by Frank Cousins at the time of the Downing Street meeting, 28 February 1967.

Ministers that the TUC's counter-plan, the Cousins proposals, was in fact an attempt by the trade union leadership to rescue the Government from *its* dilemma. Cousins sat listening to Woodcock like a proud father admiring his favourite son; there was no need for him to underline anything. He merely glowed with pleasure at the way the TUC General Secretary had seemed to demolish his former Cabinet colleagues.

Of all the series of meetings between the Government and the TUC leaders that was the toughest and most outspoken. Throughout 1967 and again in 1968, when the conflict over incomes policy was reaching a climax, the path between 10 Downing Street and Congress House began to resemble a goalmouth in mid-winter, but there was no meeting to match the candour of the session at the end of February 1967. Even so, Cousins was far from optimistic. He did not believe that the Government would retreat, despite the *tour de force* by Woodcock. He was certain that it would require a great deal more than a diversionary and alternative plan from the TUC to shift the Cabinet from its course. And he was to prove right. Nevertheless the Woodcock-Cousins alliance was now an important element which the Government could hardly ignore. The alliance was resumed almost to the effectiveness of its 1964 force and, still more significant, it was now beginning to have an important influence on the rest of the TUC General Council. Some measure of this can be assessed from the opening paragraphs of the TUC report to the special conference on 2 March :

Ever since the end of the first world war Governments have sporadically pursued policies in one form or another designed to influence the outcome of wage negotiations usually with the aim of limiting increases in wages. Only in recent years has the Government attempted to extend such policies systematically to incomes other than wages and to prices and to create new institutions for this purpose. Trade unionists have not been hostile to this development. They recognise that the development of economic and social planning and the greater involvement of Government in the direction of the nation's economic affairs make it inevitable that Governments will have regard to the relationship between incomes and productivity.

However, while trade unionists accept that planning the economy requires action on the incomes and prices fronts they also insist on the corollary that an effective incomes policy is not possible except in the context of an effective economic and social plan . . .

Implicit in these opening bars is the Cousins theme that he would support no incomes restraint outside a framework of economic and social policies related directly to socialist policies. This marked an important difference between Cousins and Woodcock since Woodcock accepted that Government (any Government) had a central role to play in contemporary economic planning and in the selection of industrial and social priorities. He regarded an incomes policy, albeit a voluntary one in which the TUC could play a decisive part, as the only serious alternative to a monetarist policy which would require a large pool of unemployment. Against this the Cousins view was altogether more ideologically motivated. His readiness to cooperate in a voluntary wages policy run by the TUC was determined by the fact that he saw it as the only viable alternative to increasing legal control by the State over the pay packets of his members. He could see no path ahead which might lead the Labour Government towards the socialist policies in which he believed and without such policies he had no intention of trading in his freedom to bargain. This difference between the two men accounted for the marked contrast in both the tone and content of their speeches at the 2 March conference. Woodcock repeatedly stressed his desire to work with the Government. And to the disgust of Cousins (who made his irritation clear during the debate) Woodcock said he did not regard the issue as a fight 'between our policy and the Government's policy'.

He continued :

Indeed, far from being an attempt to pick a fight with the Government, it [the TUC policy] fits in exactly with what I believe to be an inevitable relationship in these days between the trade union Movement and the Government of a democratic country.

Woodcock described the TUC's plan for exercising more central authority over constituent unions, somewhat lavishly, as 'the most fruitful set of proposals that has ever come from any trade union movement in any country at any time'. There was no concealing his delight at having reached this point in TUC development. But Cousins was less enchanted, certainly with the interpretation Woodcock had put on the TUC proposals. He resented any suggestion that the new strategy might offer some kind of 'partnership-in-wage restraint' to the Government. That was certainly not the way Cousins saw it. He told the conference :

We are saying that legislation is no way at all to control wages. It cannot be done . . . we are not a body to be told what the Government wants us to do. We are not agents and instruments of the Government. We refuse to be this to any Government. We are saying [to the Government] . . . away with legislation, we have had enough of it. Therefore we are talking of what we should put in place of it . . .

It was Woodcock's speech that caught the headlines. This was in fact more of a model lecture on the relationship between Government and trade unions in a modern society than a mere conference speech, and it will probably rank as one of Woodcock's outstanding performances as TUC General Secretary. He felt that his long-sought dream of providing the TUC with some real central authority, in partnership with a Government committed to a set of social and economic priorities, was now beginning to take some shape. He had no illusions about the difficulties that still lay ahead, but he saw it as the first significant, if halting, step in the direction of commitment, order and social balance. At the time the vote by that conference appeared to mark an historic advance for the TUC in its relations with member unions and their wage claims. Perhaps it was. The vote was 7,604,000 to 963,000 in favour of granting the TUC such powers.

That night on ITV's 'This Week' programme Frank Cousins was asked if he would be ready to go to jail for his beliefs. He nodded. Yes, he would be ready to do that if any action by the Government or by a 'red-robed judge' led to injustice for his members in the field of pay. Cousins's unswerving opposition to the Government's policies had not been mollified by his success at the TUC. In fact he stepped up his campaign of criticism against his former Cabinet colleagues and this led to his being invited to make many public speeches on the subject from platforms other than his own TGWU. Shortly after the special TUC conference he was asked to speak at the annual meeting of the Association of Cine, TV and Allied Technicians (ACTT), where he made such an impact that the union reprinted the speech in full as a special pamphlet.[10] In it Cousins returned to his basic assault on the Government's legal control over wages which he now saw as a permanent threat, regardless of which Government was in office.

> The Government is taking unto itself powers that it ought not to try to take. I say this as a socialist on the basis that there are areas of control which cannot be equated with democratic institutions. This is one of the things we need to look at very carefully in order to get the Government out of its misguided wage restraint policies.

Cousins did not let the matter rest there. He also questioned the 'old methods' of wage bargaining and asked whether they had really been as effective as trade unionists (including himself) had claimed in the past. There was self-criticism in his confession :

> We have to recognize . . . that we have not done all the things we needed to do in order to improve the situation, but can we improve the situation by giving more power to the TUC? I feel that we can give some tasks to our central body which will be better dealt with by a central authority.

What tasks? He listed among them working hours, holiday agreements, overtime rates, and so on. If these could be negotiated and settled centrally, he claimed, it would enable the trade union machine to work more effect-

10. 'The Economics of Injustice', May 1967.

ively at workshop level. This then was how he sought to reconcile his deep-rooted and abiding dislike for controls over wages with his recognition that some concession had to be made to the case for a greater measure of rational and central planning over pay – even though the socialist millennium had not yet arrived.

The Government White Paper was published at the end of March. There were no concessions to the TUC – except that the offensive Part IV would be allowed to lapse in August. The effect was to propose a return to the pre-freeze situation of before July 1966. In fact it consisted of a curious mixture of even tougher policies laced with an imprecision of phraseology which reflected Ministerial conflict. Instead of a $3\frac{1}{2}$ per cent 'norm' no one was to be entitled to anything at all – a 'nil norm'. This would last for another twelve months, during which time pay rises would be conceded only to those who satisfied four conditions. These were : higher productivity, more exacting work or major changes in working methods; where labour short-ages warranted changes in working practices; where wages were too low 'to maintain a reasonable standard of living'; and where the comparability between the pay of workers in corresponding grades had fallen out of line. This formula was so vague and exposed to such widely varying interpre-tations that, effectively, it transferred much of the real decision-making to the Prices and Incomes Board. Ostensibly this relieved the Government of some of the responsibility, if not the odium. It was true that the legal powers the Government were retaining were weaker than under the 1966–7 legis-lation, all of which gave the impression of a Government retreat. Yet in fact there was little of any real restraint. The Government had powers to delay any pay settlement or claim for up to seven months simply by the device of referring a claim to the Prices and Incomes Board.

The TUC found the White Paper and the subsequent Act so objection-able that they refused to discuss the details with the Government. Wood-cock's view was that the whole edifice of Government policy was largely irrelevant compared with the potential now open to the TUC. Woodcock admitted privately that but for the Government's pressure the TUC leaders would never have committed themselves even to the first step towards a more centralised authority. In twelve months the whole framework of TUC thinking on wages policy had undergone what appeared to be a major change. Whatever was said in public, whatever postures were taken up from the rostrum, the trade union leadership knew the significance of what had been done. If Woodcock was the strategist, then the driving force, the motive power, was certainly Frank Cousins.

Now Cousins approached another critical point – his last but one biennial delegate conference before retirement. True he still had one after that in

July 1969. But by then his successor would be moving into the driving seat and he would be receiving the final plaudits, the bitter-sweet handshakes. So the 1967 BDC of the TGWU was doubly important for him since it marked both his return to the trade union scene and, at the same time, his preparation for final departure. In the twelve months after his resignation from the Government and his return to the union Frank Cousins passed through an uneasy re-entry period. His severest critics – who were never far from the surface – were already preparing to write him off. They saw approaching retirement, cooling down and losing impact. Where Cousins was concerned there were rarely many neutrals. There never had been. People tended either to dislike him quite strongly, or to admire him with an undue reverence. Again, this was not an unusual phenomena for a TGWU General Secretary. Since his resignation from the Wilson Government an increasing number of observers found Cousins more enigmatic than ever. They regarded him as intellectually schizophrenic, politically and industrially less sure of his step than before October 1964. Cousins was not unaware of this, and at the 1967 union conference he tried to dispel these impressions. Indeed his performance at that conference sometimes resembled his first as General Secretary, ten years earlier, when he first set out to remodel the union and its policies. In that sense his remarkable decade had brought him almost full circle.

Cousins spent the week at Blackpool not merely in a predictable assault on Government wages policy but in seeking to revive the spirit of socialist militancy in the union. He launched demands for more nationalisation – partly by waving old and half-forgotten policy commitments under Harold Wilson's nose, but also by developing new claims for the public ownership of North Sea gas and oil, a prescient claim in 1967. He further challenged the Wilson-Brown initiative on the Common Market, though by then de Gaulle had already demonstrated that he would block the British application. Even so Cousins was careful not to isolate himself by a total disavowal of the EEC. He concentrated his attack on the manner and form of the bargaining, and at what he took to be an over-obsequious posturing by the British Government towards de Gaulle. But he resisted several more extreme demands which wanted the union to commit itself to outright opposition to the Common Market regardless of the terms that might be obtained.

Cousins also stirred a Parliamentary hornet's nest by taking a sideswipe at those MPs on the TGWU's Parliamentary panel who consistently ignored union policy. At the time the union had twenty-six sponsored MPs, eight of them members of the Government, including George Brown (Foreign Secretary), Anthony Greenwood and Robert Mellish (Housing), John Silkin (Chief Whip), Reginald Prentice (Minister of Works), and Peter Shore (Economic Affairs). Cousins did nothing to discourage the wave of criticism, often bitterly expressed, about the way some of the MPs had flouted and ignored union policy. But he did caution against any action which might be seen as a breach of Parliamentary privilege.

> We don't want to tell them what to do or what to say or what to think. What we want them to do is to come and tell us why they think they should have the workers' pennies put into a fund to help them fight the union's policies. We want them to come back and be examined. We are saying to them – come and give us an account of your stewardship.

Behind this somewhat facile explanation there was an angry Frank Cousins. He had not forgotten the campaign waged against him during the H-bomb conflict. He had ample recall of the many occasions when some members of the TGWU's Parliamentary group did their best to undermine his authority in the union by attacking his policies and frequently himself. And, most recent of all, he had no difficulty in remembering the lack of support from his own union colleagues inside the Government when he sat, so often beleaguered, in Cabinet fighting a lonely battle.

There was nothing unique, after all, about a trade union leadership requiring a review of its Parliamentary panel, certainly nothing novel about a TGWU leader keeping a watchful eye on his 'own' group of MPs. No MP in the TGWU group would have dared offend protocol under either Bevin or Deakin. Of course that was when the tide was flowing in a different direction. Inevitably the decision by the 1967 TGWU conference to 'review' its Parliamentary group membership had the effect of increasing the tension between the union's leadership and a number of their MPs who had always been critical of Cousins – not least, George Brown and Reginald Prentice. Yet no one had their sponsorship withdrawn while Cousins was General Secretary.

Cousins succeeded in re-establishing himself firmly at the 1967 BDC. My own assessment of him, at the end of that week, was published in the *Sun* at the time :

> Probably the most significant fact about the Cousins week in Blackpool is that for once he was pulling the reins of his conference to hold it back. A large section of delegates would have gone much further than he did had he given them their head. Far from writing him off I would say that Frank Cousins is now riding more confidently than ever. The question Mr. Wilson might be asking today is . . . where to?

There was reason for Cousins's confidence other than his conference success. The Confederation of British Industry that July agreed to join with the TUC in trying to encourage 'new attitudes' to wages and productivity. On the surface this appeared to give a substantial boost to the Cousins proposal for a partnership between the two major institutions on both sides of industry in order to keep the Government out of wage bargaining. The ingredients seemed to be coming together for a new compact between the two sides which might perhaps lead in the direction of a Swedish-style system of central bargaining which the TGWU leader was advocating. In fact it proved to be a somewhat cosmetic operation, though that is not what was hoped at the time.

Away from the industrial scene in Britain in that mid-summer of 1967 the world stage was occupied by a new drama, something that was to shake the foundations of international complacency for a decade to follow – the Six Day War in the Middle East which ended in a remarkable victory for Israel. One week after the Israeli-Arab truce on 17 June, China detonated her first H-bomb. Coincidental, to be sure, but a coincidence with a macabre message for the world. Where now were the hopes and pious slogans of the late 1950s and early 1960s about nuclear control and non-proliferation? Who even now can be sure how much flowed from that explosion in the Middle East? The stability of the entire western world was disturbed. The international scene, East and West, was disrupted to an extent that affected world events even more than any other single incident since Suez and Korea. Six years later, when the Middle East erupted again in the Yom Kippur war of autumn 1973, the effects of 1967 were still pervasive. That is another story, though it is not without relevance to the 'British condition', which was to take another serious lurch into deeper crisis in the winter of 1967 with the devaluation of the pound – long predicted, equally long delayed.

One of the oddities of successive British trade union hierarchies has been the way their leaders acquired the status of world statesmen. Invariably this status is unofficial or at best quasi-official, and in part the practice can be traced to Ernest Bevin's period in the Foreign Office. He was always on the look-out for an old mate whom he might invite to do a bit of foreign travel on behalf of HMG, a Victor Feather in Greece, for instance, or an old TGWU crony from Merseyside who might do a handy job in an African state. Bevin – and the Foreign Office – quickly discovered that this was frequently a rewarding ploy. So it was not exactly surprising when, in the late summer of 1967 shortly before the annual Trades Union Congress, the TUC was invited by Histadrut (the powerful Israeli trade union organisation) to send two observers to Israel to meet Ministers, Government officials and trade union leaders to discuss the aftermath of the Six Day War. Histadrut was ostensibly interested to find out what the British TUC might do to help bring about a peaceful solution in the Middle East. Clearly it was not solely concerned with establishing friendly relations with its labour counterpart in the Arab countries. What is not clear is whether this was a purely Israeli initiative, or whether other international influences played their part in using the mechanism of the British TUC. At any rate after a meeting between Histadrut and the TUC international committee it was agreed that the TUC would send two of its senior statesmen on a three-day visit to Israel. The two people were Fred (now Sir Frederick) Hayday, chairman of the international committee, and Frank Cousins. They met the Israel Prime Minister, Foreign Secretary, other Government Ministers and officials and talked with Jewish and Arab trade union leaders, in Israel. When he reported to the September Congress Frank Cousins made it clear that the Hayday-Cousins mission had been rather more than a routine visit. In fact, it was a deliberate high-level attempt to mediate in the Middle East conflict.

Cousins, following Hayday, spoke of their visit with great vividness, and asked the Congress to endorse the peace-making role which underpinned their mission, adding :

> It is not over yet [the conflict] but it will be over much quicker if we can convince the Jordanians, the Egyptians, the Lebanese and the people who are not as violently opposed to the State of Israel as are some others that their workers' interests will best be served by sitting down and talking on how the two sides can help to emancipate the total area for the benefit of the total people.[11]

The Hayday-Cousins mission was later extended to a number of visits throughout the Arab world, at the end of 1967 and in 1968. They went to Jordan and the Lebanon in December 1967, again meeting Ministers, officials and trade union leaders as well as visiting refugee camps. In March 1968 the two men visited Egypt and met the late President Nasser, who greatly impressed Cousins. Their main purpose was to try to use the international trade union movement as a possible bridge to a peaceful settlement between Israel and the Arab States. In the end there was little to show for their labours, and they both came to the view that there was such general and deep-rooted opposition, in all the Arab countries, to any direct negotiations with Israel that they were pursuing a mirage. This was especially so because both Hayday and Cousins consistently emphasised in their talks with the Arab leaders that a permanent settlement was possible only if the Arab States were prepared to recognise and accept the permanent existence of the State of Israel.

Yet though the enterprise came to nought it played a not unimportant part in the year that followed the Six Day War, and it certainly established an unusual role for trade union statesmanship even in the most critical and sensitive theatres of international conflict. It was also a novel diversion for the 1967 TUC, in helping to take their minds away from the seemingly end-

11. TUC *Annual Report*, 1967, pp. 489-92.

less dialogue over the misdeeds of the Wilson Government. Of course the March special conference had done much to defuse the battle over wages policy at the September Congress. In fact it was so defused that Frank Cousins found himself in the almost unique position of receiving support on most of the major proposals that he and the TGWU put to that Congress. In particular there was overwhelming support for the £15 a week minimum wage proposal, which gave Cousins special satisfaction. He regarded this as a considerable achievement because it signalled a general acceptance at the Congress that was unusual for him. It also meant he had overcome the hostility – or at least much of it – that had been so apparent at the previous year's Congress after his resignation.

The TGWU *Record* in its October issue celebrated the success of the £15 policy with a gleeful headline: 'The £15 Minimum: TUC's Historic Decision.' It observed with some self-indulgence:

> the unanimous decision of the TUC to back the union's proposal for a £15 nationally negotiated minimum wage was the most important decision of the annual Congress held in Brighton in September . . . the TGWU has sought TUC backing for this policy and won it. It is now the central feature of national trade union policy . . . neither the Government nor the employers can ignore this decision but the real battle now lies where it has always been – through vigorous and powerful action at the place of work and the negotiating table.

To describe the £15 minimum campaign as having become the 'central feature' of national trade union policy was to say the least something of an exaggeration. It was certainly a part of the new strategy that was beginning to unfold, but in some ways, it was still a strategy in search of a policy. The whole development was part of the 'escape mechanism' designed to release the unions from the grip of direct State interference. Of course that was a powerful lever. The plight of the lower paid worker was even more glaring than it is today, though it remains one of the central social and economic challenges facing organised labour. Cousins saw the campaign as a rallying point for his own union in terms of recruitment as well as for the trade union movement as a whole. He also believed with firm conviction that it was necessary to have a basic minimum, a floor, below which no wage should fall, in order to strengthen the campaign for a more highly paid British working class. So to that extent it was understandable that he and the TGWU regarded the success of the £15 minimum wage proposal as an important milestone.

Yet the 1967 TUC was a surprisingly placid event. After the tensions of a year of freeze and severe restraint there had been a general assumption that the Congress might explode into verbal violence, if only to ease trade union frustrations. Yet apart from some ritualistic denunciation of Government policies the mood of that Congress was, as *The Times* observed in an editorial, 'less emotional than might have been expected'. 'Perhaps', the paper added with some insight, 'it was because the critics are conscious that they themselves do not know what to do about it.' For that reason George Woodcock and Frank Cousins were able to seize and develop their initiative. 'Their own voluntary incomes policy', *The Times* continued, 'was not challenged, surprisingly enough, even by the unions who have consistently opposed it.'

Equally the Labour Party conference that year was in an unusually low key. The tone was set by a soothing, soporific speech from the Chancellor, James Callaghan, who took the brunt of trade union criticism on wages policy with the air of a man who understands intimately the problems of the shop floor but who, with the nation's budgeting and housekeeping to look after, cannot manage to do all those wonderful things he would *like* to do. No hint here of the disaster just ahead. Next day the Party leader took command in what must rank as one of his most brilliant conference performances. It was more than a mere exercise in keeping the Party flock together – it was an attempt to rekindle some of the enthusiasm for the technological revolution, to relight the flame he had ignited from the same Scarborough platform four years earlier. The spark was a little dampened by then but the speech had the desired effect of galvanising the conference. It even brought Frank Cousins to his feet to applaud the leader's performance – a point which Wilson notes in his book.

Nevertheless Cousins was not distracted from pursuing his own set-piece attack on the Government's wages policy, nor did he moderate his criticisms of the Government's handling of the Common Market question. In particular he was critical of George Brown's obsequious behaviour towards de Gaulle and the whole hierarchy of European political and economic institutions. What Cousins feared, and what he attacked, was that the British Government were now so desperately anxious to get into the EEC almost regardless of the terms, that they were in danger of debasing themselves. In his reply George Brown suggested that there was no fundamental difference between the Government's case and the TGWU. Both were concerned to ensure that certain specific conditions were met before Britain could contemplate entry into the EEC. If this was so, Brown asked, why challenge the platform? He invited Cousins to 'remit' his resolution, but the TGWU leader shook his head. On the vote Cousins's motion was lost by 3,536,000 to 2,539,000. It was a narrow-run thing, despite Brown's plea. There was no love for the EEC in the Labour Party even in 1967.

Immediately after that conference Frank Cousins, with Nance, went off to the United States as guest of the Amalgamated Transit Union of America to attend its conference in New Orleans on the way to America he did an unusual thing; he restarted his diary notes. But the diary ceased again on the day it began – 6 October. Yet in that single entry, *en route* for the USA, Cousins put on paper his innermost thoughts and reflections on the state of the Labour Movement and his views on the Party leadership. The 1967 Labour Party conference he described as having 'probably been the phoniest and most stage managed conference for many years'. He criticised the handling of the conference, especially by the conference arrangements committee, and the way in which the platform had been allowed to dominate the entire process. And he reflected somewhat bitterly on the readiness of some of his TUC colleagues to allow the Party leadership (ie, the Government) to 'use' them:

> It reminded me of the days of Arthur Deakin, Will Lawther, and Tom Williamson . . . when the platform *knew* they could always win through despite the left wing opposition of the AEU. Strangely it's now gone round to the position when they know they can beat the conference despite the opposition of the TGWU by getting the support of Jack Cooper, Bill Carron, Sidney Ford and Les Cannon. At least I give Harold credit for knowing how to invest his patronage gifts and get a quick and sure return. Give them the titles and the places on the Boards and you will never be short of supporting votes.

These observations did not detract from his admiration of Wilson's conference speech, which he described as 'masterly', though he did reflect that 'sooner or later, probably sooner, delegates will realise that Harold promised the jam before even the fruit harvest has set . . .'.

Cousins picked holes in various aspects of Wilson's technological prospectus. His diary note referred to issues that had been under debate, and controversy, before he left the Government and which he knew could not be delivered or fulfilled to match with what Wilson had told the conference.

Cousins's notes also contain fascinating glimpses of how he viewed some of his former Cabinet colleagues. He saw Jim Callaghan as

> a splendid platform performer, skilled in the art of answering points not raised and putting queries to people who are not going to be allowed to answer them. He is a very satisfying man and if he could break away from the Treasury grip could be quite a politician. But by and large the conference gave me the feeling that too many of our leaders are amateurs who will never really make the grade because they accept their departmental briefs. There are also too many little men who jump when the ringmaster [Harold] tells them to do so . . .

Cousins then returned to his favourite personality topic, George Brown, with whom he had such a curious love-hate relationship. He saw Brown as a great human dichotomy, a mixture of weakness and potential brilliance, of 'extrovertism and inferiority complex . . . he has great ability, muddled

and wasted because of his character . . . His tremendous capacity as a platform man is wasted usually because he is either trying to recover from some
escapade like the performance at the agents dance and his row with the
photographers or an over-exuberant performance related to a couple of
double whiskies . . .' (Brown objected to the photographers hounding him
on to the dance floor where he was performing in somewhat fanciful style.
This led to a great burst of Press criticism of George Brown and the following day the *Daily Mirror* and the *Sun* demanded that he should quit. The
'George Brown affair' came to dominate the rest of that Scarborough Labour
conference.)

Cousins declares that he and 'many others' came away from the 1967
conference

> with a feeling of despondency not because we lost some votes or won others
> but based on the feeling that the Government had decided to dissociate itself
> from the body of the conference, the constituency delegates, and to ally itself
> firmly with, and to rely upon, the right wing trade union vote. I cannot do
> other than feel that even in the short run this is wrong and in the long term
> it is fatal. The social democratic Labour party will wither away if it continues
> in this way.

His comment on Wilson was:

> Harold is relying on the fact that amongst his Parliamentary and Cabinet
> colleagues he is a large man amongst a group of pygmies. What he fails to see
> is that if he acted more progressively he could be a giant amongst a group of
> big men.

Cousins chose that moment, in his diary, to make some deeper observations
about his own relationship with Wilson. Much of this will already be familiar
to the reader, but the notes are worth repeating. They reflect Cousins's
conviction that he *did* have a special relationship with Wilson – a relationship which somehow went sour on both of them.

> I think it is generally known that the relationship between Harold Wilson
> and myself is a quite unusual one. I have a great deal of respect for him as a
> politician whilst at the same time being fully aware of his many failings in
> a variety of ways (perhaps it might be said – in every phase of his behaviour
> over many years). Harold is aware of this and also recognises that amongst
> his Cabinet colleagues I was perhaps the only one who didn't want his job.
> Nor in fact did I want to be Foreign Secretary or Chancellor. He knew this
> because I refused to have a change of jobs as a Minister because I felt the
> Minister of Technology had an important role to play in our modernisation
> plans.
> In these circumstances I have always been able to talk freely with him, he

recognizing my arrogance of approach and me accepting his Napoleonic beliefs.

It follows therefore that sometimes our exchanges are a little unorthodox and one of our not infrequent incidents happened at Scarborough. We both attended ASSET's cocktail party and both reached there rather early before many others had come, so naturally we both and Clive Jenkins gravitated together. After an exchange of pleasantries and quips I asked Harold (I suppose rather mischievously) why he had changed his mind about joining the Common Market after trying to persuade me to stay in the Cabinet and help fight the growing pressure from Brown and Co. to go in.

Harold answered with one word : 'Kosygin'. Then went on to explain that the USSR leader had convinced him that the only way to circumvent the growing danger from Germany was for Britain to take a part in the European development.

When I reminded him that I had been with him at the talks in Moscow and I didn't agree that K had put it like that but had rather suggested that USSR and GB should jointly take steps to prevent the growing menace of Nazi-ism, Harold promptly said : 'Oh, I didn't mean at *that* meeting. I meant when K and I met alone in March of this year (1967)'.

Cousins's caustic comment was :

> It seems that the way to win is to tell the left wing you are doing things because Russia wants us to do them, and then tell the right wing that we are doing the same things because LBJ agrees, and for the middle-of-the-roaders you get George Brown to tell them it's so that we can be a new force in the world able to lead a third block . . . what a pity our real basic supporters don't know this . . .

Cousins was recalled from his American visit to intercede in the rash of dock strikes that had broken out in the major ports following the introduction of the Devlin decasualisation scheme on 28 September. On the first day of the introduction of this historic reform dockers at London, Manchester and Hull marched out in protest – or rather in fear of what decasualisation might mean for their future jobs and security. It was the beginning of three years of strife in the docks, an astonishing paradox and a remarkable example of the way fear can inculcate perversity in human behaviour. Most of the dockers who struck on the day decasualisation started drifted back to work by the following week – except some in London and the men at Liverpool, where the strike dragged on until November. After six weeks it was finally settled by a Government inquiry under the late Sir Jack Scamp. There wasn't very much that Frank Cousins could do about the situation, but he was asked to come back partly because of a Press outcry about his absence in America and Mexico while his dockers were on strike. He returned on 18 October and immediately went into talks with Harold Wilson.

That same day he ran into a dramatic row with Ray Gunter, the Minister of Labour, who, exasperated and dismayed by the dockers' reaction to decasualisation, made a speech denouncing the whole affair as a 'Red plot'. He coupled this with a charge that the 'unions' (and by this he could only mean the TGWU) had lost control of their members. It looked like – and was certainly interpreted as an attack on Cousins, first for having been in Mexico, and secondly for the manner and style of his TGWU leadership. The Communists, Gunter alleged, were planning 'a winter of disruption'. Within hours Harold Wilson, at another public occasion, seemed to underline Gunter's message, certainly as far as the Communist threat was concerned. Cousins, supported by George Woodcock, denounced Gunter's attack and, by inference, the Prime Minister's echo. When Cousins left Downing Street that same evening after seeing both Wilson and Gunter he was at his diplomatic best: 'To suggest it is a Communist plot is quite exaggerated. I think Mr. Gunter's statement does not help.' Behind those tranquil phrases lay a blazing row he had with Gunter and Wilson, in which Cousins told them that their public statement had made a difficult situation even worse.

Cousins refused to denounce his striking dockers, despite the fact that the strike was unofficial. In Liverpool the whole port was stopped; in London there were still some 4,000 men on strike. Cousins appealed to the men to return to work and promised the union would take up all their grievances and fears. He even made a personal appeal to Jack Dash, the Communist docker who was leading the unofficial stoppage in London. He said he thought the dockers were misguided in fearing decasualisation, yet he refused to denounce them in Deakin-like style.

Cousins already sensed that the dockers' fears for their future job security was by no means groundless. Of course he supported decasualisation – with the fervour which was required and expected for such an historic, long-demanded step. But he had no illusions about the longer-term implications. Technology was already moving rapidly into the docks industry and manpower was declining. By 1967 it was down to 60,000 as against 80,000 in 1955, the year he moved into the general secretary's chair. Cousins was severely criticised for his ambivalent role in the 1967 dock strike, even by his own London region committee officials. Some dock officials in London and Liverpool would have preferred their general secretary to have publicly denounced men like Jack Dash rather than 'appeal' to them, or seek to understand what lay behind their fears. Cousins would not do that. This won him no friends among port employers, nor at the Ministry of Labour. But he was determined not to fall into the trap which, he believed, had so weakened Arthur Deakin – and the unions – to assume that a strike was wrong merely because it was unofficial.

It was said that the dock strike was the final straw which forced the devaluation of 1967, that Wilson was heard, by some Ministers, to comment on Cousins's 'responsibility' for the collapse in sterling. There is no reliable evidence to suggest that Wilson did ever suggest this, though he certainly believed that Cousins's determined opposition to Government wages policy through 1967 and 1968 led to the ultimate breakdown of Labour's incomes policy. Of course the devaluation story is quite a different matter. It would have been absurd to have suggested even half-seriously that Cousins's opposition to Government policy had, by then, reached such proportions as being capable of determining the fate of sterling. That responsibility lies elsewhere, buried more deeply in history. In any event, how vacuous the conference debates at Scarborough were made to appear within weeks. On 18 November sterling was devalued by 14.3 per cent (from $2.80 to $2.40 to the £); bank rate was increased from 6½ to 8 per cent; an IMF loan of £583 millions was secured. Public expenditure in Britain was cut back – £100 millions on defence, and another £100 millions on other sectors. A credit squeeze was imposed on consumer goods, with HP increasing and Selective Employment Tax premiums withdrawn.

To the majority of the country the devaluation was something of a surprise. After all, there had been considerable 'sunshine' talk from Ministers only a few weeks earlier, despite the dock strike. Yet it ought not to have come as a surprise. The speculation against sterling had been strong for months. In the early summer the Bank of England gossip was of imminent economic crisis.[12] In a Cabinet reshuffle in August Wilson had taken personal command of the Department of Economic Affairs, removing Michael Stewart. Peter Shore was brought into the Cabinet and put in charge of day to day affairs at the DEA, but, unusually, the Prime Minister was in effective overall command. It was clear that the economy was in serious, trouble again. Production was stagnant after a year of absolute control over pay and prices. Investment was lagging, and forward plans reflected no optimism. Wilson continued to resist devalution until the last minute, remaining convinced that it was not the right thing to do nor that it would resolve Britain's problems. He was right about the latter. But events took control and left him no option.

The eventual issue was not whether to devalue but by how much.[13] Several Ministers and a number of leading Whitehall officials advised a heavier devaluation. Indeed this became such an open secret that one of the chief difficulties *after* devaluation was to maintain the new, devalued parity. In the early months of 1968 the Government was again almost overwhelmed by continuing fierce pressures on sterling. The fight to avert another devaluation became one of Government survival as well. In the words of one Cabinet Minister :

12. See Cecil King, *The Cecil King Diaries, 1965–1970* (Jonathan Cape, 1972), p. 139.
13. Based on a conversation with a Cabinet Minister at the time.

A second devaluation at that time would have been disastrous for the Labour Government. Yet it often came very near to that in 1968. Without American support [for sterling] it would probably have been unavoidable. The movement of capital out of London reached frightening proportions. The Government simply held on grimly hoping that there would be a turn in the tide.

The period of greatest peril was in April–May 1968. Wilson was then under immense and perpetual strain. His command over the Parliamentary Labour Party was weaker than ever. His standing in the country had reached a new low, he contained himself in an unusual but palpable silence, as if hiding behind a monastic wall, while everywhere people harked back to his notorious phrase about 'the pound in the pocket'. Only Wilson's limitless tenacity kept him afloat in that period, probably the most testing of his whole Premiership. It was then that the intrigues began, in earnest, to shift him from the leadership. Intrigues which certainly involved, among others, Jim Callaghan and Ray Gunter. The clouds were moving across the Wilson era and they were never, entirely, to recede again.

Chapter Twenty-six

THE LAST LAP

The first six months of 1968 saw the Wilson Cabinet at its lowest pitch of collective morale. The lowest point of the Government's six year span. It survived as a Government because there was an automatic majority in the House of Commons, though sometimes it seemed that even this was not necessarily a complete security net. The possibility of a large left-wing revolt was always in the air. By-elections were steadily lost. The mood in the country, especially inside the Labour Movement, was one of widespread disenchantment with the politicians. Throughout industry shop-floor restiveness against the wages policy and the general restrictiveness produced a marked rise in the number and intensity of unofficial strikes, some for what appeared to be the most bizarre reasons. The cry began to rise again for 'something to be done' about strikes. The Conservative Party put the finishing touches to its industrial policy document, 'Fair Deal at Work', and prepared to legislate for an entirely new system of industrial relations. Edward Heath pledged himself, that year, to introduce this reform if the Conservatives won the next election, no matter what resistance was met.

Beyond doubt 1968 set the scene for 1970 and the Heath Government's introduction of the Industrial Relations Act. It could therefore be said that it set the scene for much else, too. Of course it is equally true that the 1960s as a whole was a period of increasing industrial tension and shop-floor upheaval. The statistics are clear on this though the dry figures alone do not adequately reveal the true dimensions of the unrest in the factories nor do they offer the full perspective of the social and political questioning that was developing so rapidly in that period. What they show is that after an explosive start to the decade there was a comparative dip in the strike figures during 1966, the year of Labour's huge overall majority followed by the summer economic crisis. But afterwards, through 1967 and into 1968, the strike figures rose sharply again and by 1969, the year of 'In Place of Strife' the explosion had reached such a level as to demonstrate that a new dimension of spontaneous militancy had been born. Inevitably the reaction from 'public opinion' was the cry for 'something to be done' about strikes. Opinion poll after opinion poll registered with monotonous predictability that sixty, seventy, even eighty per cent of this or that group believed that Government ought to introduce laws to curb the militancy on the shop floor. By 1968 the pressure on politicians (even if in *their* heads they knew better) for some form of legal curb on the powers of the trade unions was irresistible. At the same time the public standing of politicians was also at its lowest ebb. The two factors eventually came together when politicians (in the sense that both the Wilson and Heath Governments reacted to these impulses in similar form) plunged into legislative action, partly to try to restore public confidence in their political leaders. Paradoxically both actions were to prove disastrous to both Parties, and both Governments. In April 1968 an assessment of the public mood was published in *The Times* by Professor Richard Rose. He gathered together his assessment from a number of public opinion polls that had been taken over a period of years and his analysis suggested that the popularity of Harold Wilson and Edward Heath was declining simultaneously, if for different reasons; 'a situation', Dr Rose observed, 'unprecedented since opinion polls began keeping records in 1956'.

Wilson's rating fell from a peak of 69 per cent 'satisfaction level' in May 1966 to a new trough of 33 per cent in January 1969. 'In the past 23 years the Gallup Poll has only once recorded a Prime Minister's rating lower than that accorded Wilson.' Dr Rose continued: 'In October 1956 shortly before the outbreak of the Suez War Sir Anthony Eden's [Lord Avon] work was satisfactory in the eyes of only 30 per cent of the electorate.' Yet Edward Heath was faring even worse than Wilson, although in fact the statistical position for Heath looked somewhat healthier as a result of the dramatic slump in Wilson's popularity. 'What we have seen since the last general election [of 1966] is a growing dissatisfaction with the two existing party alternatives.' Dr Rose concluded: 'This has been evidenced in the by-election successes of nationalists.'

From the beginning of 1968 the impact of the continuing economic crisis took total command of events. Wilson's own leadership was the subject of many weekend soirees in the alcoves of the Establishment, and in the back streets of Labour constituencies where local party chiefs came together with their MPs. As if to set the scene for the year of hardship ahead the Cabinet met on 4 January to consider a programme of cuts in public spending which included cancelling the orders for the American F-111A – the very aircraft that had replaced TSR-2 and split the Cabinet for so many months during Frank Cousins's period in Government. Along with that cancellation there was a recasting of defence policy embracing a schedule for the withdrawal of the British presence from South-East Asia, particularly Singapore – the very policy which Wilson had resisted for so long and over which he had endlessly quarrelled with Cousins. Now, with great reluctance, Wilson agreed to backpedal – but only under pressure of continuing economic crisis, not because he had changed his judgement of the policy. The Cabinet also proposed postponing the raising of the school leaving age to 16 until 1973, and restoring prescription charges. Back to Gaitskell.

For Harold Wilson these decisions were particularly painful. Even he could not pretend that they were all part of his own planning, and he has since confessed that he was then living in constant fear of a major upheaval inside the Government, with the possibility of 'sensational resignations'. Yet it was not only the Prime Minister whose stature was diminished. The whole range of Government policies now looked threadbare. The weight, importance and emphasis put on prices and incomes policy seemed both absurdly eccentric and certainly insignificant beside the magnitude of the overall economic crisis. Yet the Government could not relax its legislative hold over wages at that juncture no matter how marginal, or even ineffective, the incomes policy was now seen to be. When it is not feasible to relax, the temptation psychologically is to tighten the grip. This is what seemed to happen when Ray Gunter, at the Ministry of Labour, stopped a pay rise of £1 a week which had already been conceded to 77,000 municipal busmen in provincial undertakings. Most of them were members of the TGWU, and the Government veto looked very much like an invitation to Frank Cousins to try his luck in confrontation with his former Cabinet colleagues.

Gunter was perfectly within his rights in stopping the pay rise because it violated a report from the Prices and Incomes Board – published one week *after* the busmen's pay deal. There is little doubt that both sides had a very shrewd idea of what the PIB report would recommend, which was an increase of 10s. a week linked with proposals for greater productivity, such as the extension of one-man-operated buses. When that report was finally published Gunter told Cousins that since the pay deal was outside the recommendations of the PIB the Government had no option but to freeze it.

No doubt Ray Gunter extracted some quiet personal pleasure from putting Cousins on the spot in this way, but from then on for virtually the rest of the year the conflict between the Government's wages policy and the TGWU rumbled on. The policy was already crumbling, but it is probably justifiable to claim that Frank Cousins's unrepentant hostility through that year contributed critically to its final collapse. Certainly Harold Wilson holds him almost personally responsible for its failure, particularly as a result of his opposition in 1967–8, though this is almost certainly carrying Cousins's responsibility too far. There were deeper social, political and economic, reasons for its collapse. Yet it is a fact that Frank Cousins's unremitting campaign against the illogicalities and even the irrelevance of the Government's wages policy helped to concentrate the force of the opposition and added the touch of personal drama. Indeed, the deadlock over the municipal busmen's wage deal came to dominate much of his final full year as TGWU General Secretary, to the point where it effectively wrecked his compact with George Woodcock in trying to turn the TUC into a really successful central authority.

Cousins recognised that the Government was as trapped by its own legislation as he was by his commitment to fight it. Nevertheless he used the dispute quite ruthlessly against his former colleagues, and he also used it to justify his retreat from continuing to support the TUC policy of a voluntary wages discipline. At that year's special conference of the TUC, held on 28 February in Croydon, the TGWU cast its vote of 1,428,000 against the Woodcock policy of voluntary pay restraint. Cousins did this because he no longer saw any reason to support it in the hope that by doing so it might persuade the Government to soften its legislative code. It is true that at that February conference the TUC policy won a majority, but of a mere 536,000 votes. The Congress split almost evenly, 4,620,000 for the policy, against 4,084,000. It was a victory which simply underlined defeat; a victory without meaning. In his speech Cousins sounded the death knell of the TUC's attempt to organise an effective voluntary policy of wage restraint. And he explained his recantation like this.

I think the Government have shown during the last few months that they are not prepared to let us do the job which we say we can do. My organisation at the last conference gave its support to the idea of doing a voluntary job. We have now been allowed to do that. We are not to be allowed to continue to try to do the job. You know that there are threats about [further] legislation. We have now been given the idea that if we vote against this report there will be legislation [ie, to tighten still further the Government's control over pay negotiations].

Cousins also pointed to the indifference shown by the Confederation of British Industry to the TUC's initiative and claimed that this, plus the attitude of the Government, effectively nullified the TUC's proposals of the previous year.

George Woodcock was a rueful and disappointed man after that conference. He knew he had lost the fight to give the TUC the power that might have turned it into an institution with new influence, and possibly with the muscle to bargain with Government in a way not previously tried. He did not reign at the TUC long enough to see that vision materialise. It was for his successors to move closer towards that objective after 1974, but then in very different circumstances. Whatever might come in the future, whatever tentative foundations had been laid (and *they were* laid), Wood-cock realised in February that they would not bear fruit in his period as TUC General Secretary. He was due to retire at the same time as Frank Cousins. Woodcock resigned himself to the consequences of history, there was little else he could do. He knew that the derisory majority he won would do no more than confirm the view, already held by the majority in the Cabinet, that the TUC could not play an effective role unaided by legislation. It had neither the will nor the capacity – at least that was the prevailing view in Government, which Woodcock had sought to contest. He knew he could no longer hope to advance his case with any conviction.

On the other hand Frank Cousins was right in pointing out that legislation was already in draft form well *before* 28 February, and that the Government was taking a somewhat cynical view of the TUC's efforts at voluntary pay policy. A new White Paper on Productivity, Prices and Incomes was issued in April and a new Bill followed on 13 May. Its main purpose was to extend and supplement the Acts of 1966 and 1967, both of which were to remain in force in conjunction with the 1968 Act providing a formidable legislative armoury. The new Bill gave the Government additional powers to delay by up to twelve months wage and price increases, to require price cuts in some instances, to limit dividends, and to control rents. Ministers still insisted that they would have preferred to rely on the TUC's volun-tary system. But after the vote at the special Congress the Prime Minister explained that it would have been far too risky to leave the policing of any wages policy to the TUC, alone and unaided. The truth is that the Govern-ment always knew there was little prospect that the TUC would secure a large enough vote at that conference to satisfy the terms and conditions which the Cabinet still attached to incomes policy, as a central feature of its economic design. The policy may have been crushed, but it had not been abandoned – largely because Ministers had no clear idea of what to put in its place. That was to come a year later with 'In Place of Strife'.

One of the interesting by-products of that special TUC conference at Croydon was a new alliance – between Frank Cousins and Hugh Scanlon, the recently elected President of the Amalgamated Union of Engineering Workers (then called the AEU or the AEF). It was far too soon to talk of a Cousins-Scanlon axis (and indeed it would have been quite wrong to do so at any time, since the alliance did not operate like that). Yet the fact remained that the combined strength of the Transport Workers and the Engineering Union was now joined against the Wilson Government's wages policy for the first time since Cousins's resignation. It looked like a formidable part-nership, and speculation about its future potential was heightened when Cousins and Scanlon joined to head up a list of 66 left-wing sponsors of a new 'Socialist Charter' programme launched by *Tribune*. The 'Charter' put forward an eight-point programme of socialist objectives for the Labour Party, which can be summarised as follows :

> Economic independence for Britain; a firm commitment to Socialist planning; a big extension of public ownership; the re-distribution of wealth; an expansion of democracy throughout industry and throughout all public bodies; ending racial, religious and sex discrimination in jobs; an independent foreign policy – and one which puts world disarmament at the centre of its focus; the re-organisation of the Labour Party's own structure along socialist and democratic lines to make it more responsive to popular control and influence.

It would be easy to be sardonic about such a list of predictable objectives. Certainly there was nothing particularly novel or unusual about this programme, which was no more than a reaffirmation of the covenant. It secured the predictable support of many left-wing MPs, academics and trade union leaders who had been traditionally on the Left. Even the support of Frank Cousins and Hugh Scanlon was not calculated to raise anyone's eyebrows. Yet the timing of the 'Charter' *was* important. With the Labour Movement, not just the Government, in considerable confusion about future policy, and widespread disenchantment, ideological uncertainty and self-questioning among socialists, the *Tribune* group believed the time was ripe for an emphatic restatement of a socialist programme. No one had any great belief that this would materially influence the Government. But it was considered necessary to set down again the broad political parameters within which the Labour Movement ought to be thinking and operating. Nor was it an act of simple caprice or chance that Frank Cousins's name was at the head of the sponsors. He had established a close connection with *Tribune*, not least because of his friendship with Michael Foot. Since his return to the union Cousins had approved the appointment of Jack Jones to the Editorial Board of *Tribune*, and the TGWU frequently responded generously to financial appeals by the paper. Recalling the political orientation of the TGWU in pre-Cousins days it is remarkable to find, in the 1968 minutes of the TGWU executive, a declaration that *Tribune* was regarded as 'the last major national newspaper firmly committed to the Trade Union and Labour Movement'.[1]

Shortly after the TUC's special conference in February the Government was shaken by an escalation of economic and political tremors which again raised the question of survival – at the least of Harold Wilson's survival as Prime Minister. (This was the period in which Cecil Harmsworth King, then chairman of the Daily Mirror Newspaper group (IPC), wrote his famous, or notorious, front-page editorial 'Enough is Enough' (*Daily Mirror* 10 May 1968). As a result he was forced to quit as the *Mirror*'s emperor while Wilson remained Prime Minister.) From early March there was a

---

1. TGWU Executive Official Minutes, Minute 34, 11 January 1968.

further run on sterling and a fresh bout of speculation about another devaluation. The gravity of these events was magnified by one of those astonishing flurries over the price of gold in world markets which threatened all the major currencies, including the dollar, and which on that occasion seemed to have been engineered by the French. It was at this point – indeed due to an incident ostensibly connected with the gold crisis – that George Brown chose to resign as Foreign Secretary. In doing so, he made it clear to the world that he could no longer serve in a Government headed by Harold Wilson.

This was not so much a climax as a prelude to still further sensations. At Easter, quickly following Roy Jenkin's first Budget as Chancellor of the Exchequer (which Wilson himself has described as 'the most punishing budget in Britain's peacetime history') a Cabinet reshuffle brought Barbara Castle to the Ministry of Labour (renamed Department of Employment and Productivity) replacing Ray Gunter, who was moved (with deep reluctance and resentment on his part) to the Ministry of Power. Gunter stayed there a mere three months before he, too, resigned from the Cabinet on the same grounds as George Brown – he could not serve under Wilson's leadership. A few weeks before his resignation the report of the Royal Commission on the unions (the Donovan Commission) had been published. Gunter had appointed that Commission, after a good deal of resistance from the TUC as well as the reluctance of several of his own Cabinet colleagues; he had steered it, nurtured it and looked upon it as his principal Ministerial task to pick up the final report and use it to develop an improved system of industrial relations. So Gunter was enraged by the decision to move him from the Ministry of Labour at that moment. When he did quit the Government he exploded with a series of denunciations of the Prime Minister and indeed the whole style and character of the Wilson Government. Eventually Gunter resigned from Parliament and indeed from the Labour Party. His articles in the Press after he resigned contained anguished examinations of the emptiness of Government, as he saw it, as well as expressions of his own personal bitterness.

In the middle of 1968 the Government was suffering from an acute crisis of confidence and confusion of objectives. Cousins knew this well enough, even if he no longer had access to the Cabinet papers. He sensed what had made Brown and Gunter explode, though he had little or no sympathy with either. He recognised in their reaction to Wilson's leadership aspects of his own frustration in Cabinet, the feeling of strangled impotence to change the course of events or, less ambitiously, to persuade the Government collectively to be bolder, more imaginative and above all to provide the nation with a dimension of leadership and vision which alone might be able to rally a dispirited and uncertain people. Cousins felt all these impulses as strongly in 1968 as he had two years earlier when he had quit the Government.

His more immediate task remained the fight over the municipal busmen's pay deadlock. But he was not itching for a full-scale battle with the Government. He saw no virtue in being baited into calling the busmen into an official strike against the pay policy. Some of the busmen's delegates were calling for official strike action, but Cousins persistently persuaded them that this would not be a sensible tactic. At first he tried to stall off the strike call by seeking legal advice on the possibility of an injunction against the municipal authorities – purely a gesture, of course. In the event legal advice urged him not to pursue this line on the grounds that it would simply amount to a costly waste of time. An article in the TGWU *Record* in March, signed by the bus section leadership, revealed the union's dilemma with great candour :

> Many of our members will want to know how the union is going to react to the challenge . . . The short answer is that we are going to resist it. But we will fight it on the ground of our own choosing not of the Government's. The union has had the experience before of finding a group of its members to bear the whole brunt of the Government's attack on wages. We found ourselves in this position in the London bus strike of 1958. Many of the municipal busmen have already been involved in industrial action (unofficially) over the wages claim last November and December. The Government no doubt calculated that public opinion, alarmed by the devaluation crisis would rally to their support if there were a major strike now in municipal transport . . . the union have decided not to move into a trap. We are resolved to defeat this attack on the living standards of our members. But we will do so in our own way and in our own grounds.

This was no more than a clarion call to retreat in the face of the Government's legislative barriers. And it once again raised the old question about Frank Cousins's bark being worse than his bite; that he was ready to wound, but afraid to kill. Indeed he did not once independently lead his troops into battle against the Government's wages policy; he resisted a frontal attack, despite all his verbal hostility to the policy. Nor is there any evidence that he was anything but cautious, and even actively restraining, when confronted with demands from his rank and file for 'more positive action'. Cousins would not lead his men into a fight he knew they would not win. Nor would he risk exposing the basic weakness of his position for the sake of a few heroic gestures.

The experience of the London busmen's strike, however fulfilling at the time, had taught Cousins several lessons. With a union as amorphous as the TGWU he knew it was essential to make sure there was at least a fifty-fifty chance of winning before starting to fix bayonets. He knew that in a frontal assault against the pay policy, given the overall political and economic climate of 1968, he could *not* win – certainly not with the municipal busmen acting as his Praetorian Guard. There was another factor in Cousins's reluctance to draw his sword against the Government – his feeling of loyalty to the Labour Movement and its Government, however much he disagreed with its wages policy. At that late stage in his career he was certainly not going to court the accusation of disloyalty. Nor was this instinct a mere rationalisation to conceal the weakness of his tactical position. Cousins was always a man deeply committted to the principles of group loyalty – from the moment he first joined a trade union as a young miner in Yorkshire, loyalty to his group was an overriding impulse. He would fight within it, but if in the end open conflict meant its possible destruction then he would flinch. Whatever the faults of the Wilson Government in 1968, or at any other time, Cousins was not prepared to go into open industrial battle against them. To have done so would have comforted and benefited the enemy. That was not part of Cousins's catechism. His dilemma was similar to that of Aneurin Bevan's in the 1950s, to attack, to criticise, fundamentally to question – but never to destroy.

I recall Cousins in April 1968 confessing to a sense of frustration at the Government's handling of the wages question and at the degree of provocation he felt he was under. Yet what could he do? Lead an open rebellion against his old colleagues in the Cabinet? In his last year of office? To be sure, he realised that a number of people, on the Left as well as his old right-wing foes, were criticising his apparent inertia. They said he was 'funking a fight', that he had 'mellowed'. Well, he reflected, let it be so, let them say what they like. He saw no purpose in taking action which might lead to the fall of the Government. Interviewed by the BBC on 28 July 1968, Cousins admitted that he felt more dispirited about the relationship between the Labour Party and the trade union movement than he had ever felt before. None the less, he did not wish to 'get into conflict with the Government,' and added, 'it is my Government'.

The usual rain of accusations – that he was a purely 'propaganda militant' – came from Left and Right. He did not like the barracking, worst of all the spuriously sophisticated derision from the editorial columns of the right-wing press. But he could do little about it, so he shut his mind to the critics, though their gibes penetrated his thin skin. In fact there was neither a sensible nor a realistic alternative to his policy.

In July the delegates representing the 77,000 municipal busmen voted 37 to 19 for a nationwide strike. They did so knowing that the union and its leaders could be fined up to £500 under the Prices and Incomes Act – or its officials jailed for non-payment. Cousins warned that meeting that a strike would be little more than an 'irritant' to the Government, but would achieve no significant success. It would be better in his view to wait until the twelve-month freeze was over then claim back-pay. Cousins's advice was rejected. The strike was fixed for 12 August. But three days before it was due to start Cousins managed to persuade the delegates to change their minds – instead of an all-out strike they agreed to press the municipalities to settle for local agreements, with productivity clauses. If these were not agreed, then it would be open to the busmen to use local pressure.

There was a series of local skirmishes through the autumn until in December, after many frustrated meetings at all levels (many of them with Barbara Castle), the busmen's dispute was settled for what the unions had been demanding all along. After three imposed delays by Government the £1 a week pay rise was agreed and back-dated to 14 December 1967. The Government had no further power to stop the increase, nor to prevent local authorities paying the back-log of pay since the original agreement of 1967. In many ways this was the final snub to its policy. At the December agreement unions and employers echoed each other in suggesting that the agreement marked the end of the incomes policy, as well as making a fair nonsense of much that had happened during the twelve months of anguished negotiations. On the other hand the Government had managed to delay an important pay claim for a year despite all the political and industrial pressure from the country's largest union and its warrior general secretary. It had not been entirely without success.

The renewed inflationary pressures in 1968, with the allied growth of industrial militancy, has been described by some analysts as being at least partly due to devaluation having been left too late. In the strictly technical sense there must be truth in this. Yet in a broader social context it is hard to see how the explosion could have been averted regardless of the timing of devaluation – at least not without the suspension of traditional freedoms enjoyed by trade unions in a liberal society. This was, as always, the dilemma. The build-up of popular expectations, the organic growth in a popular assumption of rising living standards (an assumption which not only feeds on itself but is sedulously fostered by the market economy processes) and the failure of traditional institutions in Britain (not just the trade unions) to respond to the new political and industrial challenges – precipitated by the new forces at work in society – all of these were, and remain, part of the continuing crisis. The politics of the 1960 were increasingly imprisoned by the 'more now' syndrome.

The attempts made in the first half of 1968 to tackle the problem by public expenditure cuts, modest, it is true, and a heavily deflationary Budget, were merely followed by a faster increase in money wages and a renewed burst of trade union militancy. Each development had its own generating influence on the other.

Yet merely to state that one reaction was the result of another is to oversimplify. There was a mood afoot in Britain, a mood of revolt against authority, a cynical conviction that politicians had failed and that slogans were empty : cheap goods in a faded shop window. There was a contempt for governing institutions (even the executives of trade unions) and in belief itself. The totem which beckoned with increasing allure was that of material rewards and the contagion was by no means confined to currency speculators or single-minded denizens of the market place – it infected the shop floor. And why not? By the 1970s it came to resemble a national disease – though no more so than similar diseases known to other societies. What does now seem clear is that the flowering of the weed came strongly in the later nineteen-sixties.

Yet was it primarily a British disease? Did the sickness reflect the absence of some commonly accepted, and acceptable, social-political goal? Was there in British society a profound absence of conviction and commitment? Almost certainly the answer is 'yes'. In the United States a tired and war-wearied administration under Lyndon B. Johnson was near the end of its tether, and its period. The results of Vietnam had already produced quite exceptional social problems for American society. In April 1968 the British Chancellor of the Exchequer, Roy Jenkins, was telling journalists, privately, that the whole western world faced its worst post-war economic crisis.

Jenkins believed that the British situation was, by comparison, not nearly as severe as the American condition. He saw the American economy, reflecting the state of American society, in a condition of real crisis with the world standing of the dollar mirroring that condition. Although the pound sterling was still under great pressure, and a further devaluation certainly could not be ruled out, the fact was that the pound, in the Chancellor's opinion, was under-valued against the dollar. It is an argument that has a certain familiar ring to it.

As far as the British economy was concerned it was clear, by the middle of 1968, that the merits and rewards of a formal prices and incomes policy had been practically exhausted. Certainly it was no longer regarded in Whitehall as being of real importance in medium or longer-term economic strategy. If Frank Cousins was fighting a battle on an issue that was no longer at the centre of policy then so, too, was the Government. They were all locked in their postures. The difference was that the Cousins campaign for a wages policy based on broader concepts of industrial efficiency and the redevelopment and modernisation of British industry was in fact a far sounder long-term strategy than the Government's – assuming it had one at all. In fact it is arguable whether, by the time of the busmen's settlement, the so-called incomes policy had merely become a technical ritual rather than a meaningful instrument of policy. It was tending to be used rather as an instrument of labour discipline than a piece of economic strategy. It therefore had some effect only in those areas where trade unions were at their weakest, or, as in the case of the municipal busmen, as a token resist-

ance by the Government to try to prove that something of the spirit of
incomes policy was still alive.

In several senses Frank Cousins was already preparing for his retirement
from the TGWU. His practice of visiting all the regions and speaking at
their annual 'festivals' was carried out with even more than his usual con-
scientousness. At these festivals Cousins devoted many speeches to the theme
of releasing British industry from the 'stranglehold' of legislative control
over wages, and therefore over productivity. He also urged, with increasing
vehemence, that the trade union movement should take up the drive for
industrial democracy by encouraging more shop-floor bargaining and local
productivity deals. He recognised that this would weaken the role of centralised wages bargaining and indeed perhaps further weaken the influence
of national officials, but he believed this was part of an inescapable process
already under way which the trade union leadership ought to guide rather
than resist. He was *not* saying 'all power to the shop floor'; he was saying
that power is there, is increasing and should therefore be accepted by both
sides of industry and used to the best advantage of the national economy.

Cousins believed and argued that there was immense productive potential
in a more positive use of shop-floor power and talent; the ideas and enterprise of the worker, under characteristic capitalist industrial management,
were not only wasted but discouraged. Cousins was his own mentor in this
conviction, but Jack Jones added an important and perhaps more methodical
dimension to his thinking and even to his speeches. Jones had been chairman of the Labour Party's national executive sub-committee on industrial
democracy in 1966–7, and this was the formal origin of much that has now
developed on the subject. Jones was a man with a high reputation for local
productivity bargaining in the Midlands. When he came to London as,
effectively, Frank Cousins's heir apparent, he began by acting as a kind of
national organiser, actively building up a strong force of local contacts among
rank-and-file members, shop-stewards and officials. This was the basis of
Jack Jones's strength in the TGWU: a basis which, later, was to provide
him with such an immensely powerful and influential platform. Cousins
did everything to help Jack Jones. At each regional conference in his final
year he encouraged Jones to make an increasing number of key speeches on
union and national policy. At the same time the name of J. L. Jones
appeared with greater frequency in the TGWU *Record*: sometimes to the
irritation of Jones's critics in the union, who resented the manner in which
Cousins was actively preparing the way for his successor – which usually
implied that they resented Jones's politics rather more than what Cousins
was doing.

Long before the machinery for the election of Frank Cousins's successor
was set in motion no one was in any serious doubt who would be the

next general secretary of the country's largest trade union. Quite apart from issues of personality, or even political policies, Jack Jones's imprint on the union was already seen clearly in the development of greater authority in the regional groupings of the TGWU and a distinctive move away from the traditionally commanding role played by national officials in the various trade groups. At the quarterly meeting of the TGWU executive in May 1968 the official record refers to the General Executive Council accepting Cousins's view 'that the union's policy of decentralisation of industrial nego-tiating in the direction of local officials and Lay Representation would serve the national economic growth much better than any attempt to achieve rigid governmental control.'[2]

Even more demanding was the emotional and psychological preparation for handing over to a new General Secretary. The formal preparation for the election of a new General Secretary began in May when the TGWU execu-tive agreed to the procedure governing nominations, timing of voting and eligibility. Shortly after that Cousins agreed to an appointment – his first really external commitment – as part-time chairman of the Industrial Train-ing Council, of which he was already a member and an ardent supporter. This was one of the jobs he was to retain after his retirement. He was already trying to condition himself to retirement. He knew it would be a phenom-enally difficult re-adjustment, despite his claims that he was ready to stand aside. In one sense his path to retirement was made slightly easier by the surprise appointment of Harry Nicholas as General Secretary of the Labour Party. Frank Cousins was aware of the backstage manœuvring going on to find a successor to Len Williams, the retiring General Secretary, but he was not at first aware of the nature of Harry Nicholas's involvement in the 'plot' to keep out Tony Greenwood.

Cousins knew that Nicholas was one of a number of names being con-sidered. Harold Wilson admits to mentioning Nicholas as a possibility in April 1968 to George Brown. Yet at that stage Nicholas was not regarded as a strong candidate, partly because of his age – like Cousins he was near-ing retirement age – and partly because Alfred (now Lord) Allen, Tony (now Lord) Greenwood, Sir Fred Hayday, and even Ray Gunter were all regarded as better bets. Greenwood was the favourite, because most people assumed he was the man Harold Wilson wanted in the job – though Wilson has denied this.

In the event Nicholas beat Greenwood by 14 votes to 12. That vote was the signal for a renewal burst of speculation about Wilson's future as Party leader and Prime Minister. Ray Gunter, who had resigned from the Cabinet the previous month, was one of the main architects of Nicholas's success, and Gunter's principal allies on that occasion were Jim Callaghan and George Brown. Some members of Wilson's Cabinet at that time still insist

2. TGWU Official Minutes: Minute 342, GEC, 27 May 1968, p. 96.

this was the opening shot in a fresh bid to unseat Wilson and that it very nearly came off. It has been put to me by several Ministers who were close to what was happening that the Gunter-Callaghan-Brown axis was fully mounted for the overthrow of Wilson and that Jim Callaghan was probably the main candidate for the leadership. According to Wilson's own accounts the WMG (Wilson-Must-Go) group ran a highly professional campaign and was still actively at work in April 1969, at the time of the Government's crisis over 'In Place of Strife'.

Frank Cousins was certainly aware of this intrigue. But the evidence I have suggests that his knowledge of the part played by Harry Nicholas came somewhat late in the day. At any rate, although he did nothing to discourage Nicholas's appointment it would be rash to claim that he was an enthusiastic supporter. Against this the fact remains that Nicholas's departure did clear the way, decisively, for Jack Jones's succession. The only mildly serious challenge to Jones came from Robert Davis, one of the senior national officials, who secured the next best number of nominations to Jones – 15 to Jones's 155. There was never a serious threat to Jones's succession – Cousins ensured that. Even if Nicholas had remained he would not have challenged Jones since his age was against him, despite his continuing disappointment at the way he had been brushed aside when Frank Cousins returned to the union. What can be claimed is that Nicholas's departure fragmented much of the anti-Jones (and anti-Cousins) grouping inside the top echelons of the TGWU, and to that extent made the passage for Jack Jones much easier.

What was Cousins's attitude toward the WMG plotters? He never once wavered in his belief that the intriguers should be stopped and even exposed. Cousins was characteristically opposed to intrigues of all kind. He angered and confused many of his friends on the Left of the TUC General Council because he consistently rejected their invitation that he should join with them – even lead them – in a united left-wing bloc on the TUC. His almost contemptuous dismissal of such ploys led to intense displeasure among them – most of all from the fiery Robert Willis, the printers' leader, who was convinced that Cousins threw away the chance to turn the TUC into a more powerful left-wing force by his rejection of a 'Leftist Working Together' group. Bill Jones, the left-wing chairman of the TGWU General Executive Council, and a member of the TUC General Council, frequently expressed astonishment at Cousins's refusal to join in any organised intrigue. He has told me : 'One of the strange aspects of his thinking which puzzled me and which I took up with him was his apparent inability or wish to join up with or organise if you like those who thought along with him on issues. He told me that he was against cliques and was not prepared to be a General for this purpose.'

Why should Cousins feel sympathy for Harold Wilson as the focus of intrigues in 1968–9? Partly because he regarded the alternatives as much worse than the reigning Caesar; but most of all because it was not Cousins's style. He had no stomach for the murder of political leaders to satisfy other men whose policies were secondary to their dubious personal ambitions. This was why he came to Wilson's rescue at the Labour Party conference that autumn with a show of support that astonished many observers. Despite the shattering defeat for the Government's wages policy both at the Trades Union Congress and again on the opening day of the Party conference at Blackpool, Frank Cousins thundered out a grave warning to any would-be political assassin of Harold Wilson: 'Do it at your peril.' At the Party conference he led the applause in a standing ovation for the Prime Minister after a superb Wilsonian speech to rally the Labour Party. Not since his resignation had Cousins given Wilson such a welcoming response. That night Cousins commented on his own behaviour – which was the talk of the Blackpool hotels:

> It was a demonstration of our satisfaction at his leadership and the fact that we recognise him as leader of the Labour Government and that we certainly have no wish for him to be changed for anyone else either within the Party or from another Party, as Prime Minister. If we have differences with him over legislation about incomes policy then our differences are over that – and not over his continued leadership of the Movement. You can be sure that our union will be working for the maintenance of a Labour Government.

A somewhat novel interpretation of Cousins's motivations came to me from Lord Robens (then chairman of the National Coal Board), a shrewd and experienced, if jaundiced, observer of Labour conferences:

> Cousins was determined to give Wilson a knock-out blow on incomes policy; this he achieved on the opening day of the conference with a five to one majority against the Government's policy. Having done that, and satisfied his vanity, and vindicated his beliefs, he was ready to give Wilson a helping hand. He had proved to the Prime Minister that on the issue of wages policy he, Cousins, had the unions behind him – and Wilson did not. So then Frank was ready to help his foe. It is typical of the working man. Have a scrap, then buy your opponent a glass of beer. I'll bet anything that when Frank Cousins was a lorry driver and had a punch-up he'd be the first to buy the other bloke a cup of tea in a roadside cafe. It is typical working class psychology.

It also transpired that Cousins himself had come under renewed pressure to reconsider his own position as a potential leader of the Labour Party. A number of left-wing MPs had approached him again that year, and were to do so again in the spring of 1969 during the great conflict over 'In Place of Strife', urging him to return to Parliament. Their objective was to persuade Cousins to lead the Left-wing in the House of Commons and then to make a bid for leadership in the Parliamentary Labour Party. Cousins resisted that invitation as firmly as he had rejected other intrigues against the leadership. If he was to fight Establishment views he was determined to do so with clean hands and by concentrating on policies, rather than becoming involved in a bitter, personal contest.

. Throughout 1968 Cousins was primarily concerned with the internal affairs of the union. Above all he was consumed by the traumatic sense of impending departure from his personal involvement in running this great union and the emotional conflicts which this realisation created within his own personality. Trade union leaders before him (and those who followed) have found this inner conflict quite the most difficult of all their self-reflective wrestlings. The bigger the power base the more difficult the problem. Even in his strongest and most assertive period at the Foreign Office, Ernest Bevin, virtually number two in Attlee's Cabinet, could never quite forget the fact that he had been General Secretary of the TGWU and was frequently tempted to pick up the phone to instruct Arthur Deakin how to run the union. Cousins believed he could resist this temptation, but as the final days drew closer his self-doubts increased. In particular he scanned the horizon for issues left incomplete, for sensitive areas that had been shelved. He wanted to leave the empire fit for his already defined successor, Jack Jones, to inherit, and to make sure that there were no serious impediments in Jones's path. One of these impediments was the ban on members of the Communist Party holding elected office within the TGWU. It was an issue which Cousins had ducked for long enough, not because he had any sympathy with the ban but because he had always found reasons to avoid a frontal challenge on the question.

Since 1948 Communists had, of course, been barred from holding any union post whether as lay or full-time officials. The rule, as we will recall, was drawn up during Arthur Deakin's reign as General Secretary, and despite the fact that opposition to the ban had grown since Deakin's death Cousins had never felt confident enough to make its removal a major issue. Of course he had always opposed it. Indeed his opposition to it during Deakin's period in leadership was so strong that it merely added to Deakin's suspicion that Cousins was indeed an under-cover Communist. In those days Cousins flatly rejected Deakin's assertion that the Communists were set upon a deliberate and calculated policy of industrial sabotage and were intent on using the union to achieve a narrow political objective.

Cousins's view then was that any general overall restriction of the kind Deakin imposed was thoroughly undemocratic, certainly un-socialist and, what was more important to his practical mind, counter-productive from the union's point of view. It would not remove the threat of Communist activities (if that was the motive behind the Deakin ban) but would drive those activities into different channels. If, as Deakin asserted, the Communists were a threat, then, argued Cousins, better to deal with that threat in the open. For Cousins the real test of a member's integrity and worth was his loyalty to the basic concepts and ideals of the wider Labour Movement. That was where he always stood on the issue of the Communist ban. He believed that a crude anti-communist witch-hunt was a travesty of what a trade union was supposed to be about. Moreover he had always regarded the original Deakin ban as an exaggerated, somewhat hysterical, reaction which tended to inflate the importance of the Communist Party's role in the uinon and its potential to cause trouble. So in his closing months as General Secretary of the TGWU the removal of the ban became an issue of critical importance.

Yet there remains a question of equally great importance which must be answered : why had he waited so long to face up to the Communist ban? Why was it that even in those latter days of his own powerful control over the TGWU machine did he have to be strongly urged, if not critically influenced, by Jack Jones? Because indeed that was the case.

From the moment of Cousins's election as General Secretary most senior people inside the union were convinced that he would choose to remove the ban at an early stage. Some of the older hierarchy were astonished that he let the years drift by without doing so and one or two have told me that they were all the more surprised since Cousins had confided to them, before his election, that he would lift the ban at the first convenient moment.

Why then did he shirk it for so long?

The most commonly heard answer to this question is that Cousins was too unsure of his support from the rank and file as well as from senior officials of the union to take the risk. This view (it is true that this is argued mainly by those senior officials who had been close to Deakin and in agreement with the ban) bases its strength on the fact that Cousins was over-extended in his fight to radicalise the union in his first five years as General Secretary and regarded the removal of the ban on Communists as an issue of much less political (and industrial) significance than, say, the fight for nuclear disarmament or the loosening of the reins on industrial militancy and wages policy. It is further argued that, in those first five or six years in particular, Cousins was too exposed to the taunts, especially from the still powerful Deakin-oriented union machine, that his predecessor's suspicions about Cousins's political associations might have been true. So he played it safe.

Of course Cousins knew that his was almost a lone voice among the older national officials in believing that Deakin's ban on the Communists had been a mistake. He was aware, acutely aware in fact, of the watchfulness of those officials. He felt himself to be under constant scrutiny and this made his bristling personality even more sensitive. Moreover, he did not believe the Communist issue was of such fundamental importance as to warrant making a difficult situation (it will be recalled that this was in the period of growing alienation with Hugh Gaitskell) even more difficult. So he allowed the first flush of his new leadership period to slip by. Somehow to his critics on the Left, it seemed that Frank Cousins could always find good logical reasons for shirking the issue. After the busmen's strike and the clash with Gaitskell over the Bomb came the period prior to the 1964 General Election – an especially sensitive political period with Wilson succeeding Gaitskell. Cousins reasoned with himself that to scrap the ban on Communists at that point would merely excite his critics on the Right, inside the Labour Party as well as in the Press and the Conservative Party. Inside and outside the union, as well.

There was another factor behind which Cousins sought protection. Several of the leading Communists who lost their union posts as a result of the Deakin ban had since quit the Communist Party, and, in turn, resumed full-scale activity within the TGWU. These included nationally known figures such as Bill Jones, the London busmen's leader who had been on the union executive at the time of the ban on Communists, and a full-time national official in passenger transport, Sam Henderson. Both of them resumed their earlier posts.

None the less, there are a number of critics on the Left (non-Communists as well as Communist Party members) who still claim that Cousins's failure to remove the ban before 1968 must be counted as one of his main failures. This would be the view of Bill Jones himself. Bill Jones (no relation to Jack Jones) was a constant thorn in Cousins's flesh, urging him on to bolder action. So too was Jack Jones. Both pressed him to remove the ban and both would have preferred earlier action. Even in 1968 there is evidence that it was the pressure and persuasion from Jack Jones which finally moved Cousins to scrap the ban. So the explanation that Frank Cousins deliberately fought shy of the issue must carry force. After all, what other reason could there be? He was not anti-Communist even though he had never been a Communist. He did not approve of the practical sense or the political morality of the ban. Nothing had changed in his mind since his initial opposition. So the answer must be that at first he was too unsure of himself, conscious of being surrounded by hostile critics ready to exploit any false move or mistimed step. He was ceaselessly embroiled in other major issues of time-consuming proportions. Time slipped by. There was always a reason at hand. Indeed it is possible that the ban would have remained for Jack Jones to remove had it not been for Jones's own insistence that Cousins must accept that responsibility before his retirement.

One other explanation put forward has been that Cousins was fearful of removing the ban in case it led to an explosion of left-wing power that he could not control. The advocates of this view tend to be old Deakin hands who never wanted the ban removed anyway. Theirs would seem a highly improbable theory. After all Cousins himself had released the strongest left-wing surge the trade union movement had witnessed since the war and he paved the way, consciously and deliberately, for Jack Jones to open up a further phase in that shop-floor revolution. It is hardly feasible that Cousins would believe that a removal of the ban on Communists would make his life all that more difficult. In any event, he was never the kind of leader who could be daunted by suggestions that there was a force (potential or real) in the union which could mount an effective challenge to his authority and his leadership.

No, the most attractive explanation is that Cousins had to leave it late because of the range of political battles he had chosen to fight, and having left it so late he felt genuinely embarrassed by the problem and would probably have left it to Jack Jones had his successor been prepared to accept those terms of inheritance. But Jones was not.

The removal ceremony was finally conducted at the union's rules revision conference in Belfast in July 1968 – one year from Cousins's retirement. Even then there was strong opposition from some delegates to the change in policy. Possibly this might seem in hindsight to justify Cousins's long-standing caution. But a more possible explanation is that there would have been opposition of various kinds at any stage.

Indeed, the amended rule, permitting Communists to serve again as union officials, was hedged round with all kinds of jargon-clothed qualifications. It was by no means a clear-cut expunging of the ban. What actually happened was that the rule barring Communists was replaced by a reworded clause (Clause 7 of Schedule 1) which states:

> Membership of an organisation which in the opinion of the General Executive Council is contrary, detrimental, inconsistent or injurious to the policy and purposes of the union will render the member liable to be declared ineligible to hold any office within the union either as a lay member or as a permanent or full time officer, or such other penalties as in the opinion of the GEC shall seem just.

In short, the rule was amended to give the union's executive discretion where, previously, the ban on Communists (and fascists) had been mandatory. At the time of the Belfast conference the *Record* observed: 'It was felt that this provided the union with a fair and effective system of protection against any disruptive action.'[3]

So it was done. Cousins finally, haltingly, corrected what he had always regarded as one of the more unjust and unnecessary actions dating back to the era of his old foe and predecessor, Arthur Deakin. It came late in the day. It had come after a period of delay which surprised and disappointed many of Cousins's earliest supporters and admirers.

3. TGWU *Record*, August 1968.

It was all the more surprising since Frank Cousins's outstanding quality was one of robust iconoclasm. His uneasiness over removing the ban on Communists was out of character. And it can only be explained against the bckcloth of his other, at times, overwhelming preoccupations.

· By the time Frank Cousins took his seat at the 1968 Trades Union Congress the process of electing his successor was well advanced. He was moving to the climax of his career with an increasing feeling of inner tension and anxiety, despite all the outward protestations about his readiness to accept the inevitable. In a year's time, on 8 September 1969, he would be 65. The curtain would fall with absolute precision. So the 1968 TUC, and the Labour Party conference a few weeks later, were his final functional appearances on the grand stage of the Labour Movement : the last offerings from the rostrum to the assembled activists of the socialist forum. It is true that he would still be eligible to attend the 1969 Congress, but that would be largely to take his final farewells and his Gold Badge of Congress, before slipping out of the arena. In September 1968 the final year appeared, as it does to many who have reached the pinnacle of trade union power, as a daunting shadow which he pretended not to see. Not that he would be going out with a whimper. Given the political and economic situation of 1968–9 – and indeed the character of the man – there was scant chance of that.

Everything continued to point to a final year of exceptional problems in industry and the economy in general. It was already clear to most of the TUC hierarchy that there were serious and strong pressures behind the scenes in Whitehall to stiffen the recommendations of the Donovan Royal Commission, whose proposals had disappointed those who hoped for legislation against the trade unions, especially to cure the rash of strikes. Frank Cousins already feared the emergence of a set of twin restrictions on the unions – a wages policy, bolstered by an attempt to restrict the trade union freedom to strike. He had welcomed the general tone of the Donovan Commission Report when it was published in mid-1968, but he also added a warning that there were dangers ahead if some implications of the report were carried to excess. 'In Place of Strife' was still a gleam in the eye of the Department of Employment and Productivity, but Cousins had begun to sniff danger in the air. There is no doubt that this was very much in his mind when he moved a compositive motion at the Trades Union Congress which not only condemned the incomes policy legislation and demanded its repeal but also added, in what proved to be a prescient last sentence. 'It [the Congress] also rejects any further legislation the aim of which would be to curtail basic trade union rights.'

Cousins led this new onslaught on the Government's policy with all his old vehemence and command. He had not shifted from any of his basic convictions on wages policy or in his opposition to legal controls over the unions. And after two years in which he hovered over the idea of a TUC-controlled incomes policy he now came down flatly against that, too. Not that he had an easy victory at that TUC. Ranged against him were only a few voices but they carried a good deal of influence. The most notable was the late Sir Leslie Cannon, of the Electrical, Electronic and Plumbing Trades Union, who had long argued for a consistent policy of incomes restraint within the context of economic and industrial planning. He ridiculed the concept of a wages free-for-all, especially when it was advocated by socialists committed to economic planning. But Cannon was preaching to an audience of trade union officials most of whom, by the autumn of 1968, had had enough of the restrictions. The tide was moving relentlessly against incomes policy. Indeed the railway unions had brought their opposition to the brink of a national strike in July, and were bought off by the Railways Board and the Government with a somewhat dubious productivity formula known as the 'Penzance Peace Treaty'; the engineering unions were threatening a national stoppage over their pay claim (they called a one-day strike on 21 October); and the motor car industry was racked by waves of unofficial stoppages. Very few industries in the public or private sectors were free from this mounting tension. It was scarcely a surprise to any informed observer when the Congress overwhelmingly voted to support Frank Cousins's motion No. 9, in unconditional opposition to continuing the Government's wages policy.

The vote was a disastrous one for the Government: 7,746,000 to 1,022,000, the biggest trouncing since the policy was first introduced. Cannon's motion, urging support for the principle of incomes policy and planning, was crushed by a larger vote: 8,252,000 to 360,000. In the balcony of Congress, in the front row of the visitors' gallery, sat Barbara Castle. She did not attempt to conceal her feelings and called a news conference, shortly after the vote, to insist that the Government's policy would go on in spite of everything. But she also called the Prime Minister to warn him that the incomes policy was now perilously close to collapse. That was a rough day for George Woodcock, too. Woodcock, at what turned out to be his last TUC, saw so many of his hopes crash in ruins. His passionate plea for a voluntary policy ('an inevitable part of trade union development', he told that Congress) won a modest consolation. It was agreed by 4,693,000 to 3,935,000, a majority of 758,000 compared with the February majority of 536,000. But this was of little practical value. The mood of the Congress was with Frank Cousins. His sweeping victory was total and it effectively killed the kind of incomes policy that had existed since 1966. It also provided Cousins with a great deal of personal satisfaction: it seemed a fitting sequel to his resignation from the Government in 1966.

Overall, Cousins made a significant impact at the 1968 TUC. He topped the poll in the elections for the new General Council, for the first time since he joined the TUC hierarchy twelve years earlier. Even Cousins's enemies were heard murmuring reluctant words of praise for his stamina, even if they opposed his arguments.

Shortly after the Congress the TGWU executive met to finalise the arrangements for the election of a new General Secretary and Frank Cousins, a little wistfully, offered his advice to the assembly of the union leadership. His official report to the meeting went like this:

> I am somewhat reflective as I write this report as within weeks the membership is due to elect my successor. Without wishing to influence events I feel I have to stress my profound sense of the importance of the succession. The general secretaryship is not a position any member can undertake, lacking experience, training and judgment . . . Great is the responsibility vested in the person elected to represent the host of working people in different industries and trades who unite to form this union. Their future welfare is of paramount importance and it is necessary that they recognise the vital nature of the election and understand the requirements of the job to be done in the future if further progress is to be made.

That soliloquy on the leadership of the TGWU was not lost on the general executive. Cousins mentioned no name. It was not necessary. Everyone understood the point of his argument and the name he had in mind.

The Cousins style of rule over the TGWU was by no means universally acclaimed. It had always met a strong challenge from the political Right, chiefly from the older officials associated with the Deakin era. But it had also run into difficulties with some of the younger officials, who, without always having ulterior political motives, found the Cousins style as authoritarian on the Left as Deakin's had been on the Right. They also tended to regard the union's administration as rather cobwebbed and inefficient and were critical of a certain organisational complacency which was often concealed by Cousins's stature and national impact. Even the active Left in the TGWU sometimes complained about Cousins's failure to exploit sufficiently the potential to develop the union.

Basic administrative tasks like examining potential full-time officials were generally left to others – Harry Nicholas, latterly Jack Jones, or even national officials of the various trade groups. This infuriated the Left wing, who got the impression that Cousins disregarded this crucial area because he didn't want to be accused of behaving like 'a left-wing Deakin'. In fact Cousins who was not the best of delegators felt that this was a role for which his deputies and assistants were fitted, leaving him free to concentrate on major policy issues concerning the union. Others criticised Cousins for what they described as his 'one man rule' tendencies. This was particularly evident during the election campaign for the general secretaryship when two outsiders, Alan Thomson and Larry Smith, the union's bus section national secretary and his deputy, attacked Cousins's style of leadership in their election addresses which of course went to all union members. Thomson in particular, without mentioning Cousins by name, stressed that 'no one man is able to understand or realise the aims of an organisation such as ours. To imagine this is possible is to suggest an industrial power complex [and] this is something I cannot accept.' Smith took up Thomson's theme and developed it a stage further by proposing that the office of General Secretary should be limited to a period of four years, instead of for life, once elected, and no man should hold it for more than one term. This was a rather absurd proposal, but it was by no means unpopular in some quarters despite the weight of evidence that short-term periods of office in a trade union rarely if ever produce either worthwhile policies or lasting results.

Behind the Thomson-Smith candidature was a somewhat more sophisticated campaign for the 'democratisation' of the union as well as a drive against the leadership cult as it had been experienced since the days of Bevin. This was promoted through a pamphlet written by Tony Corfield, the secretary of the union's Political, Education and International Department. And it was this pamphlet, 'Collective leadership for the TGWU', rather than the Thomson-Smith election addresses, which caused the real fuss. Corfield, an extremely able, talented young official, was highly and quite unashamedly critical of the way the union had been run, and was no more impressed by its prospect under Jack Jones than by Frank Cousins's leadership. He knew he was courting vocational suicide in the TGWU (as, no doubt, in any other organisation). Corfield was brought before the union Executive, and reprimanded. Later he resigned – or rather was pushed. The executive accused him of behaving in a manner 'inimical to the union's best interests . . .' The 'Corfield affair' was no more than a modest rumbling of discontent, but it undoubtedly reflected a much wider measure of uneasiness than the union executive would have wished the outside world to believe. All the same there is little doubt that some of Corfield's criticisms have since found their way into practical reforms in the administration of the union. But it made no difference, of course, to the result.

Jack Jones triumphed with a huge vote. He polled 334,125 compared with his nearest rival, Bob Davies, who had 28,355, votes. Alan Thomson obtained 17,118 and came ninth out of ten candidates. Larry Smith, the other arch-critic of the 'leadership style', polled 22,487 and came fifth. Jack Jones obtained 64.4 per cent of the votes cast, and 40 per cent of the union's 1,500,000 members voted in the election – an unusually high percentage. Jack Jones was the new leader of Britain's biggest union, the central powerhouse of the Labour Movement. Frank Cousins had helped to steer his chosen successor to a predictable but none the less, overwhelming victory.

Now let us for a moment turn back again to the Labour Party conference of that year – the final Party conference for Frank Cousins – one in which he repeated his triumphs of the TUC not only by confirming the defeat of the Government's wages policy, at the hands of conference, but also by enhancing his personal stature as an outstanding figure of the Labour Movement. Again it was the Transport Union motion which dominated the wages debate and it was Frank Cousins who moved it, calling for the repeal of the prices and incomes legislation and rejecting any further laws 'which would curtail basic trade union rights'. The task of trying to turn aside the almost unanimous wrath of the unions was picked up by Barbara Castle. However, it needed more than her lioness courage to try to persuade the conference to reject the Cousins motion. Almost in desperation she offered to open a completely fresh dialogue with the unions about what should follow the prices and incomes legislation when it expired in the autumn of 1969. But she could do nothing to staunch the flow of trade union feeling. Frank Cousins won that vote by 5,098,000 to 1,240,000. Bad though that was for the Government's prestige and its internal morale, it might have been still worse had the Party's National Executive Committee also voted against the Government – and they almost did. On the eve of the conference the executive split 12 votes to 12 on the Cousins motion, and only the casting vote of the chairman, Jennie Lee (Baroness Lee), Aneurin Bevan's widow, saved the Government's face, though scarcely its reputation. Indeed the news leaked out from that executive meeting that there had been an unseemly brawl between George Brown and Jim Callaghan, the Home Secretary, over the future of wages legislation. Callaghan wanted the Executive to offer the conference a promise that the legislation would be dropped the following year. George Brown rounded on him and accused Callaghan of 'ratting' on a Cabinet decision. The atmosphere between the Ministers on the platform and the delegates in the body of the conference was as tense as it had been at any time since Scarborough in 1960 – and it was broken only by the superb speech of Harold Wilson which brought Cousins to his feet in thunderous acclamation of the Prime Minister's capacity to rally a Labour Party conference – especially that conference which appeared so divided and hostile.

It was at Blackpool that autumn that Jim Callaghan sounded Frank Cousins about a post-retirement job – the chairmanship of the proposed Community Relations Commission, which was about to be established under the new Race Relations Act. Cousins had been ambivalent about a post-retirement commitment. He had been discreetly tested by the Prime Minister's office about a seat in the House of Lords, about a Governorship in one of the remaining island territories under the Crown, and other items in the list of honours and jobs for the great and the good. He rejected all such feelers. His rooted objections to accepting such decorous but ineffectual occupations (as he considered them to be) were as strong a ever, if anything even stronger. On the other hand he was not averse to retaining some kind of 'platform', provided the role was socially and politically worth while. At the same time he was tired by the unremitting pressures of public life. Occasionally a tightness across the chest, a twinge of pain, would remind him of that scarred tissue near the heart. Nance was anxious for him to retire and rest, or at least to concentrate on that inevitable garden, preferably away from the London political hub with all its temptations of work. She would frequently look at him and see the blueness of his lips and a pinched facial reflex after a particularly difficult day or an exasperating encounter. She could read the signs and feared he would push himself too far, as was his characteristic impulse.

Nance wanted to make his retirement a literal fact. Yet that was hard, very hard, for a man of such vitality, strength of will and total commitment. His private life was, as always, close to the family, with only occasional external social distractions. Watching cricket or 'Match of the Day' on TV was as much a brief holiday for him as an abiding interest. His eldest son John was then a national officer in the TGWU and there was, without doubt, a strong pride in Frank Cousins's attitude towards him. There were also voices raised in not very silent protest about the possibility of a 'Cousins dynasty' in the TGWU. Yet he resisted, and resented, any suggestion that John Cousins owed his job selection to his name rather than his ability. The gossip helped neither father nor son. None the less when John decided to allow his name to go forward as a candidate for the assistant general secretaryship, for which Harry Urwin was already an outstanding favourite, Frank did not discourage the move. (Harry Urwin was appointed Assistant General Secretary at a special session of the union's executive council on 12 March 1969. The previous day the finance and general purposes committee of the union had shortlisted three candidates – Urwin, Douglas Farrar and John Cousins.) This did nothing to allay the suspicion that Frank would have liked to see his son following in father's footsteps : certainly it did nothing to help the relationship between Frank Cousins's successor and John Cousins. These thoughts, his own reflections on future paths, crowded into Frank Cousins's mind as he contemplated his final year and listened to the offer made by Jim Callaghan. It was hard for him to make up his mind about the chairmanship of the Community Relations Commission. When he did so it was with a certain doubt about whether he was the right man for that particular job – or, indeed, whether it was the sort of job he was looking for, if indeed he was 'looking' for anything.

Frank Cousins was, of course, profoundly committed to fighting racial prejudice. The commitment went deep into his roots. The Indian doctor who once helped to restore his injured mother, the chemistry of socialist humanitarian belief which had influenced him from the beginning, his later experiences visiting Asia, Africa and the sight of so much squalor, misery, hunger and disease in countries where a dark skin was synonymous with deprivation – the mixture of instinct, conviction and experience shaped the man into an obvious symbol of aid to underpriviledged. He decided to accept Callaghan's offer. Yet he was unsure of the organisational system that was being built around the new Race Relations Act and he remained sceptical throughout. The formal invitation came before the TGWU Executive in November and the union's finance and general purposes committee approved his appointment as part-time chairman until his retirement from the union, after which he would become full-time chairman. Shortly afterwards he was also appointed as a part-time member of the National Freight Corporation, which was being set up to start in January 1969 as a co-ordinating body for State-run freight transport.

Having decided to accept the chairmanship of the Community Relations Commission it was not surprising that Cousins's last speech to the Labour Party conference – on the fourth day of the 1968 conference – was on race relations. Of course no one in the audience quite appreciated the significance of a speech that was widely acclaimed as one of Cousins's best conference performances. It was regarded as the speech of a great humanist no doubt emotively inspired by an atmosphere of 'farewell to all this . . .' As John Beavan (Lord Ardwick) observed in the *Daily Mirror* the next day the conference 'melted in sentiment' when Cousins strode to the rostrum :

> This is the end of an epoch in the turbulent life of Labour. For 13 years Cousins has been the most powerful man on the conference floor, the leader of the mighty TGWU, the man whose care carried one million votes – one sixth of the entire strength of the Labour Party . . . Over all these years he has been a leader of every Left Wing cause . . . His last speech was in the purest tradition of Socialism, a plea for the brotherhood of man, for the ending of capitalist exploitation of the coloured workers. His last words were : 'Let them be our brothers !'

When Cousins returned to his seat after that speech, the echoes of massed applause in his ears, a white-sweatered girl, pretty and chic, brought him a note. In fact the girl had earlier asked Harold Wilson for his autograph, before Cousins went to the rostrum. Harold Wilson signed it, but made a condition – that she should take a note from him to Frank Cousins congratulating him on that speech. For a moment the warmth of old associations had returned, however fleetingly.

Towards the end of 1968 there came another attack on sterling, this time, ostensibly, because of the strength of the Deutschmark. The attack was fierce and sustained and led to a further tightening of credit by the Chancellor, Roy Jenkins, which depressed both the rate of economic recovery and public opinion, and certainly upset the unions. Inevitably it intensified tension in the Labour Movement, not least because unemployment, which had begun to fall in the second half of the year, started to rise again. The renewed economic pressure came when Barbara Castle was preparing her proposals for what was to follow the Donovan Commission. The final act of the tragedy was about to unfold.

This is not the place to go over the story of 'In Place of Strife' in detail; it requires its own special study. But in considering the last months of Frank Cousins's rule as head of the TGWU it would be impossible not to reflect again on the events surrounding that White Paper and all that flowed from it.

As soon as it became clear that the Government was intending legislation on a grand scale affecting the entire range of industrial relations Frank Cousins decided that Jack Jones should be in the forefront of the talks – although he would remain alongside. At that time it seemed certain, at the turn of 1968–9, that even if the Government got its way with the legislative proposals it would take a longish time, probably until well into 1970, before anything would become law. There was nothing to suggest that the Government would try to rush through an Industrial Relations Act *before* Cousins's retirement from the TGWU.

After all, legal reforms in industrial relations had been talked about for years. The Donovan Commission appeared to discourage even the strongest advocates of the use of the law, and it did appear that Ministers could now be persuaded to take a much more sceptical view of all the pressure groups (particularly senior civil servants) who believed that legislation was the key to improved industrial relations. The origins of the Donovan Commission lay in this belief. However, those in Whitehall who had argued for many years the need for a 'legal framework' covering industrial relations were most unimpressed by the Royal Commission's Report. They still believed a legal framework was essential. Indeed the case for some form of legal intervention had long been in draft form on the shelves of the old Ministry of Labour; the problem, previously, had been to find a 'politically opportune' moment. Well before Barbara Castle was appointed to succeed Ray Gunter, the Ministry of Labour officials and Gunter were displaying disappointment at what they believed would emerge from Donovan. Perceptively, they prepared a brief to 'add to Donovan', in the event of their worst fears being justified. Barbara Castle inherited this brief when she moved into the Ministry's headquarters in St James's Square. But she was not yet convinced that the law-makers were correct. Shortly before Christmas Mrs Castle decided to organise a seminar of experts to test a wide range of views on whether Donovan should be 'added to' and if so, how. Pundits in industrial relations from both sides of industry and from the universities were called to Sunningdale, the Civil Service Staff College, for a week-end in December. The consensus was strongly against a complex catalogue of legal sanctions. Some 'tightening up' and expansion of the Donovan recommendations? Yes.

An ambitious and contentious legal framework? No. Indeed the employers'
representatives at Sunningdale were just as forceful as the union leaders on
that point.

By all accounts it would seem that Barbara Castle was almost convinced.
But the legislative hawks had captured her. They knew the Government's
need to court popular opinion, they knew, from almost every opinion poll,
that the majority of people questioned about strikes wanted 'something
done' to curb the unions, and especially unofficial strikes. They did not ask
whether it was workable – they assumed it would become so. They mainly
asked: Is it going to be popular with the electorate? The answer was self-
evident. Harold Wilson took the same view as the civil service advisers
around Barbara Castle. And looking for a way round the incomes policy
impasse he also saw anti-strike legislation as a potential trade-off for ending
legislation on prices and incomes. The strategy began to take shape. Crossman, looking back on the whole morass of incomes policy legislation, wrote
that Cousins was 'probably right in warning the Cabinet of the unworkability of the whole thing we tried to do. The unworkability of the kind of
legal mumbo-jumbo we got into with the [then] new Incomes and Prices
Bill. I am certainly now, wise after the event, more impressed by what he
said . . . than I was before.'[4]

'In Place of Strife', published on 17 January 1969 (Cmnd. 3888), contained twenty-five proposals for the reform of industrial relations. It was
an unparalleled programme for State intervention in every sphere – except
in *direct* pay issues. But since most industrial conflict is a manifestation of
the economic conflict there was hardly any need to be specific about pay
negotiations. Most of the proposals were in fact designed to strengthen the
unions and their role in collective bargaining, and many, indeed, have now
found their way into legislation. But three clauses in the White Paper stood
out like huge red lights on a snowy landscape. The first was a proposal to
give the Minister powers to enforce a 28-day 'standstill period' for any unofficial strike; the second, a clause empowering the Minister to order a ballot
of all union members where an *official* strike was threatened; and the third,
a clause enabling the Minister to impose a settlement in any Inter-union
dispute which could be resolved by neither the TUC nor the Commission
for Industrial Relations (the body proposed by the Donovan Commission to
supervise voluntary reforms). The three 'penal clauses' (as they came to be
known) were to become the heart of the matter, because they were the core
around which all the other proposals were wrapped. Indeed that core had
been even larger and more menacing in the original draft drawn up by the
civil servants. The 28-day 'cooling off' period, for example, started off as a
56-day period.

4. Richard Crossman, the unpublished diaries, 4 July 1968.

It has been said many times since then that both Harold Wilson and Barbara Castle were at first taken in by the comparatively mild reception that greeted the proposals in the early stages. George Woodcock, who was about to leave the TUC to become first chairman of the Commission for Industrial Relations, offered Barbara Castle such a moderate view when he was first told of the contents of the White Paper that the Minister mistook this for tacit approval. In fact Woodcock did regard 90 per cent of the proposals as excellent; it was the other 10 per cent that caused the trouble. But there should have been no doubt in Barbara Castle's mind about the ultimate union reaction. In my presence she was told categorically by Jack Jones, on New Year's Day 1969, that her proposals would never be accepted by the unions. Yet once she became convinced that the reforms were essential, nothing would shift her resolve to press them through. She even regarded them as laying a foundation for 'socialist' development in industrial relations. Harold Wilson was even more enthusiastic that something should be done to curb strikes. His own contribution was the proposal to enforce compulsory ballots where strikes were threatened. He identified himself completely with 'In Place of Strife', and this brought him nearer to being overthrown as Party leader than anything else in his entire period in power.

The formal talks between Barbara Castle and the TUC began on 30 December, at 11 a.m. in Mrs Castle's room in her Ministry. They ended in the Cabinet Room in the evening of 18 June 1969. During these six months the relationship between the Labour Government and organised labour came closer to rupture than at any time since a Labour government first took office in the 1920s.

Relentlessly the Government seemed to be moving along a disastrous and suicidal road. It was not merely that they had misjudged the mood of the unions and indeed the majority of the Parliamentary Labour Party: to be sure they *had* done that. But the fact was that 'In Place of Strife' came on top of a long series of actions which, rightly or wrongly, the Wilson Government had taken to try to limit the growing power and influence of rank and file militancy – which had so weakened the old trade union establishment. The progress of the incomes policy from the time of George Brown's Declaration of Intent in 1964 had been a record of friction and tension. Despite all that had been attempted Britain remained in what appeared to most people to be a state of perpetual economic crisis; devaluation, forced eventually on a reluctant Government, had not opened up any fresh escape route from the debilitating and depressing spiral of gloom. Bad luck, poor judgement, a failure of courage, a tendency to be overawed or at least overinfluenced by officials, a weakness for the quick image-making formulas – all of these, and more, went to the making of the fragile platform upon which in 1969 the Cabinet sought to build a new edifice of industrial reform. The result was inevitable, the platform collapsed.

Perhaps it would all have been different had it not been for Roy Jenkins's Budget of 15 April, which, apart from a further tightening of the taxation screw announced that the existing legislative control over prices and incomes (the 1968 Act) would be allowed to lapse at the end of the year. In its stead, the Chancellor told Parliament, would come a shortened version of 'In Place of Strife'. This 'Short' Bill (as it was later labelled) would include two of the three 'penal clauses' which had caused such bitterness. The third one, the proposal for compulsory ballots for official strikes – Harold Wilson's pet scheme – would not be pursued for the time being. Labour MPs were stunned by Jenkins's announcement – as indeed were most of the trade union leaders.

There had been no mention of the Short Bill when Harold Wilson saw TUC leaders at Downing Street four days earlier. It was then understood that the Government planned to legislate over the full range of the proposals in the original White Paper, and that this legislation would be brought before Parliament in November, included in the Queen's Speech. The TUC's General Secretary, the late Victor Feather, was told about the Short Bill only on the eve of the Budget speech – after the Cabinet had approved the switch in tactics. A complex web of reasoning lay behind the shift : the need to convince foreign opinion that the Labour Government were determined to 'do something' about Britain's record of industrial strife; the desire to demonstrate to the world that the Government *was* in control; the assumed need to replace the tottering incomes policy with a more credibly tough line against the unions – and to seize the opportunity for what looked like a useful trade-off; the belief that if the discussions on 'In Place of Strife' dragged on till November the TUC (and the backbench MPs) were more likely to succeed in blunting the cutting edge of the proposals. After all, it was reasoned, the Trades Union Congress and the Labour Party Conference would give the critics a chance to mount a huge propaganda campaign against the proposals and the Government would then be still further weakened. Better to take the plunge now, it was argued, catch the opposition (in the Labour Movement) off balance and embrace the whole package within a new budgetary strategy. It is not difficult to see why Ministers were attracted by such a scenario.

The Short Bill was to contain three clauses to help the unions as well as the two penal clauses. As Peter Jenkins observed in his well informed study of the 1969 crisis, 'the Government was hoping to make more friends than enemies'.[5] Delusion has found no loftier perch in contemporary British politics.

What part did Frank Cousins play in these critical months? From the beginning, as might be expected, he was actively engaged in fighting the whole

5. Peter Jenkins, *The Battle of Downing Street* (Charles Knight, 1970).

concept of legislative intervention. But he also believed that it was going to be a long-drawn-out dialogue between Government and TUC and that the critical time, late in 1969, would come after his retirement from the union. That is why he brought Jack Jones into the negotiations from the start, although it was Cousins, as a member of the TUC's finance and general purposes committee, who attended all the early meetings with the Prime Minister and Barbara Castle. As the negotiations reached their climax Jack Jones came more and more into the arena and in the final phase he was one of the small sub-committee of TUC leaders appointed to conclude, with Harold Wilson and Barbara Castle, the famous 'solemn and binding' pact which was to provide the TUC with greater central authority to intervene in disputes and, even more to the point, provide the Government with a formula that could help to save its face if not its political reputation at the hands of the electorate.

It was a difficult personal problem for Cousins. He wanted to be involved in the battle – and he was. But at the same time he did not want to pre-empt the role which, he knew, Jack Jones must now play. Not that there was any disagreement or difference of emphasis between them on the need to defeat the Government's proposals. They launched a series of Press interviews, articles, public speeches, attacking the penal clauses in 'In Place of Strife'. Of course they welcomed those elements in the White Paper which helped to strengthen the unions, especially the clauses covering union recognition, a workers' right to belong to a trade union, protection against unfair dismissal and the plans to extend industrial training schemes (incidentally, all these are now incorporated in contemporary legislation). Two days after the publication of Barbara Castle's White Paper Cousins was writing in the *Sunday Mirror* :

> There has been a growing belief in the ranks of even reasonably middle-of-the-road trade union members that the Labour Government has lost touch with them. They believe the Government is now displaying the absolute political aversion and dislike of trade unionists that is known to be in the minds of some members of the present Cabinet.
>
> There are obviously some proposals in Mrs. Castle's plan, such as the establishment of dismissal procedures and the guaranteeing of every worker's right to join a trade union which have been proposed by the trade unions for many years. These are fully acceptable. But it would be absolutely stupid to believe that putting the proposals in the form of a package deal will compensate for the introduction of restrictive clauses affecting strikes and relationships between members and their own trade unions . . .[6]

Cousins reflected sadly, in that article, that the whole operation was yet 'another chapter in the apparently inevitable history of the Labour Move-

6. *Sunday Mirror*, 19 January 1969.

ment. While we are very good in Opposition we immediately set out when we achieve power on a course of self-destruction, the pace of which accelerates the longer we are in office.' It was a theme he pursued, savagely, in subsequent meetings between the Prime Minister and the TUC.

Jack Jones was also writing away furiously wherever there was an outlet for his pen. In *Tribune*, immediately after the publication of the White Paper, Jones reminded the Labour Movement:

Even during the last war penal measures to restrict strikes were only taken at the height of the war in 1944. Aneurin Bevan opposed the laws from the start and Ernest Bevin who was Minister of Labour said that the legislation should be abolished as soon as possible. It didn't work anyway but did cause a lot of ill-feeling. Both Bevin and Bevan must be turning in their graves today.[7]

Both these articles were reprinted in the same issue of the TGWU *Record*.

Even before 'In Place of Strife' was officially published Cousins was already attacking supporters of legal restrictions in an article in the *Sunday Express*:

Such attempts would certainly bring the law itself into disrepute and introduce new opportunities for conflict which we are all trying to avoid . . . Naturally it is to the benefit of all of us if the time lost by strikes can be reduced. Any strike that can be avoided with justice, must be; but we should look at the causes of strikes. What can be done?[8]

Cousins proposed a series of reforms for the swift settlement of disputes by local arbitration tribunals and by modernising disputes procedures at factory level. He wanted more involvement of shop-stewards in the settling of disputes on the spot and an altogether more enlightened attitude from factory-level management. In short, Cousins saw the improvement of industrial relations as an integral part of a developing democracy on the shop floor – as did Jack Jones, whose ideas Cousins was also reflecting in these proposals. Again, it is interesting to reflect that much of this has now been incorporated in the model disputes procedures established through the new body created since that time – ACAS, the Conciliation and Arbitration Service.

But none of this was then acceptable to the Cabinet, and especially not to the Prime Minister or Barbara Castle, whose primary concern at that point was to act, and act quickly, in order to satisfy what they regarded as popular demand.

The record of the dialogue between the Government and the TUC leader-

7. TGWU *Record*, March 1969, p. 35/40.
8. *Sunday Express*, 12 January 1969.

THE AWKWARD WARRIOR

ship, especially during April, May and June, consists of an uninterrupted escalation of conflict. If one were to try to select any particular meeting which symbolised this, my own arbitrary choice would be the meeting four days before the Budget. It was held on 11 April at 10.30 a.m. in the Cabinet Room at 10 Downing Street. The Prime Minister sat in his chair in front of the marble fireplace, flanked by Mrs Castle and senior civil servants from the Department of Employment and the Cabinet Office. Eight members of the TUC finance and general purposes committee sat opposite him, ranged round the famous table – the TUC chairman, John Newton, Lord Collison, Sir Sidney Ford, Sidney Greene (now Lord Greene), George Lowthian, Sir Tom O'Brien, Frank Cousins and Victor Feather. The TUC's Deputy general secretary at the time was Lionel (Len) Murray; he too was there with two senior members of the TUC staff, David Lea, the head of the economics department, and Kenneth Graham, head of the organisation department. It was an acrimonious meeting from the start, with Victor Feather introducing the TUC's objections to the White Paper in a long, detailed and effective speech. Feather acknowledged much that was useful in the Government's proposals but then turned his fire on the 'penal clauses'. One by one he dissected the proposals to demonstrate that they would be utterly self-defeating. The TUC had spent much of March consulting the unions as to how the fabric of industrial relations would be improved by using the Donovan recommendations. The General Council, Feather told Wilson, 'were cooperating fully in discussions on the constructive parts of the White Paper'.[9]

When Harold Wilson asked for further comments from the TUC, Frank Cousins followed with a warning of the serious repercussions that could follow in relations between the Labour Party and the trade unions. 'Ministers appeared to be completely out of touch with workpeople,' Cousins told Wilson. 'The Government had to consider the effect on the total labour and trade union movement; if the political wing were to be separated he [Cousins] feared for the future of the Labour Movement.' Lord Collison, who had been a member of the Donovan Commission, echoed Cousins and warned the Prime Minister that he was wrong in assuming the proposals would help the Labour Party electorally. 'They would not win one extra vote and on the contrary they would create a very strong adverse attitude. If the Government were to fall for the idea that this might win them some Conservative votes, this also was quite wrong; these people were against the Labour Party in any case.' From Cousins, Wilson could expect vehement denunciation, but Collison was a respected Right winger, a mild and moderate man who had never been known to cause trouble. Yet it made no difference to Harold Wilson's determination to press ahead. He again

9. Quotations are taken from the official TUC minutes of the meeting, TUC F and GP Minute 12/2, 21 April 1969.

578

cited the unofficial strikes, the trouble in the steel industry and the motor car plants. As to the political reaction the Prime Minister responded : 'If we don't deal with strikes we will get the Tories anyway, and if you get the Tories you will get much more penal legislation.' He said he did not claim that the proposals would win votes for the Labour Party. What he was saying regarding the next election was this :

> if strikes continued and jeopardised the economy there would be anger against strikes and this would affect the Labour Party's position. He recalled the 1955 General Election and the dispute involving the Blue union in the Liverpool docks. This led to a fall in the women's vote for the Labour Party. This issue would therefore be a vote loser if nothing was done and nothing was seen to be done.

The Prime Minister then aded : 'The Labour Movement could be destroyed economically and politically if it did not do something about unofficial strikes.'

Frank Cousins warmed to the theme. 'If legislation were introduced,' he told Wilson, 'workpeople would protect themselves. This has been amply demonstrated by the prices and incomes legislation. The result of the control which was exercised particularly at industry level had been to shift the pressure to the shop-floor. This had shifted authority to the shop floor as well and taken away the authority of national officials.

'Any move to curb the freedom of workpeople on the shop floor directly would be abortive. The only result would be to lose the Labour Party the next election. The Government's proposals were giving big business the opportunity to destroy the Labour Movement.'

Cousins looked at Wilson and Barbara Castle and pleaded : 'Give us the opportunity to put our house in order; it will in the long run be more effective.'

Collison added : 'We're not here as your enemies, we are here as your friends.' Then Victor Feather clashed with the girl he had known as a schoolgirl in Bradford – red haired Barbara Betts, as she then was. 'Laws of the kind that were being proposed would not work in Britain even though they worked in other countries,' he said. He went on :

> The history and democratic tradition of the British people was one of the factors which distinguished them. People were guided in Britain by what was considered to be decent common behaviour and as far as law was concerned by common law rights. To decide to take action on the basis of public opinion polls [he added sardonically, glancing at Harold Wilson] was not a recipe which was applied by Government to their own behaviour generally nor was it a recipe which could be used to predict the real responses to such laws in industrial relations.

If the Government took the road they were proposing and introduced such laws and then found that they were not effective, the country would be in very serious trouble indeed.

This was a warning which in the end Wilson and the Cabinet were compelled to heed, it was also a warning which the Heath Government did not, and which in the end proved Feather to be accurate beyond even his own predictions.

A few days after that meeting, and two days after Roy Jenkins's Budget announcement of the "Short Bill", a senior civil servant who attended the Downing Street talks told me:

> Harold Wilsons' mood at last Friday's meeting was one of 'gambler's despair', as if he was playing his last ace card. He had clearly given up hope of convincing the unions and taking them along with the Government's proposals. He had decided to risk all on taking public opinion with him – regardless of the trade union reaction.

This particular civil servant was opposed to the Jenkins Short Bill because he believed it would be so rushed as to destroy the chances of a longer-term, more fundamental reform of industrial relations. He was, of course, quite right.

Throughout this period the TUC was still grappling with the problem of incomes policy. Government controls remained, enshrined in the legal curbs on prices and incomes, but they were increasingly becoming less relevant. The productivity loophole was allowing a great deal more flexibility and the average increase in earnings in 1968–9 was double that of 1967 – 3.6 per cent to 7.8 per cent. The TUC continued with its system of 'vetting' claims, trying to exert influence where it could, but no one claimed that it was a particularly impressive performance. What continued to condition the wages market was the state of the economy and to some extent the level of unemployment, hovering between 500,000 and 600,000. Nevertheless, the TUC persisted with its policy of voluntary restraint. At a special one-day conference of executives on 27 February, Victor Feather donned the mantle of George Woodcock to press forward with the policy of voluntaryism, this time setting the 'standard' pay rise at 18s. a week. Feather pursued the Woodcockian theme that incomes policy was essential to the overall trade union strategy of controlled economic expansion and social justice, although he was much less attracted by the pay-claim vetting system than Woodcock.

It was Feather's first appearance as Woodcock's successor on the TUC platform. And it is interesting to reflect that although the White Paper, was, by then, uppermost in his mind (as in the minds of all the union executives at the conference) it rated only a passing reference. Feather commented that there were good as well as bad features to 'In Place of Strife'. 'In a way,' he said with a characteristic homely touch, 'we might like to have a lick at the lollipop, but we're not going to swallow the stick.' In that phrase he had said it all.

There was much less heat and tension about that Croydon conference and the vote in support of the TUC's policy was, this time, a convincing 6,395,000 to 2,239,000 – the TGWU voting with the majority, while the engineers continued their consistent opposition to any form of interference with the processes of free collective bargaining. But it was all somewhat academic at that stage and incomes policy was in fact taken much less seriously. Frank Cousins spoke warmly of the need to support the general theme of the TUC Economic Review, which this time took a much more positive view towards productivity bargaining and economic expansion as well as a strong line on cuts in the defence programme. There was not quite the same undertone of fury against the Government's wages policy.

Events were overtaking the old bitterness about wage restraint. There was now an overriding requirement for the TUC to demonstrate as much of a united front as possible in the face of the new challenge and the Croydon vote that February reflected this factor rather more strongly than any basic shift in thinking about wages policy.

Indeed, the 'demotion' in the importance of incomes policy which the TUC sensed, and which the February conference vote clearly reflected, was pointed out two months later by the chairman of the Prices and Incomes Board, Aubrey Jones. In a bitingly critical speech in Manchester on 19 May he accused the Government of getting its economic priorities all wrong. In going for legislation against strikes, Mr Jones said, they had got the wrong perspective. The control of inflation was by far the more important issue and this meant that a prices and incomes policy was more important than trying to legislate against unofficial strikes. The fact that this was an understandable case for Mr Jones to pursue, did not make the case any less valid.

The deep ambivalence Frank Cousins felt towards his imminent retirement was not helped when he was again tempted to return to the House of Commons by the flattering musings – it is doubtful whether it would be right to describe them more precisely – of several left-wing MPs from the Tribune Group, and others who were less attached. There is no doubt that Cousins listened carefully to these siren voices beckoning him back to the glamour of Westminster. He heard the whispered undertones about the disastrous state of the Parliamentary Labour Party, the astonishing collapse of morale inside the Cabinet (this was towards the climax of the crisis on 'In Place of Strife'), and yet, in spite of all, the palpable absence of a credible alternative to Harold Wilson as leader of the Party. Or at least the absence of a name on whom a majority could agree. At that time the left-wing MPs were proposing that Cousins should return to Parliament as a leader of the

Left in the Parliamentary Party – not necessarily as a potential challenger to Wilson. That came later. The 'Come back Frank' lobby never became a serious political bandwagon, although that might be because he himself gave it not the slightest encouragement. Yet it refused to die completely. After Cousins's retirement from the TGWU, and indeed when he was already full-time chairman of the Community Relations Commission, the pressures were resumed.

They came at another critical moment in Labour's affairs – after the defeat on 18 June 1970, exactly one year to the day since the Cabinet's retreat over 'In Place of Strife'. Cousins was then approached by a similar group of left-wing MPs who this time not only urged him to rethink his refusal to return to Parliament but actually suggested that he should offer himself as a kind of 'caretaker' leader of the Party. The idea was not as outlandish as some may assume. Consider the picture of the Labour Party after that defeat of June 1970. Harold Wilson, who expected to win, was shattered to such an extent that even his closest friends and admirers were doubtful about his capacity to recover sufficiently from that blow. His personal and political confidence seemed to be destroyed. Had there been an obvious, and an agreed, alternative to Wilson in the Parliamentary Party at that time it is doubtful whether he would have survived. The Right, however, was fragmented and agreed only about whom it *did not* want to succeed. The Left had no credible candidate. Michael Foot was still a lone figure on the back benches, not yet with a place even in the Shadow Cabinet. It was put to Cousins that someone, like himself, who had identified himself so clearly and consistently with the opposition to the Wilson Cabinet's 'anti-trade-union policies' would start off, after June 1970, with great advantages. His Cabinet experience, his previous spell in Parliament, unfortunate though that may have been for him, ought not to appear as an obstacle at this time. The final point put to the man who was then chairman of the CRC, a retired trade union official, was that his age, approaching 66, was in fact an advantage since it would be seen that if he *did* return it would be purely in the role of an interim 'caretaker' leader. But none of this made rational political sense to Frank Cousins. Of course the thought lingered in his mind for a moment or two; it would have been too much to assume that such a proposal, however tentative and flimsily based, could be dismissed without even a second reflection. He was far from settled at the Community Relations Commission. Indeed, by the summer of 1970 he was already thinking of resigning the job, which he did later that year. Nevertheless, he told his admirers that it would be vainglorious of him to think in terms of leading a left-wing revolt and trying to sustain it throughout a new Parliament – even if he were to be acceptable, all round, as a 'caretaker' leader. After all, he mused, caretakers were sometimes prone to stay on; he did not consider himself physically fit enough to do the job; he had frequent recurrences of his heart trouble. At his age he did not believe it would be feasible, certainly not sensible, to take on such a task – a task that involved reviving, rebuilding, the morale of the entire Labour Movement.

He told the 'lobby' that he simply wouldn't be alive to see the job through. In his opinion the most important thing for a new leader, in 1970, would be to set down a new socialist strategy and have sufficient years ahead of him to at least see some of those political foundations established.

That was the Cousins prescription in 1970; it differed only slightly from his view in 1969. So for the third time he had turned down the idea of a return to active politics. Almost without doubt it was a judicious decision in 1970, more so than on the two earlier occasions. He was physically vulnerable. But more to the point it is improbable that he could have secured sufficient support from all sections in the Parliamentary Labour Party to have justified the attempt. To have attempted the move without that support would have endangered the unity of the Labour Party to a much greater extent than any of its existing maladies. It is inconceivable, for instance, that the Jenkinsite Right wing would have found Cousins a tolerable solution to the problem as they saw it. In that event to have forced through a 'caretaker' leader proposition would have split the Party, instead of uniting it around a new leader. Of course there were those on the Left who would not have found that situation too objectionable. But it was in Cousins's character to assist, in his retirement, what he had always striven to avoid throughout his active years as leader of the TGWU. He supported Wilson in the critical period from devaluation in 1967 onwards not because of a warm appreciation of the socialist qualities of the Prime Minister; he did it because he had no stomach to see the Party split, perhaps destroyed, by the bitterness and strife that would have followed Wilson's political assassination. In this Cousins took very much the same line as Aneurin Bevan, although they reached their views from different directions.

In short, although Frank Cousins, like Nye Bevan, had no affection or political regard for much of the Right wing in the Labour Party he saw no obvious or clear way of overcoming the obstacle they presented without inflicting even greater damage on the Labour Movement. He was prepared to live with the coalition of opposites – always provided he could retain sufficient authority to fight powerfully within it. That may not have satisfied some of the Left, but Cousins frequently regarded *their* posturings as unrealistic, just as he viewed the policies of the Right as distinctly unsocialist.

There were other factors behind the tempting proposition put to Frank Cousins in 1970. One of them, perhaps not of great historic significance though not without some value, was the impression Cousins had created by the manner and dignity of his departure from Labour's public platforms. He had deliberately set his face against rushing into newspapers or on to

TV with great 'disclosures'; he flatly refused to follow the pattern set by some of his former Cabinet colleagues and open up a public brawl about 'what went wrong' with the Wilson Governments from 1964 to 1970. He was frequently tempted, often with large sums of money, but he brushed these all aside. Sometimes the self-imposed silence became irksome, but it stuck. He would not break a lifetime of allegiance to a sacred principle – loyalty to friends and principles, even if they often drove him to distraction.

In fact he indulged in only one 'looking back' article. This attracted a great deal of interest and praise simply because it set out the Cousins philosophy with such dignity, restraint and simple honesty as to put it in marked contrast with the contributions of most other leading Labour politicians. It appeared in the *Sunday Telegraph* on the eve of Cousins's last Trades Union Congress, in 1969.[10] In one sense it was Cousins's own subjective summing up of *his* impact on the trade union movement, as well as an outline of his views and politics, present and future. His introductory paragraph, for instance, left no doubt in anyone's mind that while he would be scrupulously honest, he would not be needlessly modest.

There have been some momentous changes since I became general secretary of the TGWU in 1956 and took my seat on the General Council of the Trades Union Congress. When I arrived I found a trade union 'establishment' very firmly in control. These people believed absolutely in imposing decisions from the top.

Looking around the General Council in those days I formed the opinion that though some were men of real substance and ability the best of them tended to concentrate their effort more on their jobs as leaders of their own unions than on fashioning the TUC as the 'general staff' of the movement.

But my feeling even then was that the pattern was beginning to change. My colleagues at that time and my predecessors like Arthur Deakin of the Transport and General Workers, possessed real power within their own union structures and they used that power quite ruthlessly. For doing so they were invariably praised by the Press for what was regarded as 'responsible', ie, Right wing, leadership.

But in industry itself on the shop floor they were, already by the mid-fifties, losing the power to impose their will. Their authority had been created by the pressure of war-time and post-war centralisation. But they were increasingly remote and out of touch with their active members and it became my ambition to re-establish contact.

Now thirteen years later much of the apathy that marked official trade unionism has disappeared. There is more freedom, more open-mindedness and ordinary workers are increasingly being encouraged to demand, and to get, a bigger say in the running of their own unions and the industries in which they work.

10. *Sunday Telegraph*, 31 August 1969.

No summary of Cousins's legacy, his influence, his basic contribution to the development of the Labour Movement and to industrial affairs, could more succinctly set out his credentials. That it actually came from his own pen is less surprising than his critics might claim. He knew what he wanted to do when he took over from Deakin, and he believed he had achieved a good deal of that ambition. By no means all, by no means as effectively as he would have wished, but there was something to show for his troubles. He was immodest enough to claim credit for it – rightly so, in my view.

That article described much more, however. Cousins wrote of his long fight against wage restraint, not because he refused to understand the role wages could play, *must* play, in a planned economy, but because he saw wage restraint being used primarily for other purposes, not least to curtail the power and independence of the unions and their growing influence in society. He was suspicious of the cosy atmosphere of corporate-statism which he believed was beginning to develop a certain permanence.

> Some of my colleagues were content to go no further than to walk alongside the inhabitants of the corridors of power. But if the central authority of the trade union movement sees its main function as taking part in discussions with Ministers then it makes a grave mistake. In the last resort governments are not influenced by painstakingly prepared research documents or chats in the garden at No. 10 but by pressure.

There spoke the classic trade union bargainer, as well as the socialist.

> Look at the response exerted by the international monetary interests or the pressure of the big employers whose decisions on where to invest, and when, can make or break a government's policy on full employment or regional development or even the balance of payments.
>
> Our power [as trade unionists] is industrial and that is why the chief function of the TUC and its member unions must be to expand and sustain union activity at the place of work.

That was why, Cousins added, he believed:

> The TUC in its campaign against penal legislation is today closer to the realities of industrial life than at any time since I became a trade unionist.

He again repeated his warning that the strains imposed on the relationship between the Labour Governments and the unions during the 1969 crisis could break the 'historic link', though he did not believe that would happen. It had not happened during previous periods of great strain and tension – as, for instance, during the nuclear disarmament battles.

People tend nowadays to think that because of the continued existence of the Polaris submarines and the vestiges of the V-bomber force that those who argued for nuclear disarmament were defeated. I do not hold that view. Through the democratic processes of the Labour Party we contributed to a tremendous change in the national attitude on the whole question of nuclear and military policy. That debate was part of a process of national education.

His assessment of the effects on public opinion, and governmental policies, of that famous period was that it really had changed attitudes. But what of his joining the Cabinet in 1964 and the resultant disappointment?

Right from the election victory of 1964 when I joined the Government as Minister of Technology I felt that the answer to our problems was to change the traditional commitments accepted so long by Britain. Many of these commitments were out-dated and impossible to maintain on any rational basis. The first of these in my view was the whole financial structure. We arrived in office to face an enormous deficit run up by the Tories in the 10 years in which they never attempted to do anything radical to gear the economy to meet a changing situation with new forms of competition facing our exports and new political and economic ambitions among the countries that provide us with basic raw materials.

By permitting the unlimited export of capital for investment in other countries they [the Tories] had allowed our reserves to be dangerously depleted. From the start [of the Labour Government in 1964] a rigid freeze on the outflow of capital would have been justified together with the mobilisation of our overseas investments to boost our reserves and the introduction of import quotas. Because these things were not done we had to face the disaster of an enforced devaluation.

The second big error the Government made was in the field of defence. It took us right until the financial crisis of 1966 to take the decision to withdraw from East of Suez. Until then our frontier, officially, was still on the Himalayas . . .

Cousins developed the thesis that Britain required a great programme for national economic recovery from 1964 onwards, but that what came was always too late, too little, too reluctantly grasped. The resolve had not been there. It had been a failure of political will:

If Labour loses the next General Election – and that is by no means as certain as the Tories believe – it will be because we promised too much without being in a position to deliver. Nor in 1964, and 1966, did we tell the people what *they* would have to do to enable the promises to be fulfilled. Churchill once said rather cynically that an alternative policy was a luxury an opposition party could not afford; his own tactics from 1945 to 1951 were entirely confined to getting the Attlee Labour Government out of office. We, on the other hand, set out to promise too much and, quite frankly, we failed to deliver.

Then followed the final paragraph, which attracted so much attention among those MPs who believed that Cousins could provide the alternative leader they had been searching for :

> Whatever happens I cannot bring myself to believe that a defeat at the next election would be the ultimate disaster or that it would lead to the disappearance of the Labour Party. This Party can never be anything but a survivor. It makes terrible mistakes, usually while it is in office, and it lacks the means because of the structure of the mass media to propagate its ideas.
>
> But on our side is the gradual and inexorable and undefeatable idea that people want to change and humanise the system under which we all live.

It looked like the message of a man who, far from leaving the ship, was ready and willing to take over the helm, and, perhaps if only for a brief spell, redirect its course. That was the view taken by a number of people on the Left of the Labour Party who read it, and remembered it months after Frank Cousins had bid his farewells to the TGWU, and the TUC.

However, there was still some serious business to attend to before the day of retirement dawned. In July 1969 at the 23rd biennial delegate conference of the TGWU, in Douglas, Isle of Man, Frank Cousins began the final round of farewells. Inevitably it was going to be a protracted farewell ceremony, starting with the TGWU conference and moving on six weeks later to the Trades Union Congress, finally to the union executive's farewell dinner in London on the night of 8 September. It was all on the grand scale, though it did nothing to make the departing any easier for the awkward warrior.

The conference week was one of farewell dinners, as well as speeches from all reaches of the union. Cousins tried to treat it as just another union conference and spoke, with the traditional frequency of the TGWU General Secretary at such an occasion, on most of the major subjects. But it was impossible even for him to pretend that it was just another conference. To the last he held on to the reins of office. He was emotionally incapable of releasing the grip, but that caused no surprise. On the eve of the conference we talked into the early hours of the morning. He was in a mood of deep restlessness because he recognised how difficult it was for him to come to terms with his retirement. He was tormented by the reflection that his new job, at the Community Relations Commission, important though it was and involved though he was in its objectives, would never be an adequate substitute for the platform he had commanded for thirteen years. He admitted he was disappointed at his own behaviour and his own reactions. He had, for example, personally taken charge of the committee which arranged conference business (standing orders committee) when he ought to have left that task to Jack Jones. 'I should have been big enough to have declined the role and left it to my successor,' he acknowledged with unusual self-criticism. But the disarmingly candid confession was symptomatic of Cousins's mood. He greatly admired Jack Jones; he had indeed, as we have seen, paved the way for him. Yet, in another sense, he also resented the fact that the curtain was now rising on Jack Jones's era. Cousins was strong enough, even in that remorseful mood, to recognise his own weakness.

Perhaps, one might muse, that another great figure who left the stage in the same year, Charles de Gaulle, felt much the same way. Curiously enough, Frank Cousins, after he resigned in 1966, was compared with de Gaulle by a writer in *Socialist Commentary*, the right-wing Labour monthly journal.

In his own field Cousins has something of the same qualities and attitudes as de Gaulle. He also knows how to be awkward on the grand scale. Yet his views as expressed in his letter of resignation of July 3 [1966] on the Government's prices and incomes policy showed an old-fashioned nostalgia for the past glories of trade union battles not unlike de Gaulle's nostalgia for the past glories of France.[11]

It was not exactly the most felicitous comparison to choose, though it is hardly deniable that de Gaulle's manipulation of those 'past glories' laid the foundation for a new and effectively modern France. Still, the criticism was in the typical tradition of anti-Cousins rebukes – that he was old fashioned, rigidly in the grip of outdated ideology, autocratic, stubborn, and, most of all, irritatingly inflexible in his socialist convictions.

From the same platform where he began the tumultuous revolt against the H-Bomb in July 1959 Cousins bade goodbye to the TGWU conference with all the old defiance. He was sad, proud, joyous, humbled, hopeful, yet anxious. The Labour Government, he lamented, had failed because it believed it could 'make capitalism work better than the capitalists'.

The vote of thanks to Frank Cousins, moved by two rank-and-file-delegates, recalled, in a motion,

the courageous stand and leadership displayed by Brother Cousins in our union's fight to promote progressive economic policies designed to ensure a redistribution of the national wealth in favour of those who make the greatest contribution to society . . . [his] effective opposition to wage restraint and other legislative interference against trade unions and trade unionists [and his championing of] The cause of nuclear disarmament, international peace, and goodwill amongst the workers of the world.

11. Article by Mrs Peggy Crane, *Socialist Commentary*, August 1966, pp. 17–19.

Jack Jones compared Cousins's qualities with the 'simple socialism of Keir Hardie allied to the fire of Arthur Cook, the great miners' leader'. Frank Cousins, said, Jones, had inspired and given purpose to the union as no other man has done 'in our time'.

Amid the ovations Cousins spoke briefly; he was too overcome to spend long on his valediction. 'There has never been a man capable of running this union alone,' he said, as if replying to a hidden question. 'With you I could do anything – alone I could do nothing. What I have done for this movement is nothing compared with what you have done for me.' He broke down and in a husky whisper said : 'thank you for giving me the chance to live a worthwhile life'.

After that the other farewells were an anti-climax. He did actually move a motion at the 1969 TUC, calling on the Government to take immediate steps to implement the ILO Convention on equal pay for equal work. But that Congress was Jack Jones's launch rather more than a Cousins farewell. The Prime Minister spoke on the opening day, a speech of unrepentant courage in the light of what had happened a few months earlier. He made no apologies for his attempt to introduce anti-strike laws. Indeed he drove home his message by warning the TUC not to 'backslide' from its June agreement to curb strikes by its own voluntary system. Harold Wilson won no new friends among the union leaders at the 101st TUC at Portsmouth, but he won a good deal of respect for refusing to bend a knee. The speech was, of course, delivered with an eye on the public audience outside more than on trying to impress the Congress. It probably succeeded in doing both. Yet it was not a particularly elevating Congress for Cousins's final appearance. Apart from that one debate on equal pay he appeared only once again, to receive his gold badge. The stage was left to Jack Jones, who took it with great effect. He left no one in any doubt that his arrival would make no difference to the fighting, rebellious militant image of the Transport and General Workers' Union. The impression he made was similar to that made when Frank Cousins first took his stand at the TUC rostrum at Brighton in 1956, though the circumstances had been transformed since then.

There was a motion calling for the repeal of the Prices and Incomes Act – it was almost a ritualistic war dance, by now. It was carried by 4,652,000 to 4,207,000. The narrow margin was due to the fact that many unions considered it unrealistic for the TUC to demand the total repeal of all legislation over prices and pay from a Government that had recently capitulated so completely over strikes legislation. But the motion was pushed through by the combined strength of the TGWU and the Engineers, and the new alliance of Jack Jones and Hugh Scanlon. The force of the 'terrible twins' was born as Frank Cousins waved his goodbyes to the Congress. That

TUC was a strained and somewhat disorganised forum of immediate anxieties and uncertain objectives. The horizon was still clouded with the smoke of the June battles. The Congress was consumed by the fight against the anti-strike laws, and it seemed it scarcely had the time to think deeply about anything else. Victor Feather, with a touch of the music hall, summed up *his* feelings (it was his first full Congress as General Secretary) with the memorable comment : 'It has been said that I have been thrown in at the deep end. I don't mind that so much. But I am looking for the man who let the water out.'

On Monday 8 September the Transport and General Workers' Union executive met for its 189th session. Shortly after 10 a.m. the chairman, Len Forden, turned to the item dealing with the General Secretary's farewell dinner that evening, at the Grosvenor House Hotel, London. It was proposed that the executive should adjourn at midday to allow for everyone to prepare. Agreed. The General Secretary, Brother Frank Cousins, was then called on to report on affairs since the previous meeting of the General Executive Council. 'This,' said Cousins looking around the board room, 'this is, of course, the last report I shall be making to the council . . .' A few items later the vice-chairman of the union, Bill Jones, with his famous gravelly cockney voice, expressed thanks on behalf of the entire union membership – which, it had just been announced, now topped 1,500,000 for the first time. Cousins was handed the keys and logbook of the Rover car he had been using. And Bill Jones made the presentation with a grand flourish of brotherly sentiment. Minute No. 563a finally records :

Brother F. Cousins thereupon took his leave of the Council.

The Cousins era was over.

Chapter Twenty-seven

A POSTSCRIPT

No other man in our time, including the late Ernie Bevan, has inspired working people as much as Frank Cousins.

Jack Jones, at the TGWU conference July 1969

It is exceedingly difficult if not impossible for heroes and old soldiers to fade away. No trade union leader who has commanded the political and industrial arena as a Field-Marshal commands the battlezones can easily and suddenly toss aside the mantle and slip quietly into the folds of history. At one time Frank Cousins, a Field-Marshal of the industrial battlefield if ever there was one, could delude himself into believing that he would be able to do that, but as his retirement drew nearer he was lured into a new and unfamiliar role. He accepted the tempting invitation to become the first chairman of the newly created Community Relations Commission. As things turned out it was a mistake; it was certainly an unhappy climax to a remarkable career.

The Community Relations Commission was established in November 1968 and Frank Cousins, because he had not yet parted from his TGWU post was first of all appointed part-time Chairman. The Commission took over the functions of the former National Committee for Commonwealth immigrants which was formed in 1965 by Harold Wilson. A parallel, though somewhat different body, the Race Relations Board, had already been created under an earlier Race Relations Act of 1965 and when the 1968 Act came into force on 26 November 1968 it extended the powers of the earlier legislation and broadened the functions of the Board as well as establishing the CRC. The confusion inherent in this duality was apparent from the start. While the Board had clear and reasonably specific functions under the law the Commission's role was distinctly blurred. It was largely a propaganda body, with limited powers, an absurdly inadequate budget (Cousins

591

had a Government grant of £395,000) and only a limited direct influence over a key area of its responsibility – the appointment of community relations officers to local authorities. From the start it was a shop window operation, without muscle, and relying largely on the reputation of its impressario chairman to provide the political effectiveness and gloss which it lacked in basic organisational terms. This was certainly an unfair burden to hand to Cousins; it was equally an error of judgement by Government to establish such a commission without the necessary powers and expect it to make an impact in such a highly sensitive sphere as race relations. The Commission's task was one of education, publicity, exhortation; the spreading of a humanitarian and liberal gospel; the dissemination of goodwill and the encouragement of mutual understanding. All the virtuous clichés – but without the resources and the bite to command either regard or serious attention. Perhaps Cousins should never have accepted the task in the first place, but he found the invitation hard to resist. He certainly had no illusions about the potential difficulties or the serious limitations of the CRC. In fact when he was invited to take the job by the then Home Secretary James Callaghan, Cousins listened carefully to the job specification and finally turned to Callaghan and with characteristic bluntness observed : 'You can't bloody well win this one, Jim.' And he didn't.

Yet Frank Cousins was fascinated, and absorbed as well as deeply committed to trying to help in the fight against racial discrimination. He had led the battle against racial prejudice inside the TGWU and openly courted unpopularity, especially among the union's bus section where there had been a great deal of recruitment of immigrants. Cousins also fought against racial discrimination from the wider trade union platform, at home as well as from the international stage. Even with his awareness of the difficulties he was surely going to encounter and his strong doubts about the adequacy of the CRC he could scarcely refuse the challenge to help the Government to tackle the racial problem. In some senses it was a smaller version of the challenge he faced when Wilson invited him into the Labour Government in 1964. After all, Cousins's last major speech to a Labour Party conference was on this very issue of racial tolerance. He picked up the challenge again, but he did not fit the part.

His first problem was his part-time chairmanship. For the first nine months of the CRC's existence Cousins divided his time and energies between the TGWU, the TUC, and the Commission. Many of the full-time officials inside the new organisation resented having a part-time chairman; they did not resent Cousins himself but they believed the Commission was important enough to have had a full-time head from the beginning. When Cousins finally took over his full-time role, in the autumn of 1969, the resentment had become entrenched and a number of the Commission's staff resigned at the time. Perhaps they would have left in any event; the Commission contained a substantial element of obdurate and capricious people who required no rational reasons for exaggerating the obvious difficulties involved in such a body. Cousins's accession to full-time chairmanship seemed to provide an opportunity to raise protests about issues which did not really concern Cousins at all. Certainly he had not been responsible for the tensions that had occurred before he moved in full-time. Still, it was an unpropitious beginning. To add to the tenseness Cousins's abrasive style and mannerisms did not go down well with some of the Commission staff. They did not like his style of tough, matter-of-fact trade-union-like discipline. And for his part he found the organisation 'wooly' and very much unlike a trade union in character and outlook. Of course he was aware that the CRC had to be run in a different manner from the TGWU, but the trouble was that the Commission was quite unlike any organisation he had encountered before.

Cousins was also depressed by the lack of effective power in the Commission. It is true that he had access to the Home Secretary, yet he could hardly keep knocking on Callaghan's door.

Cousins wanted a merger with the Race Relations Board which he urged from an early stage. He did not see the sense in having two separate bodies, overlapping, in this specially sensitive area. That merging was to come about later – not in Cousins's time. In the summer of 1970, after the defeat of the Wilson Government, he came under increasing pressures from inside as well as outside the Commission. His critics seized on the Heath victory in June 1970 and assumed that this would be the signal for Cousins to resign his chairmanship. When he did not automatically do this the attacks on his leadership intensified and even spread to some of the black community groups who took criticism to the opposite extreme by accusing Cousins of 'political cowardice' – a particularly inept charge to level at him. Obviously this upset and angered Cousins. While the white, right-wing factions sneered at him for spending taxpayers money on 'the race relations industry', the black extremist groups accused him of failing to wage a sufficiently militant fight for the coloured communities. Even before the 1970 General Election Cousins came under fire from one leading figure in the black community, Mr Jeff Crawford of the West Indian Standing Committee. In March that year Crawford wrote to Cousins urging him to resign on grounds of health – he had recently suffered another heart attack. Crawford's letter contained this passage :

When I reflect on the outstanding contribution you have already made to this country and similar movements beyond these shores I would prefer to honour and remember you for what you have done so far rather than see you caught up in a situation which will almost certainly cloud your past contribution. I feel that you should consider stepping down in favour of a younger and hence more vigorous person.

By the summer of 1970 Cousins had already decided that he would leave the Commission at the end of the year. He had moved away from London to settle in a retirement bungalow at Wrington near Bristol and increasingly he was finding the commuting between London and Bristol an arduous task. His health was not good and he was plainly disappointed with the results of the Commission's work. The defeat of the Wilson Government in June clinched his decision although it was not the decisive factor. The incoming Conservative Government asked him to remain as chairman of the CRC and the new Home Secretary, Mr Reginald Maudling, tried hard to persuade him to change his mind and remain as chairman – at least until the end of 1971 when his term of office would normally have expired. But he refused. He was irritated by the constant carping – from inside and outside, and he was dismayed by the acrimony between competing groups within the immigrant communities. His own simple, clear-cut idealism was overcome by waves of petty recrimination which to Frank Cousins appeared as banal as it was self-destructive. He never lost his faith and conviction in the need to fight against racial discrimination and intolerance. But in the end he was persuaded that the task was perhaps one for a younger man. In November 1970 he resigned. Without fuss or exictement he went back to Wrighton, away from the public eye for the last time.

It was an unhappy epilogue to the career that closed in September 1969, and Frank Cousins felt deeply about it. For a long time afterwards he would not accept any other part-time roles and indeed he resigned his two remaining part-time posts (on the National Freight Corporation and the Central Training Council) shortly afterwards.

To a generation who missed the impact of Frank Cousins, the quote from Jack Jones's speech to the 1969 TGWU conference which I have used at the opening of this postscript might possibly appear as a routine overstatement of praise. But in this writer's view it is not hyperbole, it is a statement of fact. Of course, the essential point of Jack Jones's declaration was his choice of phrase – that Cousins 'inspired working people'. He did so because he spoke with their tongue, with their hopes and their ambiguities. He felt their moods and their instincts. He did not exaggerate their political idealism – except where in some instances, such as nuclear disarmament, he sought to lead rather than to follow. He had no illusions about the mountainous difficulties in his path nor the obstacles to any change in 'human behaviour'. But he felt the impulses of change and he drove his tanks forward – not with scientific clarity nor always with sophisticated political judgement, but with integrity emblazoned on his banner.

This is not an attempt to summarise or draw final conclusions. They cannot exist in precise form. Indeed, when one looks back at the Cousins era there is an impression almost of a far away period. Each epoch in modern history now seems somehow to contain elements of swifter change as if the actual fuel of time has become increasingly more volatile. For example, the span of years between 1955 when Cousins moved into his position of power and 1969 is not long by routine standards of time – a mere fourteen years. Yet in terms of the speed of events, nationally and internationally, the span of years appears to be vast in perspective. The prominent names alone (leave aside the conditions), of 1955 might, to a contemporary generation, now seem as remote as Napoleon appeared to a generation of pre-war schoolchildren. In 1955 Eden was Prime Minister, Eisenhower President of the United States; Stalin had only lately died and Nikita Khrushchev had yet to make that shattering speech to the 20th Congress of the Soviet Communist Party (a speech which split not only the Communist world but, arguably, post-war history). Hitler was only ten years dead. The TV screen was a novelty for expensive tastes; the pill was still in the test tube stage. A social revolution has swept by. Today, nothing is the same even if most is not much different.

Frank Cousins's period in power spanned that gulf – from the 1950s to the 1970s. He himself lived through one of the most momentous periods of change in modern history. When he was born the motor car and the aeroplane were much more novel than is space travel today. Britain was a great imperial power, dominant throughout the world. Cousins was schooled in the First World War, came to manhood in the post-war depression of the 1920s, developed into the militant and furious trade union advocate in the bitter 1930s. And then, in the post-war Britain of the 1950s Frank Cousins opened the door for a new generation of social and political revolt. And in so doing left his own indelible imprints on the age.

Whether he realised it or not he became a midwife of change at a critical phase in post-war Britain. He articulated the feelings and frustrations of ordinary men and women in factories, workshops and among people who service our public industries and services. His legendary verbal ambiguities were *their* ambiguities. It was as if he was articulating a strangled cry. Before he came on the trade union scene the voice of authority was the voice of the Establishment – albeit an establishment in the trade unions and the Labour Movement in general. More than anyone else he helped to transform that and open the door to change, a change which today has brought new dimensions of shop-floor power. A change that has developed more rapidly than he ever considered likely when he took over in 1955.

That is what Jack Jones meant by the reference to inspiring working people. It was also that inspiration which helped Jones himself to pick up and develop still further a quite new era of British trade union affairs, both within the unions themselves and in their relations with the State as well as with employers organisations. Trade unions *are* a new power not because they seek to dominate in the traditional sense of oligarchic power but because they do represent, however crudely it is sometimes manifest, a dimension of democratic expression by people who are only now beginning to recognise their own force and have yet to learn how to use it effectively.

When Frank Cousins took over as General Secretary of the TGWU we still lived in an era where the majority of shop-stewards knew their place and employers their certainties. Cousins didn't discover any new Einsteinian theory of power relativities, as between employed and employer, between shop floor and boardroom. But he *did* unlatch a valve. And he possessed the courage, the stamina, the physical stature (which was not unimportant), the conviction, the nerve (sometimes even the insensitivity) and above all the platform and the opportunity at a critical time in post-war British history. He was there at the right time, perhaps reinforcing Emerson's adage that 'there is properly no history, only biography'.

But of course he was as much the creature as an instrument of his time. Since Frank Cousins left the scene there have been fresh explosions both of trade union power and of confrontation between the State and the shop floor: as between the conventional form of relations between Government and trade unions and new dimensions in the power and force of organised labour. Cousins's successor, Jack Jones, also emerged as a giant of organised labour trying to grapple with these new aspects of old problems; trying to establish a fresh relationship between State and trade unions. It is an enormous task, and with each slip and skid the critics pounce to scream about the abuses of 'trade union power'. Jack Jones took over from Cousins at a moment that proved to be critical, perhaps fatal, for the Wilson Government in 1969 – when Barbara Castle's White Paper 'In Place of Strife' was published. It is almost certain that the failure of that Labour Government to come to terms with the trade unions cost Harold Wilson the election of 1970. Eventually the same became true of the Heath Government. The arrogant certainties with which the Heath administration opened in 1970, the over-ambitious absurdities of the Industrial Relations Act led, inescapably, to a new confrontation between Government and the unions. In a sense, February 1974 was an inevitable outcome given the irrationality that by then conditioned so much of the relationship between Government and unions.

The Social Contract, the agreement between a Labour Party then in opposition and the trade union leadership, was a calculated attempt to come to terms with this problem. How can the trade unions, now very much of age, work with the modern State? This is not the place to attempt any detailed answer to that question. But in a postscript to a book on Frank Cousins it is impossible to escape the question altogether. The truth is that the unions have not yet adjusted their thinking or their organisation to the new political and economic dimensions which they themselves have helped to bring into existence. I do not believe there can ever be perfect harmony between the State and the trade unions – outside a totalitarian corporatist State (and even in such a State the harmony is, largely, a political façade). It is in the nature of the trade union body to question, to challenge, to argue, possibly to rebel. Yet this is not to say that in a developing collectivist economy it is possible for the unions to remain outside the ring of responsibility. Of course their task becomes more difficult, immensely more so, but that is no justification for the unions pretending they can avoid new functions and changing roles. No doubt the shift of power to more collectivised systems will force the trade unions to adapt their *mores*. But they will also have to retain a sufficient degree of independence and integrity to satisfy their own members that they are still capable of genuine democratic expression : that they are not captive to the omnipotent State machine. That is the dilemma and the conflict always apparent in the endless dialogue about incomes policies, and so on, even between Labour Government and the trade unions. It was also always at the centre of Cousins's own dilemma.

Nor is there any easy, ideologically predetermined route through this problem. Socialists have always claimed that the role of trade unions must change to reflect the fundamental power shift that takes place within a socialist society. That is a logical enough argument. But no society is perfect and no foreseeable system is likely to be able to satisfy civilised and humanitarian standards and be without a trade union movement capable of challenging accepted wisdoms. To match these two requirements – a real shift in relationships between the unions and a democratic socialist State and, at the same time, the retention by the unions of their credibility and integrity – that surely is the major challenge of the future. So it is no bleakly critical mark against contemporary trade unions that they have not yet found their new role. It is more an indication of the immaturity of their critics that they have been, and are still being, assailed for having as yet failed to do so.

It is a basic condition of any democracy, most of all a Socialist democracy, that the unions – or whatever workers' representative bodies are called in the future – should retain their integrity, whatever the changing political and economic structure. The Communist States will have to face this problem sooner or later. And they will eventually be compelled to do so quite openly instead of trying to deal with workers' dissent under cover of secrecy, pretence and hypocrisy. Of course, all political systems contain substantial degrees of these elements. But it is precisely because Governments, whether under capitalism, socialism or a mixture of the two, cannot avoid the limitations imposed by having to choose their priorities that trade unions must remain the most effective institutions of popular dissent. It ought not to be a matter of cynical or sneering criticism that the unions have so far failed to come to terms adequately with these problems. A mature and adult society should be able to debate the issues more rationally. Power is shifting. Not so much in straight lines as between this or that class but rather in a fuzzy, often contradictory process of conflict and overlap of interests. Largely as a result of vast technological changes, no group, no system, no society is immune from another's crises; everyone is involved in the outcrop and the shifts in world power relationships. When Frank Cousins came to prominence the question, after the 1955 General Election, and the victory of the second post-war Conservative Government, was simply: 'Can Labour win again?' Twenty years on the question put was: 'Can the Conservatives govern – even if they win?' That is some measure of the shift in power.

Jack Jones has followed Frank Cousins into retirement. In so many ways the two men, in their respective historical slots have been complementary. One paved the way for the other; one opened the door, the other pushed it wide open and walked through. A trade union leader of great experience who knew and has worked with both observed to me: 'Jones has been the General; Cousins was the Messiah.'

Tomorrow's men, and women? They will need to be something of each.

> Time makes old formulas look strange,
> Our properties and symbols change,
> But round the freedom of the Will,
> Our disagreements centre still,
> And now as then the voter hears
> the battle cry of two ideas.
>
> W. H. Auden, From his 'New Year Letter' – Part III.

INDEX

Compiled by John Goodman

599

INDEX

(1948), 80–1; contests TGWU General Secretaryship (1955), 102–4; contests TGWU Assistant General Secretaryship (1955), 105–6; views on FC's early days as TGWU General Secretary, 118, 135; Labour Party and nationalisation, 146, 248; 1958 London bus strike, 165–8, 171, 184; FC's succession, 359, 478, 481, 559; FC's appointment to Labour Government, 394; appointed acting General Secretary (1964), 395; incomes policy, 451, 469; FC's return to TGWU, 490–1, 502–3; election to TUC General Council (1966), 518; 'The Cousins Plan', 524; elected Labour Party General Secretary (1968), 558–9; Labour Party leadership, 559; relationship with FC, 479
at conferences:
1963 TGWU, 361; 1965 Labour Party, 469
Noel-Baker, Philip (Lord), 300
North Atlantic Treaty Organisation, 212, 217, 219, 221, 252–3, 261, 268, 272, 295–6, 349, 425, 438, 486
Nuclear power, 416, 436, 439–43
Nuclear weapons, 132, 143–5, 349, 395, 406, 439–41, 536
Nuneaton, 408; by-election (1965), 416–8, 422; 1966 general election, 484–5; local Labour Party and FC's resignation, 480, 503–5, 512–3

O'Brien, Tom (Sir): wage restraint, 150; elected to *Daily Herald* board, 153; 1958 London bus strike, 185; nuclear disarmament, 207, 209; FC's appointment as Minister of Technology, 397; *In Place of Strife*, 578
Observer, The, 406, 416
Odhams Press, and *Daily Herald*, 208–9, 397
O'Leary, Tim, and 1962 dockers' pay claim, 319
Oliver, G., and nuclear disarmament, 299

Padley, Walter, and nuclear disarmament, 296–8
Page, Robin, 475
Pannell, Charles (Lord): nuclear disarmament, 299; as Minister of Works, 448
Patterson, Marie, 518
Pearson, Lord, 490
Peart, Fred (Lord), 203–4, 420, 462
Penney, Sir William (Lord), 430, 438–41; relationship with FC, 440–1, 478
Pensions, Ministry of, 438

Petrol tanker drivers: 1953 strike, 92–5; and 1958 London bus strike, 177, 184, 186–7, 198
Phillips, Morgan, 258–9, 270; nuclear disarmament, 208, 230; nationalisation, 248; illness, 258
Pickstock, Frank, and Campaign for Democratic Socialism, 280
Pitt, David (Lord), 522
Plowden, William, 443
Polaris, 306, 332, 349, 424, 446, 586
Poole, Lionel, 213
Powell, Enoch, 170, 470
Power workers, and 1958 London bus strike, 177, 184, 186
Prentice, Reg: nuclear disarmament, 299, and TGWU, 534–5
Press, 262, 300, 304, 363, 491, 552; hostility to FC, 140, 151, 159, 214, 257, 264, 298, 302, 307, 325, 398, 456, 467, 471, 473, 485, 542; praise for FC, 493–4, 510; 1958 London bus strike, 173, 181, 195–6; and strikes (1959), 246; Labour Party, 275, 280–1; hounds Michael Cousins, 290; and EEC, 334; hostility to Ministry of Technology, 434; seamen's strike (1966), 488
Prices and Incomes Bill/Act, 495–6, 503, 505, 508, 511–3, 533, 554, 589
Prices and Incomes Board (National Board for Prices and Incomes), 324, 450, 455, 468, 495, 548, 581
Pritt, D. N., 26
Profumo affair, 374
Public opinion polls, 197, 392, 579
Public schools, Labour Party's attitude to, 203–4

Race Relations Board, 591, 593
Racism, 301, 551, 570–1, 592
Railway Clerks' Association (now Transport Salaried Staffs' Association), 26
Railway workers: 1957–8 pay claim, 164, 171, 174–6, 179; 1958 London bus strike, 177, 187–8; 1968 dispute, 568
Randall, Leslie, 264
Ready, Yvonne and Robert, 504
Redundancies, 520; trade unions and, 94, 331–2; BMC (1956), 94, 129–32; Standard (1956), 128–9; Beeching, 338, 351
Rees-Mogg, William, 471
Rhodesia, 291, 474
Road haulage industry, 178; in 1930s, 32–9; in Second World War, 50; 1947 strike, 63–8, 94; 1949 wage claim, 86–7; 1951 strike, 90–1; problems of unionisation, 92–3

INDEX